CW00858807

Illusory Souls

By

G.M. Woerlee

Copyright © 2013 by G.M. Woerlee

Website of G.M. Woerlee: www.woerlee.org

All rights reserved.
No part of this publication can be reproduced or transmitted in any
form or by any means, electronic or mechanical, without permission in
writing from G.M. Woerlee.

Published by G.M. Woerlee

The only true voyage of discovery ... would be not to visit new landscapes, but to possess other eyes, ...

Marcel Proust, *La Prisonnière*

Contents

Chapter 8 - The Laudable Opium

Chapter 9 - Indian Arrow Poison

References

Index

Definitions of terms (in index)

x

Preface

[P.1]What is the true nature of the human mind? Do we have souls? Many religions and popular belief systems claim each individual has a separable, immortal, and immaterial soul, the vehicle of an equally immortal and immaterial mind. Belief in the human mind as something separate, immaterial, immortal and independent of the human body is so ancient, and so prevalent, that it is anchored in the very framework of our thoughts and societies. But is this belief true? After all, the human mind could just as well be a product of the functioning of the physical human brain. Determination of the true nature of the human mind is a fascinating and intriguing problem with far-reaching personal, philosophical, and even social consequences.

[P.2]One approach to this problem is to consider these differing beliefs as two theories, or models of the nature of the human mind. So this book systematically examines these two popular theories of the nature of the human mind to determine which is correct. But such an examination of the possible reality of a human soul is worthless without first precisely defining the properties of the human soul. Fortunately, there is a reasonably prolific literature dating from more than two thousand years ago to the present, providing explicit and implicit information regarding these properties. Therefore, this book first defines the almost universally accepted properties of the human soul, and subsequently tests them against the reality revealed by human experimentation published in many internationally published medical journals.

[P.3]While critical of the belief in an immaterial human soul, this book differs in one important aspect from other works skeptical of the reality of the soul. Many such skeptical works describe how extraordinary experiences supposedly proving the reality of a soul, are all explicable with natural bodily processes. Authors of these skeptical works expect such explanations will convince readers that the conscious mind is a wondrous product of the functioning of the physical brain and body. However, such a method of argument only reveals alternative ways of viewing the same physical evidence, leaving the reader with the question of which explanation is correct.

[P.4]For example, we cannot see, smell, or touch radio waves, yet these are a real and invisible phenomenon providing communication and control of many machines forming the basis of all modern societies. Likewise, the human soul is equally invisible and intangible, and the theory of an immaterial human soul as a vehicle of the conscious mind that somehow controls the very material physical body, seems to explain phenomena manifested and undergone by the mind just as well as explaining them with natural bodily processes. Speech is just such an example of a physically observable phenomenon with two alternative explanations for its generation. An area of the brain cortex called "Broca's area" controls the muscles of the physical body generating the sounds of physical speech. Damage to Broca's area means a person can think the words they want to say, but are unable to utter them as physical sounds. If the mind is a product of the functioning of the brain, then people who sustain damage to Broca's area cannot utter the words they want to say, because the mechanisms required to generate speech are damaged. Alternatively, if the mind is housed in a separable immaterial soul and controls the body through the mechanisms of the body, then damage to Broca's area has exactly the same effect—the souls of people with damage to Broca's area cannot express speech through the mechanisms of the physical body, because of damage to Broca's area. Both explanations are equally valid in this context, because both require the mechanisms of the physical body—in this example—Broca's area. No definitive differentiation between these two theories of mind is possible with this example. Therefore, this book systematically examines many medical, as well as supposedly inexplicable paranormal phenomena, to explicitly test which of the two theories of the nature of the mind provides the best explanation. This approach leaves the reader in no doubt as to which theory of mind best explains the subjective experiences and provable observed facts associated with these phenomena.

[P.5]I am not a philosopher, a psychologist, or a neuroscientist, but I am a practical physician with three decades of experience as an anesthesiologist. Anesthesiology is a medical specialism whose effective practice requires a considerable knowledge of pharmacology, as well as the alterations of body function induced by drugs, disease, injury, and surgery. Surgery is actually the application of a controlled injury for a therapeutic purpose, and the effects of surgery on the body are the same as those of any other injury. The tasks of the anesthesiologist are to minimize the deleterious effects of surgical injury, to sustain and maintain the functioning of the body during surgery, to keep the body of the patient pain-free and unconscious during surgery, and to ensure that patients leave the operating theater in the best possible condition after undergoing surgery. James Cottrell, a former president of the American Society of Anesthesiologists, pithily summarized these differences between the tasks of anesthesiologists and surgeons.

> [P.6]*Our job is to keep patients alive while the surgeon does things that could kill them. (New York Times, 8 January 2002)*

[P.7]But does the practice of anesthesiology reveal anything about the true nature of the human mind? Yes, it certainly does. Part of the work of anesthesiologists is the manipulation of levels of consciousness and mental function with a variety of drugs. This means that anesthesiologists generally have considerable practical experience observing the effects of drugs upon the level of consciousness, as well as the effects of these same drugs on the mental and bodily functioning of their patients. Furthermore, a great number of scientific studies reveal even more information about the ways drugs used to provide anesthesia alter the functioning of the mind and the body. Curiously, none of these studies pays any attention to what the effects of these same drugs reveal about the nature of the mind, and its relationship to the body. Yet when analyzed carefully, the alterations of mental and bodily function induced by drugs used in clinical anesthetic practice, clearly demonstrate multiple, hitherto unsuspected incontrovertible proofs of the illusory nature of the ancient belief in a human soul. Such an analysis truly is a *"voyage of discovery ... not to find new evidence, but to examine known evidence from a different perspective"* (paraphrased from Marcel Proust—see citation after title page).

[P.8]Examination of other phenomena known to medical science further clarifies the relationship of the human mind to the body. Ultimately, a systematic analysis of deathbed, near-death, out-of-body, paranormal, cognitive, affective, and transcendental experiences, reveals these profound experiences to be products of brain function rather than true manifestations of a separable soul. Insights from all these analyses conclusively prove the mind to be a product of the functioning of the brain and the body, as well as providing new insights into the nature of out-of-body and near-death experiences.

[P.9]Step-by-step analyses are scattered throughout this book. These analyses are such that many readers will undoubtedly comment on the fact that explanations of many mind-body interactions from the viewpoint of a separable soul, are invariably longer and more complex, than explanations from a viewpoint that the brain is the vehicle and generator of the conscious mind. This is not surprising, because materialism provides more parsimonious explanations than dualism. Indeed, during 2002 an American philosopher called Michael Potts, also once remarked on the simpler nature of physical explanations for mind-body interactions in an article discussing near-death experiences.

> [P.10]*Although one naturalistic explanation may not adequately explain a particular NDE [near-death experience], it is possible that a combination of naturalistic explanations may be able to explain every NDE. Plus physicalist explanations, which do not refer to a disembodied soul, are more parsimonious than nonphysicalist explanations. (pages 237-238 in Potts 2002)*

[P.11]Belief in the reality of a human soul is a primeval eidolon, beguiling and dominating the public and private thoughts of nearly all peoples for untold millennia. By revealing the true origin and source of the human mind, this work may help liberate us from the suffocating mental embrace of this ancient succubus. Such liberation has the potential to usher in a new age of human advancement, empowering our children, our heirs, to transcend the wretchedness of the human condition prevailing in much of our world. At the very least, it is my hope that this work will provide certainty for those grappling with uncertainty, as well as freedom for all whose minds and bodies groan under the oppressive weight of philosophical systems and religions based upon belief in a human soul.

[P.12]Finally, I would like to acknowledge my indebtedness to my intellectual opposites—people who truly believe in the reality of a human soul. Their persistent criticism was, is, and remains a wonderfully fertile source of inspiration. All serious students doubtful of the possible reality of a soul should engage in dialogue with such believers. I also wish to acknowledge the helpful criticism of my son and daughter, as well as the patience of my wife during the writing of this book.

G.M. Woerlee
Leiden, the Netherlands, 2013.

xiv

1

The Soul

[1.1]Do we have souls? Belief in the reality of the individual human soul is deeply rooted in the individual and cultural psyche of all peoples. But what is this soul? Most people believe the human soul is something separate from the physical human body, immaterial, the vehicle of the mind, and continues conscious existence forever in some immaterial universe after the death of the body. Marcus Tullius Cicero (106-43 BCE), an ancient Roman statesman, wrote a passage expressing the hope and inspiration inherent in this belief.

> [1.2]... do you think that I should have undertaken such heavy labours by day and by night, at home and abroad, if I had believed that the term of my earthly life would mark the limits of my fame? Would it not have been far better for me to spend a leisured and quiet life, free from toil and strife? But somehow, my soul was ever on the alert, looking forward to posterity, as if it realized that when it had departed from this life, then at last would it be alive. And, indeed, were it not true that the soul is immortal, it would not be the case that it is ever the souls of the best men that strive most for immortal glory. And what of the fact that the wisest men die with the greatest equanimity, the most foolish with the least? Is it not apparent to you that it is because the soul of the one, having a keener and wider vision, sees that it is setting out for a better country, while that of the other, being of duller sight, sees not its path? (pages 98-99 in De Senectute - Cicero 1996)

[1.3]Cicero penned these words more than 2000 years ago, and this belief was ancient even then. Thousands of years before Cicero, the ancient Egyptians developed a belief that the conscious mind was an immaterial and immortal "something" associated with the material body.

Furthermore, they also believed this immaterial and immortal "something" lived for an eternity in some immaterial universe together with their gods. One of the simpler funerary prayers expressing this belief, and the nature of this life after death is written in the collection of funerary supplications and prayers known as the *Papyrus of Ani* dating from about 1300 to 1350 BCE.

> [1.4]*He receives the Urrt Crown from the gods, and from the Great Company of the Gods of Anu. He thirsts not, nor hungers, nor is sad; he eats the bread of Ra and drinks what he drinks daily, and his bread also is that which is the word of Keb, and that which comes forth from the mouths of the gods. He eats what the gods eat, he drinks what they drink, he lives as they live, and he dwells where they dwell; all the gods give him their food that he may not die. Not only does he eat and drink of their food, but he wears the apparel which they wear, the white linen and sandals; he is clothed in white, and he goeth to the great lake in the midst of the Field of Offerings whereon the great gods sit; and these great and never-failing gods give unto him [to eat] of the tree of life of which they themselves do eat that he likewise may live. The bread which he eats never decays, and his beer never grows stale.* (pages 88-89 in Budge 1913)

[1.5]Ancient Egyptian pyramids were monuments to this belief, which means this belief must have existed long before their erection more than 4,500 years ago. Belief in an immortal and immaterial "something", the vehicle of the mind and all other insubstantial factors making each human unique, otherwise known as the human soul, has persisted in one form or another for many millennia.

Two theories of mind—Materialism and Dualism

[1.7]Surveys reveal that about 70% of all people living in modern Western countries believe in the reality of a human soul (Harris Poll 2008, Heald 2000, MORI 1998, Theos Ghosts Poll 2009). This belief is not only confined to the general populations of these countries. Other surveys reveal that somewhat more than 34% of university academics, other university educated people and health professionals believe that mind and body are two separate things, and believe in an immaterial soul separate from the body that survives the death of the body (Demertzi 2009). Many of these believers claim that the reality of the soul is proven by, and consistent with all the discoveries of modern science. Furthermore, believers also claim that poorly understood experiences, such as paranormal experiences, near-death experiences, and out-of-body experiences are only capable of explanation with the concept of an immaterial soul (Arnette 1992, page 18 in Carter 2010, Grossman 2002, Greyson 2010, Lommel 2010, Metzinger 2005). Most people refer to this "mind-model", or theory of the origin and nature of the mind as "dualism", because this theory proposes that each human body has a dual nature—an immaterial soul, and a material body.

[1.8]However, regarded from a strictly neutral viewpoint, dualism is no more than an ancient theory of the nature and origin of the mind. Modern science considers dualism as disproven, regarding the mind as a product of the functioning of the physical brain. "Materialism" is one of the names given to this alternative mind-model based upon physical evidence. This is a very evident and reasonable mind-model. After all, everyone knows that malfunction or damage to different parts of the brain causes changes in intellect, memory, personality, or loss of consciousness. Insights from medical practice reveal many aspects of the relationship between the mind and the functioning of the body, as well as insights into the genesis of apparently astounding experiences, such as paranormal sensory abilities, near-death, and out-of-body experiences. Even so, despite being a theory based upon more physical evidence than is available for dualism, only about 30% of all people in modern Western countries believe in the mind-model of materialism.

[1.9]Both mind-models are ancient, and arguments about the reality of these theories of mind have raged for millennia. Yet, despite the passage of all this time, no convincing proof one way or the other has yet been presented.

Belief in a separable human soul

[1.10]The fact that dualism, or belief in the reality of a separable immaterial human soul is so ancient, so pervasive, and so ingrained in the cultural psyche of all peoples, means it deserves serious study. This brings us to the first question any serious student must ask when studying the mind-model of dualism. "Why does this belief in a human soul persist in the minds of most humans if it is no more than an illusion, or even a mere delusion?" After all, an illusory or delusory belief unsupported by evidence will eventually fade away. Yet this belief has occupied the human mind for many millennia, so there must be evidence apparently supporting this belief.

[1.11]In fact, there are actually many apparent proofs of the reality of the human soul. For example, think of the writings in holy books such as the Bible, Quran, Torah, Bhagavad Gita, etc. These books are replete with wondrous apparent evidence for the reality of the soul expressed in the form of "divinely" inspired words of prophets, miraculous cures and events, prophecies, visions of holy figures, or visions of a life after death. The martyrdom of Stephen, one of the twelve apostles of Jesus, the founding prophet of Christianity, is a good example of one of the apparent proofs of the reality of the soul and an afterlife. Accused of heresy and brought before the Sanhedrin, the supreme court of ancient Israel, Stephen soundly berated and accused its members of heresy.

> [1.12]*When the members of the Sanhedrin heard this, they were furious and gnashed their teeth at him. But Stephen, full of the Holy Spirit, looked up to heaven and saw the glory of God, and Jesus standing at the right hand of God. "Look," he said, "I see heaven open and the Son of Man standing at the right hand of God."*
>
> *At this they covered their ears and, yelling at the top of their voices, they all rushed at him, dragged him out of the city and began to stone him. Meanwhile, the witnesses laid their coats at the feet of a young man named Saul.*
>
> *While they were stoning him, Stephen prayed, "Lord Jesus, receive my spirit." Then he fell on his knees and cried out, "Lord, do not hold this sin against them." When he had said this, he fell asleep [died]. (Bible, New International Version, Acts 7: 54-60)*

[1.13]So before, and while being stoned to death, Stephen had visions of the religious entities in which he believed. Fellow believers undoubtedly heard of this wondrous vision, which must have bolstered their faith in the truth of this new religious sect called Christianity. Here was proof of the reality of God, as well as proof of the divine nature of Jesus!

[1.14]Followers of Islam also report similar divine visions. Consider the "night flight", or "Miraj", of Mohammed (570-632 CE), the founding prophet of Islam. Sometime during the year 621 CE, Mohammed slept in the Kaaba, which is now the holiest sanctum of the Islamic faith. As he slept, the Archangel Gabriel provided Mohammed with a winged creature called a "Buraq", upon which he rode to the furthest mosque. The location of this furthest mosque is uncertain. It may have been in Jerusalem, a distance of about 1200 kilometers from Mecca, or it may have been in Medina, a distance of about 380 kilometers from Mecca. Regardless which of these two locations is correct, this was an impossible feat in 621 CE—a period when the fastest mode of transport was a horse—an animal whose maximum speed over a short distance is at most 70.76 km/h (43.97 mph), after which it is exhausted. After praying at the furthest mosque, Mohammed proceeded to make a lightning visit to hell and heaven where he met and spoke with Moses, Aaron, Adam, and Allah, before returning in the morning to the Kaaba in Mecca.

[1.15]*Glory to (Allah) Who did take His servant for a Journey by night from the Sacred Mosque to the farthest Mosque, whose precincts We did bless,— in order that We might show him some of Our Signs: for He is the One Who heareth and seeth (all things). (Quran, Yusuf Ali translation, 17:1)*

[1.16]This is a marvelous report of a journey at speeds impossible during 621 CE. Moreover, this journey was accompanied by visions of figures from the Islamic pantheon, as well including a visit to the immaterial universe inhabited by God.

[1.17]But these are unsubstantiated accounts in ancient holy texts. Out-of-body experiences, deathbed experiences, and near-death experiences provide more modern, secular, and apparently demonstrable evidence for the reality of a separate immaterial soul associated with the human body (Lommel 2010, Long 2010, Moody 1976, Muldoon 1973, Sabom 1998). Accounts of such secular experiences are very different to those in ancient holy texts.

[1.18]*I lost so much blood I was becoming unconscious. I felt my body separate. I was lying beside my own body. I looked over and watched the nurses and doctors working on my dead body. I myself felt very content and peaceful. I was free of pain and had a very happy feeling. I thought, if this was death it is beautiful. The thought of my family helped me to hang on to life, although I felt all my troubles were gone at the time. I couldn't feel a thing except peace and ease and quietness. (pages 67-68 in Rawlings 1979)*

[1.19]People of all cultures report undergoing such experiences. They arouse a sense of wonder, and form a body of evidence apparently proving belief in the reality of an immaterial soul capable of separating from the body. Indeed, throughout all known human history, reports of such experiences provide ostensible secular and religious "proof" for the widespread human belief in the reality of an immaterial soul.

[1.20]Massive advances made in the sciences of chemistry, physics, biology, and medicine since the latter half of the nineteenth century changed the ways many people viewed the relationship between mind and body. Paul Carus (1852-1919) was one of those who explored the relationship between these new discoveries of science and established religions. He called himself an "atheist who loved God", but nonetheless provided an interesting secular apparent proof of the human soul in a book called *The Soul of Man*. As he stated in this book, the components of the body continuously undergo change. However, the mind remains seemingly unchanged despite continuous replacement of the cells and tissues of the body, as well as the fact these tissues also adjust to age, diet, exercise, and disease.

> [1.21]*Man's soul does not consist of matter; nor can it be a substance like matter, such as are fluids or gaseous and ether-like substances. Conceptions, that materialize the soul, are the materialistic views of spiritists. It is not matter which makes of us that which we are, it is not substance, but form; and the formation of a man's life does not commence with his birth, nor does it end with his death.*
>
> *Our material existence is constantly changing, and yet we remain the same persons today that we were yesterday. How is this? It is because man's life consists not of his material presence alone, but of his formal being, and his formal being shows relatively more continuity than his material existence. There is a law of the conservation of matter and energy, but there is another law of no less importance, which I will call the law of the preservation of form. (pages 419-420 in Carus 1891)*

[1.22]There are two possible interpretations of this interesting concept. Those believing mind to be a product of body function say the substance and cells of the body may change, but their organization in the structures forming the components of body remains constant. This would explain the constant nature of the human mind. Therefore, no further discussion as to the origin of the human mind is required according to the mind-model of materialism. Believers in the mind-model of dualism view such evidence differently. Just as Paul Carus, they could justifiably claim that the constant properties of the individual human mind clearly indicates the reality of an unchanging immaterial "something", such as an individual soul coupled to, and controlling each living human body. This example illustrates an important point. The phenomenon of unchanging properties of the individual conscious human mind, as illustrated by this passage written by Paul Carus, is explicable with the mind-model of materialism as well as that of dualism. This passage provides no information enabling any provable differentiation between the mind-models of materialism or dualism. So which of these two mind-models is correct?

Differentiating between materialism and dualism

[1.23]The prime purpose of this book is an evidence-based examination and differentiation of these two mind-models. Materialism states that the physical structures and processes within the body generate all living human properties and attributes, such as consciousness and mind. However, as believers in dualism point out, it is also possible that a separate controlling influence, such as an immaterial soul, activates and controls these same physical structures and processes within the human body, to manifest human properties such as consciousness and mind. It is impossible to detect or measure anything immaterial. So the only way to demonstrate the presence of an immaterial soul, is indirectly by the manifestations of the soul through the mechanisms of the physical body.

[1.24]Simply claiming that the soul is invisible, immaterial, and separable from the human body yields no insights or methods with which to determine the reality of the soul. So the first step in the process of differentiating between the mind-models of materialism and dualism is to determine the properties of the immaterial soul as revealed by the human body. Subsequent analysis of the effects of disorders, diseases, and drugs, on the manifestations of these properties of the soul by the human body may well reveal whether dualism or materialism is the better explanation. The process of evidence-based differentiation between the mind-models of materialism and dualism in this book employs just this approach. But it is first necessary to have a careful definition of the term "soul" before commencing any study of the nature and origin of the human mind.

The names of the soul

[1.25]The first question requiring definition is what people mean and understand by a human "soul". Different people have equally many ideas about the nature of the human soul, as well as the meaning of this term.

There are several names used interchangeably to express the concept of the human "soul". These are names such as the "astral body", "non-local consciousness", "separable conscious mind", "separable consciousness", "immaterial conscious mind", "separable immaterial conscious mind", etc. All these are rather bulky terms, actually meaning no more than the ancient definition of the human soul as something invisible, immaterial, and separable from the human body. Furthermore, there is no way to determine whether the mind and the soul are one and the same, or two different things altogether. All popular belief systems, popular literature, and major religious texts indicate that the soul is the immaterial vehicle of the equally immaterial mind, or the mind itself. So I shall do away with all these wordy definitions which all mean much the same, and use the ancient and well-known term "soul" throughout this book.

Defining the properties of the soul

[1.26]What is this soul? What does it do? What is the nature of its relationship to the physical body? More importantly, what do most people believe to be the demonstrable and proven properties of the soul? Some people might quibble about the use of the term "properties" instead of "attributes". So what are the exact definitions of these terms?

- [1.27]An *attribute* is defined as "a quality ascribed to any person or thing ... an epithet or appellation in which that quality is ascribed." E.g. mercy, beauty, etc. (Shorter Oxford Dictionary, third Edition)
- [1.28]A *property* is defined as "an attribute belonging to a thing or a person ... any quality which is common to the whole of a class, but is not necessary to mark out that class from other classes." (Shorter Oxford Dictionary, third Edition)

[1.29]The gender of the human soul is unknown, and believers in reincarnation believe it may even be transferrable between animals and humans. So all we can definitely say is that the soul is an immaterial something, with properties much as the chemical and physical properties of a solid object, a gas, a liquid, or a machine. This is why the term properties is used in this book instead of the term "attributes". This book uses popular definitions of the properties of the soul. Using a popular, instead of a very scientific or philosophical definition of the soul may seem strange, but this is a definition explicitly and implicitly believed by about 70% of all people in modern Western countries. This raises the concept of explicit and implicit properties. So what are explicit and implicit properties of the soul?

- [1.30]An *explicit property* of the soul is one which is clearly described. For example, the soul can separate from the body, or is immaterial, can "hear", can "see", can report what is observed during out-of-body experiences, etc.
- [1.31]An *implicit property* of the soul is one which is not expressly stated, but which must exist if other explicit properties are present. For example, a disembodied soul must remember what it undergoes during out-of-body, or near-death experiences if the content of these experiences is subsequently reported other people. This means that memory is an implicit property of the soul.

[1.32]I call these properties "apparent", because these are the properties of the soul that are apparent to those undergoing, or hearing the various manifestations they attribute to the immaterial soul. Moreover, these are the explicit and implicit properties of the soul as expounded in innumerable religious and popular secular texts such as: the *Holy Bible*, the *Holy Quran*, the *Bhagavad Gita*, the *Upanishads*, *The Egyptian Book of the Dead* (Budge 1913), *The Tibetan Book of the Dead* (Evans-Wentz 1960), *Science and the Near-Death Experience* (Carter 2010), *The Truth in the Light* (Fenwick 1996), *The Handbook of Near-Death Experiences* (Holden 2009), *Irreducible Mind* (Kelly 2007), *Consciousness Beyond Life* (Lommel 2010), *Evidence of the Afterlife* (Long 2010), *Life after Life* (Moody 1976), *The Projection of the Astral Body* (Muldoon 1973), *Beyond Death's Door* (Rawlings 1979), *Life & Death* (Sabom 1998), and many more. So what are these properties of the soul?

Each person has an individual soul

[1.33]All accounts of out-of-body experiences, experiences in some transcendental other world such as heaven or hell, and near-death experiences, explicitly and implicitly reveal the belief that each individual human body has a separate and individual soul. This is an ancient belief dating back to a time before the building of the pyramids of Giza, more than 4500 years ago in Egypt. Ancient Egyptians first expressed this belief in pyramid and tomb texts, and later as writings on papyri placed in the coffins of the wealthier deceased. One of these texts is an explicit expression of this belief in the separate and individual nature of the soul of the scribe "Ani" in an afterlife among the gods.

9

[1.34]*Hail, O ye who make perfect souls to enter into the House of Osiris [author - the universe inhabited by the souls of the dead], make ye the well-instructed soul of the Osiris [author - Osiris was a generic name for the deceased] the scribe Ani, whose word is true, to enter in and to be with you in the House of Osiris. Let him hear even as ye hear; let him have sight even as ye have sight; let him stand up even as ye stand up; let him take his seat even as ye take your seats.*

Hail, O ye who give cakes and ale to perfect souls in the House of Osiris, give ye cakes and ale twice each day (i.e., in the morning and in the evening) to the soul of the Osiris Ani, whose word is true before the gods, the Lords of Abydos, and whose word is true with you. (pages 360-361 in Volume 2, Budge 1913)

[1.35]This is a simplistic, but very clear expression of the fact that each deceased human has an individual soul. The Islamic *Holy Quran* expresses this same ancient belief differently.

[1.36]*(To the righteous soul will be said:) "O (thou) soul, in (complete) rest and satisfaction! Come back thou to thy Lord, — well pleased (thyself), and well-pleasing unto Him! Enter thou, then, among My devotees!" (Quran, Yusuf Ali translation, 89:27-29)*

[1.37]This passage simply states that God only accepts the individual souls of the righteous into heaven. Though ancient, this belief in the individual nature of the human soul is still very contemporary. Modern accounts of near-death and out-of-body experiences reveal the same experience of apparent separation of an individual conscious mind, or soul, from the body. For example, here is an account reported by man who described his near-death experience undergone during a cardiac arrest.

[1.38]*It felt like an elephant's foot standing in the middle of my chest. I was sweating and about to vomit when I noticed that I was losing consciousness. Everything was turning black. My heart stopped beating! I heard the nurses shouting "Code 99, Code 99!" One of them dialed the phone to the hospital loud speaker. As they were doing this I could feel myself leaving by body from the headward portion, detaching and floating in the air without any sensation of falling. Then I was lightly standing on my feet watching the nurses push down on my chest. Two more nurses came in and one was wearing a rose on her uniform. Two more*

10

nurses came in and one orderly and then I noticed that they had gotten my doctor back from his visits in the hospital. He had seen me earlier. When he came into the room, I wondered why he was here. I felt fine! (pages 74-75, Rawlings 1979)

[1.39]The man reporting this account told of his individual conscious mind separating from his individual body. He made no mention of his mind uniting any sort of universal consciousness—his apparently separated mind retained its individual identity. This belief in an individual soul coupled to each individual human body is also implicitly and explicitly expressed in all secular accounts of transcendental experiences, out-of-body experiences, and near death experiences. Such a belief is contrary to another, more modern belief system claiming that the whole universe is a manifestation of consciousness (Shanahan 2005, Whitworth 2010), a sort of "virtual reality" construct as a product of some universal consciousness (Whitworth 2010).

[1.40]*While never commonly held, the idea that physical reality isn't the ultimate reality has a long pedigree. In Buddhism, the discriminated world is just an effect created by a universal "essence of mind" that underlies all. (page 224 in Whitworth 2010)*

[1.41]This concept implies the absence of individual consciousness, but that interpersonal variations in the mechanisms of each individual body through which universal consciousness is expressed and modified, gives rise to the idea of individual consciousness (Shanahan 2005). Nonetheless, this is not a popular belief. Moreover, the retention of individual consciousness during apparent separation of the conscious mind from the body during near-death, and out-of-body experiences, seems to contradict this idea. Most people simply believe in the reality of a separate individual human soul.

The soul can separate from the body

[1.42]The prior discussion of the individual human soul revealed the concept of an individual human soul, as well as the fact this soul is able to separate from the human body. Many of the accounts of near-death and out-of-body experiences cited elsewhere in this book reveal the same experiences and belief system. Many people believe that temporary separation of the soul from the body occurs during sleep, unconsciousness, out-of-body experiences, and near-death experiences. Permanent separation of the soul from the body occurs at the moment of

11

death of the body. These beliefs apparently explain the observed differences between persons who are clearly dead, and those who are unconscious, sleeping, or under general anesthesia. This ability of the soul to separate from the body is a belief beautifully expressed in the Dawood translation of the *Quran*.

> [1.43]*God takes away men's souls upon their death, and the souls of the living during their sleep. Those that are doomed He keeps with Him, and restores the others for a time ordained. Surely there are signs in this for thinking men. (Quran, Dawood translation, 39:42)*

The soul is invisible

[1.44]Millennia of human experience teaches that the soul is invisible. Proof of this is evident. For example, since time immemorial, people have raptly observed the death-throes of individuals publicly subjected to death by impaling, crucifixion, hanging, stabbing, beheading, or shooting. Yet in all these millennia, none of the millions of spectators of these sad events has ever reported seeing the souls of these dying individuals departing from their bodies. Likewise, throughout all known ages of humankind, executioners, murderers, and soldiers have never reported seeing souls departing the suddenly lifeless bodies of the countless millions of people they killed. More recently, photographic, film, and video recordings of persons dying during executions and wars never reveal souls departing the bodies of dying persons. Furthermore, no one ever reports seeing, photographing or filming the soul departing the physical body of a person undergoing an out-of-body experience (Lempert 1994, Lempert 1994a, Tart 1969, fifth study in Tart 1998). All these facts prove the invisible nature of the human soul.

The soul and the life after death are immaterial

[1.45]The next property of the soul is its immaterial nature. This is yet another of the more self-evident properties of the soul. Evidence of the immaterial nature of the soul is provided by the fact that the soul passes through solid matter such as the human body, walls, doors, and roofs without any apparent resistance. A fragment of an out-of-body experience reported by an automobile accident victim illustrates just this property of the soul.

> [1.46]*People were walking up from all directions to get to the wreck. I could see them, and I was in the middle of a very narrow*

walkway. Anyway, as they came by they wouldn't seem to notice me. They would just keep walking with their eyes straight ahead. As they came real close, I would try to turn around, to get out of their way, but they would just walk through me. (page 45 in Moody 1976)

[1.47]The apparently disembodied immaterial human soul can even pass through reinforced concrete floors without any apparent resistance. A woman reported this latter ability of the soul during an out-of-body experience she underwent while undergoing resuscitation for cardiac arrest during 1985 in the Hartford Hospital, Hartford, Connecticut.

[1.48]*She told me how she floated up over her body, viewed the resuscitation effort for a short time and then felt herself being pulled up through several floors of the hospital. She then found herself above the roof and realized she was looking at the skyline of Hartford. She marvelled at how interesting this view was and out of the corner of her eye she saw a red object. It turned out to be a shoe ... (Case 1 in Ring 1993)*

[1.49]Relatively modern, multiple story hospitals, such as the Hartford Hospital in Connecticut, have sturdy reinforced concrete floors. Seemingly effortless passage of the conscious mind through several of the reinforced concrete floors of this hospital is certainly proof of the immaterial nature of the soul and mind. The same is also true of the universe inhabited by the souls of the dead. For many millennia, people from all known civilizations have believed in the reality of such a universe. Yet no one has ever seen, photographed, filmed, or otherwise objectively detected this universe. This indicates the insubstantial or immaterial nature of this universe supposedly harboring the souls of the deceased.

The soul is continually conscious

[1.50]Since ancient times, people have believed the soul never sleeps and is continually conscious. Quintus Septimius Florens Tertullianus, otherwise known simply as Tertullian (160-220 CE), was an ancient Christian theologian. In a book entitled *A Treatise on the Soul*, he expounded current beliefs regarding the relation of dreams to the functioning of the conscious mind, which he believed to be a manifestation of the functioning of the soul.

[1.51]Meanwhile the soul is circumstanced in such a manner as to seem to be elsewhere active, learning to bear future absence by a dissembling of its presence for the moment. We shall soon know the case of Hermotimus. But yet it dreams in the interval. Whence then its dreams? The fact is, it cannot rest or be idle altogether, nor does it confine to the still hours of sleep the nature of its immortality. It proves itself to possess a constant motion; it travels over land and sea, it trades, it is excited, it labours, it plays, it grieves, it rejoices, it follows pursuits lawful and unlawful; it shows what very great power it has even without the body, how well equipped it is with members of its own, although betraying at the same time the need it has of impressing on some body its activity again. (pages 222-223, chapter XLIII in Tertullian 1918)

[1.52]These same ideas were also prevalent among other earlier Christian theologians such as Saint Augustine (354-430 CE). Saint Augustine was a Bishop in Hippo, an ancient city in Algeria, now called Annaba. He wrote the following passage in a book called *On the Soul and its Origin*.

[1.53]Now, in dreams, when we suffer anything harsh and troublesome, we are, of course, still ourselves; and if the distress do not pass away when we awake, we experience very great suffering. But to suppose that they are veritable bodies in which we are hurried, or flit, about hither and thither in dreams, is the idea of a person who has thought only carelessly on such subjects; for it is in fact mainly by these imaginary sights that the soul is proved to be non-corporeal; unless you choose to call even the objects which we see so often in our dreams, besides ourselves, bodies, such as the sky, the earth, the sea, the sun, the moon, the stars, and rivers, mountains, trees, or animals. Whoever takes these phantoms to be bodies, is incredibly foolish; [they are not bodies], although they are certainly very like bodies. Of this character also are those phenomena which are demonstrably of divine significance, whether seen in dreams or in a trance. Who can possibly trace out or describe their origin, or the material of which they consist? It is, beyond question, spiritual, not corporeal. (page 323 in chapter 25, book IV, Augustine 1874)

[1.54]In other words, the soul is supposedly continually conscious, even when the body is apparently unconscious during sleep. Reports of disembodiment of the conscious mind occurring during apparent loss of consciousness of the physical body caused by cardiac arrest, general anesthesia, head injuries, etc., seemingly confirm this property of the soul. This property of the soul raises another fascinating and obvious question. Is the soul also continuously conscious during the eternal afterlife proposed by many religions?

The soul controls the physical body

[1.55]Many people believe the soul is the source of all consciousness and properties of mind that somehow interacts with the physical body, to control the body through the mechanisms of the brain, so manifesting speech, emotions, personality, and actions on this physical world (Carter 2010, Muldoon 1973). The holy texts of Christianity and Islam also implicitly express this belief. For example, the Quran, the holy text of Islam, informs us in very graphic terms that the fate of the soul in an afterlife depends upon the control it exerts upon the body to produce thoughts, speech, and deeds during life.

> [1.56]*Say, "The truth is from your Lord": Let him who will believe, and let him who will, reject (it): for the wrong-doers We have prepared a fire whose (smoke and flames), like the walls and roof of a tent, will hem them in: if they implore relief they will be granted water like melted brass, that will scald their faces, how dreadful the drink! How uncomfortable a couch to recline on! (Quran, Yusuf Ali translation, 18: 29)*

[1.57]The Quran is replete with many similar passages all indicating the same belief—the fate of the soul in an afterlife depends upon the control it exerts over the physical body during physical life. Mohammed, the founding prophet of Islam, was not expressing a new belief. This belief was ancient even before his birth. The texts forming the *New Testament* of the Christian Bible, the holy text of Christianity, expressed this same ancient belief more than 500 years before the birth of Mohammed. A passage in the Christian Bible reveals this same belief in a passage describing the resurrection of the souls of all humans on some future "day of judgment".

> [1.58]*But the fearful, and unbelieving, and the abominable, and murderers, and whoremongers, and sorcerers, and idolaters, and all liars, shall have their part in the lake which burneth with fire and brimstone: which is the second death. (Bible, King James Version, Revelations, 21:8)*

15

1.59This passage makes it very clear that resurrected souls will not be judged only by what they may have intended, but also according to the deeds and thoughts of the bodies they controlled while alive on this world. All such statements about the fate of the soul in an afterlife unmistakably imply a belief that the soul controls the physical body. If this were not so, the immaterial soul would not be punished or rewarded in an afterlife for the speech, actions, and deeds of the physical body during life. This belief was ancient even before the lifetime of Jesus of Nazareth, the founding prophet of Christianity (30-0 BCE). The ancient Greek philosopher Plato (427-347 BCE), expressed this same belief in rather more direct terms more than 2,300 years ago in the form of a dialogue.

> 1.60*Yet once more consider the matter in this light: When the soul and the body are united, then nature orders the soul to rule and govern, and the body to obey and serve. Now which of these two functions is akin to the divine? And which to the mortal? Does not the divine appear to you to be that which naturally orders and rules, and the mortal that which is subject and servant?*
> *True.*
> *And which does the soul resemble?*
> *The soul resembles the divine, and the body the mortal there can be no doubt of that, Socrates. (page 102 in Plato 1900).*

1.61The antiquity of this belief is known to extend even further back in time, long before the building of the Giza pyramids in Egypt more than 4,500 years ago. More recently, philosophers such as Henri Bergson (1859-1941) also wrestled with the relationship of the body to the soul. The final conclusion of Henri Bergson was clear. Just as implied by the ancient writers of many holy texts, he and other contemporaries believed that the immaterial soul was the source of consciousness, the source of all attributes of mind, and the repository of all memories. Emil Wilm, an American philosopher, pithily summarized Henri Bergson's ideas on the relationship between the mind and the brain in 1914.

> 1.62*Consciousness or pure memory (as distinguished from habit) is a purely psychical mode of existence, and does not depend for its functioning upon the material dispositions of the brain. The brain does not secrete thought, as the liver secretes bile, to use an old illustration, or as heated water produces steam, it merely transmits it, as a glass window pane transmits light, or a metal rod transmits heat. (page 163 in Wilm 1914)*

[1.63]Others seized upon this same idea of the soul interacting with the body, using the body as a receiver and conduit to manifest control of the body by the soul, expressing this belief in clear and unambiguous terms.

[1.64]*This may appear paradoxical to one who is accustomed to the idea that the conscious mind is a part of the physical mechanism. In fact, the material body has no mind at all, but clings over the astral [the soul], to speak symbolically, which is the real 'Ego'— through which the conscious mind really functions. It is erroneous to believe that the astral being has a super-mentality. It has not. The conscious mind, as you know it, is the mind of the astral body. Your normal, conscious mind—everything it contains—is the YOU, you the individual, now and throughout eternity, learning as it goes. (pages 48-49 in Muldoon 1973)*

[1.65]So the body is merely the receiver, conduit, and executor of the controlling influence of the soul, much like a radio receiver is a conduit for signals from a radio station, converting them into intelligible audible sounds or music. The signal from the radio station is unaffected by factors affecting the functioning of the radio receiver, while things affecting the functioning of the radio receiver certainly affect the way the radio signal is expressed by the radio receiver (page 13 in Carter 2010). For example, if the radio receiver malfunctions, the radio may not convert the radio signal into intelligible sounds or music, but only produce garbled noise in response to the radio signal. In other words, a radio receiver modifies the radio signal in a way determined by the functioning of the receiver. The same is also true of the relationship of the controlling soul to the human body. The functioning of the soul is unaffected by the physical body, but the behavior, speech, and thoughts initiated in the physical body by the controlling influence of the soul are affected by the functioning of the body. Accordingly, this analogy opens the possibility that the functioning of the physical body under a diversity of conditions may well reveal at least some properties of the human soul.

The soul is unaffected by things affecting the body

[1.66]Even more interestingly, the soul is believed to be unaffected by anything affecting the body. We know this, because some people report periods of awareness and apparently clear consciousness, even undergoing out-of-body experiences, while "clinically dead" due to cardiac arrest, or while apparently unconscious under general anesthesia. A woman called Pam Reynolds once made an extensive report of just such an experience. She suddenly awoke while apparently unconscious during a brain operation performed under general anesthesia.

1.67The next thing I recall was the sound: It was a natural D. As I listened to the sound, I felt it was pulling me out of the top of my head. The further out of my body I got, the more clear the tone became. I had the impression it was like a road, a frequency that you go on ... I remember seeing several things in the operating room when I was looking down. It was the most aware that I think that I have ever been in my entire life ... I was metaphorically sitting on Dr. Spetzler's [the surgeon] shoulder. It was not like normal vision. It was brighter and more focused and clearer than normal vision ... There was so much in the operating room that I didn't recognize, and so many people. (page 41 in Sabom 1998)

1.68This woman was fully aware, and reported that her mental function at the time was clearer than normal, even though her physical body was ostensibly unconscious under general anesthesia. Many other people also report experiencing periods of clear consciousness, together with equally clear perceptions of their surroundings while apparently unconscious due to a variety of disorders. This was graphically illustrated by the example of a 40 year old man who underwent a near-death experience induced by cardiac arrest, during which he reported experiencing clear mental function and perceptive abilities.

*1.69A 40 year-old male patient who had an out-of-hospital ventricular fibrillation (VF) in the presence of a general practitioner and who needed 15 defibrillation attempts to establish spontaneous circulation (22 min elapsed between the call for help and restoration of spontaneous circulation (ROSC) [...] "Although I couldn't give a single sign of being alive, I wittingly went through large parts of the critical period, in a way that I heard everything. However, I was in no fear. It seemed like a beautiful mystical light (which I saw on my feet) attracted me stronger than the will to stay. That light was more than the physical light, more comprising. Not to be absorbed by that light—which seemed glorious—in order to know that I had to stay here it was necessary for me to hear the voices of my surroundings and next of kin. I also saw slides of my past."
(Martens 1994)*

1.70The lack of any apparent effect of severe cerebral hypoxia (cerebral = brain, and hypoxia = oxygen starvation of all or part of the body), on the mental function of this man in this, and many other similar cases, is often regarded as clear evidence that the soul is unaffected by disorders affecting the physical body. This belief is not new. Ancient Hindu religious texts such as the *Bhagavad-Gita*, also teach the same belief that the immaterial soul is unaffected by disorders affecting the physical body.

> [1.71] *This individual soul is unbreakable and insoluble, and can be neither burned nor dried. He is everlasting, present everywhere, unchangeable, immovable and eternally the same. (Bhagavad-Gita As It Is, 24:24)*

[1.72]The *Holy Bible*, the main Christian religious text, expresses this same belief by differentiating between killing of the body and killing the soul.

> [1.73]*And fear not them which kill the body, but are not able to kill the soul: but rather fear him which is able to destroy both soul and body in hell. (Bible, Matthew 10: 28)*

[1.74]The belief that factors affecting the functioning of the physical body do not affect the functioning of the soul is a fundamental and very evident property of the soul. However, this belief as expressed above is not entirely accurate. According to the mind-model of dualism, the soul also controls the physical body to react appropriately in response to physical sensory perceptions of the body, such as speech, sight, touch, smell, etc. This belief clearly implies the transmission of information from physical perceptions from the body to the soul, upon which the soul reacts appropriately to control the body in a manner consistent with these perceptions. Accordingly, things affecting the material body can indirectly influence the immaterial soul.

[1.75]Such a reciprocal transmission of information between the soul and the body is by its very nature subject to limitations imposed by the nature of the soul and the physical body. This means that the body filters and affects the type of information transmitted to the soul. Likewise, the functioning of the body also affects the expression of information transmitted to it by the soul. So if the body makes incorrect perceptions due to malfunction of sensory organs, or malfunction of processing of sensory information by the brain, then the soul will respond to this incorrect sensory information by activating the body to respond to these incorrect perceptions. Such responses will manifest as inappropriate, or unpredictable movements, actions, speech, behavior and deeds. This may seem an academic point, but is very relevant to any examination of the relationship between the body and the soul.

The brain filters and limits the soul

[1.76]A totally clear and fault-free interaction between something immaterial and something physical is a troublesome concept. It is always possible that disorders and the limitations of the physical body will affect or modify the expression of the immaterial soul. Ancient philosophers also implied the same in their writings. More than 2000 years ago, the ancient Roman statesman, Marcus Tullius Cicero wrote about how he viewed the relationship of the soul to the physical body.

> [1.77]*Again, you really see nothing resembling death so much as sleep; and yet it is when the body sleeps that the soul most clearly manifests its divine nature; for when it is unfettered and free it sees many things that are to come. Hence we know what the soul's future state will be when it has been wholly released from the shackles of the flesh. (page 93 in De Senectute - Cicero 1996)*

[1.78]So Cicero believed the soul is shackled and imprisoned, or at best limited in its expression by the material flesh of the body. But he was not expressing a new thought when he wrote this passage more than 2,000 years ago. This same belief was ancient even during his lifetime. More than 1900 years later, the English philosopher, Ferdinand Cannon Scott Schiller (1864-1937), reworded this same ancient belief. In a pseudonymously published book called *Riddles of the Sphinx*, he proposed that the brain is not only a conduit for the expression of the soul, but that the physical brain filters, limits, or inhibits the expression of the soul.

> [1.79]*And this gives the final answer to Materialism: it consists in showing in detail what was asserted at the outset, viz., that Materialism is a hysteron proteron, a putting of the cart before the horse, which may be rectified by just inverting the connection between Matter and consciousness. Matter is not that which produces consciousness, but that which limits it and confines its intensity within certain limits: material organization does not construct consciousness out of arrangements of atoms, but contracts its manifestation within the sphere which it permits. (page 295 in Schiller 1891)*

[1.80]At the same time as Ferdinand Schiller wrote these words, a contemporary of his, the French philosopher Henri Bergson, was also proposing the same ideas on the filtering or limiting function of the brain. The philosophy of Henri Bergson was summarized by Emil Wilm in a book entitled *Henri Bergson: A Study in Radical Evolution* (Wilm 1914), revealing that Bergson had the same ideas as Schiller.

> [1.81] *In Bergson, too, the brain's function is merely transmissive rather than productive. Just as light, heat or electricity cannot pass through matter by any path, but must take whatever route it can, whatever path it finds most pervious, so consciousness can express itself only through such forms of matter as it finds pervious to the particular kind of energy which it represents. The brain might then be thought of as composed of a kind of matter fitted to act as the carrier of consciousness, a kind which, so to speak, consciousness can penetrate.*
>
> *The main significance of the brain in Bergson, however, is not derived from the fact that it transmits ideas, but from the fact that it fails to do so! So far from the brain's being an organ of reminiscence, it is rather an organ of oblivion! It acts as a sort of mask or screen which shuts the great mass of our ideas from view. The purpose of ideas and experiences, it must be remembered, is the guidance of action. But in order that action may be effective, only such ideas must be recalled as are relevant to the situation or the problem towards which action is pointed. Without the intervention of the brain the flow of ideas would be so copious as to paralyse action. (pages 106-107 in Wilm 1914)*

[1.82]The idea of a filtering, or limiting effect of the physical brain, is actually quite a logical proposal when one considers that more than 50% of people report feelings of enhanced mental capacities during experiences of apparent disembodiment of the soul, such as near-death experiences (Greyson 1983, page 56 in Long 2010). Enhanced mental capacity during near-death experiences manifest in ways such as a feeling of cosmic unity, unusually vivid thoughts, unusually vivid senses and perceptions, sudden understanding of everything, events seem instantaneous, and unusually rapid thinking (Greyson 1983). Indeed, the separated soul appears to possess almost superhuman intelligence and understanding, as well as senses more acute than those of the physical body. Ferdinand Schiller concluded all these things were consistent with dualism, as well as being a better explanation for supernatural phenomena.

21

1.83 This explanation does not involve the denial either of the facts or of the principle involved in Materialism, viz., the unity of all life and the continuity of all existence. It admits the connection of Matter and consciousness, but contends that the course of interpretation must proceed in the contrary direction. Thus it will fit the facts alleged in favour of Materialism equally well, besides enabling us to understand facts which Materialism rejected as "supernatural." It explains the lower by the higher, Matter by Spirit, instead of vice versa, and thereby attains to an explanation which is ultimately tenable instead of one which is ultimately absurd. (page 295 in Schiller 1891)

1.84 The opinions of Bergson and Schiller are unmistakable expressions of a belief that the expression of the soul on this world is filtered, limited, or inhibited by the structures and functioning of the physical body. William James (1842-1910), an American philosopher and psychologist, considered this concept seriously. He also asked the interesting question whether the soul freed from the material body would actually possess the same properties of mind as when confined within the physical body.

1.85 Our finitenesses and limitations seem to be our personal essence; and when the finiting organ drops away, and our several spirits revert to their original source and resume their unrestricted condition, will they then be anything like those sweet streams of feeling which we know, and which even now our brains are sifting out from the great reservoir for our enjoyment here below? (pages 29-30 in James 1898)

1.86 William James developed this, and other ideas of Bergson and Schiller further (James 1898). This idea of the filtering, or limiting effect of matter on the expression of the conscious mind, has since been enthusiastically endorsed and perpetuated by other proponents of dualism ever since. Jeffrey Long, a Louisiana physician, implied the same belief based on a large database of self-reported near-death experiences.

1.87 Of 613 NDErs [near-death experiencers] surveyed, 74.4 percent indicated they had "More consciousness and alertness than normal"; 19.9 percent experienced "Normal consciousness and alertness"; and only 5.7 percent had "Less consciousness and alertness than normal." (page 56 in Long 2010)

[1.88]Doctor Jeffrey Long proposed on the basis of these statistics, that the disembodied soul has greater awareness, alertness, and intelligence than the mind in the physical body (pages 53-56 in Long 2010), as well as heightened sensory abilities (pages 60-64 in Long 2010). Other authors also claim this is the true nature of the conscious mind, as is revealed when the soul apparently separates from the physical body during near-death experiences (chapter 1 in Carter 2010, pages 160-161 in Lommel 2010).

The soul has the same mind as the body

[1.89]Nonetheless, belief in the superior intellect of the soul is by no means universal. Major religions from time immemorial have never propagated a belief in the superior nature of the soul. In fact, religious beliefs reveal something very different about the mental capacities of the soul. All religions claim that God is just and merciful. Accordingly, God would never condemn a soul to eternal torment for crimes and evil committed by the mortal body if the intelligence of the disembodied and immaterial soul was so superior, that it would never have committed these same crimes and evil for which its body merited eternal anguish. Indeed, the content of many out-of-body, and near-death experiences is often such as to prove that the soul has the same intelligence, personality and emotions as the living body (pages 48-49 in Muldoon 1973). Consider this near-death experience reported by a woman observing the resuscitation of her apparently unconscious body from the consequences of massive internal blood loss after an operation.

[1.90]*"I was brought back to my room after surgery and was speaking to my nurse," she reminisced in 1979, "when a strange separated feeling between my body and my brain occurred. High above my body I floated wondering why so many doctors were around my bed and why they were doing a venal cut-down when I told them not to." (page 222 in Rogo 1989)*

[1.91]The almost indignant reaction of the disembodied mind of this woman to the ways people were treating her body, reveals she neither knew nor understand at the time why so many doctors were standing around her bed. She even tried telling them to stop doing a venal cut-down to administer a life-saving fluid and blood transfusion. So the few words in this report clearly demonstrate that the disembodied mind of this woman possessed no more than her normal intellect and understanding. Many other spontaneous accounts of people reporting memories of the conscious experiences they underwent during experiences of disembodiment, such as during near-death experiences and out-of-body experiences, reveal the same. The intellect and personality of the disembodied human soul is identical to that of the body when normally conscious (Tiberi 1993). While this finding is inconsistent with the belief that the material substance of the body filters, limits, or inhibits the expression of the true properties of the soul, it is very consistent with popular religious beliefs of reward of the good in heaven, and punishment of the evil in hell.

The soul is the repository of all memories

[1.92]All functions of the physical brain, such as electrical brain activity and consciousness, cease 10 to 30 seconds after the heart stops beating (Aminoff 1988, Clute 1990, Rossen 1943, Visser 2001). Sudden severe brain oxygen starvation is the cause of failure of all brain functions due to all types of cardiac arrest. And while apparently unconscious during cardiac arrest, some people undergo states of disembodiment, such as near-death experiences and out-of-body experiences. Indeed, up to 18% of survivors report undergoing conscious experiences during the period of cardiac arrest and resuscitation (Lommel 2001). These people never physically tell of these experiences as they undergo them—they only report these experiences after regaining physical consciousness and the ability to speak. And because these are memories formed during a period of supposed absent brain function, as revealed by ostensibly absent consciousness at the time, proponents of dualism claim this means these survivors are reporting memories stored within their souls. Indeed, near-death experiences and out-of-body experiences during cardiac arrest, and all manner of other causes of these experiences, are the main evidence provided by the mind-model of dualism as proof that the soul not only forms all memories, but is also the repository of all memories. This is no new concept. Once again, Ferdinand Schiller formulated this same idea during 1891.

[1.93]*And again, if the body is a mechanism for inhibiting consciousness, for preventing the full powers of the Ego from being prematurely actualized, it will be necessary to invert also our ordinary ideas on the subject of memory, and to account for forgetfulness instead of for memory. It will be during life that we drink the bitter cup of Lethe, it will be with our brain that we are enabled to forget. And this will serve to explain not only the*

*extraordinary memories of the drowning and the dying generally,
but also the curious hints which experimental psychology
occasionally affords us that nothing is ever forgotten wholly and
beyond recall. (page 296 in Schiller 1891)*

[1.94]Indeed, many, many anecdotal, and some veridical accounts of near-death experiences and out-of-body experiences provide just such apparent proof of the retention of memories in the soul (Carter 2010, Lommel 2010, Long 2010, Moody 1976, Wade 1998, and many others). Consider the example of the experience of a young man who underwent an out-of-body experience caused by an automobile accident.

*[1.95]Then, I was sort of floating about five feet above the street,
about five yards away from the car, I'd say, and I heard the echo
of the crash dying away. I saw people come running up and
crowding around the car, and I saw my friend get out of the car,
obviously in shock. I could see my own body in the wreckage
among all those people, and could see them trying to get it out.
My legs were all twisted and there was blood all over the place.
(page 37 in Moody 1976)*

[1.96]This superficially simple account reveals profound insights into the memory functions of the human soul. For clarity, I will examine these in a point-by-point fashion.

- [1.97]The above short account refers to several factual and spatial memories such as estimation of distances, recognition of a car, and recognition of up and down. This is clear evidence of recognition based upon long-term memories of experiences and facts learned by his physically conscious body long before the accident. However, his mind was apparently separated from his body at the time he recognized these things, so these memories were evidently recalled from within his disembodied mind.
- [1.98]His apparently disembodied mind recognized the appearance of his body, and the appearance of his friend. This is also clear evidence of recognition based upon long-term memories of his, and his friend's appearances learned during physical consciousness and retained within his now disembodied soul.
- [1.99]His account tells of remembering the last echoes of the car crash, the situation of his body, observing people running to help, as well as all the above things. This indicates transformation of temporarily retained perceptions, observations and experiences, otherwise

known as short-term memories, into permanently retained long-term memories. Furthermore, these events occurred during a period of apparent disembodiment of his conscious mind from his physical body, indicating that transformation of short-term memories into long-term memories occurred within his apparently disembodied conscious mind, or soul.

[1.100]This man was only able to report this account to other people after recovering physical consciousness and the ability to speak. He reported this account to others with the mechanisms of his physical body, such as speech and possibly writing. Moreover, he reported this account sometime after his out-of-body experience, and certainly not during his out-of-body experience. This last fact means his report is the account of a memory of his out-of-body experience subsequently reported through the mechanisms of his physical body. Furthermore, he spontaneously recalled and reported these memories without the application of coercion, drugs, torture, hypnosis, or psychological techniques to extract these memories. This account contained old past memories, as well as new memories formed during a period of disembodiment. So this experience seemingly indicates that the soul is the repository of all memories, as well as the location where short-term memories are transformed into long-term memories.

[1.101]But periods of disembodiment are not restricted to the proximity of the physical body. During near-death experiences, the apparently disembodied conscious minds of some people are apparently transported, or translocate to an immaterial afterlife universe inhabited by the souls of the dead. Accounts of such near-death experiences reveal that apparently disembodied souls can access previous memories when transported to this transcendental afterlife universe. Such accounts also reveal that when the apparently disembodied soul is present in this afterlife universe, it is capable of forming new long-term memories (Chapters 5 and 6 in Carter 2010, Wade 1998). Consider this memory of a visit to the Christian transcendental afterlife universe undergone by a man during a near-death experience caused by a cardiac arrest.

[1.102]*There was a background of music that was beautiful, heavenly music, and I saw two figures walking toward me and I immediately recognized them. They were my mother and father, both had died years ago. My mother was an amputee and yet that leg was now restored! She was walking on two legs! (page 80 in Rawlings 1979)*

[1.103]This short account reveals all the above points. During the period the disembodied soul of this man was present in this transcendental world, his disembodied soul recognized his parents, remembered the fact his mother was an amputee, remembered the miraculous restoration of her amputated leg, as well as remembering the details of the transcendental world they now inhabited. Subsequent to his physical body recovering from the bodily effects of the cardiac arrest, he was able to spontaneously recall and relate these new memories that were formed and retained within his apparently disembodied soul through the mechanisms of his physical body to other physical people.

[1.104]The same is true of all other near-death experiences and out-of-body experiences. Memories of these experiences are spontaneously recalled memories. They are not memories detected by word association tests, drugs, hypnosis, stimulation of the brain with electrical currents, or torture. The physical bodies of these people arouse from the causes of their near-death, or out-of-body experiences, upon which they spontaneously communicate these experiences to other equally physical people using the mechanisms of their physical bodies. We have no other source of knowledge of these experiences. Furthermore, these are spontaneously recalled memories, which require adequate functioning of those mechanisms of the brain and body through which these memories are revealed as speech and writing. So interaction of the soul with the body is essential to reveal the mental activity of the soul, and memory is an essential part of the mental activity of the soul. Indeed, memory is one of the most important fundamental properties of the soul.

[1.105]Retention and formation of memories by the soul is a belief acknowledged by all major world religions such as Christianity and Islam. The roots of this belief extend back as far as ancient Egyptian religious beliefs. For many thousands of years, religions have taught, and still teach, that the fate of the soul in a life after death depends upon the thoughts, speech, and behavior of the physical body during life. After all, why should the soul undergo horrific punishments for the thoughts, speech and deeds of the physical body if it has no control over the physical body, and is not the repository of all memories?

[1.106]The holy book of Islam, *The Quran*, implicitly informs us that all thoughts, speech, and deeds of the body originate within the soul, and are remembered by the soul. Accordingly, after sinners and unbelievers die, angels seize their souls and immediately subject them to unspeakable torments for the transgressions of their bodies on this physical world as they await the Day of Judgment.

1.107If thou couldst see, when the angels take the souls of the Unbelievers (at death), (How) they smite their faces and their backs, (saying): "Taste the penalty of the blazing Fire…" *"Because of (the deeds) which your (own) hands sent forth; for Allah is never unjust to His servants: (Deeds) after the manner of the people of Pharaoh and of those before them: They rejected the Signs of Allah, and Allah punished them for their crimes: for Allah is Strong, and Strict in punishment: because Allah will never change the grace which He hath bestowed on a people until they change what is in their (own) souls: and verily Allah is He Who heareth and knoweth (all things)." (Quran, Yusuf Ali translation, 8:50-53)*

1.108The Quran contains several other passages confirming this belief (Quran, 23:99-100; 32:11). The Christian Bible contains texts antedating the Quran by 600 years and more. It says exactly the same things about the fates of the souls of good and evil persons after death. A parable told by Jesus, (the founding prophet of Christianity), about the fates of the souls of two men, the poor beggar Lazarus and a haughty rich man, is also very clear on this idea of afterlife with its punishments and rewards of the soul for the actions, deeds, and behavior of the body while alive. This passage makes implicit reference to storage of memories within the soul—clearly referring to memories of the earthly thoughts, speech, actions, and situations of the persons concerned.

1.109There was once a rich man who dressed in the most expensive clothes and lived in great luxury every day. There was also a poor man named Lazarus, covered with sores, who used to be brought to the rich man's door, hoping to eat the bits of food that fell from the rich man's table. Even the dogs would come and lick his sores. The poor man died and was carried by the angels to sit beside Abraham at the feast in heaven. The rich man died and was buried, and in Hades, where he was in great pain, he looked up and saw Abraham, far away, with Lazarus at his side. So he called out, 'Father Abraham! Take pity on me, and send Lazarus to dip his finger in some water and cool off my tongue, because I am in great pain in this fire!' But Abraham said, 'Remember, my son, that in your lifetime you were given all the good things, while Lazarus got all the bad things. But now he is enjoying himself here, while you are in pain. Besides all that, there is a deep pit lying between us, so that those who want to cross over from here to you cannot do so, nor can anyone cross over to us from where you are.' The rich man said, 'Then I beg you, father Abraham, send Lazarus to my father's house, where I have five brothers. Let him go and warn them so that they, at least, will not come to this place of pain.' Abraham said, 'Your brothers have Moses and the prophets to warn them; your brothers should listen to what they say.' The rich man answered, 'That is not enough, father Abraham! But if someone were to rise from death and go to them, then they would turn from their sins.' But Abraham said, 'If they will not listen to Moses and the prophets, they will not be convinced even if someone were to rise from death.' (Bible, Good News Translation, Luke 16: 19-31)

[1.110]The Christian Bible contains several other passages supplementing and confirming this belief in the continuation of individual consciousness and memories immediately after death (Bible, Acts 7:59; 2 Corinthians 5:8; Philippians 1:23). Going back even further in time, we read the same beliefs expressed in the ancient Egyptian funerary text, *The Papyrus of Ani*, dating back to more than 3,300 years ago (Budge 1913). Ancient Egyptians believed the soul of the deceased is weighed in the balance of good and evil, and those souls found wanting are destroyed by Ammut—the "Eater of the dead".

[1.111]*This being done Thoth reports formally to the Company of the Gods that Ani's [the deceased person] heart has been weighed, that his soul has borne testimony on his behalf, and that his heart has been found right and true by the Great Balance. Therefore Ani is sinless. He has not purloined any of the property of the gods that was under his charge officially, and he has harmed none either by word or deed. The gods then accept Thoth's report, and declare that Ani is a man true and right, and they declare that he has neither sinned against them nor done harm to them in any way. They next order that he shall not be given over to the Eater of the dead, and that he shall be endowed with an estate in Sekhet-hetepet, with an adequate supply of offerings, and with the right to enter into the presence of Osiris. (page 238 in Volume 1 in Budge 1913).*

[1.112]All these things indicate an ancient belief that the body is controlled by something immaterial that survives the death of the body, and that this immaterial something remembers the thoughts, speech and deeds of the physical body. This is why this immaterial soul must account for the deeds of the physical body in some life after death.

Punishment or reward of the soul in an afterlife implicitly requires that the soul be the indelible repository of all the memories, thoughts, words, and deeds of the body. A soul without memory is just a consciousness existing in the here and now. It would have no knowledge of a past, no awareness of the reasons of its current situation, and no memory of what transpired while in the afterlife. It would have nothing upon which to base thoughts or purpose. Indeed, a soul without memory would be very similar to the situation of a deeply demented person, reacting in the same way as a mindless animal to its situation. Punishment or reward of such a soul in an afterlife would have no purpose. Accordingly, the soul must control the body and be the repository of all memories. Furthermore, the above passages clearly indicate that the fate of the soul in an afterlife depends upon the actions, deeds and behavior of the body it controls. These are implicit and absolutely essential aspects of the ancient belief in the soul as propounded by major world religions.

[1.113]Finally, a book entitled *Science and the Near-Death Experience* written by Chris Carter contains an extensive analysis of the location of memories (Carter 2010). At the conclusion of his extensive analysis of whether memories are located within the physical brain, or in some extracerebral location such as the soul, Chris Carter summarized his findings in the following very definite statement.

> [1.114]*So the upshot from this long-winded discussion is that the notion of extracerebral memories is by no means "totally absurd." We can now see—contrary to Edwards' assertion that "it must surely be dismissed as nothing but a vague picture which is of no scientific value whatsoever"—that the theory of extracerebral memories can be considered more scientific than the mechanistic alternative. One prediction of the theory of memory traces—that they can be localized in the brain—has been convincingly proved false, and the theory is now left with the unfalsifiable ad hoc explanation that memory is stored in several places in the brain. Yet we have seen that the theory of formative causation not only has prima facie support from the available evidence but also entails several easily testable predictions. In Popper's terms, the theory of memory traces has become a metaphysical theory, and the theory of formative causation, with its notion of extracerebral memories, is the remaining scientific alternative! (page 97 in Carter 2010*

[1.115]It is evident, that Chris Carter, and many other people explicitly or implicitly believe all memories are stored within the soul. Indeed,

Edward Kelly logically states in the book, *Irreducible Mind*, that if survival of individual personality after death is a reality, then one of the most fundamental properties of the soul is that it be the repository of all memories (page 295 in Kelly 2007, see 15.111).

The soul can see and hear

[1.116]Another important property of the soul is the ability of the disembodied soul to see with light and hear with sound. There are innumerable examples of this ability during out-of-body experiences occurring as part of countless near-death experiences (see experiences cited in Lommel 2010, Long 2010, Moody 1976, Rawlings 1979, Sabom 1998). Furthermore, many people report that their sensory abilities are wonderfully enhanced when their souls are apparently separated from their bodies during near-death experiences (pages 60-64 in Long 2010).

[1.117]A man whose soul was apparently disembodied during a near-death experience induced by a period of cardiac arrest, reported a clear example of the ability of the apparently disembodied soul to see colors and the surroundings of the physical body with visible light. He described the following.

> *As Darrell [author - the patient] hovered near the ceiling [author - above his physical body], he saw Sandy [author - a nurse] wearing her pink uniform and standing at his right side, near his head. The cardiologist and two other men were clustered around his right leg, two wearing green scrubs and one wearing blue. A male nurse in blue scrubs stood at the foot of the bed on the left side. Suddenly Darrell woke up in his body. "I looked straight up and saw Sandy there." She was dressed in pink. He scanned the room and saw the others, confirming for himself what he had seen from outside of his body. (page 22 in Sabom 1998)*

[1.118]The disembodied soul is apparently also able to hear the physical sounds of speech. The best examples of these accounts are those of people who underwent out-of body experiences while evidently unconscious due to cardiac arrest, or during general anesthesia. Examples of the latter are occasionally reported in international anesthesiology literature (cases 5 and 6 in Moerman 1993, case 4 in Sebel 2004). Consider the following example.

> [1.119]*After a laminectomy a 50 year-old woman recalled explicit surgical directions which she could otherwise not have known, such as "Put the pieces of the disc into the medicine glass". She*

had no pain or discomfort and said she seemed to be out of her
body and present only peripherally as an uninvolved observer.
(case 10 in Mainzer 1979)

[1.120]The apparently disembodied soul of this woman clearly heard a fragment of a verifiable conversation. There are many other examples of "seeing" and "hearing" during out-of-body experiences. All these accounts reveal that the disembodied immaterial soul is apparently able to see with physical light seen by every physical person, and to hear physical sounds heard by all physical persons.

Summary of the properties of the soul

[1.121]Accounts related by cardiac arrest survivors telling of undergoing astonishing near-death experiences while apparently unconscious without a heartbeat, also reveal all these same properties of the soul. Sam Parnia, an eminent researcher of near-death experiences during cardiac arrest, once summarized some of his thoughts on some aspects of the functioning of the disembodied soul in the form of a question.

[1.122]*It was very interesting that we now had four independent*
studies of NDEs [Near-Death Experiences]in cardiac arrest, and
all four had raised the same questions regarding the mechanism
of causation of NDEs and the relationship between the mind and
the brain. How could thought processes, memory formation, and
reasoning be occurring at a time when there was little or no brain
function? (page 97 in Parnia 2006)

[1.123]This last short quotation is an excellent summary of one of the most fundamental properties of the soul—the soul continues conscious mental function independent of the physical body, and independent of the condition of the physical body. Finally, it is now possible to summarize the most evident explicit and implicit properties of the soul.

- [1.124]The soul is invisible.
- [1.125]The soul is immaterial.
- [1.126]The soul can separate from the physical body: temporarily separating from the body during out-of-body experiences, and separating permanently from the body upon death.
- [1.127]The soul is the vehicle of the conscious mind, or the soul and the conscious mind are one and the same thing.
- [1.128]The soul is continuously conscious.

- [1.129]The soul interacts with the physical body to control the physical body.
- [1.130]The soul is invisible and immaterial, and is therefore undetectable with any known apparatus. So the only way to detect bodily control by the soul is indirectly through the manifestations of this control, such as personality, memories, thoughts, emotions, speech, actions, and deeds.
- [1.131]The soul perceives sensations from the physical body, and subsequently controls the physical body to react appropriately to these sensations.
- [1.132]The soul is the indelible repository of all memories.
- [1.133]There are conflicting beliefs regarding the mental abilities of the human soul. Many writers claim the disembodied human soul has enhanced mental abilities, but that the physical structures of the brain and body filter, and inhibit any manifestation of these abilities on this world. Many other writers say the disembodied human soul possesses the same mental abilities as the conscious physical body. It is uncertain which of these two alternatives is correct.
- [1.134]The attributes, properties and functioning of the soul are unaffected by diseases, injuries, and drugs affecting the physical body.
- [1.135]Out-of-body experiences indicate that the disembodied soul can hear physical sounds and see with physical light.

[1.136]These are the apparent properties of the soul made evident by a multitude of wondrous experiences. The majority of people believe the soul possesses these properties. Furthermore, these apparent manifestations of the properties of the soul are also the apparent proofs employed by nearly all religious beliefs preaching the reality of a human soul, and an eternal afterlife for this soul.

[1.137]However, the fact that the soul has generally accepted properties means it may be possible to determine the reality of the soul. But how? After all, the soul is invisible and immaterial-unable to be seen, smelt, touched, or sensed in any way by humans or any instruments known to humankind at this moment. Even so, these properties of the soul reveal ways to determine its reality. According to believers in dualism, the soul must interact with the body to control the body to speak, act, and write. This is how we learn of these properties of the soul, because people relate their experiences of these properties through the mechanisms of their physical bodies to other equally physical persons by means of speech, actions, and writing. After all, if the immaterial soul has no interaction with the material body, we would have no concept, or idea of a soul.

[1.138]So interaction of the soul with the body is the key to investigating the reality of the human soul. Unlike the soul, the functioning of the body is directly affected by drugs, disease, injuries, and many other conditions. Therefore, a study of changes in the functioning of the body and conscious mind induced by these factors, may well reveal the nature and reality of any interaction between the soul and the body. Such a methodology is a very practical and objective technique of determining whether the human soul is merely an ancient illusion, or a wondrous reality. So what are the properties of the soul able to be determined by a study of the functioning of the body? Here are the most evident impossibilities and possibilities in the form of a list.

- [1.139]The soul is invisible. This is an evident property of the soul, but is not a practical method of determining the reality of the soul.
- [1.140]The soul is immaterial. This is another evident property of the soul, but is also not a practical method of determining the reality of the soul, because of the impossibility of detecting something immaterial with material instrumentation.
- [1.141]The soul is immortal. This is an impossible property to investigate.
- [1.142]The mind-model of dualism proposes that the soul is continually conscious, unaffected by anything affecting the physical body, as well as interacting with the body to control the conscious physical body to react to sensations, situations, and speech perceived by the physical body. The nature of this interaction remains speculative. We could hypothesize about hyperdimensional tachyonic information transfer, or transdimensional quantum entanglement. However, such ideas remain wild speculation until the demonstration of the reality of an interaction between the immaterial soul and the material body. Specific bodily responses involving possible transfer of information between the body to the soul, from the soul to the body, or in both directions, are the only possible method of determining the possible reality of the soul. According to proponents of the mind-model of dualism, such reciprocal interactions between body and soul do occur (see 15.10 cited from pages 13-14 in Carter 2010). Information from the physical senses of the body is processed within the brain and transmitted to the soul, which then reacts to control the body in a manner appropriate to the

perceptions transmitted to the soul. Drugs, surgery, injury and disease all affect the functioning of the physical brain, so altering the processing of many sensory perceptions of the body. A consequence of this physical reality is that the soul responds appropriately to these altered sensory perceptions, but then in a manner that is experienced and observed as unusual or abnormal. Alternatively, the subjective experiences and objective observations of persons affected by drugs, surgery, injury and disease may simply be manifestations of the soul attempting to control the body through the mechanisms of a physical body whose functioning is altered by drugs, surgery, injury, or disease. Accordingly, a study of situations where the reactions of the body reveal differences between what may be expected from materialism or dualism is a very promising method of differentiating these mind-models.

- [1.143]The mind-model of dualism proposes that the soul is continually conscious, unaffected by anything affecting the physical body, as well as being the indelible repository of all memories. This latter reveals memory to be an example of a reciprocal interaction between the soul and the body. The body perceives something to be learned with the physical senses of the body. The physical body interacts with the immaterial soul to somehow transfer the information from the physical perceptions of the material body to the immaterial soul, which then remembers these perceptions and information. Some time later, the person receives a request for this information by means of physical speech, writing, or other equally physical senses or perceptions. The physically perceived sensations of the request for information are somehow transferred from the material body to the immaterial soul. The immaterial soul responds to the request for information by recalling the information, and somehow interacting with the material body to reproduce the remembered information by actions, speech, writing, or deeds. Examples of this are learning things, actions, deeds, experiences, and interactions with other people. Moreover, the soul also learns and remembers things when apparently separated from the body such as during out-of-body experiences, or while transported to transcendental worlds outside the physical body, e.g. the Christian heaven. Such retrieval of memories is very amenable to testing by examining the multitude of international studies of memory function under many different situations.

- [1.144]A study of the many accounts of deathbed experiences, near-death experiences, out-of-body experiences, dreams, and mind-altering drugs may reveal the intellect, personality, and perceptive abilities of the human soul. But nearly all such experiences occur during mental states, and medical conditions profoundly influencing the functioning of the physical brains of those undergoing these experiences. So while these experiences may reveal clues as to the properties of the disembodied mind, the student should always take the known effects of concurrent drug use, medical conditions, and other factors, before ascribing any particular property to the soul. Nonetheless, careful study of such accounts may reveal the true nature of the human mind, or at the very least provide some clues.
- [1.145]The disembodied soul is capable of perceiving light and sound on this physical world. Moreover, the disembodied soul apparently perceives the same color spectrum, and hears the same sounds as perceived by physically conscious persons. This ability is amenable to testing by relating known physical laws to the reports of those reporting memories of their experiences of disembodiment.

[1.146]The physical determination of something as intangible and immaterial as the human soul initially seems daunting, and even physically impossible. However, a careful definition of the fundamental properties of the human soul, as proposed by the mind-model of dualism, reveals several possible ways of determining the reality of a human soul possessing these properties.

Anesthesia & the reality of the soul

[1.147]This brings us to the use of anesthesia to determine the reality of the soul. Some people may ask, "But what has anesthesia got to do with answering the question of the reality of the human soul?" Actually more than most people would imagine. Anesthesiology is unique in the world of consciousness studies, because anesthesiologists have vast practical experience in the manipulation and determination of consciousness, as well as extensive knowledge of the ways various anesthetic drugs and techniques affect the functioning of the mind and the body. Observations from the daily experience of clinical anesthesiology reveal unique ways of thinking about consciousness and mind, revealing much about the relationship of the conscious mind to the body, as well as providing extra insights enabling determination of the origin and nature of the conscious mind. Indeed, as subsequent chapters of this book reveal, anesthesia is an instrument uniquely suited for probing and revealing the true nature of several fundamental properties of the soul. Nonetheless, all these considerations fail to ask the one very important question posed below.

Why study the nature of the conscious mind?

[1.148]Insights from anesthesia and medicine provide objective evidence revealing whether dualism is correct, or whether the functioning of the brain generates the phenomenon of the conscious mind. So this book is written in the spirit of what the American neurologist, and erstwhile Surgeon General of the U.S. Army, William Alexander Hammond (1828-1900) wrote more than 100 years ago in a book entitled *Spiritualism and Allied Causes of Nervous Derangement* (Hammond 1876):

> [1.149]*There is an inherent tendency in the mind of man to ascribe to supernatural agencies those events the causes of which are beyond his knowledge; and this is especially the case with the normal and morbid phenomena which are manifested in his own person. But, as his intellect becomes more thoroughly trained, and as science advances in its developments, the range of his credulity becomes more and more circumscribed, his doubts are multiplied, and he at length reaches that condition of "healthy skepticism" which allows of no belief without the proof. (page 1 in Hammond 1876)*

[1.150]The human body is where the conscious mind manifests, and the functioning of the body reveals the nature of the conscious mind. Certainty as to the origins of the greatest wonder in our individual lives— our conscious minds—allows us to reject baseless hope and belief, as well as providing a solid basis for human social, ethical, and philosophical systems based upon fact. This is why it is important to learn the true origin and nature of the conscious mind.

2

Consciousness

[2.1]"I don't believe that stuff you're injecting will make me unconscious, so I'm going to stay awake." Some patients say this to me as I inject drugs to start general anesthesia. But no matter how much they believe in what they say, and no matter how hard they try to stay awake, all these people are unconscious within about 20 to 40 seconds. This seemingly simple chemical conquest of consciousness by anesthetic drugs reveals a fundamental property of any interaction of the soul with the body, as well as raising fundamental questions. Anesthetic drugs induce loss of consciousness by affecting the functioning of mechanisms of the physical body involved in generating consciousness, or transmitting consciousness from the soul. So induction of loss of consciousness by anesthetic drugs reveals that the soul cannot manifest consciousness in the body except through the functioning mechanisms of the physical body. Furthermore, induction of loss of consciousness by anesthetic drugs raises another two questions. Which parts of the body are necessary for the body to manifest consciousness? And most important of all—what is consciousness?

What is consciousness?

[2.2]Each working day I use drugs such as thiopental or propofol to render people unconscious, and then administer other drugs to restore them to consciousness. But even though this is my work, the only thing I know for certain about consciousness is how to tell when a person is conscious, when a person is likely to be conscious, and when a person is likely to be unconscious. Even though I have a clear idea of these aspects of consciousness, I still do not understand the phenomenon of consciousness except in terms of these manifestations. So how is consciousness defined? Here are two definitions.

2.3[Consciousness] Is the state of knowing what goes on around one… (Webster Dictionary 1991)

2.4[Consciousness means being] Inwardly sensible or aware…(Shorter Oxford Dictionary 1956)

2.5These definitions actually only define the manifestations of consciousness such as awareness and perception. They do not explain the nature of consciousness. Definitions such as the above are extensively discussed in a review article entitled *Consciousness* by Adam Zeman (2001), as well as in the very readable *Consciousness: An introduction* by Susan Blackmore (2004). Here we read extensive explanations of states of consciousness, manifestations of consciousness, and theories of consciousness. Yet even Susan Blackmore's book ends with the revealing question: "But what is consciousness?" I do not know either. So all I can do is use these definitions, as well as a very useful modern neurological definition derived from observation and clinical practice.

2.6… wakefulness refers to the sub-state that permits open eyes and a degree of motor arousal (i.e. wakefulness defines the level of consciousness); awareness refers to the sub-state that enables experience of thoughts, memories, and emotions (i.e. awareness defines the content of consciousness. Although wakefulness and awareness are intimately connected—in general, one has to be awake to be aware—it is possible to identify circumstances under which they are dissociated: … (Gawryluk 2010)

2.7This is a definition of consciousness with which it is possible to achieve something other than philosophical discussions. Indeed, clinical and laboratory studies of conscious and brain damaged persons clearly demonstrates this difference between wakefulness and awareness (Demertzi 2008, Laureys 2005a, Noirhomme 2010). One way of commencing a basic study of the phenomenon of consciousness is to examine the people and entities in which we recognize the presence of consciousness. Just look at this short list.

- 2.8A normal human is definitely conscious.
- 2.9A delirious human is definitely conscious.
- 2.10A drooling and totally demented human is definitely conscious.
- 2.11A mentally retarded human is definitely conscious.
- 2.12A cow is definitely conscious.

- [2.13]A dog is definitely conscious.
- [2.14]A cat is definitely conscious.
- [2.15]A rat is definitely conscious.
- [2.16]A hamster is definitely conscious.

[2.17]No one disputes the presence of consciousness in these very different types of people and animals. They are all very definitely conscious when awake, because they perceive and respond to their surroundings. These people and animals are very different, but the basic elements of their brains are very similar.

Consciousness and mind

[2.18]But before proceeding any further, it is first necessary to clarify the terms "consciousness" and "mind". Many popular books use these terms very loosely. Often the term "consciousness" is used to mean "mind", a usage causing confusion and uncertainty as to what is actually meant by the term "consciousness". Neurophysiologists and neurologists make a very clear distinction between the terms consciousness and mind (Gawryluk 2010, Greenfield 2002).

[2.19]To begin with, neurologists and neuroscientists define mind to mean the sum total of personality, memory, intelligence, and emotions. Mind is what we experience. Mind is what we feel—our emotions, our conscious perception of sensations, our memories, and how we think. Mind is what makes each of us an individual.

[2.20]Consciousness is that incredible "something" making mental activity manifesting as mind possible. Without consciousness, the body manifests no properties of mind, because an unconscious person manifests no properties of mind such as personality, memory, intelligence, and emotions. There are situations in which humans are conscious, but manifest no properties of mind. For example, just think of a drooling, totally demented wreck of a human. Such a person is afflicted with a dreadful disease stripping them of awareness, memory, intellect, and personality, as well as all other properties of mind making them what they once were. Yet such a person still has a sleep-wake cycle, and when awake is very definitely conscious. This is but one of many examples showing that consciousness and mind are two very different manifestations. This brings us back to the topic of this chapter.

Consciousness, the brain, and dualism

[2.21]So which parts of the brain are required for the body to manifest consciousness? Neurological studies over many decennia reveal that the reticular formation in the brainstem, and the thalamus, must function normally for consciousness to be present (Alkire 2000, Bogen 1995, Goldfine 2011, Långsjö 2012, Mashour 2008, Merker 2007, Min 2010, Noirhomme 2010, Schiff 2008, Schneider 2007, Zeman 2001). Moreover when their connections and functions are considered together with the effects of disease, injury and birth defects—the thalamus and brainstem are clearly revealed to be the generators and controllers of consciousness in humans, and all other vertebrates (Alkire 2000, Bogen 1995, Goldfine 2011, Min 2010, Schiff 2008, Schneider 2007). All manifestations of consciousness require a functioning brainstem and thalamus.

[2.22]The functioning of the thalamus and brainstem explains why people lose consciousness due to anesthesia and all other disorders. For example, anesthetic drugs induce loss of consciousness by inducing abnormal function, or even failure of the functioning of the thalamus and the brainstem. This is also true of all other disorders, injuries, and diseases causing loss of consciousness in humans and animals. They all induce loss of consciousness by the same mechanism—by inducing malfunction or failure of function the thalamus and brainstem. Accordingly, most modern neuroscientists say that consciousness is a product of the functioning of the thalamus and brainstem reticular formation.

[2.23]But most people do not share this belief. Instead, they believe the mind-model of dualism explains the nature of the conscious mind better than that of materialism. Indeed, dualism as a theory of the origin of the conscious mind is apparently consistent with many of the findings of neurological research. After all, if the physical body is merely a receiver of the controlling influence of the soul, then the mechanisms of the body manifesting this controlling influence of the soul must also function normally. So according to believers in dualism, a normally functioning thalamus and brainstem reticular formation are the indispensable conduit through which the soul expresses consciousness in the physical body.

[2.24]Even so, many people still ask themselves how it is possible for such relatively small and insignificant brain structures as the brainstem and thalamus to generate, or function as a conduit for something as amazing as the phenomenon of consciousness. I cannot answer this question. Fortunately, while I cannot answer the question of the nature

41

of human consciousness, I can review how human consciousness manifests under some of the most bizarre and seemingly unlikely circumstances, and so demonstrate the truth of the preceding discussion. Indeed, the following examples from clinical medicine clearly reveal the brainstem and thalamus to be essential for the manifestation of human consciousness.

Anesthesia of half the brain: The Wada Test

[2.25]One of the first fascinating examples from clinical medicine demonstrates how sudden selective anesthesia, or "switching-off" of large volumes of normally functioning brain tissue affects human consciousness. The Wada Test very elegantly achieves this seemingly improbable feat. A Japanese-Canadian neurologist Juhn Atsushi Wada (1924-) first described this test during 1960 (Wada 1960). For many years, the Wada Test was the main method used to determine the likely effects of extensive brain surgery (Binder 1996, Baxendale 2009), as well as to investigate the functions housed in each side of the brain.

[2.26]The basic principle of the Wada Test is simple. A small dose of a powerful anesthetic drug such as amobarbital, methohexital, propofol, or etomidate is injected into a carotid artery. This induces sudden failure of function most of the cerebral hemisphere on the side of the injection (Heller 2005, Jones-Gotman 1994, Rosadini 1967, Serafetinides 1965, Wada 1960). Most of the blood flowing through the left side of the brain, (the left cerebral hemisphere), comes from the left carotid artery, and most of the blood flowing through the right side of the brain, (the right cerebral hemisphere), comes from the right carotid artery (Silva 1999). Studies of the distribution of small doses of drugs injected into a carotid artery reveal that only insignificant amounts of the injected dose enters the thalamus, leaving it relatively unaffected and functioning normally (Hong 2000, Lee 2004, Silva 1999). Two arteries on either side of the neck vertebrae called the vertebral arteries unite at the level of the brainstem to form the basilar artery, which supplies the entire brainstem and parts of the thalamus with blood. These anatomical facts explain why only minimal amounts of a drug injected into a carotid artery enters the thalamus, while none of the injected drug enters the brainstem. This explains why injection of a small dose of an anesthetic drug into a carotid artery does not cause loss of consciousness.

[2.27]People undergoing a Wada Test do develop personality changes, altered memory function and language ability, as well as paralysis of the opposite sides of their bodies during the period of anesthesia of one half of their brains (Perria 1961, Serafetinides 1965). However, they remain conscious and continue breathing because the brainstem and thalamus are unaffected. The Wada Test clearly demonstrates how large volumes of normally functioning brain tissue can malfunction, or cease functioning altogether without affecting consciousness. But what about situations where large volumes of abnormal brain tissue are destroyed?

Removing half the brain: Hemispherectomy

[2.28]Some people require brain surgery to remove extensive amounts of abnormally functioning brain tissue. Hemispherectomy is one such operation. Hemispherectomy is the removal of a cerebral hemisphere, or one half of the brain. This dramatic operation is performed to treat extensive brain tumors invading one cerebral hemisphere, or unmanageable and invalidating epilepsy occurring in one cerebral hemisphere (Burklund 1977, Devlin 2003, Gardner 1955, Gott 1973, Griffith 1966, McClelland 2007, Smith 1966). There are various operation techniques, but all operations performed to remove half the brain always leave the thalamus and brainstem intact (Almeida 2006). Hemispherectomy does not affect the level of consciousness, but can have profound effects upon personality. For example, Gardner (1955) presented the case of a 45 year old man who underwent such an operation because of a recurrent tumor in the right side of his brain.

[2.29]*Before operation, the Wechsler-Bellevue showed a full-scale I.Q. of 118, with a verbal of 122 and a performance scale of 112. 2 months and 13 days after operation, the verbal scale yielded an I.Q. of 113, a loss of 9 points 3½ years after operation, the verbal scale gave him an I.Q. of 110, indicating an almost static intelligence level. On the memory scale, his quotient was 126. On the Rorschach [a test of personality - note by author] he gave a minimum number of responses, fatigued easily, displayed a narrow range of associations and little originality or imagination, indicating a dull intellectual functioning, and no ability for deep thinking or for adequate self-evaluation. The affect was that of a rather shallow irritability. The affect at the time of this examination was conditioned by resentment at having been asked to travel 100 miles for testing when he felt well. Patient's wife insists that he is "wonderful to live with." She describes him as patient, kind and not at all demanding. He*

43

*initiates plans for the future, he is interested in the household
budget and does not spend money foolishly. She states that her
two daughters by a former marriage are very fond of him. (Case 9
in Gardner 1955)*

²·³⁰So while removing half this man's brain had an effect on his
personality, it did not affect his intelligence or level of consciousness.
The same is true of other studies of hemispherectomy in adults whose
brain functions developed normally until extensive invasion by brain
tumors necessitated surgical removal of a cerebral hemisphere (Burklund
1977, Smith 1966). The Wada Test and hemispherectomy provide an
important lesson—they clearly demonstrate that as long as the thalamus
and brainstem function normally, consciousness is unaffected, even after
dramatically large volumes of cerebral cortex cease to function, are
removed, or damaged.

Born with nearly no brain: Hydrancephaly

²·³¹Some unfortunate children are born with a condition called
"hydrancephaly". They are born without any brain except for the
brainstem, thalamus, and immediately surrounding tissues. They possess
no brain tissue above this level, except for some vestigial pieces of
cortical tissue. Their heads look reasonably normal, but instead of brain
tissue, their skulls are only filled with fluid above the level of the
brainstem, thalamus, and hypothalamus. And because there is no brain
tissue above this level, they have an absent, or flat electroencephalogram,
except above any vestigial pieces of cortical tissue (Merker 2007,
Shewmon 1999). These children reveal that consciousness can exist
without electroencephalographic activity being recorded from the
surface of the head. A description of the brain scan (CT scan) of one of
these children revealed the following:

*²·³²Hydrancephaly was reconfirmed around 5 years 6 months,
when GLH became her neurologist. CT scan showed no
supratentorial parenchyma above the thalamus, except for a thin
left inferior temporo-occipital remnant and even less on the right.
An EEG [electroencephalogram] was isoelectric except for low-
amplitude, nondescript activity in the temporo-occipital regions.
(Case 2 in Shewmon 1999)*

[2.33]Even so, this severely handicapped child lived until 17 years of age. And while alive, this girl had a sleep-wake cycle, was able to see, and responded to music, as well as people in the following ways:

[2.34]*By age 5 years she consistently recognized certain individuals non-visually and responded to people differentially according to three categories: mother, familiar persons, and strangers. The more familiar someone was, the more she would relax, move spontaneously, and vocalize. At age 6 years a neurosurgeon described her as happy and very responsive to her mother. (Case 2 in Shewmon 1999)*

[2.35]Despite their devastating brain defects, some of these hydrancephalic children do survive until their teens. They are conscious with a definite sleep and waking cycle. Hydrancephaly clearly demonstrates that consciousness is not a function of the cerebral cortex.

Born without a brain or skull: Anencephaly

[2.36]This brings us to another dramatic and devastating birth defect. Two to seven babies in every ten thousand live births are born with a birth defect called "anencephaly". These babies are born without a brain or brainstem, and the skull is absent above the level of the eyes. This is very different to hydrancephaly where the children have a normal appearing head and skull, albeit only filled with fluid. Anencephalic babies usually never become conscious, and die shortly after birth. But sometimes an anencephalic baby is born with a brainstem and thalamus, even though the rest of the brain is absent. Such babies can live for some time, and sometimes even manifest evident consciousness (Jaquier 2006, Luyendijk 1992, Nielson 1949). Nielson (1949) once published a description of the mental and bodily functioning of an anencephalic boy who lived for 85 days after birth.

[2.37]*Most interesting to the writers was the presence of instincts and emotions. If we handled the patient roughly he cried weakly but otherwise like any other infant, and when we coddled him he showed contentment and settled down in our arms. When a finger was placed into his mouth he sucked vigorously. He would sleep after feeding and awaken when hungry, expressing his hunger by crying. (Nielson 1949)*

45

[2.38]Post-mortem examination of this unfortunate baby's brain revealed he had no brain tissue except for a spinal cord, a brainstem, cerebellum, thalamus, and hypothalamus. Nonetheless, this baby was conscious, had a sleep-wake rhythm, breathed normally, was able to express hunger, could suck as well as drink, and reacted to handling just as any other baby. Manifestations of consciousness occurring in this baby, as well as in other similar anencephalic children, reveal that breathing, feeding, and consciousness can occur without any brain tissue being present except for a thalamus and brainstem.

Brain death

[2.39]Examples of brain surgery such as hemispherectomy, and birth defects such as anencephaly and hydrancephaly, reveal that the presence of a normally functioning brainstem and thalamus are associated with the ability to breathe and manifest physical consciousness. This raises the question of what happens after total destruction of the entire brain, including the brainstem and thalamus. Such destruction is horrific and dramatic, but does occasionally occur due to a multitude of accidents and intracranial disasters. Prior to the first international consensus on the diagnosis of brain death during the 1970's (Statement of the Conference of Medical Royal Colleges 1976), some severely brain damaged persons were kept alive for prolonged periods in intensive care units before eventually dying (Kramer 1963, Mohandas 1971, Pearson 1978, Towbin 1973). The results of post-mortem examinations of the brains of some of these people can only be described as dramatic, as in the case of one unfortunate girl.

> [2.40]*This can be best demonstrated in slides derived from the brain of a 6 year-old girl suffering from tubercular meningitis (Case 1, Table 1). Artificial respiration was necessary two weeks after commencement of the disease, yet the general condition grew worse in the following 9 days and she died two months later. As far as we could ascertain the brain had been dead for two months before the heart stopped. In this period of deanimation necrotic brain substance leaked through burrholes made in the skull. (Kramer 1963)*

[2.41]The medical record of this tragic girl, as well as the post-mortem description of her brain, revealed several important points. She was not conscious, she did not breathe, and her brain, including the brainstem

46

and thalamus, was dead and decomposing long before the rest of her body died. Other persons whose bodies were kept alive long after their brains had died also revealed the same features—their brains, and in particular their brainstem structures, were extensively damaged and sometimes actually decomposing, while the rest of their bodies were still alive (Kramer 1963, Mohandas 1971, Pearson 1978, Towbin 1973)! So the example of brain death clearly illustrates that the mechanisms of the brainstem and thalamus are required for the physical body to breathe and manifest consciousness (Jørgensen 1973, Heytens 1989, Långsjö 2012, Mohandas 1971, Ropper 1984, Wijdicks 2001, Wijdicks 2008), and that the soul relies upon the functioning of these same mechanisms to manifest consciousness through the mechanisms of the physical body.

Conscious despite appearing unconscious

[2.42]The fact of consciousness raises another important question. If we look at an awake and conscious person or animal, we *know* that person is conscious. So what are the criteria used to determine the presence of consciousness? How do we determine consciousness in humans? How do we determine consciousness in animals? When you think about this question, you realize there is actually only one criterion used to determine the presence of consciousness—interaction with the environment. By this I mean: speech, facial expressions, as well as movements of other body parts in response to events in the surroundings of the conscious person.

[2.43]Even though these criteria are very useful for determining the presence of consciousness in most situations, they are woefully deficient in others. The deficiency of these criteria is revealed by the fact that some persons may appear unconscious, yet possess full and normal consciousness, despite being unable to breathe, speak, move their eyes, produce facial expressions, move or twitch a single muscle. Such people are only apparently unconscious. Consciousness under such circumstances is the daily reality for anesthesiologists, as well as being familiar to neurologists, and intensive care physicians (Sanders 2012). Let us look at some examples.

Deadly Indian arrow poison

[2.44]Curare was traditionally used to poison darts shot from the blowpipes of South American Indians. Purification and study of its effects finally lead to the introduction of curare as an adjuvant to general

47

anesthesia during 1942 by Griffith and Johnson in Montreal, Canada (Griffith 1942). Curare and more modern synthetic variants have been used in anesthesia ever since. They form a group of drugs called non-depolarizing muscle relaxants, and are an essential component of modern general anesthesia. Curare and all synthetic analogues of curare paralyze all the muscles of the body with the exception of:

- [2.45]heart muscle—otherwise everyone would have a cardiac arrest after administration of curare,
- [2.46]bladder muscles and urinary sphincters—otherwise everyone would be incontinent of urine after administration of curare,
- [2.47]intestinal and bowel muscles—these continue to function after administration of curare,
- [2.48]anal sphincters—if these were paralyzed by curare, everyone would be incontinent of feces after administration of curare.

[2.49]Curare does not enter the brain, does not induce loss of consciousness, nor cause any alteration in the state of consciousness. A sufficient dose of curare just causes total paralysis of all voluntary muscles, which is why affected people cannot breathe and cannot move, even when they make intense efforts to breathe or move. So after administration of sufficient curare without any other drugs to cause loss of consciousness, people are fully conscious and aware, but appear unconscious because they are totally paralyzed.

[2.50]During 1947, Scott Smith, an anesthesiologist working in Salt Lake City in Utah, USA, described his experiences of increasing doses of curare without any anesthesia or sedation (Smith 1947). This report is in the form of events at different times after incremental doses of curare. Despite increasing degrees of paralysis, Scott Smith was able to signal answers to questions by twitching unaffected muscles. From 2.26 pm the account described the following observations:

> [2.51]*2:26 Ability to comprehend and answer questions accurately is indicated by correctness of replies when the inquiries are restated in the negative or double negative. Indicates he desires the experiment to continue. Upon request, moves feet and hands slightly. Total of 200 units given. Some spasmodic diaphragmatic movements out of rhythm with artificial respiration. Slight snoring sound on exhalation.*
> *2:28 Can distinguish heat from cold, sharp from dull, and can feel pain pinprick.*

2:30 No further spontaneous respiratory movements. Ability to wrinkle forehead almost gone, but indicates he can hear, see, and feel touch and pain as well as ever. Pupils medium size and equal, and pupillary responses to light and accommodation unaffected. Airway inserted, and subject indicates he feels it. Jaws very relaxed. Color good. Electroencephalogram unaltered, and alpha rhythm still inhibited by pattern vision when eyelid is passively elevated. Intermittent pharyngeal aspiration started because of accumulating secretions. B.P., 130/70; pulse rate, 100. Subject indicates he desires the next 100 units rapidly, as planned.

2:32 Can no longer move feet or hands upon request, and indicates by slight remaining movement of left eyebrow that he is trying to do so. Also signals that he feels all right and that artificial respiration is satisfactory to him. Additional 100 units given rapidly; total 300 units.

2:35 Subject indicates he wants another 100 units and that the experience is not unpleasant. Answers to questions are consistent. Signals that diplopia is marked when eyelids are passively elevated and that objects are seen clearly when placed in line of gaze.

2:37 Subject signals in answer to inquiries that sensorium is normal, airway is not troublesome, and painful stimuli are felt. Additional 100 units d-tubocurarine chloride given rapidly; total 400 units. B.P., 140/80; pulse rate, 112. Electroencephalogram and electrocardiogram normal.

2:42 Ability to signal by slight movement inner aspect left eyebrow almost gone. Indicates he desires the final 100 units, that he is perfectly conscious and that his sensorium is unimpaired.

2:44 Additional 100 units d-tubocurarine chloride given rapidly; total 500 units.

2:45 Subject now unable to signal response to inquiries, due to complete skeletal muscular paralysis. Endotracheal catheter inserted with ease due to very relaxed pharynx and vocal cords, and artificial respiration continued through it. B.P., 130/84; pulse rate, 120.

2:48 Eyelids manually opened. Alpha rhythm of electroencephalogram inhibited by pattern vision (object held in line of gaze). Subject stated upon recovery that he was "clear as a bell" all this period.

[2.52]This is a vivid illustration of the conscious experience of increasing muscle paralysis due to curare, or other drugs with the same actions. Readers will have noted that the muscles around the eyes were less sensitive to the effects of curare than other muscles. Breathing failed due to paralysis of the muscles required for respiration before paralysis of these muscles around the eyes occurred. Finally, after administration of even more curare, the muscles around his eyes were also paralyzed, and he could no longer respond with even miniscule movements. At this point, the only indication of the possible presence of consciousness available to his observers was his electroencephalogram, although this was only confirmed retrospectively. This report is a clear illustration of a situation where a person is fully conscious, but appears unconscious, because of total paralysis rendering it impossible to signal the fact of consciousness.

[2.53]Every working day, anesthesiologists inject drugs similar to curare into patients undergoing operations. This is perfectly standard medical practice required to make surgery in many parts of the body possible. All these people are totally paralyzed and unable to breathe, which is why they all receive artificial respiration. At the same time, these people also receive other drugs to deaden the pain of surgery, as well as other drugs to induce unconsciousness and amnesia. However, the use of such techniques provides the anesthesiologist with a dilemma. The anesthesiologist can never be absolutely certain that a person is unconscious during all general anesthetics using curare-like drugs.

[2.54]Two Washington (USA) anesthesiologists, Sally Rampersad and Michael Mulroy, published a case report of a man demonstrating just this problem. The man was 60 years old, diabetic, morbidly obese, and had undergone prior heart surgery for clogged coronary arteries, as a result of which he had moderately poor heart function. He was brought under general anesthesia, and underwent a planned gallbladder removal because of gallstones, as well as a gastric bypass to reduce weight. The anesthesiologists reported difficulty maintaining adequate blood pressure. He was paralyzed with cistracurium, a curare-like drug, which was required to permit surgical access to the abdominal contents to perform the planned operations.

[2.55]*Cistracurium provided muscle relaxation [muscle paralysis]. Hypotension [low blood pressure], despite fluids and vasopressors, limited the use of sevoflurane. A Bispectral index® (BIS) monitor was placed before incision. The initial reading was 37, the average BIS during the surgical procedure was 44±5*

(mean SD), and the highest recorded value was 51 (Table 1).
Good signal quality was indicated throughout. His heart rates
were in the 80s throughout surgery with systolic blood pressures
ranging between 80 and 130 mm Hg (baseline, 122/55 mm Hg).
At the end of surgery, neuromuscular blockade was reversed and
sevoflurane discontinued. The patient awoke and was tracheally
extubated. When asked if he was in pain, he responded "Not now,
but I was during surgery." On further questioning, he described
no recall of intubation but vivid, painful recall of his surgery, with
"unimaginable" pain and the sensation that people were "tearing
at me." He wished he were dead and tried to communicate his
distress. He heard voices in the operating room but was unable to
recall the content of what was said, remembering only that it was
"shop talk." (Rampersad 2005)

[2.56]A dreadful experience, and profoundly upsetting for all concerned. This man's poor heart function coupled with his diabetes mellitus made him very sensitive to the effects of anesthetic drugs, which is why the anesthesiologists had difficulty maintaining a normal blood pressure with higher, standard, concentrations of anesthetic drugs. These same nervous system effects of diabetes mellitus, and his poor heart condition, combined with the effects of anesthetic drugs also explains why he did not react to the pain of the operation he underwent with sweating, high pulse rate, or increased blood pressure. Total muscle paralysis due to cistracurium, prevented him moving to signal the fact of his consciousness and pain. So his anesthesiologists relied upon the lack of these signs, as well as an internationally well-known and tested electronic monitor of consciousness, (the Bispectral index monitor), to determine whether he was conscious. He appeared unconscious, and the electronic monitor indicated he was unconscious. Nonetheless, he was conscious, felt pain from the operation, but was unable to signal this fact because of paralysis. This account is dramatic and crystal-clear evidence of how some apparently unconscious paralyzed persons may actually be conscious, even though they give no clinical signs of consciousness, and modern electronic monitors indicate they are unconscious.

The locked-in syndrome

[2.57]The locked-in syndrome is a dreadful disorder. People with this syndrome cannot breathe, cannot speak, and cannot move—yet they are conscious—locked inside an unresponsive and unmoving body

51

(Schnakers 2008). Neurologists recognize three types of locked-in syndrome: the classical type characterized by total bodily paralysis except for retention of eye movements, the incomplete type whereby some voluntary movements are retained, and the rarer total locked-in syndrome whereby even eye movements are absent (Dollfus 1990, Schnakers 2009, Smith 2005). The cause is usually injury, bleeding, thrombosis, or other diseases and disorders causing permanent damage or malfunction of a part of the brainstem called the "ventral pons". Nerve pathways from the brain controlling all movements of the body pass through the ventral pons, which is why damage, injury, or malfunction of this part of the brain effectively disconnects the body from the controlling brain (Dollfus 1990, Laureys 2005, Patterson 1986).

[2.58]The actual experience of the locked-in syndrome is a nightmare surpassing the worst dreams of those affected. They hear people talking about them. They may even hear their physicians discussing whether to turn off their life support machines. They feel everything happening to their bodies, feel the indignity of themselves being incontinent of urine and feces, feel themselves drooling, and feel the pain of all painful treatments. Worse yet, people suffering in this way often know their physicians and family do not even realize they are conscious and aware of all that is happening. They may shriek and shout in their minds that they are alive and conscious, but no sounds and no movements are evident to those about them—they are locked inside their bodies— unable to breathe, speak, or move a single muscle. A New Zealand man called Nick Chisholm, reported his initial horrific experience of undergoing the locked-in syndrome caused by a rugby injury. He graphically described his sensations, emotions, and long road to partial recovery (Chisholm 2005).

> [2.59]*All my senses are normal, if not enhanced (sight and hearing). I'm just left trapped inside this body. All my muscles wouldn't work. Basically I couldn't talk, which went first; then I couldn't walk, eat, or excrete. [...] It felt like I was in a really bad nightmare constantly for about the first three months. I could only just hear (I couldn't even open my eyes or breathe by myself); without them even knowing that I still could hear, the doctors and specialists in front of me said to my mum that I would die. They even asked my mum if she wanted them to turn the life support machine off after a few days. (Chisholm 2005)*

[2.60]However, while this description of the experience of Nick Chisholm is expressive, it still fails to reveal the truly horrid and tormented reality experienced by those unfortunate persons afflicted by the locked-in syndrome. Just as Nick Chisholm, those persons suffering the consequences of the locked-in syndrome retain normal consciousness, intelligence and mental function (Demertzi 2008, Schnakers 2008). So imagine the feelings of utter terror and total abject vulnerability of many of these people as they listen to family, doctors and nurses talking about them as if they are dead, unable to move, powerless to indicate the fact of their consciousness, helplessly drooling and incontinent—a hopeless nightmare of ceaseless anxiety, degradation, and utter helplessness. The locked-in syndrome is a dramatic illustration of how some people may appear unconscious, but actually be conscious, and unable to signal the presence of consciousness because of paralysis of all voluntary muscles.

Cataplexy and the insurance agent

[2.61]Who has not heard of the expressions: "paralyzed with fear", and "weak with laughter". These well-known expressions are normal manifestations of muscle weakness induced by powerful emotions. Some people develop a neurological disorder called "cataplexy" which is an extreme form of muscle weakness induced by emotions such as surprise, rage, laughter or fear (Cave 1931, Dauvilliers 2003, Hoed 1979, Krahn 2005). Laughter in particular, is known to inhibit the activity of nerves activating the muscles of the body (Gandevia 1999, Krahn 2001, Overeem 2004, Yokota 1992). The most extreme result of this inhibition is the generalized paralysis of cataplexy with loss of tendon reflexes (Dauvilliers 2003, Krahn 2001, Wilson 1933), but with retention of consciousness (Cave 1931, Wilson 1933). Harry Cave, a physician in San Diego, California during the 1930's, once eloquently described the experience of cataplexy (Cave 1931).

> [2.62]*Cataplectic attacks are characterized by a sudden loss of muscle tonus in the patient's skeletal musculature so that the affected muscles become weak and powerless, allowing him to sink to the ground totally helpless; after a brief period, usually from a few seconds to a few minutes, the strength and power return and the patient is able to get up unaided, feeling none the worse for his experience. (page 78 in Cave 1931).*

[2.63]This same article contains many stories of individual experiences of cataplexy. Of all the factors inducing cataplectic paralysis, laughter is the most powerful, and most common (Krahn 2005). The account of a

32 year-old insurance agent in the wonderful article by Harry Cave (1931) illustrates how laughter or excitement can induce total paralysis in a person with cataplexy.

[2.64]*About the same time he began to have attacks of momentary weakness, during which he would have to catch hold of something to prevent falling. He had fallen to the ground many times, not losing consciousness, but was able to get up again without delay. While at the table his arm often became weak and he would drop whatever he was holding. During these attacks he sat in a slumped posture, with the eyes closed and the head nodding on the chest, and was unable to answer questions or respond in any way, although he said that he knew and heard everything that went on. He had an attack which lasted for fifteen minutes during the examination. These spells of weakness came on whenever he laughed or was amused or excited, and he also felt that laughing and excitement tended to induce a sleeping attack. (Case 22 in Cave 1931)*

[2.65]This man was paralyzed and unable to move or respond to others. He appeared unconscious, but actually retained full consciousness. Accordingly, extreme cataplexy is another example of situations where consciousness is present in a paralyzed and unmoving body.

Snakebite and apparent unconsciousness

[2.66]Snake venoms from the Malayan Krait, and the South African Black Mamba, act similarly to curare—they paralyze all the muscle of breathing and voluntary movement. But there is no specific antidote for the muscle paralysis from snakebite. So until unfortunate persons recover from the venom injected during the snakebite, they cannot breathe, are unmoving and appear unconscious, even though they are actually conscious (Warrell 2010). Artificial ventilation keeps people bitten by these snakes alive until the venom is eliminated from their bodies. The first publication of this use of artificial ventilation to keep a person alive after a Black Mamba bite was from South Africa.

[2.67]*A 12 year-old Bantu boy was brought in at 3 p.m. with a history of having been bitten by a black snake approximately 4 ft. long, 1 hour previously. He had a tourniquet on the left leg, his pulse and blood pressure were normal and there was no local swelling at the site of the bite. He was given 1 ampoule of polyvalent anti-snakebite serum (this does not afford protection*

against mambas) and an antihistaminic and antibiotic.
Three hours later I was called to the ward, where the staff had
been very busy with other cases, to find him almost dead with
generalized paresis and dyspnoea. He was intubated and given
oxygen by means of a Boyle's machine and 3 ampoules (30 ml)
specific mamba antiserum intravenously and 10 ml.
intramuscularly, and 50 mg. of hydrocortisone. (There was no
evidence of bronchospasm, rash or vocal cord oedema to suggest
anaphylaxis but only marked muscular paralysis.) He was
ventilated for 1 hour with a Boyle's machine and ventilator and
then a tracheotomy was performed. It was found that with the
tracheotomy and oxygen he was able to ventilate himself and he
was nursed carefully for the next few hours. By the next day (18
hours after the bite) he was completely normal, the tracheotomy
tube was removed and the patient was discharged 2 days later.
(Case 2 in Louw 1967)

[2.68]This is yet another example of retention of consciousness in unmoving persons, who no longer breathe, and appear unconscious.

Apparent unconsciousness and the soul

[2.69]All these are examples of situations where people may appear unconscious, but are actually very conscious and alert. Furthermore, these examples all clearly demonstrate that the mind can only manifest the presence of consciousness through the mechanisms of the body, which is why these examples do not enable any differentiation between the mind-models of dualism or materialism.

Sleep and consciousness

[2.70]Sleep is a condition of apparent unconsciousness undergone by each human every night. All societies since ancient times have had a fascination with the nature of sleep, and many developed mythologies and belief systems associated with this bodily condition. James Frazer (1854-1941) was a Scottish cultural anthropologist who wrote an influential comparative anthropological work called *The Golden Bough* (Frazer 1925). This wonderful book is replete with innumerable fantastic stories from all parts of the world as it was during his lifetime—a world still inhabited by many primitive societies having minimal contact with the world outside their own. Many such societies at this time still regarded sleep as a condition of immobility of the physical body allowing the soul to continue its activities elsewhere.

[2.71]*The soul of a sleeper is supposed to wander away from his body and actually to visit the places, to see the persons, and to perform the acts of which he dreams. For example, when an Indian of Brazil or Guiana wakes up from a sound sleep, he is firmly convinced that his soul has really been away hunting, fishing, felling trees, or whatever else he has dreamed of doing, while all the time his body has been lying motionless in his hammock. A whole Bororo village has been thrown into a panic and nearly deserted because somebody had dreamed that he saw enemies stealthily approaching it. A Macusi Indian in weak health, who dreamed that his employer had made him haul the canoe up a series of difficult cataracts, bitterly reproached his master next morning for his want of consideration in thus making a poor invalid go out and toil during the night. (pages 181-182 in chapter XVIII in Frazer 1925)*

[2.72]Some cultures even extended this idea of the separation of the soul from the body during sleep, into customs and rituals related to the awakening and care of sleeping persons.

[2.73]*It is a common rule with primitive people not to waken a sleeper, because his soul is away and might not have time to get back; so if the man wakened without his soul, he would fall sick. If it is absolutely necessary to rouse a sleeper, it must be done very gradually, to allow the soul time to return. [...] Still more dangerous is it in the opinion of primitive man to move a sleeper or alter his appearance, for if this were done the soul on its return might not be able to find or recognise its body, and so the person would die. The Minangkabauers deem it highly improper to blacken or dirty the face of a sleeper, lest the absent soul should shrink from re-entering a body thus disfigured. Patani Malays fancy that if a person's face be painted while he sleeps, the soul which has gone out of him will not recognise him, and he will sleep on till his face is washed. In Bombay it is thought equivalent to murder to change the aspect of a sleeper, as by painting his face in fantastic colours or giving moustaches to a sleeping woman. For when the soul returns it will not know its own body, and the person will die. (pages 182-183 in chapter XVIII in Frazer 1925)*

^{2.74}As I mentioned earlier, almost 70% of people believe in the reality of the human soul, and often these people share many of these same ancient and primitive beliefs so beautifully described by Frazer and others. But do these ancient beliefs about sleep and dreaming, combined with modern insights into the function of sleep, reveal any insights in the nature of the conscious mind?

Types of sleep defined

^{2.75}Once again, I will begin with a few definitions, because this removes confusion. Clarity is certainly required in the matter of sleep— a subject with an enormous ancient socio-cultural baggage, and about which so much magical thinking still exists. Most adults sleep about eight hours each night. However, sleep is not a single unitary phenomenon. Sleep is a condition during which different specific variations of brain and body function occur, although these are divisible into two basic physiologically distinguishable types.

- ^{2.76}*Non-rapid eye movement sleep (NREM sleep)*: Most of the time spent sleeping is NREM sleep. This is a phase of sleep typified by a slight degree of muscle relaxation, no eye movements, and typically low frequency, (slow wave), electrical activity in the electroencephalogram. This latter is why this phase of sleep is also known as slow-wave sleep (SWS).
- ^{2.77}*Rapid Eye Movement Sleep (REM sleep)*: Each night, people typically experience four to five episodes of REM sleep. Most episodes of REM sleep last about 20 minutes, and typically occur between two to six o'clock in the morning. A nearly generalized muscle paralysis typifies this phase of sleep, with the exceptions of the muscles of breathing, the heart, the sphincters of the bladder and bowels, and most notably the muscles moving the eyes. Indeed, during this phase of sleep the eyes move around rapidly as if looking around at the events being dreamed. REM sleep produces effects upon the body fascinatingly similar to the effects of curare. As Thomas Cecil Gray remarked on the effects of curare in 1946; "In the conscious human subject the muscles of the eyes, mouth and fingers are affected first, then those of the trunk and limbs, and finally the diaphragm. Consciousness is retained, and recovery occurs in the reverse order," (page 403 in Gray 1946). REM sleep also causes paralysis of the skeletal muscles. And just as with curare, REM sleep also reduces the strength of all voluntary muscles while

leaving the muscles of the diaphragm relatively unaffected (McNicholas 2002, Tusiewicz 1977). The main difference between REM sleep and curare manifests in their differing effect on eye muscles. During REM sleep, the eyes move around rapidly, whereas lower doses of curare paralyze eye muscles.

[2.78]These are the measurably different types of sleep undergone by each of us each night. So while sleeping and apparently unconscious, we undergo variable and profound alterations of bodily function.

Sleep is a form of continuous mental activity

[2.79]While sleeping we appear unconscious and unaware of what is happening about us. Yet we do dream during sleep, and we sometimes remember these dreams. Studies performed in sleep laboratories reveal that when awoken during a period of NREM sleep, up to 86% of people recall awakening from a dream (Table 5 in Oudiette 2012). Other studies in sleep laboratories reveal that when awoken during a period of REM sleep, up to 98% of young adults recall awakening from a dream (Nielsen 2012, Oudiette 2012). Furthermore, studies of brain activity during dreaming reveal that the primary sensory areas of the brain are largely inactive, while those regions of the brain processing and bringing sensory information to the conscious brain are as active during dreaming as during normal wakefulness (Kjaer 2002, Lövblad 2003, Ogawa 2006, Rees 2002, Schwartz 2002). This means the brain is not receiving sensations from outside the body, but is spontaneously generating and processing these sensations.

[2.80]All these things mean that sleep is a bodily condition during which people appear unconscious while actually experiencing continual mental activity at varying levels of consciousness in the form of dreams (Hobson 2005, Hobson 2009, Rees 2002, Sanders 2012, Vaitl 2005, Wittmann 2004). Nonetheless, the physiological state of the body does differ between different phases of sleep, and this may manifest as different types of dreams. So do people experience different types of dreams during different phases of sleep?

Types of dreams

[2.81]Dream content does indeed differ between different phases of sleep. Most researchers recognize several different types of dreams: sleep onset dreams, dreams during NREM sleep, dreams during REM sleep, and lucid dreams. I will not discuss the neurophysiological differentiation of these different types of dreams; suffice to say this is standard work in most dream laboratories, and neurological sleep analysis centers. The most important fact about dreams is the simple knowledge about sleep each of us possesses. People lie still, and appear unconscious during sleep and dreams, and that different sleep stages are associated with different types of dreams. So what are these differences?

- [2.82]*Sleep onset dreams*: These are dreams occurring during the onset of sleep. Typically dreams in this stage of sleep consist of 64% non-visual thoughts, and 35% hallucinations (Fosse 2001). These hallucinations are usually visual and auditory, and seldom involve other sensory modalities such as smell, touch, or position (Schredl 2005). Mental activity is not self-reflective, because the dreamer does not question whether the dream is real or unreal—the dream is simply accepted as a fact (Rechtschaffen 1978).

- [2.83]*NREM sleep dreams*: Dreams occurring during NREM sleep typically contain 38% non-visual thoughts, and about 60% hallucinations (Fosse 2001). These hallucinations are usually visual and auditory, and seldom involve other sensory modalities such as smell, touch, or position (Schredl 2005). Social interactions dreamed during NREM sleep are typically self-initiated friendly interactions (McNamara 2005, McNamara 2007). Here again, mental activity is not self-reflective, because the dreamer does not question whether the dream is real or unreal—the dream is simply accepted as a fact (Rechtschaffen 1978).

- [2.84]*REM sleep dreams*: Dreams occurring during REM sleep typically contain only 22% non-visual thoughts, and 82% of the dream content consists of hallucinations (Fosse 2001). These hallucinations are usually visual and auditory, and seldom involve other sensory modalities such as smell, touch, or position (Schredl 2005). In contrast to NREM sleep, dreams of social interactions during REM sleep are more often aggressive (McNamara 2005, McNamara 2007). Once again, mental activity is not self-reflective, because the dreamer does not question whether the dream is real or unreal—the dream is simply accepted as a fact (Rechtschaffen 1978).

- [2.85]*Lucid dreams*: Lucid dreams typically only occur during REM sleep. During such dreams, people realize they are dreaming, and can even control the content of their dreams to some extent. These are

59

very vivid and often profound experiences whose properties consist of: "full awareness of the dream state: awareness of the possibility of making free decisions: clear consciousness of the dreamer: perception by all senses: full memory of waking life: full memory of all lucid dream experiences in the waking state and in the lucid dream state: awareness of the meaning of symbols" (Holzinger 2006). It is during these lucid dreams that some people experience flying dreams, or out-of-body experiences. Not only do people undergoing lucid dreams realize they are dreaming, but they can signal the fact they are dreaming. They signal they are dreaming by means of moving their eyes in a prearranged manner to generate signals on recordings of eye muscle electrical activity, or electroencephalographic activity in response to pre-arranged light or sound signals applied when they are in REM sleep (Holzinger 2006, LaBerge 2010, Voss 2009). Unlike other dreams, self-reflection is present during lucid dreams (LaBerge 2010).

[2.86]Descriptions of dreams characteristic of different sleep stages show that quiet thinking is more likely during NREM sleep. However, quiet thinking is almost totally absent during REM sleep, which is full of powerful hallucinatory material, much like hallucinations experienced by schizophrenics, or the hallucinations induced by drugs. These findings prompted the prominent neuroscientist, Allan Hobson to say, "Dreaming is therefore as hallucinatory and thoughtless (or delusional) as so-called mental illness." He concluded by aptly remarking, "These findings support the hypothesis that REM sleep is a physiological brain state that produces a distinctive and psychosis-like mental content, whereas during normal waking such properties are suppressed" (Hobson 2005). Our personal experiences of dreaming reveal the truth of these statements.

[2.87]Consider the nightmare. This is a perfect example of how internally generated body states are combined into sometimes quite terrifying dreams. Everyone has experienced at least one nightmare. Nightmares are terrifying dreams during which people attempt to escape from horrible fates, or try to warn others of fearful and terrifying things. During such dreams, dreamers may try to run, but discover their limbs feel extraordinarily heavy. They feel every movement requires enormous effort, as if they were walking through thick syrup or mud. Or they discover they cannot move at all, feeling as if they were pinned down to one place. They try to shout or scream, but little or no sound issues from their mouths. They may even feel as if they are being suffocated by a heavy weight upon their chests. Feelings of helpless despair and terror oppress and overwhelm them. They eventually awaken, and remember the imagery of their dreams, as well as their emotions of overwhelming fear and helplessness.

[2.88]Both REM sleep and curare-like muscle paralyzing drugs induce a generalized muscle paralysis, so inducing identical experiences and perceptions of paralysis in the conscious mind. The conscious sensations induced by curare-like drugs are: movement and speech require enormous effort with little or no result (Smith 1947, Topulos 1993), many people feel themselves weighted down (Gandevia 1977), and even feel as if they cannot breathe (Gandevia 1993, Topulos 1993). Paralysis due to other causes also produces the same sensations of weight and helplessness (McCloskey 1978). So rather than true experiences undergone by a disembodied soul, these nightmarish dreams are more likely internally generated sensations of the muscular paralysis of REM sleep sensed, and transformed by the conscious mind into terrifying dreams of fear and helplessness.

[2.89]Even though most dream imagery and thought is internally generated by the sleeping body and brain, sleeping and dreaming people do react to events and stimuli from outside their bodies. We know this from the simple fact that people are awakened by touch, shaking, pain, kicking, blows, sounds, and lights. These external events and stimuli are often incorporated into dreams. A dream I once had on a Sunday morning during October 1999 is a good example of a dream incorporating external sensations.

[2.90]*This Sunday morning, I was feeling lazy, and lay sleeping next to my wife who was reading a magazine and listening to the radio. While sleeping I had a vivid dream. I dreamed I was at the dentist for a regular check-up. He examined my teeth and explained that he also had to go to his dentist, but wanted to have his teeth examined before going there. I am not lazy, nor unwilling to help others, so I examined his teeth, as if this was a perfectly normal thing to do while at the dentist. As I examined his teeth, a female dental assistant came into the consulting room and said that a woman in the waiting room wanted to speak with the dentist about a near-death experience she underwent while being treated by him. Surprisingly, this dental assistant was a well-known faith healer, but I did not think this was surprising at the time. I also wanted to hear the story of this woman, so after*

61

leaving the consulting room of the dentist, I looked for her, and found her being interviewed in the middle of a busy waiting room by a psychologist. My interest in this woman's experience disappeared immediately, because I was not going to take part in this type of public "near-death experience circus". Accordingly, I left to go to my work in the adjacent hospital, where I was amazed to hear her interview broadcast over speakers throughout the hospital! My revulsion with this type of "near-death experience circus" was complete, and was sufficient to awaken me. I immediately told my wife about this dream. She laughed, and told me she was listening the radio as I lay sleeping next to her. And on the radio, she first heard an interview with a dentist, followed by an interview with this same well-known faith healer. Furthermore, this faith healer also talked about holding a special "healing session" for people who had undergone near-death experiences.

[2.91]This was a typical NREM dream with calm thinking during the dream, and with content driven by subconscious perceptions of external stimuli. These discussions teach much about the different types of sleep as well as the different types of dreams typical of the different phases of sleep. The fact that different phases of sleep are associated with different types of dreams is very strange. It means sleep and the associated dreams are not a unitary phenomenon. All the points raised in this discussion of sleep and dreaming, indicate that the experience of sleep is a useful instrument to explore whether the postulates of the mind-models of dualism or materialism correspond with reality.

Sleep and the soul

[2.92]Indeed, examination of the experience of dreaming reveals a serious problem with the mind-model of dualism. The ancient Greek philosopher, Aristotle (384-322 BCE), was one of many philosophers interested in the phenomenon of sleep and dreaming. A passage in his study of the soul called *De Anima*, poses a question related to this very problem.

[2.93]*In addition to this we must investigate the nature of dreams and explain why persons sometimes dream in sleep and at other times do not. Or shall we say that dreaming always occurs in sleep, but we do not remember our dreams? If this is true, what is the explanation? (pages 213-214 in Chapter I, "On Sleeping and Waking", in Aristotle 1902)*

[2.94]According to the mind-model of dualism, the soul is continually conscious, and dreaming is a manifestation and proof of continual consciousness of the soul. This is no new idea. For example, Marcus Tullius Cicero was an ancient Roman writer and statesman who once wrote the following passage about sleep and dreaming more than 2000 years ago.

[2.95]*Again, you really see nothing resembling death so much as sleep; and yet it is when the body sleeps that the soul most clearly manifests its divine nature; for when it is unfettered and free it sees many things that are to come. (page 93 in De Senectute - Cicero 1996)*

[2.96]The Reverend Richard Storrs once lyrically expounded the same belief almost 1900 years later during 1857, as part of a lecture given at the Brooklyn Institute in New York, USA.

[2.97]*The phenomena of Dreams are important and significant in connection with this department of our subject. Of themselves, almost, they set before us the fact I have adverted to. Consider these phenomena! [...] Its [sleep of the body] sleep is, indeed, as the ancients described it, 'the brother of Death.'*
And yet the mind, unwearied and alert, not cramped or constrained by this dullness of the body, only let forth indeed to a more free excursiveness by the transient sealing up of each physical sense, roams out every whither, in its argument and its thought. It plans disquisitions, dramas, histories; it grapples with and explicates the problems of geometry; it applies, with an intuition which is sharper than induction, the mixed mathematics, in their diverse applications. It sings to itself, with a more ethereal and triumphant utterance than it ever could attain while conscious of the body. Its invention is quick in plastic art. It feels such love for kindred and friends, for children, for the absent, as almost never inspired it before; a love so tremulous, eager, tearful, that it sometimes stirs and wakens the frame with its throbbing pulsations. It goes out over seas,—this keeneyed, liberated, exulting Soul,—and views before it, as in actual presence, the tropic islands, exuberant with their wealth of flowers and foliage, and reverberating the roll of the surf on the coral-reef; or it hovers, with shivering and stimulated sense,

through the auroral North, and traces the track of a disappearing chivalry as this pierces the ice-mountains in quest of the pole. There is no sphere of action, from the slave-ship to the throne-room, there is no sphere of life, on the earth or in the skies, that does not seem open to the access of the Soul, when the body has been benumbed by sleep, and the mind has been loosened to the ecstasy of dreams. The memory, the judgment, the imagination, the fancy, the affectionate sensibility, the conscience itself, become strangely exhilarated and energized in this state. And all that the soul wants, it would sometimes appear, is to have that state made perfect and permanent, to have its own activity entirely dissociated from that of the body, in order to gain the utmost inspiration, and an unlimited range. It is never so winged, so intuitive, so discursive, so surcharged with thought, so keenly alive to every passion, as when the body is passive and dumb, and altogether forgotten. It then vivifies the Past; incorporates the ideal; sets all actual forces in new combinations; anticipates the Future; and treads with fleet and noiseless foot aerial regions. It feels a rapture preluding Heaven. It is mastered by an anguish which hath the element of Hell in it. The Universe melts before its view, and leaves it face to face with God! (pages 313-315 in Lecture VI in Storrs 1857)

[2.98]These passages reveal a belief in the continual consciousness of the soul. Laboratory studies also reveal sleep to be a condition of continual dreaming. Nonetheless, studies of how often people can recall dreaming after spontaneously awakening from normal uninterrupted sleep, reveal something very different from laboratory sleep awakening studies. They reveal that on average, young adults can only remember dreaming between 5 to 10 times a month (Nielsen 2012), even though sleep is a condition of continual mental activity expressed as dreams. This is a stunningly low frequency of dream recall when viewed from this latter perspective. So can the mind-models of dualism or materialism explain this dramatic difference in dream recall frequency?

Dualism and dream memory

[2.99]Believers in dualism claim the soul is continually conscious during sleep (see Chapter 1). Indeed, the fact that nearly all people remember their dreams upon awakening in asleep laboratories during periods of NREM and REM sleep is very consistent with this belief. Nevertheless, the very low percentage of dream recall after spontaneously awakening from normal sleep exposes a major problem with the mind-model of dualism.

- [2.100]According to the mind-model of dualism, the soul forms all memories, and is the repository of all memories (see 1.92-1.115).
- [2.101]This means that the soul is the repository of all memories of the continuous mental activity occurring during sleep, as well as the repository of all memories of experiences undergone, and things learned while physically conscious.
- [2.102]How do people recall memories when physically awake? When asked to remember something, the physical body perceives the request. This physically perceived request is somehow transferred to the immaterial soul, which retrieves the appropriate memory, and controls the body through the conduit of the material brain to recount the memory through bodily movements, writing, or speech (see 1.143).
- [2.103]The same procedure is equally applicable to the retrieval of dream memories, as is demonstrated by the ability to voluntarily recall dreams.
- [2.104]The soul is unaffected by changes in the physical brain occurring during sleep (see 1.66-1.75).
- [2.105]The ability of the human body to recall and express memories returns to normal upon awakening. Moreover, expression of dream memories requires the same brain and bodily mechanisms regardless of whether awakening occurs purposefully as in a sleep laboratory, or spontaneously as after a refreshing night sleep.
- [2.106]Accordingly, people should be capable of recalling and recounting all the experiences and thoughts of the continually conscious soul after spontaneously awakening from normal sleep.

[2.107]This chain of logic indicates that recalling the thoughts and actions of the soul during sleep is a situation similar to recalling thoughts and actions of the physical body when awake. So according to the mind-model of dualism, sleep should not be a condition of a blank loss of consciousness, but a bodily state experienced and remembered as a period of continual consciousness. However, most people recall only very few dreams after awakening. It is true that some people do remember some of their dreams each night, and some of these people even keep dream diaries. But such recalled dreams are only fragmentary memories of relatively short periods of dreaming. People never claim recalling being continually conscious throughout the whole of the time their bodies were sleeping. This observation is very inconsistent with the claims of the mind-model of dualism. So what are possible causes of the general failure to remember the continuous conscious activity of the soul during sleep as proposed by the mind-model of dualism?

- [2.108]The cause cannot be a filtering effect of the conscious brain, because the physical brain is just as conscious after awakening in a dream laboratory as it is after spontaneous awakening.
- [2.109]Does the soul only form short-term memories during sleep? This would explain why memories of dreams are so evanescent. But the fact that some people can train themselves to remember their dreams after spontaneous awakening negates this idea, because such dream recall is a manifestation of long-term memory.
- [2.110]Does failure to remember dreams mean that the soul specifically refuses to recount dream memories? This might be the case if dreaming included "secret learning" only meant for the immaterial soul. Such a belief implies that dreaming is a sort of "secret night-school for the soul."
- [2.111]Are dream memories of the immaterial world of the soul so incredible, that they are incapable of expression or understanding in this physical universe? This might also explain why so few people remember their dreams.
- [2.112]Does the fact of spontaneous awakening from sleep automatically instruct the soul not to recount dream memories? The latter idea implies that changes occurring in the physical brain upon awakening inhibit retention of dream memories. But recall of dreams does occur on awakening in dream laboratories, and also occurs spontaneously in people who train themselves to remember their dreams.

[2.113]All these are fascinating speculations on the nature of memory, but remain speculations. Even so, all these considerations indicate a failure of dualism to explain dream recall frequency.

Materialism and dream memory

[2.114]So can the mind-model of materialism explain why people remember so few dreams after spontaneous awakening? The mind-model of materialism states that the physical brain generates consciousness, as well as all personality, thoughts, and emotions. This partly explains why differences in brain structure and function due to age (Georgi 2012, Nielsen 2012, Schredl 2009), gender (Georgi 2012, Nielsen 2012, Schredl 2008), as well as various psychological factors (Beaulieu-Prevost 2007, Parke 2009), can affect dream recall frequency. Furthermore, according to materialism, the physical brain forms all memories, and is the repository of all memories. This explains known variations in brain function during sleep and awakening are such that not all dreams are recalled (Fell 2006, Marzano 2011, Wittmann 2004a). Accordingly, physical factors related to brain structure and functioning explain the low incidence of dream recall better than the mind-model of dualism.

Dreaming and the soul

[2.115]In conclusion, even though the reality of continual conscious mental activity during sleep is apparent confirmation of the mind-model of dualism, it is not proof of the reality of this mind-model. Furthermore, the low incidence of dream recall after spontaneous awakening, and the fact that dream characteristics differ between different physiological types of sleep, reveals a failure of the mind-model of dualism, while indicating the validity of that of materialism. In other words, the low incidence of spontaneous dream recall indicates that memories are stored within the brain rather than the soul. Finally, dreaming reveals another bodily condition during which consciousness is present, even though the body appears unconscious.

Levels of consciousness

[2.116]All these discussions of the different circumstances during which consciousness manifests, as well as the anatomical and physiological basis of consciousness, finally brings us to the question of the determination of the level of consciousness.

[2.117]Consciousness manifests under the most diverse and even unlikely situations. Yet consciousness is not an all-or-nothing condition. There are different levels of consciousness. Some people are somnolent, stuporose, or even comatose. Here again we are confronted with terms describing different levels of obtunded consciousness. As usual, accuracy of communication requires definition of these standard medical terms.

- [2.118]*Obtunded consciousness*: is a reduced level of consciousness.
- [2.119]*Somnolent*: a somnolent person is excessively sleepy, manifests minimal, to no spontaneous activity, responds to calling their name, and responds to external stimuli with incoherent mumblings and uncoordinated actions.
- [2.120]*Stupor*: a person in a stupor is stuporose. A stuporose person only responds to shouting their name, repeated shaking, and reflex reactions to pain. The level of consciousness of a "deeply stuporose" person is even more obtunded. A deeply stuporose person does not respond to shouting or shaking, and only reacts to pain with reflex movements. These are reflex reactions to pain such as withdrawing, grimacing, etc. These reactions are quite distinct from directed responses to pain.
- [2.121]*Coma*: a person in a coma is comatose. A comatose person does not respond in any way to shaking, shouting, or even intense pain. They also may not manifest other basic brainstem reactions such as gagging in response to stimulating the back of the throat (gag reflex), their pupils may not respond to light (pupillary reflex), they may not close their eyes in response to touching the cornea (corneal reflex), or respond to stimulating their bronchi with a suction tube (cough reflex).

[2.122]These older terms of stupor, coma, and others, are still frequently used to describe levels of consciousness. However, they are qualitative terms, and some people interpret them very liberally. Most modern physicians now use the Ramsay Score to describe the level of consciousness. It is a simple, accurate, and easily applied clinical scoring system to define the level of consciousness, first described by the English anesthesiologist Michael Ramsay (Ramsay 1974). Six levels of consciousness are defined, and although the score has been extended and slightly modified since first published in 1974, it remains the same.

- [2.123]*Ramsay Score 0:* Normal consciousness
- [2.124]*Ramsay Score 1:* Anxious, agitated, and restless.
- [2.125]*Ramsay Score 2:* Awake, oriented, tranquil, and cooperative.
- [2.126]*Ramsay Score 3:* Sleepy, responds to commands, and opens eyes in response to loud speech or shaking.
- [2.127]*Ramsay Score 4:* Unconscious. No response to loud speech or shaking. Does respond briskly to tapping of forehead by blinking (glabellar response). Rapid response to pain.

- [2.128]*Ramsay Score 5:* Unconscious, stuporose. No response to loud speech or shaking. Responds only sluggishly to tapping of forehead. Sluggish response to pain.
- [2.129]*Ramsay Score 6:* Coma. No response to speech, shaking, tapping forehead, or pain.

[2.130]The Ramsay score is an internationally accepted system providing a standardized and general method of describing the level of consciousness. There are several other international scores of level of consciousness, but in general, these are scores designed and adapted for specific situations.

Conclusions on consciousness

[2.131]So what do all these things mean? What do these things tell us about consciousness? These various definitions, studies, and clinical phenomena all demonstrate that regardless of whether one believes in the mind-model of dualism or that of materialism, bodily consciousness is a phenomenon requiring the functioning of the brainstem and the thalamus.

[2.132]What does all this tell us about the nature of the conscious mind? To the materialist, consciousness is a product of the functioning of the brain, because the functioning of the thalamus and the brainstem generates the wondrous phenomenon of consciousness. A believer in dualism claims that the mechanisms of the thalamus and brainstem are the conduit through which the soul exercises control over the physical body such that it manifests consciousness. Both explanations of the nature of the conscious mind require the functioning of the physical mechanisms of the brainstem and thalamus. Accordingly, the anatomical and physiological basis necessary for the body to generate or manifest consciousness cannot differentiate between the mind-models of materialism and dualism.

[2.133]Even so, the common experience of dreaming during sleep does enable a preliminary investigation of the mind-models of dualism and materialism. This investigation reveals the inability of dualism to explain the low frequency of dream recall after spontaneous awakening—an indication of the failure of this mind-model. Furthermore, the discussion of dream recall raises the question of whether memory formation and retention occur within the soul or within the physical brain. Nonetheless, this discussion revealed no absolute proof of the failure of dualism. Any definitive conclusion as to which mind-model is correct requires considerable further study.

[2.134]Finally, the discussions in this chapter permits the conclusion that consciousness is a marvelous, but poorly understood phenomenon, generated or made possible by the functioning of some of the most primitive parts of the brain—the thalamus and brainstem. In practical terms, all that can be said about consciousness is that an unconscious person has no thought, will, memory, personality, emotions, or any other qualities of mind, while these attributes are present in a conscious person. This is a usable and practical way of viewing consciousness, and one expounded for many millennia by various philosophies and religions. Indeed, in the ancient Hindu holy book, the *Bhagavad Gita*, we read that the god Krishna tells the human Prince Arjuna that consciousness is the spark of light illuminating the mind, making all the properties of mind possible.

[2.135]*O son of Bharata [Arjuna], as the sun alone illuminates all this universe, so does the living entity, one within the body [the soul], illuminate the entire body by consciousness. (Bhagavad-Gita As It Is, 13:34)*

3

Subjective & Objective

[3.1]Consciousness is not always evident. The examples in the previous chapter clearly demonstrate that an apparently unconscious person may actually be conscious. Reports of people arousing from a multitude of other situations during which they appeared unconscious, repeatedly demonstrate this same fact. Moreover, even when evidently conscious, the speech, actions, and behaviors of physically conscious persons may differ considerably from what they are actually experiencing at that moment. This difference between the subjective aspects of experiences, and the externally objectively observed aspects of the same experiences requires discussion.

Subjective and objective defined

[3.2]Experiences are always conscious, because an unconscious person undergoes no conscious experiences. As discussed in the previous chapter, apparent and evident physical manifestations of consciousness are not necessary for consciousness to have been present during an experience. The effects of curare on conscious persons, the locked-in syndrome, out-of-body experiences, near-death experiences, and unintentional intra-operative awareness under general anesthesia are all good examples of conscious experiences undergone by motionless, apparently physically unconscious individuals. And consciousness is present during an experience, regardless of whether consciousness originates within the brain, or in a separable immaterial soul. Furthermore, every conscious experience has two aspects: the subjective experience itself, and the objective observation of that same experience.

- [3.3]*Subjective observation of an experience.* While undergoing an experience, an individual may observe events, persons, and other occurrences external to his or her body, perceive bodily sensations, or undergo emotions and other experiences. All such observations are subjective aspects of an individual experience.

- [3.4]*Objective observation of an experience.* Impartial onlookers may observe an individual undergoing an experience. Such impartial observers may also employ electronic or other apparatus to record the movements, actions, appearances, expressions, vocalizations, or other manifestations expressed by an individual undergoing an experience. Furthermore, observers report the circumstances under which, and during which an experience occurred. All these things are objective observations of an individual experience.

[3.5]A report of an experience undergone by an apparently unconscious individual may contain details corresponding with the external objective physical reality near that person at the time of the experience. These correspondences fix the location and time at which an experience occurred, as well as sometimes explaining the causes of the subjective aspects of the experience. Such correspondences also permit an integration of the subjective and the observed aspects of an experience.

Mary and the color red

[3.6]A short digression into a modern philosophical thought experiment is necessary prior to launching into a more medically oriented study of the differences between subjective experience and objective observation. During 1986, a philosopher called Frank Jackson, described a deceptively simple thought experiment about the experience of seeing the color red (see pages 26-27 in Rast 2012). Despite its deceptively simple appearance, this thought experiment actually reveals profoundly important facts relevant to any consideration of subjective and objective aspects of experiences. There are several variations of this thought experiment—also known as the "knowledge argument" (Beaton 2005, McGeer 2003, Vergauwen 2010). Erich Rast, a Portugese philosopher, cited the original 1986 argument of Frank Jackson.

[3.7]*Mary is confined to a black-and-white room, is educated through black-and-white books and through lectures relayed on black-and-white television. In this way she learns everything there is to know about the physical nature of the world. She knows all the physical facts about us and our environment, in a wide sense of 'physical' which includes everything in completed physics, chemistry, and neurophysiology, and all there is to know about the causal and relational facts consequent upon this, including of course functional roles. If physicalism is true, she knows all there is to know. [...] It seems, however, that Mary does not know all there is to know. For when she is let out of the black-and-white room or given a color television, she will learn what it is like to see something red, say. (Rast 2012)*

[3.8]Indeed, as Frank Jackson realized, to know all about something is very different to experiencing that something. This is an argument claiming that materialism fails to understand or describe this subjective experience. Therefore, Frank Jackson and others argue that experience is a non-physical property, and consequently this argument apparently proves the false nature of materialism. Philosophers have argued for and against this rather simplistic conclusion ever since (Beaton 2005, McGeer 2003, Rast 2012, Vergauwen 2010).

Lessons from Mary

[3.9]Philosophers are neither technicians nor physiologists. They generally ignore several crucial points in this argument relevant to the study of objective and subjective aspects of any experience. These factors are implicitly and explicitly evident in the thought experiment of Mary, and very relevant to the study of the nature of the human mind.

- [3.10]It is irrelevant whether the mind is immaterial, or a product of the functioning of the physical brain. In the example of Mary, she perceives the color red with her physical senses. The very fact of perceiving the color red by the physical senses uses different parts of the sensory apparatus, as well as those parts of the brain processing the perception of seeing the color red. Materialism then states that this process alters the functioning of the brain, which then generates the subjective experience of seeing the color red. Dualism postulates that the processed information from the brain aroused by seeing the color red is transferred to her soul, and her conscious mind in her soul responds appropriately with the subjective experience of perceiving the color red. This is a natural consequence of the reciprocal information exchange between body and soul (see 1.142). The subjective experience of perceiving the color red as undergone by a physically conscious Mary is identical in both situations. Accordingly, it is impossible to differentiate these two mind-models with this thought experiment—a point mentioned in some discussions.

- [3.11]People must first perceive a sensation before it can arouse an experience within the conscious mind. So if the physically conscious Mary could not perceive colored light at all, then she would be unable to respond with a subjective experience upon seeing the color red. Most philosophers are content to leave this as an implicitly understood fact.

[3.12]So how do experiences in response to perceptions arise? Are perceptions actually required? And is knowledge of these things relevant to this discussion of subjective and objective aspects of experiences?

Perceptions and subjective sensations

[3.13]All these things mean it is necessary to examine how a subjective experience can arise in response to a perception. I will do this step-by-step, and so demonstrate how illusions and hallucinations can occur at every step in the chain from sensation to experience.

- [3.14]Just as the scientist Mary perceived the color red with her eyes, people perceive sensations of the world outside the confines of their bodies with the appropriate sense organs. This is how people perceive sensations of movements, sounds, light, smells, taste, touch, etc. It is possible to manipulate these sensory organs to generate sensory illusions and hallucinations. Virtual reality rides in game arcades are a good example of manipulation of senses to provide wonderful illusory experiences. Another example of a wonderful sensory organ generated illusion are the vivid sensations of illusory movements generated by vibrating muscle tendons to selectively stimulate muscle sensory organs called "muscle spindles" (McCloskey 1978).
- [3.15]Sensory nerves activated by sense organs reacting to these sensations, relay these sensations to the brain as nerve impulses. Manipulation of sensory nerve function also generates hallucinations of movement and position. For example, selective electrical stimulation of sensory nerves generates illusions of position and movement (Gandevia 1985). Local anesthesia techniques such as spinal anesthesia and anesthesia of the arm result in abnormal

patterns of sensory nerve activity sensed as vivid illusions of phantom limbs, abnormal limb sizes, and abnormal limb positions (Bromage 1974, Gentili 2002, Isaacson 2000, Paqueron 2003, Paqueron 2004, Prevoznik 1964).

- [3.16]Specific dedicated areas of the brain perform primary processing of these nerve impulses. For example, the primary visual cortex performs primary processing of nerve impulses from the eyes. There is also a primary sensory cortex for each of the major senses. Stimulating these different primary sensory cortices with electrical currents generate a wide range of hallucinations depending upon the primary sensory cortex being stimulated. For example, stimulation of the primary sensory cortex subserving position, movement, and touch, generates hallucinations of these sensations (Penfield 1937, Woolsey 1979), while stimulation of the primary optical cortex generates sensations of spots of light (Dobelle 1974).

- [3.17]Processed sensory signals from the various dedicated primary sensory cortices are further processed in specific secondary, or supplementary sensory cortices which convey these sensations to the conscious mind. There is a secondary optical cortex, a secondary auditory cortex, a secondary olfactory cortex, and a secondary sensory cortex, etc. An extensive review of studies of fMRI and PET scans of the brains of hallucinating schizophrenics, reveals activation of the secondary sensory areas of the brain, as well as those regions of the brain manifesting the emotions aroused by these perceptions, yet without activation of the primary sensory areas (Font 2003). The implications are profound. It means these sensations and perceptions are generated within the brain.

[3.18]All these things mean that a conscious perception of a sensation can originate at any point in the chain of sensation perception. Knowledge and appreciation of this single fact is essential when considering differences between objective and subjective perceptions of any sensation. What a person perceives are the subjective sensations aroused by a perception. The same perception when perceived by observers, can only be termed objective when capable of confirmation by recording devices and measurement, or actually recorded by such devices and measurements. This way of viewing subjective versus objective perceptions is one way of dealing with the illusions aroused by group hallucinations, or illusions. All other perceptions are subjective, illusory, or even delusory. And regardless of whether a perception is objective, illusory, or delusory, all perceptions arouse subjective sensations and emotions. With all these facts in mind, it is now possible to examine examples of differences between the subjective and objective aspects of some experiences.

Near-death experiences: objective & subjective aspects

[3.19]Near-death experiences reveal fascinating differences between subjective and objective aspects of individual perceptions and experiences. Several of these aspects are worth examining in some detail.

Feeling of reality & illusory statistics

[3.20]Many people reporting near-death experiences say that the experience was so profound and felt so "real", that it "must be real." They even regard the visual and experiential aspects of these experiences as literal reality (pages 32-33 in Sabom 1982). Susan Blackmore devoted the whole of Chapter 7 in her book, *Dying to Live*, to an extensive discussion of the various ways the human mind develops and generates a sense of reality (Blackmore 1993). This discussion finally led her to conclude that this sense of reality was a mental model of the world generated by the mind to account for the changes in bodily sensations and perceptions during the events causing near-death experiences (page 167 in Blackmore 1993). I am not sure if this explains all aspects of the near-death experience. Nonetheless, it is certainly one of several valid explanations of the reported overpowering sense of reality. One of her concluding passages in *Dying to Live* refers to her own sense of reality undergone during a personal near-death experience.

> [3.21]*Many NDErs [Near-Death Experiencers] come back from their experiences convinced that they have seen the spirit world, convinced that they have grasped their 'overself', 'higher self' or 'ultimate being'; convinced that 'they' have met their dead loved ones and that they will live after they die. I am denying that they are right. I am not denying their experiences but I am disagreeing with the conclusions they have come to. They may, with some justification, think I am insulting them by saying 'You have not seen what you thought you saw.' I am not surprised when people come back at me with 'But I know it because I have been there.' To this I can only say—I have experienced it too and I have come to a different conclusion from you. (page 259 in Blackmore 1993)*

[3.22]As Susan Blackmore quite correctly stated—a feeling of reality is just that—a feeling. But this clear and simple observation, and all the possible alternative explanations of a sense of reality, seem not to modify the thinking of many believers in the mind-model of dualism. They believe in the literal reality of these experiences. Indeed, 17 years after the publication of *Dying to Live*, Jeffrey Long, a physician researcher in near-death experiences, clearly expressed his belief in the literal truth of the visual and experiential aspects of near-death experiences in his book, *Evidence of the Afterlife: The Science of Near-Death Experiences* (Long 2010).

[3.23]*An important NDERF [Near Death Experience Research Foundation] survey question asks 613 NDErs [Near-Death Experiencers] what they think of the reality of their experience—how they viewed the reality of their experience shortly after its occurrence and also at the time they completed the survey. In response, 95.8 percent believed at the time of completing the survey that their NDE was definitely real. Not one NDEr said that the experience they had was "definitely not real." (page 52 in Long 2010)*

[3.24]This passage is no more than the expression of a conviction based upon what Jeffery Long considered good evidence. Nevertheless, his book only presented evidence from an internet form filled in by people voluntarily responding to a public call for near-death experiences. Such an internet study is actually very biased, because people responding to such a public call for experiences on the internet are only those satisfying a number of criteria, and may actually differ considerably from the general population of persons undergoing such experiences.

- [3.25]They are people who use the internet. Not everyone has internet, and not every region in the world has internet.
- [3.26]Not everyone who has undergone a near-death experience uses internet.
- [3.27]Respondents are generally people who search the internet for near-death experience sites. They may differ from other persons, because not everyone who has undergone a near-death experience responds to such a form.
- [3.28]Usually only those people respond who have undergone a profound experience, while those persons who undergo less spectacular experiences respond less often.

- [3.29]Another problem with voluntary internet forms is whether the genders, ages, education levels, and ethnicity of the respondents to this internet questionnaire correspond in general with all people who undergo a near-death experience.

[3.30]These are but a few of the most significant problematical variables relevant to such internet surveys. It is very evident from even this short list that such random internet surveys are prone to a significant statistical bias known as "self-selection bias". However, this is not a phenomenon restricted to internet surveys. It is a well-known source of erroneous statistical conclusions from all surveys using data from self-selected volunteers, regardless of how these volunteers are recruited (Bethlehem 2009, Morton 2006, Søgaard 2004, Strandhagen 2010). Such surveys are useless for determining the true incidence of a phenomenon within a population—they only provide data relevant for determining relationships between variables within the survey data (Etter 2001). Nonetheless, many near-death experience researchers ignore such statistical niceties, and claim that all people undergoing near-death experiences believe in the literal reality of the experiences they underwent. In a book entitled the *Handbook of Near-Death Experiences* (Holden 2009), we also read that people reporting their near-death experiences regard the visionary and experiential content of near-death experiences to be "literally true", as "real experiences", even regarding them as experiences of some sort of "hyper-reality".

[3.31]*Some years later, Gabbard and Twemlow (1984) published a careful comparison of the subjective experiences of depersonalization versus OBEs [Out-of-Body Experiences] that characterize NDEs [Near-Death Experiences]. They found several fundamental differences. Whereas the subjective experience of depersonalization often includes unpleasant feelings and a sense of loss of reality, most NDEs are profoundly pleasurable and involve a sense of absolute or hyperreality. Depersonalization also involves a sense of detachment from the body that is subjectively different from the experience of near-death OBEs. Gabbard and Twemlow concluded that NDEs are distinctly different subjective experiences than depersonalization. (page 127 in Holden 2009)*

[3.32]Indeed, many of the contributors to the *Handbook of Near-Death Experiences* endorse this belief in the literal reality of the experiential

78

content of near-death experiences (see also page 187 in Holden 2009). But belief in something is not proof of the reality of that belief. After all, objective eyewitnesses of persons undergoing a near-death experience never see the transcendental universes subsequently described by these people. This means either that these transcendental universes are invisible and immaterial, or that that they do not exist except in the imagination of the persons reporting these experiences. All we know for certain is that many types of hallucinatory experiences reveal the truth of any feeling of reality to be very disputable.

Mental disorder and feelings of reality

[3.33]Schizophrenia is an incapacitating brain disease during which the persons suffer from hallucinations. About 30-50% of adult schizophrenic patients report hearing voices commanding them to perform actions and deeds, among which, acts of violence against other persons, and rather more seldom, to commit self-mutilation, or even suicide (Large 2009, Lee 2004a, McNiel 2000). Schizophrenic persons experience these "command hallucinations" as so real, that many comply with these commands, committing a variety of innocuous actions, and sometimes committing actual acts of violence against others or themselves (Hersch 1998, McNiel 2000). Genital self-mutilation is an extreme and spectacular example of compliance with the true sense of reality experienced by schizophrenic persons complying with instructions from their command hallucinations (Eke 2000, Large 2009, Ozan 2010). Erol Ozan, a psychiatrist working in Erzurum, Turkey, reported a spectacular case of command hallucination induced genital self-mutilation committed by a 55 year-old man who had suffered paranoid delusions for the 18 years prior to his act. This man experienced his command hallucinations as so real and compelling that he acted in the following way.

[3.34]*The patient indicated that 20 days prior to his GSM [Genital Self-Mutilation] he was preoccupied with the thought of cutting his penis off. He said that this thought was put into his mind by the same powerful creature. Two weeks before the GSM, the patient said he had left home without informing anyone, aiming at performing a pilgrimage. He said he traveled through many other distant cities on foot. He then decided to use the bathroom of a hospital to cut his penis off. He said he preferred a hospital bathroom to perform this act where help would be more available*

if bleeding would not stop. Despite the pain, he said he cut off his
penis and threw it into the toilet and flushed it away. During the
first psychiatric interview with him, he said that the same
powerful creature was now ordering him to cut his arm off. (Case
3 in Ozan 2010)

[3.35]This is a rare and spectacular example of the reality and compelling nature of such command hallucinations. We regard the statements and subjective experiences of this man as products of hallucinations because he acted very strangely, and no-one saw the same "powerful creature" instructing him to perform these deed. Nonetheless, his sense of the reality of the commands of this powerful creature, and the compelling necessity to comply with these commands must have been overpoweringly real to him at the time.

[3.36]Schizophrenia is not the only cause of hallucinations with an overpowering sense of reality. Intoxications due to drug overdoses, or combinations of drugs can also induce hallucinations with such an overpowering sense of reality, that affected people commit extreme acts of violence or self-mutilation. Ismail Tuwir, an ophthalmologist working in Dublin, Ireland, once reported the spectacular case of a 19 year-old man who violently removed one of his eyes while under the influence of a combination of drugs.

[3.37]*A 19 year old man was admitted following attempted*
enucleation of his right eye during an acute psychotic episode
after taking ecstasy, LSD, and excess alcohol. He described,
"seeing an army of police officers attacking him." He attempted
to remove a "bomb" which had gone into his eye using a nail
clipper and pliers. He was still in a state of psychosis running
around aimlessly and had to be held to the ground by six people
to prevent further self mutilation. (Tuwir 2005).

[3.38]This was another rare and very dramatic example of compliance with a hallucination inducing an overpowering sense of reality. The citation above refers to an "attempted enucleation", but the reality reported later in this article reveals that this man had very effectively gouged out his eye. His primary motivation for such a desperate act was a compelling sense of the "reality" of a bomb in his eye.

[3.39]Many people would quite correctly say that compliance with command, or other hallucinations, is a manifestation of some dreadful form of functional brain disorder induced by brain oxygen starvation, fever, drugs, and disease, or actual brain diseases such as schizophrenia, brain infections, brain tumors, or epilepsy. Near-death experiences occurring during cardiac arrest are also associated with a compelling sense of reality, yet they always occur during periods of abnormal physical brain function induced by varying levels of brain oxygen starvation. The same is true for near-death experiences induced by many other conditions. So why do the proponents of the literal reality of the experiential content of near-death experiences label such experiences as "true experiences of a spiritual reality", while labelling the visionary content of hallucinations occurring during brain disorders as "mere hallucinations"? After all, people reporting such experiences always feel an equally compelling sense of reality at the time. So what are the criteria for determining reality in such situations?

- [3.40]Is the criterion for reality that the hallucinations comply with current socio-cultural belief systems? Regardless of the origins of the experiential content of hallucinations, they are nearly always related to the sociocultural context in which the affected persons live. This is true for many schizophrenic and drug-induced hallucinations. Furthermore, the same is also true for the experiential content of near-death experiences (Athappilly 2006, Belanti 2008). Dependence upon sociocultural context means that experiential content reveals no fundamental properties of a soul functioning independently from the body. Accordingly, this criterion is very disputable in the situation of near-death experiences.
- [3.41]Is the criterion for the reality of a hallucinatory experience that the experiential content complies with objective reality? Such a criterion would exclude all schizophrenic, and drug intoxication induced hallucinations, as well as nearly all near-death experiences without veridical elements.
- [3.42]Is the criterion for the reality of an experience or hallucination simply that, "it feels real, therefore it must be real?" The previous examples of the man who was commanded to cut off his penis (Case 3 in Ozan 2010), as well as the man who gouged out an eye (Tuwir 2005), are extreme examples clearly illustrating the fallacy that belief in the reality of something is not necessarily proof of that belief.

[3.43]All these things reveal how belief in the compelling literal reality of hallucinations, out-of-body experiences, or near-death experiences, is not necessarily objective reality. Ivor Tuckett (1873-1942), an erstwhile critic of psychical research, once tersely summarized his findings regarding the intense belief in the reality of psychical phenomena held by many psychic researchers as an overpowering "will-to-believe" (page iii in the preface of Tuckett 1932). Indeed, belief in the reality of something is sometimes no more than a powerful expression of a belief system, and is not evidence of the reality of that belief. This is the only conclusion possible, and reveals a profound difference between the subjective and objective assessment of an experience.

Near-death experiences & enhanced mental function

[3.44]Another fascinating difference between the subjective and objective aspects of near-death experiences is that of enhanced mental function. People reporting their out-of-body and near-death experiences, often describe enhanced mental function during these experiences. These experiences of enhanced mental function are so real, so profound, and so intense, that many of those who undergo such experiences are firmly convinced of their reality. Enhanced mental function during these experiences takes various forms such as apparently increased intelligence, increased speed of thought, understanding of the universe, time expansion, and enriched hearing and vision. A woman called Pam Reynolds reported just such an example of enhanced mental function during an out-of-body experience undergone during neurosurgery performed under general anesthesia.

> [3.45]*I remember seeing several things in the operating room when I was looking down. It was the most aware that I think that I have ever been in my entire life ... I was metaphorically sitting on Dr. Spetzler's [the neurosurgeon] shoulder. It was not like normal vision. It was brighter and more focused and clearer than normal vision ... (page 41 in Sabom 1998)*

[3.46]Jeffrey Long reported the story of a man who had a prolonged near-death experience induced by a brain hemorrhage. Even though apparently unconscious, this man described his mental state as:

> [3.47]*... ; colors were electric, smells fantastic ... I was also aware of the overpowering secret to life in its truly simple form and felt and believed that nothing is real but the feeling. The experience of death has been the most real and physical experience of my life, (page 54 in Long 2010)*

[3.48]The popular and scientific literature on near-death experiences is replete with such descriptions of the apparently enhanced mental abilities and perceptions of people undergoing such experiences. But does everyone recalling undergoing a near-death experience report enhanced mental abilities and perceptive abilities?

Mental state during near-death experiences

[3.49]Bruce Greyson, a prominent near-death experience researcher, investigated the mental states undergone by 74 persons during their near-death experiences. He found that not everyone reported the same mental states or experiences while undergoing a near-death experience (Greyson 1983).

- [3.50]77% reported a feeling of peace.
- [3.51]64% reported a feeling of joy.
- [3.52]64% reported that time stopped, or lost meaning.
- [3.53]57% report a feeling of cosmic unity.
- [3.54]46% reported their thoughts were unusually vivid.
- [3.55]43% reported an unnaturally brilliant light.
- [3.56]38% reported their senses were unusually vivid.
- [3.57]30% reported a sudden understanding of everything.
- [3.58]22% reported that events seemed instantaneous.
- [3.59]19% reported that their thinking was unusually fast.

[3.60]The most common mental states were feeling of peace and serenity, joy, and time expansion. Twenty-seven years later, an analysis of 613 near-death experience accounts reported by Jeffrey Long revealed much the same, albeit in less detail (page 56 in Long 2010).

- [3.61]74.4% reported feeling more conscious and alert than normal.
- [3.62]19.9% reported normal consciousness and alertness.
- [3.63]5.7% reported less consciousness and alertness than normal.

[3.64]Evidently Bruce Greyson and Jeffrey Long asked very different questions, or questioned very different groups of people. Nonetheless, the results of such studies are clear—more than the half of all people recovering from near-death experiences report having undergone one or more aspects of apparently enhanced mental function. This feeling of enhanced mental function is often profound, intense, and convincing. Moreover, when enhanced mental function occurs during apparent disembodiment of the conscious mind, such as during near-death experiences, many people believe it cannot be anything else but a manifestation of the true nature and reality of the human soul (Cook 1998, pages 160-161 in Lommel 2010, Chapter 3 in Long 2010, Novak 2002, Parnia 2001, Wade 1998). The reasoning behind this idea is simple. People reporting a near-death experience were "very evidently unconscious" while undergoing the experience. Yet during this period of "very evident unconsciousness", they experienced clear and enhanced mental function, sometimes even while undergoing out-of-body experiences. Clear and enhanced mental function in the physical brain is impossible during unconsciousness of the body. After all, unconsciousness is a blank, a period of nothing during which the physical brain can undergo no experience. So if the body is unconscious, enhanced mental function is a manifestation of the true nature of the soul whose functioning is unaffected by the cause of the "very evident loss of consciousness" of the physical body.

[3.65]But there is a problem with this argument. Chapter 2 discusses in some detail how people may be conscious, even though they appear unconscious. Many other examples of this situation are scattered throughout this book. So are such reports of enhanced conscious awareness truly manifestations of the true nature of the soul, or are they examples of altered brain function manifesting as a belief?

Epilepsy and enhanced conscious awareness

[3.66]There are many bodily conditions associated with apparently enhanced conscious awareness. One of these is epilepsy. Epilepsy is not a single condition, but has many forms, being a product of a broad constellation of conditions such as brain tumors, injuries, hemorrhage, etc. This makes it worth discussing this condition at this point.

[3.67]I will begin with the example of enhanced vision. More than 100 years of careful neurological study reveal several instances of enhanced vision, where people report experiencing tunnel vision, or enhanced perceptions of colors just before undergoing epileptic attacks caused by brain tumors, hemorrhage, and many other types of brain damage (Bien 2000). Similarly, brain tumors and many other forms of brain disease sometimes also cause people to experience a curious type of epilepsy during which they experience states of pleasantness or ecstasy (Hansen 2003, Hermann 2004, Picard 2009), and sometimes even out-of-body experiences (Patient No. 27 in Gil-Nagel 1997). Somewhere between 0.4

and 3.9% of persons with partial epilepsy undergo religious epileptic experiences, either before, or as part of the epileptic attack (Devinsky 2008). Howard Morgan, a physician in Lubbock, Texas, reported the case of a 38 year old man with a malignant brain tumor in the right temporal lobe of his brain. This tumor caused epileptic attacks with the following features.

> [3.68]*These episodes occurred multiple times daily over the course of 2 months. A typical fit began suddenly with a feeling of irritation followed promptly by a sense of detachment. He would see a bright but not glaring light. He sensed that the light was the source of knowledge and understanding. He occasionally heard soft music. In about half of these episodes a young bearded man would appear. The man did not identify himself, although the patient assumed that this somewhat vague appearing individual was Jesus Christ. The entire episode lasted only a second or two, but to the patient it seemed much longer. His family reported that during these fits he seemed in another world and would not respond normally to them. (Morgan 1990)*

[3.69]Surgical removal of the tumor stopped recurrences of these epileptic attacks. Sadly for the man concerned, a recurrence of this same malignant brain tumor eventually caused his death 15 months after his first operation. The epileptic episodes of this man revealed several features: loss of contact with the physical world, while experiencing bright light that was the source of understanding and knowledge, hearing music, and possibly even seeing a figure from his Christian religious pantheon. A question arises in this situation. Were his experiences merely hallucinatory products of abnormal brain function due to the tumor? Or did the tumor induce changes in the brain function of this man, such that he experienced short moments when his soul was temporarily able to express its true nature through the mechanisms of his body?

[3.70]Epilepsy induced by all manner of abnormal brain function and pathology is not the only condition causing feelings of enhanced awareness, enhanced perceptive abilities, or apparently increased intelligence. Many other drugs and conditions affecting physical brain function induce these same conditions, and are discussed extensively throughout this book (see index: conscious awareness enhanced). The mind-model of materialism explains all these experiences and perceptions as products of abnormal functioning of the physical brain. This covers the explanation quite well because of the objectively demonstrable conditions inducing these experiences.

3.71However, the mind-model of dualism has rather more problems explaining these experiences. Many believers in dualism claim that the functioning of the physical brain filters the true expression of the soul as manifested by the physical body (see 1.76-1.88), and claim this filtering function may cease during some types of epilepsy. Accordingly, many believers in dualism consider the phenomena of subjectively enhanced perceptive ability and mental performance during epilepsy as manifestations of the true nature of the soul. However, epilepsy is a form of brain malfunction manifesting as a sort of electrical storm in the affected regions of the brain. In the case of the 38 year-old man cited, he was observed as physically conscious during his epileptic attacks, but his subjective experiences were very different to what his family observed (Morgan 1990). The same is true of other cases of enhanced mental function occurring during physical consciousness cited throughout this book. The mind-model of dualism can only explain such conscious experiences of subjective enhancement of mental function, as control exerted by the soul through the mechanisms of a malfunctioning brain, which means such experiences cannot be manifestations of the true nature of the soul.

Other subjective experiences and observations

3.72This brings us to a discussion of various examples of other well-known, and less well-known medical situations demonstrating the difference between subjective experiences, and observations by onlookers of the same persons as they underwent these experiences. The first medical example, and one of the most expressive, is that of delirium.

Delirium: Subjective experiences and observation

3.73Delirium is a wonderful example of the difference between subjective experience and external observation. Delirium is a conscious experience undergone during a state of altered brain function. Sudden withdrawal from chronic excessive alcohol consumption is a cause of the well-known delirium tremens. Valentin Magnan (1835-1916) was a physician at the Sainte Anne Asylum in Paris, France. He treated many patients suffering from the effects of alcoholism. Consider the following colorful report published in his book, *On Alcoholism: The Various Forms of Alcoholic Delirium and their Treatment* (Magnan 1876).

[3.74]Pierre M., aged 42 years, pigeon-feeder at the market, has been a soldier, and contracted the habit of drinking in Africa, his present occupation also gives him frequent opportunities for gratifying his taste for drink. Ordinarily he drank wine, sometimes brandy and more rarely liqueurs. He had nightmares often, and slept badly; for a long time back he had little appetite, spat and vomited sometimes in the morning white or green phlegm. Having fallen ill in consequence of fresh excesses, he was carried to the Hotel-Dieu, whence, as he disturbed the rest of the other patients, he was sent to Sainte-Anne. On admission, April 18th, he is incessantly moving; displaces everything about him, hunts in all the corners, looks behind the doors, picks up from the ground imaginary objects which he shakes and throws away immediately; strikes and rubs his foot upon the ground as if to crush insects; passes his hand before his face and blows to drive away threads and hairs, claps his hand on his thigh, and seizing his trousers, presses hard to crush, as he says, the great black spider which is creeping between the trousers and the skin; —he looks through the window— "there," says he, "is the band of La Place Maubert disguised as bears—there is a cavalcade with lions and panthers, who are looking and making grimaces—there are little children disguised as cats and dogs:" then he sees two men threatening him, and crouches quite frightened; they aim at him, he says, with their guns, they want to kill him because he has taken their daughter. He answers his comrades, he calls them, he hears disputes and wishes to run to them. It is very difficult to arrest his attention; his hands and feet are incessantly on the move to seize or repel animals and objects of all sorts. His face is covered with perspiration, the skin is moderately warm; the temperature 38.2 °C. (100.8 °F.); pulse large and compressible, 80; tongue moist. There is marked tremor of the hands, rather less of the legs, and quivering of the muscles of the face, especially when speaking. (pages 46-47 in Magnan 1876)

[3.75]This man was clearly conscious, even though his experiences were hallucinations or delusions. He recounted his experiences while undergoing them, as well as recalling them at a later more coherent moment. This account clearly illustrates the difference between subjective experience and observation by onlookers. Observers only saw a delirious man. But this man experienced something very different—he was in another parallel world undergoing attack by various people and animals.

[3.76]Such accounts raise questions about the nature of the mind. As usual, the mind-model of materialism has the most parsimonious explanation. Materialism proposes that the functioning of the conscious mind is a product of the functioning of the physical brain. Accordingly, the ravages of alcohol-induced brain damage and malfunction readily explain the hallucinations and behavior of a person suffering delirium tremens.

[3.77]Delirium tremens presents the mind-model of dualism with a major problem. If the soul is the mind, and the brain is merely the conduit of the controlling influence of the soul, then it is possible that mental experiences undergone during delirium tremens are experiences of the soul in a parallel and immaterial universe. This possibility is impossible to ignore when considering the mind-model of dualism. However, this explanation raises a question about other experiences undergone during states of altered physical brain function, such as near-death experiences, and deathbed experiences. Initiation of these experiences is often due to events causing malfunction of the physical brain. People always experience an unquestioning sense of reality while undergoing near-death experiences, deathbed experiences, and delirium tremens. The mind-model of dualism can only explain such experiences as manifestations of control by the soul exerted through the mechanisms of a malfunctioning brain. So which of these experiences are true manifestations of a parallel immaterial world experienced by the soul, or the true nature of the soul? People only decide upon the reality of an experience after recovering from the initiating cause. Subsequently, people nearly always claim that delirium tremens is simply a product of abnormal brain function, while claiming the other experiences are true manifestations of an immaterial reality, and revelations of the true nature of the soul. Nevertheless, this differentiation is only a value judgment. It is not a judgment based upon fact, because all these experiences occur during periods of abnormal brain function, and are all accompanied by an overpowering feeling of reality at the time. Accordingly, delirium tremens is an example of an experience casting serious doubt upon the validity of dualism as a mind-model, and is yet another clear illustration of the difference between objective observation and subjective experience.

Nitrous oxide: Subjective experiences and observation

[3.78]The subjective and observed effects of some drugs also illustrate differences between observation and subjective experience. Nitrous oxide is a good example of a drug with differing subjective and objective effects. Its popular name is "laughing gas", and it was one of the mainstays of general anesthesia from the 1950's to a little past the year 2000. During decades of administering anesthesia, I have personally administered nitrous oxide to many thousands of people. Some of these people did indeed begin to smile and laugh during its administration, but always had too little time to react or say any more. Nor did I ever ask these people to tell what they experienced.

[3.79]But some people such as Humphrey Davy (Davy 1800), and Peter Fenwick (page 306 in Fenwick 1996) have described their experiences of nitrous oxide inhalation. William James, the American philosopher and psychologist, once described the vivid experiences he underwent during inhalation of nitrous oxide while still physically conscious. He first published these experiences in *The Atlantic Monthly*, under the pseudonym "Benjamin Paul Blood", in an article entitled "The Anaesthetic Revelation and the Gist of Philosophy". He subsequently recounted these same experiences in his book *The Will to Believe* (James 1912).

[3.80]*The immense emotional sense of reconciliation which characterizes the 'maudlin' stage of alcoholic drunkenness,—a stage which seems silly to lookers-on, but the subjective rapture of which probably constitutes a chief part of the temptation to the vice, —is well known. [...]*
With me, as with every other person of whom I have heard, the keynote of the experience is the tremendously exciting sense of an intense metaphysical illumination. Truth lies open to the view in depth beneath depth of almost blinding evidence. The mind sees all the logical relations of being with an apparent subtlety and instantaneity to which its normal consciousness offers no parallel; only as sobriety returns, the feeling of insight fades, and one is left staring vacantly at a few disjointed words and phrases, as one stares at a cadaverous-looking snow-peak from which the sunset glow has just fled, or at the black cinder left by an extinguished brand. (paragraph 295 in James 1912)

[3.81]So while affected by nitrous oxide, but still physically conscious, he had a sense of total knowledge of the universe and the relationship of each part to the whole. However, at the same time as he underwent these astounding subjective experiences, observers would have observed him as somnolent or even apparently drunk. The experiences of William James, Peter Fenwick, and Humphrey Davy are not the only reports of such experiences due to nitrous oxide (see index). Other less illustrious persons also report similar experiences. For example, Raymond Moody also reported the story of a young woman who also had a similar transcendental and affective experience. At the time of the experience, she was physically conscious during a dental treatment, while inhaling nitrous oxide gas as a form of partial anesthesia.

> [3.82]*It was some time in my early teenage years, I was in the dentist's office for a filling and was given nitrous oxide. I was kind of nervous about taking it, because I was afraid I wouldn't wake up again. As the anesthesia began to take effect, I felt myself going around in a spiral. It wasn't like I was turning around, but like the dentist's chair was moving in a spiral upward, and it was going up and up and up.*
>
> *Everything was very bright and white and as I got to the top of the spiral, angels came down to meet me and to take me to heaven. I use the plural, "angels," because it's very vague but I'm sure that there were more than one. Yet I can't say how many.*
>
> *At one point the dentist and nurse were talking to each other about another person, and I heard them, but by the time they finished a sentence I couldn't even remember what the first of the sentence had been. But I knew they were talking, and as they did their words would echo around and around. It was an echo that seemed to get further and further away, like in the mountains. I do remember that I seemed to hear them from above, because I felt as though I was up high, going to heaven. (page 158 in Moody 1976)*

[3.83]This young woman was not undergoing resuscitation, nor was there any panic about her body at the time. The dentist and the nurse were conversing normally, working normally, and observed nothing unusual. Yet at the same time, this woman underwent wondrous transcendental and cognitive experiences aroused by inhalation of nitrous oxide. Here again is another good example of the difference between what the dentist and his assistant observed, when compared to what the woman reported undergoing during the same period. This, and other subjective experiences of nitrous oxide inhalation are another revelation of the fundamental difference between observations by onlookers, and the subjective experiences of those undergoing an experience aroused by this gas.

Fainting: Subjective experiences and observation

[3.84]The experience of fainting provides another wonderful example of the differences between external observations of a person undergoing an experience, and the subjective report of the same experience. During 1994, a group of researchers lead by a Berlin neurologist, Thomas Lempert, published an outstanding and very original study of the effects of induced fainting. This sounds like a very strange study, but actually had a very specific purpose. It is sometimes very difficult to distinguish between the convulsions induced by sudden total brain hypoxia resulting from an abnormal heart rhythm, and convulsions due to epilepsy caused by a multitude of brain disorders. Treatment of these different types of convulsions is very different. At that time there was no clear way to clinically differentiate between the convulsions originating from these two very different causes. So this study was designed to definitively answer this question.

[3.85]They asked 59 healthy young volunteers to hyperventilate for 20 seconds while squatting, and then to suddenly stand upright while forcefully exhaling through a closed larynx for 10 seconds (Lempert 1994a). This is called a "Valsalva maneuver", the effect of which is to cause a dramatic reduction of the flow of blood to the brain, so inducing sudden onset of generalized cerebral hypoxia. The effect of this sudden severe cerebral hypoxia was the induction of fainting in 42 (72%) of these volunteers, resulting in periods of apparent loss of consciousness lasting up to 22 seconds. Loss of consciousness was defined as starting at the moment the subjects fell onto thick matting placed around them, and the ensuring period of unresponsiveness. Lempert and his colleagues carefully observed and videotaped each person during this maneuver. They hoped to determine whether fainting due to such generalized cerebral hypoxia resulted in different patterns of convulsive movements, than the convulsive movements caused by epilepsy resulting from a brain disorder. Videotapes revealed each of these 42 people losing consciousness while manifesting the muscle movements listed below.

- [3.86]90% had arrhythmic muscle movements called "myoclonus".
- [3.87]79% exhibited other automatisms such as head turns with gaze deviation, lip-licking, chewing, or fumbling.

91

- [3.88]45% attempted to raise their heads, sit, or stand while still totally unresponsive.
- [3.89]40% made a continuous moaning sound lasting on average 2.7 seconds.

[3.90]Electroencephalographic recordings were successful in six subjects, and revealed that loss of consciousness occurred during slow wave theta and delta activity. Myoclonus occurred during the absence of any electroencephalograph activity in three subjects (Lempert 1994a). Ultimately this study revealed that brain hypoxia induced by fainting induced generalized convulsive twitching and jerking, while convulsions originating from an abnormal part of the brain reveals specific localizing manifestations.

[3.91]A colleague anesthesiologist called Martin Bauer was one of the several researchers involved in this landmark study of Thomas Lempert. I met with Martin Bauer quite coincidentally during 2012 at a small party at the house of a colleague, and he told me about some of the details and performance of this study. He told me that quite by chance, the first person taking part in this study reported undergoing an amazing subjective experience similar to a near-death experience during the period he was apparently unconscious. This was totally unexpected. So the researchers added a structured interview to their study: interviewing each person immediately after recovery to analyze their memories of any subjective experiences undergone while apparently unconscious. These investigators were lucky that the first person to recover made them aware of these fascinating experiences. It meant they were able to include the experiences of all subjects taking part in this study. The results were astounding! The researchers observed and recorded all the above manifestations, yet 83% of the 42 persons apparently losing consciousness recalled undergoing experiences very different to what was observed and recorded (Lempert 1994a).

[3.92]*Most subjects described the emotional experience of syncope [fainting] as pleasant, detached, and peaceful, making them unwilling to return. Some compared it to drug or meditation experiences. 2 were reminded of an earlier post-traumatic near-death experience. One participant disclosed: "I thought that if I had to die in this very moment I would willingly agree". (Lempert 1994)*

[3.93]Most of these 42 people also reported undergoing surprising subjective experiences during their brief periods of apparent loss of physical consciousness (Lempert 1994):

- [3.94]60% reported audible noises or voices
- [3.95]47% reported entering another world
- [3.96]40% reported visual perceptions
- [3.97]35% reported feelings of peace and painlessness
- [3.98]20% reported encountering preternatural beings
- [3.99]17% reported a light experience
- [3.100]16% reported an out-of-body experience
- [3.101]8% reported undergoing a tunnel experience
- [3.102]0% reported experiencing life review

[3.103]The profile of these subjective experiences is curiously very similar to that of near-death experiences reported by cardiac arrest survivors (see 12.65-12.81). This carefully performed, and well-documented study, is a beautiful illustration of how objective observations of apparently unconscious, unreactive persons, may be very different from the subjective experiences these same persons report undergoing while apparently unconscious.

A note: Difference between fainting and cardiac arrest

[3.104]The cause of loss of consciousness during fainting and cardiac arrest is the same. Both are caused by a dramatic reduction of the flow of blood to the brain, so inducing cerebral hypoxia of a degree sufficient to cause loss of consciousness. People recovering from fainting and cardiac arrest report undergoing the same experiences of peace, ineffability, out-of-body experiences, entering a transcendental world, light experiences, meeting preternatural entities, etc. (Lempert 1994, Lommel 2001). Yet even though the mechanism of loss of consciousness is identical in both situations, only 18% of cardiac arrest survivors in the prospective study of Pim van Lommel recalled undergoing any experiences during cardiac arrest (Lommel 2001), while a massive 83% of persons fainting in the study of Thomas Lempert recalled undergoing conscious experiences during their periods of apparent loss of consciousness (Lempert 1994). Chapter 12 discusses cardiac arrest and fainting, as well as reasons for this difference in considerable detail (see 12.65-12.81).

Hypnic jerks: Subjective experiences and observation

[3.105]Consider another example of the difference between external observation and subjective experience. Sometimes, just before falling asleep, people suddenly awaken with jerking movements of their limbs. These are called "hypnic jerks". Some believers in dualism say these experiences are due to the soul suddenly and forcefully reuniting with the body (pages 83-84 in Muldoon 1973). Nonetheless, these experiences are another example of the difference between observation and experience.

[3.106]Studies reveal that up to nine in ten people have had at least one such experience (Oswald 1959, Parkes 1986). Just before awakening in this manner, many people first feel as if they are floating above their bed. Then they suddenly feel themselves fall onto their bed with a jerking movement of their limbs. Dr. Oswald questioned 50 of his acquaintances about these jerks, and got the following responses as to their individual experiences.

> [3.107]*Most of those who had these jerks said that sometimes they were frightening experiences. 11 said the jerks were usually associated with a feeling of falling, and in 3 cases this was elaborated into falling downstairs, over a cliff and into a pit ("such as Joseph was cast into by his brothers"), respectively. In another, it was thought that the jerks were associated with dreaming of receiving an electric shock, in another with light flashes, or horrid faces or "spasm" over the heart. Two recent personal ones have been accompanied by a sudden light flash in one case, and in another by the sight of half a brick hurtling towards my face. Those who said they got jerks often, said that they might get several on any one night, and then none on many nights. (Oswald 1959)*

[3.108]Sometimes a person notices a bed partner suddenly awakening with jerking limb movements. And their bed partner subsequently tells them they felt their body floating and falling just before suddenly awakening with a jerk. These observations and experiences are as old as humanity. Yet throughout all these millennia of human history, no one has ever reported seeing the body of their bed partner, or the soul of their bed partner floating above the bed just before their bed partner awoke in this manner. The only conclusion from this ages-old observation is that such experiences of floating and falling just before awakening occur only in the minds of the persons undergoing them. An observer only sees someone awakening with a jerking motion of his or her limbs. This is yet another example of the difference between external objective observation, and subjective experience.

Cocaine addiction: Subjective experiences and observation

[3.109]Cocaine is one of the best-known examples of a psychostimulant drug. I will not discuss the longer-term effects of regular use of increasing doses of these drugs, nor the consequences of addiction, as this is outside the scope of this discussion. Instead, I will limit this discussion to the initial effects of these drugs.

[3.110]Cocaine (Favrod-Coune 2010, Fowler 2008, Volkow 2004), methylphenidate (Booij 1997, Freese 2012, Morton 2000, Volkow 2011), and methamphetamine (Fowler 2008), all induce a feeling of euphoria in direct proportion to the initial rising, and peak concentrations of these drugs in the brain (Volkow 2004). Not only do they induce feelings of euphoria, but also arouse a feeling of increased energy, reducing the need for rest, sleep, and food. The intense pleasure induced by larger doses of smoked, or nasal cocaine has even been called a "total body orgasm" (Favrod-Coune 2010). Observation of people using these drugs, reveal associated bodily changes such as rapid heartbeat (tachycardia), dilated pupils, sweating, agitation, tremor, and repetitive behaviors (Booij 1997, Favrod-Coune 2010, Morton 2000).

[3.111]These are the largely similar subjective and observed manifestations of these drugs. However, two fascinating studies reveal a divergence between objective reality and the effects of these drugs. The first of these two studies was that of Nora Volkow and her co-workers who published a study performed at the Brookhaven National Laboratory in New York, in the USA (Volkow 2003). Her results were confirmed by another equally fascinating study performed by Rinah Yamamoto and her group at the Massachusetts General Hospital General Clinical Research Center in Boston, USA (Yamamoto 2007). I will discuss the study of Nora Volkow in some detail, because it reveals more about the differences between observation and experience, as well as providing interesting insights into the nature of the conscious mind.

[3.112]The group of Nora Volkow subjected 25 active cocaine abusers to a different drug dosage regime on four different days. They were administered an intravenous dose of a placebo (a pharmacologically inactive substance), or methylphenidate according to a double-blind protocol whereby neither those administering the drugs, nor the experimental subjects knew what was being administered. Subsequent to drug administration, the experimental subjects scored their subjective experiences of the effects of the drug injection, as well as undergoing a brain scan. The four different regimes were:

- [3.113]Told they were administered a placebo, and were administered a placebo. This was a baseline measurement
- [3.114]Told they were administered a placebo, but actually received a dose of methylphenidate. This was a baseline measurement of the effects of methylphenidate uninfluenced by any expectation of a drug effect.
- [3.115]Told they were administered methylphenidate, but actually received a placebo. This was to measure the effect of expectation of a drug effect on the subjective experience and the objectively measured effects in the brain.
- [3.116]Told they were administered methylphenidate, and actually received methylphenidate. This was to measure whether expectation of a drug effect influenced subjective experience, and objectively measured effects in the brain.

[3.117]The effects of expectation on the observed and subjective effects induced by methylphenidate were surprising. Expectation of receiving methylphenidate increased the subjective scoring of the level of the "high" or euphoria by about 50% above that experienced when unknowingly receiving the same dose of methylphenidate. Furthermore, expectation of receiving methylphenidate increased the response of the brain as determined by the brain scan, to a level above that measured after administration of the same dose of methylphenidate when the subjects did not know they received the drug. This study demonstrated a clear difference between objective reality and subjective experience.

[3.118]This study reveals how expectation of receiving a psychostimulant drug amplifies the effects of these drugs in cocaine abusers. This is not just a revelation of a difference between objective fact, observations and subjective experience, but also reveals more aspects of the true nature of the human mind. So how do the mind-models of materialism and dualism explain these results?

[3.119]I will begin with the mind-model of materialism. Cocaine addiction, defined as chronic use of larger doses of cocaine, induces a broad range of structural and functional changes in physical brain function (Hanlon 2012). Furthermore, mounting evidence reveals that environment, together with interactions of multiple genes results in a genetic propensity for addiction to cocaine (Kreek 2005). An inherited propensity means that the brains of cocaine addicts have genetically determined structural and functional elements absent in the brains of those not addicted to cocaine. Materialism proposes that the mind is a product of the functioning of the physical brain. This means that all thoughts, together with all expectations are products of the functioning of the physical human brain. A combination of genetically and environmentally determined, as well as structural and functional changes in the physical brain due to cocaine addiction, combined with the abnormal brain function resulting from many hours of abstinence, mean that administration of the drug will relieve the consequences of abstinence. So it is not at all surprising that the brain generated effects of expectation will magnify the effects of receiving the drug.

[3.120]According to the mind-model of dualism, the soul controls the body through the conduit of the brain, controlling the physical body to speak, move, act and perform deeds in response to stimuli affecting the body, as well as in response to thoughts and other mental activity originating primarily within the soul (see 1.55-1.65). The chemical effects of drugs such as cocaine and methylphenidate affect the functioning of the physical body and the brain. These effects upon the functioning of the physical body and brain affect sensations perceived by the body and transmitted to the soul, as well as affecting the expression of control by the soul. This is the concept of the reciprocal interaction between the body and the soul as proposed by many believers in the mind-model of dualism (see 1.142, and also 15.10). And this is where some problems arise in the explanation of these results with the mind model of dualism.

- [3.121]Control of the bodies of cocaine addicts by their souls results in consciously planned and coherent physical thoughts, emotions, speech, actions, and deeds directed to obtaining the drug. Some cocaine addicts even resort to violent or criminal activities to support their habit. The consistency, the logical and planned nature of activities directed to obtaining cocaine, indicates they are purposeful manifestations of control by the soul (see 1.64). Does this mean that the immaterial soul is just as addicted as the material body to the bodily effects of cocaine, and accordingly controls the body to obtain the drug in any way possible? Such a concept is inconsistent with the belief that the human soul is unaffected by anything affecting the physical body (see 1.66-1.75).

- [3.122]The embodied souls of the cocaine addicts did not sense the presence or absence of the drug. They responded to expectations aroused by false information. Expectation even caused exaggerated reactions. This indicates that the souls of these people had no access to paranormal information about the truth or falsehood of what they were told, indicating that the soul when present in the body employs no paranormal senses.

[3.123]Accordingly, the effects of expectation in cocaine addicts are difficult to explain with the mind-model of dualism, whereas they are readily explained by materialism. This conclusion is another consequence of careful examination of differences between objective observation and subjective aspects of experiences.

Conclusions

[3.124]An external objective observer does not experience the cognitive, affective, paranormal, or transcendental experiences undergone by another person. An observer only learns that an observed person has undergone such experiences, when that person reports these experiences. This is the difference between what people subjectively experience, and what external observers perceive and measure. For example, unintentional awareness during general anesthesia, near-death experiences, and out-of-body experiences, nearly always occur when the persons undergoing these experiences are motionless and apparently unconscious. They are good examples of this difference between subjective and objective aspects of experiences. Furthermore, regardless of whether consciousness of the physical body is a manifestation of an immaterial soul, or is generated by the physical brain, uncritical acceptance of subjective experiences undergone by apparently unconscious persons as objective reality, is a fundamental fault in many studies concluding that events such as near-death experiences, and out-of-body experiences prove the reality of a soul. A passage in a book written more than 100 years ago even warns us of just such uncritical acceptance of subjective experiences as objective reality.

[3.125]*But there have always been, and probably always will be, individuals whose love for the marvelous is so great, and whose logical powers are so small, as to render them susceptible of entertaining any belief, no matter how preposterous it may be; and others more numerous, who, staggered by facts which they cannot understand, accept any hypothesis which may be offered as an explanation, rather than confess their ignorance. (page 2 in Hammond 1876)*

[3.126]Fervent believers in the reality of the literal meaning of the content of near-death experiences often confuse the intense feeling of reality associated with these subjective experiences with objective reality. And indeed, as long as their experience of the objective world about them does not clash with their belief in the reality of these subjective experiences, the worldview exposed by these subjective experiences becomes their personal reality. This is an old idea, somewhat differently, but nonetheless eloquently expressed in the book, *Beyond Good and Evil*, written by the German philosopher Friedrich Nietzsche (1844-1900).

[3.127]*What we experience in dreams, provided we experience it often, pertains at last just as much to the general belongings of our soul as anything "actually" experienced; by virtue thereof we are richer or poorer, we have a requirement more or less, and finally, in broad daylight, and even in the brightest moments of our waking life, we are ruled to some extent by the nature of our dreams. (paragraph 193, Nietzsche 1909)*

[3.128]Even a cursory examination of differences between objective observation and subjective experience in this chapter reveals some aspects of the true nature of the human mind. For example, discussions in this chapter reveal that subjective sensations of enhanced mental capacity, or experiences of a sense of reality are not necessarily objective truth. Furthermore, the objective and subjective effects of expectation in cocaine addicts reveals the illusory nature of the soul. These results are all products of a careful examination of the differences between objective reality and subjective experience.

[3.129]Finally, these discussions and examples reveal one very clear point. Any study of the nature of the nature of the human mind must account for differences between objective observations and subjective experiences. Understanding of these differences is one of the many steps on the pathway to eventual knowledge of the true nature of the human mind.

4

Mind & the Intact Brain

4.1Consciousness and mind are not the same. We all recognize the presence of consciousness in our fellow humans, cows, dogs, cats, rats, and hamsters, as well as a large variety of other animals. People and animals are conscious when awake, and while conscious, their vocalizations, movements, and behaviors reveal the mental processes occurring within their minds. Mind is the sum total of personality, and intelligence. Mind is what we experience, what we feel, our emotions, our conscious perception of sensations, our memories, and how we think. Mind is what makes each of us an individual. And consciousness is what makes mental activity manifesting as mind possible. So does the functioning of the human mind as manifested by the physical body reveal anything about the true nature of the mind?

Mental experiences: Definitions

4.2The functioning of the conscious mind is a fascinating subject, but one which first requires some careful and rigorous definitions of terms such as consciousness, awareness, various mental properties, and experiences.

- 4.3*Consciousness* is that condition of the brain making awareness and the properties of mind possible.
- 4.4*Wakefulness* defines the level of consciousness.
- 4.5*Awareness* defines the content of consciousness.
- 4.6*Mind* is the sum total of all mental processes in the conscious brain.
- 4.7*Conscious experience*. A conscious experience is an experience undergone during consciousness. (Note that conscious experiences do not only occur during evident physical consciousness.)

[4.8]These are definitions relating to consciousness and mind as defined by Gawryluk (2010) (see 2.6). But there are other states of mind and perceptive states requiring precise definition before proceeding with any further discussion.

- [4.9]An *illusion* is a perception of something objectively existing in such a way as to cause misinterpretation of its actual nature. (Merriam-Webster Dictionary).
- [4.10]A *delusion* implies an inability to distinguish between what is real and what only seems to be real, often as the result of a disordered state of mind. (Merriam-Webster Dictionary).
- [4.11]A *hallucination* is the perception of visual, auditory, tactile, olfactory, or gustatory experiences without an external stimulus and with a compelling sense of their reality, usually resulting from a mental disorder or as a response to a drug. (The Free Dictionary).
- [4.12]*Orientation* is awareness of the objective world in relation to one's self. (The Free Dictionary). Orientation is knowledge of factors such as who one is, where one is, time, date, and year.
- [4.13]*Delirium* is a temporary state of mental confusion and fluctuating consciousness resulting from high fever, intoxication, shock, or other causes. It is characterized by anxiety, disorientation, hallucinations, delusions, and incoherent speech. (The Free Dictionary).

[4.14]These are definitions of some manifestations of the conscious mind. But before commencing the discussion, it is worthwhile first defining the limits of the discussion in this chapter.

Limitations of discussion

[4.16]Materialism is a very evident mind-model. It predicts that alterations of physical brain function will change mental function experienced and manifested by the conscious physical body as thoughts, speech, actions, and behavior. The mind-model of dualism is different. Dualism proposes that the physical human body is a sort of puppet controlled by an immaterial soul. So according to the mind-model of dualism, manifestations of mind as experienced and manifested by the conscious physical body, are a result of the soul controlling the mechanisms of the physical body to produce thoughts, speech, actions and behavior. This chapter specifically examines alterations of mental function as induced in the anatomically normal brain by a variety of factors. The resulting alterations in the mental function of the conscious physical body reveal much about whether the mind-model of dualism, or that of materialism, best explains what is experienced and observed.

Hallucinogenic drugs and mind

[4.17]Many substances and drugs alter the functioning of the brain. Alcohol is the most well-known mind altering drug used since ancient times. Ingestion of enough alcohol changes the functioning of the brain such that the properties of mind are changed. Anesthetic drugs have similar effects, but will be discussed in another chapter. Mescaline is a hallucinogen contained in Peyote mushrooms, and has also long been used for its mind-altering effects. One advantage of mescaline is that the mental effects it induces occur in full consciousness, which means they can be described as they occur. As with many mind-altering drugs, objective observations and subjective experiences are very different. For example, here is an account of objective observations of a person intoxicated with mescaline.

[4.18]*It should be realized that the outward behaviour of the subject acutely intoxicated with mescaline is relatively normal. He may be absorbed in his experiences, and will talk about them freely but rationally. Only if the intoxication has become extreme may he lose control of himself and sink into a sleep-like sopor or delirium. (Mayer-Gross 1951)*

[4.19]With this in mind we can better appreciate the account of the Edinburgh physician, Weir Mitchell, who published his subjective experiences of mescaline (Mitchell 1896). After taking several doses of a tincture of mescaline, he noted:

[4.20]*At this time, also, I had a decisive impression that I was more competent in mind than in my everyday moods. I seemed to be sure of victoriously dealing with problems. This state of mind may be easily matched in the condition of some men when pretty far gone in alcohol intoxication. My own mood was gently flattering—a mere consciousness of power, with meanwhile absolute control of every faculty. I wrote a long letter of advice dealing with a rather doubtful diagnosis, and on reading it over was able to see that it was neither better nor worse than my average letter. Yet the sense of increased ability was so notable*

*that, liking to test it, and with commonsense disbelief in its
flattery, I took up a certain paper on psychology, which a week
before I had laid down in despair. I grieve to say that it was less
to be comprehended than ever. My ignorance would have
remained bliss had I not made the experiment. I next tried to do a
complicated sum, but soon discovered that my ordinary
inefficiency as to figures was not really increased. [...]
The tints of intense green and red shifted and altered, and soon
were seen no more. Here, again, was the wonderful loveliness of
swelling clouds of more vivid colours gone before I could name
them, and, sometimes rising from the lower field, and very swiftly
altering in colour tones from pale purples and rose to greys, with
now and then a bar of level green or orange intense as lightning
and as momentary. (Mitchell 1896)*

[4.21]Many believers in the reality of dualism assert that the physical
brain filters, limits, or somehow inhibits the manifestation of the abilities
of the soul. So this description of the effects of mescaline was very
revealing. For example, even though Dr. Mitchell perceived his mental
powers as increased, the reality was disappointing. No such enhancement
of mental powers was present. Worse, his mental powers were actually
reduced. This example of the effects of mescaline reveals that belief in
the filtering, or limitation of the abilities of a putative soul by the physical
brain is illusory. Also interesting in this account, was the wide
discrepancy between objective fact and subjective experience.

[4.22]More recently, another hallucinogenic drug, psilocybin, was
administered under strictly controlled conditions to 36 informed
experimental volunteers. Two different drugs were tested,
methylphenidate and psilocybin. Experimental subjects took part in two
experimental sessions, during each of which they received one of the two
drugs. They knew they would receive the hallucinogenic drug psilocybin
in one of the sessions, but did not know which session (Griffiths 2006).
None of the experimental subjects lost consciousness during the
experimental period, which means all effects of the drug on the
functioning of the conscious mind were experienced and expressed
through the mechanisms of the conscious physical body. The results of
this study were surprising.

*[4.23]It is remarkable that 67% of the volunteers rated the
experience with psilocybin to be either the single most meaningful
experience of his or her life or among the top five most
meaningful experiences of his or her life. In written comments, the*

volunteers judged the meaningfulness of the experience to be similar, for example, to the birth of a first child or death of a parent. Thirty-three percent of the volunteers rated the psilocybin experience as being the single most spiritually significant experience of his or her life, with an additional 38% rating it to be among the top five most spiritually significant experiences. In written comments about their answers, the volunteers often described aspects of the experience related to a sense of unity without content (pure consciousness) and/or unity of all things. (Griffiths 2006)

[4.24]The subjective experiences of one of the subjects in this experiment were described in more detail in another journal.

[4.25]*Her responses indicated that during the time spent in the session room she had gone through a profound mystical-like experience similar to those reported by spiritual seekers in many cultures and across the ages—one characterized by a sense of interconnectedness with all people and things, accompanied by the feeling of transcending time and space, and of sacredness and joy.*

At a follow-up visit more than a year later, she said she continued to think about the experience every day and—most remarkably—that she regarded it as the most personally meaningful and spiritually significant event of her life. She felt it had brought on positive changes in her moods, attitudes and behaviors, as well as a noticeable increase in overall life satisfaction. "It seems like the experience triggered a quickening of my spiritual unfolding or development," she wrote. "Ripples of insight still occur… [I am] much more loving—making up for the past hurts I've inflicted… More and more I'm able to perceive people as having the light of the divine flowing through them." (Griffiths 2010)

[4.26]The effect of psilocybin was to induce profound long-term cognitive and affective experiences in these conscious volunteer experimental subjects. And these experiences were considered real and profoundly spiritually significant, even though these persons knew they were aroused by a mind-altering drug (Griffiths 2008). A similar result was found in a long-term follow-up of 20 divinity students, 10 of who were administered psilocybin in a double-blind fashion prior to a lengthy church service (Doblin 1991). These results indicate that belief in the spiritual reality of an experience bears little relation to the cause.

[4.27]Careful clinical studies over many years have revealed which subjective effects truly are due to these drugs, and which are aroused by the expectation of ingesting mind-altering drugs. These studies reveal that psilocybin (Hollister 1962, Griffiths 2006, Studerus 2010, Wittmann 2007) and mescaline (Hollister 1962, Mayer-Gross 1951, Hermle 1992), induce identical dose related subjective changes in mental function. Commonly reported perceptual changes are those of perceiving colors as being more vivid than usual, with shapes sometimes being perceived abnormally. Hearing is altered, with perceptions of sounds being heightened. Synesthesias may occur. Mental changes are most commonly those of mood, which is described as happy, sad, or irritable equally. Many people also describe a sense of a deeply felt positive mood, even ineffability. Feelings of depersonalization and derealization are common, often manifesting as a feeling of being one with the universe, a transcendence of time and space, and experiencing an intuitive knowledge of everything. Altered sense of time is very common. However, some people do experience more negative emotions, expressing anxiety at the sense of derealization, and a loss of control over their thoughts that they experience as being faster than normal. These are some of the notable subjective experiences induced by these drugs in conscious persons.

[4.28]Not surprisingly for two drugs with similar effects, both psilocybin and mescaline also have a similar profile of activity on the various receptors of chemical nerve transmitters in the brain (Nichols 2004, Pytliak 2011). They also have the same effects upon brain function. Doses of psilocybin (Vollenweider 1997), and mescaline (Hermle 1998) sufficient to induce the typical subjective and objective effects of these drugs, are associated with increased nerve activity in the frontal lobes of the brain. Moreover, these subjective and objective alterations of brain and mental function are dose related (Studerus 2010, Wittmann 2007), meaning that these effects only appear above a certain minimum dose, after which these manifestations become more intense with increasing doses. The dose related nature of these subjective and objective alterations of brain function, means these drugs induce changes in the functioning of the physical brain in direct relation to their brain concentrations.

[4.29]But do these hallucinogens free the soul to express its true nature? Or does altered physical brain function induced by hallucinogens reveal something quite different?

[4.30]The materialist explanation for the mental effects of these drugs is simply that hallucinogens affect the functioning of the brain in a dose-related manner to generate these experiences. So even the most intense and profound transcendental, affective and cognitive experiences induced by drugs such as mescaline and psilocybin, are no more than products of altered brain function induced by these drugs.

[4.31]The belief system of dualism states that all thoughts, actions and speech expressed by the conscious physical body originate in, and are controlled by the soul (see 1.55-1.65). At the same time, believers in dualism also claim that physical substances such as mescaline and psilocybin only affect the functioning of the physical brain, but do not affect the soul. Therefore, transcendental, affective and cognitive experiences induced in conscious persons by mescaline and psilocybin, and expressed by the conscious physical body while under the influence of these drugs, are not necessarily manifestations of the true nature of a soul. Instead, according to the logic of dualism, such experiences are very likely manifestations of the control of an abnormally functioning physical brain by the soul (see 1.142).

[4.32]The inescapable conclusion is that remarkable transcendental, cognitive, and affective experiences induced by drugs such as psilocybin and mescaline are certainly not proof of the mind-model of dualism, but are likewise not proof of the mind-model of materialism. So do the effects of other conditions affecting the otherwise normal brain shed any more certainty as to the true nature of the conscious mind?

Oxygen starvation and mind

[4.33]"Hypoxia" is the medical term used to describe oxygen starvation of part, or all of the body. Oxygen is an essential ingredient in all vital chemical processes generating energy within the cells of the body. But there are no stores of oxygen within the body, which is why the functioning of most organs fails within seconds to minutes after oxygen supplies suddenly cease.

Eyes & brain most sensitive to oxygen starvation

[4.34]Of all the organs of the body, the retina of the eyes and the brain are the most sensitive to oxygen starvation. Failure of these organs begins within seconds after failure of normal oxygen supplies. But there are differences between the sensitivity to oxygen starvation of different parts of the eyes and brain. The retina is more sensitive to hypoxia than

106

is the cortex of the brain, and the cortex is more sensitive to oxygen starvation than are the brainstem and thalamus. We know these differences in sensitivity to hypoxia are true from the common experience of fainting.

[4.35]Fainting is a short period of loss of consciousness induced by a variety of causes that result in a sudden temporary reduction of blood pressure, severely reducing of the flow of blood to the brain. Sudden reduction or cessation of blood flow to the brain causes rapid onset of cerebral hypoxia serious enough to induce the temporary loss of consciousness called fainting. As people faint, many people notice their vision fails first. They express this after recovering from their faint by saying, "Everything went gray", or "Everything went dark", and then I woke up. What this actually means is that they were conscious at the moment their vision failed, able to perceive and understand the failure of their vision, and able to remember the failure of their vision. Accordingly, those parts of their brains necessary for perception of light, for memory of this perception, and for generating consciousness to make these things possible were functioning at the moment they perceived the failure of vision. This is proof that the retina is more sensitive to oxygen starvation than are the brain and the brainstem.

An amazing experiment

[4.36]During 1943, Lieutenant Ralph Rossen and his group published the results of an investigation that would rank as one of the boldest and most amazing I have ever read (Rossen 1943). They used a special inflatable cuff placed around the lower one third of the neck.

> [4.37]*The Kabat-Rossen-Anderson apparatus has been designed to induce temporary arrest of circulation in the human brain without affecting the respiratory tract. This is accomplished by means of a specially designed inflatable cervical pressure cuff, held down to the lower third of the neck. The pressure in the cuff rises to 600 mm. of mercury within one-eighth second. The subject himself, as well as the physician, controls the deflation of the cuff, which can be accomplished within a fraction of a second. (Rossen 1943)*

[4.38]Sudden inflation of the cuff placed in this position produced total arrest of blood flow to and from the head, without affecting breathing. The experimental subjects were observed, and monitored with electrocardiogram as well as electroencephalogram. The cuff remained inflated until evident loss of physical consciousness occurred, upon

107

which the pressure was released, and the person rapidly regained consciousness. They performed this experiment upon 126 male volunteer prison inmates in the state of Minnesota, themselves, and 11 schizophrenic patients. The likelihood of modern ethical committees ever permitting a repetition of such an experiment is almost non-existent. So the insights into the effects of sudden total cerebral hypoxia as observed by these brave men are not only dramatic, and were also a unique study of the objective observations and subjective experiences of sudden cardiac arrest in healthy persons.

[4.39]*The characteristic reactions resulting from acute arrest of the circulation in the brain for five to ten seconds were: fixation of the eyeballs, blurring of vision, constriction of the visual fields, loss of consciousness and anoxic convulsions. This response occurred with great rapidity and was uniform from subject to subject. Our procedure was to release the pressure in the cuff simultaneously with loss of consciousness by the subject. Recovery occurred quickly in every case, and the procedure was demonstrated to be free from danger. All subjects could stand, walk out of the room and go about their work within one or two minutes after the procedure, and no later effects were observed. (Rossen 1943)*

[4.40]Consciousness was lost sometime between five to eleven seconds after arrest of the cerebral circulation. Furthermore, the subjects reported experiencing altered mental function before losing consciousness.

[4.41]*Before loss of consciousness, many subjects experienced rapid narrowing of the field of vision, blurring of vision, with the field of vision becoming gray, and, finally, complete loss of vision. A number of subjects stated that they were unable to see but could still hear and were conscious. [...] Some insisted that they did not lose consciousness, [...] Although the subject was instructed to remove his finger from the jet as soon as he felt like it, and thereby release the pressure in the cuff, he failed to do so, despite loss of consciousness and an anoxic convulsion. The subject's hand thus appeared to "freeze" in that position and became incapable of voluntary or involuntary relaxation. [...] Some stated that they did not feel like bothering to release the pressure. Others stated that they tried to remove the finger from the jet but were incapable of the movement. (Rossen 1943)*

[4.42]This landmark study revealed much about the subjective mental experiences of loss of consciousness due to sudden cessation of blood flow to the head, which is the same as the effect of sudden cardiac arrest. These effects are summarized below for more clarity.

- [4.43]Loss of consciousness within five to eleven seconds after sudden and complete arrest of blood flow to the head.
- [4.44]Prior to losing consciousness, most people experience a feeling of calm indifference.
- [4.45]Some people do not remember losing consciousness.
- [4.46]Eye movements are paralyzed one second before loss of consciousness.
- [4.47]Some subjects noted that failure of vision occurred before loss of consciousness. This indicates that the retina in the eyes is more sensitive to hypoxia than those parts of the brain generating consciousness, those parts of the brain perceiving and interpreting failure of vision, as well as those parts of the brain forming and storing memories.
- [4.48]Some people reported being able to hear conversations and other sounds, even though rendered blind by the sudden arrest of blood flow to their heads. This indicates that hearing is preserved at levels of hypoxia severe enough to induce failure of vision, but insufficiently severe to cause loss of consciousness.
- [4.49]Some subjects noted they were paralyzed and unable to activate the jet to release the pressure in the inflatable cuff around their necks. This observation reveals that hypoxia causes paralysis of voluntary movements at levels of cerebral hypoxia insufficient to induce loss of consciousness.

[4.50]These observations describe and explain many of the subjective mental experiences described by people resuscitated from cardiac arrest, or other sudden extreme hypoxic episodes. However, although informative, this study employed a technique inducing such rapid onset of cerebral hypoxia, that the relation between the degree of cerebral hypoxia and mental function was unable to be determined.

Mental function during cerebral hypoxia

[4.51]So how does mental function change with the degree of cerebral hypoxia? The degree of cerebral hypoxia is impossible to measure with any degree of certainty in living humans. Instead, because mental function alters within seconds in response to changes in blood oxygen content, alterations in mental function due to cerebral hypoxia induced in normally healthy humans are directly related to arterial blood oxygen content (data derived from: pages 343-354 & 599-617 in Gastaut 1961, Gibson 1981, Goldie 1941, Hornbein 1989, Otis 1946, Refsum 1963, Shephard 1956).

- [4.52]Normal oxygen partial pressure in arterial blood (P_aO_2) = 75-100 mmHg, equivalent to a percentage arterial blood hemoglobin saturation (S_aO_2) of about 90-97%.
- [4.53]Mental function becomes increasingly abnormal below a P_aO_2 of 44 mmHg (5.9 kPa), which is equivalent to a S_aO_2 of 80%.
- [4.54]Unconsciousness is increasingly likely below a P_aO_2 less than 32 mmHg (4.3 kPa), equivalent to a S_aO_2 of less than 60%.
- [4.55]Everyone is unconscious below a P_aO_2 less than 23 mmHg (3.1 kPa), equivalent to a S_aO_2 of less than 40%.

[4.56]The reader should note that these P_aO_2 and S_aO_2 levels are not absolute, or exact thresholds for alterations of mental function induced by cerebral hypoxia. A given degree of hypoxia does not affect all people equally, because slight differences in body structure and function between individuals, means that some people are more affected by a given degree of hypoxia than others. So while a certain level of hypoxia induces an average effect across a large group of people, some people are more affected, while others are less affected. This is why interpersonal variation must always be considered when examining the effects of cerebral hypoxia in individuals.

Shorter and longer term cerebral hypoxia

[4.57]Anecdotes and studies performed over many decennia reveal the profound alterations in behavior and mental function induced by sudden onset of cerebral hypoxia.

[4.58]*Hypoxia quickly affects the higher centers, causing a blunting of the finer sensibilities and a loss of sense of judgment and of self criticism. The subject feels, however, that his mind is not only quite clear but unusually keen. He develops a fixity of purpose and continues to do what he was doing when hypoxia first began to affect him, in spite of the fact that it may lead to disaster. This*

*fixity of purpose is highly dangerous, especially when such an
individual is responsible for the lives of others, such as is true of
an airplane pilot. (page 300 in Liere 1963)*

[4.59]These same changes in mental function were also reported in a
study of rapid onset, short-term cerebral hypoxia performed by Goldie
(1941) on experienced English wartime (World War 2) fighter pilots.
Other studies of the mental effects of rapid onset, short-term cerebral
hypoxia reveal two types of initial reactions to cerebral hypoxia. Up to
59% of persons initially feel elated and hyperactive when subjected to
rapid onset cerebral hypoxia (Barach 1940, Goldie 1941, Shephard
1956), but subsequently develop a depressive dullness and blunting of
mental functions, while the remaining 41% develop a depressive
dullness and blunting of mental abilities from the very beginning of
exposure to cerebral hypoxia (Barach 1940, Shephard 1956). Barach
(1940) described these changes in a group of medical student volunteers
taking part in a study of cerebral hypoxia.

*[4.60]Ten of the 17 students (59 per cent) showed shorter or longer
periods of elation during which facial expression changed;
increased motor activity took place in the form of tapping,
singing, whistling and pressure of speech; increased productivity,
flightiness, facetiousness, heightened sense of well being were
also observed, all of these symptoms resembling the hypomanic
state. The period of elation was followed by dullness, drowsiness,
and deep sleep, from which the subject could be awakened only
after repeated attempts. Awareness of having been asleep was
generally absent, and the ability to distinguish between dream
experiences and reality showed some impairment. (Barach 1940)*

[4.61]These striking differences between initial and longer-term mental
effects of sudden onset cerebral hypoxia, as well as inter-individual
responses to cerebral hypoxia, must always be considered whenever
reviewing any accounts of the mental experiences of people who have
recovered from hypoxic episodes.

Subjective effects of cerebral hypoxia

[4.62]This brings us to a more systematic discussion of the subjective
effects of cerebral hypoxia.

- [4.63]Failure of vision occurs before loss of consciousness (Andina 1937, Cudaback 1984, Duane 1966, Rossen 1943).
- [4.64]People may initially feel cheerful, even euphoric, and believe their mental function is clearer, keener and more rapid than normal, even though none of this is true as is demonstrated by objective testing. Yet they have no insight into the reality of their mental state (Barach 1940, Cudaback 1984, Goldie 1941, page 300 in Liere 1963).
- [4.65]Many people report a sense of depersonalization and disordered body image, while some even undergo out-of-body experiences (Brugger 1999, Firth 2004).
- [4.66]"Sensed presence" is an often reported phenomenon among high altitude climbers. They cannot see anyone in their surroundings, yet sense the presence of someone, or something nearby (Brugger 1999, Firth 2004).
- [4.67]Paralysis with retention of consciousness may occur during extreme hypoxia (Doherty 2003, Lempert 1994, Rossen 1943).

[4.68]All these are the subjective mental experiences of persons suffering from cerebral hypoxia, and they should always be considered in conjunction with inter-individual differences, as well as any shorter and longer term effects.

Objective effects of cerebral hypoxia

[4.69]But what are the objective changes in mental and physical functioning determined and measured by external objective observers?

- [4.70]Memory ability is reduced. Hypoxic persons can recollect old memories, and recognize things remembered in the past. Working memory is unimpaired, but hypoxia inhibits transformation of short-term memories into long-term memories, or stops this process altogether (Barach 1940, Hornbein 1989, Hornbein 2001, pages 299 to 320 in Liere 1963, Pagani 1998, Virués-Ortega 2006, Yonelinas 2002, Yonelinas 2004).
- [4.71]Attention deficits (Bond 1998, Hornbein 2001, pages 299 to 320 in Liere 1963).
- [4.72]Reduced concentration (Hornbein 2001, pages 299-320 in Liere 1963).
- [4.73]Slowed reaction times (Hornbein 1989, Hornbein 2001, pages 299-320 in Liere 1963, Virués-Ortega 2006).

- [4.74]Diminished ability to perform tasks (Otis 1946, Hornbein 1989, Hornbein 2001, pages 299-320 in Liere 1963).
- [4.75]Reduced ability to perform mental arithmetic (Goldie 1941, Koller 1991).
- [4.76]Reduced visual contrast discrimination (Otis 1946, pages 299-320 in Liere 1963).
- [4.77]Paralysis of conscious voluntary movements during severe hypoxia (Lempert 1994, pages 299-320 in Liere 1963, Rossen 1943).

[4.78]So just as with the effects of the hallucinogenic drugs mescaline and psilocybin, there is a difference between the subjective experience and objective observation of people suffering from cerebral hypoxia. The appearance of a person experiencing cerebral hypoxia says absolutely nothing about their subjective mental state.

Cerebral hypoxia & the filtering effect of the brain

[4.79]Hypoxia is a physical event, and therefore cannot affect the soul, although hypoxia profoundly affects the functioning of the physical brain. Proponents of the mind-model of dualism claim that the physical brain limits, inhibits or filters the expression of the true nature of the soul (see 1.76-1.88). Earlier I cited passages where researchers found that cerebral hypoxia induces a state of mind where people feel their minds are clearer than normal, their senses keener, as well as feelings of happiness and euphoria.

[4.80]So does this mean that cerebral hypoxia removes some of the limiting or filtering influences of the physical brain on the expression of the soul? This would then mean that cerebral hypoxia enables the soul to express its true enhanced consciousness through the medium of the physical body. But there is absolutely no evidence for this. Despite experiencing apparently enhanced conscious mental function, persons suffering from cerebral hypoxia actually manifest reduced concentration, and reduced ability to perform mental arithmetic. Then we come to the ability of the supposedly unfiltered and uninhibited hypoxic conscious mind to make correct decisions. Hypoxic persons feel their minds are clear, and their intellect keener than before, but this is an illusion, as was convincingly demonstrated by experimental studies of cerebral hypoxia in English wartime (World War 2) fighter pilots.

[4.81]*At saturations of 80% a change in behaviour becomes obvious; the subject fidgets, becomes irritable and will not cooperate in simple experimental procedures. There is a considerable impairment in the performance of simple mental tasks, such as making calculations or reading codes; at the same time the subject is convinced of his good condition and that he is carrying out his tasks with skill and accuracy, and when his mistakes are pointed out he often becomes abusive and accuses the observer of miscounting his scores. The handwriting forms an excellent index of the degree of anoxia, and after recovery is a convincing proof to the subject of his incapability while anoxic, which otherwise he finds difficult to believe. The absence of self-criticism engendered by oxygen lack has, of course, important practical applications; it is necessary that the pilot should not be allowed to use his own judgment as to when oxygen is necessary, as he is unable to recognize the symptoms of anoxia owing to his euphoria and may thus defer taking oxygen until his performance has fallen so far as to have disastrous results. (Goldie 1941)*

[4.82]Cerebral hypoxia induces a subjective feeling of enhanced mental abilities in physically conscious persons. This is supposedly due to a reduction of the filtering or limiting effect of the brain on the expression of the soul. Yet experiment after experiment only reveals reduced mental abilities. This is yet another illustration of the fact that altered brain function, supposedly enabling the soul to manifest its enhanced awareness and intellect, only reveals the belief in the superior mental properties of the human soul to be an illusion. So how do the differing mind-models of materialism explain the effects of cerebral hypoxia, and especially the effects of cerebral hypoxia on long-term memory formation?

Materialism, cerebral hypoxia, and memory

[4.83]Materialism explains that cerebral hypoxia affects multiple aspects of brain function, among which the processes forming long-term memories. Further evidence for this effect is indicated by the fact that the degree of amnesia is directly related to the severity of cerebral hypoxia. Furthermore, differences in inter-individual responses to cerebral hypoxia, as well as differing levels, and duration of hypoxia between different persons explains the variations in the effects of hypoxia on memory formation (see also 12.111-12.119).

Dualism, cerebral hypoxia, and memory

[4.84]Of all the effects of cerebral hypoxia, the effects on long-term memory formation are the most interesting. Believers in dualism claim that experiences occurring during physical consciousness form long-term memories within the soul. But increasing degrees of cerebral hypoxia increasingly inhibit the formation of new long-term memories (see previous pages). This is very strange when considering the following facts.

- [4.85]Believers in dualism claim that the soul controls all thoughts, speech, actions and deeds of the physical body (see 1.55-1.65).
- [4.86]Short periods of cerebral hypoxia, during which the S_aO_2 is less than 80%, but higher than 60%, do not induce loss of consciousness. Short periods of cerebral hypoxia at these levels cause no brain damage, but do temporarily affect the functioning of the physical brain, which returns to normal upon the disappearance of cerebral hypoxia.
- [4.87]The fact that experimental subjects are able to cooperate with experimenters, and perform tests during cerebral hypoxia, means that the perceptions required for the appropriate reactions are transmitted to the soul, which then controls the physical body to make the appropriate reactions in speech, actions, and deeds. If this did not occur, the soul would be unable to control the body to react appropriately.
- [4.88]The soul is unaffected by cerebral hypoxia or anything else affecting the physical brain (see 1.66-1.75).
- [4.89]All brain and memory functions return to normal after the body completely recovers from the effects of cerebral hypoxia.
- [4.90]The soul is supposedly the indelible repository of all memories, meaning it is the repository of all memories of the perceptions and reactions of the conscious body (see 1.92-1.115). So after restoration of normal cerebral oxygenation, people should be able to spontaneously recall and recount all the perceptions, thoughts, speech, actions, and deeds that occurred during a period of cerebral hypoxia (see 1.143).
- [4.91]But despite the fact that information transfer to the soul does indeed occur during cerebral hypoxia, formation and recall of memories is inhibited during periods of short-term cerebral hypoxia when the S_aO_2 is less than 80% (Barach 1940, Gibson 1981, Goldie 1941, Yonelinas 2002, Yonelinas 2004).

- [4.92]Memories of actions, speech, and deeds performed in response to requests and questions of others while under the influence of cerebral hypoxia, are not memories of secret things only available to the immaterial soul. Instead, such memories are public, containing nothing requiring secrecy. So according to the logic of dualism people should be able to recall all speech, actions, and deeds while consciously experiencing cerebral hypoxia. But most people do not recall these things, a fact indicating that memory is stored in the physical brain rather than the soul.

[4.93]These effects of cerebral hypoxia upon memory, prove that memory is a function of the physical brain, and not the soul. Accordingly, if each person has a soul, then the properties of this soul are very different to those proposed by the popular mind-model of dualism (see Chapter 1).

The Wada Test and the mind

[4.94]Hypoxia is one way of temporarily affecting the functioning of the otherwise normal physical brain. The Wada Test is more selective. It renders one half of a normally functioning, fully developed adult brain temporarily nonfunctional with a small dose of an anesthetic drug injected into a carotid artery (see also Chapter 2). People do not lose consciousness, and are able to cooperate with the neurologist, even though paralysis of the affected side of the body does occur while undergoing this test (Lee 2004, Silva 1999, Wada 1960). So if the physical brain truly does filter or limit the expression of the soul, then this may be apparent during a Wada Test.

[4.95]Yet in the more than 50 years since this test has been used, no neurologists have described enhanced mental abilities, or paranormal experiences being reported by patients undergoing this test, regardless of which cerebral hemisphere is anesthetized (Kelley 2002, Levin 1994, Perria 1961, Serafetinides 1965, Wada 1960). Patients only demonstrate the neurological deficits consistent with the areas of brain rendered non-functional by the test. This is further indication that destruction, or blocking the functioning of even massive quantities of functioning brain tissue, does not remove any putative limiting or filtering effect of the physical brain on the expression of the soul.

[4.96]According to believers in dualism, the soul is the indelible repository of all memories. So the Wada Test may reveal whether memories are stored in the physical brain, or in the soul. Memory function is indeed abnormal in conscious persons undergoing a Wada Test (Andelman 2006, Branco 2006, Buchtel 2002, Dupont 2010, Kelley 2002, Loring 1992, Loring 1994, Ojemann 2002, Takayama 2004). However, this finding has two possible interpretations. It may be proof that memory is a function of the physical brain. Alternatively, the abnormal brain function induced by the Wada Test may prevent retrieval and expression of memories.

[4.97]So the Wada Test yields both dubious and very evident conclusions. It does not reveal any lifting of a filter function of the physical brain, nor does it reveal whether memories are stored in the physical brain, or in an immaterial soul. However, the clear fact of temporary paralysis resulting from anesthesia of affected areas of brain is very revealing. Drugs injected during the Wada Test are at such low dosage that they only affect some areas of the brain, but do not affect the spinal cord, nerves going to the muscles of speech and movement, nor the muscles themselves. All these things are functionally intact. If the soul could activate the muscles of speech and movement directly, the Wada Test would cause no paralysis. Therefore, the Wada Test clearly reveals and proves that the soul can only manifest its presence in this material world through the mechanisms of the brain, and nothing else.

Electrical stimulation of the brain

[4.98]Prior to the availability of effective drugs to treat epilepsy, brain surgery to remove the diseased area of brain was the only therapy available for those with intractable epilepsy. Brain scans and electroencephalography did not exist in this long past era. The neurologist would first diagnose which was the likely part of the brain causing epilepsy in the affected patient. Subsequently, the neurosurgeon would operate on the patient under local anesthesia, so that the patient was fully awake and cooperative during the operation. After opening the skull and exposing the brain, the neurosurgeon would administer small graduated electrical shocks to various areas of the brain to find the exact region causing the epilepsy. The diseased area of brain was then removed, and often the patient would be cured, or experience fewer epileptic attacks. Such electrical stimulation of the brain affected not only diseased areas, but also revealed the functions of normal regions of the brain. Such surgery revealed an enormous body of knowledge about the functions of different regions of the brain. Wilder Penfield (1891-

117

1976) was a famous, and much lauded Canadian neurosurgeon who performed groundbreaking fundamental studies during such surgery. The development of brain scans, electroencephalography, and effective drugs for epilepsy, has not removed the necessity for performing some types of brain surgery under local anesthesia. There are still several other reasons why patients must undergo neurosurgery under local anesthesia, and be cooperative during electrical stimulation of their brains.

4.99Believers in the mind-model of dualism claim that all thoughts and all properties of mind occur within the soul (see Chapter 1). They also believe that electrical stimulation of the physical brain cannot affect the soul. However, electrical stimulation of the physical brain may change brain function sufficiently to alter the expression of the soul through the physical mechanisms of the brain. This system of thought has fascinating implications when viewing results of studies of electrical stimulation of the brains of conscious people undergoing neurosurgery under local anesthesia. For example, stimulation of the temporal lobe of the brain can arouse memories of music heard in the past. Penfield's descriptions of the experiences of two patients reported provide interesting insights.

4.100*D.F. heard an orchestra playing a certain song when a point on the superior surface of the right temporal lobe was stimulated after removal of the anterior half of the lobe. The hearing seemed to her so realistic that she thought a gramophone had been turned on. The point was restimulated many times and each time she heard the same orchestra which seemed to begin playing at the same place in the same piece. When she was warned falsely, and stimulation was withheld, she heard nothing; when stimulated, with or without warning, she heard it. When she hummed, accompanying thus the music in her mind, the tempo was about what might have been expected of an orchestra. The continued repetition of the stimulation seemed to facilitate this particular response rather than other possible responses. It was not a song that she knew very well and she could not recall when it was that she had "heard it that way before".*

M.G. said, when the first temporal convolution on the right side was stimulated, "I hear people coming in—I hear music now, a funny little piece." Stimulation was continued and she went on to explain that the music she was hearing was the theme song of a children's programme. (Penfield 1955)

4.101These patients were awake, "hearing this music", and were able to hum to the tune and talk about the music they heard at the same time.

118

Similarly, a study by Gloor (1982) revealed that stimulations of the amygdala of another patient could evoke childhood memories.

4.102The patient immediately opened his mouth with an astonished look on his face, sat up, and said that now he knew what is was: it was the feeling of being at a picnic in Brewer Park in Ottawa. "A kid was coming up to me to push me into the water. It was a certain time, a special day during the summer holidays and the boy was going to push me into the water. I was pushed down by somebody stronger than me. I have experienced that same feeling when I had 'petit mals' before." Again no after discharge was noted. When questioned, he said that this had been a true event in his life which occurred when he was about 8 years old, probably shortly before his seizures started. A "big fellow" had pushed his head under the water at that time. When questioned whether he actually saw himself being threatened by the "big fellow" he said no, but it was a feeling as if he were there and was being chased. (Gloor 1982)

4.103Penfield (1955) also demonstrated that electrical stimulation of the brain could arouse other experiences, such as hallucinatory conversations with persons far away.

4.104J.T. exclaimed that he heard his cousins, who were actually in South Africa, talking. He was laughing, he said, at something with them and yet he knew at the same time that he was also in the operating room. Though he made the effort, he could not recall what they were laughing at. (Penfield 1955)

4.105Again, these patients were awake at the same time as they perceived these memories and hallucinations. Even more surprisingly, electrical stimulation of the angular gyrus, a part of the cerebral cortex at the junction of the parietal, occipital and temporal lobes, can generate out-of-body experiences in such a way that the affected persons are conscious, and can relate the details of their out-of-body experiences at the same time as they view themselves from a position outside their physical bodies.

4.106The stimulating current was shut off and the electrocorticogram showed that a slow wave 4 per second generalized rhythm had been set up as an after-discharge. While this was continuing the patient exclaimed: "Oh God! I am leaving my body." Dr. Karagulla, who was observing him, said he looked

terrified at the time of the exclamation and made gestures as
though he sought help. (Penfield 1955)

[4.107]And a more recent experience was published by Olaf Blanke
during 2002.

[4.108]*Initial stimulations (n = 3; 2.0-3.0 mA) induced vestibular*
responses, in which the patient reported that she was "sinking
into the bed" or "falling from a height". Increasing the current
amplitude (3.5 mA) led to an OBE ("I see myself lying in bed,
from above, but I only see my legs and lower trunk"). Two further
stimulations induced the same sensation, which included an
instantaneous feeling of "lightness" and "floating" about two
metres above the bed, close to the ceiling. [Note: an OBE is an
out-of-body experience] (Blanke 2002)

[4.109]These are amazing experiences aroused by tiny electrical currents
passing through the appropriate parts of the brain. What they actually
demonstrate is a form of apparent dual consciousness. In these examples,
the persons concerned had conscious experience of a memory of music
at the same time as they were consciously aware of their surroundings
and communicating with the doctors. Similarly with the memories of
past life events, electrical stimulation of the brain aroused memories at
the same time as they were consciously aware of their surroundings and
communicating with those about them. Even more surprisingly, some
people undergoing stimulation in the region of the angular gyrus found
their consciousness dissociated from their bodies, viewed their bodies as
if from a position outside their bodies, yet at the same time were
conscious of their surroundings, and were able to communicate with the
people around them using physical speech. These studies and the
resulting experiences have far-reaching consequences for the two mind-
models discussed in this book.

Electrical brain stimulation: Two minds?

[4.110]Does this seeming dual consciousness occurring during electrical
stimulation of out-of-body experiences mean there is a conscious mind
of the physical brain, as well as that of the soul? If this concept is true,
then it would be impossible to decide which thought, which decision, or
which memory originates from the physical conscious mind, or from the
soul. However, we know one fact for certain, the seemingly disembodied
conscious minds of people during out-of-body experiences, and near-
death experiences, have the same memories, and the same personalities

as those of the physical persons concerned (see Chapter 1). They are one and the same.

Memories aroused by electrical brain stimulation

[4.111]This brings us back to the matter of memories aroused by electrical stimulation of the physical brain. Believers in dualism claim that the soul is the repository of all memories (see 1.92-1.115). Patients to whom such electrical brain stimulation is applied are conscious. So according to the logic of dualism, while physically conscious, their souls control their physical brains during such electrical stimulations. Electrical currents applied to the physical brains of these physically conscious people arouse these memories without any voluntary effort from the persons concerned. But why should electrical stimulation of physical brain arouse random irrelevant memories?

[4.112]The mind-model of materialism explains this observation with the fact that random electrical stimulation of the brain will only arouse random memories stored within the physical brain. According to the mind-model of dualism, the mechanisms of the brain transmit signals to the soul, which then transmits control signals to the physical brain, so controlling the body to respond appropriately. Electrical stimulation of the physical brain cannot directly affect the soul. Nonetheless, electrical stimulation of the brain induces some unpredictable nervous activity within the physical brain. Such unpredictable and random electrical activity aroused within the physical brain, is identical to nerve impulses arising from perceptions which may well be interpreted by the soul as instructions from the physical body to retrieve specific memories. The soul retrieves these memories, and controls the body to express them. This is a manifestation of an indirect influence of the body upon the manifestations of control exerted by the soul over the physical body. In this situation, the soul reacts appropriately in response to incorrect information from the body (see 1.142-1.143). Indeed, the author Chris Carter cites Rupert Sheldrake who proposed just such an explanation.

[4.113]*Finally, Penfield's experiments, in which he invoked vivid memories by electrically stimulating the temporal cortex of patients, are sometimes considered as evidence in support of the trace theory of memory. But Sheldrake points out that "here again, this need not mean that the memories are actually stored inside the nerve tissue. If one stimulates the tuning circuit of a radio or a TV set, the tuning may be changed such that*

121

transmissions from a different station are picked up; but this would of course not mean that these new programs are stored inside the components of the tuning circuits that were stimulated." (page 96 in Carter 2010).

[4.114]This explanation by believers in the mind-model of dualism, is an elegant alternative explanation of why electrical stimulation of some parts of the physical brain arouses random and irrelevant memories.

Disembodiment aroused by electrical brain stimulation

[4.115]Electrical stimulation of the physical brain not only arouses old memories, but can also arouse out-of-body experiences. The angular gyrus is the region of the physical brain integrating position and movement signals from the body. So it is not surprising that electrical stimulation of this region of the brain elicits hallucinations of altered position and movements relative to the body, such as out-of-body experiences. People undergoing such out-of-body experiences are within their bodies, only the relation of their body images to their physical bodies is distorted, arousing hallucinations of separation and movement independent of the physical body. During this electrical stimulation induced "separation" from their bodies, they may view their bodies as if from a position outside their bodies, while at the same time they are able to feel sensations from their bodies, and physically communicate with those around them. They manifest a consciousness which is apparently in two places at the same time. This is very similar to a report of an out-of-body experience that occurred during resuscitation from a cardiac arrest, during which the person concerned (Mr. B.) viewed his body from a position outside his body, while at the same time feeling severe pain from the cardiac massage machine.

[4.116]*Interviewer: No, okay. By the way did he [Mr. B.] describe that he could see anything at the same time as he felt pain. Was there a combination ...?*
TG: He [Mr. B.] saw himself lying under the heart massage pump, and that was incredibly painful. And in between he also saw me busy with him ... (Rivas 2008)

[4.117]In this fragment, TG the male nurse who reported this experience to the interviewer described what the patient had told him of his near-death experience. And this report is similar to the reports of some mountaineers in life-threatening situations who perceive bodily sensations at the same time as they undergo out-of-body experiences. One mountain climber vividly described his experience.

> [4.118] *"I felt myself projected from the rock where I was standing and flying several meters through the air. It was more than mere imagination or daydreaming; the feeling of being up there was as real as the simultaneous feeling of standing on this rock and holding the rope" (subject 6, while watching his companion's fall at an altitude of approximately 3000 m). (Brugger 1999)*

[4.119]These reports indicate that spontaneous out-of-body experiences, as well as out-of-body experiences induced by brain electrical stimulation are actually variants of the same types of experiences. They cannot be due to separation of the soul from the body, because the conscious mind perceives sensations from the body at the same time as it undergoes an out-of-body experience. Moreover, the conscious mind is able to communicate with physical speech at the same time as it is apparently displaced out of the body. The belief that out-of-body experiences are due to separation of a soul from the physical body does not explain these observations. These observations are only explicable by a displacement of body image generating a hallucination of displacement out of the body (Blanke 2005, Blanke 2005a, Bünning 2005, Easton 2009). It is true that this explanation does not explain out-of-body experiences in all situations. Nonetheless, these explanations do mean it is impossible to distinguish between out-of-body experiences aroused by abnormal sensory and brain function, and out-of-body experiences due to separation of the soul from the body. All these things mean that out-of-body experiences are not proof of a separable conscious mind.

Concluding remarks on electrical brain stimulation

[4.120]In conclusion, electrical stimulation of the brain is inconclusive as to whether the soul, or the physical brain is the repository of all memories. Furthermore, electrical stimulation induced out-of-body experiences are equally well explained by dualism as by materialism. This fact means it is impossible to distinguish between dualism or materialism as an explanation for experiences arising from electrical stimulation of the brain. Nonetheless, this conclusion does mean that experiences aroused by electrical stimulation of the brain cannot be considered proof of the mind-models of either dualism or materialism.

Brain structure is influenced by mind

[4.121]Social and emotional development, as well as skills training provide even more surprising revelations revealing the relationship of the conscious mind to the physical brain. Recent developments in different brain scanning techniques have unleashed a flood of information about the relation between mind and brain. Such studies clearly demonstrate that the brain to be a dynamic organ, capable of development and change at all ages (Wittenberg 2009). Some of the most interesting studies are those revealing how social and mental development, emotional and physical neglect, sexual abuse, and training affect brain structure.

- [4.122]The corpus callosum is a thick and broad bundle of nerve fibers exchanging information between the right and left sides of the brain. The amygdala is a part of the brain involved in the processing and memory of emotional reactions. Children raised in an environment of mental, emotional, and physical neglect have an amygdala (Mehta 2009), and corpus callosum significantly smaller than those of less deprived children (Teicher 2004).
- [4.123]People with a history of "early life stress", such as violence, sexual abuse, divorce, sustained conflict, frequent surgery, etc, have structural and functional alterations in the corpus callosum (Paul 2008).
- [4.124]Women with an early life history of sexual abuse not only have significant neuropsychological differences compared with other women (Navalta 2006), but also have a thinner frontal cortex, as well as a smaller corpus callosum and amygdala than normal (Anderson 2008).
- [4.125]The hippocampus is a part of the brain transforming temporary memories into permanent memories. Furthermore, the rear, or posterior part of the hippocampus is necessary for spatial memory and spatial memory processing. Official taxi drivers in London, (England), are required to pass a test of their knowledge of the streets of London, and be able to mentally map out routes using this knowledge. Brain scans reveal that the posterior hippocampus of London taxi drivers to be larger than normal, and that the degree of enlargement is directly related to the number of years working as a taxi driver (Maguire 2000).
- [4.126]Piano playing is a skill learned with much practice. There are measurable structural changes in different parts of the brains of

persons with years of piano practice, compared to the brains of persons without piano training (Ying Han 2009).

- [4.127]There are measurable structural changes in different parts of the brains of people who have practiced various forms of meditation for many years (Lazar 2010, Luders 2009).

[4.128]The list is long. Life experience and training are associated with changes in brain structure. However, are these changes caused by the events with which they are associated, or are these meaningless coincidental associations? Some of these questions cannot be answered. After all, subjecting children to years of neglect and sexual abuse just so as to study their adult brains would truly be the apex of immorality and inhumanity. Fortunately, other studies do reveal that training does affect brain structure and function.

- [4.129]Serial scans of the brains of children who studied piano playing for fifteen months revealed significant differences in development of multiple regions of the brain compared with other children who did not study piano over the same period (Hyde 2009).
- [4.130]Serial scans of the brains of people studying juggling reveal changes in the brain pathways related to the skills required for juggling (Scholz 2009).
- [4.131]Strokes can cause damage to the speech areas of the brain. Provided the brain damage is not too devastating, serial scans reveal that speech therapy induces changes in alternative pathways in the brain related to speech (Schlaug 2009).
- [4.132]Serial scans of the brains of people undergoing meditation training reveal measurable changes in various brain structures after periods as short as one month (Hölzel 2011, Tang 2010).

[4.133]These fascinating studies teach that conscious mental effort induces changes in brain structure, revealing the brain to be a more dynamic and changeable organ than hitherto suspected. Furthermore, these studies reveal the likelihood that many inter-individual differences in adult brain structure may well be partly due to differences in upbringing. This is anatomical confirmation of what has been suspected from years of observation and study.

[4.134]Just as exercise causes functional and structural changes in the heart and muscles of the body, the training of skills, as well as the effects of emotions and behavior also induce functional and structural changes in the brain. This is the explanation of materialism. Nonetheless, believers in dualism claim that changes in brain function and structure induced by upbringing and training, are products of the influence of the soul on the structure and function of the physical brain. Accordingly, they claim these changes in physical brain function and structure are proof of the reality of this belief. However, neither explanation is conclusive proof of dualism or of materialism.

Ethnicity, culture, gender & the brain

[4.135]This conclusion also finds support in the differences in brain function between peoples raised in different cultures, as well as between men and women of the same race raised in the same sociocultural environment. Upbringing is an aspect of culture. So it comes as no surprise to learn that while brain structure and function is essentially identical between people of different races and cultures, recent neuroradiological studies reveal significant differences in the functioning of the brains of people from different ethnic backgrounds and cultures (Ansari 2009, Aron 2010, Balram 2009, Chiao 2008, Demorest 2010, Gutchess 2010, Han 2008, Ng 2010, Zhu 2007). Furthermore, while the structure and function of the brains of men and women are essentially the same, there are measurable anatomical differences (Brun 2009, Cosgrove 2007, Xu 2000, Zaidi 2010), and functional differences (Cosgrove 2007, Grön 2000, Han 2008) between the brains of males and females with identical cultural and racial backgrounds. Gender, racial, and cultural differences in brain function and anatomy provide intriguing discussion points.

Different races: different near-death experiences

[4.136]Ethnic background, culture, upbringing, language, and environment cannot directly affect the immaterial soul (see 1.66-1.75). Nonetheless, the visionary content and transcendental worlds encountered during near-death experiences do differ between peoples from different races and cultures (Abramovich 1988, Carter 2010, Kellehear 2001, Knoblauch 2001, Lundahl 1993, Murphy 2001, Osis 1986, Pasricha 1986, pages 33-34 in Evans-Wentz 1960). What is the explanation for this observation? Believers in dualism and reincarnation might, and sometimes do say, that souls are reincarnated in bodies and cultures suited for the further spiritual development of each soul. This latter is no new concept. An ancient Hindu holy text called the

Khandogya Upanishad, colorfully expounds this very same concept of progressive spiritual development.

[4.137]*Those whose conduct has been good, will quickly attain some good birth, the birth of a Brahmana, or a Kshatriya, or a Vaisya. But those whose conduct has been evil, will quickly attain an evil birth, the birth of a dog, or a hog, or a Kandala. (V Prapathaka, 10 Khanda, 7, in Müller 1879)*

[4.138]This passage clearly implies that the souls of males and females, persons of different social classes, races, and animals, are at different levels of spiritual evolution. An astounding concept, and one immediately raising the question of how this is all managed. Is there some celestial clearing house—an accounting and management bureau directing the souls of the recently deceased to their next incarnation in the body of the appropriate gender, race, social class, or type of animal? Or does each soul individually select its subsequent incarnation in a physical body suited to furthering its spiritual development? This latter concept implies that each soul has such a degree of insight into correct behavior, that reincarnation for purposes of spiritual development would actually be superfluous. More importantly, the concept of a soul undergoing spiritual development, requires the soul to possess memory ability—for without memory, there is no learning, and therefore no spiritual development.

[4.139]Another fascinating question raised by this philosophy is that of which gender, race, culture, or animal has the spiritually most advanced souls. Are the souls of women more spiritually advanced than those of men? Or is the opposite true? Then what about the souls of peoples of different races, cultures, and upbringing? Is the soul of a Ukrainian street prostitute who supports her disabled parents spiritually less developed than that of an Islamic suicide bomber? Is the soul of a Canadian wheat farmer less advanced than that of a Sahel nomad? Is the soul of a Catholic priest less advanced than that of a Buddhist monk or a Wahhabite Imam? What about the difference between the spiritual development of the soul of a vapid Sydney socialite and that of a Columbian cocaine farmer? These are unendingly fascinating speculations, and a list of such comparisons is endless. Such comparisons also raise the question of whether the near-death experiences of persons with spiritually advanced souls differ from those of persons with spiritually undeveloped souls. Indeed, a comparison of the near-death experiences of different sociocultural groups and genders may well reveal which genders, which races, and which sociocultural groups possess the spiritually more advanced souls. Such an investigation could even herald the beginning of an era of NDE-racism, (NDE = near-death experience), resulting from comparison of the near-death experiences of peoples of different genders, races and cultures. Fascinating speculations … However, despite the intriguing nature of these speculations, they remain just that—wild speculations, albeit intriguing.

Gender, race, and brain function

[4.140]This brings us to a major problem. Are the physical bodies of men, women, Chinese, Norwegians, Kalahari bushmen, Italians, Amazonian Indians, or other races, controlled by different types of souls specific for each gender, race, or level of spiritual development?

[4.141]For believers in dualism, the phenomenon of enhanced conscious awareness undergone during experiences of apparent disembodiment of the soul, means that any such distinction is nonsense. It is no more than nineteenth century twaddle regarding the supposed mental superiority of one ethnic or cultural group over the other. Differing genetic makeups and diets of peoples of different genders, races and cultures result in subtle differences between brain structures of people from different genders, races and cultures. These subtle differences between brain structures result in differences in responses to control by the soul, so explaining why the expression of attributes and properties of the soul by the physical body differs somewhat between persons of differing genders, races and cultures.

[4.142]Materialism explains these same facts differently. The detailed structures and functioning of the brains of peoples of differing genders, races and cultures are formed and modified by their genetic backgrounds, diets, cultures, environments, languages and life experiences (Fagiolini 2009, Gräff 2008, Petronis 2006). These effects are reflected in differences in mental function as expressed by the physical body. Accordingly, materialism is an equally adequate explanation for these observed differences. So these observations cannot be considered proof of the mind-models of dualism or materialism.

Children and diversity

[4.143]These discussions of the effects of upbringing, life experiences, culture, and race upon the structure and functioning of the brain teach clear and important lessons for all humanity. In fact, these observations have far-reaching implications for the functioning and organization of societies. Our future depends upon our children. They are our gift to the future, our keepers in our dotage, and the medium of our personal and communal immortality. To ensure the best possible future, children should receive individually optimal upbringing and education to ensure maximum development of their full neurological potential. Furthermore, the effects of language, race, culture, and upbringing upon brain structure and function, teaches us the lesson of neurological diversity of peoples. Just as diversity in animals and plant species has proven its worth, such neurological diversity is another valuable and hitherto relatively unused property of humanity. Just imagine what might be possible with creative utilization of neurological differences resulting from differing cultures and races. Who knows, perhaps future societies will regard neuro-diversity as a valuable resource?

Mind is a product of brain function

[4.144]Most of the phenomena discussed in this chapter are explicable with either dualism or materialism. One consequence of this observation is that dualism and materialism are alternative, equally adequate mind-models in these situations. However, some objectively observed phenomena do permit of definite conclusions regarding the true nature of the mind.

- [4.145]The Wada Test conclusively proves that the soul is unable to directly influence the nerves, muscles, and other tissues of body. Therefore, the Wada Test conclusively proves that the soul can only manifest its presence in this material world as speech, actions, behavior, and deeds, through the mechanisms of the physical brain.
- [4.146]Mescaline and cerebral hypoxia induce states of mind where people consider their mental process to be clearer, more rapid, and more efficient than normal. This is a subjective experience. According to the mind-model of dualism, such enhancement of mental function is due to a reduction of the filtering, or limiting effect of the physical brain on the expression of the soul (see Chapter 1). However, objective testing of the mental functioning of people experiencing such states of mind reveals the illusory nature of such subjective feelings. Such objective studies prove the supposed "filtering" or "inhibiting" effect of the physical brain on the expression of the soul to be no more than an illusory subjective experience.

- [4.147]Many people reporting experiences of disembodiment such as near-death experiences, or out-of-body experiences, also report their mental function was clearer than normal, feelings of omniscience and understanding of the workings of the universe. But these people do not undergo objective testing during such experiences. So are such subjective experiences of enhanced mental function during such mental states, true or illusory?

- [4.148]Cerebral hypoxia clearly reveals the physical brain to be the repository of long-term memories—a fact totally at variance with the mind-model of dualism (see Chapter 1). This fact has profound consequences for belief in the reality of disembodiment of the soul during near-death experiences and out-of-body experiences. But the soul forms no long-term memories. Therefore, formation and retention of memories within the physical brain reveals the illusory nature of such experiences. Accordingly, such experiences are not proof of the reality of a human soul.

[4.149]The totality of all these facts reveals the absence, and illusory nature of a soul with the properties believed by most people (see Chapter 1)—proving that mind is a product of the functioning of the brain.

5

Mind & the Abnormal Brain

[5.1]The previous chapter examined the consequences of changes in the functioning of the anatomically normal brain for the mind-models of dualism and materialism. But what does the functioning of the abnormal brain reveal about these mind-models? By abnormal brains, I mean the brains of persons whose brains are congenitally abnormal, or the brains of people affected by disease, injury, or surgery. The effects of all these things are intriguing, yielding fascinating insights into the origin and nature of the human mind. However, before examining the effects of abnormal brain structure, it is first necessary to examine conceptions about the relation of brain volume and weight to intelligence and other mental faculties.

Brain and mind

[5.2]Brain volume and weight correlate quite well with skull volume, otherwise known as "cranial capacity", in persons with normal brain structure and development. Many nineteenth scientists believed brain volume and weight correlated directly with intelligence and other properties of the mind. Accordingly, many nineteenth century scientists diligently collected skulls and brains of deceased persons to examine the relationship between boney structures, brain size, brain weight, and mental attributes.

Brain volume and intelligence

[5.3]In fact, this interest developed into a scientific rage. Nineteenth century scientists collected the skulls of peoples of all races to determine how the evident external differences between different genders, races, and different individuals of the same race correlated with the underlying boney structures, but also to determine relationships between skull volumes, skull conformation, and mental function. This interest was not just restricted to the indiscriminate collection of skulls of deceased persons of all levels of society. Many scientists also collected the brains and skulls of eminent persons, to examine how the structures of their brains correlated with the mental abilities of these persons while alive. Collection and examination of brains was certainly more relevant to determining a relationship between brain structures and attributes of mind than just examining the hollow skulls of these persons. Some scientists even formed mutual societies dedicated to this purpose.

[5.4]*It is owing to the courage and wise forethought of certain advanced thinkers and fruitful contributors to science that the brains of members of the American Anthropometric Society have become available for scientific study. Occasionally an individual has directed his nearest of kin to arrange for the preservation of his brain; such men were Tiedemann, Grote and the two Seguins. But not until the Mutual Autopsy Society of Paris was founded in 1881 was this most legitimate claim of science met by the establishment of an association formed for the express purpose of securing elite brains for scientific study. On this side of the Atlantic, the American Anthropometric Society was the pioneer association founded on similar lines, followed by the Cornell Brain Association under the leadership of Prof. Burt G. Wilder. (Spitzka 1907)*

[5.5]However, fresh brains were not always available for study, but skulls were available, and provided a method of indirectly determining brain volume and weight. The volume of the skull occupied by the brain, or "cranial capacity", was measured by filling the skull cavities of deceased people with small lead pellets (lead shot), or any other convenient substance such as dry "Calais sand". Brain weight was then calculated from a known relationship between cranial capacity and brain weight. The outcomes of these studies, and the resulting attitudes were epitomized in the writings of scientists such as the English anthropologist and statistician Francis Galton (1822-1911), in a book first published in 1869 called *Hereditary Genius* (Galton 1869). Similar ideas were published by American ethnologists such as Samuel Morton (1799-1851) in books entitled *Crania Americana* (Morton 1839), and *The Races of Man* (Morton 1868). Of all the works appearing during this time period, one of the most fascinating was a book called *Lectures on Man: His Place in Creation and in the History of the Earth,* written by the German-Swiss zoologist and geologist Carl Christoph Vogt (1817-

1895). Carl Vogt compared the personalities and intellectual capacities of Negroes with whites, using cranial capacity as an implicit measure of intelligence.

> [5.6]*I must not omit to draw your attention to a point worthy of particular notice. According to Aitken Meigs' measurements, the cranial capacity of Negroes born in Africa is considerably more than that of the American slaves. Is this the effect of that cursed institution which degrades men to the condition of chattel, and deprives them of that liberty which alone can lead to a higher development? As slavery exercises an equally injurious influence on the master, it might perhaps be possible, by a comparative examination, to show a similar relation as regards the cranial capacity of the inhabitants of the free and of the slave states of North America. The recent tremendous butcheries may afford abundant materials for such investigations. Let the materials, then, be made use of before they find their way into the bone mills and manufactories of artificial manure. [Author's note: By "recent tremendous butcheries" Vogt was referring to the American of Civil War, 1861-1865] (page 92 in Vogt 1864)*

[5.7]Stunned amazement is the only possible reaction of most modern Western Europeans to the last sentence! Using war victims as fertilizer? Carl Vogt must have been a very "interesting" man. The rest of this paragraph is quite conventional for the time. He referred to the skull measurements of James Aitken Meigs, who found that the cranial capacities of Negroes born and raised in slavery in the USA were "considerably" smaller than those of free Negroes living in Africa. This latter was a form of tendentious misreporting, or a total lack of any understanding of the true meaning of statistical analysis.

[5.8]James Aitken Meigs (1829-1879) was a Philadelphia physician ethnologist who published a book called *Catalogue of Human Crania* during 1857 (Meigs 1857), in which he detailed the skull types and cranial capacities of many races. Table III on page 17 of this book, provides a wealth of data on the cranial capacities of peoples of diverse races. In this table, we find that the average cranial capacity of American Negroes born in slavery was found to be 80.8 cubic inches. This average was based upon a study of the skulls of only 12 deceased American Negro slaves of unmentioned gender and origin. The lead shot measurement technique used by Meigs was accurate, but the conclusions drawn from these data were very misleading. After all, women generally have a smaller cranial capacity than men, but that does not make them less intelligent. Moreover peoples of different tribes and races have different cranial capacities (Meigs 1857), and Negro slaves in the USA came from many different tribes and regions of Africa. Furthermore, Meigs used cranial capacity measurements from only 64 Negro skulls of unmentioned African tribe, race, and gender, to conclude that the average cranial capacity of Negroes born in Africa was 83.7 cubic inches. This was the source of Carl Vogt's information, and this was the "considerable" difference in cranial capacity alluded to by Carl Vogt: 80.8 versus 83.7 cubic inches! In the same Table III of this book, we read that a study of skulls of Caucasian citizens of the USA, (again without mention of gender), revealed that Caucasians had an average cranial capacity of 93.5 cubic inches, versus the 80.8 and 83.7 cubic inches cranial capacity measured in the skulls of Negro slaves and Africans of unknown gender or tribe. This was "proof" of the inferior mental capacity of Negro slaves, and all other African Negro peoples in general. Meigs' data on cranial capacities are accurate and interesting, but the non-existent quality of the conclusions drawn from these data can immediately be consigned to the rubbish heap of history. However, at the time these data did confirm the feelings of innate superiority held by many Caucasian people living in the USA, providing them with a biological basis for perfidious institutions such as slavery and racial inequality.

Brain weight and intelligence

[5.9]Not only did nineteenth century scientists actively collect and measure skulls, but they also collected and studied the brains of recently deceased the brains of eminent, famous, and intelligent persons. The weights of the brains of these persons were even published as a sort of ranking of real intelligence. One result of this was that eminent persons whose postmortem brain weights were lower than average were assumed to be actually intellectually less gifted than assumed during life. So some prominent persons, afraid their brains might be smaller than those of other illustrious persons, took measures to prevent possible postmortem public humiliation by ensuring their skulls and brains were never removed after death.

[5.10]Too much reliance is still placed on the now very old researches on the weights of brains made by RUDOLPH WAGNER (1805-1864), of Gottingen. He furnished by far the largest number known, and not many have been added since. He

measured and weighed so many brains of renowned men, that a weight below the normal, i.e., average, gave rise to the suspicion that the man was after all not so clever as was thought during his lifetime. This alarmed some of his renowned contemporaries so much, that they thereupon had a clause inserted in their wills, forbidding a postmortem examination of their brains. (page 67 in Hollander 1920, Volume 2)

[5.11]However, as the passage below indicates, such brain weights were often not very accurate, as the circumstances of the measurement were never standardized.

[5.12]Of more recent brain weights taken, the lowest recorded was that of Ignaz von Dollinger, the celebrated Catholic theologian, which weighed 1207 grammes, and the heaviest was that of Turgenieff, the Russian novelist, which was 2012 grammes. How unreliable—without the fullest details-these brain—weights are, is shown by the careful weight taken of the brain of HELMHOLTZ, distinguished for his wonderful researches in optics. ("Zeitschrift für Psychiatrie," 1899). The weight of his brain, including the blood coagulum, was 1700 grammes. This being removed, the brain weighed 1540; but so much blood remained that it was estimated that 100-120 grammes should be deducted. This would reduce the brain weight to 1420-1440 grammes. Helmholtz had therefore a brain not much above the average weight; but how do we know that in the cases of those very heavy brain weights recorded allowance was made for the quantity of blood, as was made in the case of Helmholtz? (page 66 in Hollander 1920, Volume 2)

[5.13]Edward Anthony Spitzka (1876-1922) was an American neurologist who published an exhaustive study and review of the brain weights of eminent men in relation to those of the less prominent during 1903 (Spitzka 1903, Spitzka 1907). He found that the brains of prominent intellectuals, military and political leaders weighed on average 75 to 125 grams more than their contemporaries belonging to the same gender and race. However, brain weight is not the only factor determining intelligence and other mental attributes. This is clearly demonstrated by the fact that women's brains are generally smaller than men's brains, and the weights of brains of peoples of different races also differ considerably (Davis 1868).

Modern insights on brain size and intelligence

[5.14]Modern studies of the brain reveal only a weak relationship between different measures of intelligence and brain size (Witelson 2006). Other recent studies and reviews demonstrate that important factors determining intelligence are not only brain size, but also the degree of interconnectivity, as well as the efficiency of communication between different parts of the brain (Deary 2010, Gläscher 2010). Intelligence is a complex totality of the trade-off between brain size, interconnectivity, and efficiency of communication within the brain. These three factors explain why peoples of differing genders and races manifest similar intelligence despite differing cranial capacities (Fox 2011). Nonetheless, the final conclusion is that a certain minimum of brain tissue is required for intelligence to manifest, and that there is a correlation, albeit weak, between brain size and intelligence.

Manifestation of intelligence and mind by the brain

[5.15]Intelligence, personality, emotion, memory, and all other properties of mind are manifest to other persons through the medium of the speech, actions and behavior of the physical body. Consider the examples of consciousness in persons who are totally paralyzed as discussed in Chapter 2. A conscious, but totally paralyzed person may be intelligent, possess the full gamut of human emotions, as well as an individual personality. But such a person cannot communicate any of these things to others, because total paralysis prevents use of the physical mechanisms of the body required to communicate these aspects of mental function to others on this physical world.

[5.16]The conclusion of this undeniable fact for the mind-models of dualism and materialism is identical. According to the mind-model materialism, destruction of some brain mechanisms results in an inability to generate or manifest the properties of mind generated by the destroyed regions of the brain. Similarly, the mind-model of dualism also predicts that destruction of some brain mechanisms means the soul cannot express the properties of mind manifested by these destroyed brain regions. After all, the soul cannot activate or control destroyed, damaged, or malfunctioning physical bodily mechanisms. In conclusion, manifestation of any attributes and properties of the mind by the physical body, such as consciousness, personality, memory, emotion, intelligence, etc., require that the physical mechanisms of the body expressing these functions be present and functional.

5.17Broca's aphasia is a good, albeit tragic example of how failure or damage of a region of brain affects physical expression of the properties of the mind. Broca's area of the cortex of the brain is a part of the primary motor cortex controlling voluntary movements, and Broca's area controls the complex coordinated movements of mouth, tongue, and breathing required to utter speech. There is also lateralization of Broca's area in most people, such that the left side of the brain is dominant side. This is why strokes affecting the primary motor cortex on the left side of the brain often also affect Broca's area. Persons afflicted by this type of neurological disaster are often also paralyzed on the right side of their body. People suffering a stroke damaging Broca's area can understand speech, can formulate a response in their minds, but cannot express themselves with speech, because the neurological mechanisms in Broca's area controlling the muscles generating speech no longer function. Hollander (1920) reported a classic example of a case of Broca's aphasia resulting from a stroke.

5.18*In 1896, at the age of twenty-seven years, an apparently healthy young woman suddenly was seized with a stroke of paralysis and fell to the ground, remaining unconscious for ten hours. On recovering consciousness, she was found hemiplegic [paralyzed] on the right side and to have lost all power of speech. Before the stroke she had been able to speak four languages, French, German, Italian, and Spanish, but from that moment and afterwards she was unable to pronounce anything more than the two simple words, "Oh non." A slight degree of word-blindness, which was remarked, disappeared after a few months. The patient came under the observation of Professor Déjèrine at the Salpêtrière, who considered the case very striking, the intelligence being of a very high order and other cerebral functions being to all appearance intact. Her condition remained practically unchanged for ten years. Re-examination by M. Briand, in May, 1908, showed the existence of a spastic right hemiplegia—with exaggerated reflexes on that side. Spontaneous speech was nil, except for "Oh non," used correctly and in its proper sense. The patient was unable to repeat words on request. With the letters of the alphabet before her, she was able to spell out any word in any of her four languages, either spontaneously or to order. There was not the slightest trace of word-deafness in any of these languages. Writing was perfectly performed with the left hand, spontaneously and to dictation, and copying was* *accurate. There was neither mind-blindness nor mind-deafness; no astereognosis or apraxia. There was no indication whatever of intellectual defect; the patient was well aware of her surroundings, of events in her life; memory, attention, and judgment were unimpaired. The case appeared to be one of pure motor aphasia. On May 15th, 1909, death occurred from renal causes and a necropsy was secured. (page 401 in Hollander 1920, Volume 1)*

[5.19]Similarly, damage to other regions of the brain also affects manifestations of the control exerted by the mind, regardless of whether the mind is a product of the functioning of the brain, or whether it an aspect of the soul. But this is not the whole story.

Recovery and neuroplasticity of the brain

[5.20]Damage to parts of the brain caused by injury or disease is sometimes not as permanent, or profound as that displayed by the unfortunate woman with the Broca's aphasia above. Furthermore, depending upon the cause, location, and extent of damage to the brain, recovery or shifting of certain functions within the brain does occur. Such reallocation of functions to other regions of the brain is called "neuroplasticity", and occurs in children and adults (Desmurget 2007, McClelland 2007, McFie 1961, Rosenberg 2008, Smith 1966, Vanlancker-Sidtis 2004). A man with a slow growing tumor in the dominant left side of his brain clearly demonstrated such neuroplasticity.

[5.21]*We describe a 28 year-old, right-handed male diagnosed with a left temporo-frontal glioma. It was decided to manage him expectantly due to the low level of suspicion of malignancy and the close proximity of the lesion to critical language function centers. Language functional MRI (fMRI) tests were performed twice within the ensuing 2 years before surgical intervention. Regional brain activation was measured within the temporal and frontal lobes. Laterality index (LI) was calculated based on the corresponding number of activated voxels. The main finding is that over time, prior to resection of the enlarged tumor, the inferior frontal gyrus (IFG) changed from being strongly left lateralized in the first fMRI exam to being bilateral in the second fMRI exam, mainly due to larger activation in the right hemisphere. By that time, although the patient was not aphasic, his language performance was significantly below average. These findings suggest that a slow growing tumor in an adult language-related area might result in a functional reorganization by recruiting the right hemisphere. However, the contribution of such reorganization to the preservation of language performance remains equivocal. (Rosenberg 2008)*

[5.22]The somewhat equivocal last sentence in this abstract did not reveal the whole story. Later in the body of this same article, the authors reported, "In fact, he was able to communicate well enough to keep a high functioning level at work and in his daily life up to and after his second operation." (page 471 in Rosenberg 2008). So he was able to continue working, because of transfer of many expressive speech functions subserved by the Broca area on his dominant left side, to the right side of his brain.

[5.23]Unfortunately, the extent of recovery or transfer of functions from diseased or injured areas of the brain to other regions is often neither predictable, nor always complete. Both factors must be taken into account whenever considering the effects of congenital brain abnormalities, or the effects of injuries and disease. These last words finally bring us to a discussion of what abnormal brain structures and functions teach about the differences between the mind-models of dualism and materialism.

Amount of brain tissue and the conscious mind

[5.24]During any discussion of the relationship between mind and brain, someone almost inevitably comes up with the statement that: "Intelligence is not a property of the brain, because some super-intelligent university students have been found with only a thin shell of brain in a head otherwise filled with only water... " The more well-read persons will proceed to cite an article by Eugene Berger in which a pediatrician called John Lorber (1915-1996) remarked upon one of his study persons.

[5.25]*Professor John Lorber speaks of the CT scan of a hydrocephalic brain. "When we did a brain scan we saw that instead of the normal 4.5 centimeter thickness of brain tissue between the ventricles and the cortical surface, there was just a thin layer of mantle measuring a millimeter or so. His cranium is filled with cerebrospinal fluid." Can you imagine being alive with* *a brain 1/450th of normal? That's no brain at all. But there is more. The brain scan with a 1 millimeter rim of cerebrum was that of a young student at Sheffield University who had an IQ of 126, gained a first class honors degree in mathematics, and was socially completely normal. The student's physician at the university noticed that the youth had a slightly larger than normal head and so referred him to Dr. Lorber, simply out of interest. Can you imagine an IQ of 126 and no brain? That does not fit my idea of the way this universe works. (Berger 1983)*

5.26This remarkable fact certainly did not accord with the world-view of Eugene Berger, nor does it correspond with the world-view of many other people. Some people regard this and similar cases as positive proof of the reality of the mind-model of dualism, because here is an example of a person with normal mental function and above normal intelligence, despite possessing almost no brain (Smit 2011)! Yet both Berger and some of those believing in the mind-model of dualism display a curious blind spot in their thinking, as well as ignoring a number of very relevant and proven medical facts.

The inconsistent position of dualism?

5.27Studies of the weight of the brain discussed in the beginning of this chapter reveal only a weak relationship between intelligence and brain weight. Furthermore, as discussed earlier in this chapter, even the most fervent believers in the mind-model of dualism acknowledges that brain mechanisms are required to express manifestations of mental function on this world by means of the physical body. This concept is extensively discussed throughout the book *Science and the Near-Death Experience* (Carter 2010). Yet on the other hand there are those who consider it possible for the mind to express itself through the medium of the physical body without the intermediary of any physical neurological control mechanisms. Consider the following citation referring to the case of the intelligent hydrocephalic young man reported by John Lorber.

5.28*… the fact that some virtually brainless people can be highly intelligent and social, leads to an almost unavoidable conclusion: that consciousness is not a product of the brain. Rather, consciousness will make use of the brain, or won't even use a brain in case of the brain's virtual absence, but will then express itself through other—as yet unexplained pathways. (pages 485-486 in Smit 2011)*

[5.29]This is a curious argument contradicting all that has been learned about the functioning of the body for many decennia.

- [5.30]We know the physically conscious minds of people totally paralyzed with curare or the locked-in syndrome cannot speak, move, perform actions, or deeds, even though they consciously try to do these things.
- [5.31]We know physically conscious people suffering from the consequences of permanent damage to parts of their brains due to surgery, tumors, injuries, strokes, or temporarily due to a Wada Test, cannot move the paralyzed parts of their bodies, even though they still possess considerable amounts of normally functioning brain tissue.
- [5.32]We know physically conscious persons suffering from a stroke affecting Broca's area cannot speak, even when they try to do so. Yet these people also possess normal intelligence and mentation (see example in this chapter).
- [5.33]The mental disintegration seen in persons with brain diseases such as Alzheimer's disease, and other causes of severe and eventually lethal dementias are also revealing. They reveal the requirement for functioning mechanisms of the physical brain to generate the attributes and properties of the mind, or to act as a conduit for the soul.
- [5.34]The bodies of brain-dead persons can be kept alive and in a functionally perfectly normal state, by using drugs to support the circulation, and a mechanical respirator to support the breathing. All that is missing is a brain, which is dead in these unfortunate individuals. According to the mind-model of dualism, the souls of such brain-dead persons are now totally freed from the filtering, or inhibiting influence of the physical brain. But there is a very conspicuous absence of any evidence of control exerted by a soul over the living and perfectly functional bodies of brain-dead persons. So brain death reveals the fallacy of belief systems claiming that the soul "won't even use a brain in case of the brain's virtual absence, but will then express itself through other—as yet unexplained pathways." (Smit 2011).

[5.35]All these things clearly prove that the mechanisms of the brain are required to express speech, behaviors, actions, and deeds through the mechanisms of the physical body. Persons with congenital hydrocephalus have no special celestial dispensation exempting them from this requirement. Accordingly, the argument that properties of mind, such as intelligence, of people with hydrocephalus can be expressed without the intermediary of the mechanisms of the physical body is patently foolish. So how is it possible to explain the mental function and intelligence of the young man described by John Lorber, as well as that of other persons with hydrocephalus?

Explaining hydrocephalic mental function

[5.36]Hydrocephalus is a condition in which an abnormal amount of fluid accumulates within the ventricles (fluid filled cavities) of the brain. It may be congenital or caused by disease. The effect of this accumulation of fluid in the ventricles is to press and flatten the brain against the hard skull. This is why the cortical thickness of the brains of survivors of congenital hydrocephalus may be considerably reduced, as in the case of this university student. However, this flattened brain material does function to a greater or lesser degree, as is shown by the example of the university student (Berger 1983), and by the fact that electroencephalographic activity occurs over the whole surface of the flattened brains of people with compensated hydrocephalus (Greenberg 1977). In fact, the presence of electroencephalographic activity over the entire skull of hydrocephalics is what differentiates hydrocephaly from hydrancephaly.

[5.37]John Lorber was a pediatrician who conducted considerable research on people born with hydrocephalus in the Sheffield area of the United Kingdom during the 1960's and 1970's (Lorber 1984). This young man was referred to him because his head circumference was larger than normal, which made him a likely candidate to have been born with hydrocephalus (Wilson 2008a). Some people born with hydrocephalus (congenital hydrocephalus, infantile hydrocephalus), have a head size slightly larger than normal, develop relatively normally, and seldom manifest any neurological problems until later in adult life (Wilson 2007, Wilson 2008a). So this story also shows this was an unusual young man, because untreated congenital hydrocephalus is usually fatal, and those that do survive childhood usually have below normal intelligence (Chi 2005, Feuillet 2007).

[5.38]*The natural history of untreated hydrocephalus involves either early death or poor intellectual development in survivors. In 1962, Laurence and Coates reviewed 182 patients with infantile hydrocephalus and found that nearly 66% of untreated patients died by 18 months, and 80% died by 20 to 25 years of age. Only 46% of untreated patients survived infancy, and only 38% had normal intelligence in childhood. (Chi 2005)*

[5.39]But why do people die of hydrocephalus, and what happens when it is untreated? The brain is not a solid organ jammed inside the hard bones of the skull. Instead, the brain is about 1200-1500 grams of jelly-like nervous tissue floating in a bath of fluid inside the skull. This fluid is called "cerebrospinal fluid", and is continually produced by specialized tissue within the brain called the "choroid plexus". Cerebrospinal fluid is continually produced, and an equal amount is continually removed. This keeps the pressure inside the head constant, and ensures the brain and spinal cord are always bathed in fresh cerebrospinal fluid. Hydrocephalus occurs when the passages through which cerebrospinal fluid flows are blocked, or when it is no longer removed as fast as it is produced. This may be the result of congenital abnormalities, or diseases affecting the brain at any age. When cerebrospinal fluid is no longer removed as fast as it is produced, the pressure inside the head increases, causing compression of brain tissue, reducing blood flow within the brain, as well as traction of various parts of the brain. The final result is a decreasing level of consciousness, altered mental function, urinary incontinence, inability to walk and move normally. Eventually brain function is so severely compromised that death occurs (Hasan 1989, Hurley 1999). This is the mechanism of malfunction and death due to hydrocephalus at any age.

[5.40]But babies are different to adults. Their skull bones are separate, connected to each other by tough fibrous tissue. This allows flexibility of the skull during birth, and also allows the skull to expand during the first two years of life. After two years of age, the skull bones of children fuse into the single hard adult skull size and form. So the skulls of babies born with hydrocephalus expand with the expanding pressure inside the skull until expansion is no longer possible, or until achieving a balance between production and removal of cerebrospinal fluid. The latter mechanism is why this intelligent young hydrocephalic man described by Dr. Lorber survived untreated congenital hydrocephalus. We know he must have had hydrocephalus at birth, or as an infant, because the larger than normal head of this young man proved he had a hydrocephalus before the bones of his skull fused together as a child (Wilson 2007, Wilson 2008a). And the increased cerebrospinal fluid pressure inside his skull flattened the tissues of his developing brain into a one millimeter thick layer before an equilibrium between production and removal was achieved.

[5.41]This brings us to the matter of the high intelligence of the hydrocephalic young man described by Dr. Lorber. While most persons with untreated congenital hydrocephalus have a below normal intelligence, about 38% have an intelligence quotient (IQ) above 85 (Table 14 in Laurence 1962), and 3.7% even have an IQ of 120 and above (Figure 11 in Laurence 1962). Moreover Laurence (1962) found that the fewer the other bodily disabilities associated with hydrocephalus, the higher the intelligence (Figure 15 in Laurence 1962). But intelligence is not an easily defined property of the mind. Instead, intelligence is a measurement whose definition depends upon whether one is measuring verbal, mathematical, or social intelligence, etc. This is also reflected by the fact that there is only a weak relationship between different measures of intelligence and brain size (Witelson 2006). Modern studies actually reveal that the most important factors determining intelligence are the degree of interconnectivity, as well as the efficiency of communication between different parts of the brain (Deary 2010, Gläscher 2010).

[5.42]More than anything else, the intelligent young man with hydrocephalus reported by Dr. Lorber, reveals the fundamental plasticity of the developing infant human brain. Indeed, the mind-models of dualism and materialism both require neuroplasticity, whereby this young man made up for his lack of brain tissue by developing a spectacular degree of interconnectivity, as well as efficiency of communication between the remaining different parts of his brain. The same is true of all other of the 3.7% intelligent persons with hydrocephaly. Intelligence and other manifestations of mind in a hydrocephalic brain are equally well explained by dualism as by materialism. Dualism explains this by claiming the presence of sufficient adequately functioning brain tissue to enable the manifestation of these properties of the soul through the mechanisms of the physical brain present inside the hydrocephalic skull. Materialism claims the functioning mechanisms of the brain tissue present inside the skulls of these hydrocephalic persons are sufficient to generate these manifestations of mind. Accordingly, the example of intelligence existing in persons with hydrocephalus, does not demonstrate whether the mind-model of dualism or materialism best explains the manifestation of intelligence and other manifestations of mental activity by the physical body.

Anencephaly and the conscious mind

[5.43]Even so, many believers in dualism continue to claim the case of the young man presented by Dr. Lorber definitively proves the conscious mind is separate and independent of the physical body. But this is a very simplistic view of the properties of the conscious mind. Taken to extremes, it implies that a person can possess normal mental function when no brain is present beyond that needed to sustain consciousness and breathing.

[5.44]The sad infant malformation called "anencephaly" is a perfect example of the extreme consequences of such a belief. Anencephaly is a birth defect occurring in 0.38 to 5.9 babies per 1000 births (Canfield 1996, Horowitz 1969). Anencephalic babies are born without a brain, often also having no head above eye level. This condition is invariably fatal: about 20% are stillborn, 67% die within 24 hours (Jaquier 2006), but some do survive for several days (Jaquier 2006, Nielson 1949), sometimes even up to 237 days (Luyendijk 1992).

[5.45]Studies of the brains of those anencephalic babies surviving many days in relation to the anatomy of the structure of their brains reveals they possess brainstem structures enabling breathing and swallowing, even though the rest of the brain is absent. The mental functioning of these survivors consists of no more than basic spinal reflexes, and basal consciousness (Luyendijk 1992, Melnick 1987, Nielson 1949). This is at a level far below that of babies with normal brains. For example, the infant described by Dr. Luyendijk who survived a remarkable 237 days revealed the following neurological function.

[5.46]*The anencephalic infant showed all the outward characteristics of the malformation: a sturdy build and remarkably coarse hands, and a Buddha-like face. Instead of the calvarium a lobulated triangular reddish area is seen, which is sharply delimited from the surrounding scalp. The eyes have a divergent position and the pupils are middle wide and unreactive to light. The sucking reflex is present; oral application of a quinine sulphate solution causes some smacking of the tongue and lips, although it is not followed by any facial expression. A loud sound results in a twitching movement of the head and stiff closing of the eyes. Compensatory head-positioning is slightly indicated and rotation of the child in a vertical position causes deviation of the head but does not cause eye movements. Caloric stimulation was negative. When the cerebrovascular area is touched the mero-anencephalic child*

shows a smiling expression which involves the mouth and eyelids.
Pressure in the posterolateral parts causes a twitching movement
of the head followed by a rotation to the heterolateral side,
sometimes in combination with some irregular breathing.
(Luyendijk 1992)

[5.47]This child had only reflexes sufficient for feeding, and a few other functions. Otherwise, this level of development is far below that of a corresponding six month old infant. Subsequent study of the brain of this child revealed it possessed a brainstem, but no other brain tissue (Luyendijk 1992).

[5.48]Anencephalic babies never grow to childhood or adulthood, and never manifest normal mental function. This extreme example of absent brain tissue reveals that conscious humans need more than just a brainstem to survive, and manifest normal mental function. Accordingly, the example of anencephaly indicates that survival and the manifestation of normal mental function also requires the presence of cortical and subcortical structures. However, it might also be argued that the necessity for cortical and subcortical structures is unproven by the example of anencephaly, because anencephalic babies die shortly after birth, and so never get the chance to manifest the mental properties of their souls as proposed by the mind-model of dualism.

Hydrancephaly and the conscious mind

[5.49]I discussed the birth defect of hydrancephaly in Chapter 2 (see 2.31-2.35). Hydrancephalic children possess only a brainstem, thalamus, and some vestigial pieces of cortex. The rest of their normal skulls are filled with fluid. There is no electroencephalographic activity measureable over their skulls, except for that above pieces of vestigial brain tissue (Merker 2007, Shewmon 1999). Such unfortunate children survive only until about 17 to 20 years of age. They have a normal sleep wake cycle, but are profoundly mentally retarded, and incapable of independent existence. An article discussing the philosophical and medical aspects of consciousness in these children, also contained a detailed description of the development and findings in four of these unfortunate children, among which, the following individual.

[5.50]*At age 10 years, the patient required a permanent*
tracheostomy for airway obstruction due to macroglossia. CT
scan at that time showed occipital-lobe remnants but no other

cerebral cortex. Posterior fossa structures were normal. Since then, he has remained in excellent general health. Puberty began around 13 or 14 years.

At ages 9, 12, 14, and 17 years, this subject was evaluated with the Vineland Adaptive Behavior Scales. Age-equivalent scores ranged initially from 4 to 10 months and recently from 1 to 5 months, with a decrease in the daily living domain related to inability to take food orally.

DAS [Dr. Shewmon] visited the patient when he was 17 years old. His head circumference was 57 cm, his pupils reacted to light, and his eye movements were roving and nystagmoid without fixation or following. Extremities had fixed contractures, and reflexes were hyperactive with sustained clonus. Facial expression and slight head turning were his only means of communication. (Case 4 in Shewmon 1999)

[5.51]This unlucky child was a perfect example of almost total absence of brain cortex and subcortical structures, but with a functioning thalamus and brainstem. I discussed the example of the intelligent hydrocephalic young man found by Dr. Lorber, who had only a minimal shell of cortical and subcortical structures (see above). The example of this young man has prompted some believers in dualism to propose that expression of the soul in this physical world is independent of the presence and quantity of cortical and subcortical brain structures. The example of hydrancephaly demonstrates that consciousness is possible even in persons with no more cortical material than a vestigial remnant occipital cortex. Yet in the above case of hydrocephaly—at 17 years of age, this boy was profoundly spastic, required gastrostomy feeding, and had an intelligence level assessed at the equivalent of 4 to 10 months (Case 4 in Shewmon 1999). This, and other examples of hydrancephaly, demonstrate the reality that normally functioning cortical and subcortical structures are required for the body to manifest normal mental function, in addition to just manifesting the consciousness made possible by a functioning thalamus and brainstem.

[5.52]Another aspect of the mind-model of dualism is the belief that the physical brain somehow inhibits or filters manifestations of the soul, impairing the full expression of its true nature (see 1.76-1.88). Hydrancephaly is an example of a condition where a person is conscious, but has a truly minimal amount of cortical and subcortical tissue to filter, or inhibit the expression of the true nature of the soul. The logical consequence of this belief is that persons with hydrancephaly should possess at least normal mental function. Furthermore, because of the absence of subcortical and cortical tissue to filter the manifestations of the mind, some of these children might even express the unfettered power of their souls, manifesting enormously enhanced mental abilities far beyond those of normal persons. But these sad children possess none of these attributes and abilities. Their mental abilities and life expectancies are severely curtailed by their unfortunate and dreadful congenital abnormalities.

[5.53]The conclusion from the example of hydrancephaly is evident. Any expression of the true nature of the conscious mind requires a minimal amount of normally organized cortical and subcortical material. But does hydrancephaly reveal any new insights into the differences between the mind-models of dualism and materialism? In the mind-model of dualism, the mechanisms of the brain are required as a conduit for the expression of the properties of the soul, while for the materialist the conscious mind is a product of the functioning of the brain. The same physical brain mechanisms are necessary in both situations. So do other forms of abnormal brain structure and function reveal new insights?

Brain surgery and mind

[5.54]Damage or injury to various parts of the brain is known to alter mental function. The same is also true for brain surgery. Before the introduction of the first therapeutically active antipsychotic drugs in the 1950's, psychiatric institutions were filled to overflowing with patients unable to function in society. This sad state of affairs was summarized in a review by George Mashour in 2005.

> [5.55]*In 1937, over 400,000 patients lived in approximately 477 American psychiatric institutions. Over half of the hospital beds in the United States were used by psychiatric patients, and by the 1940s, US$1.5 billion was required to treat mental illness. (Mashour 2005)*

[5.56]This situation continued to deteriorate, so physicians welcomed all therapies that might possibly alleviate the enormous burden of psychiatric disease with open arms. Psychosurgery, a form of brain surgery changing the mental function of people, was one of the therapies employed at the time. Walter Jackson Freeman (1895-1972), a neurologist, and his neurosurgical colleague James Winston Watts (1904-1994), were fervent advocates of psychosurgery such as prefrontal lobotomy and leucotomy. They did much to popularize psychosurgery for psychiatric disorders (Black 1982, Mashour 2005). Statistics at the time revealed psychosurgery to be an effective treatment, allowing up to 47% of people to be discharged from mental institutions, and 20% to resume employment (Black 1982). So it is not surprising that many tens of thousands of psychiatric patients in the USA and the UK underwent diverse forms of prefrontal lobotomy and leucotomy during the heyday of psychosurgery from 1935 to 1955 (Black 1982, Christmas 2004, Mashour 2005).

[5.57]Transorbital leucotomy was one of the most popular techniques during the 1950's in the USA. In essence, this is a technique where the eyelid is lifted up, and an instrument driven upwards through the thin bone of the upper orbit (eye-socket) into the frontal lobe of the brain. Sweeping the blade of the instrument left and right severs the fibers connecting this part of the frontal lobe cortex to the rest of the brain. Just read the description of this procedure as published by Walter Freeman in 1949.

> [5.58]*Transorbital lobotomy seems to be more successful when carried out in conjunction with electroconvulsive shock than when it is done under ordinary anesthesia. [...] The function of the electroshock is primarily to produce generalized disruption of cortical activity. Transorbital lobotomy can then be performed in the postconvulsive coma without further anesthesia. It has been my custom to administer two convulsive shocks at an interval of one or two minutes in order to prolong the stage of coma, because a patient coming too quickly out of coma might dislodge the instrument and endanger his life. No preparation of the operative field is necessary, since the conjunctival sac is normally sterile, and the tears flow freely after the electrical discharge. After the second convulsion subsides a towel is placed over the nose to prevent contamination by saliva or nasal secretions. The eyelid on one side is then elevated and the point of the instrument inserted into the conjunctival sac, being careful not to touch the skin. The point of the instrument is moved around against the vault of the orbit until it sets properly, and the shaft is then brought into position parallel with the bony ridge of the nose. [...] The point is then driven through the orbital plate by gentle blows of a hammer until the 7 cm. mark on the shaft of the instrument reaches the edge of the upper eyelid. Maintaining the instrument parallel with the bridge of the nose, the handle of the instrument is moved*

149

laterally about 15° and then medially about the same, is returned to the mid position and withdrawn. [...] Within an hour some patients can get out of bed, talk, use the bedpan, and take liquids. (Freeman 1949)

[5.59]Wow ... is the first instinctive reaction of most modern physicians and non-physicians when reading the details of this operative procedure. Most modern physicians could not even dream of performing procedures such as this under these conditions. Nonetheless, at the time, this procedure was popular among psychiatrists, because according to Walter Freeman, neither neurosurgeons nor anesthesia were required. Psychiatrists could perform this procedure after administering electroconvulsive shocks with minimal apparatus and practically no sterility. No need for troublesome dialogues with neurosurgeons—and it worked (Black 1982)! Not surprisingly, neurosurgeons refused to associate themselves with this procedure, prompting Walter Freeman to say disparagingly:

[5.60]*Watts, who now employs that method almost exclusively, long ago said that "the surgeon sees what he cuts but does not know what he sees." (Freeman 1958)*

[5.61]Not surprisingly, this type of unsterile and uncontrolled neurosurgery had a significant risk of serious complications such as infection, bleeding, and a two percent mortality (Black 1982). Moreover the operation sometimes resulted in serious personality changes due to overenthusiastic severing of the connections of the prefrontal cortex with the rest of the brain.

[5.62]*Much has been written about these serious personality changes. To epitomize, it may be said that they represent the Boy Scout virtues in reverse. [A Scout is trustworthy, loyal, helpful, friendly, courteous, kind, obedient, cheerful, thrifty, brave, clean and reverent.] They are likely to be particularly prominent in the early phases after lobotomy and to disappear progressively with the passage of time. (Freeman 1958)*

[5.63]The effect of transorbital leucotomy is now known to be due to severing the orbitofrontal neural circuit located in the prefrontal cortex just above the eye sockets, which has an important controlling influence on behavior and personality (Cummings 1993, Mashour 2005). Severing the fibers of this circuit causes personality changes such as becoming more outspoken, worrying less than normal, irritability, elevated mood, emotional lability, and tactlessness. Moreover, these people also show alterations in interest, initiative, or conscientiousness (Cummings 1993).

[5.64]The history of psychosurgery is fascinating, repeatedly revealing what simple observation of brain-damaged persons reveals to us all— brain disease, injury, and surgery can cause changes in mental function without affecting the level of consciousness. But does psychosurgery aid in differentiating between the mind-models of dualism and materialism? Unfortunately not. According to the mind-model of materialism, surgery changes the structure of the brain, so altering the properties of mind generated by the brain. However, the mind-model of dualism teaches that psychosurgery alters the structure of the brain, so changing the physical expression of the control exerted over the physical body by the soul. Accordingly, psychosurgery fails to differentiate between materialism and dualism.

Brain tumors, epilepsy, and mind

[5.65]Brain tumors affect the functioning of the brain by destroying the areas of brain tissue they occupy, by pressure and traction of adjacent areas of brain tissue, as well as by causing localized epilepsy affecting adjacent areas of brain tissue, or even the whole brain. Tumors affecting some areas of the brain can also affect mental function. For example, brain tumors in some areas of the brain can generate visual hallucinations (Norton 2000, Teeple 2009), while tumors affecting the prefrontal lobes alter social functioning (Burns 2003, Hoffer 2007). A very unusual case was that of a man who developed sociopathic impulsive sexual behavior and pedophilia due to an orbitofrontal tumor (Burns 2003). Religious conversion is another unusual alteration of mental function sometimes resulting from temporal lobe tumors. An example of this was described by a bus conductor.

> [5.66]*The patient's first conversion experience occurred in 1955 at the end of a week in which he had been unusually depressed. In the middle of collecting fares, he was suddenly overcome with a feeling of bliss. He felt he was literally in Heaven. He collected the fares correctly, telling his passengers at the same time how pleased he was to be in Heaven. When he returned home he appeared not to recognize his wife, but she did get from him a somewhat incoherent account of his celestial experience. [...] On admission to St. Francis Hospital Observation Unit, he was constantly laughing to himself; he said that he had seen God and*

that his wife and family would soon join him in Heaven; his mood was elated, his thought disjointed and he readily admitted to hearing music and voices: 'I wish they would tell me I could go to earth. Look at you cooped up here. I could give you a game of tennis.' He remained in this state of exaltation, hearing divine and angelic voices, for two days. (Case 1 in Dewhurst 1970)

5.67The list of changes in mental function due to brain tumors is endless, as are the changes in mental function due to injuries, disease, or abnormalities in areas of the brain known to be involved in the generation and expression of aspects of mind. More recently, studies of epileptic activity manifesting during consciousness reveal other fascinating subjective experiences providing insights into the nature of the conscious mind. A woman once described the experiences she underwent during epileptic seizures caused by a tumor in the left temporal lobe of her brain.

5.68*She added: "During the seizure it is as if I were very, very conscious, more aware, and the sensations, everything, seems bigger, overwhelming me." [...] These episodes influenced her life, "It is a big happening in your life to have these seizures. Thanks to these experiences, I do not fear death anymore. I see the world differently, every sensation is stronger; for instance I see more colours than before, and I have more detailed perceptions, particularly when listening to music." (Case 1 in Picard 2009)*

5.69She was conscious, and able to listen to music during these experiences at the same time as she felt herself to be more conscious and aware than normal. Similar experiences of enhanced conscious mental function were described by a man during epileptic seizures caused by a tumor in the right temporal lobe of his brain.

5.70*"I feel rooted to the spot with a more developed consciousness. I feel a stronger consciousness of the body and the mind, but I do not forget what is around me." According to the notes the patient made about his feelings during the auras: "My inner body rises from an unalterable bliss. I escape into the time space of my body. It is a moment of fullness in the loophole of time, a return to myself. It is an unconditional, privileged moment of inhaled sensations. My body and my head may interact differently to what every human knows. It is a sensation that is not common, something to discover." (Case 2 in Picard 2009)*

[5.71]And after surgery for a brain tumor, one man developed very interesting conscious epileptic experiences in the scarred brain tissue adjacent to the site of the operation on his brain.

[5.72]*Three shorter episodes (about 1 min) characterized by accelerated thinking, ultrarapid calculation, heightened consciousness, and euphoria were also noted, but were never associated with disembodiment, vestibular, or somatosensory sensations. These experiences started 6 months after surgery and increased in frequency. (Lopez 2010)*

[5.73]The experiences of enhanced conscious mental function aroused by these episodes of epilepsy occurred during full consciousness, and were profound subjective personal experiences. Yet objective examination with brain scans and electroencephalography, and subsequent treatment with surgery and drugs, proved them to be products of brain malfunction, rather than a lifting of any putative filtering effect of the physical brain. Here again we see a difference between subjective personal experience and external objective observation. These personally profound subjective experiences raise fascinating questions related to the origin of the conscious mind.

[5.74]Religious experiences, heightened and more rapid conscious awareness, and heightened perceptive abilities, are subjective experiences. The mind-model of materialism states such experiences are products of abnormal brain function. However, the mind-model of dualism claims these experiences are manifestations of the true nature of the soul. Nevertheless, these are subjective experiences occurring in brains with abnormal structures, during moments of demonstrably abnormal brain function. Moreover, surgery and antiepileptic drugs terminate the occurrence of these experiences. We could argue that these abnormalities of brain structure and function enable the soul to manifest its true nature, and that treatment with surgery and drugs prevents this occurring again. But these displays of the supposedly true nature of the soul manifest through the medium of demonstrably abnormal brain tissue, with equally abnormal function. So according to the logic of dualism, these displays of altered thinking and heightened conscious mental function, are actually expressions of an interaction between the soul and abnormally functioning brain tissue, rather than manifestations of the true nature of the soul itself. Accordingly, epilepsy and brain tumors reveal that marvelous transcendental, cognitive and affective experiences are not necessarily proof of the reality of a human soul.

Concluding remarks on mind in an abnormal brain

[5.75]Most of the phenomena discussed in this chapter cannot definitively distinguish between the mind-models of dualism and materialism. Nonetheless, some of the objectively observed manifestations of mental function in persons with abnormal brains do reveal some important aspects of the true nature of the conscious mind.

- [5.76]The first most evident fact revealed by these objective phenomena, is that any expression of the properties of mind such as intelligence, memory, emotion, etc, requires the presence of functioning brain tissue and structures performing these functions. Dualism and materialism both require the presence of the same functioning brain structures.
- [5.77]The presence of brain damage, injury, or the effects of surgery alters the mechanisms of the brain through which the soul expresses itself in this physical world. This is a situation similar to that of a damaged, but still functioning radio receiver. Damage and malfunction of the radio set does not affect the signal from the radio station, but does affect the transformation of the radio signal by the radio set into the sounds transmitted through the medium of the radio signal. The soul cannot directly control the body directly, but must act through the mechanisms of the physical brain to produce speech, actions and deeds. So just as with the metaphor of the radio set receiving a radio transmission, damage, injury, disease and drugs do not affect the soul and controlling influence, but do alter the way the conduit of the brain transforms the controlling influence of the soul into speech, actions, and deeds.
- [5.78]The fact that the soul must act through the mechanisms of the physical brain to manifest in this physical universe has profound consequences. For example, some people with epilepsy secondary to brain surgery or injury, undergo subjective experiences during full physical consciousness such as religious experiences, heightened and more rapid conscious awareness, heightened perceptive abilities, accelerated thinking, and ability to perform ultra-rapid calculation. But no one ever performs objective tests of the reality of these subjective experiences, so all that is available as to their reality are the subjective experiences themselves. So are these experiences manifestations of the true nature of the soul? Or are they manifestations of the soul acting through malfunctioning or damaged brain tissue? On the other hand, are they simply experiences

generated by abnormally functioning brain tissue? It is impossible to differentiate between these possibilities. Nevertheless, the reality of multiple explanations means these experiences are neither proof of the reality of a human soul, nor revelations of the true nature of the soul.

[5.79]In conclusion, mental function manifested by persons with abnormal brains reveals dubious, as well as definitive differences between the mind-models of dualism and of materialism. The following chapters continues the search for proof of which of the two mind-models better explains the origin and nature of the mind.

6

The Gas

[6.1]God was the first anesthesiologist. The Bible of the Christians tells us that God acted as anesthesiologist and surgeon to excise a rib from Adam, the first man. From this rib, God created a woman as a companion for Adam. Modern medical knowledge allows us to speculate that this was a primordial method of harvesting stem-cells from the marrow of the excised rib to clone a female companion for Adam. At least, this is all we can infer from this terse operation report in the Bible.

> [6.2]*And Adam gave names to all cattle, and to the fowl of the air, and to every beast of the field; but for Adam there was not found an help meet for him. And the LORD God caused a deep sleep to fall upon Adam, and he slept: and he took one of his ribs, and closed up the flesh instead thereof; And the rib, which the LORD God had taken from man, made he a woman, and brought her unto the man. And Adam said, This is now bone of my bones, and flesh of my flesh: she shall be called Woman, because she was taken out of Man. (Bible, King James Version, Genesis 2: 20-23)*

[6.3]General anesthesia subsequently fell into disuse for innumerable millennia until October 16 in 1846. It was on this day that William Morton gave the first successful public demonstration of general anesthesia in the Massachusetts General Hospital. This latter event was a momentous occasion. Finally, humankind was freed of the necessity to endure the pain of surgery! Passages in the holy books of two major world religions inform us that there were undoubtedly many inscrutable divine reasons why untold ages had to elapse between the first general anesthetic administered by God, and the subsequent first public demonstration by Morton. Both the Bible and the Quran reveal this in no uncertain way. For example, we read in the Bible that:

$^{6.4}$*A man's heart deviseth his way: but the LORD directeth his steps. (Bible, King James Version, Proverbs: 16:9)*

$^{6.5}$This same concept is expressed in the Quran.

$^{6.6}$*It is true thou [Mohammed] wilt not be able to guide every one, whom thou lovest; but Allah guides those whom He will and He knows best those who receive guidance. (Quran, Yusuf Ali translation, 28:56)*

$^{6.7}$It is wonderful how great world religions always come up with identical concepts satisfying the profoundest needs and questions of the human spirit. Such passages in these holy books reveal that only God knows why anesthesia was not revealed or discovered earlier in human history. Moreover, these passages also clearly state that God even determined why anesthesia was not revealed, or discovered earlier in human history. So does the delayed discovery of anesthesia mean that humans living before the discovery of general anesthesia were more sinful, and therefore more hateful to God, than people born afterwards? Perhaps God wanted people to die unnecessarily of dreadful surgically correctable diseases and injuries, as well as to suffer the horrid pains of primitive surgery for those millennia between the creation of Eve from Adam's rib, and the re-discovery of general anesthesia in 1846. These are fascinating speculations. They almost totally absolve humans from any lack of observation and association, as well as from ignorance and even simple stupidity! Nonetheless, however fascinating, such intriguing theological discussions and speculations are not the main purpose of this book. Now it is time to enter into the domain of anesthesia history.

Revelations from the history of anesthesia

$^{6.8}$But why delve into the history of general anesthesia? After all, the main theme of this book is the relationship between the body and the mind as revealed by anesthesia and other branches of medicine. The answer is twofold. History is often fascinating, and I happen to enjoy learning the history of even the most mundane things. More importantly, it is an unfortunate fact that all modern studies of the subjective mental effects of general anesthetic drugs, simply provide colorless, insipid, bare, and emotionless measurements and data about the effects of anesthetic drugs, but omit to tell of the sometimes wondrous and profound mental experiences induced by these same drugs. Yet it is just these fascinating experiences that reveal so much about the origin and nature of the mind.

[6.9]Returning to the history of general anesthesia, William Morton was the first to publicly demonstrate the reality of general anesthesia to make pain-free surgery possible. Nonetheless, Morton was not the first to successfully administer general anesthesia for surgical procedures. He received the credit, but it was actually a general practitioner called Crawford Long who administered the first general anesthetic for a surgical procedure.

Who was Crawford Long?

[6.10]Crawford Long (1815-1878) was a physician who started a general practice during 1841 in the town of Jefferson, in the state of Georgia, in the USA. At the time, Jefferson was a small, relatively isolated country town inhabited by "only a few hundred people". Entertainment was scarce in such country towns. So many people took to pastimes such as drink, religion, hunting, taxidermy, taffy-pulling, quilting, knitting, embroidery, etc. Nitrous oxide inhalation and "ether frolics" were also popular diversions, and Crawford Long along with other young male inhabitants of Jefferson were enthusiastic occasional users.

[6.11]*In the month of December, 1841, or January, 1842, the subject of the inhalation of nitrous oxide gas was introduced in a company of young men assembled at night in this village [Jefferson] and several persons present desired me to prepare some for their use. I informed them I had no apparatus for preparing or preserving the gas, but I had a medicine (sulphuric ether) which would produce equally exhilarating effects; that I had inhaled it myself, and considered it as safe as the nitrous oxide gas. [...] The company were all anxious to witness its effects. The Ether was introduced: I gave it first to the gentleman who had previously inhaled it, then inhaled it myself, and afterwards gave it to all persons present. They were so much pleased with the exhilarating effects of Ether, that they afterwards inhaled it frequently, and induced others to do so, and its inhalation soon became quite fashionable in this county, and in fact extended from this place through several counties in this part of Georgia. (pages 36-37 in Boland 1950)*

[6.12]But as Crawford Long noted, exhilaration was not the only effect of ether. He also noted that people felt no pain from falls or blows while under the influence.

[6.13]*On numerous occasions I have inhaled Ether for its exhilarating properties, and would frequently, at some short time subsequent to its inhalation, discover bruises or painful spots on my person, which I had no recollection of causing, and which I felt satisfied were received while under the influence of Ether. I noticed my friends, while etherized, received falls and blows, which I believed were sufficient to produce pain on a person not in a state of anesthesia, and on questioning them, they uniformly assured me that they did not feel the least pain from these accidents. These facts are mentioned that the reasons may be apparent why I was induced to make an experiment in etherization. (pages 36-37 in Boland 1950)*

[6.14]And so it was, that on 30 March 1842, that Crawford Long administered ether anesthesia to facilitate the excision of an unsightly sebaceous cyst from the back of the neck of James Venables. This was the first known use of ether to provide general anesthesia for a surgical procedure. Crawford Long's country practice was not large, which is why he seldom performed surgical procedures. This was one of the reasons why his account of his experiences was only published several years afterwards during 1849 (pages 36-47 in Boland 1950).

[6.15]His delay in publishing cost him international fame as the first to administer a gas for surgical anesthesia. This fame was reserved for two dentists further north in the state of Massachusetts—Horace Wells, and William Morton. These two men were business partners for about four weeks during 1843 in a short-lived dental prosthetic practice in Boston. This brief association was cordially, but very firmly dissolved by Wells during November 1843. A letter Wells wrote to his mother eight months later, clearly reveals in no uncertain way that the dubious character of Morton was the real reason for dissolving this partnership as soon as possible (pages 40-41 in Wolfe 2000).

[6.16]*I found him [Morton] to be a fellow without any principle whatsoever [...] I was not at all surprised when report came that he was in the daily habit of visiting grog shops. Aside from that, he was the most deceitful man, I ever knew, he would not scruple [sic] to tell direct falsehoods when he knew he must be detected in a lie within a few hours. He is now married. I attended his wedding at Farmington a few weeks since and if I ever pitied a body, I truly pitied that girl. (page 42 in Wolfe 2000).*

[6.17]Even so, it was William Morton who subsequently successfully demonstrated the reality of general anesthesia with ether in 1846. So how did this brief association finally result in the successful and famous demonstration of surgical anesthesia in the Massachusetts General Hospital on 16 October 1846? I will begin with the background to this discovery—the studies performed by Humphrey Davy of the properties of nitrous oxide.

Humphrey Davy and gravy

[6.18]Humphrey Davy (1778-1829) was an eminent English chemist who published the first serious studies of the effects of nitrous oxide on humans during 1800. He also performed many other chemical researches, among which the discovery of the alkali metals potassium and sodium. This latter discovery was immortalized in a small rhyme I somehow never managed to expunge from my memory since first hearing it at junior high school.

[6.19]*Humphrey Davy*
abominated gravy
He lived in the odium
of having discovered sodium.

[6.20]As was common for scientific research at the time, Humphrey Davy tested the effects of nitrous oxide upon himself. The subjective mental effects of this gas were such that he gave nitrous oxide its better known name of "laughing gas".

[6.21]*I had now a great disposition to laugh, luminous points seemed frequently to pass before my eyes, my hearing was certainly more acute and I felt a pleasant lightness and power of exertion in my muscles. [...] I felt a sense of tangible extension highly pleasurable in every limb; my visible impressions were dazzling and apparently magnified, I heard distinctly every sound in the room and was perfectly aware of my situation. By degrees as the pleasurable sensations increased, I lost all connection with external things; trains of vivid visible images rapidly paired through my mind and were connected with words in such a manner, as to produce perceptions perfectly novel. I existed in a world of newly connected and newly modified ideas. I theorised; I imagined that I made discoveries. [...] As I recovered my former state of mind, I felt an inclination to communicate the discoveries I had made during the experiment. I endeavoured to recall the ideas, they were feeble and indistinct; one collection of terms, however, presented itself: and with the most intense belief and prophetic manner, I exclaimed to Dr. Kinglake, "Nothing exists but thoughts! —the universe is composed of impressions, ideas, pleasures and pains!" (pages 487-489 in Davy 1800)*

[6.22]These mental effects were so pleasurable, that Davy even held laughing gas parties he called "hilarious evenings", where invited persons could inhale nitrous oxide. He also popularized his experiences with nitrous oxide in a book published during 1800 entitled, *Researches, Chemical and Philosophical; Chiefly Concerning Nitrous Oxide, or Depholgisticated Nitrous Airs and its Respiration* (Davy 1800). So the effects of nitrous oxide were widely known and popular, which brings us to the first medical use of this drug by Horace Wells.

The unhappy Horace Wells

[6.23]Quincey Colton (1814-1898) was a travelling showman, who while a medical student, realized that travelling shows were more profitable than the practice of medicine. So he stopped his medical studies to engage in the more profitable occupation of public demonstrations of the then new, and marvelous, medical and electrical wonders. In the beginning of December 1844, Colton circulated an advertisement in Hartford, Connecticut, for a public "scientific" demonstration of the effects of nitrous oxide.

[6.24]*The effect of the Gas [nitrous oxide] is to make those who inhale it either Laugh, Sing, Dance, Speak or Fight, and so forth, according to the leading trait of their character. They seem to retain consciousness enough not to say or do that which they would have occasion to regret. (page 94 in Duncum 1947)*

[6.25]Horace Wells (1815-1848) had a dental practice in this very same town, and attended a private demonstration of nitrous oxide inhalation given by Quincey Colton on 11 December 1844. During this demonstration a young man called Samuel Cooley, became so wild and uncoordinated under the influence of nitrous oxide, that he injured himself by falling and running against furniture. Yet when he recovered his senses, he stated that he had felt no pain whatsoever when he injured himself. Wells was an observant man, always searching for ways to improve his dental practice. The standard of dental hygiene at the time was appalling. Many young people had infected or bad teeth, and aside from prostheses, extraction was the only real, but sometimes horrendously painful "treatment" offered by dentists. Wells spoke with Colton about the manufacture and application of nitrous oxide. Finally, he induced Colton to bring some nitrous oxide to his office, where he inhaled the gas, and while under its influence had a tooth painlessly extracted by his colleague Dr. Rigg. Upon recovering his senses, Wells was heard to exclaim; "A new era in tooth pulling!" (page 95 in Duncum 1947).

[6.26]As an interesting aside, the reader should note that while nitrous oxide always induces significant pain relief, the other mental effects do vary somewhat from person to person. Some people experience a reduced level of consciousness, others begin to laugh or become exhilarated, while others report experiencing profound transcendental, affective and cognitive mental states. More than 100 years after Horace Wells, Peter Fenwick, an English neurologist, once took part in an experiment during which he had to perform certain tasks while breathing 40% nitrous oxide in oxygen. He reported his experiences of the mental effects of nitrous oxide.

[6.27]*The world suddenly became full of meaning, and I knew that I had obtained a universal symbol which contained all knowledge. When I completed the experiment and as the mask was taken from me I called to my colleagues, I have it! The answer to all knowledge! And I held up two fingers in a V sign. (page 306 in Fenwick 1996)*

[6.28] Horace Wells was not interested in transcendental, affective, or cognitive experiences. He was only interested in the pain relieving effects of this gas. So after his personal experience of nitrous oxide, Wells administered this gas to several of his patients to painlessly extract teeth. Convinced he had a wonderful discovery—the use of inhalation of nitrous oxide to relieve the ghastly pains of surgery—he contacted his old business partner, William Morton.

[6.29]At this time William Morton had a flourishing dental prosthetic practice in Boston, while at the same time studying medicine at the prestigious Harvard medical school. Morton introduced Wells to two surgeons, who arranged for him to provide a lecture on his discovery, as well as arranging for him to use nitrous oxide on a patient who was to undergo an amputation. But the patient decided at the last moment not to undergo the operation, so the waiting physicians and medical students asked Wells to demonstrate the use of nitrous oxide on one of the medical students to relieve the pain of a tooth extraction. Unfortunately, due to the unreliable method of nitrous oxide administration used by Wells, the medical student did feel some pain during the tooth extraction, although he later stated that it was less than otherwise. Nonetheless, the audience was not convinced, and Wells departed an unhappy man after many called his method of pain-free surgery to be "a humbug affair" (page 96 in Duncum 1947).

[6.30]This failure and the resulting public scorn, must have affected Wells deeply. Several months later, he became ill, and after recovering, gave up the practice of dentistry entirely. Subsequently, he busied himself with several occupations (page 121 in Duncum 1947). Sometime during late 1847 to early 1848, he became addicted to chloroform, another newly introduced anesthetic drug. His character changed for the worse. Finally, he was arrested and interred in a New York police cell on the charge of "vitriol-throwing" at women, (spattering random women with sulphuric acid). It was here that he was subsequently found dead in a pool of blood after having slashed a femoral artery with a razor. But what was the cause of this tragic event?

[6.31]The story of his suicide was published in all its lurid details in the local newspapers, as well as in an anonymous editorial published in the *Provincial Medical and Surgical Journal* on 31 May 1848. The text of the announcement of his suicide is so poignant, and gives such a vivid image of the depths of his degradation and desperation, as well as of the times in which he lived, that I feel I must quote some details. How did he ever descend to depravity as vile as vitriol-throwing? The sad story published in this editorial was derived from one of the letters lying on the bloody floor of the cell of the deceased Horace Wells.

[6.32] *... he says he became acquainted with a young man who frequented his office, as a dentist, that his friend called and said he would thank him (Dr. Wells,) for some vitriolic acid [suphuric acid], with which to pay back a loose female, who injured his (the friend's,) dress—that he complied with the request of the young man, and that they prepared a phial to squirt the acid, by cutting a groove in the cork-stopper thereof. The letter goes on to say, that they then sallied out into Broadway—that they met the female, on whose person vengeance was to be doled out—and that*

163

his acquaintance did so avenge the former injury. (Editorial 1848)

^{6.33}But this was not the end. Horace Wells refused the invitation of this acquaintance to "continue the sport", and went home. There he continued his habit of inhaling chloroform to produce sensations of exhilaration. Two evenings after the above events, while recovering full awareness of his deeds in a police cell, he wrote of his experiences after awakening from a marathon chloroform binge in which he indulged subsequent to assisting his acquaintance.

^{6.34}*I lost all consciousness before I removed the inhaler [of chloroform] from my mouth. How long it remained there I do not know, but on coming out of the stupor I was exhilarated beyond measure, exceeding any thing I had ever before experienced, and seeing the phial of acid, I seized it and rushed into the street and threw it at two females, and may have thrust it others, but I have no recollection farther than this. The excitement did not leave me for some time after my arrest. (Editorial 1848)*

^{6.35}Arrested, interred, disgraced, and horrified beyond measure at his actions, Horace Wells decided to commit suicide. He saturated a silk handkerchief with chloroform, stuffed it into his mouth, and tied another around his mouth and neck to hold it in place. While thus rendered pain-free and half-anesthetized, he slashed one of his femoral arteries with a razor and bled to death. Such was the tormented end of one of the founding fathers of modern anesthesia.

Nitrous oxide and mental function

^{6.36}It is strange that a substance with so simple a chemical structure as nitrous oxide, (two nitrogen atoms bound to one oxygen atom), can produce such profound subjective effects. Experimental studies with human volunteers over many years have verified the wide variety of subjective and objective mental effects of nitrous oxide. To begin with, inhalation of nitrous oxide at concentrations below 50% neither induces sleep nor loss of consciousness.

Subjective mental effects of nitrous oxide

[6.37]So individuals inhaling such lower concentrations of nitrous oxide are awake and cooperative as they experience, and describe the following subjective manifestations of nitrous oxide inhalation.

- [6.38]Subjective experiences of nitrous oxide include: hilarity, inhibition of emotions, can arouse indescribable feelings of having achieved universal knowledge, an understanding of the relationship of all parts of the universe to the whole (pages 487-489 in Davy 1800, page 306 in Fenwick 1996, page 294 in James 1912).
- [6.39]Nitrous oxide can also induce changes in body awareness and image, as well as experiences of a dreamy, detached reverie state during which about 70% of people report experiencing a happy, euphoric mental state (Block 1990).
- [6.40]Nitrous oxide produces sedation in many people (Korttila 1981, Parkhouse 1960).
- [6.41]People often experience a sense of dissociation from their surroundings during nitrous oxide inhalation (Parkhouse 1960).
- [6.42]People generally feel themselves to be in control of their thoughts and in control of their bodies during nitrous oxide inhalation (Zacny 1994).
- [6.43]Nitrous oxide inhalation can cause time sense to slow down, i.e. a sense of time dilation, or a feeling that an instant lasts a long time (Block 1990, Robson 1960).

Objective mental effects of nitrous oxide

[6.44]All the above are subjective mental effects of nitrous oxide. So what are the measurable objective effects induced by nitrous oxide inhalation?

- [6.45]Pain threshold increases with increasing nitrous oxide concentration (Duarte 2008, Parkhouse 1960).
- [6.46]Short-term memory ability is reduced (Duarte 2008, Galinkin 1997, Henrie 1961, Korttila 1981, Parkhouse 1960, Robson 1960).
- [6.47]Nitrous oxide inhalation inhibits the formation of long-term memories (Galinkin 1997, Henrie 1961).
- [6.48]Procedural memory is unaffected by nitrous oxide, even at concentrations of 45% (Robson 1960).

- [6.49]Lengthening of reaction times to various stimuli (Duarte 2008, Zacny 1994).
- [6.50]Reduced speed and accuracy when performing mental arithmetic (Korttila 1981).
- [6.51]All tests of mental ability degrade in a concentration related manner, becoming increasingly less efficient with increasing nitrous oxide concentrations above 20% (Parkhouse 1960).
- [6.52]Time sense becomes increasingly disordered with increasing nitrous oxide concentrations (Robson 1960).
- [6.53]Inhalation of nitrous oxide increases the flow of blood through the brain, while at the same time altering the metabolic rates of various parts of the brain (Gyulai 1996, Lorenz 2001, Reinstrup 1997, Reinstrup 2008).
- [6.54]These same studies of regional brain blood flow and metabolism also reveal that nitrous oxide significantly increases nervous activity in the anterior cingulate gyrus on both sides of the brain (Gyulai 1996). This is a fascinating observation, because transcendental meditation (Cahn 2005, Short 2010, Travis 2009), as well as the transcendental experiences of Carmelite nuns (Beauregard 2006) also activate the anterior cingulate gyrus. Does this mean that nitrous oxide somehow acts to induce a form of chemically induced transcendental meditation? The anterior cingulate gyrus is known to mediate the use of language, spontaneous movement, and spatial relationships (Allman 2001, Davis 2005), as well as that marvelous emotional and cognitive process known as romantic love (Bartels 2000).

Materialism and nitrous oxide

[6.55]The influence of nitrous oxide on mental function increases with increasing inhaled concentration, indicating that the effects of this gas on mental function are products of the effects of this gas upon the functioning of the physical brain. Accordingly, the mind-model of materialism claims these concentration-related effects are proof of the materialist model of the conscious mind.

Dualism and nitrous oxide

[6.56]So how does the mind-model of dualism explain these marvelous effects of nitrous oxide inhalation? Proponents of dualism claim that the physical brain filters and limits the full expression of the soul (see 1.76-

166

1.88). So the amazing subjective experiences aroused by nitrous oxide inhalation are ostensibly manifestations of the true nature of the soul, released by nitrous oxide from the filtering and limiting effect of the brain to express its true nature. However, there are major problems with this belief.

- [6.57]Believers in dualism claim that the soul is the origin of all thoughts, emotions, speech, actions and deeds of the conscious physical body (see 1.55-1.65). While breathing nitrous oxide, some physically conscious people report experiencing enhanced awareness, transcendence, and omniscience. Believers in the mind-model of dualism claim these experiences are made possible by nitrous oxide removing the limiting, or filtering effect of the physical brain on the expression of the true nature of the soul. However, all human studies clearly demonstrate that inhalation of increasing concentrations of nitrous oxide increasingly alters the functioning of the conscious physical brain. This has profound consequences for the mind-model of dualism. One way of viewing this phenomenon is to use the radio signal-receiver analogy of Chris Carter (pages 13-14 in Carter 2010). A radio signal is unaffected by malfunction of the radio receiver, but malfunction of the receiver changes the way the radio signal is expressed by the receiver, while revealing nothing of the true nature of the signal. So according to the logic of dualism, these amazing states of mind are more accurately defined as manifestations of altered expression of the control exerted by the soul through the mechanisms of a physical brain whose functioning is altered by nitrous oxide, rather than an expression of the true nature of the soul.
- [6.58]This brings us to the proposed filtering and limiting effect of the physical brain as claimed by believers in dualism (see 1.76-1.88). While inhaling nitrous oxide, the conscious physical body is still under control of the soul, and may experience enhanced mental abilities such as enhanced awareness, transcendence, omniscience, as well as insight into the workings of the universe. So if inhalation of nitrous oxide removes the limiting or filtering effects of the physical brain, then the enhanced awareness of a physically conscious person breathing nitrous oxide should be able to perform mental tasks, such as mental arithmetic, more efficiently and accurately than normal. But quite the reverse is true. Instead of being more efficient and accurate, the mental abilities of a physically

conscious person inhaling nitrous oxide actually degrade with increasing inhaled nitrous oxide concentrations (see 6.46-6.51). This is very inconsistent with the belief that these nitrous oxide induced experiences reveal the true nature of the unfettered, superior intellect of the soul, by releasing it from the limiting, or filtering effect of the physical brain. Accordingly, the experience, or sensations of enhanced awareness and intellect reported by persons inhaling nitrous oxide do not correspond with objective reality—such sensations are hallucinations.

- [6.59]Believers in dualism claim that the soul is the origin of all thoughts, emotions, speech, actions and deeds of the conscious physical body (see 1.55-1.65). Furthermore, according to the mind-model of dualism, the soul is the indelible repository of all memories (see 1.92-1.115), and unaffected by anything affecting the functioning of the body (see 1.66-1.75). So if memories are stored in the soul, then nitrous oxide should not affect memory. A physically conscious person inhaling nitrous oxide cooperates, and reacts appropriately to speech and their surroundings. According to the belief of dualism, this means that physical perceptions of speech and surroundings are transferred normally to the controlling soul of this person; otherwise, the soul could not control the body to respond and behave appropriately. So memories of these things should be indelibly stored in the soul of that person, and available for spontaneous recall after the effects of nitrous oxide on the physical brain have disappeared (see 1.143). But increasing concentrations of nitrous oxide increasingly inhibit the formation, or subsequent recall of new short and long-term memories of events, speech, and actions occurring while inhaling nitrous oxide. This fact is totally incompatible with the belief system of dualism. It indicates that the soul is not the repository of memories, but that memories are stored in the physical brain.

[6.60]These effects of nitrous oxide on the functioning of the brain reveal clear and unequivocal conclusions. The effects of nitrous oxide on the human brain reveal two fundamental properties of the soul—the filtering effect of the brain, and the location of memories—to be illusory.

- [6.61]The effects of nitrous oxide reveal the physical brain to be the repository of long-term memories, and not the soul as purported by the mind-model of dualism (see 1.92-1.115).

- ^{6.62}The effects of nitrous oxide on the functioning of the brain reveal the "filtering effect" of the physical brain on the expression of the soul to be illusory (see 1.76-1.88).

^{6.63}These are consequences of the known objective experimental effects of nitrous oxide on human brain function. As with any theory, if a theory does not explain the objective observations, then another theory or model is required. Therefore, the effects of nitrous oxide on brain function prove the illusory nature of a soul with the properties defined in Chapter 1 of this book!

^{6.64}This brings us to the position of nitrous oxide within the field of anesthesia. It possesses analgesic properties, but these are insufficient to permit pain free surgical procedures. So nitrous oxide is relegated to the position of a supplementary analgesic gas, used together with other anesthetic gases during general anesthesia. More commonly, it is used to provide conscious analgesia, (analgesia = pain relief), for dentistry, during childbirth, and in ambulances. Such is the current status of nitrous oxide in modern anesthetic practice. But what about anesthetic gases and the introduction of general anesthesia by William Morton?

The dubious William Morton and etherization

^{6.65}William Thomas Green Morton (1819-1868) was the son of a bankrupt property speculator. He left home at 18 years of age, and after a period of 18 months as a clerk in a general store, he went into business for himself. Morton's business dealings revealed a dishonest and opportunistic character, as most of his many businesses were fraudulent, or simply criminal. For example, he obtained goods on credit by fraudulent means, as well as forging promissory notes and postage stamps. A newspaper article published on September 30, 1840, in the St. Louis *Daily Evening Gazette* revealed the general low esteem in which he was held by many people in that city, as well as in New Orleans, Rochester, and Cincinnati. It described all his fraudulent dealings in these cities in great detail under the heading: "BEWARE A VILLAIN".

> ^{6.66}*It is quite evident from these, and a great many other circumstances, of different grades of atrocity, that there is no point of villainy at which conscience would induce him to pause. His mind must be constantly occupied in concocting schemes of deliberate rascality, so elaborately planned, and so atrocious in their nature, that the mind of an honest man must regard them*

with equal horror and astonishment. There is a retribution here,
as well as hereafter, and it cannot be long before his career is
ended by the penitentiary or the gallows; (page 32 in Wolfe 2000)

[6.67]Morton finally ceased his dubious business ventures, and studied dentistry from 1841 to 1842. Although he never completed his studies, he started a dental practice in Framingham, and later in Boston where he also had a short-lived association with Horace Wells. Morton subsequently set up his own dental practice in Boston, and also started to study medicine. Eventually he built up a reasonably thriving dental prosthetic practice, which was one of the principal reasons for his interest in methods of providing pain relief for dental procedures.

Dental practice in the nineteenth century

[6.68]Extraction of diseased teeth, and broken stumps of teeth, was necessary to provide a better fitting denture. But the dreadful pain associated with extracting even rotted dental elements was enough to deter many potential clients. Morton was familiar with the ideas of Horace Wells of using gases to provide pain relief during dentistry and surgery. So during 1844, Morton consulted with one of his teachers at the Harvard Medical School, the eminent chemist and geologist, Professor Charles Thomas Jackson (1805-1880), as to suitable substances to provide insensibility (page 115 in Duncum 1947). Jackson suggested ether because it could render a tooth insensible with a local application, as well as rendering people insensible when inhaled. This latter was general knowledge, because many people knew that inhalations of too much ether during the then popular "ether frolics" induced stupefaction.

Experimentation with ether and success!

[6.69]Morton only really began seriously experimenting with ether in July 1846. He tried the effects of ether inhalation upon his dog, himself, as well as one of his assistants, T.R. Spear. Late in September 1846, Morton had another meeting with Jackson where he learned where to obtain the purest ether, as well as getting some hints as to how ether could be reliably applied (pages 100-105 in Duncum 1947). Morton experimented further with the effects of ether on himself. Finally, on the evening of September 30, 1846, he successfully employed ether anesthesia to painlessly extract a tooth from Eben Frost (page 105 in Duncum 1947). He subsequently approached John Collins Warren

(1778-1856), an eminent surgeon at the Massachusetts General Hospital, for permission to demonstrate the use of ether to relieve the pain of surgery. And so it was on Friday, 16 October 1846, that Morton successfully administered ether anesthesia to a young man, Edward Abbott, to enable the painless removal of a vascular neck tumor. Edward Abbott was partially conscious during the whole operation, and repeatedly told Dr. Warren during the procedure that he felt no pain at all. In response to further questioning by Dr. Warren, he replied "that he knew of the operation, and comparing the stroke of the knife to that of a blunt instrument passed roughly across his neck." Finally, Dr. Warren made his famous remark; "Gentlemen, this is no humbug." (page 110 in Duncum 1947). This single public and famous event heralded the beginning of surgical anesthesia, a medical advance making much of modern medicine possible.

[6.70]This first successful demonstration proved the value of the idea of anesthesia to the world. As a practicing dentist, aware of the pain associated with dental procedures, Morton fully realized the potential of anesthesia. So immediately after this successful demonstration, Morton decided to patent the idea and his method of administering ether for general anesthesia. Horace Wells also claimed priority for the idea of administering anesthesia by gaseous inhalation, but his claim was generally considered irrelevant (pages 18-20 in Morton 1880). Professor Jackson had a different claim. He not only wanted financial compensation for his advice, but also claimed priority for the idea of ether anesthesia on the basis of his advice. A priority battle ensued.

The Morton versus Jackson priority battle

[6.71]Professor Jackson claimed he invented the idea of general anesthesia, saying that Morton was simply a person he had instructed to apply the technique, much as a doctor instructs a nurse (page 123 in Duncum 1947, pages 17-18 in Morton 1880, pages 137-142 in Wolfe 2000). This latter was a patently ridiculous claim. Nonetheless, this inconsistency did not prevent him writing a letter about his prior knowledge to a friend in France, Elie de Beaumont, in a letter dated November 13, 1847.

[6.72]*Five or six years ago I recognized the peculiar state of insensibility into which the system is plunged by the inhalation of the vapour of pure sulphuric Ether, which I breathed in great quantity, at first as an experiment and later at a moment when I*

171

had a severe cold caused by inhalation of chlorine. (page 123 in Duncum 1947)

[6.73]This means Jackson claimed to have known of the anesthetic properties of ether sometime around 1841-1842. But this was not something he had discovered. Instead, this was knowledge published in an internationally consulted standard chemical-medical text entitled *The Elements of Materia Medica and Therapeutics*, written by Jonathon Pereira, and first published during 1838 (page 16 in Morton 1880). The relevant passages on the properties of ether contained the following statements.

[6.74]*If the air be too strongly impregnated with ether, stupefaction ensues. (page 375 in Pereira 1842)*

[6.75]*The vapour of ether is inhaled in spasmodic asthma, chronic catarrh, and dyspnoea, hooping cough, and to relieve the effects caused by the accidental inhalation of chlorine gas. (page 376 in Pereira 1842)*

[6.76]The curious correspondence between the letter of Jackson and the prior writings of Periera is very suggestive. It seems to suggest that Jackson was simply lying to Elie de Beaumont so as to claim prior discovery for the anesthetic properties of ether. The evident conclusion is that he, along with many others at the time, did not connect this knowledge of the properties of ether with the relief of surgical pain. After all, as a respected professor at the Harvard Medical School, he certainly had the connections and authority to ask a surgeon to aid him with performing a demonstration of ether anesthesia. But there is no record of his ever having approached, or requested any of his surgical colleagues to test whether ether could be used to relieve the pain of surgery. Instead, it was Morton who took the initiative to experiment with the anesthetic properties of ether, it was Morton who personally arranged the first demonstration of ether anesthesia on 16 October 1846, and it was Morton who bore personal responsibility for possible failure. Jackson's embarrassing responses to public questioning demonstrated these facts in no uncertain manner.

[6.77]*"Did you make one little experiment?" said the late Professor Louis Agassiz to Dr. Jackson at a meeting of the Boston Academy of Arts and Sciences, adding dryly, after receiving a negative reply, "It would have been better if you had." On another occasion Professor Agassiz said, "If Dr. Morton had killed his first patient, would you [Jackson] have accepted the blame just as now you ask for the honor?" Dr. Jackson was silent. (footnote on page 16 in Morton 1880)*

[6.78]Nonetheless, despite all evidence to the contrary, Jackson persisted with his claims. Morton finally came to an agreement with Jackson, and together they were granted a patent for the use of ether with the special inhaler of Morton. But this patent proved totally unenforceable. Ether was generally available, and not under any patent whatsoever. Furthermore, administration of ether anesthesia with a simple sponge, or towel, was safer and more efficient than when using the inhaler designed by Morton. All that remained for Morton was to gain recognition for priority in his discovery. He now commenced petitioning the federal government of the USA for acknowledgement of his priority in the discovery of the practical application of ether for general anesthesia.

Morton's claim against the government and demise

[6.79]His Boston dental practice waned and finally failed due to lack of supervision. So Morton gave up dentistry during 1847 to take up farming. He continued petitioning the USA federal government for recognition of priority for his discovery, and started legal action against the same government for financial compensation because of patent infringement. His claim was that the same federal government that granted, guaranteed, and protected his patent, also flagrantly infringed this very same patent, by permitting the application of ether anesthesia in all military establishments without any recognition of his patent rights whatsoever. Legal costs associated with this lawsuit ruined Morton. He and his family now lived in varying degrees of poverty and comfort on their farm (Wolfe 2000). Finally, while visiting New York City in the middle of a heat wave during 1868, Morton suddenly died of an apoplexy (pages 128-129 in Duncum 1947).

[6.80]So how should we view the contribution of Morton to the relief of pain during surgery? His critics, and the victims of his earlier fraudulent business dealings, were all unanimous in agreeing with a statement of Rev. Dr. Lange of St. Louis, who stated in an affidavit published in the *National Police Gazette* during 1852, that:

[6.81]*"I have since been greatly surprised by learning that Morton is assumed to be the discoverer of the property of Ether, in preventing pain in surgical operations. I know nothing of chemistry, but in Morton I had discerned a degree of general*

*ignorance which would make a scientific discovery by him appear
to be little less than miraculous. That he was shrewd enough to
pursue his frauds, I attributed rather to his want of consciousness
than to his intellectual ability." (facsimile on page 275 in Wolfe
2000).*

[6.82]This may all be true of the character of Morton. Yet he was shrewd
enough to defraud, and fool people during multiple dubious and
sometimes elaborate business deals. So he certainly possessed more
intelligence than just ordinary "rat cunning". He became familiar with
the concept of relieving dental and surgical pain with inhalation of gases
during his prior association with Horace Wells. He also knew that while
nitrous oxide inhalation provided pain relief during dentistry, the
analgesia was not always reliable or sufficient. Just as Crawford Long
before him, he too realized that another popular recreational drug, ether,
might well provide dental and surgical anesthesia. However, although
priority for administering the first ether anesthetic belongs to Crawford
Long, he worked unknown and unrecognized in a small town in Georgia,
and no one knew of this fact until he published his experiences in 1849,
three years after Morton's successful public demonstration in 1846.
Others, such as Charles Jackson may have known of the anesthetic and
analgesic effects of ether before 1846, but never made the mental leap of
applying these effects to relieve the pain of dentistry and surgery.
Moreover, Morton dared to experiment with ether upon himself and
others. He also dared risking public humiliation with his demonstration
of the effects of ether before a critical audience, even though memory of
the failure and humiliation of Horace Wells just one year earlier was still
fresh in the public mind. Morton was the man who alerted the world to
the reality of general anesthesia to relieve the pain of surgery on 16
October 1846, and is therefore justly renowned for making this great
discovery known to the world.

Building on the great discovery

[6.83]Within a year after the public demonstration of general anesthesia
by Morton, James Young Simpson (1811-1870) reported the anesthetic
effects of chloroform during November 1847 (Simpson 1847).
Chloroform was a more powerful and rapidly acting agent than ether, but
associated with a higher mortality due to cardiac arrest. Within a few
very short years, both chloroform and ether were used all over the world

174

to provide general anesthesia for surgical procedures. General anesthesia had arrived.

[6.84]Prior to the advent of anesthesia, surgeons had to limit the duration of any procedure to minimize surgical pain. Surgical pain meant that many people refused operations, preferring deformity or death to surgical torment. Anesthesia, by eliminating pain, made surgery a realistic alternative. Furthermore, anesthesia made more extensive and protracted surgical procedures possible, stimulating a veritable explosion of advances in surgery and dentistry. This was the boon of anesthesia.

[6.85]No new general anesthetic agents were developed or discovered during the 60 years after the discovery of ether and chloroform anesthesia. The only significant developments during these decades were the development of various masks, inhalers, and vaporizers. But the administration of anesthesia remained essentially unchanged since the days of Morton and Simpson. Furthermore, the administration of anesthesia was usually left to untrained nurses, medical students, and even hospital porters. Anesthesia was considered no more than a necessary adjunct to surgery, and no one thought of also actively sustaining vital functions, or carefully monitoring the depth of anesthesia. So it was not surprising that general anesthesia was associated with a significant mortality.

[6.86]The twentieth century saw the development of a plethora of other anesthetic gases such as vinyl chloride, ethyl chloride, cyclopropane, methoxyflurane, trilene, halothane, enflurane, isoflurane, desflurane, sevoflurane, etc. Eventually, decades of experience with modern gases of good chemical purity, and systematic studies by specialist anesthesiologists revealed accurate information about the effects of anesthetic gases. Surprisingly, despite their differing chemical compositions, the mental effects of these gases are largely similar to ether. So what are the effects of anesthetic gases?

Effects of anesthetic gases

[6.87]I will ignore discussions of the details of administration of general anesthesia, and will only discuss the effects of these anesthetic gases on consciousness and mental function. John Snow (1813-1858), was an English physician and epidemiologist. He was also the first English physician to become a professional anesthesiologist, and described five stages of anesthesia (page 133 in Lee 1968).

175

Guedel stages of anesthesia

[6.88]Subsequently, other systems of describing the depth of anesthesia with ether and chloroform were developed, but the most successful classification was that published during 1937 by Arthur Guedel (1883-1956). This was a system for determining the depth of ether anesthesia using clinical signs such as: level of consciousness, breathing, pupil diameter, etc (pages 133-138 in Lee 1968). Guedel divided the depth of ether anesthesia into four stages.

- [6.89]*Stage 1 - Analgesia:* From beginning of anesthesia to loss of consciousness. Patients may pass through a phase where they are conscious, but have varying degrees of analgesia and voluntary control of movements.
- [6.90]*Stage 2 - Delirium & Uninhibited:* Patients become delirious before losing consciousness. Uncoordinated and involuntary movements, vomiting, and breath holding may occur. Loss of voluntary control of movements.
- [6.91]*Stage 3 - Surgical Anesthesia:* Patients are unconscious, breathing is regular and automatic. Surgical anesthesia is present. There are three subdivisions in this plane of anesthesia.
- [6.92]*Stage 4 - Medullary Paralysis:* Patients are comatose. Pupils are wide open. Muscles are all paralyzed. Breathing ceases due to paralysis of the medullary respiratory center. Death occurs unless respiration is assisted and anesthesia is lightened.

[6.93]These different stages of anesthesia correlate with the modern Bispectral Index (BIS), which is an integrated electroencephalographic measure of depth of anesthesia. The BIS scale varies between 0 to 100, where 100 is fully awake, and zero is no brain electrical activity whatsoever. About 95% of people are definitely unconscious at a BIS of 50 (Drummond 2000), which is why a BIS under 50 is normally considered to indicate unconsciousness. The Guedel stages of anesthesia are clearly reflected in the BIS at different stages of ether anesthesia (Bhargava 2004).

- [6.94]**Stage 1** - Analgesia: associated with a BIS of about 75.
- [6.95]**Stage 2** - Delirium: uninhibited movements and excitation is associated with a BIS of 100 due to increased nerve and muscle electrical activity.

- [6.96]**Stage 3** - Surgical anesthesia: is associated with a BIS varying between 41 to 25.

[6.97]Stage 1 of Guedel's classification is the most interesting anesthetic stage when studying the relationship between general anesthesia, paralysis, and mental activity.

Stage-1 anesthesia and conscious paralysis

[6.98]Consider the experience of William Morton on the evening after his second talk with Jackson on 30 September 1846. After his discussion with Jackson, Morton returned to his rooms and inhaled ether from a handkerchief. Initially he noticed:

> [6.99]*I felt a numbness in my limbs, with a sensation like a nightmare, and would have given the world for some one to come and arouse me. [...] I attempted to raise from my chair, but fell back. Gradually, I regained power over my limbs, and full consciousness. (page 67 in Wolfe 2000)*

[6.100]He was conscious at the time he noted his paralysis, indicating that ether can cause paralysis of voluntary movement at concentrations too low to induce loss of consciousness. Further evidence for the reality of this phenomenon comes from rather more tawdry experiences. Shortly after ether and chloroform anesthesia came into popular use for dentistry and surgery, some patients reported dreaming of sexual experiences, or actually undergoing sexual assault by their physicians or dentists while under the influence of ether or chloroform (Strickland 2007). Consider this case reported less than one year after the first public demonstration of ether anesthesia on 16 October 1846.

> [6.101]*The first reported case of alleged sexual abuse during anesthesia occurred in Paris, France, in 1847. [...] A Parisian dentist was accused of using Ether to assist in sexually assaulting two girls on successive days. [...] The second girl was able to recall details of her assault, but at the time she felt that she was unable to resist because of the effects of the Ether, stating that she "felt paralyzed, her limbs were heavy, and she was unable to fight off" the dentist. (Strickland 2007)*

[6.102]It was uncertain whether this assault was real or hallucinatory. Regardless of the reality of the accusation, this is also a report of the feeling, or experience of paralysis of voluntary movement induced by ether. But there is more. During stage-1 of anesthesia, most people report being pain free, even though awake and able to sense the operation being performed. So here we have the observation that the first stage of anesthesia includes consciousness, a feeling of muscle paralysis or weakness, together with a degree of analgesia.

Artusio and different levels of Stage-1 anesthesia

[6.103]Joseph Artusio, a New York anesthesiologist, published a paper during 1954 in which he subdivided Guedel's stage-1 of ether anesthesia into three different sub-planes (Artusio 1954). People are awake throughout stage-1 of ether anesthesia. Artusio described the mental state during the third plane of stage-1 anesthesia as:

[6.104]*In stage I-plane 3, memory for past events remains acute but recent memory is dulled, response to spoken voice is prompt and cerebration is excellent. Eyes focus well on command, primary colors can be distinguished and total analgesia is present. This plane is characterized by the completely comfortable, cooperative patient. (Artusio 1954)*

[6.105]These same stages of anesthesia are applicable to all other gases used in anesthesia. So just before losing consciousness due to anesthetic gases, people in this first stage of anesthesia are awake, feel no pain, can hear and see, as well as feel weak or paralyzed. Studies of brain function during light anesthesia reveal that anesthetic gases reduce the functioning of the whole brain cortex, which explains the feelings of paralysis or difficulty moving, as well as the feelings of calm. Furthermore, low concentrations of anesthetic gases also suppress the responses of the sensory cortex to touch and mild pain (Heinke 2002).

Subanesthetic concentrations and statistics

[6.106]Concentrations of anesthetic gases inducing loss of consciousness do just what is stated. They induce loss of consciousness, during which no conscious mental activity occurs. Lower inhaled concentrations of anesthetic gases insufficient to induce loss of consciousness are called "subanesthetic concentrations". The same also applies to blood concentrations and doses of other anesthetic drugs. However, these are average concentrations and doses. There is considerable variation between individuals as regards the concentration of an anesthetic drug or gas causing loss of consciousness. The same is also true for all other anesthetic drug effects. This concept is best illustrated by an examination of the concentrations of anesthetic gases at which people awaken from general anesthesia.

[6.107]For example, consider the concentration of ether at which people awaken. When ether is used as sole anesthetic agent, people awaken at an average lung ether concentration, (alveolar concentration), of 1.4±0.22% of one standard atmosphere (Stoelting 1970). This figure is in the form of an average plus and minus one standard deviation in the Gaussian, or Normal statistical distribution. What it means is that 50% of people are asleep, and 50% of people are awake at a lung ether concentration of 1.41%. Furthermore, it means that 15.8% of people are awake at a lung ether concentration above 1.41 + 0.22 = 1.63%, while 2.2% are still awake at a lung ether concentration above 1.41 + (2 x 0.22) = 1.85%. This phenomenon of variation of anesthetic gas effect between individuals is true for all anesthetic gases.

[6.108]Accordingly, when discussing the mental effects of subanesthetic concentrations of anesthetic gases, the reality of considerable inter-individual variation mean it is more accurate to speak of "subanesthetic gas effects", rather than "subanesthetic concentrations". These same considerations are equally true for "subanesthetic concentrations" and "subanesthetic doses" of injected anesthetic drugs. Even so, the fact that subanesthetic drug and gas effects are directly related to the concentrations and doses of anesthetic drugs, render the terms "subanesthetic concentrations", and "subanesthetic doses" both useful and practical.

Subanesthetic gas concentrations and the mind

[6.109]Subanesthetic concentrations of anesthetic gases may induce states of excitement or "exhilaration". Ether was known to induce such a state of excitement or exhilaration long before it was ever used as an anesthetic drug. Indeed, prior to its use as an anesthetic drug from 1846 onwards, ether was freely available from pharmacies, and was even used as a nineteenth century "party drug", as is evident from this description of an "ether frolic" in Georgia during 1839.

[6.110]*Dr. Wilhite says that from the time he was ten years old (1832), he was familiar with the use of ether by inhalation as an excitant; that the boys and girls in his neighborhood near Athens, Georgia, were in the constant habit of using it; that there was hardly ever a gathering of young people that did not wind up with*

an ether frolic. Old fashioned "quiltings" was very common at that time, and in the evening the boys and young men would go to these for the purpose of a dance or an ether frolic.
On one occasion he met several young people at Mr. Ware's, about five miles west of Athens, at a quilting. The girls and boys all finished the evening by inhaling ether. Some would laugh, some cry, some fight, and some dance, just as when nitrous oxide gas is inhaled. It was in the Fall of 1839. Wilhite was a romping boy of seventeen. All the boys and all the girls had inhaled the ether. Some of them more than once. (Sims 1877)

[6.111]Likewise, soon after its introduction into anesthetic use in 1847, chloroform was also known to cause exhilaration or excitement, as was beautifully described during 1865 by Ernest Sansom, an early English anesthesiologist.

[6.112]*There is generally a bright expression of face; the tendency is usually to cheerfulness, and while unconsciousness is yet unaffected, there is frequently an inclination to laughter. (page 28 in Sansom 1865)*

[6.113]Induction of "exhilaration" with inhalation of subanesthetic doses of these drugs was the reason for the early use of ether as a party drug, as well as the basis for chloroform addiction. At this, and slightly deeper levels of anesthesia with chloroform, some people report experiencing enhancement of the sense of hearing and other senses, "life review", hallucinations, or even singing while influenced by subanesthetic concentrations of chloroform.

[6.114]*The distinctive sleep, therefore, commences—the narcosis. The senses become affected; frequently the sounds in the room are exaggerated in their intensity, the ticking of the clock becomes like the falling of a ponderous hammer. The surrounding objects become dim, and as it were dissolve in light, and then a veil enwraps them all. There is very frequently still an exhilaration, a disposition to laugh, talk, or sing. Dreams and fancies occur— temporary mental impressions which are effaced and forgotten when the narcosis is prolonged. A strange effect is the production of the phenomena of narcotic reminiscence. Events of the past life may be recalled, conversations may be repeated, and actions reproduced. A sailor will go through, with imaginary shipmates, his nautical manoeuvres, or sing his sea songs. I have heard a young girl, throughout the whole course of a surgical operation,* sing *"Beautiful Star"* correctly, word for word and note for note. Hymns and prayers are often given with distinct utterance. (page 29 in Sansom 1865)

[6.115]Other early writers on the effects of anesthetic gases reported even more spectacular effects. For example, the philosopher William James, also reported upon the profound cognitive, affective and transcendental experiences sometimes aroused by inhalation of anesthetic gases such as chloroform in his book, *The Varieties of Religious Experience.* An experience reported by a Mr. Symonds was especially dramatic.

[6.116]*After the choking and stifling had passed away, I seemed at first in a state of utter blankness; then came flashes of intense light, alternating with blackness, and with a keen vision of what was going on in the room around me, but no sensation of touch. I thought that I was near death; when, suddenly, my soul became aware of God, who was manifestly dealing with me, handling me, so to speak, in an intense personal present reality. I felt him streaming in like light upon me ... I cannot describe the ecstasy I felt. (page 391 in James 1902)*

[6.117]He told of arousing from the anesthetic a profoundly disappointed and disillusioned man.

[6.118]*Then I flung myself on the ground, and at last awoke covered with blood, calling to the two surgeons (who were frightened), "Why did you not kill me? Why would you not let me die?" Only think of it. To have felt for that long dateless ecstasy of vision the very God, in all purity and tenderness and truth and absolute love, and then to find that I had after all had no revelation, but that I had been tricked by the abnormal excitement of my brain. (page 391 in James 1902)*

[6.119]Mr. Symonds was an intelligent and articulate man, who then raised a fundamental question about the nature of his and other similar drug-induced experiences.

[6.120]*"Yet, this question remains, Is it possible that the inner sense of reality which succeeded, when my flesh was dead to impressions from without, to the ordinary sense of physical relations, was not a delusion but an actual experience? Is it possible that I, in that moment, felt what some of the saints have said they always felt, the undemonstrable but irrefragable certainty of God?" (page 392 in James 1902)*

[6.121]More than one hundred years later, similar experiences are reported with inhalation of subanesthetic concentrations of modern anesthetic gases. And just as in the nineteenth century, these same experiences are reasons why all anesthetic drugs may become drugs of addiction in susceptible persons (Spencer 1976, Yamashita 1984).

Subjective effects of subanesthetic gas concentrations

[6.122]In general, inhalation of subanesthetic concentrations of all anesthetic gases induces both subjective, as well as objective effects. Some of the subjective effects of subanesthetic concentrations of anesthetic gases have already been discussed, and here are some others revealed by human experimental studies.

- [6.123]Sedation, confusion, feelings of being carefree, loss of control of thoughts and the body, as well as floating feelings (Galinkin 1997, Janesewski 1999, Zacny 1994).
- [6.124]People may feel euphoric, dreamy and detached, experience changed body awareness, feel "high", say they "enjoy the experience of the gas" (Beckman 2006, Parbrook 1989)
- [6.125]Many people report loss of memory for events and actions performed during inhalation of subanesthetic doses of anesthetic gases (Hosick 1971).

Objective effects of subanesthetic gas concentrations

[6.126]Reports of modern human experimental studies of anesthetic gas effects rarely include accounts of subjective mental effects of anesthetic gases. However, there are many reports of objectively determined mental effects of subanesthetic gas concentrations.

- [6.127]Loss of muscle control also occurs at concentrations of anesthetic gases too low to cause loss of consciousness (Kammer 2002).
- [6.128]Lengthening of reaction times in direct proportion to inhaled anesthetic gas concentrations (Beckman 2006, Cook 1978, Galinkin 1997, Zacny 1994).
- [6.129]Psychomotor performance degrades in direct proportion to the inhaled concentrations of anesthetic gases (Beckman 2006, Cook 1978, Galinkin 19987, Janezewski 1999).
- [6.130]Time distortion increases with increasing inhaled concentrations of anesthetic gases (Galinkin 1997).

- [6.131]Short and long term memory function increasingly degrade with increasing inhaled concentrations of anesthetic gases (Cook 1978, Dwyer 1992, Galinkin 1997).
- [6.132]Brain imaging studies reveal that even subanesthetic concentrations of anesthetic gases affect the functioning of the physical brain (Heinke 2001, Kerssens 2005).

Materialism and subanesthetic gas effects

[6.133]The fact that these measurable changes in conscious mental function are related to the inhaled concentration of anesthetic gases indicates that mental function expressed by the physically conscious mind is directly related to the functioning of the brain. This relationship between concentration and mental function provides significant support for the mind-model of materialism.

Dualism and subanesthetic gas effects

[6.134]But what if the conscious mind is immaterial and separate from the body as proposed by dualism? Anesthetic gases do not directly affect the soul (see 1.66-1.75), but do affect the mechanisms of the physical brain through which the soul controls the body. According to the mind-model of dualism, the thoughts, speech and deeds of an evidently physically conscious person inhaling subanesthetic concentrations of an anesthetic gas are under the control of the soul. The inhalation of even subanesthetic concentrations of anesthetic gases induces demonstrably abnormal physical brain function. And it is during the inhalation of subanesthetic concentrations of anesthetic gases that we learn of these extraordinary transcendental, cognitive, and affective experiences induced by these gases, because people tell of them as they undergo them. Therefore, just as with nitrous oxide inhalation, such experiences undergone by a person inhaling subanesthetic concentrations of anesthetic gases, are actually expressions of an abnormally functioning brain responding to control by the soul, rather than manifestations of the true nature of the soul. This fact has profound implications. It means that transcendental, cognitive and affective experiences are products of abnormal brain function, and not necessarily manifestations of the true nature of a putative soul as proposed by the mind-model of dualism.

[6.135]This brings us to another problem with the mind-model of dualism as revealed by anesthetic gases. Believers in dualism claim that the soul is the repository of all short and long-term memories (see 1.92-1.115).

However, even a cursory study of the effects of inhaling subanesthetic concentrations of anesthetic gases reveals the true location of memories in a very direct and evident manner.

- [6.136]Believers in dualism claim that the soul controls the body to produce speech, actions and deeds when it is physically conscious (see 1.55-1.65).
- [6.137]Physically conscious persons inhaling subanesthetic concentrations of anesthetic gases cooperate fully with the persons around them, reacting and speaking in an appropriate and purposeful manner.
- [6.138]This means that during inhalation of subanesthetic concentrations of anesthetic gases, the physically conscious body somehow transmits perceptions to the soul, which subsequently controls the body to produce appropriate speech, actions and deeds.
- [6.139]Believers in dualism claim that all memories are indelibly stored within the soul (see 1.92-1.115).
- [6.140]The soul is unaffected by anything affecting the tissues of the body, including anesthetic gases (see 1.66-1.75).
- [6.141]Therefore, according to the logic of dualism, memories of events, perceptions, experiences, thoughts, speech and actions while the physical body is conscious during inhalation of subanesthetic concentrations of anesthetic gases are all stored in the soul.
- [6.142]After cessation of inhaling anesthetic gases, and recovery of all normal brain and memory functions, people should be able to recall and relate memories of all that transpired during inhalation of subanesthetic concentrations of anesthetic gases (see 1.143).
- [6.143]But all studies of the effects of inhalation of increasing subanesthetic concentrations of anesthetic gases, reveals a concentration related impairment of formation and recall of long-term memory of events occurring while under the influence of these gases (Chortkoff 1995, Cook 1978, Dwyer 1992, Galinkin 1997, Hosick 1971, Wang 2011).

[6.144]According to the mind-model of dualism, memory function should be unaffected in conscious cooperative persons breathing subanesthetic concentrations of anesthetic gases (see 1.143). However, subanesthetic concentrations of anesthetic gases do affect memory, and in particular, formation and recall of memories. Materialism readily explains this observation with the effects of subanesthetic gases on the processes of formation and recall of long-term memories. However, not all people have amnesia for the periods their minds were affected by these gases. But this observation is readily explained by the well-known fact of inter-individual variation in response to the effects of these gases. Taking all these factors and chain of logic into account leads to only possible conclusion. Memories are not stored in the immaterial human soul, but in the physical human brain.

Conclusions on anesthetic gases and the soul

[6.145]Objective and subjective mental effects of inhalation of subanesthetic concentrations of anesthetic gases reveal several important aspects of the mind-body interaction at variance with dualism.

- [6.146]Subanesthetic concentrations of anesthetic gases only degrade mental performance, in spite of people experiencing feelings of omniscience, of clearer, faster, and better thought processes than normal. If people can experience such mental states due to the effects of drugs—when are such feelings due to other states of mind reality, and when are such feelings not illusory?
- [6.147]Transcendental, cognitive and affective experiences may occur during inhalation of subanesthetic concentrations of anesthetic gases. Likewise, the effects of inhalation of anesthetic gases on the functioning of the brain also reveal these experiences are not necessarily a result of lifting the "filtering effect" of the physical brain on the expression of the soul. Instead, such experiences are manifestations of the interactions of the mind with a brain malfunctioning due to anesthetic gases. This raises the question of when such experiences truly are manifestations of a human soul.
- [6.148]Inhalation of subanesthetic concentrations of anesthetic gases reveals that long-term memories are stored in the physical brain, and not in the soul.

[6.149]Subjective and objective observations of the effects of anesthetic gases have profound consequences for the mind-model of dualism. Of these effects, the effect of subanesthetic concentrations of anesthetic gases on memory formation has very evident consequences. Believers in the mind-model of dualism claim that the soul has the ability to form memories when separated from the body, such as during out-of-body, and near-death experiences. However, the effects of inhalation of

185

subanesthetic concentrations anesthetic gases on mental function prove that memories are stored within the physical brain, and not in the soul. Accordingly, memories of out-of-body, and near-death experiences are not memories of disembodiment retained in an immaterial soul, but illusions and hallucinations generated within the physical body. Furthermore, the absence of memory function in the soul also reveals the illusory nature of the popular belief in spiritual development of a soul in a series of repeated reincarnations—a soul without memory cannot undergo spiritual development in a series of reincarnations. So the mental effects of inhalation of subanesthetic concentrations of anesthetic gases prove belief in the reality of the soul to be no more than an ancient communal illusion, or that the soul has very different properties to those believed for many millennia.

7

In the Vein

[7.1]Administration of general anesthesia remained essentially unchanged for almost a century after 1846. It was always induced, and maintained, with a vapor inhaled though a mask or other apparatus. The introduction of rapidly acting barbiturate drugs administered directly into a vein, (intravenous administration), changed all this. Anesthesia could now be administered within seconds by injecting a drug into a vein. Intravenous administration of anesthetic drugs meant no more inhalation of smelly gases, and no more terrifying and claustrophobic masks. Hexobarbital (Evipan®) was the first such rapidly acting barbiturate drug used for intravenous anesthesia. It was introduced in Germany during 1932, and thiopental (Pentothal®), another rapidly acting intravenously administered barbiturate anesthetic drug, was introduced in the USA during 1934. However, World War 2 (1939-1945) and its aftermath, finally resulted in the more general availability, and consequent greater international popularity of thiopental.

[7.2]Anesthesiologists rapidly embraced both drugs because of the speed with which they acted, as well as their efficacy. But the way these drugs were used when first introduced into anesthesia practice was very different to their current use. Anesthesiologists initially used them as total anesthetics, administering doses sufficient to induce coma. Comatose people do not react to pain (see 2.121), which is why this comatose state was initially called "general anesthesia". Indeed, thiopental was once used as an anesthetic drug for just about any operation. It was the anesthetic drug of choice for many years for short procedures such as curettage, hemorrhoidectomy, and fracture reduction. It was once even recommended as single drug anesthesia for military use, because of portability and ease of administration (page 285 in Lee 1968).

Anesthesia and Pearl Harbor

[7.3]The latter use of thiopental for military anesthesia is the origin of an old, and still prevalent anesthesia myth—that American anesthesiologists killed more American servicemen with thiopental in the aftermath of the surprise Japanese air attack on the American Pearl Harbor naval base on Hawaii, on 7 December 1941, than did the bombs and machine gun fire of the attackers. So what is the origin of this myth?

[7.4]The numbers of wounded resulting from the Japanese attack exceeded the capacity of the local military medical services. So local civilian doctors and medical facilities were drafted under emergency regulations to aid with treating the large numbers of wounded. Subsequently, an American surgeon, F.J. Halford, published an alarming article describing his observations of the deaths of some of these wounded people as a result of anesthesia with intravenous hexobarbital and thiopental.

> [7.5]*I was fortunate enough to have been called as a civilian surgeon to a military hospital in Honolulu on December 7. A number of patients were given evipal [hexobarbital] by competent anesthetists only to have respiratory failures, some of which ended in death. [...] In several cases when as small an amount as 0.5 Gm. of pentothal sodium [thiopental] solution had been administered, there suddenly appeared a "cyanosis decolletage" which was the inevitable and irremedial predecessor of death. (Halford 1943)*

[7.6]This was indeed dramatic. Modern anesthesiologists reading this passage immediately understand what most likely happened to the unfortunate people observed by this surgeon. Many of these people were severely injured due to bomb blasts, bullets, flying debris, etc. Many had also lost large volumes of blood. These severely injured people sometimes died when a dose of thiopental as "small" as 0.5 gram was administered. Anesthesiologists think quite differently nowadays. Such a dose of thiopental is large by modern standards, even when administered to healthy persons. And when a dose of 0.5 gram thiopental is administered to severely injured people who have lost a lot of blood, the end result is almost inevitably severe shock, and eventual death if the resulting low blood pressure and heart failure are not adequately treated. Most surgeons and practitioners od anesthesia at the time did not fully appreciate this fact, so F.J. Halford concluded his article with the bombastic statement:

188

[7.7]As Admiral Gordon-Taylor of the British Navy has so aptly said, "Spinal anesthesia is the ideal form of euthanasia in war surgery"—then let it be said that intravenous anesthesia is also an ideal method of euthanasia. (Halford 1943)

[7.8]This article is the source of the anesthesia legend that American anesthesiologists caused more deaths with thiopental than did the Japanese bombs and bullets at Pearl Harbor. Belief in this legend continued until the 1995 publication of an extensive analysis of the mortality statistics of the Pearl Harbor attack. Study of the actual statistics of this sad event revealed that only a small number of injured persons died as a result of anesthesia administered after the Japanese raid on Pearl Harbor. By far the majority of persons dying as a result of this raid were killed by the direct and indirect effects of bombs and machine gun fire (Bennetts 1995). Furthermore, this study of anesthesia mortality at Pearl Harbor revealed that very few servicemen actually received intravenous hexobarbital or thiopental anesthesia in the aftermath of the Pearl Harbor attack. Most received open-drop ether, which is a much safer technique when dealing with injured people who have lost significant volumes of blood.

Intravenous induction agents

[7.9]Thiopental and hexobarbital are examples of intravenously administered short acting drugs that induce sedation, unconsciousness, or coma depending upon dose. Modern anesthesiologists inject these drugs into a vein to rapidly induce loss of consciousness at the start of general anesthesia. This is why these types of drugs are called "intravenous induction agents". Loss of consciousness occurs within 15-60 seconds after injection of these drugs, and lasts from about 6 up to 20 minutes (Flaishon 1997, Korttila 1992). Subsequently, anesthesiologists employ other drugs and gases to maintain and supplement general anesthesia until the operation is finished.

[7.10]Many different drugs have been, and still are used as intravenous induction agents. These drugs do not only induce rapid loss of consciousness, at subanesthetic doses they also induce sedation, as well as other alterations of conscious mental function.

Mental effects of thiopental

[7.11]Thiopental and hexobarbital belong to a class of drugs called barbiturates. Various barbiturate drugs have been used throughout the years, but thiopental remains the intravenous anesthetic induction agent against which all others are compared. So I will restrict all further discussion of barbiturates to thiopental, because this is the barbiturate drug most commonly used worldwide. In common with all other drugs, administration of thiopental induces both subjective and objective effects. I will first deal with the subjective effects. These have been investigated and described since the introduction of this drug during 1934.

- [7.12]The first thing most people notice after injection, is the taste of garlic, as blood mixed with thiopental flows through their tongues and stimulates their taste buds. This is absolutely characteristic for thiopental.
- [7.13]Sensations reported by people administered subanesthetic blood concentrations of thiopental, or recovering from a single dose of thiopental, vary from sedated to "high", to dizziness (Young 1997).

[7.14]The objective effects of thiopental have also been subject to intensive study during the 80 years this drug has been used in psychiatry, neurosurgery, and anesthesia.

- [7.15]The degree of sedation, or diminution of level of consciousness, is directly proportional to the blood thiopental concentration (Veselis 1997, Veselis 2004a).
- [7.16]Coordination ability degrades in direct proportion to the thiopental blood concentration (Korttila 1992).
- [7.17]Thiopental also affects memory. Increasing blood concentrations of thiopental are associated with increasing degradation of short and long term memory (Osborn 1967, Veselis 2004a), although these effects are less than those induced by propofol (Veselis 1997). Curiously, the memory deficits induced by thiopental are greater for emotionally positive things than for emotionally negative things (Pryor 2004).
- [7.18]Mental concentration degrades in direct relation to the thiopental blood concentration (Korttila 1992).

190

- [7.19]Attention is reduced in direct relation to the thiopental blood concentration (Korttila 1992).
- [7.20]Psychomotor functioning degrades in direct relation to the thiopental blood concentration (Korttila 1992, Young 1997).
- [7.21]Time perception is increasingly distorted with increasing thiopental blood concentration (Young 1997).

[7.22]I will discuss the implications of these experimental results in the last part of this chapter. Thiopental is not the only intravenous anesthetic induction agent used in modern anesthesia practice. Several other drugs are in common clinical use. Propofol is one of these drugs.

Propofol & "dancing the white rabbit"

[7.23]Since its introduction during 1986, propofol has rapidly replaced thiopental as the induction agent of choice in most Western_European countries and the USA. Propofol is relatively insoluble in water, so it is dissolved in a mixture of soya milk and water, giving it the appearance of milk. Older anesthesiologists, such as myself, with years of experience administering thiopental, immediately noticed the remarkable difference between people awakening after propofol or after thiopental. Many people experience awakening from propofol as extremely pleasant—as a euphoric "high"—awakening refreshed and full of energy (Zacny 1992a). This is why, soon after the introduction of propofol into routine anesthetic practice, some patients would specifically ask for anesthesia with propofol, asking for anesthesia with "that white stuff", because acquaintances, friends and family told them it felt so wonderful. Studies reveal that the effects of propofol upon brain function mimic those of refreshed awakening from a deep sleep after a period of sleep deprivation (Nelson 2004), which may explain why people awaken feeling so wonderful after arousing from propofol administration.

[7.24]One author speculated that this very same effect may be the reason why propofol is an attractive drug of addiction for people whose occupation includes regular periods of sleep deprivation (Nelson 2004). One study of the abuse potential of propofol clearly demonstrated that about one half of people found the effects of low dose propofol to be very pleasant, expressing their experiences of propofol in the words:

[7.25]*kind of a nice buzz ...*
felt good ...
liked feeling from the drug, relaxing ...

very pleasant, liked it, rush was intense, very warm, relaxed ...
(Zacny 1993)

[7.26]So, not only does low dose propofol arouse pleasant feelings in some people, but it also simulates the effects of sleep recovery in sleep deprived people. Indeed, this may be why propofol abuse among anesthesia workers is becoming an increasingly well-known phenomenon. It has even acquired the name "dancing the white rabbit". One study of propofol abuse in university departments of anesthesiology during 2007 revealed that of 25 known addicts, seven had died directly as a result of propofol abuse—a death rate of 28% (Wischmeyer 2007)! The usual technique of propofol abuse is to inject 50-100 mg intravenously, experience the effects, and after recovering consciousness, repeat the injection, sometimes up to 10-15 times a day (Follette 1992). Unfortunately there is a very narrow margin between a euphoric dose, and a dose causing potentially lethal respiratory system obstruction or actual respiratory failure. These latter are the subjective effects of propofol. But what are the known objective effects?

- [7.27]Propofol has no pleasant garlic taste. Instead it has a really quite disgusting taste and aftertaste. Fortunately, only a few patients notice the taste, and comment upon it just before they fall asleep and then forget it.
- [7.28]Just as with all other intravenous induction agents, propofol also induces dose, and blood concentration related changes in the level of consciousness (Shafer 1988, Vuyk 1992).
- [7.29]Retention of memories degrades in direct proportion to propofol blood concentration (Cork 1996, Lysakowski 2000, Roode 2000, Veselis 2004a, Veselis 2006). Propofol affects retention of memories associated with negative emotions to a greater degree than memories associated with positive emotions (Pryor 2004).
- [7.30]Ability to perform mental arithmetic degrades with increasing blood propofol concentration (Okawa 2002).
- [7.31]Psychomotor function is impaired in direct proportion to propofol blood concentration (Grant 2000, Korttila 1992, Zacny 1992a).
- [7.32]Propofol and thiopental affect the level of consciousness through much the same mechanisms, but otherwise affect different parts of the brain (Veselis 2004).

[7.33]As with thiopental, I will reserve discussion of the implications of the subjective and objective changes in mental function induced by propofol to the last part of this chapter. This brings us to a discussion of ketamine, another, but very unusual intravenous anesthetic drug.

Ketamine, also known as "Special K"

[7.34]Ketamine was introduced into anesthetic practice during 1965. When injected intravenously at doses of more than 2 milligrams per kilogram body weight, ketamine rapidly induces loss of consciousness. However, unlike thiopental or propofol, ketamine is also a powerful analgesic drug, which is why it can also be used as a sole general anesthetic agent for many surgical procedures (Reich 1989). Ketamine also exerts a powerful analgesic effect even when administered at doses insufficient to induce loss of consciousness. This latter property is one of the reasons why ketamine is currently enjoying a resurgence of popularity, being used to manage an ever increasing range of painful disorders (Himmelseher 2005, Hocking 2007).

[7.35]However, ketamine at doses sufficient to relieve pain, but insufficient to cause loss of consciousness, also induces notable subjective mental effects, the most notable of which are psychedelic experiences. Ketamine also induces other experiences such as feeling tired and sedated, difficulty with concentration, distorted time perception, sensations of disembodiment, narrowing of visual fields, etc. The intensity of these sensations are directly related to the blood and brain concentrations of this drug (Bowdle 1998, Oye 1992, Pfenninger 2002, Pomarol-Clotet 2006). After administration of doses of ketamine insufficient to induce loss of consciousness, most people report unusual disturbances of perception such as:

[7.36]*Visual experiences of this type took a variety of forms, ranging from changes in sharpness: 'Things don't look right, cabinets don't look hard, everything looks rounded, edges not sharp', or 'I couldn't make out the outline of things', or 'Colours are blurred into one', to loss of depth: 'You appear like a 2D image', and alterations in size and shape: 'My hands look small, but the fingers are really long', or 'My legs look very big and funny shaped, like another person's'. One participant described a more complex visual perceptual change where the interviewer, who was heavily pregnant, gradually came to look more and more like a dome with a pair of eyes on top.*
There were also perceptual distortions in other modalities: 'Things feel more liquid when I touch them', or 'I am feeling like I

*am made of sandpaper', or 'I feel like I'm shrunken inside', or
'Each limb seems separate, detached from each other', or
'Disconnected from arms'. Several people described feeling as if
parts of their body or objects they were holding were moving or
not in the position they knew they were in; for example, the
keyboard was continually sliding off their lap, or their foot was
sliding across the floor, their arms felt like they were crossed
when they were by their sides or they were slouched forward
when they were sitting upright. (Pomarol-Clotet 2006)*

[7.37] Barbara Collier studied the effects of ketamine administered for anesthesia required for minor surgical procedures in 131 patients (Collier 1972). She reported the following subjective experiences in one subgroup of 11 patients administered 40 to 60 mg ketamine intravenously. Of these 11 patients:

[7.38]*10 experienced a sensation of floating in space.
9 felt the 'spirit' or mind rise from the body.
4 saw coloured or white patterns with their eyes closed. In one
case the room turned green.
3 were able to 'look down' on their bodies lying on the trolley and
note the exact time the 'spirit' re-entered it, i.e. a few moments
after the return of light pinprick.
1 subject 'became' one of a pile of boxes.
2 experienced the 'mind' moving very rapidly in one direction
through a vacuous space with a loss of time and light concepts.
Such a remarkable phenomenon of awareness relates to
'Fundamental physical laws of Nature'—Galileo's primary
mechanical law of inertia and Newton's 1ˢᵗ law of motion. (Collier
1972)*

[7.39]Usually people are not at all upset by these perceptive and cognitive disturbances. But this is not all. About 10% of people report experiences of dissociation, nightmares and hallucinations after ketamine administration such as transcendental experiences, the experience of falling into a black hole, (the "K-hole" experience), out-of-body experiences, and even near-death experiences.

[7.40]*It [ketamine] can reproduce all features of the NDE [near-
death experience], including travel through a dark tunnel into
light, the conviction that one is dead, "telepathic communion with
God", hallucinations, out-of-body experiences and mystical
states. If given intravenously, it has a short action with an abrupt*

end. Grinspoon and Bakalar (1981, p34) wrote of ... becoming a disembodied mind or soul, dying and going to another world. Childhood events may also be relived. The loss of contact with ordinary reality and the sense of participation in another reality are more pronounced and less easily resisted than is usually the case with LSD. The dissociative experiences often seem so genuine that users are not sure that they have not actually left their bodies. (Jansen 1997)

[7.41]About 30% of people administered ketamine undergo such intense and profound experiences, that they refuse to believe they were anything else but actual experiences of a real transcendental world (see page 10 in Jansen 1997). Indeed, the powerful sense of reality aroused by hallucinations induced by ketamine are revealed by the quotations of some users cited by Jansen (2000).

[7.42]*I was actually God. I distinctly felt the universe watching for my signal to see if it should cycle through itself once again, as it had an infinite number of times, or should it simply conclude. It felt so beyond unquestionably real, it was just as plain and crisp as it could be, not some hallucination ... (page 423 in Jansen 2000)*

[7.43]Such hallucinatory effects are part of the several reasons why ketamine is an attractive recreational drug for many people, who describe it with expressive names such as "Special K", "Ket", and "Vitamin K". These are the subjective effects of ketamine, but what are the objective effects of ketamine at doses and blood concentrations insufficient to induce loss of consciousness?

- [7.44]The degree of mental disorder induced by ketamine increases with increasing blood ketamine concentration (Bowdle 1998, Honey 2005, Krystal 1998, Malhotra 1996, Oye 1992).
- [7.45]Memory function becomes increasingly abnormal with increasing blood ketamine concentration (Honey 2005, Malhotra 1996, Oye 1992, Pfenninger 2002).
- [7.46]Psychomotor dysfunction induced by ketamine is directly related to the blood ketamine concentration (Krystal 1998).
- [7.47]Ketamine induces a disturbed "sense of body ownership", or feelings of dissociation (Morgan 2010).

^{7.48}All these surprising and profound effects of ketamine are explained by the effects of this drug upon the mechanisms of the brain.

^{7.49}*The psychic sensations reported during emergence from ketamine anesthesia have been characterized as alterations in mood state and body image, dissociative or extracorporeal (out-of-body) experiences, floating sensations, vivid dreams or illusions, "weird trips," and occasional frank delirium. The vivid dreams and visual illusions usually disappear immediately upon wakening, although recurrent illusions (flashbacks) have been reported several weeks after ketamine administration in adults and children.*
Recent cerebral glucose utilization studies in animals indicate that ketamine produces depressive action on the inferior colliculus (a primary acoustic relay nucleus) and the medial geniculate (a visual relay nucleus). It would appear that psychic emergence reactions occur secondary to ketamine-induced depression of these auditory and visual relay nuclei, leading to misperception and/or misinterpretation of and auditory and visual stimuli. Furthermore, the loss of skin and musculoskeletal sensations results in a decreased ability to feel gravity, thereby producing a sensation of bodily detachment or floating in space. (White 1982)

^{7.50}This beautifully succinct explanation by Paul White explains the hallucinations induced by ketamine. Moreover, it is supplemented by the fact that ketamine does not seem to cause actual loss of consciousness, as is revealed by increases in electroencephalographic measures of consciousness used in anesthesia, such as the Bispectral Index (Hans 2005, Wu 2001), and the Spectral Entropy (Hans 2005). All these measures of consciousness paradoxically indicate a lightening of consciousness after ketamine administration, so rendering these measures of the level of consciousness useless. These electroencephalographic studies mirror other studies of brain function showing that ketamine has very different effects on the brain than do propofol and thiopental. Unlike the latter two drugs, ketamine actually increases the total flow of blood to the brain, specifically increasing brain activity in parts of the brain such as the anterior cingulate gyrus, the thalamus, and frontal cortex (Långsjö 2003).

^{7.51}Finally, just as with thiopental and propofol, I will defer discussion of the implications of these effects of ketamine for the two mind-models

discussed in this book to the last part of this chapter. And this brings us to the last drug I want to discuss in some detail.

Wondrous midazolam

[7.52]Midazolam is seldom used as an intravenous induction agent. Instead, its main use is as a sedative to reduce anxiety during medical procedures. Lower doses of midazolam allow the useful combination of sedation and retention of consciousness, such that patients retain the ability to speak and cooperate with their physicians while undergoing stressful investigations, or procedures under local anesthesia. In addition, midazolam has the added advantage of a relatively short duration of action after intravenous administration of small doses. All physicians notice that people sedated but conscious after administration of midazolam, often forget what happened during the period of evident sedation, despite being conscious and cooperative at the time. Anesthesiologists also regularly administer midazolam to sedate or reduce anxiety prior to administering spinal anesthesia, as well as during the period of the subsequent operation. Most patients are definitely conscious and cooperative after intravenous administration of a standard 2.5-5 mg dose of midazolam. Yet many of these patients report afterwards that they were under general anesthesia, or remember absolutely nothing of the time they spent in the operating theater. Midazolam very clearly induced amnesia in these people, blocking the formation of long-term memories during the periods their brains were affected by sedative doses of midazolam. Not only anesthesiologists, but many other different physicians have employed these same conscious sedation and amnesic actions of midazolam since its introduction during the 1980's (Bosch 2004, Chudnofsky 1997, Fröhlich 1995, Lipscomb 1998, Macken 1998, McQuaid 2008, Patkl 2011, Swann 2011).

[7.53]The most notable effect of midazolam is its effect on the formation of memories. Many studies reveal midazolam has no effect upon past memories, or short-term memory, but does inhibit the formation of long-term memories (Bulach 2005, Reder 2006, Veselis 2009). Indeed, the higher the dosage of midazolam, the more profound these effects on memory formation (Bulach 2005, Langlois 1987, Roode 2000, Tian 2010, Veselis 1997). Just as with the other drugs discussed in this chapter, I will defer discussion of the relevance of the effects of midazolam to the last part of this chapter.

Other intravenous induction agents

[7.54]Etomidate is another commonly used drug for inducing unconsciousness at the beginning of anesthesia. But I will not discuss this drug because the mental effects are more or less similar to those of thiopental. During my career, I have used several other intravenous drugs used for rapidly inducing sleep at the beginning of general anesthesia, such as propanidid, alphathesin, and methohexital. These were effective and good drugs. But they have fallen into disuse for various reasons. For example, propanidid and alphathesin were provided in a solution of polyethoxylated castor oil (Cremophor EL®), which is a substance inducing an unreasonable number of severe allergic reactions. Methohexital possesses no real advantages above thiopental or hexobarbital, which is why this drug also eventually disappeared from the anesthetic arsenal.

[7.55]Gamma Amino Butyric Acid (GABA), diazepam, and several others have also been tested, and even used for short periods. These drugs also demonstrated no real advantages above the old and trusted thiopental, which is why they too fell into disuse. So I will not discuss these drugs any further, and will leave them to molder in the vaults of anesthesia history.

Asleep in ten seconds?

[7.56]Now we come to the fascinating differences between the perceptions of observers and those undergoing anesthesia. One aspect of these differences is the speed people remember losing consciousness at the start of general anesthesia. Another aspect is the actual memory of loss of consciousness due to anesthesia. These two points may seem trivial, but are sometimes a source of confusion to some patients, and mild amazement at the foibles of the human mind to the attending anesthesiologists.

Time to loss of consciousness

[7.57]Many patients tell me they lost consciousness within ten seconds after intravenous administration of thiopental or propofol at the beginning of a previous general anesthetic. Or they say this was the speed which a family member remembered losing consciousness at the beginning of general anesthesia. This is a wonderful illustration of the way personal experience differs from objective observation. The person remembers only that it took them about ten seconds, or counting to ten, to lose consciousness. However, the anesthesiologist looking at the clock will always report that loss of consciousness took longer than ten seconds. What is the reason for this discrepancy between the subjective experience of the patient, and the objective observation of the anesthesiologist?

7.58The answer lies partly in the time intervals between the point of injection of a drug and the arrival of that drug at any part of the body. These transit times, called "circulation times", have been extensively measured for many different parts of the body. Anesthesiologists nearly always inject intravenous anesthetic drugs into an arm vein, and it takes about 10-20 seconds for a drug injected into an arm vein to arrive in the brain (pages 121-124 in Altman 1959). However, injection of a dose of an intravenous induction agent sufficient to cause loss of consciousness is never instantaneous, but is done slowly over a period of about 10 to 30 seconds. Furthermore, people do not lose consciousness, or experience mental effects due to a drug, because of the action of that drug on blood inside blood vessels. People experience these effects, because drugs diffuse out of the blood vessels into the surrounding brain tissue where they exert these effects. So an intravenous induction agent must first arrive in the blood vessels of the brain. Then the drug must diffuse out of the blood vessels into the tissues of the brain in sufficient quantities in order to exert an effect on the brain, such as induction of loss of consciousness. These processes take time. So while an intravenous induction agent may indeed arrive in the brain within ten seconds, it still takes several seconds after arrival of the drug in the brain before loss of consciousness occurs. The reality of these facts is revealed by the times it takes patients to lose consciousness after starting to inject effective doses of various intravenous induction agents:

- 7.59Thiopental - 38.6-60 seconds (Kashtan 1990, Maltby 1980).
- 7.60Propofol - 48.6 seconds (Kashtan 1990).
- 7.61Etomidate - 65 seconds (Lallemand 2003).
- 7.62Ketamine - 60 seconds (Wu 2001).
- 7.63Midazolam - much longer than 60 seconds.

7.64After an intravenous induction drug arrives in the blood vessels of the brain, it starts diffusing into the tissues of the brain. In the seconds prior to losing consciousness, people experience the mental effects of increasing brain concentrations of these drugs. Amnesia for events while

199

under the influence of these drugs, is among the many mental effects exerted on the conscious brain by drugs such as thiopental (Veselis 2004a), etomidate (Vinson 2002), and especially by propofol (Roode 2000, Veselis 2004a, Veselis 2006). All this means that people simply forget their last few seconds of consciousness, because they form no long-term memories in the last few seconds before losing consciousness. This is why patients only remember ten seconds to loss of consciousness, and why anesthesiologists observe times longer than ten seconds. This explains the difference between the subjective time to loss of consciousness reported by patients, versus the time to loss of consciousness observed by anesthesiologists.

No memory of loss of consciousness

[7.65]Upon awakening from general anesthesia, patients sometimes ask, "When is the operation going to start?" Or, "Is it finished? I thought you had to start ..." When you think about it, you realize these patients are actually saying they cannot remember when they lost consciousness, or even that they lost consciousness. They are then amazed to hear that the operation is finished, and that they have just awoken from a period of general anesthesia. This is a manifestation of absent long-term memory of the experience of losing consciousness.

[7.66]Most people cannot remember losing consciousness at the beginning of general anesthesia. However, the term "most people", means there are also some others who do remember losing consciousness due to general anesthesia. This observation has several consequences. Persons claiming they were continually conscious during general anesthesia may be telling the truth. Or these persons may simply have forgotten the periods of unconsciousness, and just like threading beads on a necklace, unthinkingly combined separate periods of consciousness into one coherent story. This latter is typical of accounts of people reporting continual consciousness during general anesthesia, which is why claims of continual consciousness during general anesthesia require more evidence than simply claiming the experience.

Intravenous induction agents and the mind

[7.67]Do the effects of other intravenous induction agents reveal anything about the true nature of the conscious mind, or soul? They certainly do. Intravenous induction agents reveal answers to several fundamental questions such as the relationship of the soul to the body, the way the soul interacts with the body, as well as answering the question of whether memories are stored within the brain or the soul.

The soul cannot bypass the mechanisms of the body

[7.68]A materialist would claim that the proven relationship between drug dose, brain drug concentration, and drug effect, is a strong indication that conscious mental function is a product of the functioning of the brain. According to the mind-model of dualism, the soul controls the physical body through the mechanisms of the physical brain. Therefore, the mind-model of dualism also predicts that the control exerted by the soul over the mechanisms of the brain becomes increasingly abnormal with increasing dosages, and brain concentrations of drugs affecting brain function. These effects actually prove that the soul cannot bypass the mechanisms of the body when interacting with the physical world. In the case of materialism, these brain mechanisms are necessary to generate these properties of mind, while in the case of dualism, these same brain mechanisms are the necessary conduit for the physical expression of these properties of mind. Accordingly, these manifestations of the mind by the physical body cannot distinguish between the mind-models of dualism and materialism.

Ketamine and the mind

[7.69]About 30% of people truly believe in the reality of the cognitive, affective, and transcendental experiences they underwent while under the influence of ketamine (see page 10 in Jansen 1997). According to the postulates of dualism, physically conscious persons relating their experiences are under the control of their individual souls. Ketamine produces very real changes in the functioning of the physical brains of conscious people (White 1982). Therefore, according to the logic of believers in dualism, conscious experiences undergone while the brain is affected by ketamine are actually manifestations of the control exerted over the conscious physical body by the soul through the abnormally functioning mechanisms of the physical brain, and not necessarily a manifestation of the true nature of the soul.

[7.70]The mind-model of materialism is somewhat simpler. It states that experiences induced by ketamine are products of the effects of this drug on the functioning of the physical brain.

[7.71]So belief in the reality of ketamine experiences raises the very real problem of how to distinguish between a so-called "real paranormal experience", from what might be termed a "mundane drug-induced hallucination." This is not just a theoretical question. It means that what people perceive as "real" near-death experiences, out-of-body experiences, or enhanced consciousness during ketamine administration, are indistinguishable from these same experiences induced by the effects of this drug upon the functioning of the brain. Accordingly, seemingly paranormal experiences aroused by ketamine are not proof of the reality of a human soul.

Induction agents and memory

[7.72]Induction agents affect mental function in a dose and brain concentration related manner. Midazolam and propofol are especially notable for their effects upon the formation of memories. They have no effect on old memories, but inhibit formation of new long-term memories. For example, a person under the influence of these drugs may be sedated, but conscious and cooperative, able to perform tasks requiring short-term memory, and also able to remember all details from the distant and recent past, yet is later unable to remember anything said and done while under the influence of these drugs. These effects on memory have profound implications for the mind-model of dualism, and are worth examining in some detail.

Midazolam proves we have no souls

[7.73]The immaterial soul and the mind are one. Regardless of the correctness of this concept, most people believe the soul can somehow separate from the living body-for example, during out-of-body experiences. And we know that people remember what they experience while the soul is apparently disembodied during out-of-body experiences. Such experiences indicate that short-term and long-term memories are stored within the soul. So let us examine in a point-by-point fashion whether dualism or materialism better explains the amnesic effect of the drug midazolam on the formation of long-term memories. I only discuss midazolam because its effects on memory are a wonderful illustration of the effects of all other intravenous anesthetic induction agents on memory function.

Materialism and the amnesic effects of midazolam

[7.74]The mind-model of materialism reveals its parsimony in the explanation of the amnesic effects of midazolam. Midazolam affects multiple processes in the functioning of the physical brain. One of these effects is an effect on the processes involved in the formation and recall of long-term memories. Nevertheless, not all people have amnesia for the periods their minds were affected by midazolam. Materialism readily explains this fact with the well-known inter-individual variation in response to the effects of this drug. In fact all clinicians recognize the wide inter-individual variation in midazolam effects. For example, some people fall asleep after as little as 2.5 milligrams of midazolam, while others require more than 15 milligrams.

Dualism and the amnesic effects of midazolam

[7.75]How does the mind-model of dualism explain the amnesic effects of midazolam? The explanation is somewhat more complex, so I will put it into the form of a list.

- [7.76]The mind-model of dualism states that the physically conscious body of a person is a sort of mindless robot under the control of the soul (see 1.55-1.65).
- [7.77]Midazolam administered at doses sufficient to cause amnesia does not induce loss of consciousness. After such doses of midazolam, most people are somewhat sedated, yet perceive and react appropriately to their surroundings. They are cooperative, talk normally, answer questions appropriately, and otherwise react appropriately with speech and movements.
- [7.78]According to the logic of dualism, the physical body transmits perceptions of speech, sight, touch, and surroundings in some way to the soul, which then controls the body to speak, move, and act appropriately in response to others and the situation (see 1.142).
- [7.79]Believers in the mind-model of dualism claim that the soul is the indelible repository of all memories (see 1.92-1.115).
- [7.80]The mind-model of dualism states that the soul is unaffected by drugs affecting the physical brain (see 1.66-1.75).
- [7.81]Therefore, according to the mind-model of dualism, memories of thoughts, speech, actions, deeds, and perceptions made while sedated with midazolam, but physically conscious and cooperative, are all indelibly stored within the soul (see 1.143).

- [7.82]All physical brain functions return to normal after the body eliminates all the administered midazolam.
- [7.83]Memories of the perceptions, speech, sounds, and events occurring around the conscious physical body while under the influence of sedative doses of midazolam, are public memories. They are memories much like hearing and remembering a conversation, hearing a sound, or remembering a snippet of news from a newspaper. They are public memories—not memories of anything secret, intended only for the use of immaterial beings or souls.
- [7.84]Therefore there is no conceivable reason why people cannot recall conscious actions and speech during procedures performed under midazolam sedation.
- [7.85]So if the soul is the indelible repository of all memories, then all people should be able to remember all that occurred while sedated, but physically conscious and cooperative (see 1.143).
- [7.86]But most people remember nothing of what they thought, said, did, or perceived during the period their physical brains were affected by midazolam.

[7.87]This observation is repeated daily, all over the world wherever midazolam is employed for both its conscious sedation and amnesic effects. It is the daily reality of myself, and all other physicians administering midazolam to the patients we treat. The only explanation for all these repeatedly observed facts is that the soul is not the repository of memories, but that the physical brain forms and retains all memories.

Midazolam proves the absence of a soul

[7.88]Accordingly, formation, retention and recall of long-term memories all occur within the physical brain, and not within an immaterial soul. Memory is one of the fundamental properties of the soul proposed by believers in dualism (see page 295 in Kelly 2007, see citation at 15.111). So the effect of midazolam on memory actually proves the illusory nature of a human soul with the properties defined by the mind-model of dualism in Chapter 1!

Intravenous induction agents and the soul

[7.89]Intravenous induction agents reveal important information relevant to this study of the true nature of the mind. Indeed, subjective and objective experiences induced by intravenous induction agents are windows revealing the true nature of the human mind.

[7.90]Loss of consciousness due to intravenous induction agents is one of these objective phenomena. Many people struggle to stay awake after administration of intravenous induction agents, but they all lose consciousness after a few seconds. Loss of consciousness is due to failure of the thalamic and brainstem mechanisms necessary for generation of consciousness in the physical body. The mind-model of materialism states that these are the neurological mechanisms generating consciousness, while the mind-model of dualism states that the normal functioning of these neurological mechanisms is necessary to act as a conduit for the consciousness of the soul. Regardless of which mind-model is correct, the mechanisms of the thalamus and brainstem are required for consciousness to manifest. Loss of consciousness due to intravenous induction agents proves that the soul cannot arouse consciousness in the physical body, except through the medium of the appropriate brain mechanisms. This fact supplements proof provided by the Wada Test, as well as the effects of brain surgery, brain injury, and brain diseases, that the soul can only manifest its nature in this physical world through the mechanisms of the brain (see Chapter 5).

[7.91]The effects of intravenous induction agents such as propofol, and especially of midazolam on memory, clearly indicate that the immaterial soul is not the repository of memories. This is the opposite of what is claimed by proponents of the mind-model of dualism, and has profound implications for several aspects of this mind-model.

- [7.92]A soul without the ability to form memories cannot recall what it experiences during periods of disembodiment. Accordingly, accounts of apparent disembodiment during out-of-body experiences, or near-death experiences, are memories of hallucinations of disembodiment occurring within the physical brains of people subsequently reporting such experiences.
- [7.93]The holy books of Christianity and Islam tell us that the souls of the dead remember their thoughts speech and deeds, and are appropriately punished or rewarded for an eternity in an everlasting afterlife inhabited by the souls of the dead. However, absence of memory function in a separable immaterial conscious mind means that everlasting punishment or reward of the immaterial soul has no function. Without memory, punishment or reward are visited upon a conscious mind with no memories of anything transpiring more than

a few seconds in the past. It would serve no real purpose. A soul without memory experiences no heaven, nor can it experience hell—heaven and hell simply do not exist for a soul without memory.

- [7.94]Absence of memory in the soul means that the reincarnated soul learns nothing during each reincarnation. After all, without memory, a soul learns no lessons in each successive incarnation, a fact destroying this fundamental postulate of the philosophy of reincarnation.
- [7.95]Absence of memory function in the soul means that the soul, if it exists, has properties very different to those believed by most proponents of dualism.

[7.96]Absence of memory function in the soul is conclusive proof of the illusory nature of a human soul with the explicit and implicit properties claimed by religious and popular belief systems (see Chapter 1). Nonetheless, it is still worth examining other aspects of the interactions of this putative soul with the physical body as revealed by anesthesia and other medical phenomena.

8

The Laudable Opium

[8.1]*In Xanadu did Kubla Khan*
A stately pleasure-dome decree:
Where Alph, the sacred river, ran
Through caverns measureless to man
Down to a sunless sea.

[8.2]These few simple words evoking such wondrous transcendental imagery were dashed off by the poet during a moment of opium-induced inspiration. Unfortunately for those anxious to learn more than the scant fifty lines composed about this stately pleasure-dome, "a person on business from Porlock" interrupted the poet's feverish flow of inspiration (Sykes 1908).

The unhappy Samuel Coleridge

[8.3]Samuel Coleridge (1772-1834) was the name of the poet. During 1798 he lived in a farmhouse in Exmoor near the village of Porlock. It was here that he wrote the poem entitled "Kubla Khan" while under the influence of an opium tincture, (Laudanum), taken to treat a bout of diarrhea. Coleridge's sickly constitution provided him with more than sufficient reasons for using opium—a chronic use finally ending in a hopeless addiction to Laudanum sometime about 1803 (pages 133-179 in Day 1868). His letters revealed he suffered chronic low fever since childhood (pages 136-137 in Day 1868), regular pain from an infected tooth (page 137 in Day 1868), and chronic illness subsequent to hospitalization for rheumatic fever during 1788-1789 (page 138 in Day 1868). Moreover, during November 1796 he developed hellish facial pain. His eloquent description of this pain in a letter to his friend Festus, leaves the medically trained in no doubt as to its cause.

8.4I am not mad, most noble Festus! But in sober sadness I have suffered this day more bodily pain than I had before a conception of. My right cheek has certainly been placed with admirable exactness under the focus of some invisible burning-glass, which concentrated all the rays of a Tartarean sun. My medical attendant decides it to be altogether nervous, and that it originates either in severe application or excessive anxiety. My beloved Poole, in excessive anxiety I believe it might originate. I have a blister under my right ear, and I take twenty-five drops of Laudanum every five hours, ... (pages 134-135 in Day 1868)

8.5This is a masterly description of pain due to a Herpes Zoster virus infection of the trigeminal nerve. He elaborated further on his pain to another friend.

8.6A devil, a very devil, has got possession of my left temple, eye, cheek, jaw, throat, and shoulder. I can not see you this evening. I write in agony. (page 135 in Day 1868)

8.7But this was not the end of his problems with the affliction of his trigeminal nerve. A letter written by Coleridge during 1803 revealed he suffered from chronic pain around his right eye as a result of the damage caused by the infection of his trigeminal nerve during 1796 (trigeminal neuralgia), as well as from other less well defined rheumatic problems (pages 139-140 in Day 1868).

8.8In January, 1803, he says: "I write with difficulty, with all the fingers but one of my right hand very much swollen. Before I was half up the Kirkstone mountain, the storm had wetted me through and through. In spite of the wet and the cold I should have had some pleasure in it, but for two vexations; first, an almost intolerable pain came into my right eye, a smarting and burning pain; and secondly, in consequence of riding with such cold water under my seat, extremely uneasy and burdensome feelings attacked my groin, so that, what with the pain from the one, and the alarm from the other, I had no enjoyment at all!" (page 139 in Day 1868)

8.9This brings us back to the interruption by a "person on business from Porlock" of his flow of inspiration while writing the poem of Kubla Khan. There is much speculation, but no-one is sure who this may have been. Either this was Coleridge's excuse for a lack of inspiration to finish the poem of "Kubla Khan", or it was the pharmacist from Porlock delivering a new supply of opium tincture.

Opium, Laudanum, and Paregoric

[8.10]Opium is the milky fluid, or latex, from the seed case of the poppy flower. Dried opium latex is a brownish substance containing a mixture of various compounds such as codeine, thebaine, papaverine, and up to 10% of morphine by weight (Schiff 2002). Morphine is a powerful analgesic drug, with a multitude of other effects upon the functioning of the brain, breathing, intestines etc.

[8.11]Various opium preparations were used in the past, such as pills, powders, and solutions. The most popular and well known of these was Laudanum, an opium preparation first introduced and popularized in England by Thomas Sydenham (1624-1689), an eminent physician at that time (Schiff 2002). Laudanum is an alcoholic solution of opium containing 10% opium by weight, resulting in a strong solution of morphine with a concentration of about 1 gram = 1000 milligrams of morphine/100 ml Laudanum. Powerful stuff… Laudanum must never be confused with Paregoric, another popular opium containing drink used throughout the nineteenth century. Paregoric is a camphorated tincture of opium with a morphine concentration of about 40 mg/100 ml (Schiff 2002). Indeed, many deaths due to morphine overdose occurred due to confusion between the properties of Paregoric and Laudanum. People to whom the same volumes of Laudanum were administered as Paregoric, received a dose of morphine 25 times higher than expected, often with lethal result.

[8.12]Massive use and abuse of opium preparations was common throughout Europe and the USA from about 1700 to 1930. A few nineteenth century medical men wrote of the social disruption, the individual tragedies, and terrible effects of such misuse (Hawkins 1867), but few people took much notice. Eventually, the social and medical climate changed during the beginning of the twentieth century as the dangers inherent to addiction, and unregulated use of opium preparations gained more public recognition.

Why did our ancestors use so much opium?

[8.13]Why did our ancestors use so much opium? There were many reasons. Public health measures to minimize infection, to ensure clean drinking water, provide healthy housing, as well as safe disposal of sewage and other wastes, were minimal until the beginning of the twentieth century. At the same time, agriculture yielded minimal surpluses, which were inefficiently stored and unequally distributed. Medical practice was also relatively primitive, with very limited therapeutic options available to physicians until the 1930's. The sum total of all these things was an accepting, almost abject helplessness in the face of a truly appalling burden of disease, of unequal supplies of adequate quantities of safe food and water, as well as minimal public health measures. All these things are reflected in the truly shocking, (by today's standards), high child mortality, and generalized poor adult survival during the early nineteenth century. For example, a census conducted in England during 1838 revealed that 30% of all live-born babies died before 10 years of age, and 50% of all people had died by 45 years of age (Lifetables 2010). These are horrifying statistics by modern standards, but were no better or worse than those for other European countries at that time.

[8.14]Opium relieved many of the woes afflicting our forefathers. Opium relieved pain of all types. Opium slowed and stopped the unpleasant manifestations of the frequent diarrheal diseases. Opium relieved the symptoms of anemia, which was very common at the time. In an age when tuberculosis and other lung infections of all sorts were rife, it suppressed the cough, as well as relieving many other unpleasant symptoms of these disorders. Opium calmed fretful and crying children. Opium relieved and reduced the symptoms of anxiety and depression. Opium induced calm and sleep. Opium made people feel happy and at peace with the world. Opium was a panacea in a world without effective medication and solutions for a multitude of problems. Just after the Civil War in the United States (1861-1865), Horace Day eloquently expressed many of these reasons in a book called *The Opium Habit*.

[8.15]*Professional and literary men, persons suffering from protracted nervous disorders, women obliged by their necessities to work beyond their strength, prostitutes, and, in brief, all classes whose business or whose vices make special demands upon the nervous system, are those who for the most part compose the fraternity of Opium-eaters. The events of the last few years have unquestionably added greatly to their number. Maimed and shattered survivors from a hundred battlefields, diseased and disabled soldiers released from hostile prisons, anguished and hopeless wives and mothers, made so by the slaughter of those*

who were dearest to them, have found, many of them, temporary
relief from their sufferings in Opium. (page 7 in Day 1868)

[8.16]Yet this passage failed to describe all the reasons for opium
addiction or abuse. Most addicts were actually poor working people.
Their wages were a pittance, barely sufficient for the necessities of life.
In return for this pittance, they often endured ten to twelve hour working
days of mind-numbing, backbreaking labor. Many sought relief from this
hell of soul-destroying drudgery in alcohol. Others found relief in the
even cheaper, and readily available Laudanum, or pills made of raw
opium. Thomas de Quincey described the wide availability of cheap, raw
opium pills in the industrial midlands of England during the early years
of the nineteenth century.

> [8.17]... , *some years ago, on passing through Manchester*
> *[England], I was informed by several cotton manufacturers that*
> *their work people were rapidly getting into the practice of Opium-*
> *eating; so much so, that on a Saturday afternoon the counters of*
> *the druggists were strewed with pills of one, two, or three grains,*
> *in preparation for the known demand of the evening [one grain =*
> *60 mg opium = 6 mg morphine]. The immediate occasion of this*
> *practice was the lowness of wages, which, at that time, would not*
> *allow them to indulge in ale or spirits;... (page 7 in Quincey*
> *1823)*

[8.18]But even this is not the full explanation for the widespread opium
and morphine addiction during the nineteenth century. The condition of
women in most parts of the world before the latter half of the twentieth
century was not enviable. Smaller body size and strength, together with
the biological consequences of reproduction, pregnancy and child care,
all combined to form a biological iron straitjacket limiting their social
options. Subjugation, repression, frustration, and misery were the lot of
many women—the unhappy genetic fate of half the world population
(Heinzen 1891). Religious and legal systems, as well as socioeconomic
structures, even confirmed and enforced the role of women as second-
class citizens (Kenny 1879). All manner of psychological problems
resulted, which were often described as hysteria by nineteenth century
physicians. Not surprisingly, many women turned to opium for relief,
with the resulting consequences so condescendingly described in the
following passage.

> [8.19] *The patient was a woman of thirty-seven, mother of five*
> *children, and subject to morphinomania since the age of thirty-*

*one. Always of somewhat hysterical temperament, she had been
since the age of twenty-six a hysteric of the most advanced type;
violent attacks, anaesthesia of left side and of pharynx, diminution
of visual field, etc.; then insistence on keeping her bed, and
constant druggings with ether, chloroform, chloral, finally with
injections of morphia every few hours. Exhaustion; lividity; cold
sweat and hallucinations if the injection was deferred. (page 464
in Appendix 530A, Myers 1903)*

[8.20]What a sad story. This was a disturbed and desperate woman. Was
her condition simply a manifestation of mental disease, or was it a
reaction to her social situation? And to think that many people refer to
the nineteenth century as "the good old days" …

[8.21]Towards the end of the nineteenth century, worldwide abuse of
opium and its derivatives occurred on a massive scale. Turkey, Persia,
and China all produced massive quantities of opium, but the British
Empire was the largest producer and supplier of opium for international
trade. Indeed, the financial interests and armies of the British Empire
encouraged and enforced the drugging, debilitation, and financial ruin of
China, from the first Opium War in 1839 until the Chinese government
finally brought a halt to English opium exports to China between 1907
to 1917 (Merwin 1908, Report of the International Opium Commission
1909). But the Chinese were not the only consumers of opium and its
derivatives at this time. Both the United States and the United Kingdom
also consumed opium and its products on a massive scale. An
examination of the per capita opium consumption in these countries
reveals the staggering scale of opium consumption and addiction around
1900.

- [8.22]The population of the United Kingdom during 1901 was 41.46
  million (census data), and the annual opium consumption was
  117,934 kilograms (page 613 in Volume 7 of Chambers
  Encyclopaedia 1901), which means an annual per capita opium
  consumption of 2.84 grams of opium for every man, woman, and
  child per year.
- [8.23]The population of the United States during 1907 was 87 million
  (census data), and the annual opium consumption was 270,362
  kilograms (page 92 in Dunn 1920), which means an annual per capita
  opium consumption of 3.11 grams of opium for every man, woman,
  and child per year.

- [8.24]The population of the China during 1906 was 413.65 million, and the annual opium consumption was 22.95 million kilograms (page 130 in Volume 20 of the Encyclopaedia Britannica 1911), which means an annual per capita opium consumption of 55.5 grams of opium for every man, woman, and child per year.

[8.25]These figures reveal a truly stunning magnitude of opium use or abuse by modern standards. These countries were awash with opium and opium products. But if the United Kingdom and the United States of America were awash with opium and its products, then China was drowning in them! When you consider that not everyone in these countries used opium, or opium products, this means that some people consumed astounding quantities of these substances. This fact and the preceding discussion about the role of English exports of opium to China, give a colored picture. Of all the opium consumed each year in China, only one seventh was provided by English exports to China—the rest was produced within China (page 130 in volume 20 of the Encylopaedia Britannica 1911). While this fact is interesting, it does not change the main problem revealed by the statistics of opium consumption in China at the beginning of the twentieth century. The level of opium consumption in China around 1906 simply beggars description. According to Alexander Hosie, a commercial attaché to the British Legation in Peking at the time:

[8.26]*I am well within the mark when I say that in the cities fifty per cent, of the males and twenty per cent, of the females smoke Opium, and that in the country the percentage is not less than twenty-five for men and five per cent, for women. (page 10 in Merwin 1908)*

[8.27]Alexander Hosie also travelled extensively in China in the years 1910 to 1911, subsequently writing an extensive report of his travels (Hosie 1914). However, even prior to these travels, he had intimate knowledge of the effects of opium upon the peoples of the "Opium provinces" of Yunnan, Shansi, Kansu, and Kueichou. "Opium provinces" were sad and desperate regions, where opium growing was the main agricultural industry. This was why, even before his extensive further travels, he supplemented the statement above, as recorded by Samuel Merwin in 1907.

[8.28]*In regard to another so-called "Opium province", Yunnan, we have the following statement: "I saw practically the whole population given over to its abuse. The ravages it is making in men, women, and children are deplorable... I was quite able to realize that any one who had seen the wild abuse of Opium in Yunnan would have a wild abhorrence of it." (page 11 in Merwin 1908)*

[8.29]Samuel Merwin also travelled through the "Opium province" of Shansi. Opium smoking was so prevalent in Shansi, that he was jokingly informed that, "eleven out of ten Shansi men are opium-smokers" (page 59 in Merwin 1908). When you consider that the population of China in the period around 1900, was about 400 million, this means that the level of opium addiction, abuse, or usage in China at this time was simply staggering, surpassing all imagination! Just as Alexander Hosie, Samuel Merwin also observed firsthand the socioeconomic ravages and human tragedies wreaked by opium addiction: inanition, inability to work, inability to think clearly, poverty, starvation, villages of recently built houses falling into decay. He commented on the typical opium addict.

[8.30]*Everywhere along the highroad and in the cities and villages of Shansi you see the Opium face. The Opium-smoker, like the Opium-eater, rapidly loses flesh when the habit has fixed itself on him. The colour leaves his skin, and it becomes dry, like parchment. His eye loses whatever light and sparkle it may have had, and becomes dull and listless. The Opium face has been best described as a "peculiarly withered and blasted countenance." With this face is usually associated a thin body and a languid gait. Opium gets such a powerful grip on a confirmed smoker that it is usually unsafe for him to give up the habit without medical aid. His appetite is taken away, his digestion is impaired, there is congestion of the various internal organs, and congestion of the lungs. Constipation and diarrhoea result, with pain all over the body. By the time he has reached this stage, the smoker has become both physically and mentally weak and inactive. With his intellect deadened, his physical and moral sense impaired, he sinks into laziness, immorality, and debauchery. He has lost his power of resistance to disease, and becomes predisposed to colds, bronchitis, diarrhoea, dysentery, and dyspepsia. (pages 64-65 in Merwin 1908)*

[8.31]China was a thrall of the poppy from 1839 to 1907. Not only was China enslaved by a drug it did not want, but many of its people were starving, because extensive areas of fertile agricultural ground were

214

given over to poppy cultivation to support this debilitating habit. From 1907 to 1917 the Chinese government resolutely made, and enforced international agreements to reduce and stop opium imports (Report of the International Opium Commission 1909, Dunn 1920, Willoughby 1925). The result was a reduction of local opium growing, and addiction to a fraction of previous levels, finally ending the ghastly enslavement of China to opium (Dunn 1920, Willoughby 1925).

Opium abuse and the relation of mind to body

[8.32]The history of opium use and abuse is fascinating. But what made this drug so attractive that it once enslaved whole nations? No one becomes addicted to a drug that only offers sedation and death. Nor do people hurl themselves into a vile cesspit of human degradation: willingly accepting loss of employment, loss of possessions and homes, sink into the most depraved and lowly criminal activities, or even willingly sell their wives and children into slavery to get more of the drug. Accordingly, opiates such as opium, morphine, and heroin must induce such wonderful mental experiences and effects, that people are willing to endure such miseries. The reader should note that the conscious physical bodies of addicts perpetrate all these depravities— depravities purposefully and consciously directed to obtain more of the drug—which means that the souls of these conscious addicts control their physical bodies to do all these things (see 1.55-1.65). This raises the question of whether the souls of these addicts are addicted to opium. A fascinating concept—immaterial souls addicted to the effects of opium upon the material bodies of addicts. This is but one aspect of the effects of opium and opiates in relation to the soul. And indeed, the bodily and mental effects of opium and opiates reveal much more about the functioning of the conscious mind, so further enabling a differentiation between the mind-models of materialism and dualism.

Sites of action of opiates

[8.33]Any fuller understanding of the mental effects of opiates requires an understanding of how opiates exert their effects. These effects are mediated by specific groups of opiate receptors distributed throughout the brain and spinal cord. So what are the various types of opiate receptors in the brain and spinal cord, and what occurs when they are activated by opiates?

215

- [8.34]*delta receptors:* Antidepressant effect, pain relief, opiate dependence.
- [8.35]*kappa receptors:* Dysphoria, sedation, narrowing of pupils, pain relief (at spinal cord level).
- [8.36]*mu-1 receptors:* Pain relief, opiate dependence.
- [8.37]*mu-2 receptors:* Euphoria, respiratory depression, narrowing of pupils, opiate dependence.

[8.38]Activation and blocking of these different receptors explain all the many effects of opiates, as well as the variability of the mental effects ascribed to morphine in particular, and all other opiates in general. Opiate receptors are structures formed of several protein subunits, coded for by specific genes. This implies that genetic differences between individuals are possible. And indeed, genetic variations in opiate receptor subunits do occur in humans (Dahan 2009). Moreover, the densities of the different types of opiate receptors at each part of the body and brain differs somewhat between different people, between the young and old, as well as between men and women (Dahan 2008, Sarton 2000, Zubieta 1999). Slight inter-individual differences in opiate receptor densities and types explain why different individuals experience different effects after the same dose of the same opiate. These differences reveal the fallacy in saying that the clinical and mental effects of any given opiate at a particular dose are identical for all people, although a group will experience an average effect. Nonetheless, the effects and experiences revealed by stimulation of the various opiate receptors reveal much about the true nature of the conscious mind.

Opiate effect: Respiratory depression

[8.39]Respiration, or breathing, is a basic vital function driven and regulated by the levels of oxygen and carbon dioxide in the body. Failure of adequate respiration means insufficient carbon dioxide is eliminated from the body. Failure of adequate respiration also means insufficient oxygen enters the body to support all the energy generating chemical reactions so essential for life. And failure of respiration means failure of life. Morphine and all other opiates disrupt the control of respiration by reducing the sensitivity of regulating systems responding to oxygen and carbon dioxide concentrations in the blood and tissues of the body. Such disruption, or down-regulation of respiratory control, occurs after administration of single doses of opiates (Babenco 2000, Dahan 2010, Ladd 2005, Mildh 2001), as well as during chronic opiate administration

(Teichtahl 2005). Administration of sufficiently high doses or concentrations of opiates causes total cessation of respiration (Stanley 1977, Streisand 1993). This lethal effect of opiates has been known for a long time. Indeed, during 1867 an English physician wrote that inappropriately high doses of commonly available morphine preparations, such as Paregoric and Laudanum, administered by ignorant parents were a significant cause of infant death and disability.

8.40Can we then wonder, after what I have narrated, that there should be so great a mortality amongst the infants of this country, or such miserable, feeble, and brownish yellow countenances so striking amongst many of its inhabitants? What can or should be done to discourage this almost wholesale murder amongst infants, and contamination amongst adults? (Hawkins 1867)

8.41Opiate-induced respiratory depression is the main cause of death due to opiate overdoses. Alexander Marcet published one of the first successfully "treated" cases of morphine overdose during 1806. The person concerned was an 18 year old man who had ingested six ounces (about 170 ml) of Laudanum. This is a dose of Laudanum containing about 1700 mg of morphine—a gigantic and certainly lethal dose! Treatment was simple: the young man was continually walked around the room, regularly shaken, shouted at, given tea and coffee to drink, and administered emetics such as copper sulphate. Administration of a "glyster", which is an old term for an enema administered by a large syringe, almost "certainly" contributed to the success of this treatment. The young man survived these torments and his morphine overdose, although he was groggy for some days afterwards (Marcet 1806). Other treatments recommended for the treatment of morphine overdose during the nineteenth century were flagellation, hot irons applied to the epigastrium, electric shocks, cold showers, walking, coffee, strychnine and atropine (pages 192-194 in Kane 1880). During 1880, a Dr. H. Kane published a graphic and colorful description of the use of an early description form of artificial respiration to treat respiratory failure induced by a morphine overdose.

8.42The patient was supported in the sitting posture, by an assistant kneeling on the bed at his back and holding his head erect between his hands; two other assistants, standing on each side of the patient, now took charge of an arm each, holding the limb firmly at the elbow and upper part of the forearm; the tongue was now pressed down by the handle of a spoon, or the fingers introduced into the mouth; the assistants having charge of the arms were now directed to elevate these limbs simultaneously, carrying them above the head at an angle of about forty-five degrees, and dragging upon them so as to slightly lift the patient; the arms were then depressed and brought down close against the sides of the thorax so as to compress the chest.

The effect of these movements was the following: at each attempt at lifting the body by the arms in this way, forcible traction outwards was made on the walls of the chest, through the pectorales major and minor muscles, the serrati and parts of the two latissimi dorsi muscles giving rise to expansion of the walls of the thorax; the air was thus caused to enter forcibly into the lungs, and thus inspiration was completed. The arms were then brought steadily down and pressed against the sides of the thorax and abdomen compressing them and expelling the air forcibly from the lungs and effecting expiration. Under the use of the artificial respiration, the appearance of the patient was much improved. The color was restored to the face, the lips became redder, and the countenance more natural, though the relaxation of the muscular system was by no means lessened; if the head was left unsupported for an instant, it fell forward as suddenly and forcibly as that of a dead man. The artificial movements were continued for more than an hour, and though the color of the patient was improved and the heart's action became normal, still, when they were omitted, there was found no improvement in the natural respirations, these being still but four in a minute, as before artificial respiration was applied. (pages 210-211 in Kane 1880)

8.43These passages also echo the practical experience of all anesthesiologists, anesthetic nurses, and recovery room nurses. It is a common observation that people who have undergone extremely painful operations, may be fully conscious and breathe normally after administration of doses of opiates that would normally cause breathing to stop altogether (Combes 2000). These old observations that shouting, shaking and pain may reverse the effects of opiate-induced respiratory depression are as true today as more than 100 years ago. Even so, many people remain comatose and do not breathe after large doses of morphine or other opiates, despite application of aggressive shaking, attempts to walk them around, torture, or even major surgery (Quintin 1981, Stanley 1973, Stanley 1979, Waller 1981).

[8.44]Large doses of opiates are required during general anesthesia to prevent reactions to the pain of surgery. Upon termination of general anesthesia, some people are awake and respond to questioning, but do not breathe. When instructed to breathe, they take a breath, slowly breathe in and out on command, and then do nothing until instructed to breathe again. If left unattended, these people stop breathing altogether, develop severe hypoxia, go into cardiac arrest, and ultimately die. This is a phenomenon regularly observed by all anesthesiologists and recovery room nurses. When asked about their subjective experiences during this period, these people report feeling calm, indifferent, and even happy. They were undismayed about not breathing, did not realize they were not breathing, did not even think about breathing, and had no urge to breathe. They only breathed on command because they were continually "nagged" in loud and commanding tones. Subsequently some of these people even complain bitterly about the continual "nagging" orders to breathe.

[8.45]Lack of any spontaneous urge to breathe, whereby each breath must be consciously activated, is a manifestation of opiate actions upon the human body known as "Ondine's Curse". This eponymous name is derived from the Germanic legend of an immortal water nymph called Ondine. She fell in love with a mortal man who reciprocated her feelings. Both swore each other eternal fidelity. Ondine lost her immortality after bearing a child to her mortal husband. One sad day, Ondine discovered her husband in the embrace of another woman. Unfortunately for her straying husband, Ondine's loss of immortality did not mean loss of her magical powers. So she cursed him by removing automatic control over his breathing. He managed to stay awake for several days, but finally fell into an exhausted sleep, upon which his breathing stopped forever. Such was the curse of Ondine.

Opiate effect: Sedation and anesthesia

[8.46]This brings us to the next important effect of opiates—sedation. Opiates of all types induce sedation (Evans 1974, Paqueron 2002), and even general anesthesia (Stanley 1973, Stanley 1979, Streisand 1993). Indeed, general anesthesia using only 100% oxygen and a high dose of a single opiate such as morphine (Stanley 1973), fentanyl (Quintin 1981, Stanley 1979, Streisand 1993), or sufentanil (Gilron 1996), was once a popular method of administering general anesthesia for patients undergoing cardiac operations during the 1970's and 1980's. The main reason for this popularity was the exceptional stability of heart function and circulation during cardiac operations performed under such anesthesia. However, when concurrent administration of drugs inducing sleep or amnesia is omitted, up to 50% of people may be awake and aware of their surroundings while undergoing cardiac operations with this technique of "general anesthesia" (Hilgenberg 1981, Lowenstein 1971, Streisand 1993). Fortunately, none of these patients report experiencing pain during such high dose opiate "anesthesia", just consciousness, and awareness of their surroundings (Gilron 1996, Hilgenberg 1981, Lowenstein 1971). Periods of awareness during high dose opiate anesthesia are regularly reported.

[8.47] *Her recount began with her description of hearing discussion of the adverse outcome of a patient who could not be weaned from CPB [cardiopulmonary bypass] on the previous day and of the complexity of her own operation. She denied pain or anxiety when she was aware but did sense "touching and pressing" on her chest. The patient tried to indicate that she was awake by unsuccessfully attempting to open her eyes, vocalize and move her arms. Finally, she was able to move her left foot laterally. She also described technical details discussed by the surgeons such as inspecting "the back of the heart" and placing pacemaker wires. Her last recollection from this period was hearing the surgeons discuss sternal closure. This entire recount was unequivocal and corroborated by staff present during the operation. The only factual error made was regarding the position of her arms which she claimed were at 90 degrees from her body when, in fact, they were tucked in by her sides. (Gilron 1996)*

[8.48]This account contains a number of interesting elements. She heard the surgeons and assistants speaking, she felt the operation, she felt no pain, she felt calm, she tried to move and speak but could only move her left foot slightly, and her image of the positions of her limbs was abnormal. All these things are also elements found in the reports of people who tell of undergoing near-death experiences during cardiac surgery. This raises questions for people who believe that the near-death experience is due to separation of an immaterial soul from the body during such experiences. They must ask themselves which aspects of such an experience are due to anesthetic drug effects, and which are actual aspects of the near-death experience itself.

[8.49]This brings us to the fascinating relationship between pain relief, sedation, and loss of consciousness induced by opiate drugs. The fact that some people may be awake, but free of pain during operations performed under high dose opiate anesthesia suggests that sedation and pain relief due to opiates may be two quite different effects exerted by opiates. Dr. Xavier Paqueron reported a study confirming just this suspicion. He found that sedation induced by opiates did not automatically indicate adequate pain relief, because even sedated people still reported experiencing pain when aroused (Paqueron 2002). The differences between the effects of the different opiate receptors reveal why sedation and pain relief are two quite different effects of opiates. Examination of the effects induced by the different opiate receptors reveals that only kappa receptors mediate sedation, while pain relief is mediated by delta, kappa, and mu receptors. Accordingly, opiates causing significant kappa activation will induce sedation as well as varying degrees of pain relief. On the other hand, opiates preferentially activating delta and mu receptors are opiates capable of inducing powerful pain relief, but less sedation. This explains why people can be awake during surgery performed under high dose opiate "general anesthesia" yet feel no pain due to the operation.

8.50Altered levels of consciousness, varying from sedation to unconsciousness, are another one of the mental effects of opiates. However, opiates also induce other, even more fascinating mental effects.

Mental effects of opiates

8.51Most modern descriptions of the mental effects of opiates are colorless and insipid. Only older lyrical descriptions of the subjective experiences of opiate injection, inhalation, or ingestion, enable a beginning of any understanding why individuals are even now slaves of these drugs, and why whole nations were once thralls of the sap of the poppy. These descriptions are as true for opium, as for all other opiates such as morphine, heroin, fentanyl, sufentanil, alfentanil, piritramide, etc. Just read this expressive late nineteenth century description of the first experiences of subcutaneously administered morphine.

8.52*The seeming increased intellectual activity, the apparent*
enlargement of mental capacity and power which are felt by the
Morphine inebriate during the first stages of his experience, are
real to him, beyond question. To his own consciousness there is
no illusion in the visions which he beholds, no deceitfulness in the
inspiration which he feels. As he lies steeped in a "tranced calm"
the tides of thought seem to roll into his brain from some

221

exhaustless ocean, —the horizon of his daily thinking seems to lift its curtains, revealing infinite reaches of sublime speculation He believes himself to have passed into a new world. It is a real world to him. It is not a portion of his nature only which is under the mystical charm, but all of it. He himself is under the power of the spell. His faculties of perception and feeling, his will, every part and power of his nature are wrought upon by the wonderful witchcraft. There is no central or secret quality of will or judgment that is not influenced by the drug. (page 13 in Keeley 1881)

[8.53] A physician from the same period related his personal experiences of the effects of morphine he injected subcutaneously to relieve his exhaustion.

[8.54] I say dreams, because there was one after another, and one chased into the other; then they would get mixed up in a queer fashion, but they were all delightful and bewitching. Now, I was in the midst of flowers whose fragrance fairly intoxicated me; then among airy—like structures, whose towers and minarets pierced the crimson and purple cloud islands that floated high in a sky of deepest blue. Forms of enchanting loveliness passed in and out, while music from unseen voices was as the songs of angels. The scene changed rapidly without shock to my highly sensitized nerves; the impossible and unusual became substantial and natural. I stood on an island of emerald green, looking out upon an opalescent sea of sublime tranquility, upon which men of stately mien walked as upon dry land; then I was suddenly transferred to a mountain peak, where I saw all the kingdoms of the world, with their pleasures and riches, without a suggestion of the sorrows and afflictions that beset humanity. I saw the faces of loved ones lit up with ineffable happiness as they pleasantly conversed with me; it did not occur to me until after the waking that these were the forms of those who had been called hence during my childhood, youth, and younger manhood. They were living and real; yet their manner and speech were not those of the living. These and a thousand other visions floated before the dream eyes of the quickened but disordered brain; but the sensations were in the highest degree pleasurable and the delirium was one of ever-changing joy. (pages 103-104 in Cobbe 1895)

[8.55]These passages are poetry. They reveal most modern descriptions of opiate effects to be woefully pallid and drear, devoid of all emotions and evocative qualities enabling non-addicts to understand the seduction of opiates. In addition, these passages reveal several significant, fascinating, and amazing facets of the mental effects aroused by opiates. Note in these passages: the belief in the reality of the dreams, the transcendental worlds and experiences, the feeling of ultimate knowledge, of calm sublimity, and of power, as well as meeting with the spirits of deceased known persons. (N.B. Note the similarity of these opiate experiences to near-death experiences.) Opiate addicts often describe these effects as aspects of their initial experiences of these drugs. This is the awesome power of all opiates—the seductive experiences driving some people to try more and more, to relive these initial almost divine experiences again and again. But with repetition comes physical addiction and desensitization, after which the addict requires increasingly higher doses of opiate to induce the same experiences again. At the same time, the consequences of physical addiction are the same for all opiate addicts—they must inject, smoke, or ingest the opiate regularly to prevent withdrawal symptoms. These facts inspired William Cobbe more than 100 years ago to say of opiates; "Opium is the Judas of drugs; it kisses and then betrays" (title page in Cobbe 1895).

[8.56]The reader should note that these marvelous experiences are conscious experiences. An unconscious person is just that—unconscious. An unconscious person experiences nothing. Unconsciousness is a blank space of no experiences, much like a dreamless sleep. A person reporting undergoing incredible experiences during a period of unresponsive unconsciousness induced by opiates, was actually conscious during this period of unresponsiveness. They were only apparently unconscious.

[8.57]I will not discuss the "betrayal of opium", such as the dreadful medical and psychosocial problems associated with opiate addiction. Nor will I discuss the medical use of opiates for severe chronic pain, and the attendant physical addiction. This book confines itself to the short-term effects of these drugs. So let us look more rigorously at some of the differences between the subjective mental effects of different opiates, and the differing mental effects induced by the same opiate in different individuals.

[8.58]A careful double blind study performed by Louis Lasagna in 1955 revealed that both heroin and morphine induce euphoria in 40-45% of people, and dysphoria in about 50% of persons (Lasagna 1955). Other studies reveal similar results (Angst 2012, Haemmig 2001, Jasinski 1986). Furthermore, higher doses, and more rapid administration produce more profound and intense mental effects (Marsch 2001). As regards the addictive potential of various opiates—this varies from one opiate to another. For example, heroin, oxycodone, and morphine demonstrate higher addictive potential than do buprenorphine or fentanyl (Comer 2008).

Subjective mental effects of opiates

[8.59]So what are some of the most relevant subjective effects of morphine and its analogues as revealed by modern research?

- [8.60]Opiates induce feelings expressed as a "high", liking, or "good effect", "coasting", or "spaced-out", and whose intensity is in direct proportion to the administered dose (Foltin 1992, Jasinski 1986, Jones 1999, Marsch 2001, Martin 1961, Walker 1998, Walker 1999, Zacny 1997, Zacny 1998).
- [8.61]Opiates induce either dysphoria or euphoria, the intensity of which is in direct proportion to the dose (Haemmig 2001, Jasinski 1986, Kaiko 1981, Marsch 2001, Smith 1962).
- [8.62]Feelings of "floating" are experienced in proportion to opiate dose (Walker 1999, Zacny 1997, Zacny 1998).
- [8.63]About 25-33% of people administered opiates report feelings of "increased mental activity" (Table 5 in Smith 1959, Smith 1962).
- [8.64]More than one half of people administered opiates report feelings of "clouded" mental function (Table 5 in Smith 1959, Smith 1962, Walker 1999, Zacny 1997, Zacny 1998).
- [8.65]One half of people administered opiates feel "sluggish" or weary, and have no desire to move (Smith 1959, Walker 1998, Zacny 1997, Zacny 1998).
- [8.66]Subjective mental effects change with the duration of exposure to opiates. Even during a period as short as a single administration, many people report initially experiencing euphoria, which subsequently change with time to feelings of dysphoria and sedation (Angst 2012, Mirin 1976, Zacny 1992). This difference between the initial short-term, and longer-term effects, must always be taken into account when studying any account of subjective experiences induced by opiates.

8.67These are the subjective mental experiences relevant to this study of the nature of the conscious mind as proposed by theories such as dualism and materialism.

Objective mental effects of opiates

8.68But what are the objective mental effects of opiates relevant to this study of the human soul?

- 8.69The pain relieving or analgesic effect of opiates is directly related to their dosages and blood concentrations, and is present at concentrations that do not cause loss of consciousness (Austin 1980, Dahan 2004, Gourlay 1988, Kaiko 1981, Lemmens 1988).
- 8.70The sedative effect of opiates is directly related to their dose and blood concentration (Veselis 1994, Walker 1999).
- 8.71Psychomotor ability decreases with increasing dose (Marsch 2001, Smith 1962a, Veselis 1994, Walker 1999, Zacny 1997, Zacny 1998).
- 8.72Memory impairment occurs after opiate administration, but is not as severe as with midazolam or propofol (Veselis 1994, Zacny 1997).
- 8.73Various brain scanning techniques reveal that opiates administered at doses insufficient to induce loss of consciousness, but sufficient to cause pain relief and affect mental function, do alter the functioning of the brain (Adler 1997, Becerra 2006, Firestone 1996, London 1990, Wagner 2001).

8.74These studies reveal very little difference between the mental effects of different opiates. Most interestingly, these studies actually demonstrate profound differences between the subjective experiences induced in different people by the same dose of the same opiate. For example, morphine can induce either dysphoria or euphoria. So what are the differences between the effects of opiates observed in clinical practice?

Variable effects of opiates in medical practice

8.75Everyday anesthesiology practice confirms the reality of these studies. Furthermore, there are also other variations in the effects of opiates regularly observed in clinical practice.

Opiates administered to pain-free adults

[8.76]Anesthesiologists, anesthetic nurses, and recovery room nurses have considerable experience with the immediate effects of opiates administered intravenously to patients without pain, as well as to those in pain. The mental effects of opiates are noticeable within seconds to minutes after intravenous injection, and differ considerably between these two groups of patients. Healthy persons about to undergo general anesthesia for planned operations are not in pain when commencing anesthesia. Nearly all modern anesthesiologists administer a dose of an opiate equivalent to 10-15 milligrams of morphine about 30-60 seconds prior to induction of loss of consciousness. This reduces the dose of intravenous induction agent required to induce loss of consciousness, as well as reducing the sometimes major changes in blood pressure occurring due to subsequent introduction of tubes and catheters. Within seconds, many of these people make their subjective reactions to this initial dose of an opiate known. For example, an interesting study of the mental effects of the short acting opiate, remifentanil in Asian patients, revealed that a constant intravenous infusion of this drug induced sensations of warmth in 39%, floating sensations in 17%, dizziness in 27%, and sleepiness in 17% of the 70 persons studied (Haba 2011). Opiates induce a wide range of other mental effects. Many people report experiencing dysphoric mental effects such as; "I feel awful." "I'm anxious / terrified." "Ugh, that does not feel good." Other people experience something quite different. They report euphoric reactions such as: "Wow, that's better than whisky!" "Cool!" "I feel good." "Good trip! Where can I get this stuff?" These are a few of the reactions I have personally heard.

Opiates administered to adults in pain

[8.77]However, in contrast to this group of pain-free patients, those persons receiving intravenous injections of opiates to treat pain, often feel better because of less pain. They seldom report dysphoric effects. This difference between the situations in which opiates are administered, illustrates how medical condition and situation influences the subjective mental effects of opiates.

Women are more sensitive to opiates than men

[8.78]Anesthesiologists, and other physicians regularly administering and prescribing opiates recognize a clear gender difference in sensitivity to opiates. Women are more sensitive than men to the pain relieving and respiratory depressant effects of opiates (Sarton 2000). This is why anesthesiologists and surgeons prescribe lower doses of opiates to women than to men for pain management after operations.

Redheads and opiates

[8.79]The brain produces a hormone called "Melanocyte Simulating Hormone" (MSH), which induces cells in the skin and hair roots to produce a dark pigment, called Melanin. This is why many people have darker hair and skin color. MSH does this by activating special receptors on the cell surfaces of these pigment producing hair root and skin cells. These MSH-receptors are made of proteins, whose structure is coded for by inherited genes. But one or more of the genes coding for the MSH-receptor is abnormal in persons with red hair, which is why the MSH produced by their bodies has no effect on their hair and skin color, resulting in red hair, pale skin, and light colored eyes (Mogil 2003). These same MSH receptors are also found in the brain, where they modulate the activity of some of the opiate receptors in the brain. Reduced activity of these brain opiate receptors is the reason why redheaded people experience more fear of pain (Binkley 2009), have a lower pain threshold (Liem 2005), and require deeper anesthesia than people with other hair colors (Liem 2004). Anesthesiologists know this from experience, and take it into account when administering opiates and general anesthesia to redheaded people.

Different people and different opiates

[8.80]Not all opiates stimulate the different receptors equally. Each specific opiate stimulates these receptors to a greater or lesser degree. On average, everyone's brain is identical, because brain structure and function is the same for each human. Even so, there are subtle variations between people as regards the distribution, density, and types of opiate receptors. Anesthesiologists and recovery room nurses notice this regularly as variable responses of people to opiates. Recovery rooms are special places where people go to recover after undergoing anesthesia and surgery. Here they also receive pain-relieving drugs when needed, so they can return pain-free to the regular hospital wards. Safety and economy in hospital recovery rooms, requires that each patient receives a standard opiate drug to manage their pain after surgery. Many recovery rooms use morphine for this purpose. Morphine is a very predictable, effective, and useful drug. But some people experience minimal pain relief after even repeated morphine injections. The anesthesiologist usually does one of two things in response to this observation. He prescribes a different sort of drug to enhance the pain relieving effect of the morphine, or he switches to another opiate. In this latter situation, instead of continuing the administration of morphine, the recovery room nurse will now administer a different opiate. Such "opiate switching" is often effective, because of slightly differing distribution profiles of opiate receptors between people, as well as the differing receptor activation profiles of different opiate drugs. "Opiate switching" is a clinical practice revealing how opiate receptor distribution, density, and types can vary from one person to another (Bart 2004, Bond 1998, Gerra 2007, Landau 2004, Zubieta 1999).

Genetically determined differences in opiate effects

[8.81]The very fact that some people experience euphoria, while others experience dysphoria from the same opiate administered under exactly the same conditions, indicates a possible genetic basis for these differences. And indeed, a wonderful large scale monozygotic and dizygotic twin study, revealed a genetic basis for the variability in opiate effects between different people. There is a significant heritable component for the respiratory depressant, nausea inducing, and drug disliking effects of opiates, while there is a strong familial correlation for the drug liking, sedative, and dizziness inducing effects of opiates (Angst 2012).

[8.82]The above twin study, as well as other studies, confirms an inherited susceptibility for opiate addiction (Bart 2004, Bond 1998, Gerra 2007, Tsuang 1998). But this genetic basis is not as simple as saying; "One of your parents is/was a heroin addict; therefore you will be a heroin addict." The inheritance of such a propensity for opiate, and other addiction, is rather more complex.

[8.83]Louis Lasagna once summed up the variability of opiate mental effects between individuals in a comment made during 1955.

[8.84]*There has, for example, been a strong tendency for textbook writers to describe the central nervous system effects of a drug like Morphine in oversimplified terms and sweeping generalizations, as if Morphine produced certain set effects that were evident in all persons at all times, or at least most persons at most times. It is obvious that the subjective effects of drugs, no less than the objective effects, are dependent on the situation in which the drug is administered. It is also likely that the production of a given mental state, even in the same situation, will not prove equally pleasant to all persons. In addition, of course, there are such problems as the effects of dosage, route of administration, and duration of treatment. (Lasagna 1955)*

[8.85]This can be all summed up with the statement that not everyone reacts in the same way, or undergoes the same subjective experiences when administered morphine or other opiate drugs. And this passage is as true now as when it was written.

Opiates and the soul

[8.86]Many of the subjective effects of opiates are strikingly similar to those reported by people recounting their near-death experiences. So do the effects of opiates reveal anything about the true nature of the conscious mind, and the origin of these experiences? Can these effects differentiate between the mind-models of dualism and materialism?

Materialism and opiate effects

[8.87]Materialists explain that opiates demonstrably alter the functioning of the brain, so generating all the subjective and objective experiences reported subsequent to opiate administration. Indeed, the fact that the magnitudes of effects induced by opiates on the functioning of the brain are proportional to opiate dosage and blood concentration, indicates a physical substrate for these effects. So according to the mind-model of materialism, the effects of opiates are yet another demonstration that the conscious mind is a product of the functioning of the brain.

Dualism and opiate effects

[8.88]The position of dualism is somewhat different. Some believers in dualism might claim that higher doses of opiates release the soul from the filtering, limiting, or inhibiting effects of the physical brain, so permitting the expression of the true nature of the soul. But there is a problem with this concept, as the point by point explanation below demonstrates.

229

- [8.89]The mind-model of dualism claims that the bodies of physically conscious persons are under the control of their individual souls (see 1.55-1.65).
- [8.90]The mind-model of dualism also claims that the soul expresses itself in this material world through the physical mechanisms of the body.
- [8.91]Opiates alter the functioning of the physical brain, and exert no direct effects upon the soul. However, altered brain function induced by opiates can modify the processing of bodily perceptions within the brain. This in turn alters the perceptions and sensations transmitted from the brain to the soul. The soul receives this abnormal information, and responds by controlling the physical body accordance with this abnormal information. The final result is the expression by the physical body of all the wondrous subjective and objective effects manifested by people affected by opiates (see 1.142).
- [8.92]Altered brain function induced by opiates can also alter the manifestations of control exerted by the soul over the brain. This is a phenomenon similar to a damaged radio set—the radio signal is unchanged but its expression by the damaged radio set is a garbled mish-mash. According to the mind-model of dualism, this means that marvelous experiences induced by opiates in some physically conscious persons, such as euphoria, increased speed of thought, floating feelings, visions of transcendental worlds, meeting deceased relatives, life review, etc, are actually manifestations of an interaction between the controlling influence of the soul, and a physical brain whose functioning has been altered by opiates, rather than an expression of the true nature of the soul (see 1.65, 1.142).

[8.94]A major problem with the explanations of dualism is that these manifestations of a possible controlling soul are very demonstrably expressed through the mechanisms of an abnormally functioning conscious physical brain. Therefore these expressions of the controlling influence of a soul, reveal nothing about the true nature of any putative human soul. In fact, opiate induced abnormal brain function in physically conscious persons actually obscures any manifestation of the true nature of the controlling human soul. Nonetheless, such considerations fail to disprove the possible reality of a controlling human soul. Instead, the reality of such experiences reveals that any controlling human soul has properties very different to those proposed by believers in the mind-model of dualism in Chapter 1.

Concluding remarks on opiates and the soul

[8.94]Opiates are capable of arousing the same marvelous transcendental, affective, and cognitive experiences in physically conscious persons as occur during experiences of apparent disembodiment of the soul, such as during out-of-body experiences and near-death experiences. As explained above, the mind-models of dualism and materialism provide several possible alternative explanations for these experiences. But there is no way of conclusively demonstrating which of these alternative explanations is correct. However, the fact that there are several theoretically valid alternative explanations means that it is incorrect to claim these experiences are manifestations of the unfettered true nature of the soul. The same is equally true for the alternative, but more parsimonious explanation of materialism. Notwithstanding these seemingly indecisive conclusions, the effects of opiates do indicate that the properties of any human soul are very different to those proposed by dualism in Chapter 1. So it is worthwhile continuing with our examination of the mental effects of other drugs and experiences occurring during anesthesia to examine what they reveal about the nature of the conscious mind.

9

Indian Arrow Poison

9.1Nothing now remained to show that life was still within him, except that his heart faintly beat and fluttered at intervals. In five-and-twenty minutes from the time of being wounded he was quite dead. His flesh was very sweet and savoury at dinner. (page 142 in Waterton 1879)

9.2This was no cannibal feast, but a description of eating an ox killed with curare—the deadly arrow poison of the South American Orinoco Indians. Orinoco Indians had no idea their use of curare would eventually unleash a revolution in general anesthesia, as well as providing new insights into the nature of the conscious mind.

A short history of curare

9.3The first report of mysterious deadly South American arrow poisons to reach the English speaking world was from an account of the voyage of Sir Francis Drake (1540-1596) to the Caribbean in 1585-1586. During 1586, Drake attacked and plundered the Spanish city of Cartagena on the north coast of present day Columbia. The Spanish defenders were aided by Indian allies firing poisoned arrows.

9.4They had joined with them many Indians, whom they had placed in corners of advantage, all bowmen, with their arrows most villainously empoisoned, so as if they did but break the skin, the party so touched died without great marvel. Some they slew of our people with their arrows; some they likewise mischiefed to death with certain pricks of small sticks sharply pointed, of a foot and a half long, the one end put into the ground, the other empoisoned, sticking fast up, right against our coming in the way as we should approach from our landing towards the town, whereof they had

*planted a wonderful number in the ordinary way; but our keeping
the sea wash shore, missed the greatest part of them very happily.
(pages 242-243 in Payne 1880)*

[9.5]This was amazing! A mere scratch with a poisoned arrow caused
the scratched person to quietly die! Ten years later the English courtier
and privateer, Sir Walter Raleigh (1552-1618), made a voyage to Guiana
in search of Eldorado, the fabled city of gold. He did not find it, but did
encounter Indians firing poisoned arrows from their bows. His account
of these encounters was as fanciful as that of the rest of his voyage.

[9.6]*There was nothing whereof I was more curious than to find out
the true remedies of these poisoned arrows; for besides the
mortality of the wound they make, the party shot endureth the
most insufferable torment in the world, and abideth a most ugly
and lamentable death, sometimes dying stark mad, sometimes
their bowels breaking out of their bellies, which are presently
discoloured as black as pitch, and so unsavory as no man can
endure to cure or to attend them. And it is more strange to know
that in all this time there was never Spaniard, either by gift or
torment, that could attain to the true knowledge of the cure,
although they have martyred and put to invented torture I know
not how many of them. But everyone of these Indians knew it not,
no, not one among thousands, but their soothsayers and priests,
who do conceal it, and only teach it but from the father to the son.
(pages 369-370 in Payne 1880)*

[9.7]The nature of the poisons used on the arrows in this fantasy rich
account from the voyage of Raleigh is uncertain. In any case the poison
was certainly very different to that described in the annals of the voyages
of Sir Francis Drake ten years earlier. These men died a horrible death,
in all likelihood due to some sort of ghastly sepsis, (blood poisoning),
caused by a horridly putrescent substance smeared on the arrow tips.
However, these accounts do reveal that the Spanish conquerors of South
America were well aware of poisoned arrows. This fearful "flying death"
of South American Indians remained the stuff of legends until the
researches of Alexander von Humboldt (1769-1859). While travelling in
South America during 1799-1804, he was particularly interested in the
famous "curare" arrow poison used by the Indians living around the
Orinoco River. This was about 200 years after the reports of Drake and
Raleigh, and European knowledge of curare was still a matter shrouded

in fearful legend and fable as is illustrated by the following fanciful anecdote.

[9.8]The missionaries Gumilla and Gili had not been able to penetrate into the country where the Curare is manufactured. Gumilla asserts that this preparation was enveloped in great mystery; that its principal ingredient was furnished by a subterranean plant with a tuberous root, which never puts forth leaves, and which is called specially the root (raiz de si misma); that the venomous exhalations which arise from the manufacture are fatal to the lives of the old women who (being otherwise useless) are chosen to watch over this operation; finally, that these vegetable juices are never thought to be sufficiently concentrated till a few drops produce at a distance a repulsive action on the blood. (pages 438-439 in volume 2 of Humboldt 1852)

[9.9]The truth was rather more mundane. Bark from the vines and roots from which the curare poison was extracted, were crushed to provide a yellow colored juice, from which the fibers were removed by filtration. Subsequent boiling removed most of the water and concentrated the toxin. The concentrated toxin was then mixed with a gum to stick it to arrows (pages 439-442 in volume 2 of Humboldt 1852). A few years later during 1812-1814, Charles Waterton (1783-1865) also travelled through the same regions along the Orinoco as Humboldt. He too was interested in curare, and described animal deaths due to curare, as well as an account of an Indian who accidently killed himself with a curare poisoned arrow.

[9.10]The Arowack Indian said it was but four years ago that he and his companion were ranging in the forest in quest of game. His companion took a poisoned arrow, and sent it at a red monkey in a tree above him. It was nearly a perpendicular shot. The arrow missed the monkey, and in the descent, struck him in the arm, a little above the elbow. He was convinced it was all over with him. "I shall never," said he to his companion in a faltering voice, and looking at his bow as said it, "I shall never," said he, "bend this bow again." And having said that, he took off his little bamboo poison box, which hung across his shoulder, and putting it together with his bow and arrows on the ground, he laid himself down close by them, bid his companion farewell, and never spoke more. (page 144 in Waterton 1879)

[9.11]Death is quiet, and the speed of death is evidently related to the dose of the poison (page 143 in Waterton 1879). Humboldt, and subsequently Waterton, both agreed on the nature of death due to curare, as well as making fascinating remarks about the meat of animals killed by arrows or darts poisoned with curare. It was Waterton who remarked on the sweet taste of the meat of an ox killed by curare (see 9.1), while several years before, Humboldt noted that Orinoco Indians preferred to eat meat killed with curare.

[9.12]*Scarcely a fowl is eaten on the banks of the Orinoco [river] which has not been killed with a poisoned arrow; and the missionaries allege that the flesh of animals is never so good as when this method is employed. Father Zea, who accompanied us, though ill of a tertian fever, every morning had the live fowls allotted for our food brought to his hammock together with an arrow, and he killed them himself; for he would not confide this operation, to which he attached great importance, to any other person. Large birds, a guan (pava de monte) for instance, or a curassao (alector), when wounded in the thigh, die in two or three minutes; but it is often ten or twelve minutes before life is extinct in a pig or a peccary. (page 444 in volume 2 of Humboldt 1852)*

[9.13]How fascinating! The meat of animals killed by curare apparently tastes better than the meat of animals killed by other methods. The actions of curare on the body explain this fascinating observation.

The action of curare

[9.14]Nerves do not activate muscles directly. Instead there is a small cavity, or space called a "synaptic cleft", between a nerve ending and the membrane of the muscle cell activated by that nerve ending. Signals transmitted along a nerve to a muscle release the chemical "acetylcholine" from the nerve ending into the synaptic cleft. This activates specific acetylcholine receptors on the nerve membrane of the adjacent muscle cell at that point, causing the muscle fiber to contract. Curare, and drugs with an action similar to curare, combine with these acetylcholine receptors to interfere with, or block this action of acetylcholine. The result is that nerve signals no longer activate muscle fibers (Fagerlund 2009). The most evident effect of this blockade of muscle acetylcholine receptors is paralysis of all muscles of voluntary movement, together with paralysis of the muscles of respiration. Death due to curare is caused by paralysis of the muscles of respiration, and the subsequent failure of oxygen supply to the tissues of the body. This is why people administered curare can be kept alive by means of artificial respiration.

[9.15]Indeed, if a person or animal "poisoned" with curare is kept alive with artificial respiration, the paralysis of curare eventually vanishes. The disappearance of curare induced paralysis is a product of normal bodily processes such as: distribution of curare throughout the tissues of the body, excretion of unchanged curare in the urine and bile, and metabolism of curare in the liver. All these normal physiological processes eventually result in the curare concentration at nerve endings becoming so low, that the curare-induced paralysis disappears. Curare, and drugs similar to curare, are used by anesthesiologists all over the world as part of the drug mixtures used to provide general anesthesia. Every day, all over the world, anesthesiologists administer curare, or other drugs with a curare-like action, to untold thousands of patients undergoing surgery, using artificial respiration to keep them alive during general anesthesia. Nevertheless, curare does not affect all muscles and body tissues in exactly the same way.

Different muscles: different sensitivities

[9.16]Acetylcholine receptors are made of groups of proteins positioned within cell membranes. But the structure of acetylcholine receptors differs somewhat from one tissue to another. This explains the differential actions of curare on the tissues of the body. Acetylcholine receptors on the diaphragm and skeletal muscles of the body are different to those in the brain, which in turn are different to the acetylcholine receptors in nerve ganglia, heart muscle, on bowel muscle, on urinary bladder muscle, or other muscles of the body. Differences between acetylcholine receptors explain why curare does not cause: unconsciousness due to any action of curare on the brain, incontinence of feces due to paralysis of intestinal and rectal muscles, incontinence of urine due to paralysis of bladder and other urinary sphincter muscles, or cardiac arrest due to paralysis of heart muscles.

[9.17]Curare and curare-like muscle paralyzing drugs such as tubocurarine, toxifarine, gallamine, pancuronium, pipercuronium, vecuronium, rocuronium, atracurium, cistracurium, etc., all paralyze skeletal muscles by the same mechanism. However, even though the acetylcholine receptors on these muscle fibers are very similar, there are still subtle differences between these different muscle groups. These subtle differences explain the observation made by Thomas Cecil Gray (1913-2008) during 1946. He remarked that some skeletal muscle groups are more sensitive to the effects of curare than are others.

[9.18]*In the conscious human subject the muscles of the eyes, mouth and fingers are affected first, then those of the trunk and limbs, and finally the diaphragm. Consciousness is retained, and recovery occurs in the reverse order. (page 403 in Gray 1946)*

[9.19]All curare-like drugs cause paralysis of all the skeletal muscles of the body, but have much less effect on the muscle fibers of the diaphragm (Foldes 1961, Foldes 1971, Gal 1981, Smith 1947). This is why lower doses of curare can cause total paralysis of all limb and trunk muscles, but with retention of adequate breathing using the relatively curare resistant muscles of the diaphragm (Foldes 1961, Foldes 1971, Gal 1981, Smith 1947). Higher doses of curare, and curare-like drugs, also induce paralysis of the diaphragmatic muscles, causing breathing to fail altogether.

[9.20]Curiously, just like the muscle fibers of the diaphragm, the muscle fibers of the forehead are also relatively unaffected by curare. This is why people, conscious but paralyzed with these drugs, can move their eyebrows or wrinkle their foreheads, even though they are otherwise totally paralyzed and unable to breathe (Smith 1947). This is also why the Bispectral Index of consciousness may also be affected by the electromyographic signal of the forehead muscles (Messner 2003), rendering this measure of consciousness useful, but not 100% accurate as a measure of consciousness (Avidan 2008).

Curare, respiratory failure, and anesthetic safety

[9.21]Differences between the effects of curare on the various muscle groups of the body, explains the earliest use of curare as an adjuvant drug to provide muscle relaxation of limb and abdominal muscles in spontaneously breathing patients under general anesthesia (Gray 1946, Harroun 1946, Prescott 1946, Whitacre 1945). However, it became obvious during the 1950's that the use of curare without adequate attention to the adequacy of respiration was associated with a definitely higher death rate than normal (Beecher 1954, Cullen 1959). In one extensive review published during 1954, the death rate of patients receiving curare during general anesthesia was 1:370, while that of patients receiving general anesthesia without curare was 1:2100 (Table XIII in Beecher 1954)! The response of anesthesiologists to these disastrous 1950's statistics was to provide assisted respiration, or complete artificial respiration, (otherwise known as controlled respiration or ventilation), to compensate for paralysis of muscles of respiration due to curare (Dundee 1952, Gray 1952, McAleavy 1961).

[9.22]Subsequent evolution and application of assisted and controlled respiration to patients receiving curare-like drugs, has made general anesthesia with curare to provide muscle paralysis, about ten times safer than many common surgical procedures. Compare the mortality of modern general anesthesia with that of several common operations.

- [9.23]Mortality directly caused by general anesthesia is about 10-16 deaths per 100,000 persons in Western Europe (Arbous 2001, Lienhart 2006).
- [9.24]Mortality due to undergoing an operation to remove the womb (hysterectomy) under general anesthesia is about 120-160 deaths per 100,000 operations (Bachman 1990).
- [9.25]Mortality due to undergoing an operation to remove the gallbladder under general anesthesia is about 150-1400 deaths per 100,000 operations, depending upon the health of the patients and technique of operation (Feldman 1994, Hannan 1999).
- [9.26]Mortality due to undergoing an operation to remove the large bowel for cancer under general anesthesia is about 800-5000 deaths per 100,000 operations, depending upon the health of the patients and technique of operation (Nelson 2006).

[9.27]Some people are still horrified by these statistics of the safety of general anesthesia, forgetting that most of those who die as a result of general anesthesia are generally very sick persons who are likely to die anyway. Even so, some young and healthy people do die as a result of general anesthesia, although exact statistics of this are not available. One way to gain some perspective here is to examine the mortality of pregnancy. Pregnancy is a profound life event, often welcomed and considered "safe" by many people. Yet the various complications of pregnancy ultimately cause the deaths of about 5-10 young women per 100,000 pregnancies in the USA and Western Europe (Chang 2003, Hill 2005). This mortality is comparable to that of general anesthesia. It is curious—most people welcome pregnancy, but many fear general anesthesia.

[9.28]Curare conveys so many advantages that its use is justified. The profound paralysis of muscles surrounding the organs of the body makes operations easier and safer. Curare enables a lighter level of anesthesia, making general anesthesia safer for people with poorly functioning hearts. However, administration of curare during general anesthesia does mean that respiration must be assisted, or completely controlled so as to ensure an adequate supply of oxygen to sometimes desperately sick patients.

[9.29]Hospital wards in hospitals all over the world are staffed with dedicated, hardworking nurses. But each nurse must care for a number of patients, and cannot spend all her or his time with just one patient. But a person just awakening from an operation performed under general anesthesia requires just such one-on-one care, and the lack of such care makes the recovery period unsafe. All modern hospitals now provide this almost one-on-one care in recovery rooms adjacent to the operating theaters. However, such recovery rooms were uncommon until the 1970's. The more rapid and safer recovery period conferred by the use of curare, was the basis of the following remark made by Dr. Cecil Gray in an article published during 1946.

> [9.30]*It is on return to the wards that the biggest price is so often exacted. But in these patients the essential reflexes are fully recovered prior to leaving the theatre, and within half an hour they are co-operative, able to do breathing exercises, to cough and expand their chests, and can be left with safety to look after themselves. This has meant a tremendous reduction in postoperative pulmonary morbidity. (page 406 in Gray 1946)*

[9.31]The use of curare, or similar drugs, enabled the rapid return of adequate reflexes, and normal breathing. This was a vast improvement on the earlier practice of sending half-anesthetized patients back to the hospital wards, while still partly under the influence of anesthetic drugs affecting consciousness, breathing, and other reflex activity. These same considerations are as true now as in 1946. The appropriate use of curare, or curare-like drugs, enables a shorter recovery period, as well as enabling better and safer operations.

Sweet and tasty meat

[9.32]However, none of these facts explains why the meat of animals killed with curare is sweeter, and tastier than meat from animals killed by other means. Understanding of why this is so, requires a short explanation of what happens inside the mouth when eating starches.

[9.33]Starches are long chains of various sugar molecules. Starches do not taste sweet initially, but when held for a short while in the mouth they do taste sweet. This common observation is due to the action of an enzyme called "amylase" contained in human saliva. Amylase breaks down the long chains of sugar molecules in starch into sweeter tasting smaller molecules. But what about meat?

[9.34]Meat is muscle tissue, and besides the normal proteins, fats, electrolytes and water, muscle cells also contain a starch called glycogen. Muscle glycogen is composed of groups of glucose molecules bound together in various conformations, and functions as a rapidly available energy store for muscle cells. Bovine bull muscle glycogen content is about 0.8 to 1.0% of wet muscle weight, and just as with all other starches, amylase in saliva breaks glycogen in the mouth down into the sweeter tasting double glucose molecule called maltose (Roberts 1960).

[9.35]Hunted animals rapidly deplete their muscle glycogen stores while attempting to escape from their hunters (Klont 1995, Munoz 2007), as do struggling restrained animals (Apple 1995). Administration of curare to animals reduces muscle glycogen depletion, because muscle paralysis prevents the use of glycogen to power muscle contraction (Bendall 2006, Glenn 1987).

[9.36]These facts explain the sweet taste of the meat of the ox described by Waterton so long ago. The ox was paralyzed with curare, so it could not struggle or run away. Muscle paralysis meant it could not use its muscles to escape. So none of the glycogen contained within its muscles was consumed in struggle or attempting to escape. As a result its muscle tissue contained nearly normal amounts of glycogen in the meat subsequently pronounced as "sweet and savoury" by Waterton and his companions. Likewise, the muscles of the fowl killed with such care with curare by Father Zea for the delectation of Alexander Humboldt and his party, were also not subjected to chasing, exercise, or struggling before dying. Accordingly, their muscles also contained nearly normal amounts of glycogen. So it is very likely that the nearly normal muscle glycogen content in the meat of animals eaten shortly after killing with curare, explains why the meat eaten by the Waterton and his party tasted sweet.

Central nervous system effects of curare

[9.37]This is fascinating material, but do the effects of curare teach us anything about the nature of the conscious mind? Does curare have any mental effects? Curare and curare-like drugs are highly ionized, fat-insoluble molecules, and cannot diffuse out of brain capillaries to enter the substance of the brain. This explains why people totally paralyzed by high doses of curare, and curare-like drugs are still fully conscious with normal mental function, even though they cannot move, breathe, or speak. During the 1940's several anesthesiologists experimented upon themselves, and clearly demonstrated the truth of this fact (Prescott 1946, Smith 1947). I have detailed the experiences and perceptions of Dr. Smith in Chapter 2 (see 2.50-2.51). A similar, but more dramatic experience of total paralysis with a high dose of curare was reported in 1946 by Frederick Prescott (Prescott 1946).

[9.38]*A dose of 30 mg given intravenously next produced, within two minutes, complete paralysis of the muscles of the face, neck, limbs, and abdomen, and the subject was unable to open the eyes, move, speak, cough, or swallow. Within three minutes the intercostals were paralysed, and breathing became rapid and shallow. Spirometer measurements with the subject breathing pure oxygen then recorded 25 respirations per min. (control 11 per min.) and a tidal air of only 160 c.cm. (control 750 c.cm.). For the next two minutes respiration became more and more difficult and the feelings of the subject can only be described as terrifying. To be conscious yet paralysed and unable to breathe is a very unpleasant experience. [...] No analgesic action was observed with a dose of 30 mg of d-tubocurarine chloride. Strips of adhesive plaster torn from a hairy part of the body still produced considerable pain. (Prescott 1946)*

[9.39]This was true fundamental research! All studies of the effects of curare, and curare-like drugs reveal the same properties. Higher doses of curare and curare-like drugs cause total paralysis of all voluntary muscles of the body, as well as the muscles of breathing, but do not affect consciousness and sensations of pain in any way (Foldes 1961, Foldes 1971, Gal 1981, Gandevia 1993, Messner 2003, Topulos 1993).

Curare and sensations of weight and position

[9.40]However, curare, and curare-like drugs do affect other bodily sensations such as those of position and movement. Some people report experiencing a loss of body image, and body position while paralyzed. One person even reported feeling "totally dissociated, without any body image" (see 10.2), while another person said she felt "disconnected from my body ... It's not the same as lying totally relaxed." (Topulos 1993). Such sensations are dramatic, but are not reported very often. Attempts to move while totally paralyzed with curare, or curare-like drugs, requires enormous mental effort and results in minimal to no movement, but does produce unusual sensations of illusory movements (Gandevia 1993).

> [9.41]*All reported strong sensations of effort accompanying attempted movement of the limb, as if trying to move an object of immense weight. Subjective difficulty in sustaining a steady level of effort for more than a few seconds was experienced, partly because there was no visual or auditory feedback that the effort was appropriate, and because all subjects experienced unexpected illusions of movement. As examples, attempted flexion of the fingers produced a feeling of slight but distinct extension which subsided in spite of continued effort, and attempted dorsiflexion of the ankle led to the sensation of slow plantar flexion. Further increases in effort repeatedly caused the same illusory movements. An attempt to describe these sensations diagrammatically was made by subject 3 in the debriefing interview. Efforts such as trunk flexion, maximal inspiratory efforts or handgrip produced more complex illusions. (Gandevia 1993)*

[9.42]So how do curare, and curare-like drugs, affect sensations of position and movement, possibly even generating sensations of disembodiment such as out-of-body experiences?

Curare and muscle spindles

[9.43]Special muscle fibers called "muscle spindles" are sandwiched between the fibers of all muscles of the body (Fitz-Ritson 1982). Muscle spindles signal the degree of stretch of muscles, and being muscle fibers themselves, they also shorten and relax together with the surrounding muscle fibers. However, muscle spindles also independently tense and relax relative to the surrounding muscle fibers, so altering their sensitivity to stretch, as well as generating other sensory signals. Despite there being very few muscle spindles relative to the numbers of surrounding muscle fibers, they are the most important sensory organs providing the nerve signals needed to sense body position, limb positions, together with sensations of weight and movement (McCloskey 1978, Proske 2009, Proske 2012, Winter 2005), as well as providing some of the sensory information generating body image (Proske 2012). Muscle spindles are encased within an extra membrane separating them from the surrounding muscle fibers—an anatomical fact with important consequences for understanding the sensory phenomena aroused by curare (Luu 2009). This extra membrane encasing muscle spindles means that when curare, and curare-like drugs, diffuse out of the capillaries in between muscle fibers, they act relatively rapidly on the acetylcholine receptors in the surrounding muscle fibers, but their action on the muscle spindles is delayed because of the necessity to first diffuse through the membranes surrounding muscle spindles before they can affect acetylcholine receptors on muscle spindles. The reverse occurs when curare is eliminated from muscle tissues—it takes longer for curare and curare-like drugs to be removed from muscle spindles than from the surrounding muscle fibers, because these drugs must first diffuse though the membrane surrounding muscle spindles before they can be removed by blood flowing though muscle capillaries (pages 3141-3143 in Luu 2009). These facts explain the sometimes contradictory results of studies of the effects of muscle spindles on sensations of movement and perceptions of weight.

Curare and illusory sensations

[9.44]The preceding discussion reveals that the anatomical presence of a membrane surrounding muscle spindles indicates that the effects of curare on perceptions of weight, position, and movement may be divided into two phases—early and subsequent.

[9.45]Shortly after the administration of curare, or curare-like drugs, the muscle fibers surrounding muscle spindles may be paralyzed, while the muscle spindles remain active, are more tensed than the surrounding muscle fibers, and sending signals to the brain. This difference in muscle spindle versus surrounding muscle fiber tension, explains why some experiments show that people feel everything feels lighter than normal (Luu 2009), possibly even causing sensations of floating. Furthermore, at this same time, even though the surrounding paralyzed muscle fibers do not move in response to immense mental effort, muscle spindles may well contract, so producing sensations of illusory movements (Gandevia 1993).

[9.46]After the passage of some more time, the muscle spindles are also paralyzed by curare, cease their activity and send no more signals to the brain. This generates the well-known effects of partial paralysis expressed as more mental effort being required to produce movements. Furthermore, people affected by these drugs perceive body parts as heavier than normal, as well as experiencing abnormal perceptions of the positions of partly paralyzed body parts (McCloskey 1978). Some people partially paralyzed by curare report feeling a "tightness around the chest", or feeling that something heavy is pressing on their chests (Prescott 1946). A feeling of suffocation due to curare-induced respiratory insufficiency causing carbon dioxide accumulation may exacerbate this feeling of tightness, or of a great weight (Gandevia 1993). Aaron Kopman and his colleagues described the following experiences and observations of the effects of partial paralysis with a curare-like drug (Mivacurium).

> [9.47]*At TOF ratios <0.75, all subjects were uncomfortable. Most reported that speaking required great effort and that swallowing was becoming difficult. Most found it impossible to sip water through a straw because they could not maintain a tight seal with their lips. Finally, all subjects at this level of block had the same "flat" expression. We believe that this was a reflection of significant involvement of the facial muscles. (Kopman 1997)*

[9.48]These are the sensations of partial and total paralysis due to curare, and curare-like drugs.

Curare and conscious sleep paralysis

[9.49]Many of the sensations produced by curare are similar to those described by people during conscious sleep paralysis. We are all familiar with the dreams we call nightmares. During sleep, the body is paralyzed; otherwise we would move and act out our dreams. But some people awaken, and find themselves still paralyzed, because the paralysis of sleep did not disappear synchronously with the return of consciousness (Liddon 1967, Mahowald 1990). This is called "conscious sleep paralysis", and about one in twenty persons, and possibly more, experiences one or more episodes of sleep paralysis during their lifetime

(Browne-Goode 1962, Cheyne 2004). Episodes of conscious sleep paralysis are not only associated with the unpleasant feelings of paralysis, but are also frequently associated with hallucinations of "sensed presence", where the experiencer feels the proximity or presence of someone, known or unknown, or even that of entities such as the "incubus", or the "succubus" (Cheyne 2004, Cheyne 2005, Lorenzi 2004, Sharpless 2010). But sensed presence of intruders, demons, evil beings , succubi, or incubi, are not the only hallucinations reported during conscious sleep paralysis. Many people also report undergoing out-of-body experiences during conscious sleep paralysis (Cheyne 2004, Cheyne 2005, Sharpless 2010).

[9.50]Henry Guy de Maupassant (1850-1893) was a prolific French writer. He wrote one of the most dramatic and harrowing descriptions of conscious sleep paralysis combined with a nightmarish sensed presence in his short story, "The Horla".

> [9.51]*I sleep—a long time—two or three hours perhaps—then a dream—no—a nightmare lays hold on me. I feel that I am in bed and asleep—I feel it and I know it—and I feel also that somebody is coming close to me, is looking at me, touching me, is getting on to my bed, is kneeling on my chest, is taking my neck between his hands and squeezing it—squeezing it with all his might in order to strangle me.*
>
> *I struggle, bound by that terrible powerlessness which paralyzes us in our dreams; I try to cry out—but I cannot; I want to move—I cannot; I try, with the most violent efforts and out of breath, to turn over and throw off this being which is crushing and suffocating me—I cannot!*
>
> *And then suddenly I wake up, shaken and bathed in perspiration; I light a candle and find that I am alone, ... (Maupassant 1903, "The Horla")*

[9.52]Such unexpected paralysis is terrifying. People experience fear and anxiety because they find themselves unable to move or shout. All these are sensations and perceptions aroused by the muscle paralysis of sleep in dreaming, awake, or half awake persons. And these are the same sensations induced by paralysis due to curare, or curare-like drugs.

Curare and the soul

[9.53]The bodily and experiential effects of curare provide a number of profound lessons relevant to this study of the true nature of the conscious mind. These lessons are not immediately apparent, but become evident when applying physiological principles to the mind-models of dualism and materialism.

Submission to chemical reality

[9.54]Curare does not affect consciousness or the functioning of the mind. Instead, curare uncouples the brain from the body, by blocking the signals from the brain to the voluntary muscles of the body. To consciously experience total paralysis due to curare, is to experience helpless imprisonment inside the body—to be locked inside the body—an experience of total submission to the chemical reality of the functioning of the body. Neither the conscious mind, or soul can bypass this chemical blockade of nerve signals to the voluntary muscles. So the effects of curare teach that regardless of its origin and nature, the conscious mind and the soul must use the mechanisms of the body to express its will in the physical world as speech, expressions, actions, and deeds.

Dualism and curare

[9.55]Brain function is unaffected by curare. Likewise, the functioning of the soul is also unaffected by curare. Nevertheless, when people are fully conscious, and their minds are evidently present within their bodies while paralyzed with curare, they do experience hallucinations of position, weight, and movement. These hallucinations are products of the effects of curare upon the sensory mechanisms of the body detecting sensations of position, weight, and movement (see 9.40-9.46. This implies that when the soul is evidently present within the physical body, the soul relies upon information from the senses of the body to perceive sensations of position, weight, and movement. However, descriptions of out-of-body experiences reveal something very interesting—they reveal that the apparently disembodied soul also senses position, weight, and movement in the physical world. Here is an example of just such perceptions reported by Margot Grey in her book, *Return from Death*. She reported an out-of-body experience occurring during the near-death experience of a student who nearly asphyxiated due to croup.

9.56My eyes were popping out of my head and I was aware I was being asphyxiated. I can remember trying to rouse my sister who was asleep in the same room with me, but as I couldn't breathe this wasn't possible. I told myself to relax and accept that I was unable to breathe and just lay there waiting to die. By this time I was unable to close my eyes. Then I realised that I was starting to move upwards towards the ceiling and I thought I was going to bang myself on the ceiling at any minute and turned to avoid hitting the ceiling and as I did so I saw myself lying on the bed and I thought I looked very ill, terrible with great bags under my eyes. I felt weightless and I somehow moved through the ceiling which was no longer important. I was aware of going faster and faster. (pages 38-39 in Grey 1985)

9.57This account reveals that the disembodied soul of this person felt sensations of: moving upwards, turning, seeing his body at a distance from the point of observation, feeling weightless, moving faster and faster. Other examples of out-of-body experiences where apparently disembodied souls remember feeling sensations of position, weight, and movement are scattered throughout this book (see 1.38, 1.48, 1.51, 10.36). All these accounts contain clear descriptions of sensations of position, weight, and movement in this physical world. According to the mind-model of dualism, such sensations of position, weight, and movement cannot originate within the body, because the soul is separated from the body during an out-of-body experience, and is supposedly unaffected by anything affecting the physical substance of the body (see 1.66-1.75). Therefore, sensations of position, weight, and movement sensed by the disembodied soul clearly imply that the immaterial soul also possesses parallel non-physical sensory systems capable of providing the soul with these sensations during periods of disembodiment. When you think about it, the concept of a soul able to sense position, weight, and movement in this physical world is rather strange—after all,the soul is unaffected by the physical world. So does all this mean that the disembodied soul can somehow sense gravity? Furthermore, does this idea of parallel immaterial organs capable of sensing position, weight, and movement correspond with any sort of physical or non-physical reality?

9.58A search of the medical literature reveals several reports of out-of-body experiences occurring during forms of general anesthesia in which curare and curare-like drugs were employed (see paragraphs 1.119, 10.36, 10.38, 10.45). These patients also experienced the changeable

247

effects of curare upon their perceptions of weight, movement and position. Accordingly, these physical sensations cannot be excluded as a cause of the sensations of weight, motion and position reported by these patients as they underwent their out-of-body experiences. Furthermore, other drugs employed during general anesthesia may also arouse out-of-body experiences. Accordingly, out-of-body experiences undergone during general anesthesia are not necessarily proof of disembodiment of a soul. Such experiences may also be products of the effects of anesthetic drugs on the brain. As a supplement to the effects of curare, the effects of local anesthesia reveal that the conscious mind, regardless of whether it is embodied or disembodied, only perceives sensations of position, weight, and movement with the physical senses of the body (see Chapter 11). Combine these facts with the proven reality that the soul has no ability to form memories—as is clearly described in several chapters of this book—so even if the soul could separate from the body, it would be unable to remember what it experienced while disembodied. All these facts indicate dualism fails to explain the experiential aspects of out-of-body experiences undergone while under the influence of curare administered as a component of general anesthesia.

Materialism and curare

[9.59]Sensations aroused by curare include illusory movements and sensations of disembodiment. Therefore, during a period of awareness during general anesthesia, these sensations need not only be products of the effects of other anesthetic drugs, but may also be illusory perceptions due to the effects of curare on the functioning of muscle spindles.

[9.60]Finally, the above discussion teaches that materialism is clearly the more parsimonious and better explanation of all observations. It explains all subjective and objective aspects of experiences aroused by the administration of curare—alone—or in combination with other anesthetic drugs. All these things mean that the brain is the generator and vehicle of the mind, and relies upon the physical senses of the body for all sensations of position, weight, and movement, as well as sensations of disembodiment. Sensations of disembodiment aroused by the effects of curare are illusions and hallucinations due to misinterpretation of sensations generated by physical bodily sensors affected by curare. This is the lesson of curare.

10

Awareness

[10.1]Anesthesiologists monitor many different body functions during general anesthesia to determine whether the patients under their care are in good physical condition. They administer extra doses of different types of drugs when required to provide extra muscle paralysis, pain relief, or to adjust the depth of anesthesia, while at the same time ensuring that patients under their care remain unconscious. Nonetheless, despite all this, some people do awaken to experience some form of awareness, or actual full conscious awareness during general anesthesia. Some reports of unrecognized full conscious awareness during general anesthesia are truly horrible.

[10.2]*My first reaction to this was an irrational surge of fear and panic and the absolutely desperate necessity to move. I felt I had to insert some of my own will on the situation. The closest parallel I can think of is of being in a coffin, having been buried alive. It was only then that I realized I didn't have a body to move. I searched for my feet, and couldn't find them. I nevertheless made a massive effort to move my nonexistent right foot—I didn't realize that I had succeeded until a voice about 10 feet away (i.e. near my feet) said: "She's moving her toes, it's time you got her to sleep." I immediately realized that what I had done was to invite more pancuronium [a muscle paralyzing drug similar to curare], and I made no further attempt to move (until after the pain started). I somehow felt I should conserve any power to move that I still had. I remained in this state of mind (horizontal and supine) but otherwise totally dissociated, without any body image; continuously filled with fear, listening to every word, every sound in the theatre, quite compos mentis and fully appreciating my position. One pint of beer would have dulled my mind more than the "anaesthetic". (Anonymous editorial 1979)*

^{10.3}This was part of the dreadful experience of an anesthesiologist who was fully conscious as she underwent a cesarean section performed under general anesthesia. Many people have heard similar stories of people who awoke during an operation performed under general anesthesia. Some of these are horrific tales similar to that of this woman—stories of people who awaken during surgery to find themselves unable to move or speak, yet conscious and aware, and fully able to feel the dreadful pain of the operation they are undergoing. Such experiences rival the torments of the damned in hell as are so gloatingly described in some holy books.

^{10.4}Reports of consciousness, or awareness occurring during general anesthesia are generally called: awareness experiences, unintended or unintentional intraoperative awareness, or anesthetic awareness. The term consciousness is usually omitted, because people must be conscious in order to be aware. General anesthesia is not one single technique, but the result of a wide range of drugs and drug combinations. Indeed, an apocryphal remark by an anesthesiologist about the wide range of drugs and substances with which general anesthesia can be administered states, "You can even administer anesthesia with airplane glue, as long as you know what you are doing!" The result of this diversity is that several different types of awareness experiences may occur during general anesthesia. Nevertheless, regardless of the nature of these differing awareness experiences, the question remains of how it is possible for people to be conscious and aware under supposedly adequate general anesthesia. Part of the answer lies in the differences between individuals, as well as the types of surgery.

Sensitivity to anesthetic drugs varies

^{10.5}Anesthetic drug doses and anesthetic drug concentrations used in anesthesia are averages. For some reason, many people do not apply normal common sense to anesthetic drugs. However, you can always view it in the same way as you view the height of people. For example, the average height of American men is 5 feet 10 inches (178 cm). But this does not mean ALL American men are exactly 5 feet 10 inches tall, and not one fraction of an inch taller or shorter. There are many men taller than 5 feet 10 inches, and many men are shorter than 5 feet 10 inches. Everyone understands this reality. Clinical experience and laboratory studies reveal that this same concept of averages is also true for anesthetic drug doses, as well as anesthetic gas concentrations. Not

everyone manifests a certain response to a drug at exactly the same dose or blood concentration of a drug. A large group manifests a certain response at an average dose or blood concentration of a drug, but there is considerable variation above and below this average.

[10.6]Reasons for these differences between individual sensitivities to anesthetic drugs vary from age of patients, gender differences, genetic differences, the effects of concurrent diseases, as well as prior abuse of alcohol or other drugs (ASA 2006, Orser 2008). Furthermore, different types of surgery also have an influence. For example, a person undergoing a painful major operation generally requires a higher opiate dosage, than does a person undergoing a minor and less painful operation. These differences mean that some people may well be awake while under presumably adequate general anesthesia (Avidan 2008).

Awareness and types of general anesthesia

[10.7]As mentioned earlier, general anesthesia is not a single technique, with only one drug, or only one drug mixture, with standard predictable effects. Many different drugs are used to induce and maintain general anesthesia, and there are many different ways of using the same drugs and drug combinations. Furthermore, techniques of general anesthesia and anesthetic drugs have continuously evolved and changed since the first demonstration of general anesthesia with ether by William Morton in 1846. Modern anesthesiologists administer different types of general anesthesia tailored to fit the requirements of each patient. Furthermore, different patients managed by the same anesthesiologist, may receive very different anesthetic drugs, and different techniques of general anesthesia for the same operation. As if this were not enough variation, different anesthesiologists may employ very different general anesthetic techniques on patients undergoing the same operation.

[10.8]Insights and research result in continual evolution of anesthetic techniques. Just as with all other branches of medicine, continual evolution of insights sometimes result in popular systems of general anesthesia, making a saying of the eminent German surgeon, August Bier (1861-1949), very applicable to anesthesia.

[10.9]*The practice of medicine is like a woman's boudoir. It changes with fashion. (page 103 in Vogeler 1942)*

[10.10]Nonetheless, despite the continual evolution of general anesthetic techniques, some remarks can be made about which groups of patients and techniques are associated with a higher risk of awareness.

- [10.11]The "Liverpool Technique". This was a system of general anesthesia named after the city of Liverpool in the United Kingdom. It was a popular system of anesthesia used in the United Kingdom and Australia during the 1950's until the late 1970's. Patients were hyperventilated with only a mixture of oxygen and nitrous oxide, received minimal amounts of opiates, and no anesthetic vapors. This system of anesthesia was associated with an incidence of awareness in the region of 2% to 4% (Ghoneim 1992).
- [10.12]General anesthesia for cesarean section is associated with a higher than normal incidence of awareness in the mothers. There is a reason for this high incidence of awareness. Drugs administered to induce and maintain general anesthesia in the mother, cross the placenta and also affect the as yet unborn baby. This is why babies are in better condition after delivery by cesarean section performed under spinal or epidural anesthesia, than babies delivered under general anesthesia (Gordon 2005). But sometimes clinical necessity requires that cesarean section be performed under general anesthesia. So anesthesiologists attempt to balance the requirement of general anesthesia for the mother, with the necessity to give the child as little anesthesia as possible. The result is that patients undergoing cesarean section under general anesthesia have a high incidence of awareness ranging from about 2.5% up to 25% (Ghoneim 1992).
- [10.13]General anesthesia for cardiac surgery has its own special requirements. All anesthetic drugs further depress the functioning of an already malfunctioning heart. So anesthesiologists always try to use combinations of drugs causing as little depression of heart function as possible. This usually translates into a higher chance of awareness during general anesthesia administered for cardiac operations varying between 1% to as high as 23% depending upon the general anesthetic technique employed (Ghoneim 1992, Phillips 1993).
- [10.14]General anesthesia for injured or very sick people is a problem. All anesthetic drugs depress, or impair the functioning of the heart as well as the ability of the body to maintain an adequate blood pressure. This problem is accentuated by severe, life threatening

Awareness

medical disorders, loss of blood, and injuries. Therefore anesthesiologists tend to reduce the doses and concentrations of anesthetic drugs in such cases so as to sustain blood pressure and heart function. Unfortunately, this delicate balance between the requirement for general anesthesia, and the low blood pressure and reduced heart function caused by injury and concurrent disease, results in a chance of awareness varying from 11% up to 43% (Ghoneim 1992).

[10.15]This list tells us that certain types of surgery are more likely to be associated with anesthetic awareness. Furthermore, the clinical situation of seriously injured and sick people means that only lower concentrations and doses of anesthetic drugs can be administered without causing death or disability. People also differ from each other, which is why different persons undergoing exactly the same operation with the same general anesthetic technique, may have widely differing anesthetic drug requirements. A combination of these factors, combined with the great variety of general anesthetic techniques and drugs, the variation in general anesthetic drugs and techniques between different hospitals and anesthesiologists, all explain why people who awaken while apparently unconscious under general anesthesia may report very different types of awareness experiences.

Different types of awareness experiences

[10.16]Indeed, the experience of awareness during general anesthesia has several forms. Many experiences of awareness during general anesthesia are fragmentary and dreamlike, and not all of those reporting awareness describe feeling pain at the time. Some people describe a period of complete awareness during general anesthesia. Yet others describe ecstatic experiences. A few people report undergoing out-of-body experiences, and there are even a few rare cases of people reporting undergoing near-death experiences while under general anesthesia (Errando 2008, Orser 2008, Pollard 2007, Ranta 1998, Sandin 2000, Samuelsson 2007, Sebel 2004).

[10.17]Any understanding of these different experiences of anesthetic awareness requires a basic knowledge of the drugs used during general anesthesia. Since the introduction of curare into anesthesia in the 1940's, anesthesiologists frequently administer general anesthesia with three basic groups of drugs.

253

- [10.18]Sleep-inducing drugs and anesthetic gases are used to keep people asleep and remove all memory of events occurring during the operation. These drugs also affect mental function at doses and blood concentrations insufficient to induce loss of consciousness (see Chapters 6 & 7).
- [10.19]Muscle paralyzing drugs are administered to paralyze all the muscles of the body. These muscle paralyzing drugs only paralyze the muscles of the body, but do not affect the functioning of the brain, which is why a person can be paralyzed by these drugs but fully conscious (see Chapter 9).
- [10.20]Opiates are administered during general anesthesia remove the pain of operations. Opiates affect mental function and induce pain relief at doses and blood concentrations insufficient to cause loss of consciousness (see Chapter 8).

[10.21]Combinations of different concentrations of these three different groups of drugs explain the horrific experiences, the partially conscious experiences, the fully conscious experiences, as well as the sometimes even wondrous conscious experiences of people under general anesthesia. So what are these different experiences?

- [10.22]*The person was awake, was able to move, but felt no pain.* These people have adequate concentrations of painkilling drugs in their body, but insufficient concentrations of muscle paralyzing or sleep-inducing drugs in their bodies.
- [10.23]*The person was awake, was unable to move, but felt no pain.* These people have adequate concentrations of painkilling and muscle paralyzing drugs in their bodies, but are awake because of insufficient concentrations of sleep-inducing drugs in their brains.
- [10.24]*The person was awake, was able to move, and felt the pain of the operation.* These people have inadequate concentrations of all three groups of drugs in their bodies.
- [10.25]*The person was awake, felt the pain of the operation, but was unable to move, speak, or do anything.* This is due to inadequate brain concentrations of sleep-inducing and painkilling drugs, but the person is still paralyzed by the muscle paralyzing drug. It is a terrible situation—like the torments of hell visited upon the living. This is a disaster, a situation that all anesthesiologists dread having happen with their patients. Usually this situation is immediately recognized and appropriately dealt with, but some people react so minimally to

the pain of their operations that the situation is not recognized. These people then suffer the torments of the damned. Profoundly upsetting to the patients and the anesthesiologists—horrible … This was the experience of the woman cited at the beginning of this chapter (see 10.2).

[10.26]Accounts of experiences of unintentional awareness during general anesthesia clearly reveal these facts. For example, an 82 year old woman reported an experience of unintentional awareness during a gallbladder operation performed under general anesthesia. Her experience clearly reveals the effects of therapeutic and subanesthetic concentrations of the drugs administered to provide general anesthesia.

[10.27]*Heard discussions, felt something done in her stomach; recurring pressure of blood pressure cuff on her arm; no pain (Case 5, Ranta 1998)*

[10.28]This woman was conscious and aware, because she reported hearing the discussions occurring about her—meaning that the concentrations of anesthetic drugs in her brain were too low to induce loss of consciousness. She felt the surgical manipulations inside her body, but felt no pain, because the concentrations of analgesic drugs in her brain were evidently sufficient to block the pain of surgery. She did not report anxiety—indicating that the therapeutic concentrations of opiates, and the subanesthetic concentrations of drugs used to induce loss of consciousness induced their characteristic anxiolytic effect. Therefore, this episode of unintentional intraoperative awareness reveals the fact of consciousness, as well as the subjective and objective effects of subanesthetic brain concentrations of drugs administered to provide general anesthesia.

Transcendence and ecstasy during anesthetic awareness

[10.29]Some people report undergoing transcendental and ecstatic experiences during unintentional awareness during general anesthesia. Such experiences are hardly surprising when one considers the mental effects of subanesthetic brain concentrations of many drugs used to administer general anesthesia (see discussions in Chapters 6, 7, 8). For example, opiates are known to cause cognitive, affective, and transcendental experiences in some people (see Chapter 8). Consider the effects of opium as poetically described by Thomas De Quincey in his classic work, *Confessions of an English Opium-Eater* published in 1821.

^{10.30}The sense of space, and in the end the sense of time, were both powerfully affected. Buildings, landscapes, etc., were exhibited in proportions so vast as the bodily eye is not fitted to receive. Space swelled, and was amplified to an extent of unutterable infinity. This, however, did not disturb me so much as the vast expansion of time; I sometimes seemed to have lived for 70 or 100 years in one night—nay, sometimes had feelings representative of a millennium passed in that time, or, however, of a duration far beyond the limits of any human experience.

The minutest incidents of childhood, or forgotten scenes of later years, were often revived: I could not be said to recollect them, for if I had been told of them when waking, I should not have been able to acknowledge them as parts of my past experience. But placed as they were before me, in dreams like intuitions, and clothed in all their evanescent circumstances and accompanying feelings, I recognised them instantaneously. (pages 69-70 in Quincey 1823)

^{10.31}These are also the effects of the morphine like drugs used in anesthesia, because opium is no more than a morphine containing gum extracted from poppies. Modern anesthesiologists usually first inject a dose of a morphine-like drug such as morphine, pethidine, fentanyl, sufentanil, remifentanil, etc, prior to inducing sleep with another drug. What they and I notice is that while some patients report unpleasant sensation, others feel fantastic, or even wonderful. These are the same cognitive, affective, and transcendental experiences as reported by Thomas De Quincey, and by all opiate addicts.

^{10.32}And then there are other people who report similar experiences during anesthesia. During 1980 a young physician Ernst Rodin reported his experiences while undergoing general anesthesia for diagnosis of possible lung cancer, tuberculosis, or cancer elsewhere in his body. He confessed to being anxious, and told that he would prefer to die on the operating table if he had cancer.

^{10.33}I remember lying down on the operating table, the needle for the anesthetic being placed into my arm, and directing a last request to the Deity: "If it is a metastasis, please let me stay on the table." The next thing I knew was a feeling of tremendous bliss accompanied by the knowledge, "It was a metastasis; I have died and now I am free." There were no other sensory experiences, only absolute certainty: "It's over and it's wonderful." There was no shadow of a doubt that this was,

*indeed, death rather than just near-death. The next event was my
utter shock and dismay at finding myself in a hospital bed with my
wife standing over me. (Rodin 1980)*

[10.34]This was a dramatic and extremely profound experience, indelibly
inscribed in his memory. The exact cause of such experiences is unlikely
to be exclusively pharmacological. Such reports actually reveal how
pharmacological and psychological effects combine to produce
individual awareness experiences during general anesthesia.

Out-of-body experiences during anesthetic awareness

[10.35]Out-of-body experiences are one of the most remarkable
experiences reported by some people after awakening from general
anesthesia. People who undergo such out-of-body experiences
sometimes report hearing actual conversations occurring at the time, as
well as other visual and auditory details, at a time they were apparently
unconscious under general anesthesia. When I reviewed the
anesthesiology literature dealing with awareness during general
anesthesia, I found several references to out-of-body experiences during
general anesthesia (case 10 in Mainzer 1979, cases 5 and 6 in Moerman
1993, case 4 in Sebel 2004). These are often described in a rather
summary fashion.

[10.36]*The patient reported an "out-of-body experience" at some
point during the surgery with her floating out of her body and
watching the surgery from above. She thought it was very
"weird." She thought frequently about it. (Case 4 in Sebel 2004)*

[10.37]During 1994, a young woman once told me of an out-of-body
experience she underwent during a nose operation for which I
administered general anesthesia. Her experience also contained veridical
aspects indicating she truly was conscious at the time.

[10.38]*She told me that she awoke during her nose operation. She
saw her body as it lay upon the operating table, as if she was
standing outside her body in a position at the right-hand side of
the foot of the operating table. She realized it was she who lay
upon the operating table, but felt no alarm or consternation upon
realizing that she was apparently standing outside her body. She
saw the surgeon operating upon her nose, but felt neither the
operation, nor any pain from the operation. She saw the assistant
of the surgeon. She saw the anesthetic assistant sitting next to the*

anesthetic machine located at the left hand side of her body. And she remarked that she could not see the faces of any of these people.

[10.39]This report fascinated me, because I finally had an account of an out-of-body experience where I knew all the circumstances surrounding the reported observations. So what happened to this woman before, during, and after her operation? She was fully conscious when brought into the operating theater. General anesthesia was induced. Her blood pressure, blood oxygen content, heartbeat, as well as the concentrations of inhaled, and exhaled oxygen, carbon dioxide, nitrous oxide and anesthetic gases were continually measured. She was aroused from the general anesthetic upon completion of the operation. We brought her to the recovery room only after she was fully conscious. And there she reported undergoing a short out-of-body experience during her operation.

[10.40]Her blood pressure, blood oxygen concentration, and blood carbon dioxide concentration remained normal throughout the operation. No-one in the operating theater observed anything unusual during the operation. No-one saw her soul standing next to the operating table. Her body remained upon the operating table during the operation. She could not move, breathe, or speak during the operation, because she had received a curare-like drug that almost totally paralyzed all the muscles of her body, and was being mechanically ventilated through a tube placed between her vocal cords. But shortly before the end of the operation, when the effects of all the drugs she received were partly worn off, she made slight movements of her arms and legs. So, just in case she was awake, the anesthetic assistant promptly administered an extra dose of a powerful sleep inducing drug. Otherwise there was no reason to think she was conscious at any time during the operation. She was only capable of speaking after she awoke from the general anesthetic.

[10.41]The observations she made during her out-of-body experience were correct. But physical sensory and mental functions explained all her observations. She was fully conscious when brought into, and out of the operating theatre, so she saw the people in the operating theatre, their clothing, the instruments, and the anesthetic machine at the left hand side of the operating table. She saw all these things before, and after her operation. She was apparently conscious for a short time at the moment when she moved slightly. But at that moment, her eyes were taped shut, while her brain and the rest of her body were still affected by the local and general anesthetic drugs she had received. So she felt no pain from the operation she was undergoing, nor was she able to speak and tell people what was happening at that moment. In fact she did not even think of speaking during the experience. Curare-like muscle paralyzing drugs can cause people to lose the sense of body image (Topulos 1993). The effects of subanesthetic concentrations of general anesthetic drugs, combined with this known effect of the curare-like drug she had received, caused her sense of body position to function abnormally. So she interpreted her abnormal sensory nerve signals in such a way that she perceived herself as being outside her body, as well as generating an autoscopic hallucination. Finally, she was able to spontaneously recall her experience after awakening.

[10.42]Out-of-body experiences during anesthesia are remarkable experiences. Nonetheless, careful analysis reveals that even these apparently paranormal experiences are explicable with the pharmacological effects of anesthetic drugs and physiology.

Near-death experiences during anesthetic awareness

[10.43]Even more remarkably, some people report undergoing near-death experiences during general anesthesia. These are profound, often life changing experiences. Such experiences are rarely reported in scientific anesthesiology literature. They are mainly found in popular books on near-death experiences. This does not mean these experiences are any less real or profound. It just means they are less likely to be subjected to rigorous scientific analysis, often to be dismissed as "hysterical attention seeking fantasies", or relegated to the terrain of "new age" cranks and gullible believers in all manner of weird and fantastical things. This is a pity, because many of these experiences are well worth studying, simply because they tell us more about the functioning of the human body under some circumstances.

[10.44]One near-death experience occurring during a well documented general anesthetic was reported during 2006. A 15 year old boy reported undergoing a near-death experience when 12 years old during an operation performed under combined general and epidural anesthesia. His experience was a typical near-death experience together with an out-of-body experience.

[10.45] *'I was sleeping and suddenly I felt awake and had the impression that I was leaving my body through my head. I could see from above my whole body lying on the back on the operating table, (on request he answered that his body had no deformities)*

259

and surrounded by many doctors. I felt as being above my physical body and I was lying face down. I was like a spirit without my own arms and legs, and I was floating under the ceiling of the room. Initially, while feeling detached from my real body (which was lying on the operating table), I felt a little bit scared and weird, but then I had a sensation of lightness and I felt relaxed and comfortable. I had the impression that everything was real. I distinguished the operating room and the surgeons. I then saw a dark tunnel in front of me and I felt attracted to it. I passed through the tunnel very fast and at its end I saw a bright light that did not hurt my eyes. As I was passing through the tunnel, I heard noises which sounded like when you are watching TV without a program, then these noises became voices. Suddenly I felt again attracted to my body (which was still lying on the operating table), in which I went again through my head. (Lopez 2006)

[10.46]This is an amazing experience, which many would even consider paranormal. However, those reporting this episode performed a thorough analysis confirming the possible medical and physiological origins of the experiences reported by this boy.

[10.47]All these things indicate the diversity of experiences of unintentional awareness during general anesthesia. But how common are experiences of unintentional awareness during general anesthesia, and what are the relative frequencies of the different types of awareness experience?

How common are different types of awareness?

[10.48]Unintentional awareness during general anesthesia is rare. This fact necessitates large scale prospective studies to reveal the true incidence, and the relative frequencies of different types of awareness experience. However, there are very few publications of large scale prospective studies of awareness—a fact necessitating a meta-analysis, which is an analysis of the combined results of several smaller studies.

[10.49]A meta-analysis of various prospective studies reveals the incidence of unintentional awareness in adults undergoing general anesthesia for non-cardiac surgery, as well as the relative frequencies of different types of awareness. This meta-analysis reveals that 132 out of 40,654 (0.32% = 3.2:1000) adult patients report unintentional awareness during general anesthesia (data from: Errando 2008, Ranta 1998, Sebel 2004, Sandin 2000, Samuelsson 2007). Of these 132 persons reporting unintentional awareness experiences during general anesthesia, the relative frequencies of the different types of awareness experiences were:

- [10.50]39.3% (52/132) were aware, experienced anxiety, and felt pain.
- [10.51]19% (25/132) were aware, experienced anxiety, but felt no pain.
- [10.52]41% (54/132) were aware, but experienced no anxiety or pain.
- [10.53]0.7% (1/132) was aware, felt no anxiety or pain, and underwent an out-of-body experience.

[10.54]This meta-analysis reveals that contrary to popular belief, about 60%, or most people feel no pain during an episode of unintentional awareness while under general anesthesia. So how do these statistics translate to the situation in the USA, where we know that about 20 million people underwent general anesthesia during 2004? This meta-analysis tells us that about 3.2 people per 1000 undergo an awareness experience during general anesthesia, which means up to 64,000 people will have experienced some form of unintentional awareness while undergoing general anesthesia administered for non-cardiac surgery in the USA during 2004.

- [10.55]39.3% of these 64,000 persons experienced pain with, or without anxiety during their period of awareness, which means about 25,152 people had such an awareness experience in the USA during 2004.
- [10.56]19% of these 64,000 persons experienced anxiety, but without feeling pain during their period of awareness, which means about 12,160 people had such an awareness experience in the USA during 2004.
- [10.57]41% of these 64,000 persons experienced feelings of calm indifference and no pain during their period of awareness, which means about 26,240 people had such an awareness experience in the USA during 2004.
- [10.58]0.7% of these 64,000 persons underwent an out-of-body experience without feeling pain during their period of awareness, which means about 448 people had such an awareness experience in the USA during 2004.

[10.59]These can only ever be approximate statistics, but do reveal, that significant numbers of people undergo experiences of unintentional awareness under general anesthesia each year in the USA. Extrapolate these figures to the whole world, and you realize that each year, large numbers of people undergo all manner of unintentional awareness experiences while under general anesthesia. Interestingly, such statistics also reveal that worldwide, considerable numbers of people undergo out-of-body experiences during periods of awareness under general anesthesia each year. Very curiously, we hear very little of these experiences. This raises the question of whether many people do not report such experiences for fear of being considered insane.

Psychological consequences of awareness

[10.60]Some people report suffering psychological after-effects varying from minor to severe after undergoing experiences of unintentional awareness during general anesthesia. But does a period of unintentional awareness always cause such mental distress that people inevitably develop significant psychopathology? Large scale retrospective studies of awareness all indicate that awareness experiences are dreadful, and almost invariably associated with pain and distress (Mashour 2010, Domino 2012). A large scale retrospective study to determine the psychological sequelae of these experiences, reported an incidence of psychological sequelae in 52% of patients reporting awareness, and late psychological consequences in 22% (Ghoneim 2009). Dr. Moerman (1993) reported a very good retrospective study of 26 patients referred for further investigation of experiences of unintentional awareness during general anesthesia (Moerman 1993). He found that 70% of these patients suffered shorter and longer term psychological aftereffects. Most interestingly, examination of the anesthetic records of 12 of these 26 patients by independent anesthesiologist assessors who did not know whether they were examining the charts of those reporting, or those not reporting awareness experiences, revealed that a possibility, or suspicion of anesthetic awareness, was evident in the anesthetic chart of only one of these 12 patients (Moerman 1993). This latter finding confirms the experience of most anesthesiologists—the occurrence of awareness during apparently adequate general anesthesia is usually only discovered after the persons concerned awaken and are in a condition to report their experiences.

[10.61]Large scale prospective studies of awareness during general anesthesia, after which people reporting awareness experiences are specifically followed up to determine psychological sequelae are uncommon. Such studies are exacting and time consuming. However, data from several such prospective studies do reveal that of 40 patients with confirmed unintentional awareness during general anesthesia, only 12 (30%) reported shorter and longer term psychological aftereffects (Errando 2008, Lennmarken 2002, Wennervirta 2002). This is very different from the 52-72% of people reporting shorter and long-term psychological aftereffects in retrospective studies of self-reported unintentional awareness experiences (Domino 2012, Ghoneim 2009, Kent 2013, Moerman 1993). This difference indicates a bias in retrospective studies of self-reported awareness experiences, undoubtedly caused by the fact that people are more likely to report unintentional anesthetic awareness experienced as painful and horrible, than people who underwent pain-free experiences of awareness in a state of calm indifference (Kent 2013, Lennmarken 2007). All this means that any study of the true incidence of psychological aftereffects of unintentional awareness during general anesthesia, requires prospective studies, and not data from retrospective self-reporting of experiences.

Detecting awareness during general anesthesia

[10.62]Detection of possible consciousness in a person under general anesthesia is not always easy. Some people are conscious and aware while under general anesthesia, yet give absolutely no indication of consciousness (Orser 2008). Absolute certain determination of the presence of consciousness in an unmoving, unresponsive, apparently unconscious person under general anesthesia is difficult. Many years ago, I heard one person colorfully comparing the difficulty of determining consciousness under these circumstances with the metaphor: "like trying to grab an eel in a bucket of snot." So unless the patient actually moves, there is no certain way to be absolutely sure a person is actually unconscious. This is why even now the mainstays of awareness detection during general anesthesia remain: suspicion, the bodily reactions of the person, and supplementation of these observations with diverse electronic monitors.

Clinical signs of awareness

[10.63]Anesthesiologists always carefully and regularly check the condition of the patients they manage under general anesthesia. They check to see whether the patients have an adequate circulating blood volume, whether the heart function and blood pressure are within acceptable limits, whether the oxygenation and respiration are adequate, and whether there are any signs of other problems such as inadequate anesthesia or awareness. Signs of possible awareness during general anesthesia are suspicion, plus any one or more of the following: movement, widened pupils, perspiration, rapid pulse, and elevation of blood pressure. However, these clinical signs of awareness under general anesthesia are also the same as those of inadequate general anesthesia, or other problems such as: sudden extra intense surgical pain, massive blood loss, or pre-existing psychological stress. Patients undergoing operations may move in response to surgical pain, or to signal awareness. So the anesthesiologist must always make a careful assessment of the likely causes of these signs from clinical experience, suspicion, assessment of the situation, supplemented where possible with other techniques.

[10.64]However, clinical assessment of consciousness is not infallible (Jensen 2004), because some people undergo periods of awareness during general anesthesia without anyone knowing, or even suspecting it until after the operation (Moerman 1993). This is why clinical monitoring is often supplemented with other monitoring techniques of the level of consciousness.

Isolated forearm technique

[10.65]The isolated forearm technique is an effective clinical method to detect whether a person is awake under general anesthesia. The technique is essentially very simple. After induction of general anesthesia, but before injecting any muscle paralyzing drugs, a pneumatic tourniquet is inflated around an upper arm to a pressure of about 200-250 millimeters of mercury (mmHg). This effectively stops any subsequently injected muscle paralyzing drugs from entering and paralyzing the arm. Sensation and muscle power in the arm remains for up to 20 minutes before lack of oxygen in the arm causes nerve and muscle malfunction (Tunstall 1977). A modification of the technique is to deflate the tourniquet after 15-20 minutes, after which sufficient muscle power often remains to allow a patient to signal awareness (Wang 1995). Awake and aware persons under general anesthesia can move and signal with this non-paralyzed arm when requested. For example, a person who is apparently unconscious under general anesthesia can be requested to respond by squeezing the hand of the researcher three times for a "yes" response, and two times for a "no" response if actually conscious. Many other combinations of responses are thinkable, as long as they are responses uneqivocally requiring conscious effort (Andrade 2008, Baraka 1989, Byers 1997, Gaitini 1995, Russell 2001, Wilson

1980). And indeed this does happen, making the isolated forearm technique one of the most reliable methods of detecting unintentional and intentional awareness in persons undergoing general anesthesia (Russell 1995).

Electronic detection of awareness

[10.66]Suspicion, experience, and reactions of the person's body to surgery are now often supplemented with electronic monitors purporting to accurately measure the level of consciousness, or depth of anesthesia. Unfortunately, none of these highly advanced pieces of electronics is absolutely accurate. This is why some people experience awareness during general anesthesia, even though these devices may indicate they were unconscious (Avidan 2008, Avidan 2009, Bruhn 2006, Drummond 2000, Messner 2003). So while professional associations of anesthesiologists in all countries acknowledge the utility of these measures of consciousness, they never recommend they be absolutely relied upon to determine the absence or presence of consciousness. Instead they encourage anesthesiologists to use these devices together with experience and clinical insights, supplemented with common sense, to gauge the likelihood of consciousness (ASA 2006, Jensen 2004, Pandit 2013).

Intentional awareness: The wake-up test

[10.67]Up till this point the discussion has been restricted to unintentional awareness experiences undergone during general anesthesia. But some experiences of awareness during general anesthesia are intentional. This may sound surprising, but intentional awareness is necessary during some forms of surgery performed under general anesthesia. Some young people require corrective surgery of abnormal curvatures (scoliosis) of their spines. Scoliosis surgery involves placing metal rods next to the spine. After anchoring these rods to the bones of the spine above and below the level of deformity, they are tensioned to stretch the misaligned bones of the spine in between, so correcting the alignment of the spine. Such stretching can also stretch the nerves and spinal cord contained within the spinal canal to such a degree, that paralysis of the legs occurs. Therefore, after tensioning the rods to realign the bones of the spine, tests are performed to determine the functioning of the possibly affected nerves and spinal cord.

[10.68]One of the standard tests used during such operations is the "wake-up test" (Dorgan 1984, Grottke 2004, Imani 2006). After tensioning the rods parallel to the spine, and while the extensive and large wounds in the back are still open, patients are aroused from general anesthesia, kept calm and pain free. At this time they usually have received such high doses of opiates that they are pain-free, but cannot breathe, and therefore receive artificial respiration with a machine. They are also unable to speak because of the tube in their trachea (windpipe) necessary to provide artificial respiration. Nonetheless, they are conscious. Patients are first asked to make purposeful hand movements in response to commands and questions, because the arms are not paralyzed by back surgery. For example, they may be asked to squeeze the hand of the investigator twice for a "yes" answer, and three times for a "no" answer. All variations on this type of yes-no questioning with hand movements are possible. Subsequently, the ability to purposefully move legs and feet on command proves the absence of paralysis due to excessive stretching of the spinal cord and nerves. General anesthesia is then recommenced and the operation completed. This is intentional awareness during general anesthesia.

Lessons from anesthetic awareness

[10.69]A person who says they were conscious during an operation performed under general anesthesia is not hysterical or insane. They may very well have been conscious. Careful study of each story, together with an analysis of the anesthetic chart and the surgical procedure, often reveals the time period during which the period of consciousness occurred, as well as the likely causes of the experience.

[10.70]Even so, some people report verifiable periods of awareness during general anesthesia without demonstrating any of the clinical signs of awareness. Some of these people may have even been continuously monitored with apparatus measuring the level of consciousness, and this apparatus may have indicated they were continually unconscious during general anesthesia. But in all such cases, people with verifiable accounts of awareness during general anesthesia were definitely conscious during their experiences, despite apparently adequate general anesthesia, and despite what any monitoring apparatus may have indicated at the time. This is the reality of clinical anesthesia. All such experiences are wonderful illustrations of the ways the functioning of the bodies of different individuals interact with the effects of surgery and anesthetic drugs.

[10.71]Observations made by people reporting their spontaneous, or accidental experiences of awareness during general anesthesia raise some fascinating questions. About 40% of people reporting undergoing an experience of unintentional intraoperative awareness during general anesthesia were neither anxious, nor felt any pain from the surgical procedure undergone at the time. Some people even report experiencing clear consciousness during awareness under general anesthesia, undergoing out-of-body experiences, as well as other cognitive, affective, paranormal, or transcendental experiences.

[10.72]Believers in dualism say that the soul is unaffected by drugs or anything affecting the functioning of the body, and that it expresses itself in this material world through the mechanisms of the body. However, during general anesthesia, the bodily mechanisms through which the soul expresses itself are supposedly inoperative due to the effects of anesthetic drugs upon the body. So according to the belief system of dualism, the actions of general anesthetic drugs upon the body, liberates the soul from limitations imposed by the filtering effect of the material substance of the body. And while thus liberated from the body, the soul can undergo amazing cognitive, affective, transcendental, and paranormal experiences revealing its true nature. These experiences are remembered by the soul, and subsequently related to other persons when the mechanisms of the body required for bodily consciousness and speech recover sufficiently after cessation of general anesthesia. Many believers in dualism claim this is the only possible explanation for these experiences, because these people were under general anesthesia, and therefore supposedly unconscious or incapable of clear consciousness due to the drugs used for general anesthesia. But is this a true explanation of the facts?

[10.73]Unfortunately, proponents of dualism nearly always ignore the fact that subanesthetic concentrations of anesthetic drugs do measurably alter the functioning of the brain. Indeed, subanesthetic concentrations of anesthetic drugs sometimes even induce apparently paranormal experiences. Examples of some of the mental effects of subanesthetic concentrations of anesthetic drugs and techniques are: calm indifference, absence of pain sensations, "clear" consciousness, inability to move, loss of body image, as well as other cognitive, affective, paranormal, and transcendental experiences. So do experiences of intraoperative awareness provide insights into the reality of the mind-models of dualism and materialism?

The isolated forearm technique and the soul

[10.74]The isolated forearm technique of detecting awareness during general anesthesia reveals something totally irreconcilable with the mind-model of dualism. According to proponents of dualism, the soul is continually conscious, even during general anesthesia (see 1.50-1.54). Furthermore, the conscious physical brain is controlled by the soul (see 1.55-1.65). Believers in dualism also claim that drugs used to provide general anesthesia only affect the functioning of the brain, but have no effect upon the soul (see 1.66-1.75). So the brains and bodies of people evidently manifesting consciousness with the isolated forearm technique are controlled by their souls.

[10.75]There are relatively few high quality published studies of the isolated forearm technique. So any study of the effects of this technique necessitates a meta-analysis of the published results. A meta-analysis of data from 423 persons included in several prospective isolated forearm studies reveals several fascinating and revealing facts (data from: Andrade 2008, Baraka 1989, Byers 1997, Gaitini 1995, Russell 2001, Tunstall 1977, Wilson 1980).

- [10.76]16.7% (71/423) of persons were unequivocally conscious and aware while undergoing surgery under general anesthesia.
- [10.77]Of these 71 persons discovered to be conscious during these studies, only 23 were questioned as to whether they felt pain while conscious and undergoing operation. Of these 23 persons 3, (3/23 = 13%), replied that they felt pain while unequivocally conscious and aware while undergoing surgery under general anesthesia.
- [10.78]2.8% (2/71) of persons remembered being conscious and aware, even though they were unequivocally conscious and aware while undergoing surgery under general anesthesia.

[10.79]Even though 16.7% of people are unequivocally conscious during general anesthesia, only 2.8% of these demonstrably conscious persons can actually remember being conscious. This failure to recall periods of awareness and conscious responses to commands during isolated forearm technique testing, has profound consequences for the popular belief in the mind-model of dualism. But how?

- $^{10.80}$Prior to taking part in these isolated forearm studies, participants were instructed beforehand as to the purpose of these studies. They also received instruction in the responses required of them, as well as how these responses would be requested. These instructions were given at a time these people were normally conscious, with normally functioning physical brains and normal memory function.

- $^{10.81}$Believers in dualism claim that the soul is the repository of all memories. So according to the mind-model of dualism, memories of these instructions are indelibly stored in the souls of the participants (see 1.92-1.115).

- $^{10.82}$Believers in dualism claim that the physical bodies of conscious and aware persons are under the control of their souls (see 1.55-1.65).

- $^{10.83}$Anesthetic drugs only exert their effects on the physical brain and body, and do not affect the functioning of the soul (see 1.66-1.75).

- $^{10.84}$The physical bodies of people are both conscious and aware when purposefully responding to instructions during testing with the isolated forearm technique, which means they are under the control of their souls at the time.

- $^{10.85}$Commands to elicit responses during isolated forearm studies are verbal. Participants hear these commands with their physical ears, and subsequently transmit these commands in some way to their souls. Subsequently the souls of these people transmit commands to their physical bodies to perform the desired actions with their isolated forearms (see 1.142).

- $^{10.86}$According to the mind-model of dualism, all these things mean that memories of the situation during the isolated forearm test, memories of the instructions, and the actions performed in response to these instructions, were all indelibly retained in the souls of those people who consciously responded.

- $^{10.87}$Physical brain function and memory functions, all return to normal after awakening and full recovery from general anesthesia. So after recovering from general anesthesia, participants are in a condition where they should be able to recall and express memories formed and retained in the soul while physically conscious and responding during the isolated forearm technique (see 1.143). Such memories are not memories of something so secret that the soul is forbidden to repeat, because the "material world is not yet ready for such revelations." Instead, recalling such memories is no different to recalling a telephone number, the date of a birthday, or where you ate yesterday evening. These memories are public knowledge and nothing secret.

• [10.88]Nevertheless, only 2.8% of people making conscious responses during isolated forearm studies can recall responding or even being conscious. But if memories are indelibly stored within the soul, then why can only 2.8% of persons spontaneously recall consciously responding to instructions during isolated forearm studies?

[10.89]Believers in the mind-model of dualism claim memory is an essential property of the soul (see Chapter 1, page 295 in Kelly 2007, see also 15.111). But the mind-model of dualism cannot explain amnesia for unequivocally proven periods of consciousness during isolated forearm studies. However, the mind-model of materialism readily explains results from the isolated forearm test as being due to the dose-related amnesic effects of anesthetic drugs on the formation and recall of memories within the physical brain (e.g. see for nitrous oxide 6.46-6.47, for ether 6.131, for thiopental 7.17, for propofol 7.29, for ketamine 7.45, for midazolam 7.53). Nevertheless, not all people have amnesia for the periods their minds were affected by anesthetic drugs. Materialism readily explains this fact with the well-known phenomenon of inter-individual variation in response to the effects of anesthetic drugs. But this repeatedly confirmed experimental result of amnesia for periods of purposeful conscious awareness during general anesthesia, is totally at variance with the mind-model of dualism. Amnesia for events, speech, actions, and deeds occurring while under the influence of subanesthetic doses and concentrations of drugs used for anesthesia proves memories are retained within the physical brain, and not in any separable human soul.

The wake-up test and the soul

[10.90]The wake-up test discussed earlier also has profound implications for belief in the reality of a human soul. Prior to undergoing spinal surgery to straighten a severe scoliosis, patients are instructed they will be awoken during the procedure, and asked to move their hands and feet to test the integrity of their spinal cord function after the spine has been straightened with tensioning rods. Prior to performing the wake-up test, gases and drugs to maintain an unconscious state are stopped, as are all muscle paralyzing drugs. High doses of opiates reduce anxiety and prevent these patients feeling any pain.

[10.91]A meta-analysis of 318 patients who underwent a wake-up test during spinal surgery performed under a wide variety of anesthetic techniques reveals that all 318 patients were awake and responded unequivocally to commands to move their hands and feet during their operations. Questioning of these 318 patients after completion of surgery, revealed that only 36 (11.3%) spontaneously recalled undergoing the wake-up test. Only two of these 36 persons remembered feeling any pain during the wake-up test, all others reporting feeling pain-free, calm, and composed while undergoing the test (data from: Blussé van Oud-Alblas 2008, Dorgan 1984, Grottke 2004, Kazemi 2006, McCann 2002, Seol 2012, Ting 2004). The difference of percentage recall between the isolated arm technique (2.8%), and the wake-up test (11.3%), is explained by the fact that anesthetic drug and gas concentrations are higher during the isolated forearm technique, so resulting in lower chance of recall.

[10.92]Materialism explains these observations with the amnesic effect of anesthetic drugs on the formation of memories within the physical brain. However, the mind-model of dualism is unable to explain why so few people can spontaneously recall undergoing the wake-up test. According to this mind-model, the separable immaterial soul is the controller of all conscious thoughts, emotions, actions, and deeds of the physical body, as well as the repository of all memories. Therefore, the souls of all persons should retain long-term memories of cooperating with the wake-up test. But they do not. This means the physical brain is the repository of all memories, and not the soul, a finding contradicting one of the most fundamental tenets of the mind-model of dualism. So just as with the isolated forearm technique, the wake-up test also proves belief in a separable immaterial soul to be no more than an ancient communal illusion.

Awareness experiences & the soul illusion

[10.93]The most important lesson from awareness studies is the effect of subanesthetic concentrations and doses of drugs used to provide general anesthesia upon memory. Indeed, this more than anything else, proves that memories are stored in the physical brain, and not in any separable immaterial soul. This fact clearly demonstrates, and proves the illusory nature of a key property of the soul proposed by the mind-model of dualism. And absence of any memory function in the human soul has several profound implications.

271

- [10.94]Memories of apparent disembodiment during out-of-body experiences, and of transcendental worlds visited during near-death experiences, are memories formed within the physical brain. Therefore, memories of events occurring during experiences of disembodiment are products of perceptions made by the body, together with hallucinations induced by the events causing these experiences, as well as hallucinations originating within the psyches of those individuals subsequently reporting these experiences.
- [10.95]A soul without memory has no concept of punishment or reward. It exists in the here and now, without any concept of what has passed, or what is. Accordingly, absence of memory function within the soul, means there is no heaven, and no hell.
- [10.96]Absence of memory function within the soul, means that a soul learns nothing during successive reincarnations. Absence of memory function does not dispose of the idea of reincarnation of a possible soul, it just means that a possible soul undergoes no spiritual development in successive reincarnations.

[10.97]The conclusion of studies of unintentional and intentional awareness during general anesthesia is evident. The soul is not the repository of all memories as proposed by the mind-model of dualism— a finding proving the illusory nature of the human soul as defined by the mind-model of dualism in Chapter 1. So if individual humans do have an immaterial soul, then this human soul has properties very different to those proposed by the current popular mind-model of dualism (see Chapter 1).

11

Local Anesthesia

11.1 Borne on the wings of two Coca leaves, I flew about in the spaces of 77,438 worlds, one more splendid than another. I prefer a life of ten years with Coca to one of a hundred thousand without it. It seemed to me that I was separated from the whole world, and I beheld the strangest images, most beautiful in color and in form that can be imagined. (page 30 in Mariani 1892)

11.2 Not only do people ingesting cocaine sometimes undergo transcendental experiences, but they always feel themselves invigorated and more alert than normal. Cocaine was, and still is the source of energy enabling Andean peoples to perform exhausting physical labor, or make long treks at high altitudes with little food and water. The 1878 edition of the Encyclopaedia Britannica even contains a strange and fantasy rich paean to these effects of the coca leaf, in which a South American Indian not only addresses Incan gods, but also classical Greek gods.

11.3 Our Varicocha first this Coca sent,
Endow'd with Leaves of wondrous Nourishment,
Whose Juice succ'd in, and to the Stomach tak'n
Long Hunger and long Labour can sustain;
From which our faint and weary Bodies find
More Succour, more they cheer the drooping Mind,
Than can your Bacchus and your Ceres join'd.
Three Leaves supply for six days march afford
The Quitoita with this Provision stor'd
Can pass the vast and cloudy Andes o'er.

11.4 South American Indians regularly chew coca leaves to alleviate the harsh reality of grinding poverty, hard physical labor, and oxygen deprivation at high altitudes in the Andes mountains. But this is not all, coca leaves have also been used since time immemorial for their aphrodisiac and medicinal properties.

[11.5]The Peruvian Indians employ Coca to stimulate uterine contractions and regard it as a powerful aphrodisiac. Leopold Casper, of Berlin, considers Coca one of the best of genital tonics, and many modern observers concur in this opinion. Vecki says that Cocaine internally to a man aged fifty six invariably occasioned sexual excitement and cheerfulness. (page 429 in Mortimer 1901)

[11.6]The rapidly increasing popularity of coca preparations resulted in increasing imports of coca leaves into the USA during the latter half of the nineteenth century. An American physician, W.S. Searle published an essay which was little more than a song of praise extolling the virtues of coca (Searle 1881). He regarded coca as a panacea for almost all major and minor ills and discomforts afflicting humankind. And among many others at the time, Searle claimed coca was a cure for then current scourge of morphine addiction.

[11.7]Professor Palmer, of the University of Louisville, Kentucky, has an article upon this subject in the Louisville Medical Journal, for 1880, and he therein narrates three cases in which he found the Coca a complete and easy substitute for the Opium or Morphine which had been habitually taken. One sufferer had been in the habit of taking thirty grains of Morphine daily [an amazing 1800 mg/day], and yet abandoned that drug wholly, and at once, and without the slightest difficulty, by resorting to the fluid extract of Coca whenever the craving attacked him. (page 130 in Searle 1881)

[11.8]Not only was coca apparently a good way to cure morphine addiction, but it was also more invigorating than coffee or tea, a wondrously effective remedy for weariness and exhaustion.

[11.9]An eminent lecturer has, by my advice, taken a teaspoonful of the fluid extract before going upon the platform, and informs me that it very largely prevents his customary fatigue.
A lady who was so reduced in strength by uterine haemorrhage as to be unable to walk more than a single block, took two bottles of the Coca bitters (a preparation which contains only a little alcohol in addition to the Coca) and she informs me that it enabled her to accomplish miles without fatigue.

Other ladies who were accustomed to experience great fatigue after shopping or visiting expeditions, report a great increase of power and endurance. (pages 124-125 in Searle 1881)

11.10 Searle went even further with his gushing paean of praise of cocaine to ultimately conclude: "… the introduction of this substance into general use is a matter of exceeding importance, and its employment should be fostered by every true physician." (pages 137-138 in Searle 1881)

11.11These are wonderful descriptions of cocaine's mental effects, and I do not apologize for their antiquity. Their enthusiasm and flavor is redolent of an age of innocence when everything was fresh and new. The mental effects of cocaine remain unchanged with the passage of more than one hundred years, only the prose now used to describe these effects is threadbare, evoking none of the vivid verbal imagery and innocence of this bygone age. Cocaine is arousing, invigorating, and pleasurable. Moreover, ever-increasing doses are required to induce the same mental effects. These facts make cocaine a very addictive substance. Recreational use of cocaine became a major world problem during the later nineteenth century, and remains so even now at the beginning of the twenty first century. During 1910, Sir Edward Grey, a British Foreign Minister, once wrote of his concern about the epidemic of cocaine and morphine addiction to the American ambassador to England.

11.12 *… spread of morphia and the Cocaine habit, is becoming an evil more serious and more deadly than Opium smoking, and this evil is certain to increase … (quoted in Karch 1999)*

11.13When Stephen Karch wrote this passage, the total annual world production of cocaine was about 10 tons, while during 1996 it was estimated at about 700 tons (Karch 1999). During 1910 the total world population was 1,750 million people, which means an annual worldwide cocaine availability of about 5.7 milligrams cocaine per person per year. However, during 1996 the total world population was 5,713 million people, which means an increase of annual worldwide cocaine availability to about 123 milligrams cocaine for every man, woman, and child in the world per year. Access to cocaine was, and is limited in most parts of the world, which means that relatively few people actually consume this drug. So this calculation implies that relatively few people manage to consume simply enormous quantities of cocaine each year. So while the cocaine problem was worrisome in 1910, the growth of cocaine production means that the world in 2010 was veritably awash with cocaine!

Cocaine: the first local anesthetic

[11.14]But cocaine is not only a drug with pronounced pleasurable and psychomimetic effects. Cocaine was also the first effective local anesthetic drug. Humankind suffered the horrid pains of surgery for uncounted millennia until the international introduction of general anesthesia in 1846. But general anesthesia is not suitable for everyone, or for every type of surgery. Even so, for many years general anesthesia remained the only reliable form of anesthesia. Professor Schroff was a pharmacologist who reported his experiences with cocaine during 1862.

[11.15]*Schroff was one of the first to experiment with the new alkaloid. He observed that Cocaine produces a slight anaesthesia of the tongue, and gives an agreeable sense of lightness of the mind with a condition of cheerfulness and well being, followed by lassitude and an inclination to sleep. From augmented doses he remarked giddiness, buzzing in the ears, dilatation of the pupils, impaired accommodation, headache, restlessness, and a feeling as though walking upon air. (page 412 in Mortimer 1901)*

[11.16]Curiously, very few people at the time realized the import of this well-known observation of surface anesthesia of the tongue. Nonetheless, some physicians did realize the usefulness of this property of cocaine, and employed the local anesthetic effect of cocaine to treat a few patients.

[11.17]*In 1865, Dr. Fauvel, of Paris, used a preparation of Coca which had been prepared for him by Mariani as a local application, to relieve pain in the larynx, and this treatment was continued in England by Dr. Morrell Mackenzie and in the United States by Dr. Louis Elsberg, who had remarked the beneficial effects of this application in Fauvel's clinic. (page 412 in Mortimer 1901)*

[11.18]Even so, the thought of applying the local anesthetic effects of cocaine to permit painful, or surgical procedures remained relatively unknown and unconsidered (Calatayud 2003). During 1880, the St. Petersburg born physician Vassily von Anrep (1852-1927), published an extensive study of the pharmacology of cocaine. He also mentioned the local anesthetic effect of cocaine, as well as the potential use of this local anesthetic effect for surgical procedures (BMJ 1885, Yentis 1999). For some reason, this work remained relatively unknown, and no physicians acted upon this knowledge until the young Viennese ophthalmologist, Karl Köller (1857-1944), recognized the potential of cocaine for local anesthesia in eye surgery. After a few brief animal and human experiments, Köller successfully applied the local anesthetic properties of cocaine to eye surgery (Calatayud 2003, Reis 2009). Apparently Karl Köller was the right man at the right time, with the right insights into the potential of local anesthesia. His initial experiences with cocaine were published during 1884, after which international interest in the local anesthetic applications of cocaine exploded (Calatayud 2003, Reis 2009).

[11.19]During 1885, just one year after the publication of the effects of cocaine by Karl Köller, Professor Knapp, a New York ophthalmologist, published some of the American experiences using local anesthesia with cocaine (Knapp 1885). These experiences varied from the use of cocaine local anesthesia in ophthalmology, to urology, gynecology, ear nose and throat surgery, to general surgery. One report by Knapp of a particularly heroic operation performed with cocaine local anesthesia stands out. This was the drainage of a large hydatid abscess from the liver of an otherwise very sick man. It reveals what is possible with primitive apparatus and diagnostic tools. This was epic surgery, and it is for this reason that I cite the report in its entirety.

[11.20]*The condition of the patient was such that the effects of any general anaesthetic were greatly feared. Therefore it was determined to perform the operation under the effects of Cocaine. The skin over the tumor was carefully cleansed with soap and water, and then the four percent solution was rubbed in for half an hour. Prof. J. Williston Wright, Dr. Stone, and Dr. Ashton assisting, we then made the incision. The skin and subcutaneous fat were passed with trivial pain. Reaching the muscles we found such sensitiveness as to necessitate the use of the Cocaine. In five minutes after a free application we passed without pain to the peritoneum. This proved the most sensitive of all the tissue we encountered, but a free application of the remedy speedily anesthetized it, so that we cut through it without pain. Contrary to expectation, no adhesions were found between the tumor and the abdominal wall, but its tissue was so little sensitive, a few minutes application of the Cocaine prepared it for incision. Partially emptying the sac with an aspirator, its walls were seized and held against the abdominal incision while we made a free opening. Passing in the fingers we stitched the edges of the cut in the tumor to the wound in the abdominal wall. As many as eight sutures were thus placed, each being passed through all the layers of the abdominal wall, thence into the sac. This was done without the slightest pain to the patient. Next the sac was emptied and washed out, one gallon of pus and broken down hydatids being removed. Then the usual dressing was applied. A careful examination of the patient, made by all the gentlemen present, showed that his condition was much better than when the operation began. (pages 86-87 in Knapp 1885)*

[11.21]Heroic surgery indeed! Just imagine the stench of one gallon, (about four liters), of pus and broken down hydatids, (hydatids are parasitic tapeworms). The attention to detail during this operation was excellent. For example, the opening of the liver abscess was stitched to the opening in the abdominal wall, so preventing the contents of the abscess flowing into the abdominal cavity and causing a lethal peritonitis. Even so, the man died 23 days after the operation because his bile ducts no longer functioned. However, at the time, this operation was this man's only chance of survival.

[11.22]Many other applications of local and anesthesia were developed using cocaine before the arrival of other, safer local anesthetic drugs. In fact, just about all the local and regional anesthetic techniques in current use, were developed before 1900. The names of the inventors and developers of these techniques are too numerous to mention, but include illustrious names such as Maximillian Oberst (1849-1925), George Crile (1864-1943), William Halsted (1852-1922), Carl Schleich (1859-1922), August Bier (1861-1949), Heinrich Braun (1862-1934), and many others. So let us examine the history of one of the most significant forms of local anesthesia developed at the end of the nineteenth century—spinal anesthesia.

Spinal anesthesia: a history

[11.23]Spinal anesthesia was one of the most significant local anesthetic techniques developed in the last years of the nineteenth century. It is a deservedly popular form of anesthesia of the lower half of the body, and in the right hands is as safe, if not safer than general anesthesia. The spinal cord extends from the base of the brain down to the twelfth chest vertebra. The brain and the spinal cord are bathed in spinal fluid (cerebrospinal fluid) contained inside a sack (dural sac) enclosing the whole brain and spinal cord, and extending to the pelvis. A spinal anesthetic is performed by inserting a needle between two vertebrae, piercing the dural sac to inject a local anesthetic drug into the cerebrospinal fluid bathing the spinal cord and nerves. The local anesthetic drug anesthetizes all nerves around and below the level of injection, enabling pain-free surgery to be performed in the lower half of the body.

Accidental discovery

[11.24]During 1885, just one year after Karl Köller unleashed an international tsunami of interest in local anesthesia with cocaine, John Corning (1855-1923), a New York neurologist, reported the discovery of what he called "spinal anesthesia" (Corning 1885). Corning was searching for an effective method of treating pain originating from the spinal cord. He realized that administration of painkilling medicines near to the spinal cord could be a very effective method of relieving this type of pain. After preliminary experimentation on a dog, he reported his first experience of treating a patient with urinary problems and "spinal weakness" with a spinal injection.

[11.25]*To this end I injected thirty minims [1.85 milliliters] of a three percent solution of the hydrochlorate of Cocaine into the space situated between the spinous processes of the eleventh and twelfth dorsal vertebrae. As there was no numbness, tingling, or other evidence of modified sensibility after the lapse of eight minutes, I again injected thirty minims of the solution at the same spot and in the same manner. About ten minutes later the patient complained that his legs "felt sleepy"; and, on making a careful examination with the wire brush [part of an electrical stimulating device], I found that sensibility was greatly impaired. Currents which caused lively sensations of pain and reflex contractions in the upper extremities were disregarded and barely perceived in the lower limbs. [...] The passage of a sound [through the urethra], though usually accompanied by considerable pain, remained almost unperceived, and an urethral electrode caused no inconvenience, even when strong currents were used. The sensibility of the scrotum and glans penis was also impaired to a marked degree, as proved by repeated tests with the electric brush. (Corning 1885)*

[11.26]From the perspective of a modern anesthesiologist, it is somewhat uncertain as to where the local anesthetic solution was actually injected in this particular patient. The volumes of the solution used were small, but the cocaine concentration of 3% was very much higher than the 0.5% to 1.0% solutions employed to produce true spinal anesthesia in studies performed by August Bier during 1898 (Bier 1899). So the conclusion of most authors is that this was not true spinal anesthesia, but epidural anesthesia, where the local anesthetic solution is injected just outside the dural sac surrounding the spinal cord (Oehme 1998). Regardless of the exact placement of the local anesthetic solution, this was a landmark event in local anesthesia. Corning's concluding remark was farsighted.

[11.27]*Whether the method will ever find an application as a substitute for etherization in genitourinary or other branches of surgery, further experience alone can show. Be the destiny of the observation what it may, it has seemed to me, on the whole, worth recording. (Corning 1885)*

[11.28]No other physicians took notice of this observation, because no other studies of spinal anesthesia were reported for several years afterwards. However, Corning continued applying spinal injections in his neurological practice. After further consideration of the anatomy of the spinal cord and vertebrae (pages 247-250 in Corning 1894), he finally described the application of true spinal anesthesia with cocaine for relief of neurological pain in human patients in his book entitled *Pain in its Neuro-Pathological, Diagnostic, Medico-Legal, and Therapeutic Relations* (pages 251-254 in Corning 1894).

[11.29]After this the potential of spinal anesthesia remained unknown and ignored for several years until 1898. On the 16th of August 1898, August Bier, a surgeon at the Royal Surgical Hospital in Kiel, Germany, successfully applied spinal anesthesia for an operation performed on the tuberculous ankle of a 34 year old laborer (Bier 1899). During the days afterward he used spinal anesthesia for several other operations. But Bier did not learn of spinal anesthesia from the publications of Corning. Instead, he developed the idea of spinal anesthesia quite independently, because of the coincidental presence of another physician, Heinrich Quincke (1842-1922), a colleague internist working at the same hospital. Quincke had done much research on the use of lumbar puncture, (spinal tap), to remove cerebrospinal fluid for diagnosis and treatment of a multitude of brain and nervous diseases, as well as mentioning the possibility of injecting therapeutic substances (Oehme 1998). Many eminent German surgeons at the time were very active developing and promoting local anesthesia with cocaine. So it was a small step for August Bier with his surgeon's knowledge of anatomy and the local anesthetic effects of cocaine, to consider injecting cocaine with a lumbar puncture to anesthetize the nerves of the spinal cord.

[11.30]After these initial successful tests of spinal anesthesia upon his surgical patients, Bier decided to perform some scientific tests of the nature of anesthesia provided by this technique. So it was that on the 24th of August 1898, that August Bier and his assistant August Hildebrandt (1868-1954), met at the house of Bier to study the effects of this technique of anesthesia upon each other. Bier was the senior surgeon, and very sportingly allowed Hildebrandt to perform spinal anesthesia upon himself first. The lumbar puncture was successful, but due to lack of standardization of syringe and needle couplings, Hildebrandt was unable to connect the syringe to the needle and inject the cocaine solution. Then it was the turn of Hildebrandt to undergo spinal anesthesia. Bier successfully performed spinal anesthesia upon Hildebrandt, and proceeded to perform scientific studies of the degree, intensity and nature of the anesthesia. He carefully noted the times and the effects of different stimuli:

[11.31]*- After 13 minutes: A burning cigar applied to the legs was felt as heat, but not as pain. Ether produced a feeling of cold.*
- After 15 minutes: Tickling the sole of the foot was no longer felt as such but only as movement. Pinching the leg was felt as light pressure but pinching the upper chest was very painful.
- After 18 minutes: Strong pinching was hardly felt at all below the nipples.
- After 20 minutes: Avulsion of pubic hairs was felt simply as elevation of a fold of skin, but avulsion of chest hair above the nipples on the contrary was very painful. Strong hyperextension of the toes was not unpleasant.
- After 23 minutes: A strong blow to the shin with an iron hammer did not provoke pain.
- After 25 minutes: Strong pressure and traction on the testicles was not painful.
- After 32 minutes: Tickling the sole of the foot was perceived as faint touch. Needling down to the femur and strong pressure on the testicle were not painful.

281

*- After 40 minutes: Strong blows on the shin did not hurt. The
entire body began to perspire gently.
- After 42 minutes: Constriction by a rubber tube tourniquet
around the thigh produced no pain, but around the upper arm was
very painful. (Bier 1899, translated in Wulf 1998)*

[11.32]Epic stuff! This was heroic medical research! After the effects of
the anesthesia had worn off, and experiencing no ill effects from their
scientific studies, the two men proceeded to celebrate the success of their
experiment by dining, drinking wine, and smoking several cigars (Bier
1899). The publication of these studies in Germany during 1899
unleashed worldwide interest in spinal anesthesia, and the technique
rapidly became part of the anesthetic armamentarium. Spinal anesthesia
did not enter clinical use as a result of the publications of John Corning,
but August Bier, just as Karl Köller before him, was evidently the right
man at the right time with the right message. Spinal anesthesia had
arrived!

Spinal anesthesia priority battle

[11.33]A curiously protracted priority battle subsequently ensued
between Bier and Corning. August Hildebrandt was one of the main
reasons for the long duration of this priority question. Possibly
embittered at not being a co-author of the article announcing the use of
spinal anesthesia, even though Bier frequently acknowledged his
assistance in the article itself (Bier 1899), he regularly contested August
Bier's priority in the discovery of spinal anesthesia in publications, at
medical congresses, and in public. He further fuelled the priority
controversy by claiming Bier knew of the publications of Corning, but
refused to acknowledge this fact, preferring instead to claim credit for
the independent discovery of this technique for himself. All this finally
resulted in Hildebrandt being expelled from the Berlin Medical
Association (Berliner Ärtztenverein) sometime before 1913 for behavior
unworthy of a colleague, ("incollegialen en standesunwürdigen
Verhaltens"). Perhaps other personality problems also contributed to this
behavior. Werner Forssmann (1904-1979), the 1956 Nobel Prizewinner
for medicine, was a junior physician at the same hospital as August
Hildebrandt during 1929. In his autobiography he described that
Hildebrandt was generally known as a "reckless egoist". Forssmann also
tells that the villa of Hildebrandt resembled a Chinese museum, being
filled with valuable temple and palace treasures plundered while he was

a military surgeon during the multinational European suppression of the Chinese Boxer rebellion of 1900. Even during 1929, thirty years after the original publication by Bier in 1899, Hildebrandt was still regularly contesting August Bier's priority to the discovery of spinal anesthesia at medical congresses and in public (page 87 in Forssmann 1972).

[11.34]One curious fact remains in this story of the priority battle between Bier and Corning. In his 1899 article, August Bier makes no mention of prior experimental work, or reasoning to establish the volume and concentration of cocaine solution needed to provide spinal anesthesia. The volumes and cocaine concentrations used were just stated as is—no prior reasoning, and no prior experimentation (Bier 1899). So where did the ideas for these concentrations and volumes arise? A study of the volumes and cocaine concentrations used by Bier for spinal anesthesia to perform operations on six patients between the 16th to the 27th of August 1898, reveals some variation between concentrations and volumes (pages 362-364 in Bier 1899). One likely explanation is that Bier was cautiously experimenting with concentrations and volumes, using his knowledge of the effects of cocaine local anesthesia on anesthesia of single nerves as propounded by German surgical contemporaries such as Oberst, Schleich, Braun, and many others.

[11.35]The conclusion of history is that Corning was the first to lay the theoretical basis and practical application for spinal anesthesia. However, his suggestion to use spinal injections of cocaine for surgical anesthesia languished, unappreciated and forgotten for several years on shelves in medical archives (Corning 1885, Corning 1894). The role of Bier was to independently develop the same theoretical and practical application of this technique, but had priority for the successful worldwide introduction of spinal anesthesia for surgery (Oehme 1998).

Surgeons, anesthesiologists and spinal anesthesia

[11.36]Curiously, spinal anesthesia and most other local anesthetic techniques were developed by surgeons. Practically no anesthesiologists at the time took part in the development of local or regional anesthesia. This latter fact was not altogether surprising at the time. Surgeons were the physicians who spoke with, and diagnosed the patients at the outpatient clinics. Surgeons managed these patients in the wards. Surgeons performed the operations, and directed the nurses and junior doctors providing general anesthesia for these operations. And surgeons maintained contact with the patients and their families after performing the planned operations. Up to 60 years ago, most professional

283

anesthesiologists simply administered general anesthesia, and had no more association with the management of patients than that. Moreover, general anesthesia was associated with consequences such as frequent nausea and vomiting after anesthesia with ether or chloroform, a reasonable chance of developing a lung infection after operation, cardiovascular collapse was common in seriously ill patients, and there was a relatively high mortality after surgery performed under general anesthesia. So it is not at all surprising that surgeons sought ways to eliminate the necessity for general anesthesia. Moreover, because of these differing degrees of responsibility up till 60 years ago, many surgeons were very disdainful of anesthesiologists. A disparaging remark made in 1909 by the Romanian surgeon, Professor Thomas Jonnesco (1860-1926), expressed this attitude beautifully.

[11.37]*General spinal anaesthesia is infinitely superior to inhalation anaesthesia. Owing to its simplicity, it is within the reach of all, and as there is no contraindication it may be employed with any patient. As it can be performed by the surgeon himself it does away with the attendance of a person often inexperienced, and never responsible. (Jonnesco 1909)*

[11.38]This remark was certainly relevant to the situation on continental Europe and the USA at the time. Anesthesia on continental Europe and the USA at that time was typically administered by inexperienced nurses, students, or even hospital orderlies under the direction of the surgeon. The situation in England at the time was different. English law required general anesthesia to be administered by a physician. However, in reality, many physician anesthesiologists at the time in England may also have been relatively inexperienced or unknowledgeable, as was revealed by remark of an English surgeon, Arthur Barker (1850-1916), during 1908. His comment about spinal anesthesia was equally disparaging to the anesthesiologists of the time, but with a promise of the future situation.

[11.39]*These considerations may ultimately result in the procedure [spinal anesthesia], should it prove really useful and safe, as I believe it to be, drifting into the hands of the professional anaesthetists in large towns just as general anaesthetics have in this country. But this can only come about when they have devoted as much attention to the study of spinal analgesia in all its aspects as they have done during the last sixty years to Chloroform, Ether, etc. Still, the surgeon can quite well carry out the whole procedure single handed, though in some cases he would be glad to have the time free for other matters connected with preparation for operation. (Barker 1908)*

[11.40]Indeed, this was the prevailing attitude for some time. One army surgeon even proposed that spinal anesthesia was an ideal form of anesthesia for military surgery.

[11.41]*Tropacocaine spinal analgesia has its place in military surgery, especially field work in time of war, because it offers the following advantages: (1) It obviates the necessity for the storage and transportation of the bulk of general anesthetics. (2) Is much more economical than general anesthesia. (3) The immense saving of time and attention in its administration. (4) The saving in operative personnel, dispensing with the necessity of anesthetizers. (5) The saving in the number of attendants for individual patients—after operation under spinal anesthesia the patient does not require such attention as under general anesthesia. (6) The saving of a number of bearers—under spinal anesthesia, patients are much more able to assist themselves. (page 465 in Allen 1920)*

[11.42]In the following paragraph, Carroll Allen remarked that such statements were wildly optimistic, and even dangerous, because of the well-known problem of lethal shock caused by administration of spinal anesthesia to persons suffering from massive blood loss, or severely infected wounds (pages 465-466 in Allen 1920). Allen's remarks reflected the statement of Admiral Gordon-Taylor, an English surgeon commenting upon his experience treating soldiers wounded in the trench warfare of Flanders during World War 1, that "spinal anesthesia is the ideal form of euthanasia in war surgery" (see 7.7). Indeed, when applied by persons ignorant of the consequences of spinal anesthesia, these statements are as true today as when made more than 90 years ago.

[11.43]Much has changed since these comments were made. Surgeons and anesthesiologists now work as a team complementing each other. Patients and their surgeons now rely on the expertise of anesthesiologists to provide restful adequate anesthesia, to manage and treat the consequences of surgery, such as pain and loss of blood, while at the same time managing and treating any concurrent serious medical conditions. The result is that modern surgeons are temporarily freed from managing the patient, and can fully concentrate, employing their expertise to perform the required operation to the best of their abilities.

And this brings us to an illuminating study of the actions, and failures of local anesthesia.

Actions and failure of local anesthesia

[11.44]Some patients say that local anesthetic drugs do "not work on them", or that they were paralyzed by the local anesthetic, but still felt the pain of the operation, while others tell of feeling their anesthetized limbs in impossible positions. The mechanisms of action of local anesthetic drugs explain all these conscious manifestations of local anesthesia as perceived by persons undergoing operations under local anesthesia.

Incorrect placement as a cause of failure

[11.45]One cause of failure of all local anesthesia techniques is simply the incorrect placement of the local anesthetic. A local anesthetic drug must be injected in the appropriate place if it is to anesthetize the region to be operated. Placement of local anesthetic drugs for many types of local anesthetic techniques is a skill which takes much practice to perform accurately. Even then, success is not always absolutely certain at all times. Unfortunately some people interpret this failure as "local anesthetics don't work on me."

Altered tissue chemistry as cause of failure

[11.46]Another reason for failure of local anesthesia is infection or inflammation of the tissues to be anesthetized. All local anesthetic drugs such as cocaine, procaine, chlorprocaine, prilocaine, articaine, lidocaine, bupivacaine, and ropivacaine, share similar properties and cause local anesthesia by the same mechanism. They are all weakly alkaline substances, which are termed "weak bases" by chemists. When dissolved in water, and watery tissues such as blood, and the fluids inside as well as outside cells, some of the local anesthetic molecules interact with the acids and bases in these fluids, and dissociate to form positively and negatively charged ions. This is a reversible chemical reaction, which means there is always an equilibrium between the proportion of ionized and unionized molecules.

[11.47]The degree of acidity or alkalinity of a fluid is expressed as the "pH" of the solution. A solution with a pH = 7.0 is neutral, being neither alkaline nor acid. A solution with a pH less than 7.0 is acid, and is more acid as the pH decreases to the minimum of zero. And a solution is termed alkaline when the pH is greater than 7.0, and becomes increasingly more alkaline as the pH increases to a maximum of 14.

[11.48]Blood, and the fluids in between the cells of the body have a pH of about 7.4, which means the fluids outside the cells of the body are slightly alkaline. But the fluids inside cells have a pH of about 6.9, which means these fluids are slightly acidic. All local anesthetic drugs are weakly alkaline, which means that increasingly higher proportion of local anesthetic molecules are ionized as the fluid in which they are dissolved become more acidic. And an increasingly higher proportion of local anesthetic molecules are non-ionized as the fluid in which it is dissolved becomes more alkaline.

[11.49]This has important practical consequences for local anesthetic drugs. Nerve fibers, or rather nerve "axons", are actually no more than long extensions of nerve cells conducting nerve signals from one part of the body to another. And a nerve is a bundle of such nerve axons. Now a local anesthetic is always injected into the fluids outside nerves, never inside nerves, and never inside nerve cells. The injected local anesthetic drug diffuses through the tissues of the nerve to reach the axons of the nerves. But local anesthetics do not cause local anesthesia by an action on the outer surface of nerve axons. Instead, local anesthetic molecules must diffuse through the axon cell membrane, where they block the action of sodium channels on the inside surface of the cell membrane. This action of local anesthetics on the sodium channels blocks nerve signal propagation at that point of the axon. And when this happens for all axons forming a nerve, then no signals from the brain to the body are conducted past the anesthetized part of the nerve to activate the muscles served by that nerve. Likewise, no sensory signals from that part of the body are conducted past the anesthetized part of the nerve to the brain.

Local anesthetics don't work on me

[11.50]Many people say that "local anesthetic drugs don't work on them." However, upon questioning, these people nearly always tell of going to a dentist with an infected tooth or gums. Infected and inflamed tissues are more acidic than normal. Accordingly, a higher proportion of local anesthetic molecules are ionized than normal in infected or inflamed tissues, so reducing the quantity of non-ionized local anesthetic molecules able to diffuse inside nerve axons. The result is that infected and inflamed tissues are very difficult, if not impossible to adequately anesthetize with local anesthetic drugs. The dentist injects local

287

anesthetics as usual, and in the correct places. Yet these unfortunate people feel pain, despite local anesthesia, because the local anesthetic drug was injected in inflamed or infected tissue. This is another reason why some people say that "local anesthetics don't work on them."

I was anesthetized, but still felt pain...

[11.51]Some people say they were anesthetized by a local anesthetic, but still felt the pain of the operation. One cause of such experiences is that not all the nerves supplying the operated area were anesthetized. This is a very evident explanation of such experiences. Another explanation is related to the mechanism by which individual nerves are anesthetized by a local anesthetic.

[11.52]A nerve is composed of bundles of nerve fibers (or axons), much like a thick telephone cable with many hundreds or thousands of wires bundled together to form one cable. Local anesthetic drugs are never intentionally injected directly inside nerves. This can cause actual damage to nerves into which local anesthetic drugs are injected. Instead, local anesthetic drugs are injected in the tissues and spaces surrounding the nerves to be anesthetized, so as to bathe the nerves concerned in the local anesthetic drug. The local anesthetic drug then diffuses from the outer surfaces of nerves into the nerves concerned. Accordingly, nerve fibers near the surface of the nerve are first anesthetized, and the centrally located nerve fibers are anesthetized last.

[11.53]This is not just an interesting theoretical aspect of local anesthesia, but has very practical clinical consequences. For example, spinal anesthesia is often used for operations on the ankles. Sometimes patients administered spinal anesthetics are anesthetized such that they are unable to move or feel anything around their hips and knees, yet feel pain when the surgeon begins to operate on their ankles. The reason for this phenomenon is that nerve fibers from the ankles are more centrally located inside the nerves to be anesthetized, than those from the hips and knees. So either the anesthesiologists and surgeon have not waited long enough for the local anesthetic drug to diffuse into the nerve fibers supplying sensation to the ankle, or the concentration and amount of local anesthetic drug in the region of the nerves concerned was insufficient to totally anesthetize the nerve fibers concerned. This is another reason why some people say that local anesthetics do not work on them.

Phantoms and loss of body image

[11.54]Local anesthesia also reveals some of the mechanisms by which our minds perceive our bodies. A very common example illustrating this is local anesthesia at the dentist's office. Many people have undergone minor dental procedures performed under local anesthesia. No pain or anything unusual is noticed during the procedure, but as the local anesthetic wears off, many people feel that a lip or a cheek is massively swollen. They look in the mirror, but see their lips and cheeks are quite normal. This surprising, but common observation is the result of partial activity of the sensory nerves. As the local anesthetic wears off, some nerves are still anesthetized, while others have recovered their ability to send sensory information to the brain. The resulting abnormal mix of sensory signals going to the brain is interpreted as massively swollen lips or cheeks. Such changes of body image also occur due to other local anesthetic techniques (Paqueron 2003).

[11.55]Spinal anesthesia is the injection of local anesthetic around the nerves leaving the lower part of the spinal cord. This anesthetizes the lower half of the body. All the nerves providing movement and sensation to an arm can be anesthetized by an injecting a local anesthetic where these nerves are bundled together just above the collar bone (clavicle). Both spinal anesthesia and local anesthesia of an arm provide even more interesting observations. I often administer spinal anesthesia for knee operations. When the anesthetized leg is raised to disinfect the skin, many patients exclaim, "Is that my leg?" This simple observation has far-reaching implications. These people do not feel their anesthetized legs, they have no idea where their legs are in relation to their bodies. In fact, their legs are dissociated from their body images (Paqueron 2003). I personally underwent spinal anesthesia for a meniscus operation during 2007, and also experienced all these phenomena. It was a fascinating experience.

[11.56]People undergoing spinal anesthesia or local anesthesia of an arm make other surprising observations. They often remark that their anesthetized limbs are in the last position of the limb before the local anesthetic took effect. People undergoing spinal anesthesia often say they feel as if they are sitting, even though they are lying flat on the operating table, because spinal anesthesia is often performed in the sitting position (Isaacson 2000, Paqueron 2003). Similarly, people undergoing local anesthesia of an arm often say their arm is lying in various hallucinatory positions, even though their arms are lying next to their bodies, or in the position required by the surgeon (Dirksen 2000, Gentili 2002, Paqueron 2004).

[11.57]People undergoing spinal anesthesia or local anesthesia of an arm, are unable to move the anesthetized parts of their bodies, no matter how hard they try. They may even look at the anesthetized parts of their bodies, and try to induce movement, but this also fails. All they notice is a sensation of dissociation from their now senseless and immobile limbs. This fact indicates that the conscious mind cannot bypass the effect of local anesthesia. Furthermore, these phenomena prove that the conscious mind uses the mechanisms of the body, not only to activate the body, but also to receive sensations from the body, so as to know the position of the body and its parts in space.

Local anesthesia, consciousness and the soul

[11.58]Many believers in the mind-model of dualism seemingly cannot conceive of the mind as a product of the functioning of the physical brain. Local anesthesia cannot affect the soul, because it only affects the material body. Moreover, expressions of the physically conscious brain and the soul are unaffected by local anesthesia of nerves outside the brain. All these things mean that local anesthesia reveals interesting aspects of the relationship between the conscious mind and the body.

Altered body image

[11.59]When an anesthetized leg of a patient under spinal anesthesia is raised so that the patient can see the anesthetized leg, they often exclaim, "Is that my leg?" These people know they have a leg, but have no idea where it is. People undergoing spinal anesthesia, or local anesthesia of an arm, also often experience phantom limb positions. Usually they sense their anesthetized limbs in the last position they were in before anesthesia was complete (Bromage 1974, Gentili 2002, Isaacson 2000, Paqueron 2003, Paqueron 2004, Prevoznik 1964). Such hallucinations of position after local anesthesia are common. About 86-100% of people hallucinate unreal arm positions after local anesthesia of their arms (Bromage 1974, Dirksen 2000, Gentili 2002), and almost all people hallucinate their hips as being flexed after spinal anesthesia, when the local anesthetic was injected in the sitting position (Bromage 1974, Prevoznik 1964). This is not all. People also have abnormal perceptions of the sizes and shapes of body parts whose sensory nerves are anesthetized with local anesthesia (Dirksen 2000, Paqueron 2003).

[11.60]Such hallucinations of position, abnormal body image perception, and loss of body image are products of altered sensory signals from sensory nerves which are fully or partially anesthetized by local anesthesia. Such observations prove that the conscious mind receives information about limb position relative to the body, as well as information about limb size and shape, from the sensory nerves transmitting this information to the brain. This phenomenon is mirrored in the effects of limb amputation, after which more than 85-98% of people develop sensations of a phantom limb (Manchikanti 2004). Amputation does not affect the brain, yet people sense a phantom limb after amputation, often in strange positions, and 70% experience pain in a phantom limb (Melzack 1992).

[11.61]Do these phenomena aid in differentiating between the mind-models of materialism and dualism? Materialism explains the phenomenon of phantom limbs after amputation with the measurable changes in brain structure and function (Karl 2001, Lotze 2001). As regards the effects of local anesthesia, administration of local anesthesia induces changes in the patterns of sensory nerve signals arriving in the brain. These things explain the perceived sensations of phantoms. Believers in the mind-model of dualism also have an explanation for the perception of phantoms by the soul. They explain phantoms as products of abnormal sensations from affected nerves transmitted via the brain to the soul, which then interprets these abnormal signals as indicating abnormal positions, or altered body image (see 1.142). This explanation is actually really no different to that of materialism. Accordingly, these observations prove that the physically conscious mind, as well as the embodied soul, only perceive position and size information from the body through the sensory mechanisms of the body.

Sensory information and conscious mind

[11.62]An important supplement to the above is provided by the fact that no sensory information from anesthetized body parts reaches the conscious mind. We know this to be true, because operations are possible on parts of the body under local anesthesia without the person even realizing the operation has begun, or feeling the operation. This observation, when combined with the known effects of local anesthesia on the sensations of body position and body image, proves once again that the physically conscious mind, or embodied soul, is totally dependent upon sensations from the body for information about what is happening to the body. This is as true for the soul, as for a conscious mind originating as an epiphenomenon of brain function.

Local anesthesia and reduced consciousness

[11.63]People undergoing local anesthesia of the lower half of the body with spinal and epidural anesthesia experience sedation (Pollock 2000, Doufas 2004), and reduced electroencephalographic activity (Antognini 2003, Ariskaka 2008). This is most likely due to a reduction of sensory nerve signals from the anesthetized lower half of the body activating the reticular formation of the brainstem (Antognini 2003, Ariskaka 2008, Doufas 2004, Pollock 2000). In other words, local anesthesia indirectly changes brain function. Such indirectly reduced levels of consciousness are as easily explained by both mind-models—both require the functioning of the appropriate mechanisms of the brain to manifest consciousness in the physical body.

Conclusions from local anesthesia

[11.64]These perceptions and insights from the effects of local anesthesia reveal that the physically conscious mind, as well as the embodied soul, builds its image of the body, and the world about it from sensations generated by the physical senses of the body. And when sensory information from anesthetized body parts is blocked by local anesthesia, the anesthetized body part entirely disappears from the conscious body image, or the conscious mind perceives a phantom with abnormal position, size and shape.

[11.65]Proponents of dualism claim that the physical body is merely an unthinking conduit for control by the soul (see 1.64). Nonetheless, the preceding discussion teaches that when the soul is evidently located within the body, it is just as dependent upon the senses of the body for information about the body and the world about the body, as if it were it a product of the functioning of the brain. So while the effects of local anesthesia provide insufficient evidence to determine the nature and origin of the conscious mind, the effects of local anesthesia prove that the sensory mechanisms of the body are the source of all sensory perceptions of the conscious mind, regardless of the nature of this conscious mind.

[11.66]However, the mind-model of dualism has a major problem with sensations perceived while the soul is apparently disembodied. The discussion in this chapter, as well as that of the effects of curare in

Chapter 9 (see 9.54), reveal that while evidently embodied, the only source of information about body movements, weight, and position available to physical mind and the soul, is derived from the sensory systems of the body. But a problem arises during disembodiment, such as during out-of-body experiences, and near-death experiences. During such experiences, the soul feels motion, position, and other sensations similar to those experienced by the physical body. An example of such sensations was reported as part of a near-death experience undergone by a woman during a general anesthetic administered for a tooth extraction.

[11.67] *During this time I found myself out of my body, standing beside the dentist, and I remember feeling frightened looking down at my body and thinking I must be dead. Then everything went black and I felt myself rushing through the blackness at such speed that it's impossible to compare it to anything. (page 42 in Grey 1985)*

[11.68] This, and many other comparable experiences, appears to indicate that the disembodied soul possesses a parallel set of immaterial sensory organs sensing movements, weight, and position (see 9.55-9.57). Such a concept of a parallel, but immaterial set of sensory systems possessed by the soul that come into action when disembodied, adds an extra level of complexity to the mind-model of dualism.

[11.69] Indeed, this latter level of complexity indicates that the mind-model of dualism becomes less and less probable. However, improbability does not mean impossible—improbability means just that—unlikely. Nonetheless, the improbability of a second immaterial set of sensory organs in the soul finds support in a study of emotions and sensations experienced during out-of-body experiences reported by Emilio Tiberi. This study revealed that the apparently disembodied souls of 7% of persons reporting these experiences sense pain within their bodies (Tiberi 1993). This report also finds confirmation in some isolated case reports, such as that of a man who underwent an out-of-body experience during a cardiac arrest. While dissociated from his body, this man observed the machine administering cardiac massage, and felt severe pain due to the cardiac massage. Titus Rivas, a Dutch parapsychologist, reported in an interview with this man:

[11.70] *He was a hardworking rebar worker and he told me what happened. He began to tell what he saw ... From a corner of the room he saw me busy with him, with the heart massage. That he was placed under a device that was very painful. I can imagine that the compressions from the heart massage pump are more painful than chest compressions administered by a person. It was a pneumatic apparatus that works by using high pressure compressed air to push a piston on the chest. He described me taking the denture out of his mouth and placing it on a shelf of a cart with all bottles on it. And he also heard the clinking of the bottles. [NB. Author's translation] (Rivas 2008)*

[11.71]Such reports indicate that the soul perceives at least some sensations from the physical body when disembodied. This raises the question of which sensations the soul actually perceives with any possible immaterial sense organs. Previous chapters reveal that the disembodied soul possesses no memory abilities. The effects of local anesthesia, and these observations, indicate that the soul derives all sensory information from the sensory organs of the body when embodied, as well as when apparently disembodied. Only one conclusion is possible—a human soul with the properties claimed by the current mind-model of dualism is an untenable illusion.

12

Cardiac Arrest & Consciousness

[12.1]Survivors of cardiac arrest sometimes report undergoing conscious experiences, such as near-death experiences, during the periods they were undergoing resuscitation. Some even report making veridical perceptions during such experiences—perceptions made at a time when they were "evidently" unconscious and without any detectable heartbeat. Near-death experience reports from cardiac arrest survivors are surprising, and often regarded as inexplicable. Indeed, many researchers in the field of near-death experiences regard such experiences as the strongest proof for the reality of the mind-model of dualism. Pim van Lommel, a cardiologist, is one such researcher. He stated as much in the discussion of the results of his landmark prospective study of near-death experiences occurring during cardiac arrest.

> [12.2]*With lack of evidence for any other theories for NDE [Near-Death Experience], the thus far assumed, but never proven, concept that consciousness and memories are localised in the brain should be discussed. How could a clear consciousness outside one's body be experienced at the moment that the brain no longer functions during a period of clinical death with flat EEG [electroencephalogram]? Also, in cardiac arrest the EEG usually becomes flat in most cases within about 10s from onset of syncope. Furthermore, blind people have described veridical perception during out-of-body experiences at the time of this experience. NDE pushes at the limits of medical ideas about the range of human consciousness and the mind-brain relation. Another theory holds that NDE might be a changing state of consciousness (transcendence), in which identity, cognition, and emotion function independently from the unconscious body, but retain the possibility of non-sensory perception. (Lommel 2001)*

^{12.3}Subsequently, Bruce Greyson, another eminent physician researcher in the field of near-death experiences, stated much the same, albeit in somewhat different wording.

^{12.4}The paradoxical occurrence of heightened, lucid awareness and logical thought processes during a period of impaired cerebral perfusion raises particularly perplexing questions for our current understanding of consciousness and its relation to brain function. As prior researchers have concluded, a clear sensorium and complex perceptual processes during a period of apparent clinical death challenge the concept that consciousness is localized exclusively in the brain. (Greyson 2003)

^{12.5}Sam Parnia, another physician whose main field of research is also that of near-death experiences occurring during cardiac arrest also stated much the same.

^{12.6}The occurrence of lucid, well structured thought processes together with reasoning, attention and memory recall of specific events during a cardiac arrest raise a number of interesting and perplexing questions regarding how such experiences could arise. As seen these experiences appear to be occurring at a time when global cerebral function can at best be described as severely impaired, and at worse non-functional. (Parnia 2007)

^{12.7}This perception of the impossibility of clear consciousness during the loss of consciousness induced by cardiac arrest has continued to this day. More recently, Bruce Greyson and his co-authors, Emily Kelly, and Edward Kelly, in Chapter 10 of the *Handbook of Near-Death Experiences* (2009), penned another similar statement to this effect.

^{12.8}The issue is not, however, whether there is any brain activity, but whether there is the type of brain activity that is considered necessary for conscious experience. Such activity is detectable by EEG, and it is abolished both by anesthesia and by cardiac arrest. In cardiac arrest, even neuronal action potentials, the ultimate physical basis for coordination of neural activity between widely separated brain regions, are rapidly abolished. Moreover, cells in the hippocampus, essential for memory formation, are especially vulnerable to the effects of anoxia. Thus it is not plausible that NDEs under anesthesia or in cardiac arrest can be accounted for by a hypothetical residual capacity of the brain to

*process and store complex information under those conditions.
(page 228 in Holden 2009)*

[12.9]As if this were not enough, during 2010 Pim van Lommel reiterated his belief that consciousness never occurs during manual external cardiac massage applied for cardiac arrest in a book called *Consciousness Beyond Life: The Science of the Near Death Experience*.

[12.10]*Research has shown that external heart massage cannot pump enough blood to the brain to restore brain function. Nobody has ever regained consciousness during external resuscitation of the heart. (page 167 in Lommel 2010).*

[12.11]These are the thoughts and conclusions of several physician researchers on the relation of brain function to near-death experiences occurring during cardiac arrest. But are these clearly stated beliefs true? Many people uncritically accept the authority of these physicians. Nonetheless, there are many situations during which people appear unconscious, yet are very conscious (see Chapter 2)—and near-death experiences are definitely conscious experiences, even though they occur during cardiac arrest at a time when people appear unconscious. So is this belief in the impossibility of consciousness and apparently clear thought processes during cardiac arrest and resuscitation based upon physiological fact?

Mechanism of loss of consciousness due to cardiac arrest

[12.12]The first step in the analysis of this problem is to understand the mechanism of loss of consciousness due to cardiac arrest. A constant supply of oxygen is essential for the normal functioning of the body, and the beating of the heart performs the essential task of pumping oxygen enriched blood to all parts of the body. Cardiac arrest means that the heart suddenly stops beating altogether, or no longer effectively pumps oxygen enriched blood around the body. Oxygen is not stored in any tissue of the body, and different tissues consume oxygen at different rates. The retina and the brain have very high rates of oxygen consumption in relation to their weights. This is why sudden failure of circulation caused by cardiac arrest causes rapid development of severe hypoxia in these tissues, resulting in failure of function manifesting as loss of vision, and loss of consciousness within seconds after cardiac arrest.

How long to loss of consciousness?

[12.13]So how long does it take to lose consciousness after cardiac arrest? The most definitive answer to this question was provided by a remarkable and audacious study published by Lieutenant Ralph Rossen and his co-workers during 1943 (see 4.36-4.50). This extraordinary study revealed that 56% of persons lose consciousness within 6-7 seconds, and 95% lose consciousness within 9-10 seconds after sudden total cessation of blood flow to the brain (Rossen 1943). However, this was a dramatically sudden cessation of brain blood flow. In the real world of cardiac arrest, various studies show that people become unresponsive, or apparently unconscious, about 9-21 seconds after onset of various common causes of cardiac arrest (Aminoff 1988, Gastaut 1957). This means that many people experience several seconds of consciousness after cardiac arrest. The mental experience of cardiac arrest is very similar to that of fainting. People first experience darkness due to failure of retinal function, before failure of brainstem function causes loss of consciousness (see 4.34-4.35). The report of a woman describing her experience of cardiac arrest beautifully illustrates these points.

[12.14]*Suddenly, I was gripped by squeezing chest pains, just as though an iron band had been clamped quickly around the middle part of my chest and tightened. My husband and a friend of ours heard me fall and came running in to help me. I found myself in a deep blackness, and through it I heard my husband, as if he were at a great distance, saying, "This is it, this time!" And my thoughts were, "Yes, it is." (page 27 in Moody 1976)*

[12.15]People have up to 21 seconds of consciousness after cardiac arrest begins, and this period may be even longer with some types of arrhythmia such as ventricular tachycardia. But if a functional heartbeat not restored within five minutes after cardiac arrest, increasing degrees of brain damage occur, and death is almost certain after ten minutes if cardiac resuscitation is not started (Berek 1995, Böttiger 2001, Safar 1988). Cardiac massage is an essential part of cardiac resuscitation, and if efficiently applied, will sustain life for long periods of time until an effective heartbeat is restored. But can cardiac massage also restore and sustain consciousness during cardiac arrest when the person has absolutely no heartbeat?

Cardiac massage

[12.16]There is no circulation of blood through the brain during cardiac arrest. However, effective application of cardiac massage during cardiac arrest generates a pumping action of the heart, pumping blood around the body, keeping the brain and other vital organs supplied with life giving, oxygen enriched blood, until normal heartbeat and circulation can be restored with drugs and electric shocks. This is the purpose of cardiac massage. And this is why people can survive periods of cardiac arrest lasting longer than five minutes without developing brain damage. In clinical practice there are three different methods of applying cardiac massage.

- [12.17]*External cardiac compression / massage.* This is the most commonly applied technique. A person forcefully compresses the sternum 60-80 times per minute.
- [12.18]*Mechanical external cardiac compression / massage.* Here a machine performs the work of compressing the sternum. This is a more effective form of cardiac massage, generating a greater flow of blood and blood pressure than external manual cardiac massage.
- [12.19]*Internal cardiac massage.* The chest is opened, and the operator regularly squeezes the heart, so generating a flow of blood around the body. This is the most dramatic, but also the most effective form of cardiac massage, generating the greatest flow of blood and blood pressure.

[12.20]Indeed, the employment of cardiac massage to pump blood around the body until restoration of an adequate heart rhythm, indicates the heart is no more than a pump whose purpose is to pump oxygen enriched blood around the body. The modern practice of heart transplantation during the last few decades proves this to be fact. People require heart transplantation because their hearts function so badly that they are barely able to stay alive. Some of these heart transplantation candidates die while awaiting a suitable human transplant heart. So several technically advanced medical centers in the USA remove the diseased hearts of some of these people, and replace them with pneumatically driven mechanical hearts to keep these people alive while they await suitable transplant hearts. Such mechanical hearts not only keep these people alive, but also enable them to resume a reasonably normal life while awaiting a transplant heart (Copeland 2004). In other words, these people no longer have a biological heart. Instead, they just have a mechanical pump, pumping blood around their bodies. The fact that a mechanical pump totally replacing the heart can sustain life, consciousness, mental, and physical activity, reveals that the heart has nothing to do with these functions. Instead, the successful implementation of mechanical hearts proves the heart is no more than a pump, albeit a pump made of meat instead of metal.

How much blood must the heart pump?

[12.21]The example of cardiac massage, and especially of mechanical pumps to replace the heart, raises an interesting question. How much blood must be pumped around the body each minute to sustain evident consciousness in adult humans? By this, I mean physical consciousness together with the ability to move and to speak.

[12.22]First, it is necessary to define some terms. The amount of blood the heart pumps per minute is known as the "cardiac output". Its unit is liters/minute (l/min). Another measurement is known as the cardiac index. Cardiac index is the cardiac output divided by the body skin surface area. Its unit is liters/meter^2/minute (l/m^2/min). There are good reasons to prefer the measure of cardiac index over cardiac output, but this is a discussion too technical for this book.

[12.23]Many studies have been performed to determine the accuracy of different techniques to measure the amount of blood the heart pumps per minute. One reason for the veritable plethora of such studies is to determine the accuracies of these techniques at cardiac output levels ranging from low to high. These studies reveal that adult humans are evidently conscious even when cardiac output is as low as 1.7 to 2 liters/minute (l/min) (Gabrielson 2002, Grondelle 1983, Hoeper 1999, Yung 2004). This means consciousness is possible at surprisingly low cardiac output levels. So can cardiac massage generate a flow of blood around the body at, or above this level of 1.7 to 2 l/min, and so sustain consciousness, or even restore consciousness?

Cardiac output generated by cardiac massage

[12.24]Unless patients are undergoing heart or lung operations at the time of cardiac arrest, the technique of cardiac massage used is almost invariably external cardiac massage. As mentioned earlier, external cardiac massage was developed by the electrical engineer, William Kouwenhoven (1886-1975) and his medical colleagues, and introduced into regular medical practice during 1960 (Kouwenhoven 1960).

Unfortunately, relatively little research has been performed on how much cardiac output is generated by external cardiac massage in humans. The reason for this relative dearth of information is understandable. Cardiac resuscitations are often very hectic situations. Accurate measurement of cardiac output is often a technically exacting procedure requiring significant time that is simply not available. This is why cardiac output is almost never measured during cardiac resuscitations performed upon persons who have a chance of surviving. Consequently, ethical constraints have meant that most human research on cardiac output generated by external cardiac massage has been performed upon recently deceased persons.

[12.25]Even so, by combining the data from various studies, we do know the distribution of cardiac outputs achieved during manual external cardiac massage applied during cardiac arrest. Cardiac output data in most of these studies are expressed in terms of the cardiac index. Cardiac indices achieved during cardiac massage administered during cardiac arrest are (data from: Del Guercio 1965, Fodden 1996, Liu 2002, MacKenzie 1964, Oriol 1968):

- [12.26]Manual external cardiac massage applied during cardiac arrest generates a cardiac index greater than 2 $l/m^2/min$ in 43% of persons.
- [12.27]Manual external cardiac massage applied during cardiac arrest generates a cardiac index greater than 2.5 $l/m^2/min$ in 40% of persons.
- [12.28]Manual external cardiac massage applied during cardiac arrest generates a cardiac index greater than 3 $l/m^2/min$ in 23% of persons.

[12.29]The average adult body surface area of women is about 1.6 m^2, and of men is about 1.9 m^2, and people are conscious with a cardiac output above 2 l/min (see above). So these studies indicate that cardiac outputs greater than 1.7-2 l/min are achieved in more than 40% of persons undergoing external cardiac massage applied for cardiac arrest.

Blood pressure generated by cardiac massage

[12.30]But cardiac output is not the only factor required for consciousness. Blood pressure is also needed to keep the blood vessels open and to drive the blood around the body. Blood pressure generated by manual external cardiac massage has been the subject of some considerable human research (data from: Del Guercio 1965, McDonald

1982, Oriol 1968, Swenson 1988, Wei 2006). Combining the data from the 68 measurements in these studies reveals the following:

- [12.31]Manual external cardiac massage generates mean arterial blood pressures at, and above 30 mmHg in about 24% of people.
- [12.32]Manual external cardiac massage generates mean arterial blood pressures at, and above 40 mmHg in about 15% of people.
- [12.33]Manual external cardiac massage generates mean arterial blood pressures at, and above 50 mmHg in about 9% of people.

[12.34]Several very good studies have determined the lowest blood pressure limits at which normal consciousness without cerebral hypoxia is sustained in healthy adults, as well as in adults with high blood pressure (Finnerty 1954, Harmsen 1971, Strandgaard 1976). These human volunteer studies consisted of lowering the blood pressure in conscious adult volunteers until signs of cerebral hypoxia occurred, but revealed no absolute value at which cerebral hypoxia occurs. What Finnerty (1954) and Harmsen (1971) did demonstrate, was that the mean arterial blood pressure level at which cerebral hypoxia occurs, is related to the usual resting mean arterial blood pressure level for each individual.

[12.35]The technique used by these scientists was in principle relatively simple—they lowered the blood pressures of volunteer subjects until they began to experience manifestations of cerebral hypoxia. Ethical considerations prevented them lowering the blood pressures of their volunteer subjects further to induce loss of consciousness. Nonetheless, these studies provide data very relevant to this study of the efficacy of cardiac massage. Finnerty (1954) reported that the average threshold low arterial blood pressure inducing cerebral hypoxia in 17 aged and young persons with normal blood pressure was 31.5±8.5 mmHg (Tables IA and IB in Finnerty 1954). Strandgaard (1976) used much the same methodology and reported that the average threshold low blood pressure inducing cerebral hypoxia in 10 persons with normal blood pressure was 43±8 mmHg (Table 5 in Strandgaard 1976). These studies mean that many people are conscious, with or without manifestations of cerebral hypoxia, at mean arterial blood pressures as low as 30-40 mmHg. This fact, together with an examination of blood pressures generated by manual external cardiac massage, predicts that manual external cardiac massage generates sufficient blood pressure to sustain some form of consciousness in about 24% of persons suffering from cardiac arrest. Nevertheless, this figure of "about 24%" is theory based upon data from experimentation, and ignores the reality that many people must also recover from severe cerebral hypoxia after institution of cardiac massage. So can cardiac massage actually restore and sustain consciousness?

Brain oxygenation during cardiac massage

[12.36]Cardiac massage applied for cardiac arrest generates a pumping action of the heart. This pumps blood through the lungs where oxygen chemically combines with blood, which then flows into the left heart from where it is pumped into arteries, to eventually flow through capillary blood vessels in the substance of the brain. Oxygen then diffuses from blood flowing through the capillaries of the brain into the substance of the brain. This is how cardiac massage provides a flow of blood and oxygen to the tissues of the brain. But does cardiac massage actually generate a sufficient pumping action of the heart to transport enough oxygen into the brain to sustain viability, or even consciousness?

[12.37]Near infrared spectroscopy provides a measure of brain oxygen partial pressure (Tobias 2008). This technique has only relatively recently been introduced into clinical practice, and is not yet in common use. Clinical reports of a few persons who suddenly developed a cardiac arrest while undergoing near infrared monitoring of brain oxygenation, reveal that brain oxygenation declines precipitously within seconds after cardiac arrest. Application of efficient manual external cardiac massage restores brain oxygenation to some degree (Imberti 2003, Martens 2010, Nagdyman 2003). So the pumping of blood generated by efficient external cardiac massage does indeed provide oxygen to the brain, but the exact quantities remain a subject for future research.

Electroencephalogram during cardiac massage

[12.38]But is the amount of oxygen supplied to the brain by cardiac massage sufficient to restore brain electrical activity as revealed by the electroencephalogram? The electroencephalogram only displays the electrical activity of the nerve cells near the brain surface. Reports of people undergoing cardiac arrest and resuscitation while attached to an electroencephalograph are rare. There are very good reasons for this. Electroencephalographic apparatus is not available in all parts of a hospital. Moreover, electroencephalographic apparatus requires careful attachment to the body if it is to yield usable results. Yet disappearance of any electroencephalogram signal, (flatline), occurs about 5-30 seconds after the flow of blood to the brain suddenly stops (Aminoff 1988, Clute 1990, Rossen 1943, Visser 2001). Accordingly, most patients suffering cardiac arrest would be either dead or successfully resuscitated long before the arrival and attachment of any electroencephalographic monitoring. These things make the electroencephalogram unusable in the hectic situation of cardiac arrest and resuscitation events. Furthermore, loss of consciousness occurs before total failure of the electroencephalogram, and even for experts, interpretation of an electroencephalogram is not always clear.

[12.39]The few known studies of cardiac resuscitation performed upon people suffering from cardiac arrest while undergoing electroencephalographic monitoring, do demonstrate that cardiac massage can restore brain electrical activity, or electroencephalogram (Elton 1961, Losasso 1992). Nonetheless, restoration of electroencephalogram is not instantaneous. While efficient cardiac massage does restore a measure of blood circulation as well as transporting oxygen into the tissues of the brain, oxygen must first diffuse from the blood capillaries into the small metabolic powerhouses within brain nerve cells called mitochondria, before it has any effect on brain function. For it is within these mitochondria, that oxygen is an essential substrate in a series of vital energy generating chemical processes providing the energy driving brain nerve cell activity. This is not an instantaneous process, which is why clinical case reports show that electroencephalographic activity does not return until about 15-25 seconds after instituting effective internal cardiac massage (Case 5 in Elton 1961), and external cardiac massage (Losasso 1992). But does restoration of cardiac output, blood pressure, brain oxygenation, and brain nerve cell activity as manifested by the electroencephalogram, mean that some people can actually regain consciousness during efficient cardiac massage?

Consciousness during cardiac massage

[12.40]Many proponents of the mind-model of dualism claim that consciousness is impossible during external cardiac massage. However, case reports in reputable international medical journals reveal that people sometimes do regain consciousness while undergoing external cardiac massage applied during cardiac arrest (Bihari 2008, Grogaard 2007, Lewinter 1989, Tobin 2009). For example, during 2009, Joshua Tobin and his colleague Frederick Mihm published the case of a 62 year old man with a prior heart transplant, whose heart suddenly no longer pumped blood despite generating electrical activity (Tobin 2009). This is a situation known as "pulseless electrical activity", or by its older name of "electromechanical dissociation" (Bocka 1988). Vigorous manual external cardiac massage was applied, and the man regained consciousness. When cardiac massage was stopped, he lost consciousness, only to regain it when manual external cardiac massage was started again.

[12.41]*As chest compressions continued at a rate of approximately 100 per minute, the patient's mental status improved to the point where he reached for the endotracheal tube [used for artificial ventilation]. When chest compressions were held to check for a pulse, however, the patient no longer made purposeful movements.*

Upon resumption of chest compressions, the patient again reached for the endotracheal tube. He was told that he was receiving life sustaining chest compressions after his heart had stopped and that he had been intubated to assist with ventilation. The patient appeared to understand this and refrained from reaching for the endotracheal tube again. He was now able to wiggle his toes and give a "thumbs up" to command. Throughout the emergency, the patient was told what was happening in a reassuring manner by the team member at the head of the bed. (Tobin 2009)

[12.42]This continued for two hours, during which this man was clearly conscious during the application of manual external cardiac massage. Unfortunately, his condition was such that nothing could be done for him. So after all medical possibilities were explained and discussed with him, he agreed with his doctors that further resuscitation efforts were senseless, consented to their termination, and died. He was extensively monitored while conscious and undergoing manual external cardiac massage, and it was found that this man was conscious when his mean arterial blood pressure was above 50 mmHg (Tobin 2009).

[12.43]The mean arterial blood pressure of 50 mmHg, above which consciousness was restored and sustained, was echoed in two other similar reports (Bihari 2008, Lewinter 1989). These case reports indicate consciousness may be restored, and sustained, during efficient external cardiac massage generating a mean arterial blood pressure above 50 mmHg. An examination of the statistics of blood pressures generated during manual external cardiac massage, reveals that a mean arterial blood pressure of 50 mmHg or more is measured in about 9% of people undergoing such cardiac massage. The reader should note that this figure of 50 mmHg is derived from three patients with a poor prior medical condition, and does not necessarily apply to all persons suffering from cardiac arrest. Nonetheless, the final conclusion is that efficient manual external cardiac massage potentially generates sufficient blood pressure, as well as cerebral blood flow, to restore and sustain some form of consciousness in significant numbers of persons undergoing cardiac massage.

Consciousness during cardiac arrest

[12.44]So some people are conscious during cardiac arrest. Indeed, consciousness generated by the brain may be retained, restored, or return at several periods during, and after cardiac arrest.

*   [12.45]When losing consciousness at the start of cardiac arrest.
*   [12.46]While undergoing cardiac massage during cardiac arrest.
*   [12.47]While regaining consciousness after successful resuscitation.

Conscious experiences during cardiac arrest

[12.48]A short period of consciousness remains for up to 21 seconds after cardiac arrest. In addition, partial or full consciousness is possible in 24% of persons undergoing efficient manual external cardiac massage for cardiac arrest. These facts mean that remembered periods of consciousness during a period of cardiac arrest and massage might originate from the period before loss of consciousness, as well as from a period of effective cardiac massage. However, fewer than the expected 24% of people will actually remember conscious experiences undergone during cardiac arrest. This is because even though consciousness may have been present during cardiac arrest, many survivors will have undergone periods of cerebral hypoxia sufficiently severe to inhibit the formation of long-term memories (see index: hypoxia and memory dysfunction). This explains why only 10-18% of people recall undergoing various conscious experiences, including near-death experiences, during cardiac arrest (Greyson 2003, Lommel 2001, Parnia 2001, Schwaninger 2002). The reality of possible consciousness during cardiac arrest is fascinating. It means no one can ever be entirely sure whether a person suffering from cardiac arrest is conscious or unconscious. Even more interestingly, the phenomenon of consciousness during cardiac arrest reveals more information enabling a differentiation between the mind-models of dualism and materialism.

Duration and intensity of conscious experiences

[12.49]People remain conscious for up to 21 seconds after cardiac arrest. However, some abnormalities of heart rhythm enable a longer period of consciousness, e.g. ventricular tachycardia. Yet even these few seconds are sufficient to undergo quite profound experiences, such as near-death experiences. The truth of this was clearly demonstrated by the experiences of those who survived attempting suicide by jumping off the Golden Gate Bridge in Los Angeles in the USA. Depending upon the tides, the road deck of the Golden Gate Bridge varies between 76 to 82 meters (250-270 feet) above sea level, which means a fall time of about four seconds before impacting with the water below at about 118-121 kilometers per hour (73.6-75 miles per hour). During these few seconds, the few interviewed survivors had quite intense and life changing experiences.

> [12.50]*The experience of jumping for all six of the survivors was described as tranquil and peaceful and not frightening or terrifying as one might suspect. This is similar to the account mountain climbers give after they have survived accidental falls from great heights. One survivor said, "It was a good feeling—no screaming. It was the most pleasant feeling I've ever had. I saw the horizon and the blue sky and I thought how beautiful it was." Another survivor said that at first he had a peaceful feeling and then he felt like he went into a "dream": ... "I never felt I was dying." One subject stated that he experienced "a sense of relief" and "peace" on the way down. One subject said he "caught a glimpse of San Francisco ... thoughts of goodbye—leaving San Francisco is like leaving the world. I felt like a bird flying—total relief. In my mind I was getting away from one realm and going to another. I did not struggle. I gave up. I was looking forward to what was to come. Even now I'm symbolically still looking for the better world-I'm still in that place between the bridge and the water." Another reported that his descent was "like eternity-beautiful—I enjoyed the sensation." (Rosen 1975)*

[12.51]Such accounts reveal a profound sense of time dilation, during which these survivors underwent profound experiences perceived as lasting longer than the few seconds required to fall and enter the water below.

[12.52]In the landmark study of Thomas Lempert, 42 persons underwent induced periods of loss of consciousness lasting up to 22 seconds (Lempert 1994a, see paragraphs 3.84-3.103 for an extensive description of this study). During these few seconds of loss of consciousness, 83% reported undergoing profound conscious experiences including: out-of-body experiences, entering transcendental worlds, tunnel experiences, meeting preternatural beings, feelings of peace and painlessness, visual perceptions, etc. (Lempert 1994). This is yet another demonstration that the brevity of an experience bears no relation to the subjective duration and intensity of the experience.

Consciousness can return during cardiac massage

[12.53]Blood pressure and cardiac output generated by efficient cardiac massage, does supply the brain with oxygen, enabling the resumption of electroencephalogram activity, and the return of clear and evident consciousness in some people undergoing internal cardiac massage (Miller 1961), during machine external cardiac massage (Grogaard 2007, Lewinter 1989), and during manual external cardiac massage (Bihari 2008, Tobin 2009). But while evident consciousness may return during efficient cardiac massage in some people, others may appear unconscious, even though conscious and aware—a fact not always evident to observers in some studies (Greyson 2003, Lommel 2001, Parnia 2001, Schwaninger 2002).

Mind-models and consciousness during cardiac arrest

[12.54]Dualism and materialism explain consciousness during cardiac arrest equally well. Both agree that efficient cardiac massage can restore brain function to a degree such that the body can manifest consciousness. Materialism explains that cardiac massage restores sufficient brain function to generate consciousness. The mind-model of dualism explains the reason for consciousness during cardiac massage differently. An eminent English educational psychologist, Cyril Burt (1883-1971), indirectly expressed the basic explanation for consciousness during cardiac massage from the viewpoint of dualism in a statement quoted, and enthusiastically endorsed by Chris Carter.

[12.55]The brain is not an organ that generates consciousness, but rather an instrument evolved to transmit and limit the processes of consciousness and of conscious attention so as to restrict them to those aspects of the material environment which at any moment are crucial for the terrestrial success of the individual. In that case such phenomena as telepathy and clairvoyance would be merely instances in which some of the limitations were removed. (page 18 in Carter 2010)

[12.56]So dualism explains that if efficient cardiac massage can restore sufficient function to the mechanisms of the physical brain—the physical brain will once again act as a conduit through which the soul manifests consciousness in this physical world. Nonetheless, cardiac arrest always causes cerebral hypoxia, and this modulates conscious experiences undergone during cardiac arrest. This brings us to a discussion of the role of hypoxia in the generation of near-death experiences occurring during cardiac arrest, a topic discussed in some detail later in this chapter. The excellent study published by Pim van Lommel during 2001 is a good point to start this discussion.

The Pim van Lommel study

[12.57]Pim van Lommel, a Netherlands cardiologist, performed a well structured landmark study of the incidence of recall of near-death experiences in 344 survivors of proven cardiac arrest in the region of Arnhem in the Netherlands (Lommel 2001). The data collected in this study reveals invaluable insights into the true incidence of the recall of such experiences. However, closer examination of this excellent study reveals part of the analysis to be grossly simplified. The data in this study reveals three medically very distinct groups among the 62 out of 344 cardiac arrest survivors recalling undergoing a near-death experience. A careful examination of the data related to these three groups reveals even more information on the matter of near-death experiences during cardiac arrest (Lommel 2001).

- [12.58]30 patients developed a cardiac arrest while undergoing investigations of the functioning of their hearts in a specialized electrophysiological laboratory. Part of the testing in such laboratories is by stimulating the conduction systems of the heart with electrical currents, and cardiac arrest occurs as a complication of the procedure. Resuscitation is immediate and rapid in such situations, because all resuscitation apparatus and medicines are ready for immediate use. These persons experienced less than one minute of cardiac arrest, and less than two minutes loss of consciousness. Of these 30 persons, eight recalled undergoing a near-death experience = 8 / 30 = 26.7% (about 27%). These people experienced the shortest period, and least severe degree of cerebral hypoxia of all the patients included in this study.

- [12.59]204 patients survived resuscitation from cardiac arrest occurring somewhere within the hospital in which they were admitted. About 80% were resuscitated within two minutes of cardiac arrest, and 80% of these regained consciousness within five minutes. A response time of less than two minutes means that most of these patients were in a coronary care unit, or an intensive care unit, where their heart rhythms were continuously monitored. Such a speedy reaction to cardiac arrest generally does not occur in a general hospital ward. This explains why about 20% of persons in the study of Pim van Lommel underwent a period of cardiac arrest lasting longer than two minutes, and 20% underwent a period of loss of consciousness lasting more than five minutes. This longer period of unconsciousness is the result of a more severe degree of cerebral hypoxia due to cardiac arrest. Of the survivors in this group = 62 - 21 = 41 recalled undergoing a near-death experience. This is a near-death experience recall frequency = 41 / 204 = 20%.

- [12.60]110 patients survived resuscitation from cardiac arrest occurring outside hospital. About 80% had a period of cardiac arrest lasting longer than two minutes, and 56% were unconscious for periods longer than ten minutes. This group of people survived the most severe and prolonged degree of cerebral hypoxia resulting from their cardiac arrests. Of these survivors, 13 reported undergoing a near-death experience (Table 3 in Lommel 2001). This is a near-death experience recall frequency = 13 / 110 = 11.8% (about 12%).

[12.61]Even though these differences are not statistically significant, these data do place the following statement of Pim van Lommel in the discussion of his article in a very strange light: "If purely physiological factors resulting from cerebral anoxia caused NDE [near-death experience], most of our patients should have had this experience" (page 2043 in Lommel 2001). But the data from this article reveal just the opposite. They demonstrate that recall of near-death experiences decreases with increasing duration of cardiac arrest and duration of cerebral hypoxia. So the data of Pim van Lommel (2001) are actually in full agreement with decades of studies revealing that increasing severity and degree of brain hypoxia due to cardiac arrest do affect those parts of the brain involved in recall of memories (Grubb 1996, Grubb 2000, Liere 1963, Mecklinger 1998, Mlynash 2010, Shadden 1992).

[12.62]The other fascinating aspect of the study of Pim van Lommel, is the clear demonstration that the subjective intensity of a near-death experience is unrelated to the duration of the actual experience. The 26.7% of persons reporting a near-death experience during the very short period of cardiac arrest during electrophysiological studies clearly revealed this fact—their experiences were as profound as those of people with longer periods of cerebral hypoxia. The effect of these short periods of cardiac arrest on the brains of these people (Lommel 2001) were identical to short periods of syncope induced in the study of Thomas Lempert (Lempert 1994, Lempert 1994a). Both studies indicate that the profundity of an experience is unrelated to its brevity.

[12.63]All these things explain how profound near-death experiences may occur during the few seconds before consciousness is lost after cardiac arrest. This brings us to a more general discussion of near-death experiences during cardiac arrest.

Near-death experiences during cardiac arrest

[12.64]Cardiac arrest is a disaster causing rapid onset of profound cerebral hypoxia. This is why people who lose consciousness due to cardiac arrest all suffer from the short and long-term effects of varying degrees of cerebral hypoxia. Cerebral hypoxia does not always present with disorientation and disorganized thought processes. Nor does cerebral hypoxia always cause loss of memory for events occurring during the period of hypoxia. Moreover, sudden onset cerebral hypoxia induces the same affective, cognitive, and transcendental subjective experiences as those described as occurring during near-death experiences—very different to the average effect of long lasting cerebral hypoxia, which does induce blunted and disorganized thought processes (see 4.57-4.61). However, many believers in the reality of the mind-model of dualism dispute whether cerebral hypoxia generates or initiates near-death experiences occurring during cardiac arrest, even though the data of researchers such as Pim van Lommel clearly reveal this fact (Lommel 2001).

Thomas Lempert: short-term cardiac arrest

[12.65]The landmark syncope study of Thomas Lempert (1994) discussed in Chapter 3 (see 3.84-3.103), is actually identical to a prospective cardiac arrest study. Induction of loss of consciousness was by sudden severe reduction of blood flow to the brain (see subjects and methods in Lempert 1994a). These people underwent only a few seconds of reduced to absent cerebral blood flow. This is identical to what occurs during cardiac arrest, only the experimental subjects of Thomas Lempert awoke within seconds after losing consciousness, while persons suffering cardiac arrest undergo much longer periods of reduced or absent blood flow to the brain. So the study of Thomas Lempert can rightly be considered a prospective study of short-term cardiac arrest. The frequencies of experiences undergone by the 42 persons in the Thomas Lempert study were (Lempert 1994):

- [12.66]35% reported feelings of peace and painlessness.
- [12.67]47% told of entering another world.
- [12.68]20% reported encountering preternatural beings.
- [12.69]17% experienced encountering or entering "light".
- [12.70]16% underwent an out-of-body experience.
- [12.71]8% had a tunnel experience.
- [12.72]0% reported undergoing life review.

Pim van Lommel: longer term cardiac arrest

[12.73]Now compare these results with the data from longer term cerebral hypoxia reported in the equally wonderful study reported by Pim van Lommel and his group. Pim van Lommel (2001) reported that 62 of the 344 patients included in his landmark study of conscious experiences undergone during cardiac resuscitation for cardiac arrest, remembered undergoing some form of conscious experience. These people underwent longer periods of cardiac arrest than did the experimental subjects of Thomas Lempert. The reported frequencies of experiences were:

- [12.74]55% reported feelings of peace and painlessness.
- [12.75]29% told of entering another world.
- [12.76]32% reported encountering preternatural beings.
- [12.77]23% experienced encountering or entering "light".
- [12.78]24% underwent an out-of-body experience.
- [12.79]31% had a tunnel experience.

- [12.80] 13% reported undergoing life review.

[12.81] These two studies reveal that sudden onset of cerebral hypoxia caused by fainting and cardiac arrest induces a similar constellation of subjective experiences, albeit with differing frequencies. An explanation for the differences in percentages of experiences reported lies in the differences between the persons studied, and the severity of the cerebral hypoxia undergone. The cardiac arrest survivors interviewed by the team of Pim van Lommel were older, were expecting possible death, underwent periods of loss of consciousness due to cerebral hypoxia for two minutes or more, and were sometimes interviewed many days after resuscitation from cardiac arrest (Lommel 2001). This was a very different group of persons to the healthy young volunteer subjects taking part in the study of Thomas Lempert. These were all healthy young volunteers who lost consciousness due to cerebral hypoxia for a period no longer than 22 seconds, were certainly not expecting possible death, and were interviewed within minutes after regaining consciousness (Lempert 1994, Lempert 1994a). These differences are very likely the reason why 83% of persons involved in the study of Thomas Lempert recalled undergoing these experiences (Lempert 1994a), and why only 12-27% of the patients in the study of Pim van Lommel recalled undergoing any experiences (Lommel 2001), as well as explaining differences in the constellation of experiences between his and Thomas Lempert's results.

Expectation and near-death experiences

[12.82] Furthermore, as Bruce Greyson pointed out during 1985, the expectation of possible death in the cardiac arrest survivors almost certainly contributed to the differing reported percentages of experiences, such as entering another world, meeting preternatural beings, entering the light, and life review.

[12.83] *Cluster analysis of 89 near-death experiences yielded three discrete types of such experiences: transcendental, affective, and cognitive. Demographic variables did not differentiate individuals having these different types of experiences, but cognitive near-death experiences were less frequent following anticipated near-death events. (Greyson 1985)*

[12.84] The prospective studies of the different teams of researchers lead by Thomas Lempert and Pim van Lommel reveal the important fact that

313

cerebral hypoxia generates, initiates, or at least modulates, near-death experiences occurring during cardiac arrest.

Blood oxygen content and transport

[12.85]Nonetheless, the beginning of this chapter is replete with citations from physicians who generally dismiss the idea that near-death experiences during cardiac arrest are products of cerebral hypoxia (page 217 in Holden 2009, Lommel 2010, Long 2010, Moody 1976, Sabom 1982, Sabom 1998). Furthermore, others such as Chris Carter, the author of a book entitled, *Science and the Near-Death Experience: How Consciousness Survives Death*, wholeheartedly agree with these physicians.

[12.86]*Explanations for the NDE [near-death experience] in terms of anoxia have also been dealt a blow by a medical study of the NDE occurring in patients whose blood gases were being monitored during the resuscitative effort. [...] , it is nevertheless interesting that patients in the group that reported an NDE had higher oxygen levels than those in the control group. (page 163 in Carter 2010)*

[12.87]Chris Carter was referring to the study of Sam Parnia published during 2001. This was a study of 63 survivors of cardiac arrest, of whom four reported undergoing a near-death experience. The arterial blood oxygen pressures of these four patients were found to be higher than normal (Parnia 2001). Later, in this same book he also referred to a patient described by Michael Sabom, who "saw" blood being sampled from one of his femoral arteries during a near-death experience. The arterial oxygen partial pressure was also normal in this sample (page 244 in Sabom 1982). So it is well worth discussing the matter of blood oxygen content to tissue oxygen content in some further detail.

[12.88]Several studies of oxygen partial pressures in the arterial blood of patients undergoing cardiac massage for cardiac arrest have been published since the 1970's (Fillmore 1970, Prause 1998, Steedman 1992, Weil 1986). All these studies confirm that the arterial partial pressure of oxygen is often nearly normal, and sometimes even above normal during efficient cardiac resuscitation.

[12.89]But oxygen does not enter the tissues of the brain from arteries. Arteries are no more than thick walled blood vessels whose function is to transport oxygenated blood pumped by the heart to the tissues of the body. Once within their target tissues and organs, arteries branch into thin walled capillaries, from which oxygen diffuses from blood into the cells of the surrounding tissues. So these articles actually indicate that arterial partial pressure of oxygen during cardiac resuscitation is a measure of the efficiency by which oxygen enters blood from the lungs (Fillmore 1970). However, the partial pressure of oxygen in arterial blood says nothing about whether this oxygen is actually being supplied in sufficient quantities to organs such as the brain. This is a very fundamental fact of physiology, which several physicians writing popular books on the subject of near-death experiences seem to have ignored or forgotten (pages 306-311 in Fenwick 1996, pages 114-116 in Lommel 2010, pages 65-66 in Long 2010, pages 19-21 in Parnia 2006, page 244 in Sabom 1982).

[12.90]The following very simplified, but nonetheless useful formula, clearly reveals the relationship between arterial blood oxygen content and oxygen supply to the body.

$$Oxygen\ Flux = 0.134 \times [Hb] \times S_aO_2 \times CO$$

Explanations for the symbols are:

- *Oxygen Flux* = milliliters oxygen pumped by the heart into the body per minute (ml/min). The average resting adult consumes oxygen at a rate of about 200-300 ml/min at a cardiac output of about 4-5.5 l/min.
- *[Hb]* = hemoglobin concentration in grams/100 milliliters (g/100 ml).
- S_aO_2 = percentage saturation of hemoglobin with oxygen in arterial blood. Hemoglobin is 90% saturated at an oxygen partial pressure of 8 kilopascals (kPa), or 60 millimeters of mercury (mmHg). The maximum percentage saturation of hemoglobin during administration of 100% oxygen at sea level atmospheric pressure is 97%.
- *CO* = cardiac output, which is the volume of blood pumped by the heart each minute, expressed as liters/minute (l/min).
- *0.134* = a constant based on the fact that 1.0 gram of hemoglobin can transport, or bind with a maximum of 1.34 milliliters of oxygen. The convention of expressing hemoglobin concentration as g/100 ml necessitates multiplication of this constant by 10, and the use of percentage saturation of oxygen requires division by 100. The final result is a constant whose value = 0.134.

315

[12.91]Cardiac massage generates a pumping action of the heart, which means this equation explains how hypoxia manifests during cardiac massage applied to persons with a cardiac arrest.

- [12.92]The brain of a person with normal hemoglobin and blood oxygen content, will receive more oxygen with a higher cardiac output, i.e. more efficient cardiac massage.
- [12.93]Anemia means a low blood hemoglobin concentration. The brain of an anemic person requires a higher cardiac output, or more efficient cardiac massage than a person without anemia in order to provide the brain with sufficient oxygen. For example, at the same oxygen levels in arterial blood, a person with a hemoglobin concentration of 5 g/100 ml will need two times the cardiac output of a person with a hemoglobin concentration of 10 g/100 ml to sustain consciousness or prevent cerebral hypoxia.
- [12.94]A person with lower oxygen content in their blood requires more efficient cardiac massage to generate sufficient cardiac output to supply the brain with enough oxygen to sustain consciousness.
- [12.95]A person with a maximal oxygen content in their blood may still experience cerebral hypoxia if the cardiac output is too low, meaning during less than efficient cardiac massage. This explains why the patients described by Michael Sabom (page 244 in Sabom 1982), and Sam Parnia (Parnia 2001), were able to remember their near-death experiences. They had normal, to higher than normal oxygen levels in their blood, but still suffered cerebral hypoxia as evidenced by the occurrence of near-death experiences. Nonetheless, people with a higher than normal, or normal oxygen partial pressure in their arterial blood during near-death experiences are less hypoxic at any level of cardiac output, which means they have a higher chance than otherwise of being able to remember the mental manifestations of cerebral hypoxia.

[12.96]These are some of the implications of the above equation. All these things explain why arterial blood oxygen partial pressure is an inadequate measure of brain oxygen supply during cardiac arrest.

Adolf Fick and tissue hypoxia

[12.97]The more mathematically and physiologically educated person can use this equation to calculate other factors. In this chapter, the most interesting use of this equation is to calculate the minimum cardiac output compatible with normal oxygen supply to the body and consciousness at rest. However, the calculation does require some basic facts.

- [12.98]Blood flows into the brain through arteries, and flows out of the brain through the Jugular veins. The place where the Jugular vein on each side exits the skull to bring blood back to the heart is called the "Jugular Bulb". Studies in healthy humans reveal that cerebral hypoxia manifests when the level of oxygen saturation in the venous blood in the Jugular bulb ($S_{jv}O_2$) drops below 33-40% (Schell 2000).
- [12.99]Blood oxygen saturation levels in normal healthy adults in various parts of the circulation are: S_aO_2 is about 95-97%, $S_{jv}O_2$ is between 54-75%, and right ventricular or pulmonary venous oxygen saturation (S_vO_2) is between 60-80%.
- [12.100]Normal resting adult human oxygen consumption at rest is about 200 to 300 milliliters oxygen per minute (VO_2).
- [12.101]Normal blood hemoglobin concentrations in healthy adults are in the range 13.5-17 g/100 ml for men, and 12-15 g/100 ml for women.

[12.102]Substituting factors such as VO_2 and S_vO_2 into the oxygen flux equation, and rearranging, yields the following expression.

$$VO_2 = 0.134 \times [Hb] \times CO \times (S_aO_2 - S_vO_2)$$

[12.103]Rearranging for cardiac output yields the well-known "Fick equation", first published in 1870 by the German physiologist Adolf Eugen Fick (1829-1901). These parameters and the Fick equation are still the "golden standard" with which to calculate cardiac output, and is the method against which other techniques of cardiac output measurement are compared.

$$CO = VO_2 \div (0.134 \times [Hb] \times (S_aO_2 - S_vO_2))$$

[12.104]Substituting resting normal adult human values into this equation such as: $VO_2 = 200$ ml/min, [Hb] = 14 g/100 ml, $S_aO_2 = 97\%$, and $S_vO_2 = 33\%$ as a minimum below which bodily and cerebral hypoxia occurs yields a cardiac output = CO = 1.67 l/min. This reveals that for a resting adult with a low basal oxygen consumption, a surprisingly low cardiac output of 1.67 l/min is sufficient to sustain a body oxygen supply with normal consciousness, and without any cerebral hypoxia. This relatively simple exercise in mathematical physiology reveals profound consequences very relevant to this discussion.

- [12.105]It explains how it was possible for some resting people to be fully conscious, despite a surprisingly low cardiac output level of 1.7 l/min reported in some studies of cardiac output measurement techniques (Grondelle 1983, Hoeper 1999, Yung 2004).
- [12.106]Efficient manual cardiac massage generates a cardiac output at, or greater than 1.7 l/min in 43% of persons undergoing manual external cardiac massage for cardiac arrest. However, many persons undergoing cardiac resuscitation will not recover consciousness at these cardiac output levels, because they suffer the residual effects of cerebral hypoxia. But even so, some do regain consciousness, as is revealed by the clinical reports cited in this chapter.
- [12.107]Less efficient cardiac massage will result in cardiac output levels causing cerebral hypoxia, although not always with loss of consciousness. Such persons will experience cerebral hypoxia while conscious, and may even undergo near-death experiences.

[12.108]All this explains how people can be conscious during external manual cardiac massage applied during cardiac arrest, as well as cardiac output levels enabling near-death experiences.

Hypoxia and control by the soul

[12.109]The effects of cardiac arrest on the body are purely physical. In the case of cardiac arrest, rapid failure of consciousness of the body is a result of failure of sudden failure of the supply of oxygen to the brain. Restoration of consciousness of the body depends on the restoration of adequate circulation to supply the brain with sufficient oxygen to support consciousness. Brain function sufficient to generate consciousness (materialism), or to manifest the transmission of consciousness (dualism), is a physical chemical process. There are gradations of hypoxia, and people may be physically conscious and aware, even when suffering such severe cerebral hypoxia that they appear unconscious because of generalized muscle paralysis (see 4.67, 4.77).

[12.110]Believers in the mind-model of dualism say that the individual souls of people control the brains and bodies of conscious people (see 1.55-1.65). In addition, people are most definitely conscious while undergoing near-death experiences. Therefore, according to the mind-model of dualism, memories of near-death experiences undergone during cardiac arrest are actually memories of the interaction of the soul with a hypoxic, malfunctioning physical brain during the period of cardiac arrest (see 1.142).

Cardiac arrest and memory

[12.111]Varying degrees of neurological, cognitive defects, and memory malfunction are common, albeit very variable in intensity, among cardiac arrest survivors (Grubb 1996, Grubb 2000, Liere 1963, Mecklinger 1998, Mlynash 2010, Shadden 1992). So the fact that near-death experiences are spontaneously recalled long-term memories reveals supplementary evidence enabling us to distinguish between the mind-models of materialism and dualism. Prospective studies reveal that 10-18% of survivors of cardiac arrest report experiencing clear consciousness or near-death experiences while apparently unconscious during a period of cardiac arrest and resuscitation (Greyson 2003, Lommel 2001, Parnia 2001, Schwaninger 2002). Survivors only report near-death experiences undergone during cardiac arrest after they recover evident physical consciousness and the ability to speak. No torture, coercion, hypnosis, psychological cues, or drugs are used to elicit these memories of near-death experiences. So these reports are spontaneously recalled memories of a period of apparently clear consciousness during cardiac arrest and resuscitation.

[12.112]No electroencephalographic recordings were made of the brain activity of any of the patients during cardiac arrest and resuscitation in the studies reported by physicians such as Bruce Greyson (Greyson 2003), Pim van Lommel (Lommel 2001), Sam Parnia (Parnia 2001), and Janet Schwaninger (Schwaninger 2002). Even so, this did not prevent these physicians assuming these people could have had no form of brain function during their periods of cardiac arrest and resuscitation. This is why these authors implicitly, and even explicitly, suggest such experiences are memories of experiences undergone by the souls of these people during a period of absent brain function. So let us critically examine the phenomenon of spontaneous recall of memories of near-death experiences undergone during cardiac arrest using the mind-model of dualism.

- [12.113]Many near-death experience researchers claim that people have minimal, to no physical brain function during cardiac arrest (Greyson 2003, Lommel 2001, Parnia 2001, Schwaninger 2002).

- [12.114]According to the mind-model of dualism, cardiac arrest only affects the physical brain, and has no effect upon the soul (see 1.66-1.75). So the soul remains conscious after cardiac arrest causes the physical body to lose consciousness (see 1.50-1.54).

- [12.115]The souls of people are capable of making veridical observations of physical events, as well as undergoing cognitive, transcendental and affective experiences while their physical bodies are "evidently unconscious" during cardiac arrest (Greyson 2003, Lommel 2001, Parnia 2001, Schwaninger 2002).

- [12.116]Believers in dualism claim that memories are indelibly stored within the soul (see 1.92-1.115).

- [12.117]According to the investigators in the study of Pim van Lommel, only 2% (1/62) of the cardiac arrest survivors reporting near-death experiences had any memory problems, whereas 14% (40/282) of the survivors who did not report a near-death experience did experience memory problems (Table 3 in Lommel 2001). This means that $1 + 40 = 41 = 12\%$ of the 344 cardiac arrest survivors studied by the Pim van Lommel group had any memory problems or deficits. So according to Pim van Lommel, about 88% cardiac arrest survivors interviewed in this study experienced absolutely no memory problems. The implicit conclusion of Pim van Lommel is that the brain regions of cardiac arrest survivors required for recall and expression of memories, such as those of near-death experiences, functioned normally after recovering from cardiac arrest.

- [12.118]Accordingly, if the soul remains conscious during cardiac arrest, as well as being the repository of all memories, and the physical mechanisms of the brain required to recall and express memories all function normally after recovery from cardiac arrest, then all cardiac arrest survivors recovering consciousness without memory problems should be able to relate experiences undergone during cardiac arrest. But only 10-18% of cardiac arrest survivors ever recall experiences undergone during cardiac arrest, instead of the 88% of survivors who recover without any memory problems (Greyson 2003, Lommel 2001, Parnia 2001, Schwaninger 2002).

[12.119]Explanations based upon the mind-model of dualism fail to explain why only 10-18% of people recall experiences undergone during cardiac arrest. However, the mind-model of materialism does explain this statistic. Previous chapters clearly demonstrate that the physical brain is the repository of all memories. Furthermore, cerebral hypoxia inhibits the formation of memories in direct proportion to the severity and duration of hypoxia (see 4.70). The short period of consciousness remaining after the start of cardiac arrest, restoration of consciousness by efficient external cardiac massage, together with the residual effects of cerebral hypoxia explains why only 10-18% of people are able to remember conscious experiences undergone during cardiac arrest.

Cardiac arrest & proof of materialism

[12.120]All these things mean that people recalling undergoing near-death experiences during cardiac arrest and resuscitation, must have been conscious, even though they appeared unconscious at the time, and had brain function sufficient to support formation of memories of the experiences they subsequently reported. Consequently, according to the mind-model of dualism, near-death experiences recalled by cardiac arrest survivors are not true manifestations of the true nature of the soul. Instead, these experiences are expressions of the soul acting through the mechanisms of a conscious physical brain whose functioning is affected by hypoxia (see 1.142). Therefore, the mind-model of dualism predicts the same as that of materialism—reports of near-death experiences undergone during resuscitation for cardiac arrest are products of the effects of cerebral hypoxia. They are not manifestations of the true nature of the soul.

[12.121]But people never tell of undergoing near-death experiences during cardiac arrest. Instead, they only tell of undergoing near-death experiences after recovering physical consciousness and the ability to speak. So people spontaneously reporting near-death experiences undergone during a cardiac arrest are actually recalling long-term memories of these experiences. Discussions throughout the preceding chapters clearly demonstrate that the physical brain, and not the soul, is the repository of all memories. This fact has far reaching implications for the belief that near-death experiences undergone during cardiac arrest are manifestations of disembodiment, or continued consciousness of the soul. After all, if near-death experiences undergone during cardiac arrest were products of mental activity in the continually conscious soul, then no-one would ever recall these experiences because the soul possesses no memory ability. But some people do recall these experiences...

[12.122]Accordingly, near-death experiences undergone during cardiac arrest, are mental experiences occurring within the physically conscious brains of apparently unconscious persons. The hypoxia affected brains of these persons are capable of recalling these experiences at a later moment. The role of any putative soul in this type of experience is minimal, because the experience occurs within the brain. However, this argument cannot exclude a sort of modulating role of the soul on these experiences, although the nature of any such modulation is unknown and difficult to conceive. So instead of near-death experiences during cardiac arrest being proof of the reality of the soul, these experiences actually mean that any putative immaterial human soul has properties very different to those proposed by the mind model of dualism.

13

Soul & Psi

[13.1]Many people claim paranormal abilities are indirect proof of the reality of a human soul, and the reality of a life after death (Glicksohn 1990, Irwin 1993, Thalbourne 1996, Voracek 2009), as well as the fundamental truths espoused by many religions (Irwin 1993, Lindeman 2012, Orenstein 2002, Rudski 2003, Wain 2007). So it is impossible to disregard paranormal beliefs when considering the relationship of the mind to the body, and the possible reality of a human soul. Indeed, many believers in the mind-model of dualism claim the soul uses just such paranormal abilities to perceive and interact with the physical world.

[13.2]The out-of-body experience is the most relevant phenomenon providing ostensible proof of paranormal abilities. Many of those believing in the reality of separation of the soul from the body during out-of-body experiences, postulate that non-physical, or paranormal sensory abilities explain perceptions recalled by persons recounting what they observed during these experiences. Janice Holden, one of the co-editors, and author of Chapter 7 in the *Handbook of Near Death Experiences: Thirty Years of Investigation*, wrote just such an explanation.

[13.3]*For reasons discussed here later, NDE [near-death experience] researchers and others have shown particular interest in what I am calling apparently nonphysical veridical NDE perception (AVP). In AVP, NDErs report veridical perception that, considering the positions and/or conditions of their physical bodies during the near-death episodes, apparently could not have been the result of normal sensory processes or logical inference—nor, therefore, brain mediation—either before, during, or after those episodes. Thus, AVP suggests the ability of consciousness to function independent of the physical body. (page 186 in Holden 2009)*

[13.4]In this passage, Janice Holden claims that some perceptions reported by persons recalling their out-of-body experiences could not have been made with physical senses, or be products of subconscious logical inference. By inference, she invokes perceptive abilities other than those of the physical senses. Emily and Edward Kelly, together with Bruce Greyson are the authors of Chapter 6 in the book *Irreducible Mind* edited by Edward and Emily Kelly (Kelly 2007). They were much more explicit regarding the possible modes of perception.

> [13.5]*Nevertheless, the large numbers of claims of veridical OBEs [out-of-body experiences], both corroborated and uncorroborated, suggest the need for a response more robust than "quietly dropping" them.*
> *An alternate explanation for these veridical cases might be, not that the person's consciousness in some sense literally left the body and traveled to the distant location, but that the person learned about the event in question by some psi process such as telepathy or clairvoyance, and then incorporated that knowledge into the OBE, which was simply an added hallucination. The evidence for psi from both experimental and field studies is sufficient to make this a plausible theory for many, perhaps even most, of the veridical cases. (page 401 in Chapter 6 of Kelly 2007)*

[13.6]Here the authors clearly propose paranormal perceptive abilities such as telepathy, or clairvoyance, as an explanation for otherwise inexplicable veridical perceptions made during out-of-body experiences. It is an elegant way of getting around the possibility that no such thing as disembodiment of the soul occurs. In this system of thought, the embodied soul uses paranormal perceptive abilities to perceive events outside the body, and the sensations of disembodiment are a hallucination generated by bodily sensations plus these paranormal perceptions. These possibilities necessitate a discussion of the relevance of possible human paranormal perceptive abilities to the mind-models of dualism and materialism.

Types of paranormal abilities defined

[13.7]So is there any proof for the reality of human paranormal abilities? Belief in, and experience of paranormal abilities, has been reported in all societies since ancient times. A wave of public interest in all manner of paranormal experiences during the nineteenth century was the impetus for the founding of the Society for Psychical Research in England during 1882, and the American Society for Psychical Research the USA during 1885. This was the dawn of modern research into these phenomena. Extensive studies and developing insights since 1882 revealed fundamental types of paranormal experiences and phenomena. The book, *Parapsychology: Frontier Science of the Mind*, written by one of the founders of modern American parapsychological research, Joseph Banks Rhine (1895-1980), defines these various types of fundamental paranormal phenomena into sensory and motor aspects.

- [13.8]*Extrasensory perception:* "the knowledge conveyed in a parapsychical occurrence concerns events external to the subject, technically the mental process is properly called a perception. Since the senses are not involved (and, with no physical mediation from the object to the percipient such, as characterizes sensory perception, they could not be) these cognitive phenomena of parapsychology are called extrasensory perception or ESP." (pages 7-8 in Rhine 1957) [author's note: "parapsychical" is an old term for paranormal]
- [13.9]*Telepathy:* "is the transfer of thought from one mind to another without the intermediation of the senses." (page 9 in Rhine 1957)
- [13.10]*Clairvoyance:* "is defined as the extrasensory perception of objects or objective events, as distinguished from the mental states or thoughts of another person." (page 9 in Rhine 1957)
- [13.11]*Precognition:* "is the perception of a future event by means of extrasensory perception." (page 10 in Rhine 1957)
- [13.12]*Psychokinesis:* "in which, again without physical intermediation, some personal influence produces a physical effect. Such direct mental operation on a material body or a physical energy system is called psychokinesis or PK. This is the same as the familiar popular concept of mind over matter." (page 8 in Rhine 1957)

[13.13]These various aspects of paranormal phenomena are bundled into the general descriptive term "psi". The definition of psi is as follows.

[13.14]*But as the reader becomes familiar with the nature of these capacities and their way of functioning he will find it easy and convenient to use a general term to designate the whole range of parapsychical phenomena, and for this the Greek letter psi has come into general use. This is a device of convenience and does not imply that it is known that there is only one basic underlying type of process. (page 9 in Rhine 1957)*

[13.15]Almost 40 years later, a newer definition of psi further clarifies some of the properties of this collection of apparently paranormal phenomena.

[13.16]*The term psi denotes anomalous processes of information or energy transfer, processes such as telepathy or other forms of extrasensory perception that are currently unexplained in terms of known physical or biological mechanisms. The term is purely descriptive: It neither implies that such anomalous phenomena are paranormal nor connotes anything about their underlying mechanisms. (Bem 1994)*

[13.17]Daryl Bem's definition of psi is actually very interesting. It states that psi abilities are poorly understood forms of anomalous perception. Such a definition opens the future possibility of incorporating these abilities into the gamut of presently known, and well-defined, human sensory and motor abilities.

How common are paranormal experiences?

[13.18]One extensive review indicates that somewhat more than 50% of all people report personal experience of paranormal abilities such as telepathy, clairvoyance, precognition, or psychokinesis (page 222 in Targ 2000). However, closer examination reveals that only about 10-15% of all people undergo what actually could be defined as true psi, or paranormal experiences (Kennedy 2005). Even so, this means that psi experiences are really quite common. This was the basis of the initial belief of the founders of the Society for Psychical Research during 1882. They also thought that because these phenomena were relatively common, that definitive proof of their reality would require only a few months or years. But did this happen? Has research since 1882 convincingly established the reality of paranormal phenomena, or psi?

No definitive proof for psi

[13.19]About 10-15% of the general population has had personal experience of apparently paranormal sensory perceptions. Indeed, the fact that psi abilities are so common, means that proof would be so evident as to require no complicated statistical analysis—simple experiments and equally simple statistical analyses would reveal the evident reality of such abilities. Nevertheless, many years of research by extremely capable and dedicated scientists since the founding of societies for psychical research has yet to conclusively prove the reality of any of these psi abilities (Alcock 2003, Bauer 1984, Hyman 1988, Kennedy 2001, Meehl 1956, Milton 1999, Milton 2001). So what are some of the reasons for this claim for a lack of definitive proof for psi abilities?

Decline effect and failure of training

[13.20]Rhine was the first to publish the surprising observation that scores in tests of psi abilities were better in the initial phase of an experiment, and declined as the experiment progressed. He called this phenomenon the "decline effect", and considered it as one of the most conclusive proofs of psi abilities (pages 60-62, 89, 90 in Rhine 1957).

[13.21]*Another suggestion offered by Rhine to address the issue of deception was paying attention to the "signs of psi," or specific features of the subject's performances. This included psi missing and decline effects, which he believed "could serve as evidence against experimenter deception when it was discovered later by another analyst". Such signs were seen by Rhine as hidden indicators of the presence of psi in the data unlikely to be faked. (page 94 in Alvarado 2011)*

[13.22]Even though Rhine considered decline effects as a sign of the presence of psi, results of completed experiments in which a decline effect is evident, often reveal no evidence of psi abilities (Alcock 2003, Dunne 1994, Kennedy 2003, Rhine 1957). Decline effects also diminish with increasingly rigorous and sophisticated experimental methodologies to determine the existence of psi abilities (Kennedy 2003). Other researchers also find no evidence that the decline effect is proof of any psi abilities (Dunne 1994, page 38 in Grim 1984).

[13.23]More interestingly, the reality of a decline effect reveals something very puzzling indeed. People taking part in experiments testing psi abilities are actually training themselves to use such abilities—much as a musician trains by continually practicing a piece of music, or in the use of an instrument. However, instead of the psi abilities of participants taking part in psi experiments improving with such training—the psi abilities of participants in psi experiments actually decline with training (Meehl 1956). This is an effect never observed with the training of any other human senses or abilities. Therefore, the decline effect is not a proof of psi abilities, or actually reveals that psi abilities are stranger than any other known sensory or motor ability.

Meta-analyses fail to prove the reality of psi abilities

[13.24]Then we come to the very controversial matter of large scale meta-analyses of multiple studies of psi abilities. A meta-analysis is a statistical technique combining results of several similar studies to identify patterns, relationships, and differences. Parapsychologists often employ this statistical technique because of inadequate sample sizes in many studies of psi abilities. Such meta-analyses of psi abilities have been a major source of contention between proponents and skeptics of psi abilities. For example:

- [13.25]"Ganzfeld" is a German term meaning "whole field". Ganzfeld studies are a technique in parapsychological experimentation subjecting people to unpatterned visual and auditory sensory stimuli. This produces a situation similar to sensory deprivation by reducing the effects of environmental noise, so allowing perception of weaker psi signals. Until now, Ganzfeld studies of psi abilities yield the most positive evidence of psi abilities such as telepathy and clairvoyance. Several meta-analyses of Ganzfeld studies yield quite spectacular results seemingly proving the reality of psi abilities (Bem 1994, Storm 2001, Storm 2006, Storm 2010, Williams 2011). However, equally well performed meta-analyses of the data from these same studies question the validity of such seemingly spectacular results (Hyman 1985, Hyman 1988, Milton 1999, Milton 2001).
- [13.26]Meta-analyses of many studies of precognition also yield spectacular results seemingly proving the reality of this psi ability (Bem 2011, Honorton 1989). Even so, other equally sophisticated meta-analyses of the data from these same studies fail to reveal any evidence of precognition (Ritchie 2012, Wagenmakers 2011).
- [13.27]Meta-analyses of many psychokinesis experiments by some researchers reveal apparently impressive evidence of the reality of this psi ability (Girden 1962, Jahn 1982, Radin 1989, Rhine 1957). Yet other equally well executed meta-analyses of the data from these same studies fail to reveal any evidence of psychokinesis (Bösch 2006, Hyman 1988).

[13.28]So what do such equally well executed, but conflicting analyses using the same datasets reveal? The most glaringly evident revelation is a failure of sophisticated statistical analyses of these extensive datasets to unequivocally demonstrate the existence of paranormal abilities. This same failure of meta-analyses to conclusively prove the reality of psi abilities was also discussed by the noted parapsychologist, James E. Kennedy (2003, 2004, 2005, 2006). He was very clear about the value of meta-analyses in parapsychological studies.

> [13.28a]*One of the most revealing properties of psi research is that meta-analyses consistently find that experimental results do not become more reliably significant with larger sample sizes as assumed by statistical theory (Kennedy, 2003b; 2004). This means that the methods of statistical power analysis for experimental design do not apply, which implies a fundamental lack of replicability.*
>
> *[...]*
>
> *Further, for the past two decades, the debates about the reality of psi have focused on meta-analysis. The evidence that psi experiments typically do not have properties consistent with the assumptions for meta-analysis adds substantial doubts to the already controversial (Kennedy 2004) claims about meta-analysis findings in parapsychology. (pages 266-267 in Kennedy 2005).*

[13.29]As mentioned earlier in this chapter, paranormal experiences are relatively common. After all, one review states that about 10-15% of all people have undergone at least one apparently paranormal experience (Kennedy 2005). Complex statistical analyses are unnecessary to prove the reality of common abilities—their reality should simply be evident. But many years of parapsychological research reveals no consistently unequivocal, and irrefutable proof for the reality of psi abilities. Such proof is singularly absent. This state of absent to equivocal proof may indicate psi abilities are no more than an ancient illusion. An alternative explanation is that psi abilities are actually very different to those tested for by parapsychological researchers. But all these studies, and all these analyses, are products of formal parapsychological research. Are there any alternative sources of evidence for the reality or illusory nature of psi abilities?

Blindness and the paranormal

[13.30]One method is to examine whether people with severe sensory deficits manifest psi abilities. This is a technique similar to Ganzfeld studies, only using people with long-term sensory deficits such as blindness and deafness, instead of the short-term effects of a Ganzfeld study. Blindness is a perfect example of a sensory deficit severely handicapping those affected. So do blind people develop paranormal abilities to compensate for their serious sensory deficit? For the practical purposes of this discussion, we can divide blindness into four different types according to cause. Blindness can be induced suddenly by simply blindfolding a sighted person, babies can be born blind due to a large number of congenital causes, injury and disease of areas of the brain processing visual signals can cause blindness, and eye diseases can cause blindness. So it is very instructive to investigate whether the phenomenon of blindness reveals anything about the reality of psi sensory abilities.

[13.31]But is a discussion of blindness relevant to a this discussion of psi abilities? The answer is an unqualified, "Yes!" Many people believe psi abilities can be trained and developed. Hundreds of books purport to teach people how to develop their supposedly dormant psi abilities. Equally many people and organizations offer courses teaching people to develop these same supposedly dormant paranormal senses. Furthermore, we know blind people develop the use of their remaining senses to compensate somewhat for their loss of sight. This begs the very logical question of whether blind people develop any of the psi sensory abilities believed to be dormant in all humans. And if such abilities are not dormant in all humans, they are at least present in the 10-15% of humans known to have experienced psi phenomena (Kennedy 2005). Therefore, an analysis of the occurrence of psi sensory abilities in blind people should be very revealing.

Blindness due to blindfolding

[13.32]Blindfolding a sighted person is a method of instantly inducing temporary blindness. Common personal experience, and the experiences of blindfolded people throughout millennia, reveals only that blindfolded people do not suddenly develop psi perceptive abilities compensating for sudden loss of sight. Blindfolded people are effectively blind, and compensate for the sudden disappearance sight with their remaining senses. Some proponents of the reality of psi perceptive abilities, might claim that sudden blinding with a blindfold may yield too little time for development of any dormant psi abilities. This would be a very strange claim, because Ganzfeld studies also do not last long either. However, an answer to this possible objection is available. Persons blindfolded for several days do sometimes report visual hallucinations, but reveal no evident psi perceptive abilities (Zuckerman 1964).

Congenital and childhood blindness

[13.33]Childhood blindness includes hereditary disorders of brain and eye development, as well as infections and vitamin deficiencies. A publication of the World Health Organization during 2004 analyzed the worldwide causes of blindness for the year 2002. Table 4 on page 848 of this publication reveals that childhood blindness, with its multitude of causes related to disease or congenital abnormalities of the eyes and brain, accounts for only 3.9% of all causes of blindness worldwide (Resnikoff 2004). I will not discuss childhood blindness because this affects development and function of the brain during growth of the child to adulthood (Büchel 1998, Ortiz 2011, Qin 2013), and this abnormal brain development may well affect development of psi abilities in unknown ways.

Adult acquired blindness

[13.34]According to *Fact Sheet No. 282* on *Visual Impairment and Blindness*, published by the World Health Organization, there were about 314 million people alive on this world with a visual impairment during 2009, of which 45 million were totally blind (WHO 2009). And uncounted millions of blind people have lived and died prior to 2009. Of course, this figure of 45 million says nothing about the causes of blindness. An earlier World Health Organization publication during 2004 analyzed the worldwide causes of blindness for the year 2002. Table 4 on page 848 of this publication reveals that the major causes of adult blindness are: cataract 47.8%, glaucoma 12.3%, macular degeneration 8.7%, corneal opacities 5.1%, diabetic retinopathy 4.8%, trachoma 3.6%, and Onchocerciasis 0.8% (Resnikoff 2004). These are all causes of blindness due to eye diseases. Adding all these percentages reveals that worldwide, more than 83% of all persons who became blind during adulthood became that way because of eye diseases. Furthermore, these are all eye diseases occurring in people who possessed normal vision for many years. This means that those regions of the brain required for processing nerve signals from the eyes, and translating them into conscious visual imagery, developed normally in these unfortunate people. Accordingly, because the brains of these people developed normally while sighted, the structures and functioning of the brains of these blind people would be the same as the brains of sighted people.

Blind people develop no paranormal abilities

[13.35]Many believers in the reality of paranormal perceptive abilities claim these abilities are latent in all people, and can be trained and developed. Total, helpless blindness is a wonderful stimulus to develop all remaining perceptive abilities, including paranormal perceptive abilities. Just imagine if blind persons did develop paranormal perceptive abilities. Blind clairvoyant, telepathic, and precognitive people would be wonderfully successful and wealthy. Just imagine how successful such a person would be as a poker player. They would be able to guess which card they would get, and know the cards of the others. At blackjack, they would know which cards they would receive. At roulette, they would know which numbers to bet upon. But gambling casinos are not overrun with rich blind gamblers, fleecing sighted gamblers with their paranormal perceptive abilities. The stock market is another field in which paranormally gifted blind persons would dominate. But there are no obscenely wealthy paranormally gifted blind stock market investors. You could go on and on with more such examples. But the reality is that no-one expects a blind person to develop paranormal sensory abilities, even though paranormal sensory abilities are supposedly dormant in each person, and purportedly able to be trained and developed.

[13.36]Development of remaining physical senses fails to compensate for loss of sight, because the blind are still considerably handicapped. So what do we know about any dormant psi perceptive abilities possessed by blind people? The above conditions eventually result in total blindness over periods of months to years, which means persons suffering these disorders have more than enough time to gradually develop any dormant paranormal perceptive abilities. However, blind people never receive courses to train any dormant psi abilities. Blind people also do not spontaneously develop any dormant psi perceptive abilities, even though 10-15% of all people report spontaneous experiences of psi abilities (Kennedy 2005). In addition to this popular knowledge, formal parapsychological studies also reveal that blind people develop no psi abilities compensating for their lack of sight (Storm 2001a, Storm 2007).

[13.37]All these things are part of ages-old knowledge why no one seriously expects blind people to navigate safely across traffic filled streets, drive automobiles, or fly aircraft. Indeed, if people knew they would develop psi abilities after becoming blind, they might even rejoice upon being so afflicted.

[13.38]*Ask yourself what your reaction would be upon hearing that a loved family member, such as a father, a son, or a brother, has suddenly become totally blind. Would you say; "Joyous news! Oh happy day! He has been blessed with blindness. He will no longer be hindered by the gross material sense of physical sight. Now he will be able to develop his dormant paranormal senses, and these will enable him to 'see' without seeing. He will be able to perceive people as they really are, to learn and to understand the motives underlying their every word, and their every action. He will be able to perceive the world around him as it really is. He may even be able to perceive the future. Oh lucky, lucky man! Let us feast and celebrate!" (modified from page 82 in Woerlee 2005)*

[13.39]Such a reaction is unheard of. No-one throughout all history, or in any known human society, has ever reacted to such news in this way. The normal reaction upon hearing such news is of pity, of sorrow, and of compassion for the enormity of the calamity afflicting the loved family member. Becoming blind is not regarded as a wonderful opportunity to develop any dormant psi abilities. Instead, everyone knows that a family member afflicted with blindness will be permanently handicapped. And the afflicted family member, living in his now dark world, dependent upon help from others, knows this best of all. Common knowledge from millennia of human experience teaches us that blind people live in a dark world. Their information about this world, and their perceptions of this world, are derived only from their remaining physical senses, modified by their memories of the world as they experienced it when they still possessed sight. The blind are living proof that people possess no paranormal sensory abilities as defined by parapsychology, and this knowledge supplements the absence of conclusive experimental proof of the reality of psi perceptive abilities after more than 100 years of intensive research.

Heinrich Hertz and Psi

[13.40]All these things reveal psi abilities are very unlikely, or at best very different to what most people believe. Compare the lack of evidence for psi abilities to that of radio waves. Electromagnetic radio waves received by televisions, radios, and cellular telephones are just like the sensations people claim to perceive with paranormal sensory abilities. They are invisible, and cannot be sensed with the physical senses of the body. The renowned Scottish physicist James Clerk Maxwell (1831-1879) predicted the existence of radio waves in 1873. Heinrich Rudolf Hertz (1857-1894), a German professor of physics at the University of Karlsruhe in Germany, detected and confirmed the reality of radio waves in 1887. The explosive development of radio technology and science since 1887 has resulted in the ubiquitous application of radio waves throughout all facets of modern society. Devices based upon the application of radio waves: such as radios, televisions, microwave ovens, satellite navigation, cellular telephones, and many other applications, are what make modern society possible.

[13.41]Contrast the development of radio technology with the situation of proof of the reality of psi abilities. As yet no unquestionable proof of the reality of psi abilities has been presented, despite more than a century of intensive research since 1882, (a date preceding the first discovery of the reality of equally invisible radio waves in 1887), and despite the fact that psi experiences are reported by 10-15% of all people (Kennedy 2005). So the existence of psi abilities is illusory, or at best very unlikely.

[13.42]However, such negative proof does not constitute absolute proof of the absence of psi abilities. It is a negative proof, much like saying; "I cannot find proof, therefore it does not exist." Such a negative proof does not exclude the reality of psi abilities. Negative proof may simply be an indication that all investigations conducted thus far used incorrect methods for detecting the existence of psi abilities. Nonetheless, as discussed above, even a cursory examination of the world about us reveals definitive proof of the absence of psi abilities such as psychokinesis, clairvoyance, telepathy, and precognition.

Perception and control by Psi?

[13.43]Even so, many people still believe in the reality of these psi abilities, either because of personal experiences, or because of the experiences of others. These reasons were, and still are the main reasons for belief in the reality of psi abilities. So just for the sake of argument, do psi abilities manifest in objectively measureable ways when viewed from the perspective of the mind-body relationship? This is an idea well worth examining, even if only because of the widespread belief in psi abilities, and the possibility that paranormal, or other unknown phenomena may somehow be involved in the control of the brain and the body by an immaterial human soul.

Materialism and psi

[13.44]The position of materialism, or rather a pragmatic analysis of the negative results of parapsychological research, is very clear. Psi abilities are illusory. Sense organs perceive sensations. Mental activity generated by the brain controls movements. Consciousness and mental activity are products of brain function.

Dualism and psi

[13.45]However, imagine what would happen if the soul does indeed possess wondrous psi abilities. A combination of the mind-model of dualism and psi abilities opens several possibilities. The soul could employ psi abilities such as telepathy and clairvoyance to sense the world around the physical body, and psychokinesis to activate the body. So what are some objectively observable consequences of such a situation?

- [13.46]Imagine if the souls of many deaf persons could perceive the world with paranormal senses such as clairvoyance and telepathy. Just as with blindness, deafness due to afflictions of the physical body would not exist. But just as in the situation of blind persons, the deaf also remain deaf. This ancient observation may indicate the impossibility of training latent psi abilities present in many deaf people. It may indicate that psi abilities are exceedingly rare, which contradicts studies indicating that 10-15% of people undergo paranormal experiences during their lives (Kennedy 2005). It could also indicate the illusory nature of psi abilities.
- [13.47]Proponents of the mind-model of dualism claim that the soul is continually conscious (see 1.50-1.54), and is unaffected by drugs, diseases, disorders, and injuries affecting the physical brain (see 1.66-1.75). An out-of-body experience is ostensibly due to disembodiment of the soul. So the fact that some people undergo out-of-body experiences while seemingly unconscious during general anesthesia, appears to confirm belief in continual

335

consciousness of the soul. Imagine that the soul also possesses psi perceptive abilities. This would mean that during general anesthesia, the soul would continually perceive sensations about the body with psi sensory abilities such as clairvoyance or telepathy. Proponents of the mind-model of dualism also claim that the soul is the repository of all long-term memories (see 1.92-1.115). The functioning of the brain required to recall and express memories returns to normal after the effects of general anesthetic drugs fade away (see 1.143). So according to this chain of logic, most people awakening after general anesthesia should be able recall veridical events and speech occurring near their bodies while they were physically unconscious under general anesthesia. But they do not, and discussions throughout this book even reveals that the soul possesses no memory abilities. All this indicates the irrelevance of any putative psi perceptive abilities possessed by the soul during periods of general anesthesia, or any other of the myriad causes of loss of consciousness of the physical body.

- [13.48]What if the soul perceives veridical events and sounds near a person undergoing an out-of-body experience with psi abilities? One fact is certain, veridical perceptions made during out-of-body experiences are verifiable physical perceptions confirmed by other physically conscious persons, as well as by physical recording apparatus. However, extensive discussions throughout this book reveal that the soul possesses no memory abilities. So even if the soul could perceive veridical physical events with psi perceptive abilities during out-of-body experiences, the soul would be unable to remember these events, and therefore unable to recount these memories at a later moment. Accordingly, there is no possibility that the apparently disembodied soul employs psi perceptive abilities during out-of-body experiences.

[13.49]All these things indicate that paranormal perceptive abilities are absent during these situations, indicating the rarity of psi perceptive abilities, their illusory nature, or that they are very different to what most people believe. However, what are the consequences if the soul employs psychokinesis to affect and control physical body functions? Proponents of the reality of psychokinesis claim that people are able to affect the working of electronic random number generators and computers (Girden 1962, Jahn 1982, Radin 1989), as well as the movements of physical objects as large as falling dice (Rhine 1957). The magnitudes of these experimental effects are such that if the soul possesses psychokinetic abilities, then it should be able to affect some chemical reactions within bodily tissues, or affect the functioning of nerves. So if the soul possesses any psychokinetic abilities, then many persons will objectively demonstrate psychokinetic control of body functions during several medical conditions. Let us examine some of the more dramatic examples.

- [13.50]Brain death is a dramatic and tragic event resulting from a multitude of causes. But the end result is always the same—the physical brain is dead. Physical consciousness and brainstem reflexes are absent in brain dead persons. Jørgensen (1973) reported a very thorough study of brain death in 63 persons in whom the diagnosis was very definitely confirmed by the demonstration of, "neither supratentorial- nor infratentorial circulation on serial angiography performed twice at an interval of more than 20 min" (page 260 in Jørgensen 1973). Translated into non-technical language, this statement means there was no flow of blood inside the skulls of these unlucky persons, meaning their brains were definitely dead. Diagnosis of brain death and brainstem death was therefore very definite in these unfortunate patients. Their brains were dead, but their spinal cords still functioned, generating sometimes quite spectacular forms of spontaneous movements such as the "Lazarus sign". The Lazarus sign is a spinal reflex described in brain dead persons who suddenly raise their arms and cross them over their chests (Heytens 1989, Ropper 1984). Nevertheless, none of these spectacular movements are responses to commands, nor are they driven by physically conscious activity. Near-death experiences ostensibly reveal that the soul is unaffected by death of the physical brain. So if the soul possesses psi abilities such as psychokinesis, why can it not activate the evidently still functioning spinal cord, nerves, and muscles outside the brain to indicate the fact of consciousness? After all, if psychokinesis generates sufficient energy to affect electronic circuitry, or the movements of falling dice, then it could certainly activate a nerve controlling a muscle. If this is true, then a neurologist could ask a brain dead person to move a finger, or twitch a muscle in response to a command or question. But studies of 65 persons with angiographically confirmed brain and brainstem death reported above only reveal a total lack of conscious activity, or conscious responses manifested by the body (Jørgensen

1973, Heytens 1989, Ropper 1984). This may indicate that the soul possesses no psychokinetic abilities. Another possibility is that the soul only interfaces with the body through the brainstem, which is also dead in brain dead persons. It could also indicate the illusory nature of the belief in psychokinesis.

- [13.51]Spinal cord injury can result in total paralysis of the lower body. The unfortunate person remains normally conscious, their brains, and the functioning of their minds are unaffected. In other words, according to the logic of the mind-model of dualism, the interaction between the souls of these unfortunate people and their bodies is unaffected. So if the souls of these unlucky persons possess psychokinetic abilities, why are they unable to directly activate the nerves below the damaged level of the spinal cord, or induce healing and neuroplasticity in the spinal cord resulting in a restoration of control over the paralyzed lower body? The brainstem, or likely interface of the soul with the body, is intact in these persons. So there is no reason why this would not occur if the soul possesses psi abilities such as psychokinesis. This indicates a lack of psychokinetic abilities in the many millions of paraplegic persons who have lived, and are now alive.

- [13.52]Shortly before death, some deeply demented, or brain damaged persons exhibit moments or periods of clear lucidity. Such lucid intervals sometimes give rise to rather fuzzy and illogical ideas proposed by some believers in the mind-model of dualism such as Nahm (Nahm 2009) and Smit (Smit 2011). For example, Smit (2011) invokes "other—as yet unexplained—pathways" to explain this phenomenon. After all, according to the mind-model of dualism the soul is unaffected by any of the many causes of dementia (see 1.66-1.75). So is psychokinesis a mechanism explaining these lucid intervals? As discussed throughout this book, the soul only expresses itself in this material world through the mechanisms of the physical body (see 5.27-5.35). This means there is no evidence of psychokinetic activity driving such lucid intervals. Instead, temporary restoration of reasonably normal functioning of these diseased brains explains the phenomenon of lucid intervals better than any paranormal phenomena (see discussion in Cobb 2000).

[13.53]All these, and many other medical conditions reveal a spectacular absence of any manifestations of psi abilities such as psychokinesis, clairvoyance, or telepathy. So the conclusion regarding the relevance of paranormal abilities to the relation of the mind to the body is evident—the functioning of the human body reveals no evidence for psi abilities.

Psi is not meant to be used for personal gain

[13.54]Nonetheless, even though the discussions in this chapter reveal the illusory nature of psi abilities, some people are not satisfied with such a conclusion. Some even make a final attempt to disregard the absence of psi abilities in medical conditions, by making specious statements such as; "Aha, but psi abilities are not intended for personal purposes or personal gain." Such a statement is very strange, and raises the question of who made this ruling. Nonetheless, I have personally heard more than one person making this statement. As one of the characters in a book entitled *The Unholy Legacy of Abraham* explains (Woerlee 2008), people always use psi abilities for personal gain.

[13.55] *"That's strange, if you read the paranormal experiences most people report, then you realize they are nearly all very personal. Many paranormal experiences are dreams or premonitions of events, illnesses, or accidents occurring to the persons making these reports, or to their near family members. Many gamblers attribute a streak of luck to paranormal abilities, and gamblers most definitely work for personal gain. Throughout thousands of years, magicians, sorcerers, shamans, witch-doctors, astrologers, oracles, and fortune-tellers have exploited their paranormal abilities for very personal gain to earn a living. Some even became very wealthy. And you tell me that you are not supposed to use paranormal abilities for personal benefit, financial or otherwise, when this is precisely what everyone does, and has done for tens of thousands of years. So tell me, who says you are not supposed to use paranormal abilities for personal gain? Is it God? This is very unlikely, because the God of the Jews, the Christians, and of Islam, permits one quarter of the Western European population to experience paranormal events for just these purposes of personal benefit or profit. Perhaps this ruling not to use paranormal abilities for personal gain comes from other gods, such as the gods of ancient Greece, from the gods of the Eskimos, the gods of ancient Persia, the gods of India, the gods of the Australian aboriginals, or those of the Aztecs? Do angels regularly descend to earth with flaming swords to order humankind not to use paranormal abilities for personal gain? Or is this simply good advice from little green men from outer space visiting our humble little planet? You tell me." (pages 88-89 in Woerlee 2008)*

[13.56]Viewed in this way, the idea that psi abilities may not be used for personal gain is patently ridiculous. People making such a statement seem to forget that practitioners of psi such as astrologers, tarot readers, palmists, dowsers, and many others, often use their abilities for personal gain. The reality is that for many millennia, people have always employed psi abilities for personal gain, sometimes personal, sometimes financial. Accordingly the argument that psi must not be used for personal gain is manifestly ridiculous.

Is psi relevant to the study of the soul?

[13.57]Psi perceptive abilities and psychokinesis as proposed by parapsychology and popular belief do not exist. Nonetheless, millennia of belief in, and reports of apparently paranormal experiences seem to indicate something is happening. Indeed, the very fact that people sometimes make observations incapable of clear explanation reveals clues to expanding our knowledge of human sensory and interpretive abilities. But what abilities are we talking about?

- [13.58]Are many apparently paranormal psi perceptive abilities and psychokinetic phenomena manifestations of as yet poorly understood psychological, physiological and physical phenomena? For example, psi perceptions may be a product of subconscious integration of subliminal, otherwise disregarded perceptions, and known information. However, if psi is no more than a name for such as yet poorly understood processes, then such apparently paranormal perceptive abilities are irrelevant when considering the relationship between the body and the soul.
- [13.59]Spontaneous apparent psi sensory abilities and phenomena are quite common, because about 10-15% of people report having experienced such perceptions. Yet the reality of psi sensory abilities and phenomena remains unproven despite more than 120 years of fruitless attempts to unequivocally prove the reality of these sensory abilities and phenomena. This raises the question of whether popular belief in psi perceptive abilities and psychokinetic phenomena are no more than ages-old mass illusions. Indeed, this is the most likely explanation after more than 120 years of failure to unequivocally

prove the reality of these phenomena. This explanation also means that psi abilities are irrelevant when considering the relationship between the body and the soul.

- [13.60]Do the extensive statistical studies of these phenomena truly reveal the reality of "something"? Unfortunately for this idea, manifestations of this "something" are fickle, are marginally present, and only revealed by sophisticated statistical meta-analyses. Furthermore, a statistical "something" that is fickle, random, and marginal, cannot explain the perceptions and effective control of the body by an immaterial soul. This also means that psi abilities are irrelevant when considering the relationship between the body and the soul.

Conclusion: psi is irrelevant

[13.61]The reality of psi abilities with the properties proposed by parapsychology is no more than a popular illusion. Therefore, as regards the relevance of psi to differentiating which mind-model is correct—the conclusion is equally evident. Psi abilities are most likely products of ages-old collective illusions, or simply products of poorly understood subconscious sensory and integrative processes. However, regardless of the putative reality of any possible psi abilities, they are irrelevant to any understanding of whether the mind-models of dualism or materialism better explain the true nature of the human mind.

14

Out of the Body?

14.1Some people report undergoing experiences during which they sense themselves displaced out of their physical bodies, such as during out-of-body experiences, or find themselves transported to transcendental worlds, such as during near-death experiences. Frequently, other transcendental, affective, or cognitive perceptions accompany such experiences. Michael Marsh, the author of a book entitled *Out-of-Body and Near-Death Experiences* (Marsh 2012), has coined the useful term "extracorporeal experiences" for such experiences. This covers both experiences of disembodiment to the vicinity of the physical body, as well as apparent transport to transcendental worlds. Many people consider such experiences as proof of the reality of a human soul. But are such extracorporeal experiences truly manifestations of a separation of the soul from the body? Or are they unusual manifestations of altered body function?

Extracorporeal experiences during anesthesia

14.2Some people report undergoing such experiences during general anesthesia. Jeffrey Long cites some very profound near-death experiences in his book *Evidence of the Afterlife* (Long 2010). One of them was that of a young woman who underwent a second heart valve replacement within six months.

14.3*During my surgery I felt myself lift from my body and go above the operating table. The doctor told me later that they had kept my heart open and stopped for a long time, and they had a great amount of difficulty getting my heart started again. That must have been when I left my body because I could see the doctors nervously trying to get my heart going. It was strange to be so detached from my physical body. I was curious about what they* *were doing but not concerned. Then, as I drifted further away, I saw my father at the head of the table. He looked up at me, which did give me a surprise because he had been dead now for almost a year. (page 98, Long 2010)*

[14.4]This is a superficially astonishing and wondrous story. Her heart did not beat. Furthermore, her chest was open, so she could not breathe. Yet there was her conscious mind, calmly observing all these things from a position outside her "clinically dead" body. Nevertheless, this idea of so-called "clinical death" is a misnomer. A machine called a ventilator inflated and deflated her lungs during this phase of her operation. Only her heart was not beating during her experience. However, in between attempts to restart her heart, the surgeons would have applied internal cardiac massage to sustain a circulation of blood around her body. Efficient internal heart massage can restore brain electroencephalographic activity (Case 5 in Elton 1961), as well as restore consciousness (Miller 1961). At the same time, the anesthesiologist would have stopped administering any anesthetic drugs, to eliminate the known depressive actions of these drugs on heart function. This latter was most likely the reason she awoke and underwent an unusual extracorporeal experience—in this case a combined out-of-body and near-death experience. As I mentioned earlier in this book, up to 23% of people report experiencing a period of unintentional intraoperative awareness at some point during a heart operation performed under general anesthesia (see 10.13).

[14.5]Many proponents of dualism do not believe such out-of-body experiences and near-death experiences are unusual cases of awareness during general anesthesia. They claim that general anesthetic drugs always cloud and reduce the level of consciousness, saying this is "proof" these wondrous experiences cannot be episodes of awareness during general anesthesia. As further evidence for this claim, they report that about 83% of people undergoing near-death experiences during general anesthesia, have a level of consciousness described as "more consciousness and alertness than normal" (page 102 in Long 2010). For further emphasis, they also point out that that these people report their conscious minds were displaced outside their bodies during their moments of awareness. Subsequently these people report "hearing" verifiable conversations, and "seeing" verifiable events and colors. Accordingly, they claim such remarkable extracorporeal experiences are proof of the reality of a separable immaterial consciousness, or soul.

[14.6]This is a claim that has the advantage of being plausible to people unfamiliar with the different types of unintentional awareness experiences occurring during general anesthesia (see 10.17-10.25). Nonetheless, the extensive discussions in preceding chapters of this book, more than adequately demonstrate that the soul has no memory function. So these superficially amazing experiences are actually no more than memories of hallucinations induced by the mental effects of subanesthetic concentrations of the drugs used to provide general anesthesia, combined with real perceptions.

Anesthetic drugs and extracorporeal experiences

[14.7]Many drugs used to induce general anesthesia are also drugs of addiction. People do not abuse drugs, or become addicted to them, because they induce unpleasant feelings, stupor and grogginess. Instead, people become addicted to drugs because these substances induce experiences, emotions, or other states of mind they consider so desirable that they are willing to become slaves to these substances (Robinson 2000). For example, subanesthetic concentrations of drugs used to provide general anesthesia can induce wonderful feelings of euphoria and relief of anxiety (Table 5 in Lutsky 1994), marvelous expansion of conscious awareness, as well as other transcendental, cognitive, and affective experiences (see Chapters 6,7,8). Such emotions, altered perceptions, and states of mind are certainly part of many extracorporeal experiences occurring during general anesthesia.

[14.8]For example, opiates are a well-known class of addictive drugs, known to induce a plethora of euphoric, extracorporeal, transcendental, cognitive and affective experiences in susceptible persons (see 8.51-8.55). Opium was the crude forerunner of all opiates, followed by morphine extracted from opium, and later the semisynthetic heroin more than 100 years ago. Opium products were more or less freely available until the beginning of the twentieth century, and opiate addiction was common. Opium and its modern semisynthetic and synthetic opiates are common drugs of addiction, but stricter controls restrict their general availability. However, physicians are in a unique position to gain access to these drugs, and several surveys reveal some physicians are addicted to opiates such as meperidine, hydrocodone, oxycodone, fentanyl, alfentanil, and sufentanil (Booth 2002, Farley 1992, Lutsky 1994, Ward 1983).

[14.9]As for anesthetic gases—subanesthetic concentrations of these gases also induce euphoric, extracorporeal, transcendental, cognitive and affective effects. Indeed, nitrous oxide has been used for its euphoric and other effects since 1800 (Davy 1800), and it is still a reasonably popular party drug (Garland 2009, Rosenberg 1979), as well as being a drug of addiction (Booth 2002, Garland 2009, Shulman 2007, Wilson 2008). These same effects are also why ether (Krenz 2003), and chloroform (Weinraub 1972), have been used as drugs of addiction since before 1850. Strict controls and limited availability, severely reduce the possibility of addiction to modern anesthetic gases. Nonetheless, there are reports of addiction to modern anesthetic gases such as halothane (Booth 2002, Kaplan 1979, Spencer 1976, Wilson 2008), isoflurane, sevoflurane, and desflurane (Wilson 2008).

Extracorporeal experiences are illusions

[14.10]The effects of subanesthetic concentrations of drugs used to provide general anesthesia (see Chapters 6,7,8), are indistinguishable from what people recall undergoing during extracorporeal experiences. This means it is impossible to determine whether amazing experiences recalled by people awakening from general anesthesia, are due to periods of unintentional intraoperative awareness while their brains were affected by subanesthetic concentrations of anesthetic drugs, or whether these experiences truly were unfiltered manifestations of the soul. Accordingly, such apparently amazing experiences are definitely not proof of the reality of the soul, and the mind-model of dualism. Furthermore, extensive studies of the effects of drugs used during anesthesia reveal that the soul is not the repository of all memories—the physical brain is the repository of all memories. The soul forms no memories, and can therefore remember nothing of any activities while apparently disembodied. Accordingly, memories of extracorporeal activities are illusions and hallucinations generated by the functioning of the body, as well as conscious interpretations and interpolations of ambient perceptions. This brings us to a discussion of out-of-body experiences.

Out-of-body experiences

[14.11]Out-of-body experiences are an ostensibly amazing type of extracorporeal experience. But are they explicable with physiology and medical science? One way of examining this question is to study the apparently veridical reports of persons recounting such experiences. This is a technique frequently employed in popular works describing these experiences. However, more than a century of such anecdotal studies has done more than inculcate a sense of wonder at the superficially "medically inexplicable" nature of such experiences. The first part of any examination of any experience is to examine the situations under which they occur.

When do out-of-body experiences occur?

[14.12]The medical conditions and bodily states during which out-of-body experiences occur may reveal clues to any possible physiological explanation of such experiences. One of the earliest studies was that of a USA psychiatrist Stuart Twemlow and his co-workers during 1982 (Twemlow 1982). This was a purely descriptive study of the various state of mind and bodily conditions during which these experiences occurred. Twemlow found that out-of-body experiences occurred during states of mind varying from depression to excitation. Out-of-body experiences mostly occurred during states of relaxation, but also occurred during exhaustion, cardiac arrest, severe pain, childbirth, during accidents, high fevers, general anesthesia, near-death experiences, and even sexual orgasm (Twemlow 1982). In fact, only 10% of out-of-body experiences occur during near-death experiences (Twemlow 1982), a fact indicating the possibility that out-of-body experiences may not be part of the near-death experience, but an experience induced by the cause of the near-death experience. Other reports reveal out-of-body experiences occurring due to epilepsy due to multiple sclerosis (Arias 1996), meningitis, brain tumors, and epilepsy (Blanke 2004), as well as electrical stimulation of the temporoparietal junction of the brain (Blanke 2002, Ridder 2007).

[14.13]These inducing causes and associated conditions are so diverse, that no conclusions as to the cause of these experiences are possible. For example, out-of-body experiences cannot only be due to abnormal brain function, because most such experiences occur in persons with normal brain function. Out-of-body experiences also cannot be only due to states of relaxation, because they also occur during childbirth, extreme pain, and even sexual orgasm. More information as to the properties of these experiences is required. Another approach is to study the properties of the apparently dissociated mind.

Properties of the apparently disembodied mind

[14.14]Despite the myriad situations inducing out-of-body experiences, or situations during which such experiences occur, the properties, or attributes of the apparently disembodied mind are very similar. Indeed, these properties of the apparently disembodied mind reveals a good deal about the nature of these experiences. An extensive analysis of the properties of the separated consciousness during an out-of-body experience is listed in chapter 10 of the book *Mortal Minds* (Woerlee 2005). Here we read that the properties of the separated consciousness during an out-of-body experience are:

- [14.15]The out-of-body experience is a conscious experience, because persons undergoing these experiences are conscious, even though they may appear unconscious to onlookers.
- [14.16]The disembodied conscious mind is apparently displaced outside the body. That is why it is called an out-of-body experience.
- [14.17]The apparently disembodied conscious mind is invisible. No one can see, film, or photograph the disembodied conscious mind of a person undergoing an out-of-body experience (see 1.44).
- [14.18]The disembodied conscious mind is immaterial. It can pass though solid walls and concrete floors (see 1.47-1.49).
- [14.19]The attributes of the disembodied soul, such as intelligence, memory and personality, are the same as those of the conscious mind of the person undergoing the out-of-body experience. Many accounts of out-of-body experiences prove that the mental processes and intelligence of people undergoing these experiences are no different to what they manifest when in their physical bodies (see 1.89-1.91).
- [14.20]The disembodied soul is unable to control the body during an out-of-body experience. There are many accounts of people telling of trying to speak and move during out-of-body experiences. But they all report being unable to arouse movements in their bodies, nor can they generate speech. In other words, the will of the disembodied consciousness cannot activate the physical body to move or speak. The only exceptions to this rule are out-of-body experiences aroused by direct electrical stimulation of the brain (Blanke 2002, Penfield 1955, Ridder 2007).
- [14.21]The disembodied soul is capable of detailed perceptions. For example, the disembodied soul can "see" with physical light, and describe veridical colors and events, as well as "hear" verifiable

spoken words and other physical sounds (see 1.116-1.120). The disembodied soul also perceives weight, motion, and has a sense of position (see example 9.55-9.57). Furthermore, about 7% of all disembodied souls feel pain from disorders affecting their individual bodies (Tiberi 1993).

- [14.22]While disembodied during an out-of-body experience, the conscious mind retains its sense of individual identity (see 1.33-1.39).
- [14.23]The out-of-body experience is almost always a remembered experience, because no one tells of undergoing an out-of-body experience during the experience itself. The only exceptions to this rule are out-of-body experiences aroused by direct electrical stimulation of the brain (Blanke 2002, Penfield 1955, Ridder 2007). People only report undergoing out-of-body experience after their conscious minds have returned to their bodies. This means that nearly all out-of-body experiences are long-term memories of experiences, spontaneously recalled and recounted after recovering physical consciousness and the ability to speak. Accordingly, out-of-body experiences seemingly reveal that the soul is the indelible repository of all memories (see 1.92-1.115).

[14.24]This list of properties is identical to those of the separable immaterial soul as defined in Chapter 1 (see 1.123-1.135). This list also makes it possible to determine whether out-of-body experiences truly are due to separation of the conscious mind from the body, or whether they are simply marvelous hallucinations. When considering these possibilities, the first question immediately coming to mind, is how something invisible and immaterial can hear and see physically verifiable events.

Hearing and seeing during out-of-body experiences

[14.25]The soul is invisible, able to effortlessly pass through solid concrete floors and other objects, as well as being unaffected by anything in this material world. Yet people recounting their out-of-body experiences sometimes tell of seeing subsequently physically verified events and colors, or of hearing subsequently verified sounds and conversations during their experiences. They make these observations from a perspective outside their physical bodies: either from a perspective floating above, or standing next to their bodies at the time of these experiences. Such observations astonish many people, some of whom subsequently claim these reports are certain proof of the reality of a soul, because verifiable observations were made while the conscious minds of these people were located outside their physical bodies. But how can an invisible and immaterial soul "hear" the sounds of speech and other things, or "see" colors and objects with visible light during an out-of-body experience?

The "hearing" soul

14.26I will begin with the apparent ability of the disembodied soul to "hear" the physically verifiable sounds of speech and other sounds. Penny Sartori, a near-death experience researcher, once published an account of her interview of a man resuscitated for cardiac arrest in the hospital where she worked. This man described hearing verified spoken speech while his conscious mind was apparently disembodied during an out-of-body experience.

> 14.27*Penny: On the monitor next to your bed was something hidden on top. Could you see what it was?*
> *[Patient:] No, I'll be honest with you, Pen, I didn't look. I didn't twist my head back that way; I was just looking at my side. I could see you and the doctor and two to three others around me. Pen, if that's death, it's wonderful, there's no pain at all.*
> *Penny: Do you recall hearing anything while in this state?*
> *[Patient:] Only the words that my father spoke, and the gentleman saying, "He isn't ready yet." Going back ... I heard voices down below but couldn't make out what they were saying. Only thing ... something about my eye, life there. ... I don't know what he meant by that.*
> *Penny: I remember that. It was the consultant actually, and he looked in your eye and he shone a torch and he said, "'Yes they are reacting, but unequal."*
> *[Patient:] Yes, something like that, and then to my father, "He isn't ready yet; he's got to go back." (page 74 in Sartori 2006, square brackets [Patient:] inserted by author for clarity)*

14.28We already know many of the properties of the human soul. So we know that the disembodied soul of a person undergoing an out-of-body experience does not interact with physical matter at all, because it can effortlessly pass through the solid matter of the body, as well as through solid walls and even reinforced concrete floors (Case 1 in Ring 1993, see also 1.47-1.49). Sounds forming speech and other sounds are no more than air pressure variations varying in intensity from subtle to powerful. We hear these air pressure variations as sound, because the eardrums of our physical ears move back and forth in response to these pressure variations. But if disembodied souls can pass effortlessly through the very dense and solid physical matter of reinforced concrete, this means that the separated soul is unresponsive to pressure variations transmitting and forming sounds in air. Accordingly, the disembodied soul is effectively deaf to physical sounds such as speech, music, or other sounds transmitted through air.

The "seeing" soul

[14.29]This brings us to a discussion of the apparent ability of the supposedly disembodied soul to "see" physically verifiable colors and events with visible light. An example of such "sight" was reported in a book written by Michael Sabom entitled *Light & Death*, in which a man called "Darrell" reported veridical visual observations he made during an out-of-body experience induced by a period of severe failure of heart function.

[14.30]*As Darrell hovered near the ceiling, he saw Sandy wearing her pink uniform and standing at his right side, near his head. The cardiologist and two other men were clustered around his right leg, two wearing green scrubs and one wearing blue. A male nurse in blue scrubs stood at the foot of the bed on the left side. Suddenly Darrell woke up in his body. "I looked straight up and saw Sandy there." She was dressed in pink. He scanned the room and saw the others, confirming for himself what he had seen from outside of his body. (page 22 in Sabom 1998)*

[14.31]He reported "seeing" the actual pink color of the uniform of a nurse called "Sandy", as well as the color of the clothing of others near his bed during a period of disembodiment. Subsequently he verified this after "returning" to his body. This is a clear veridical visual observation. The apparently disembodied soul of this man made correct and verified observations of the situation around his body at the time, as well as describing the colors of the clothing of people around his bed as perceived with visible light. But how it is possible for the disembodied soul to perceive visible light?

[14.32]Visible light is electromagnetic radiation in the wavelength range of 380 to 740 nanometers. So if the disembodied soul of a person undergoing an out-of-body experience perceives the surroundings in the same colors as physically conscious bystanders, this means that the disembodied soul only interacts with, and perceives light in the wavelength range of 380 to 740 nanometers. This is an evident physical fact. We know this, because addition or subtraction of other wavelengths of light changes the colors perceived. For example, everyone knows from practical experience how colored filters and different colored light changes the colors perceived. Furthermore, perception of visible light by the soul means that light must interact with some aspect of the soul— otherwise the soul could not make any observations with physical light. This fact determines the possible properties of the "light sensitive aspect" of the apparently disembodied soul, as well as limiting the possible forms of interaction with light. So what are the ways the soul can interact with physical light so that it could "see" with physical light? These are (see also pages 120-123 in Woerlee 2008):

- [14.33]*Totally or partially blocking light passing through the whole or part of the soul.* This would mean that the disembodied soul would be perceived as a distinct form, a shadow, or partially transparent something. Regardless of which of these things is the reality, all people would be able to see the disembodied soul, and it would be able to be photographed and filmed.
- [14.34]*Refracting or reflecting light in the vicinity of the soul.* The disembodied soul might interact with light by refracting or reflecting visible light in its vicinity. This is also something readily seen by all people, as well as being able to be photographed and filmed.
- [14.35]*Changing the color of light passing through or around the soul.* The disembodied soul might interact with light by altering the colors of light passing through it, or in its vicinity. Likewise, this too is something readily seen by all people, as well as being able to be photographed and filmed.

[14.36]Nevertheless, none of any of these things has ever been described by observers of people subsequently reporting near-death experiences or out-of-body experiences. The disembodied soul is invisible to all human observers, photographic, film, or video cameras.

[14.37]However, some believers in dualism might say that people near persons undergoing near-death experiences or out-of-body experiences were not specifically looking for the disembodied soul at the time, because their attention was diverted or directed at other things, and this is why they did not see the souls of these people separating from their bodies. This is a tendentious argument. The soul supposedly separates from the human body upon the death of the body, and people have carefully observed the dying for countless millennia. Throughout all known ages of humankind, spectators of public executions have keenly observed the death throes of individuals put to death by strangulation, crucifixion, hanging, impalement, beheading, shooting, etc. Executioners, murderers, and soldiers often observe the dying moments of those they kill. For countless thousands of years, people have attended dying family members at their deathbeds. Yet throughout all these millennia, none of the countless millions who have attentively observed the death throes of the dying, has ever told of seeing the souls of these persons departing from their bodies at the moment of death. This is the result of ages of careful observation. So the soul as proposed by the mind-model of dualism is invisible, which means the soul has no interaction with visible light.

[14.38]More recently, photographic, film and video recordings of people undergoing death by murder, or during wars and executions, also reveal no souls, or separable immaterial consciousness departing the bodies of the dying. As if this were not enough proof, there is also specific observation. For example, during 1994, Thomas Lempert published a careful videometric study of the convulsive movements of persons with self-induced sudden cerebral hypoxia (Lempert 1994a), during which seven (16%) of 42 experimental subjects reported undergoing an out-of-body experience during the ensuing period of loss of consciousness (Lempert 1994). All persons taking part in this study were continually observed by the neurologists performing the study, as well as having continual video recordings being made of their bodies by two high speed cameras, from the period before loss of consciousness until after regaining physical consciousness (see "subjects and methods" in Lempert 1994). These researchers observed these people continually, as well as making video recordings of their bodies before, during, and after their out-of-body experiences. Yet they did not report seeing, or making video recordings of anything departing from, or returning to the bodies of those persons subsequently reporting undergoing an out-of-body experience (Lempert 1994, Lempert 1994a), a finding confirming an earlier study reported by the parapsychologist Charles Tart (Tart 1969, fifth study in Tart 1998). However, if the soul can see colors and objects with visible light, then some interaction with visible light on this physical world is necessary. Such an interaction means that visual observations, video, film, and photographic recordings would confirm the reality of the soul. But no such evidence is available. The results of millennia of visual observation and modern studies are unequivocal—the disembodied soul is invisible. And invisibility has very clear consequences for the ability of a soul to perceive light perceptible to physically conscious humans. A letter by Ed Wysocki on page 62 in the July/August 2013 edition of the *Skeptical Inquirer* makes this fact even more abundantly clear for the situation of totally invisible humans, ghosts, or souls.

> [14.39]*We may first consider that if the lens in each eye of the invisible person had the same refractive index as air, it would not focus the image to the retina. At the very least, the person would see a blurred image. But we may go even further. We are able to see because the photons impact the photoreceptors in the retina. If all components of the eye are totally transparent, there will be no impact and no signals will be sent to the brain. (page 62, July/August 2013, Skeptical Inquirer)*

[14.40]Therefore, an invisible disembodied soul undergoing an out-of-body experience cannot perceive light seen by physically conscious humans. A disembodied soul is effectively blind to visible light waves.

[14.41]However, the ability of the physical body to "see" during out-of-body experiences is explicable with the integration of a combination of factors as was suggested by Krishnan in a very perceptive letter published during 1993 (Krishnan 1993). Krishnan suggested that sight during out-of-body experiences was likely due to a combination of direct vision, blindsight, and synesthesia all combining to provide sensory inputs whose totality generates the veridical visual experience during apparent disembodiment (Krishnan 1993).

[14.42]People whose primary optical cortex no longer functions are blind, even though their eyes function normally. They no longer consciously perceive light and visual images. Yet persons who have become blind due to disease of the primary visual cortex still have the use of other areas of the brain used to process visual information. This is called blindsight. Blindsight is the ability to see when the primary visual cortex no longer functions, and has been the subject of considerable scientific research (Ro 2006, Stoerig 1997, pages 1276-1277 in Zeman 2001). Blindsight enables people blinded due to primary visual cortex malfunction, to non-visually navigate their way through crowded rooms, perceive simple shapes, objects, movements, color, orientation of lines, and even facial emotions (Gelder 2010). Blindsight does not only occur in people blinded due to visual cortex malfunction. Unconscious visual perceptions using the same neural pathways in the brain as blindsight,

353

also affect the way even normally sighted persons perceive visual imagery (Lau 2006, Tamietto 2008).

[14.43]Krishnan (1993) and Terhune (2009) suggest synesthesia as another possibility by which people could apparently visually perceive events in their vicinity. Synesthesia is a curious ability possessed by some individuals who translate the perception of one sensation as the perception of quite a different sensation, e.g. touch being interpreted as a visual sensation, smells as sound, smells as visions or light, etc. (Hubbard 2007, Ramachandran 2003). Furthermore, synesthesia is an inherited, genetically transmitted neurological condition or ability (Asher 2009, Hubbard 2007), manifesting in about 1 to 4% of all people in Western Europe (Hubbard 2007, Simner 2006), which means that synesthesias of all types are reasonably common. So during out-of-body experiences, some people may translate heard sounds, movements, and touching as visual inputs used to construct a verifiable "visual" image of their surroundings. Finally, many people reporting subsequently verifiable visual events, may simply have seen these things with their eyes, or been informed of them, before reporting their stories. All these factors unconsciously combined and integrated into understandable visual imagery, explain the ability of some people to report verifiable visual imagery of their vicinity during out-of-body experiences.

The soul cannot "hear" and cannot "see"

[14.44]It is evident that the soul can neither hear physical sounds, nor see visible light. Nonetheless, believers in the mind-model of dualism might argue that the disembodied soul has a rather more "subtle interaction" with physical visible light and sound, and that such a subtle interaction— while invisible to physical eyes—makes it possible for the soul to see and hear. The real, but totally invisible flood of subatomic particles, such as neutrinos produced by the sun and other stars, passing unnoticed through our physical bodies every minute is an example of such an interaction. Every now and then a neutrino interacts with a physical particle to produce a reaction, but these reactions are rare and invisible. By analogy, believers in dualism might argue that some sort of hitherto unknown form of transdimensional quantum entanglement, or another form of fantastical interaction between the immaterial and the material, explains the ability of the soul to hear with physical sounds, and see visible light. Such a contrived explanation cannot be excluded.

[14.45]But blind people cannot "see" visible light, and deaf people cannot "hear" physical sounds. The clear absence of any such transdimensional, or other form of quantum entanglement in the embodied souls of the blind, and the deaf, is proof that the embodied soul only perceives its surroundings through the physical senses of the body. Any other senses would manifest as apparent paranormal perceptive abilities in the blind and the deaf. But these do not exist—the blind remain blind, and the deaf remain deaf—they do not see, and they do not hear. Furthermore, as is more than adequately demonstrated throughout this book, the soul forms no memories. So even if the disembodied soul could perceive ambient sights and sounds with abilities such as paranormal perceptive abilities, transdimensional quantum entanglement, or whatever perceptive ability some people claim the soul may possess, the soul would have no memory of what it saw. It could be claimed that when disembodied, the soul transmits such information to the physical brain, which then remembers these ambient sights and sounds. But many believers in dualism also claim that many veridical observations made during near-death experiences occur during periods of totally absent brain function. However, information transfer between a conscious perceiving disembodied soul, and a physically non-functioning brain is impossible, because a non-functioning brain cannot process or store any information. All these things mean that possible explanations using dualism are inconsistent with any physical, or even non-physical reality.

14.46Physical laws are adamant, unchanging, and provable. These same physical laws mean it is impossible for an invisible, disembodied soul capable of passing through concrete floors and other solid matter to hear sound waves transmitted through air, or to see light at visible electromagnetic wavelengths. The implications of these facts are evident—the soul cannot "see" light at visible electromagnetic wavelengths, and cannot "hear" sound waves transmitted through air. So if there is a soul as proposed by believers in the mind-model of dualism, then it can only perceive light and sounds perceptible to other physically conscious humans through the senses of the body. This is a logical conclusion derived from known physical laws, the mind-model of dualism, and the behavior of the apparently disembodied soul during out-of-body experiences. But this raises the question of how the conscious mind perceives veridical perceptions during out-of-body experiences.

The brain generates out-of-body experiences

14.47The preceding discussion, and other discussions throughout this book, makes it possible to draw several conclusions about out-of-body experiences. Paranormal psi perceptive abilities such as clairvoyance and telepathy do not exist, or at best are irrelevant to any discussion of the functioning of the soul (see discussion Chapter 13). Veridical perceptions of light and sound are only possible through the sense organs of the body (see discussion above). The intelligence, emotions, and personality of the apparently disembodied soul are the same as that of the physically conscious body (see Chapter 1, and discussion this chapter). More importantly, discussions throughout this book conclusively prove that memories are stored in the physical brain, and not in the soul. So if the out-of-body experience were an experience undergone by a disembodied soul, then no one would be able to recall the experience, because the soul possesses no memory ability. Accordingly, the sense organs of the physically conscious body perceive veridical perceptions made during out-of-body experiences, the mind of the physically conscious body processes these perceptions, and the physical brain remembers these perceptions. The only logical conclusion is that the functioning of the physical body generates out-of-body experiences.

[14.48]Out-of-body experiences arise as a result of a vast number of illnesses, types of brain pathology, drugs, altered brain function, and different types of mental function. This clearly indicates there is no single mechanism by which the body can generate out-of-body experiences. So what are the general bodily mechanisms generating out-of-body experiences? An analysis of the bodily systems contributing to the genesis of these experiences reveals they do not always have a single cause, and may be products of one or more bodily mechanisms (page 152 in Woerlee 2005).

- [14.49]*Altered muscle spindle function.* A person may perceive sensations of abnormal body position, flight, and weightlessness when their muscle spindles tense or relax to a different degree than the surrounding muscle fibers (see 9.43-9.46). For example: when riding a Harley-Davidson motorcycle, self-induced out-of-body experiences, during powerful bodily vibrations induced by other factors.
- [14.50]*Altered function of the angular gyrus.* The angular gyrus is a part of the brain acting as a nexus integrating sensory information about position and movement of the body. Abnormal function of this region of the brain generates out-of-body experiences (Blanke 2002, Ridder 2007). For example: during epilepsy affecting this region of the brain, brain tumors, severe hypoxia, toxic effects of drugs etc.

- [14.51]*Altered brain function.* Misinterpretation of sensory nerve signals from the body due to altered brain function may arouse autoscopic hallucinations, dreams of flying, as well as out-of-body experiences. For example: during hypoxia, the effects of subanesthetic concentrations of anesthetic drugs, epilepsy, mental states such as meditation, etc.
- [14.52]*A combination of factors.* Altered muscle spindle function, together with altered brain function may also generate perceptions of out-of-body experiences. The same is also true of other combinations of factors.

[14.53]This explains the genesis of out-of-body experiences and the nature of the recalled perceptions. The out-of-body experience is an experience undergone in a conscious physical brain, and the experiential content is a product of physical perceptions integrated within the physical brain into a hallucination of displacement of the conscious mind to a location outside the physical body. This concept of the generation of the out-of-body experience is not new. Susan Blackmore proposed this idea in 1993 for the visual and auditory perceptions reported by people reporting their out-of-body experiences.

[14.54]*The answers include prior knowledge, fantasy and lucky guesses and the remaining operating senses of hearing and touch. Add to this the way memory works to recall accurate items and forget the wrong ones, and we have the basis for an alternative account of why people are able to see what is going on. (page 115 in Blackmore 1993)*

[14.55]Extensive subsequent neurophysiological studies and reviews reaffirm this concept of out-of-body experiences.

[14.56]*Along similar lines, non-visual sensory stimuli may be associated with particular visual phenomenological features of an OBE [out-of-body experience]. For instance, whereas somatic, tactile and vestibular information may contribute to the visual representation of one's physical body, exogenous cues such as auditory stimuli may be utilized in the representation of environmental objects and other persons. In this respect, the visual complexity of an OBE may be a function of the number and vividness of non-visual sensory inputs concurrently available to a percipient. (Terhune 2009)*

357

[14.57]Indeed, since 2002, the study of out-of-body experiences has developed into a respectable field of neurophysiology (Arzy 2006, Blanke 2002, Blanke 2004, Brugger 2009, Lopez 2008, Marsh 2012, Ridder 2007, Schwabe 2007, Terhune 2009). Such studies provide ever more insights into the ways we perceive our bodies and the relationships of our bodies to the world about us. This brings us to a discussion of near-death experiences.

Near-death experiences

[14.58]A few people report undergoing near-death experiences during anesthesia, cardiac arrest, and an infinitude of other conditions. During these experiences, they tell of meeting deceased relatives in transcendental worlds, of viewing all the incidents of their lives, of passing through a tunnel to enter light. Many proponents of the mind-model of dualism regard near-death experiences as proof of an immaterial soul, and proof of a life after death. But what actually defines a near-death experience?

Near-death experiences defined

[14.59]Raymond Moody was the first person to define the nature of near-death experiences in a book called *Life after Life* (Moody 1976). He defined ten components of the near-death experience, which he also described as occurring in the following sequence:

- [14.60]A feeling of peace and calm.
- [14.61]The sense that death was imminent or had occurred.
- [14.62]Hearing a noise or music.
- [14.63]The experience of entering a tunnel or darkness.
- [14.64]The experience of leaving one's body.
- [14.65]Meeting figures, strangers, deities or deceased relatives.
- [14.66]Meeting a being of light, or entering into a brightness or light.
- [14.67]A review of the major events of one's life.
- [14.68]The experience of encountering a border, or limit, the passing of which means certain death.
- [14.69]The conscious decision to return to the body.

[14.70]Subsequent analysis revealed that not all those reporting near-death experiences actually undergoes each of these components. Interestingly, the chance of undergoing each of these components is relatively constant regardless of the initiating cause of the near-death experience. Pim van Lommel published an analysis of the relative frequencies of each of these components in 62 out of 344 prospectively studied cardiac arrest survivors reporting undergoing near-death experiences during resuscitation for cardiac arrest (Lommel 2001).

- [14.71]56% experienced a feeling of peace and calm.
- [14.72]50% experienced a sense that death was imminent or had occurred.
- [14.73]32% met figures, strangers, deities or deceased relatives.
- [14.74]31% felt themselves entering a tunnel or darkness.
- [14.75]24% underwent an out-of-body experience.
- [14.76]23% met a being of light, or enter into a brightness or light.
- [14.77]13% underwent a review of the major events of their life.
- [14.78]8% experienced encountering a border, or limit, the passing of which means certain death.

[14.79]This is a very interesting and accurate list. It is very different to retrospective studies of self-reported near-death experiences resulting from a large range of causes. The Pim van Lommel study was unique, because of its prospective nature, with specific questioning of cardiac arrest survivors within a week after arrest (Lommel 2001). There was no spontaneous reporting of memories years after the event. Accordingly the relative frequencies of these experiences as reported by Pim van Lommel is a true reflection of the incidence and relative frequencies of near-death experiences induced by a single cause—cardiac arrest. Very interestingly, this list clearly indicates that not everyone undergoes each component of the near-death experience. In other words, while there are many shared experiences, each person may undergo a unique combination of these experiences during an individual near-death experience. Another near-death experience researcher, Bruce Greyson, reasoned that elements of near-death experiences strongly related to one another are component elements of the near-death experience, whereas elements unrelated to any of the other elements were more likely due to the cause of the near-death experience. During 1983 he published a study, expanded upon in 1985, revealing four different clusters of experiences truly belonging to the near-death experience, and defined these groups of experiences as: affective, cognitive, transcendental, and paranormal (Greyson 1983, Greyson 1985). So how are these different types of experience defined?

- [14.80]*Cognitive experiences:* time seems to speed up, thought is very clear and rapid, review of scenes from the past, understanding of the universe, oneself and others.
- [14.81]*Affective experiences:* a feeling of relief, peace or pleasantness, a feeling of joy or happiness, a sense of harmony or unity with the universe, seeing, or being surrounded by bright light.
- [14.82]*Paranormal experiences:* senses are more vivid than usual, extrasensory perception, seeing scenes from the future, separation from the body.
- [14.83]*Transcendental experiences:* entering a mystical or unearthly world, encountering a mystical being or presence, seeing figures from a religious pantheon, seeing deceased relatives or friends, coming to a barrier, or point of no return.

[14.84]Curiously, Bruce Greyson found that the well-known experiences of altered time perception and of passing through a tunnel were unrelated to all other components of the near-death experience. He concluded that even though experiences of altered time perception, and passage through a tunnel, occurred frequently during near-death experiences, they were unrelated to other components, and therefore are not actual components of the near-death experience (Greyson 1983). Subsequent studies reveal the "tunnel experience" only occurs in some cultures, which is why some researchers regard it as a "cultural contaminant" (Athappilly 2006, Kellehear 1993). Furthermore, the out-of-body experience occurs in only 25 % of near-death experiences, and is a hallucination aroused by the functioning of the physical body. All these facts have implications for the way we view near-death experiences.

Near-death experiences are products of body function

[14.85]Indeed, the above observations raise the question of which aspects of the near-death experience are products of the functioning of the body, and which are possibly manifestations of a possible soul. However, one fact is certain: near-death experiences are remembered experiences, and memory is a function of the physical brain (see 1.92-1.115). This means it is impossible for a person to remember near-death experiences undergone during periods of absent brain function, e.g. as is claimed occurs during cardiac arrest. An evident conclusion of this fact is that the near-death experience cannot be a manifestation of disembodiment, or continued consciousness of the soul during periods of absent brain function, as is proposed by the mind-model of dualism. After all, if the

360

near-death experience is something only undergone by the soul, then no-one would remember these experiences. This fact does not exclude a role for a soul in the genesis of these experiences. However, it does limit the role of the soul to that of modulation of the experiential content of an experience occurring within, and remembered by the physical brain. Accordingly, near-death experiences are products of abnormal brain function in physically conscious persons. People undergoing near-death experiences may appear unconscious, but they are conscious because unconscious persons undergo no conscious experiences. Moreover, the brains of persons undergoing near-death experiences function sufficiently well to lay down long-term memories of these experiences, which they subsequently relate to others. There are more problems with the explanations of dualism. Near-death experiences are not a unitary phenomenon—no two near-death experiences are identical. So how is it possible to explain such a diverse group of experiences?

Near-death experiences are results of a "common pathway"

[14.86]Near-death experiences occur during a multitude of conditions, states of mind, and disorders. For example, near-death experiences occur during the following conditions.

- [14.87]During conditions of extreme fear, or anxiety.
- [14.88]During general anesthesia and other drug intoxications. For example during ketamine administration, local anesthetic toxicity, and general anesthesia.
- [14.89]During cardiac arrest.
- [14.90]During blood loss resulting from injuries or surgery.
- [14.91]During high fevers.
- [14.92]Hypoxia in its myriad forms is a common initiating cause.
- [14.93]Brain tumors, or scars from brain operations.
- [14.94]Many, many other conditions.

[14.95]Yet even though these many causes differ, they all generate similar groups of affective, cognitive, and transcendental experiences, as are reported by people recalling their near-death experiences. This repeated observation is indicates that these multitudinous initiating causes all act, and exert their effects through the same bodily systems, or "common pathway", to generate the relatively consistent constellation of experiences labeled the "near-death experience".

361

[14.96]So what do I mean by a "common pathway"? Each of these causes, or triggers of near-death experiences, including psychological causes, produces its own constellation of effects upon the functioning of the brain. But some of the neural pathways of the brain through which these triggers act upon the functioning of the brain, are also those generating the constellation of experiences called the near-death experience. And these same pathways are activated by each of the triggers inducing near-death experiences. This is a shared, or "common pathway" by which all these diverse and apparently unrelated triggers act to generate near-death experiences.

[14.97]Karl Jansen once proposed that NMDA (N-Methyl-D-Aspartate) receptor mediated pathways in the brain are the "common pathway" through which many of these triggers mediate the near-death experience (Jansen 1997). However, this NMDA model suffers from one major drawback—it fails to explain all aspects of the genesis and manifestations of near-death experiences. We know this, because even though near-death experiences have many similar elements, not everyone has exactly the same experience. For example, not everyone enters and experiences a transcendental world. Not everyone meets deceased relatives, or the gods of their personal religious pantheon. Not everyone experiences life review. Not everyone has the experience of a barrier. You can go on and on. In other words, the situation is not that of a simple single common pathway phenomenon. This means near-death experiences are a complex of manifestations resulting from a multitude of individual causes, possibly acting through several common pathways.

[14.98]Juan Saavedra-Aguilar and Juan Gomez-Jeria published a very sophisticated multiple pathway model during 1989. They proposed a complex interaction of psychological and physical factors resulting in temporal lobe dysfunction, hypoxia, and neuropeptide/neurotransmitter imbalance (Saavedra-Aguilar 1989). After some extensive and partly constructive comment during 1989 (Saavedra-Aguilar 1989a), interest in this model seemed to disappear, even though this model accounted for many aspects of the near-death experience, as well as the multiple inducing causes. Olaf Blanke and Sebastian Dieguez proposed another variant of a multiple common pathways based on studies of studies of the brains of patients who made complete recovery from cardiac arrest.

[14.99]*Based on the selective sites of brain damage in cardiac arrest patients (with excellent recovery) and the associations of key NDE phenomena to some of these same areas we would like to suggest that two main types of NDEs [near-death experiences] exist, depending on the predominantly affected hemisphere. We propose that type 1 NDEs are due to bilateral frontal and occipital, but predominantly right hemispheric brain damage affecting the right TPJ [temporoparietal junction] and characterized by OBEs [out-of-body experiences], altered sense of time, sensations of flying, lightness, vection, and silence. Type 2 NDEs are also due to bilateral frontal and occipital, but predominantly left hemispheric brain damage affecting the left TPJ and characterized by feeling of a presence, meeting of and communication with spirits, seeing of glowing bodies, as well as voices, sounds, and music without vection. We expect emotions and life review (damage to unilateral or bilateral temporal lobe structures such as the hippocampus and amygdala) as well as lights and tunnel vision (damage to bilateral occipital cortex) to be associated with type 1 and type 2 NDEs. (page 321 in Chapter 23 in Blanke 2009)*

[14.100]This is an interesting model, in that while it proposes no specific mechanisms of neurotransmitter, it does propose a differentiation in pathways inducing these experiences. Such near-death experiences are always products of cerebral hypoxia, and inter-individual regional differences in brain blood supply are part of this explanation of the observed phenomena. However, this model is more limited than that of Juan Saavedra-Aguilar and Juan Gomez-Jeria (1989), because it only deals with near-death experiences reported by cardiac arrest survivors. So what about other models?

[14.101]Bruce Greyson's seminal articles describing four basic types of near-death experiences reveals more parts of the puzzle (Greyson 1983, Greyson 1985). He found that while near-death experiences could be classified as predominantly affective, cognitive, or transcendental: no one has a predominantly paranormal near-death experience, even though each of these three different groups of near-death experiences may contain paranormal elements. All this indicates the possibility of three fundamental, partly overlapping "common pathways" in the brain, through which the myriad different causes of near-death experiences act in varying degrees to produce each individual near-death experience. This would explain the differences, and the overlapping components observed in individual near-death experiences. However, this says nothing about neurotransmitters, the regions of brain, or neural pathways involved.

[14.102]Other studies provide more clues. A study presented by both James Council and Bruce Greyson during 1985, reveals that the transcendental component of near-death experiences was unrelated to manifestations of cognitive, affective, or paranormal components of near-death experiences (Council 1985). Does this mean that pathways in the brain using opiate receptor mediated, or modulated transmission, are part of a common pathway generating transcendental near-death experiences (see 8.51-8.55)? Speculating further—is the common pathway for extracorporeal experiences and paralysis of voluntary movement, mediated by the same neurological mechanisms as mediate rapid eye movement sleep (Nelson 2006a, Nelson 2007)? These are almost certainly the same neurological mechanisms as mediate cataplexy (Cave 1931, Dauvilliers 2003). Rapid eye movement sleep intrusion and cataplexy certainly explain why persons undergoing near-death find themselves unable to move or speak. Other neurological mechanisms explaining near-death experiences have been suggested (Blackmore 1993, Wettach 2000, Woerlee 2005). But all these individual explanations fail to explain the enormous range of conditions generating near-death experiences, as well as failing to explain the full spectrum of differing near-death experiences. Indeed, the sheer diversity of factors triggering of near-death experiences, together with their expression in a common set of experiences, reveal near-death experiences to be a manifestation of several "common pathways", together with the manifestations of the many individual causes. Viewing near-death experiences as common pathway experiences opens a way to further theorize, and eventually solve the neurobiological basis of these fascinating and profound human experiences.

The "core" near-death experience

[14.103]Near-death experiences are not a consistently homogeneous set of experiences. Bruce Greyson realized this, and analyzed a large group of near-death experiences to separate the fundamental elements of near-death experiences, from the manifestations of the multitude of events inducing them (Greyson 1983). His studies indicated that near-death experiences differ between people, as well as according to the disorders inducing them (Greyson 1983, Greyson 1985). This implies that near-death experiences cannot be considered in isolation from their causes. Unfortunately, no subsequent research has followed-up the profound implications of these studies.

[14.104]This brings us back to general anesthesia, and the effects of anesthetic drugs. Why anesthetic drugs? The effects of drugs used to provide general anesthesia are well defined by decennia of study. Moreover, recording of parameters revealing the physical conditions of persons undergoing general anesthesia is more frequently and exactingly recorded than anywhere else within a hospital, or any other setting during which near-death experiences occur. Comparison of the components of near-death experiences with the effects of anesthetic drugs yields an evident conclusion. The mental and bodily effects of subanesthetic concentrations of anesthetic drugs explain nearly all of the subjective and objective mental and sensory components of near-death experiences undergone during general anesthesia.

[14.105]So subtraction of the effects of the drugs used during a specific general anesthetic from the experiences reported by a patient who underwent a near-death experience during that general anesthetic, may well reveal a fundamental "core" near-death experience. The same method is also applicable to near-death experiences due to all other causes. Subtraction of the mental, and bodily effects of the inducing causes of individual near-death experiences, may well enable the definition of a true "core" near-death experience. Alternatively, this technique may simply confirm the reality of several overlapping common pathways generating overlapping experiences.

Culture and near-death experiences

[14.106]Many people undergoing near-death experiences report experiences of disembodiment, and while in this state, entering transcendental worlds inhabited by the souls of deceased relatives, as well as the deities of their socio-culturally determined religious beliefs. The visionary content of each of these transcendental worlds apparently revealing a future life after death is strangely parochial. It differs between peoples from different cultures, and has a visionary content similar to that of the culture in which a person lives (Abramovich 1988, Carter 2010, Kellehear 2001, Knoblauch 2001, Lundahl 1993, Murphy 2001, Osis 1986, Pasricha 1986). Indeed, this same phenomenon is reported within the *Tibetan Book of the Dead* (pages 33-34 in Evans-Wentz 1960, see 15.71).

[14.107]Socio-cultural patterns and expectations are deeply rooted within the mind of each person. They are products of the upbringing and the culture inhabited by each individual, and result in measurable changes in brain structure and function (Ansari 2009, Aron 2010, Balram 2009,

Chiao 2008, Demorest 2010, Gutchess 2010). Such socio-cultural imprinting in the physical brain, and the fact that memories are stored within the physical brain, explains why the visionary content of these transcendental afterlife worlds differs between peoples of different cultures.

[14.108]All these facts are inconsistent with the mind-model of dualism, and mean that near-death experiences are not manifestations of the true nature of the human soul. Instead, near-death experiences are experiences undergone within the conscious physical brain. The remembered sensory and visionary content is a product of the effects of the inducing causes of these experiences, interpretations of actual physical perceptions made during these experiences, as well as the modulating influences of individual expectation, and socio-cultural influences.

[14.109]Nonetheless, staunch advocates of the mind-model of dualism may reject this explanation. So let us look at these experiences from a slightly different viewpoint.

Near-death experiences and the soul

[14.110]Bruce Greyson defined the affective, paranormal, transcendental, and cognitive mental states undergone by persons reporting near-death experiences in two seminal articles (Greyson 1983, Greyson 1985). By demonstrating that near-death experiences consist of several groups of related experiences, these studies revealed a key to a beginning of understanding their genesis. Nonetheless, there are several ways of viewing these descriptions of near-death experience components. They may be viewed as a useful definition of near-death experiences, as an instrument aiding the study of the genesis of near-death experiences, or simply as a description of components of a literal reality that must be present before an experience can be classified as a near-death experience. As regards this latter aspect, many proponents of the mind-model of dualism believe in the literal reality of the experiential content of these experiences, and claim they reveal the true nature of the soul (Grossman 2002, Hastings 2002, Potts 2002, Rivas 2003).

[14.111]But this belief is very problematical. This book reveals the soul possesses no memory. Therefore, as discussed earlier in this chapter, near-death experiences are actually products of abnormal brain function in physically conscious persons capable of remembering these experiences, and recalling them some time later. Consider the fact that these mental states, and near-death experiences, also occur during altered states of conscious physical brain function, such as are induced by attempted suicide (Rosen 1975), fear of death (Rodin 1980), and meditation (Beauregard 2006, Cahn 2005). Likewise, oxygen starvation (Brugger 1999, Cudaback 1984, Firth 2004), hyperventilation and fainting (Lempert 1994), subanesthetic concentrations of anesthetic gases such as chloroform and nitrous oxide (Chapter 6), morphine and morphine-like drugs (Chapter 8), and anesthetic drugs such as ketamine (Jansen 1997), also induce the same gamut of mental states and experiences. Affective, paranormal, transcendental, and cognitive experiences induced by all these events and drugs are in no way different to those undergone by people reporting near-death experiences induced by these very same causes. This indicates that near-death experiences induced by these multiple causes are also likely to be manifestations of abnormal conscious physical brain function induced by these multiple causes and drugs. It is true that explaining these experiences with the effects of the inducing conditions, and drugs, uses known and provable phenomena. Nevertheless, in the interest of strict logic, there is no clear way of distinguishing the influence, or modulating effect of the soul on these experiences. However, this uncertainty means that near-death experiences cannot be considered as proof of the reality of the human soul.

Deathbed experiences and the soul

[14.112]Fortunately, a category of near-death experiences called deathbed experiences, provides another approach to determining the role of the soul in modulating these experiences. Deathbed experiences are a constellation of affective, paranormal, transcendental, and cognitive experiences identical to near-death experiences. Only in the case of deathbed experiences, people are clearly physically conscious as they undergo these experiences during their last days, hours, or minutes of life. They are a unique category of near-death experience, because people undergoing such experiences report their perceptions and visions to their attendants at the same time as they perceive and experience these things. And because no memory is involved, no distortion of these experiences by errors of memory function occurs. This means these experiences may reveal the true nature of the soul better than near-death experiences.

[14.113]One of the best and most extensive studies of deathbed experiences was that of two parapsychologists, Karlis Osis and Erlendur Haraldsson. These researchers reported a detailed study of the dying moments of 471 people in the book called *At the Hour of Death* (Osis 1986). Table 1 on page 223 of this book gives a statistical breakdown of the intervals between the reporting of transcendental apparitions of deceased people, deities and saints, and the moment of death in these 471 people.

- [14.114]12% reported apparitions 0-10 minutes before death
- [14.115]15% reported apparitions 11-60 minutes before death
- [14.116]20% reported apparitions 61 minutes to 6 hours before death
- [14.117]15% reported apparitions 7-24 hours before death
- [14.118]38% reported apparitions for a longer period before death

[14.119]Many of these 471 dying people also reported mood elevation, or seeing transcendental worlds prior to death. The primary causes of death in these 471 people were (see Table 12 on page 237 in Osis 1986):

- [14.120]17% died of cancer.
- [14.121]24% died of heart and circulatory disease.
- [14.122]21% died of injuries and postoperative disorders.
- [14.123]10% died due to brain injury, brain disease, and uremia.
- [14.124]22% died of infections and respiratory disease.
- [14.125]6% died from other miscellaneous lethal disorders.

[14.126]All these diseases significantly affect brain function in persons dying of these disorders. The reasons why these disorders affect the functioning of the physical brain vary from a reduction of the supply of oxygen to the brain in about 90% of all dying people, to a direct toxic effect on the brain in somewhat less than 10% of all dying people (Murray 1997). During their terminal periods of failing body function, these dying people were communicating their affective, paranormal, transcendental, and cognitive experiences to those around their deathbeds at the very same time as they were undergoing them. An example of such a deathbed experience is that of a woman dying of heart failure during 1924, shortly after giving birth in the Mothers' Hospital in London, England. The mother of this unfortunate young woman wrote of the death of her daughter, Doris, (also referred to as Mrs B.):

[14.127]*The wonderful part of it is the history of the death of my dear daughter, Vida, who had been an invalid some years. Her death took place on the 25th day of Dec., 1923, just 2 weeks and 4 days before her younger sister, Doris died. My daughter Doris, Mrs.*

*B., was very ill at that time, and the Matron at the Mothers'
Hospital deemed it unwise for Mrs. B. to know of her sister's
death. Therefore when visiting her we put off our mourning and
visited her as usual. All her letters were also kept by request until
her husband had seen who they might be from before letting her
see them. This precaution was taken lest outside friends might
possibly allude to the recent bereavement in writing to her,
unaware of the very dangerous state of her health.
When my dear child was sinking rapidly, at first she said, 'It is all
so dark; I cannot see.' A few seconds after a beautiful radiance lit
up her countenance; I know now it was the light of Heaven, and it
was most beautiful to behold. My dear child said, 'Oh, it is lovely
and bright; you cannot see as I can.' She fixed her eyes on one
particular spot in the ward, saying, 'Oh, God, forgive me for
anything I have done wrong.' After that she said, 'I can see
Father; he wants me, he is so lonely.' She spoke to her father,
saying, 'I am coming,' turning at the same time to look at me,
saying, 'Oh, he is so near.' On looking at the same place again,
she said with rather a puzzled expression, 'He has Vida with him,'
turning again to me saying, 'Vida is with him.' Then she said,
'You do want me, Dad; I am coming.' Then a very few parting
words or sighs were expressed-nothing very definite or clear.
With great difficulty and a very hard strain she asked to see 'the
man who married us': this was to her husband, who was standing
on the opposite side of the bed. (pages 13-14 in Barrett 1926)*

[14.128]This experience reports several familiar near-death experience elements such as darkness, and the experience of light, mood elevation or exultation, seeing transcendental figures of deceased persons, (her father and sister), and the apparently paranormal vision of her sister Vida, of whose demise she supposedly knew nothing. Believers in dualism claim such experiences are manifestations of the true nature of the soul, as well as the reality of a life after death. But is this true? What is the reality of deathbed experiences?

[14.129]The souls of dying persons undergoing deathbed experiences are definitely located within their physical bodies, because people who tell of their experiences at the same time as they undergo them are definitely physically conscious. This means they express their affective, paranormal, transcendental, and cognitive deathbed visions and experiences to observers through the mechanisms of their physical bodies—using the physical bodily mechanisms of speech, expression, and movement. The physical bodies of dying persons are malfunctioning—otherwise they would not be on their deathbeds. So according to the mind-model of dualism, this means that deathbed experiences as communicated to observers, are products of a controlling soul expressed through the mechanisms of a malfunctioning physical body. This is a situation analogous to using a malfunctioning television to tune into a television signal—the malfunctioning television transforms the original uncorrupted signal into something garbled and different. The same is true of the controlling influence of the soul expressed through the malfunctioning mechanisms of the physical body of a dying person (see 1.142). So according to the logic of the mind-model of dualism, a deathbed experience is actually a product of the interaction of the soul with a malfunctioning physical body, rather than a manifestation of the true nature of any possible human soul.

Conclusion—a filtered soul

[14.130]The discussion above reveals that the mechanisms of the malfunctioning human body affect the expression of the human soul—in the case of deathbed experiences, such that any controlling influence of the putative soul manifests affective, paranormal, transcendental, and cognitive experiences (see 1.142). These latter experiences are therefore not manifestations of the true nature of the human soul. So are the properties of the soul, as expressed through the medium of the healthy conscious physical body, manifestations of the true nature of the soul? According to proponents of the mind-model of dualism, the normally functioning healthy human body also filters, and limits the expression of the true nature of the human soul (see 1.76-1.88). Therefore, neither the healthy, nor the abnormally functioning human body reveals manifestations of the true unfiltered nature of the soul. The true nature of the human soul remains hidden in both situations. Nevertheless, this discussion still does not disprove the possibility of a soul controlling the physical human body in some way—only that the true nature of this soul is very different to that proposed by many proponents of the mind-model of dualism (see 1.123-1.135). Furthermore, analysis of extracorporeal experiences and deathbed experiences, reveal that the origins and manifestations of these amazing, and superficially paranormal experiences, actually prove the illusory nature of an immaterial soul with the properties defined in Chapter 1!

15

Freedom from Heaven

[15.1]Almost 70% of all people living in modern Western countries believe each individual person has a soul (Harris Poll 2008, Heald 2000, MORI 1998, Theos Ghosts Poll 2009). Furthermore, they believe the soul separates from the physical body at death, to somehow continue existing for an eternity in a parallel immaterial universe inhabited by the souls of the dead. The dualism articulated in this belief has withstood millennia of common sense and observation, and may even be impervious to explanations offered in the preceding chapters. Such an attitude is understandable, for it gives many people the dubious comfort of false hope, as expressed by the ancient Roman statesman and philosopher, Marcus Tullius Cicero, more than 2000 years ago.

> [15.2]*And if I err in my belief that the souls of men are immortal, I gladly err, nor do I wish this error which gives me pleasure to be wrested from me while I live. (page 97 in De Senectute, Cicero 1996)*

[15.3]False hope is just that—false hope. And as Cicero stated in this passage, there is absolutely nothing wrong with false hope if it provides personal meaning, comfort, or even pleasure. But when regressive and repressive social structures are coupled to this false hope, such as still happens in many parts of our little planet, then it is time to seriously address the reality of this belief. So this chapter analyzes other aspects of the mind-model of dualism, concentrating especially on the consequences of belief in a life after death. These discussions and arguments also permit some final and definite conclusions about the nature of the conscious mind. I will begin with possible reasons why people find belief in a soul so attractive and plausible.

Lifespan & oppression fuel belief in a soul

[15.4]Those lucky enough to live in modern wealthy Western countries with good governments can expect to live a long life. This is very different to the life expectancies of our ancestors even 150 years ago. In England during 1838, about 30% of all people died before their tenth birthday, and about 40% of all people died before attaining 30 years of age (Lifetables 2010). When you look at such survival figures, you realize that life must have been no more than a brief period of diseased consciousness for many people at the time. Belief in a separate incorruptible soul that lives for eternity in some sort of paradise after death is certainly a comforting belief in the face of such a massive burden of disease. Yet the modern world of 2010 is not much different in some regards. There are still massive inequalities within, and between many parts of the world.

[15.5]For example, consider the situation of Zimbabwe during 2010. Zimbabwe is an African land whose population was once about 13 million. Government mismanagement and political unrest during the years prior to 2010, produced economic misery together with massive food shortages, resulting in a massive diaspora of more than three million Zimbabweans to adjacent lands, and in particular to South Africa (Mutangi 2008). A cursory comparison of the differences in mortality between Zimbabwe and the USA during 2008 reveals dramatic differences (WHO 2010). Zimbabwe has a high child mortality rate. About 10% of all Zimbabwean children die before attaining ten years of age. But this is not the worst. About 50% of all inhabitants of Zimbabwe die in the economically active and child-caring age range of 30 to 50 years (WHO 2010)! The main cause of this horrific mortality is an epidemic of Human Immunodeficiency Virus (HIV) infection affecting 7 to 33% of the population (UNAIDS 2008). HIV infection exacerbates the mortality of the multitude of other infectious diseases rife in Africa, such as parasitic infections, hepatitis, tuberculosis, and diarrheal diseases. Furthermore, HIV infection also exacerbates the effects of starvation due to poverty and food shortages. This apocalyptic backdrop is certainly one of the many reasons why membership of the congregations of Christian churches in Zimbabwe has increased since the year 2000.

[15.6]Islam and Christianity are religions practiced by more than half the world population. These two religions share so many fundamental beliefs, that their differences are more a matter of form than belief. Consider the example of Christianity. Christianity teaches that the diseased, the oppressed, and the enslaved can all look forward to an eternal life in paradise after death—as long as they perform their duties, are well behaved, and obedient while alive. This comforting belief in an eternal life after death in paradise for those helpless to change their situations of deprivation, disease, and oppression, certainly contributes to the worldwide popularity of Christianity.

[15.7]Organized versions of Christianity also have an important social function. Actively participating members of a particular Christian congregation often provide beneficial mutual aid and social cohesion. For example, an employer may prefer to employ a fellow congregation member. Church members with powerful positions outside the church may well exert influence to aid fellow congregation members. Furthermore, mutual cohesion within the active membership of a church often results in the provision of significant housing, food, clothing, and other material aid to socially and economically weaker members of the congregation. These are but some of the reasons why Christianity flourishes in regions where deprivation, starvation, disease, poor education, ignorance, and government mismanagement are rampant.

Why do educated people believe in a soul?

[15.8]But oppression, poverty, deprivation and ignorance do not explain why about 70% of the generally healthy, and well educated populations of Western countries believe in the reality of the human soul. This belief in a soul is more precisely formulated as a belief in an individual soul that survives the death of the body. So why do generally healthy and well educated people believe in the reality of a human soul?

[15.9]The answer to this question lies in the wondrous and seemingly inexplicable nature of lucid dreams, in reports of experiences of awareness during general anesthesia, as well as in stories of out-of-body, and near-death experiences. Reports emphasizing the astounding and inexplicable nature of these experiences spread from one person to another, as well as in newspapers, magazines, books, radio, and television programs. These experiences all share one common feature—consciousness is astonishingly and inexplicably present during periods when the individuals concerned are supposedly unconscious, or even apparently dead. Furthermore, this separated consciousness is apparently capable of thoughts, perceptions, and actions independently of the physical body. So it is quite understandable that people from ancient times until the present, have concluded that the conscious mind is something invisible and immaterial, separable from the material body—or in other words, that humans possess an invisible, immaterial and separable soul. Moreover, the experiences of those reporting near-death experiences are such that many people also conclude that the soul continues to exist after the material body dies. Chris Carter expressed this ancient belief in the mind-model of dualism in modern terms in the book, *Science and the Near-Death Experience.*

[15.10]*However, this conclusion is not based on the evidence alone. There is an implicit, unstated assumption behind this argument, and it is often unconsciously employed. The hidden premise behind this argument can be illustrated with the analogy of listening to music on a radio, smashing the radio's receiver, and thereby concluding that the radio was producing the music. The implicit assumption made in all the arguments discussed above was that the relationship between brain activity and consciousness was always one of cause to effect, and never that of effect to cause. But this assumption is not known to be true, and it is not the only conceivable one consistent with the observed facts mentioned earlier. Just as consistent with the observed facts is the idea that the brain's function is that of an intermediary between mind and body—or in other words, that the brain's function is that of a receiver-transmitter—sometimes from body to mind, and sometimes from mind to body. (pages 13-14 in Carter 2010)*

[15.11]Discussions in earlier chapters revealed several objective phenomena totally at variance with this belief in a human soul. So Chris Carter is incorrect when he says it is impossible to distinguish whether the conscious mind is a product of the functioning of the brain, or whether the brain is merely the receiver, conduit, and executor of the instructions of the separable and immaterial soul. Moreover, this ancient and pervasive belief in a human soul is associated with some very thorny problems seldom consistently addressed by believers. So let us look at some of these problems with logic and common sense, as well with as insights from modern medical studies.

Belief versus proof

[15.12]About 70% of people believe in the mind-model of dualism, or the reality of the human soul. Many people are convinced their conscious minds truly were separated from their bodies during out-of-body, and near-death experiences. Veridical perceptions made while undergoing such experiences even provide apparent proof of the reality of this belief. During these experiences, some people also report feelings of intense ineffability, a realization that their consciousness was "clearer than normal", as well as a total understanding of functioning of the world and universe. The profundity of the emotions experienced during these mental states is almost universal among those reporting such experiences. And because they all report similar intense convictions and emotions, their collective opinion is that these experiences must be true examples of the separation of the conscious mind from the body, or true manifestations of the workings of the human soul.

[15.13]An amazing claim! A lawyer would say that the burden of proof rests upon the person who makes an amazing claim, and not on the person who does not share this belief. But I am not a lawyer. So all I can say is that the functioning of the human body explains the generation of consciousness, as well as all the properties of the mind with provable and measurable facts. Even apparently paranormal phenomena such as out-of-body, and near-death experiences are explained by the functioning of the body. Furthermore, as is extensively discussed throughout this work, basic clinical observation of medical reality disproves one of the most fundamental propositions of the mind-model of dualism—the extracorporeal location of memory. And when all these things are explained, believers in dualism can offer no other proof except their intense belief in the reality of the human soul.

[15.14]So does the fact that almost 70% of all people truly believe in the reality of a human soul mean that the mind-model of dualism is true? The concept that if most people believe something is true, then it must be true, is based upon two factors: ignorance, and overestimation of the mutual critical capacity of large groups of people.

[15.15]Ignorance as a foundation for a belief, always reminds me of a wonderful little footnote in a surgical textbook once popular among medical students in Australia and England during the 1960's and 1970's. In the chapter describing the different types of swellings of the scrotum, the authors remark that a particular type of swelling called a "spermatocele" may sometimes be as large as a testicle, so giving the illusion of a third testicle. This once resulted in a very interesting petition to the Pope during the middle-ages.

[15.16]*Sometimes the patient may believe that he has a third testicle. It is recorded that in the fourteenth century the Pope granted a*

petition from a gentleman to marry two wives because he
possessed three testicles. (page 1327 in Rains 1981)

[15.17]This example may seem frivolous. Nonetheless, it is a superb example of how ignorance of basic medical knowledge, coupled with a particular religious belief system, resulted in a decision now considered hilarious. The same is also true of many phenomena once considered paranormal or having a divine origin. This is the origin of the "God of the gaps" concept first propounded by Henry Drummond (1851-1897) in his *Lowell Lectures* published during 1896.

[15.18]*There are reverent minds who ceaselessly scan the fields of Nature and the books of Science in search of gaps—gaps which they will fill up with God. As if God lived in gaps? What view of Nature or of Truth is theirs whose interest in Science is not in what it can explain but in what it cannot, whose quest is ignorance not knowledge, whose daily dread is that the cloud may lift, and who, as darkness melts from this field or from that, begin to tremble for the place of His abode? What needs altering in such finely jealous souls is at once their view of Nature and of God. (page 333, Chapter 10, in Drummond 1908)*

[15.19]In essence, practitioners of the "God of the gaps" belief state; "Something, or an event, cannot be explained by science, therefore God must be the cause." The same is also true of belief in the paranormal; "Science cannot explain this perception, or that occurrence, therefore the cause must be paranormal." These gaps in knowledge are getting ever smaller with the advance of science and critical observation. So the century-old advice of Henry Drummond, as well as that of most present day philosophers and scientists, is simply that if something is inexplicable at this moment, more observations, knowledge and improved theories will eventually render these previously mysterious events explicable.

[15.20]The idea that popular belief is always correct also reminds me of the classic saying; "One hundred thousand lemmings can't be wrong!" But lemmings are animals, not humans. Unfortunately, large human groups possess similar attributes. For example, for many millennia, people believed the earth was flat, and that the Sun and the stars moved around the sky in patterns determined by the gods. This belief was even official Christian church doctrine in some countries of Europe until about 1650. Indeed, to say otherwise at the time was regarded as a vile heresy requiring punishment with the full might of the church. This is why the

Italian scientist Galileo Galilei (1564-1642) was convicted of heresy, and even narrowly escaped being condemned to death for stating that the earth was not flat, and that the planets orbited around the Sun. Yet during the lifetime of Galileo, and in the preceding millennia, simple observations proving many of the statements of Galileo were known to all. For example, the appearance of ships as they disappeared over the horizon, was a well-known phenomenon proving the shape of the earth. The posthumous publication of the heliocentric model of Nicolaus Copernicus (1473-1543) preceded the birth of Galileo, and was known to him. In fact, the heliocentric model of Copernicus was considered a convenient mathematical fiction by the Christian church at the time, because it greatly simplified astronomical calculations of the paths of the planets and sun. However, the church considered it just that—a mathematical fiction without any relationship to reality. In other words, the observations proving the statements of Galileo were known long before his lifetime, but very few people had tested whether observation corresponded with popular belief before Galileo made his statements.

[15.21]All this is an astounding revelation of how popular belief can sometimes blind large numbers of people to observed facts, or cause people to hold beliefs at variance with common sense and observation. Similarly, popular belief in something without any observable and measurable physical proof, is just that—an unfounded belief unless it corresponds with all measurable and observable facts. So let us examine other inconsistencies associated with belief in a human soul.

Material or immaterial—which is more likely?

[15.22]About 70% of people believe in a conscious mind that is separable, immaterial, and survives death of the body to live for an eternity in a universe inhabited by the souls of the dead. But is this theory of a soul more likely than the theory of the conscious mind as a product of the functioning of the material brain? Without any medical knowledge, there are actually very few ways to distinguish between these two theories of the origin of the conscious mind. So is it possible to establish which is more likely without any recourse to medical knowledge whatsoever? The answer to this question was indirectly suggested by a correspondent who asked me the following question:

[15.23]*Can you, or any other materialist enlighten me as to how a thought (and more importantly an original thought such as a completely new invention) is generated by a lump of meat, albeit*

rare meat?
Where is 'I' (or me) In what part of my skull do 'I' reside?
How can the flowing of mere electrons hither and thither, account
for the human condition of empathy, for instance? Electrons don't
appear to have an intelligence that we could ever quamtify, so why
should several billion joined together? (Question on an internet
forum by "Mr Ed")

[15.24]I am indebted to "Mr Ed" for asking this question. It forced me to think more deeply upon the matter. And the answer to this very fundamental question is equally fundamental. The first part of the answer is to carefully distinguish between consciousness and mind.

[15.25]Briefly stated, consciousness makes mind and all the properties of mind such as empathy, memory, emotion, etc., possible. Consciousness can even exist without mind. And consciousness is something quite amazing. All my personal professional experience as an anesthesiologist, all I have learned from others, all the studies and books I have read on consciousness come to the same conclusion—we know when it is present, and often when it is not—but no one is sure what it is. All that is known is that some process generates consciousness.

[15.26]The dispute between the mind-models of dualism and materialism is whether this process occurs in the lump of meat called the brain, or in some separate immaterial "something" that somehow interacts with, and controls this physical lump of meat. One fact is certain—absence of any organized process is chaos without any of the properties of mind. This is why both mind-models require consciousness and the properties of mind to be the result of some organized process. According to materialism, the functioning of the physical brain generates consciousness and mind by the organized physical processes of electronic currents, and myriad chemical reactions within the intricate structures of the physical brain. The advantage of this materialist view is that science is steadily unraveling the provable electrical, physical, and chemical processes occurring within the brain generating consciousness and all the properties of mind. Similarly, according to dualism, an immaterial soul must also function by some organized process, otherwise it simply would not exist. But absolutely none of the processes generating the phenomenon of an immaterial soul are known or understood. All we are told by believers is that they are immaterial, and that they must occur if individual souls truly exist. The reader should note, that in the interests of strict logic, the fact that these postulated immaterial processes are unknown does not mean they do not exist. All that can be said about these postulated immaterial processes is that they are simply unknown at this time. And regardless of whether the processes generating the conscious mind are material or immaterial, all such organized processes are equally marvelous, because they result in the phenomenon of the individual conscious mind.

15.27Belief in a human soul is made difficult by the fact that this mind-model requires the immaterial soul to somehow interact with the substance of the very material physical brain to control all thoughts, deeds and speech of the physical body. Yet we know from the phenomenon of out-of-body experiences, that an immaterial soul does not interact with physical matter because it is capable of passing though the human body, reinforced concrete floors, and brick walls (see 1.47-1.49). Nonetheless, this fact does not mean that an immaterial soul cannot interact with the physical brain. We have the example of neutrinos, gamma rays, X-rays, and radio waves that can pass through these things and also interact with physical objects. For example, X-Rays pass through solid objects, but are slightly absorbed, more in some parts than others, to reveal X-Ray pictures of the body and other objects. Nonetheless, radio waves, X-Rays, gamma rays, neutrinos, etc., are physical waves and particles, which explains their interaction with physical matter. But the soul is immaterial, which explains its undetectable nature. So who knows by what unknown mechanisms the soul interacts with the physical brain? I certainly do not know.

15.28The conclusion of this line of thought is evident. A theory of the conscious mind as a product of the functioning of the physical brain requires no leap of faith. However, a huge leap of faith, and some considerable belief is required when postulating that the individual conscious mind is a product of some unknown immaterial process, which somehow interacts with the material brain to control all thoughts, actions, and speech. A material origin of the conscious mind is simply more likely than an immaterial origin. However, while this discussion reveals materialism is likely to be the correct explanation of the nature of the human mind, it is not proof of materialism. So what about other questions raised by the mind-model of dualism?

Origin of the soul, predestination, and purpose

15.29Two of the first questions springing to mind in the matter of a possible human soul, are the nature of its origin and its purpose. Many religions and belief systems also couple belief in an immaterial soul with concepts such as predestination, and reasons why the immaterial soul requires union with a physical body. So is there a finite supply of souls created at the beginning of the universe, each awaiting eventual union with a single physical body? Is there a finite number of souls in the universe being endlessly recycled by means of reincarnation in a series of physical bodies? Is there an infinite number of souls awaiting eventual union with a single physical body? Or is the soul an immaterial product of the material fertilization of an ovum by a sperm? These questions are impossible to answer, except possibly with religious beliefs based upon divine inspiration. The ancient Jewish pseudoepigrapha provide a colorful legend supporting the concept that all the souls that will ever unite with a human body reside within some heavenly repository until required.

[15.30] With the soul of Adam [the first man] the souls of all the generations of men were created. They are stored up in a promptuary, in the seventh of the heavens, whence they are drawn as they are needed for human body after human body.

The soul and body of man are united in this way: When a woman has conceived, the Angel of the Night, Lailah, carries the sperm before God, and God decrees what manner of human being shall become of it—whether it shall be male or female, strong or weak, rich or poor, beautiful or ugly, long or short, fat or thin, and what all its other qualities shall be. Piety and wickedness alone are left to the determination of man himself. Then God makes a sign to the angel appointed over the souls, saying, "Bring Me the soul so-and-so, which is hidden in Paradise, whose name is so-and-so, and whose form is so-and-so." The angel brings the designated soul, and she bows down when she appears in the presence of God, and prostrates herself before Him. At that moment, God issues the command, "Enter this sperm." The soul opens her mouth, and pleads: "O Lord of the world! I am well pleased with the world in which I have been living since the day on which Thou didst call me into being. Why dost Thou now desire to have me enter this impure sperm, I who am holy and pure, and a part of Thy glory?" God consoles her: "The world which I shall cause thee to enter is better than the world in which thou hast lived hitherto, and when I created thee, it was only for this purpose." The soul is then forced to enter the sperm against her will, and the angel carries her back to the womb of the mother. Two angels are detailed to watch that she shall not leave it, nor drop out of it, and a light is set above her, whereby the soul can see from one end of the world to the other. (pages 56-57 in Ginzberg 1913)

Predestination of the soul

[15.31]The above passage is a very colorful example of belief in predestination. The Jewish God had formed the souls of each person for a specific life at the very creation of the universe. So God knew these specific individuals were going to be born, despite all the cumulative randomness introduced into the world because each individual is free to choose a path of evil or righteousness. Accordingly, this legend clearly indicates that the idea of so-called "individual free choice" of persons to choose a path of evil or righteousness, is only a cheap charade to make believers think they have a choice. This perfidious belief in predestination is also clearly expounded in the holy books of more recent major world religions, such as Christianity and Islam. Just look at this example from the New Testament of the Christian Bible.

[15.32]*The beast that thou sawest was, and is not; and is about to come up out of the abyss, and to go into perdition. And they that dwell on the earth shall wonder, they whose name hath not been written in the book of life from the foundation of the world, when they behold the beast, how that he was, and is not, and shall come. (Bible, American Standard Version, Revelation 17:8)*

[15.33]In other words, at the very creation of this universe, a long, long time before each of us was born, God determined the number of souls, as well as the fates of each of these souls (see also Bible, Matthew 25:34, Acts 13:48, Romans 8:28-30 & 9:11-13, Ephesians 1:3-6 and 1:11, Revelation 13:8). The implications of this belief are startling. It means that at the very creation of the universe, God planned every miscarriage and every abortion, and every death due to infanticide, accident, old age, murder, wars, pogroms, natural disasters, famines, epidemics, and disease. If this were not so, then God would not know the exact numbers of souls required, and for whom. Predestination interpreted in this strict manner means humans have no free will. After all, if humans had the smallest bit of free will, the cumulative results of this free will would render the future unpredictable, altering the sequence of events in the world such that many persons would die, not be born, or many more children would be born. The Holy Quran, the holy book of Islam, another major world religion, echoes this same repellant philosophy.

15.34Naught of disaster befalleth in the earth or in yourselves but it is in a Book before We bring it into being Lo! That is easy for Allah (Quran 57:22)

15.35Other passages in the Holy Quran expound this same belief (see also Quran 6:2, 11:6). And if the reader thinks this idea of heavenly predestination is confining and depressing, the Christian prophets were apparently inspired by their God to tell humankind even more about the unbelievably repulsive nature of divine predestination.

15.36Nay but, O man, who art thou that repliest against God? Shall the thing formed say to him that formed it, Why didst thou make me thus? Or hath not the potter a right over the clay, from the same lump to make one part a vessel unto honor, and another unto dishonor? What if God, willing to show his wrath, and to make his power known, endured with much longsuffering vessels of wrath fitted unto destruction: and that he might make known the riches of his glory upon vessels of mercy, which he afore prepared unto glory, (American Standard Version Bible, Romans 9:20-23)

15.37So the merciful Christian God actually creates people whose explicit function is to reveal the "glory of God" by living lives of malevolent and vile wickedness! Then this just and merciful God presumably dooms them to everlasting torment in a life after death because they revealed the "Glory of God!" Yet other passages in the Christian Bible supplement this same concept of people predestined for lives of evil and disobedience to God (see Bible, Romans 9:17, Revelation 17:17). This raises an interesting question about horrific leaders and rulers such as Attila the Hun (406-453), Vlad Tepes of Romania (1431-1476), Ivan the Terrible of Russia (1530-1584), Adolf Hitler of Germany (1889-1945), Idi Amin Dada of Uganda (1925-2003), Pol Pot of Cambodia (1925-1998). According to Saint Paul, one of the founders of the Christian religion, God ordained and placed these monsters as rulers of their countries, as well as placing our current rulers above us.

15.38Let everyone be subject to the governing authorities, for there is no authority except that which God has established. The authorities that exist have been established by God. Consequently, whoever rebels against the authority is rebelling against what God has instituted, and those who do so will bring judgment on themselves. For rulers hold no terror for those who do right, but for those who do wrong. Do you want to be free from fear of the one in authority? Then do what is right and you will be commended. For the one in authority is God's servant for your good. But if you do wrong, be afraid, for rulers do not bear the sword for no reason. They are God's servants, agents of wrath to bring punishment on the wrongdoer. Therefore, it is necessary to submit to the authorities, not only because of possible punishment but also as a matter of conscience. (NIV Bible, Romans 13:1-5).

[15.39]So did God purposefully place these paragons of monstrous evil as rulers of nations—as "vessels of wrath fitted unto destruction"—in order that God could make his "glory" known to all? If this is true, then these malevolent creatures truly were "godsends" to humankind, and just as much victims of the inscrutable nature of God, as were the many millions murdered by the willing, and unwilling slaves of their vile and repellant ideals. This is a thought provoking concept—the Christian Bible preaches the divine introduction of unspeakable and malignant evil to demonstrate the "glorious nature of God!"

[15.40]Nonetheless, despite such horridly fascinating considerations, the concept of predestination implicitly implies the creation of a finite number of souls. Now holy books are supposedly the inspired writings of prophets. But there is absolutely no physical proof of the truth of any such divine inspiration, except for the profound belief of the followers of these religions. Therefore, such revelations in holy books cannot be considered proof of a finite number of souls. It is just as defensible to conceive the possibility of an infinite number of souls. And this brings us to the purpose of an immaterial soul.

Purpose of the soul and reincarnation

[15.41]Many people believe the soul possesses superior intelligence and knowledge to what it manifests in the physical body (see 1.76-1.88). But why should something immaterial, mentally superior, as well as immortal, need to unite with something as short-lived, corruptible, and frail as a physical human body? However, there is also evidence demonstrating that the soul possesses the same intelligence and mental capacities as the physical body with which it is united (see 1.89-1.91). This latter possibility partly explains why the soul must undergo mortal life in a physical body, so as to learn lessons only possible within the form of a physical body.

^{15.42}Religions such as Christianity and Islam implicitly propose the soul learns these lessons within a single human lifespan. Other beliefs and religions such as Hinduism and Buddhism, propose an endless cycle of birth-life-death, and reincarnation. During each incarnation, an immaterial soul learns new lessons, and its behavior during an incarnation determines its fate, and the nature of the body in which it is reincarnated. Indeed, this belief even goes so far as to propose that some people will even be reincarnated as dogs or pigs (V Prapathaka, 10 Khanda, 7, in Müller 1879, see citation at 4.137). In other words, this belief plainly states that vertebrate mammals such as dogs and pigs also have souls which may be reincarnated as humans. What a fascinating concept! Human and animal souls are apparently one and the same, and interchangeable in this belief system! This is an interesting and important concept I will discuss later in this chapter.

^{15.43}There is another interesting idea arising from the belief in reincarnation only occurring in a body appropriate for the further development of the soul. Does this mean that the development of the soul of a person can be deduced from the content of near-death experiences? For example, people whose souls are at a lower stage of spiritual development would be expected to have near-death experiences with a content quite different from people whose souls are at a higher level of spiritual development. Do such differences occur?

^{15.44}There are more problems associated with the concept of learning lessons from life in a physical body. To begin with, reincarnation is unable to be proven despite many attempts to do so. And the concept of learning during an incarnation in a physical body is equally unable to be proven. Nonetheless, just assume that it does occur, then this passage from the *Khandogya Upanishad* teaches that each individual soul learns different lessons from a physical life, and that each individual soul is reincarnated in a physical body appropriate to learning such lessons. The most obvious question arising from this belief is how the soul determines the most appropriate reincarnation. For example, consider the situation of an evil underdeveloped soul. According to the *Khandogya Upanishad*, such a soul would be relegated to reincarnation in a dog, hog, or other lowly animal (see 4.137). Such a soul is clearly lacking in any sort of insight into its condition. How would such a soul choose the most appropriate reincarnation? The solution to this problem implies some form of celestial bookkeeping, whereby underdeveloped souls are simply directed to their subsequent reincarnations. Is this likely? It would

certainly add an extra improbable layer of complexity to belief in reincarnation and the mind-model of dualism.

[15.45]Belief in the necessity of reincarnation to learn lessons on this physical world, as well as the determination of the nature of the subsequent body in which a soul is reincarnated, has other truly fascinating consequences. Combine belief in reincarnation with modern neurophysiological studies demonstrating that the physical brains of people of different genders, different races, and different sociocultural backgrounds respond differently to the same stimuli. This repeatedly confirmed physical observation has profound implications for belief in reincarnation. It implies that different types of physical bodies provide different platforms for specific lessons learned in each reincarnation. In other words, the degree of spiritual advancement of each individual soul determines the gender, race, culture, and socioeconomic status of any subsequent reincarnation (see 4.135-4.142). So do these observable differences in brain function mean that one gender is spiritually more advanced than the other, or that there is a gradation of spiritual advancement between different genders, races or sociocultural groups? Such a system of thought, coupled with neurophysiological studies, could even be the basis of a new form of racism whereby one gender, race, or culture is considered more spiritually advanced than the other. This is one of the more interesting consequences of belief in reincarnation, but is incapable of any sort of proof one way or the other.

[15.46]However, even though popular, reincarnation is not a viable belief system. Reincarnation requires a soul with memory, for without memory, a soul cannot learn lessons from a physical life enabling spiritual development. Yet the soul, if it exists, possesses no ability to remember anything, and therefore cannot learn anything. Accordingly, belief in reincarnation is no more than a pitiful and desperate hope for eternal life, and a manifestation of hopeful fantasies replacing logic.

Paradise, hell and heaven

[15.47]Believers in dualism claim that the soul continues to exist after death in some immaterial afterlife inhabited by the souls of the dead. Various names and concepts have been ascribed to this immaterial universe inhabited by the souls of the dead: the underworld, paradise, hell, and heaven. Many people believe that those reporting their near-death experiences have had a glimpse of this afterlife, but returned to life

385

because it was not yet their time to die. This belief in an afterlife raises several interesting questions.

Are there hamsters in heaven?

[15.48]One of the more interesting questions is the presence of animals such as hamsters in heaven. Are there hamsters in heaven? This sounds absurd, but is actually a very serious question. Many people believe the reality of a separable, immaterial, and immortal conscious mind is proven by out-of-body, and near-death experiences. Hamsters and other animals manifest consciousness and many attributes of mental activity similar to humans, all of which satisfy the criteria for consciousness and mind discussed and defined earlier in this book (see 2.6). So do hamsters and other animals have souls—and do the souls of these animals enter an eternal afterlife as proposed by many believers in dualism? These are fascinating questions well worth examining in some more detail.

[15.49]To begin with, consciousness and mind are not the same. Consciousness makes all the attributes of mind possible, but mind does not make consciousness possible. A repetition of the short list earlier in this book (Chapter 2) illustrates how we view consciousness in humans and animals.

- [15.50]A normal human is definitely conscious.
- [15.51]A mentally retarded human is definitely conscious.
- [15.52]A drooling, incontinent, and totally demented human is definitely conscious.
- [15.53]A cow is definitely conscious.
- [15.54]A dog is definitely conscious.
- [15.55]A cat is definitely conscious.
- [15.56]A hamster is definitely conscious.

[15.57]No one would deny these different types of humans, or these different animals are definitely conscious, yet their minds differ enormously. I have absolutely no idea what transpires in the conscious mind of a cow, dog, cat, or hamster. I am not even sure I would even want to know. Yet these animals are just as conscious as humans, and they definitely possess similar mental properties. Just consider the various properties of the conscious minds of dogs. A conscious dog is aware of, and interacts with its surroundings with emotions and behavior recognizable to humans.

- [15.58]*Memory.* Dogs remember people. They remember those who treated them well, those who are friendly, as well as those who abused them. Dogs remember places they have visited before.
- [15.59]*Learning.* Learning requires memory, the ability to learn, as well as the ability to put what is learned and remembered into practice. Dogs can learn, Dogs are trained as guide dogs for the blind. Dogs are trained to assist physically handicapped persons. Dogs are trained as guard dogs, Dogs are trained to perform tricks and dances.
- [15.60]*Emotions.* Dogs show a full range of emotions. Dogs are joyful on the return of a loved master. Dogs are affectionate with a loved master. Dogs are clearly content and happy, when they can lie in the proximity of a loved master after having exercised and eaten. Dogs are clearly happy when able to please their masters. At other times dogs are fearful and afraid, while at other moments dogs may be aggressive, angry, or enraged.
- [15.60]*Personality.* Dogs have personalities. Some dogs are very social, and happy to meet other dogs and people. Other dogs may be more reserved, or even asocial except with their masters.

[15.61]The same is true to a greater or lesser degree with many other animals. All these things are not altogether surprising, because the brains of animals possess the same basic structures as human brains. Cells forming the brains of animals also have identical structures and metabolic processes, as well as functioning in the same way as human brain cells. Consciousness and all the properties of mind are made possible by identical or similar structures in all these different human and animal brains. So is not the conscious mind, or soul, of a cow, dog, cat, or hamster just as identical, separable, immaterial, and immortal as that of a human? This means we should expect to see cows, dogs, cats, hamsters, and other animals in an afterlife. The immaterial universe of the afterlife would not only be filled with the souls of humans, but also with the souls of contentedly mooing cows, happily sniffing dogs, purring cats, and cuddly little hamsters.

[15.62]Look at it another way. People living in the USA eat a lot of meat compared to many other countries. According to the Wikipedia Encyclopedia on the internet, the average American adult consumes meat equivalent to approximately 1/10th of a cow, about 1/3rd of a pig, around 27 chickens, and one turkey per year. So during an active adult life of 50 years, the average USA adult will have eaten meat equivalent to about 5 cows, 18 pigs, 1350 chickens, and 50 turkeys. Now if the separable conscious mind of each of these animals also goes to the same afterlife as human souls, then the American afterlife will be a cacophony of happily mooing cows, grunting pigs, cackling chickens, and gobbling turkeys. There would be more animals in heaven than humans in an American afterlife. If you look at the figures above, there would be 5 + 18 +1350 + 50 = 1423 animal souls for every human soul in an American afterlife. This sounds more like a zoo than heaven. Regardless of the accuracy of these statistics, meat eating humans consume many animals during a normal lifespan, so there will always be more animal than human souls in an afterlife. Imagine spending an eternity in an afterlife surrounded by the souls of the animals you ate during your earthly life. Just imagine your uneasy feelings of guilt as one of them occasionally interrupts its frolicking, to gaze melancholically and plaintively at you with that one question in their sad eyes; "Why did you eat me?"

[15.63]Animals such as cows and pigs also possess conscious minds. Moreover, consciousness in animals is just as amazing as is human consciousness. So what is the functional difference between the conscious mind of a drooling, incontinent and demented human, and the conscious mind of an intelligent dog? There is no real difference. Both are conscious, and both manifest properties of mind. The soul supposedly passes into an immaterial universe after death, yet the afterlife reported by people returning from near-death experiences is spotlessly clean and sterile. There are no multitudes of animals. Instead, the afterlife is a universe inhabited only by gods, other holy entities, and the souls of deceased humans whose intelligence, personalities, and physical appearances match those of their physical bodies at their prime. Another curious fact is that no-one ever reports meeting mentally retarded souls, or baby souls in the afterlife. So at what age, at what intelligence level, and at what point on the evolutionary tree do conscious beings qualify for admission to the afterlife? How do believers in dualism explain this inconsistency?

Why are there no extraterrestrials in heaven?

[15.64]This brings us to another important question about the afterlife. Why does no-one ever report seeing extraterrestrial souls in the afterlife? Our Sun is no more than a very average star near the rim of a galaxy made up of at least 200-400 billion stars. And our planet orbits this very average star. Relatively recent observations reveal more than 400 planets, called "exoplanets", orbiting stars in our astronomical vicinity (Lammer 2010, Sasselov 2010). More recent studies report that each star in our galaxy has on average about 1.6 planets (Cassan 2012), which means about 200-400 billion planets in our galaxy alone. Furthermore, smaller Earth-size planets are more common than large Jupiter size planets (Cassan 2012). This means that solar systems with other planets not too unlike ours are common in our galaxy. Our galaxy is but one of countless millions in the visible universe. So the universe must contain countless billions of other planets similar to ours—and many of these will contain intelligent life forms. This is no longer speculation, but a certainty.

[15.65]More than 200 years ago, Thomas Paine (1737-1809) speculated that each of the myriad stars in the night sky were suns around which planets orbited (page 60 in Paine 1831). And to think, this was in a time period that people were still discovering the planets of the solar system— they had no concept of galaxies, or of the distances to stars outside the solar system. In retrospect, Thomas Paine was a visionary with ideas far ahead of his time. He also proposed that many such planets contained intelligent life forms with hopes, aspirations, and viewpoints similar to ours.

[15.66]*But it is not to us, the inhabitants of this globe, only, that the benefits arising from a plurality of worlds are limited. The inhabitants of each of the worlds of which our system is composed, enjoy the same opportunities of knowledge as we do. They behold the revolutionary motions of our earth, as we behold theirs. All the planets revolve in sight of each other; and, therefore, the same universal school of science presents itself to all.*
Neither does the knowledge stop here. The system of worlds next to us exhibits, in its revolutions, the same principles and school of science, to the inhabitants of their system, as our system does to us, and in like manner throughout the immensity of space. (page 61 in Paine 1831)

[15.67]Paine also proceeded to speculate whether these multitudes of different intelligent life forms on other planets were denied the "privilege" of the Christian faith, as well as what was necessary should Christianity even now be present on all planets with intelligent life forms (pages 61 and onwards in Paine 1831).

[15.68]*From whence then could arise the solitary and strange conceit that the Almighty [God], who had millions of worlds equally dependent on his protection, should quit the care of all the rest, and come to die in our world, because, they say one man and one woman [Adam and Eve] had eaten an apple! And, on the other hand, are we to suppose that every world in the boundless creation, had an Eve, an apple, a serpent and a redeemer? In this case, the person who is irreverently called the Son of God [Jesus], and sometimes God himself, would have nothing else to do than to travel from world to world, in an endless succession of death, with scarcely a momentary interval of life. (page 62 in Paine 1831)*

[15.69]When Thomas Paine wrote this passage more than 200 years ago, people seriously believed in the tenets of Christianity, and either shunned or laughed at those propounding such "insanely foolish" heresies. This is a truly fascinating and confrontational speculation for all believers in Christianity. Similar arguments are possible for all other religions. These arguments of Thomas Paine were no more than mere speculation during his lifetime. So if there are more than 400 large, Jupiter sized planets orbiting suns in our astronomical vicinity, there must be countless billions of as yet unknown and undetected smaller planets similar to ours spread throughout the universe. Some of these are almost certainly inhabited by intelligent life forms. The sum total of the populations of these myriad worlds would vastly outnumber that of our single planet. After dying, the souls of all these intelligent beings would presumably also cross over into the universe inhabited by the souls of the dead. But people recovering from near-death experiences never report meeting multitudes of extraterrestrial beings in the universe inhabited by the souls of the deceased, even though they meet many other deceased human souls. Does this fact mean extraterrestrials have their own heavens? Or, as is speculated by more anthropocentric types, are humans the only intelligent creatures in the universe with souls?

Heavenly hallucinations

[15.70]The *Bardo Thödol*, better known as the *Tibetan Book of the Dead*, is a collection of Tibetan Buddhist texts dating from sometime before 1500 CE. It describes the passage of the deceased into the afterlife as well as the form in which the afterlife appears to the soul of the deceased (Evans-Wentz 1960). It also answers the question of why we see no mentally retarded souls, no animals, and no extraterrestrials in this transcendental and immaterial universe inhabited by the souls of the dead. One passage is particularly relevant.

[15.71]*Accordingly, for a Buddhist of some other School, as for a Hindu, or a Moslem, or a Christian, the Bardo experiences would be appropriately different: the Buddhist's or the Hindu's thought-forms, as in a dream state, would give rise to corresponding visions of the deities of the Buddhist or Hindu pantheon; a Moslem's to visions of the Moslem Paradise; a Christian's, to visions of the Christian Heaven, or an American Indian's to visions of the Happy Hunting Ground. And, similarly, the materialist will experience after-death visions as negative and as empty and as deityless as any he ever dreamt while in the human body. In other words, as explained above, the after-death state is very much like a dream state, and its dreams are the children of the mentality of the dreamer. Rationally considered, each person's after-death experiences, as the Bardo Thödol teaching implies, are entirely dependent upon his or her own mental content. (pages 33-34 in Evans-Wentz 1960)*

[15.72]This passage is amazing. It clearly states that the souls of the dead undergo a life after death in a transcendental world inhabited by the dead in an environment of their own making, an environment of their own imagining, and in an environment whose content is determined by their own sociocultural upbringing and mental content! And indeed, the visionary content of near-death experiences of people from different cultures is in full agreement with this old text (Abramovich 1988, Carter 2010, Kellehear 2001, Knoblauch 2001, Lundahl 1993, Murphy 2001, Osis 1986, Pasricha 1986). So human souls spend eternity in an infinitude of individual human heavens. Extraterrestrial beings spend eternity in an infinitude of extraterrestrial heavens. And cuddly little hamsters spend eternity in hamster heaven. This explains why no one reports seeing mentally retarded souls, why no one reports seeing animals, and why no one reports seeing extraterrestrial life forms in the transcendental world inhabited by the souls of the dead.

[15.73]But this very concept of a socioculturally, and individually determined content and form of a life after death has a serious flaw. What is the difference between such an afterlife and a drug-induced hallucination, a wild fantasy, or a simple hallucination induced by any other cause? When you think about it for a while, you realize there is no difference. The afterlife as described by the *Tibetan Book of the Dead* is actually no more than an eternal hallucination whose content is determined by each person's individual personality, upbringing, and culture. Such a parochial afterlife contains no possibility of personal development. Even worse, an afterlife does not last one year, or 100 years, or a mere 1,000 years. No, an eternal afterlife lasts millions of years, an eternity. Imagine living the same self-induced hallucination for countless millions of years—for all eternity. Just imagine spending a million years, an eternity, in the company of your insufferably pious in-laws ... Such an afterlife is eventually doomed to become a tedious hell of eternal repetition. A horrid thought. This is yet another one of those curious and interesting inconsistencies implicit in the idea of the immortality of the separable and immaterial human soul. Nevertheless, some people dispute this idea, claiming this concept proposed within the *Tibetan Book of the Dead* indicates that individual consciousness is a localized manifestation of an all-encompassing universal consciousness.

Individual versus universal consciousness

[15.74]Some believers in the idea of an immaterial nature of individual consciousness claim the universe is a manifestation of some sort of universal consciousness (Levin 2011, Manousakis 2006, Shanahan 2005, Whitworth 2010). The individual soul, or consciousness, is then no more than a localized manifestation, singularity, or irregularity in the stream of universal consciousness. Some mention of this concept has been made throughout this book. But is it a believable or viable concept? Several experiences and observations actually contradict this belief. For example, the mental experiences of people when apparently separated from the body, the belief that the soul is the repository of memories, and the consequences of expectation in cocaine addicts.

[15.75]All reports of near-death experiences, out-of-body experiences, and transcendental experiences reveal the individual always retains a sense of "self" and individuality during these experiences. The same retention of individual self during afterlife experiences is reported in ancient Egyptian funerary texts, as well as in the citation from the centuries-old *Tibetan Book of the Dead* earlier in this chapter. The afterlife state may be hallucinatory, but it is an individual hallucination. Elsewhere, the *Tibetan Book of the Dead* describes this same retention of individual self in an "after-death experience".

[15.76]*About this time [the deceased] can see that the share of food is being set aside, that the body is being stripped of its garments, that the place of the sleeping-rug is being swept; can hear all the weeping and wailing of his friends and relatives, and, although he can see them and can hear them calling upon him, they cannot hear him calling upon them, so he goeth away displeased. (pages 101-102 in Evans-Wentz 1960)*

[15.77]More modern near-death experiences reported after successful resuscitation from cardiac arrest reveal the same. Many believers in the mind-model of dualism say that because persons suffering a cardiac arrest have no heartbeat, do not breathe, and are unconscious, they are truly "clinically dead". After rapid successful resuscitation, these persons are once again alive and conscious, and retain normal memory function (Lommel 2001). However, no persons successfully resuscitated from proven cardiac arrest ever report disintegration of the sense of self, or merging with a universal consciousness. Instead, they only report retention of the sense of individual self, as do all other persons reporting their near-death experiences.

[15.78]The same is true for other experiences of disembodiment, such as out-of-body experiences. Indeed, people never tell of losing the sense of individual self during out-of-body experiences. This would be a very logical consequence of such experiences. After all, if the individual conscious mind is merely a manifestation of a universal consciousness, then it is very reasonable to expect disintegration of the sense of individual self during out-of-body experiences. A very few people do indeed report a sense of universal consciousness, but even these persons still retain the concept of individual self during such experiences. Accordingly, the concept of a universal consciousness finds no support in experiences of disembodiment, such as out-of-body experiences.

[15.79]Then there is the matter of memory. The mind-model of dualism claims that the soul, some non-local consciousness, or some other manifestation of a universal consciousness forms all memories, and is the repository of all memories. Furthermore, this mind-model proposes that the physical brain is merely a conduit for learning, recalling, and recounting memories. Out-of-body experiences supposedly reveal that the disembodied soul can form memories independently of the physical brain. Indeed, accounts of out-of-body experiences made by physically conscious people recounting their experiences to others, ostensibly prove that memories made by the disembodied soul are accessible to the physically conscious brain (see 1.143). These aspects of the mind-model of dualism not only have profound and testable consequences for belief in an individual soul, but also for the concept of a universal consciousness, or non-local consciousness.

Anesthesia and universal consciousness

15.80Consider physical loss of consciousness due to general anesthesia. Brain mechanisms required to learn, recall, and recount what is learned, all return to normal after full recovery from general anesthesia. We know this is true, because people recovering physical consciousness from general anesthesia are able to learn new things, to recall what they learned, and to recount what they learned. A universal consciousness is supposedly unaffected by general anesthesia, and consequently remains fully conscious during general anesthesia. This means it makes observations, undergoes experiences, and forms memories of all these things while the physical body is unconscious under general anesthesia. Near-death experiences and out-of-body experiences teach that memories formed in a disembodied universal consciousness, or soul, should be just as accessible to the conscious physical body as are all other memories. So why is it that so very few people can recall and recount experiences of the universal consciousness, during general anesthesia? Does this mean that the universal consciousness, is also unconscious during general anesthesia? Does this mean the universal consciousness does not always undergo disembodiment during general anesthesia, and therefore has the same lack of perceptions as the unconscious physical body during general anesthesia? Does this mean the non-local, or universal consciousness lacks sentience—and being conscious without sentience, can have no experiences, and therefore remembers no experiences? Alternatively, it could also mean that the body is the repository of all memories. Nevertheless, regardless of all these considerations, one fact remains. No one ever recalls conscious experiences undergone by a universal consciousness during general anesthesia, even though physically conscious people are capable of recalling memories formed within their individual disembodied minds during out-of-body, and near-death experiences. This fact more than anything else, reveals the untenable nature of the concept of the soul, a non-local consciousness, or a universal consciousness acting as a repository of memories.

Reincarnation and universal consciousness

15.81Reincarnation in a series of physical bodies is a belief held by many people. Indeed, the concept of a universal consciousness seems to accord well with this belief. Nevertheless, neither an individual soul, nor a universal consciousness, has any ability to store memories. As this book reveals, the physical body is the repository of all memories. A universal consciousness without memories is no more than a blank consciousness without mind or personality, because these attributes require memory. If such a universal consciousness underwent repeated incarnations in a physical body, no learning, and no spiritual advancement would occur—just a repeated, blind mechanical imbuement and activation of a series of physical bodies with consciousness. Viewed in this way, lack of memory in a soul, or universal consciousness, is conclusive proof of the illusory nature of reincarnation as currently proposed by believers in this philosophy. These facts are all evidence for failure of the concept of a universal consciousness.

People only use 10% of their brains

[15.82]Many courses claiming to develop and train dormant paranormal powers, nearly always mention the "fact" that "medical science reveals that people only use 10% of their brains." "Golly! Wow! Awsome...!", are some of the more usual reactions of many believers in the paranormal upon hearing this "scientific fact." By implication, this means the unused 90% of the brain may well house the ability for paranormal abilities—an implication willingly embraced by naïve believers as "scientific" justification for their beliefs.

[15.83]But is this true? What is the source of this knowledge of the functioning of the brain? It certainly does not originate in any known scientific medical literature. A review of this belief written by Robynne Boyd (2008) revealed this idea apparently originated sometime during the early twentieth century, a period at the very beginning of studies of the functioning of the human brain (Boyd 2008). Even a cursory examination of neurological texts dating from around 1900 CE, reveals that really very little was known about the functions of most of the brain at the time this idea originated. So this idea is a very reasonable misinterpretation if neurologists at this time stated that the functions of only 10% of the volume of the human brain were known, while the functions of the other 90% of the brain were unknown. But knowledge of the functioning of the brain has increased with leaps and bounds since the beginning of the twentieth century. The introduction of Computerized Axial Tomography scanning apparatus into medical use in the mid 1970's, was the beginning of an unbelievably rapid, even explosive growth of knowledge about the functioning of the human brain. Computerized Axial Tomography is now supplemented by other brain imaging techniques such as Positron Emission Tomography, Single Photon Emission Computed Tomography, Magnetic Resonance Imaging, functional Magnetic Resonance Imaging, Diffusion Tensor Magnetic Resonance Imaging, etc. All these techniques reveal the functioning of even the deepest parts of the brain, as well as the connections between different parts of the brain (Catani 2006, Fields 2004, Hagmann 2007, Hagmann 2008, Heine 2012, Insel 2010, Niu 2012, Posner 2006, Thompson 2001). Research with these instruments reveals the truth of what Boyd pointed out in her article—all parts of the brain have a function, and all parts of the brain are active during a 24-hour period (Boyd 2008). Only one conclusion is possible. The idea that people only use 10% of their brain is no more than a 60 to 100 year old myth—a myth based upon hearsay and misunderstanding of the deficiencies of equally old studies of the human brain.

Impossible to prove or disprove?

[15.84]This brings us to the matter of proof of the reality of a human soul. August Bier, the surgeon, was a devout believer in the reality of the immortal and immaterial soul. He even wrote a book about it called *De Seele* ("The Soul" by Bier 1939). During 1897 he performed some experiments on pigs to demonstrate the control exerted by the soul over the body, as well as the seat of the soul within the body.

> [15.85]*I used anesthetized pigs on whose white skin you can see every change of blood color and filling of blood vessels, just as in humans, and cut off a leg while leaving only the blood vessels attached. I then carefully cut the blood vessels and connected the severed ends with glass tubing so that the normal circulation to the severed limb was maintained. (author's translation of page 43 in Bier 1939)*

[15.86]He then wound a tight rubber bandage around the whole leg to squeeze all the blood out of the severed limb for several minutes. Subsequently which he unwound this rubber bandage and observed what happened. What he found was that the blood vessels on the severed and isolated limb reacted in exactly the same way as the blood vessels on the legs of a normal intact pig. After releasing the rubber bandage, they dilated, resulting in a larger flow of blood through the isolated limb. He called this reaction "Blutgefühl" (blood feeling). But he was at a loss to explain how it could occur in the absence of any nerves to control the widening and narrowing of the blood vessels in the severed limb. He proceeded to explain this as the action of the soul, which he presumed to be present throughout the whole body, even in the living severed limbs of these pigs. Nowadays we know this reaction is secondary to formation of acidic products of metabolism in the blood-deprived limb—a purely metabolic reaction that has nothing whatsoever to do with a soul (Ho 1992, Girardis 2000).

[15.87]But this leaves us with the same question. How does an immaterial soul exert any control over the material body? Only one conclusion is possible. Regardless of whether the conscious mind is located in an immaterial, separable soul, or whether it is a product of the functioning of the brain, the conscious mind can only act through the mechanisms of the body. This is a fact everyone can personally verify by examining how disease, injury, and drugs alter the control exerted over the body by a supposedly immaterial soul.

- [15.88]Injury to the primary motor cortex on one side of the brain causes paralysis of the opposite side of the body. No amount of mental effort can cause the paralyzed body half to move.
- [15.89]Damage to Broca's speech area on the left side of the brain causes a total inability to speak. Affected persons can form words in their minds, but cannot express them. And damage to Wernicke's speech area causes failure to even form words, or understand language.
- [15.90]Damage or removal of the prefrontal lobes changes personality.
- [15.91]Drugs such as ketamine, mescaline, LSD, and alcohol definitely change mental function, intellect and personality.

[15.92]According to the belief system of dualism, the brain is merely the receiver and conduit of the thoughts and will of the soul. We know from practical experience, and the above observations that the conscious mind only acts through the mechanisms of the body. The mind-model of dualism also claims that the soul is unaffected by anything affecting the material body. This belief is explicitly expressed in the *Bhagavad Gita* (see 1.71).

[15.93]The implications of this are truly ghastly for the soul. Imagine that a peaceful and good person is unknowingly administered mind altering drugs, and subsequently commits acts of violence and general mayhem while under their influence. The functioning of the mechanisms of the brain are altered by the effects of these drugs, so when the soul gives instructions to do something, the effects of these drugs on the brain causes the instructions to be interpreted wrongly as acts of violence and mayhem. The soul can only look on with helpless despair at the incorrect interpretation of all its instructions. This is an interesting idea, especially when you realize that the fate of the soul in the afterlife promised by religions such as Christianity and Islam depends upon the actions of the physical body, and not those of the soul. A fascinating theological conundrum.

[15.94]Such examples are endless. But what can we conclude from all this? Any control exerted by the soul over the body is exerted through the mechanisms of the body, and any control exerted by the soul over the body is affected by the functioning of the mechanisms of the body. However, it is also possible to explain all these observations of the effects of changes in body and brain function by saying that the functioning of the physical brain generates the phenomenon of the conscious mind. This would mean that the conscious mind is not separate from the body, but that the brain is the generator and the vehicle of the conscious mind. Yet the result is the same—changes in the functioning of the physical brain affect manifestations of the expression of the conscious mind by the body. This means it is actually impossible to differentiate between the mind-models of dualism and materialism with this line of reasoning.

Amazing experiences are not proof of a soul

[15.95]This book contains extensive discussions on the subjective experiences aroused by many drugs. The subjective effects of many of these drugs include all manner of transcendental, affective, cognitive, and paranormal experiences. These observations also raise some fascinating questions.

- [15.96]What happens when a drug addict injects heroin, and then reports undergoing a variety of transcendental, affective, cognitive, and paranormal experiences while under the influence of the drug? The almost invariable reaction of most people is that the drug addict is simply reporting drug-induced hallucinations that have nothing whatsoever to do with any manifestation of the true nature of the human soul. Nonetheless, the experiences undergone by the drug addict are identical, just as intense, and just as profound as those reported by people after near-death, or out-of-body experiences. So are these drug-induced experiences manifestations of the true nature of the soul? Alternatively, are they simply drug-induced hallucinations?

- [15.97]Studies with two hallucinogenic drugs, ketamine (Collier 1972, Jansen 1997) and psilocybin (Griffiths 2006), on volunteers who knew they were receiving these drugs, revealed something surprising—amazing even. Many of those receiving these drugs underwent profound mystical, spiritual, or paranormal experiences. Yet even though they knew these experiences were drug-induced, they still believed in the reality and spiritual significance of these experiences. The significance of this observation is profound. It means that the cause of such an experience is irrelevant, but the intensity of the psychological impact of the experience is what makes it so personally believable and enriching.

- [15.98]Consider a theoretical extension of these ketamine and psilocybin studies. For example, imagine the surreptitious administration of ketamine or psilocybin to someone ignorant of the effects of these drugs, or the fact of their surreptitious administration. While under the influence of one of these drugs, the person may undergo a variety of transcendental, affective, cognitive, and paranormal experiences just as identical, intense, and profound as during any undergone by persons reporting spontaneous near-death, or out-of-body experiences. Imagine that even after returning to normalcy, that person never learns of the surreptitious drug administration, but undergoes a spiritual transformation due to this experience, believing only that something astounding has occurred. The person concerned may well believe these experiences were a true and profound spiritual event. But what would be the reaction of others who knew of the surreptitious drug administration upon learning of the experiences and transformation undergone by this person? Would they simply dismiss these experiences and subsequent spiritual transformation as drug-induced hallucinations, or would they consider them as true manifestations of the soul made possible by these drugs? This example highlights the difference between the profound belief of the unknowing experiencer in the reality of the spiritual nature of the experience, and the possible dismissal of the spiritual nature of the same experience by the knowing.

- ^{15.99}Similarly, a person rendered immobile and apparently unconscious by subanesthetic concentrations of anesthetic drugs may also undergo a variety of transcendental, affective, cognitive, and paranormal experiences. After recovering, the person reports their memories of these experiences undergone while apparently unconscious. Are these experiences merely anesthetic drug-induced hallucinations? Alternatively, are they manifestations of the true nature of the soul made possible by the effects of these drugs?

- ^{15.100}Drugs, surgery, injury and disease have no effect upon the soul, but do affect the functioning of the physical brain. For example, a sleep inducing drug acts by exerting a chemical effect upon those parts of the brain regulating the level of consciousness. For example, subanesthetic doses of anesthetic drugs, opiates, hallucinogens, etc., all alter the functioning of the brain. Such drugs can also induce near-death experiences, out-of-body experiences, or other affective, cognitive, and transcendental experiences in some people. The mind-model of materialism explains these seemingly amazing experiences as products of the effects of these drugs upon the functioning of the brain. Dualism approaches this problem differently. People are conscious during such experiences. This means their bodies are supposedly under the control of their souls while affected by these drugs. So according to the mind-model of dualism, this means that such experiences are not true manifestations of the soul, but are instead expressions of the soul acting through an abnormally functioning brain. Alternatively, it could be said that drugs, surgery, injury and disease alter the nature of the physical perceptions of the body transmitted to the soul, and that the soul reacts appropriately to control the body in accordance with these abnormally processed perceptions (see similar situation here 4.112-4.113). Consequently, such experiences are not proof of a human soul, because the observable and experienced results of the effects of drugs, surgery, injury and disease are indistinguishable from the consequences of a soul trying to control a malfunctioning body (see also 1.142).

^{15.101}All the above considerations and examples mean that belief in the reality of profound spiritual, cognitive, affective, or transcendental experiences is just that—a belief in the immaterial reality of the experience, but not necessarily the objective reality. Nonetheless, believers in the experiential reality of out-of-body experiences, near-death experiences, and deathbed experiences, say these experiences are

so intense, and so profound they must be revelations of the true spiritual nature of the soul. They claim that people can distinguish between experiences induced by psychoactive drugs such as ketamine and psilocybin, by anesthetic drugs, by many other different drugs, or by the myriad causes of oxygen starvation, by carbon dioxide accumulation, by fevers, and even those induced by psychological stress.

> [15.102]*Consequently, contrary to Nelson, Mattingly, Lee, and Schmitt's assumption that NDEs [Near-Death Experiences] have a "neurophysiological basis" (p. 1003) or "physiological basis" (p. 1004), most NDErs believe their experiences involved elements that were spiritual in origin and, thus, cannot be explained in purely physiological/medical terms. In Wilber's (2000) terms, NDEs may be transpersonal experiences that cannot be reduced to exclusively biological or prepersonal causes. (Long 2007)*

[15.103]The phrase: "most NDErs believe their experiences involved elements that were spiritual in origin and, thus, cannot be explained in purely physiological/medical terms" says it all. Their belief is their proof! But studies of the mental experiences induced by psychoactive drugs such as ketamine and psilocybin, by anesthetic drugs, by many other different drugs, by the myriad causes of oxygen starvation, by carbon dioxide accumulation, by fevers, and even those induced by psychological stress, proves this belief to be fundamentally incorrect. Changes in the functioning of the brain induced by a multitude of factors can induce intense transcendental, affective, cognitive, and paranormal experiences which those undergoing them believe to be real. Therefore, belief in the spiritual nature of an experience is not proof of the spiritual or immaterial origin of an experience.

[15.104]Moreover, no observer can see the content of these experiences. Observers do not see the conscious minds of people departing their bodies during out-of-body experiences, do not see the tunnel, do not see the bright light, do not experience ineffability, do not see the transcendental worlds, do not experience the life review, etc. Observers do not see these things because they occur only within the conscious minds of those undergoing these experiences. This is the difference between observers and those undergoing a subjective experience. Observers only learn of these subjective experiences through the medium of physical speech generated by the physical bodies of those who undergo these experiences. And observers only learn of these experiences, because those undergoing them report them as they occur, or spontaneously report their memories of these experiences after recovering the ability to speak.

Conclusive evidence—there is no soul!

[15.105]This book reviews many phenomena, experiences and medical observations, as well as drawing some clear conclusions. Now it is time to summarize evidence for the statement that the conscious mind is not something immaterial and separate from the body—evidence proving we have no souls. The totality of all evidence for the idea that consciousness and mind are products of the functioning of the brain and body is overwhelming and physically provable. This is evidence derived from observations repeatedly confirmed during anesthesia, observations during medical procedures, observations of the world about us, as well as observations made by those believing in the reality of a human soul. Alternative explanations, theories and arguments without provable facts remain just that—alternative explanations, theories and arguments—and are not proof one way or the other. For the sake of purity of argument, these proofs are both absolute and supplementary.

- [15.106]An *absolute proof* is one incapable of an alternative explanation, and proves the illusory nature of the human soul.
- [15.107]A *supplementary proof* is one that supports and supplements an absolute proof, but is not itself an absolute proof.

[15.108]So what are the relevant absolute and supplementary proofs revealing the illusory nature of the soul as defined by millennia of popular belief?

The soul cannot see or hear

[15.109]People report hearing and seeing verifiable events in their vicinity during out-of-body experiences. The disembodied soul can pass through reinforced concrete floors (Case 1 in Ring 1993, see also 1.47-1.49). But something invisible and immaterial with the ability to pass through concrete floors cannot hear physical sounds and cannot see physical light. These sensations are only possible through the physical sense organs of the material body. Paranormal sensory abilities are no solution to this problem, because "hearing" and "seeing" with paranormal abilities is also no more than a popular illusion (see Chapter 13). Invocation of some form of subtle transdimensional quantum entanglement, or other form of quantum weirdness to explain perception of visible light and physical sound is also not a viable alternative explanation (see Chapter 14). So the very experiences supposedly proving the reality of the separable and immaterial nature of the conscious mind, actually prove the impossibility of a soul with the ability to "see" with physical light, and to "hear" physical sounds. This is absolute proof of the absence of a soul with the properties claimed by the mind-model of dualism (see 1.123-1.135).

The soul cannot form memories

[15.110]The ability of the disembodied soul to recall memories, and to form new memories, is a truly fundamental property of the soul (see 1.92-1.115). A soul without memories cannot remember anything about its life, body, surroundings, family, or relatives while disembodied during out-of-body experiences or near-death experiences. A soul without memory is simply incapable of recalling what it underwent during out-of-body experiences, or near-death experiences. A soul without memory is incapable of remembering evil and good performed during mortal life, so rendering any punishment or reward in the eternal afterlife promised by many religions a mockery visited upon these souls by a malignant God. Similarly, retention of memories within the soul is essential for the belief system of reincarnation, where lessons learned during mortal life determine the nature of a subsequent reincarnation. All these things mean memory determines the reality of the soul as proposed by believers in the mind-model of dualism. This was stated in no uncertain terms by Alan Gauld in Chapter 4 of the book, *Irreducible Mind: Toward a Psychology for the 21st Century* (Kelly 2007).

[15.111]*Any attempt (not least Myers's) to systematize and interpret the ostensible evidence for human survival of bodily death has to take on board the empirical facts, so far as they are known, of the relationship between memory and the brain. Most modern neuroscientists regard memory as totally a function of the brain, a view which if justified (and it was widely enough held in Myers's own time) is fatal to the possibility that memory and related features of personality might survive death as Myers hoped, believed, and argued. It is curious how many subsequent persons who have discussed the evidence for survival and its interpretation have failed to take this crucially relevant question fully on board. (page 295 in Kelly 2007)*

15.112Studies in many laboratories and countries reveal the inhibition of spontaneous recall of dreams after awakening from sleep. Many other multinational studies reveal the inhibition of spontaneous recall of conscious experiences undergone while under the influence of cerebral hypoxia, midazolam, propofol, subanesthetic concentrations of anesthetic gases, the isolated forearm test, and the wake-up test. All these many studies prove conclusively that the physical brain is the repository of all memories, and not the soul. This is proof of the illusory nature of the ancient belief in the soul as an immaterial something with the capacity to form and retain memories, and therefore absolute proof of the illusory nature of a human soul with the properties claimed by the mind-model of dualism (see 1.123-1.135).

Cocaine addiction proves the absence of a human soul

15.113Cocaine addicts manifest clear differences between observed and measured reality, as well as observed effects, and subjective experiences when administered an expected dose of cocaine or methylphenidate. The mind-model of dualism cannot explain these differences (see 3.111-3.123). Accordingly, objective and subjective effects exhibited by cocaine addicts expecting to receive cocaine or other psychostimulant drugs, are absolute proof of the illusory nature of a human soul with the properties claimed by the mind-model of dualism (see 1.123-1.135).

Sensation and movement prove the absence of a soul

15.114Humans possess no paranormal sensory abilities (see Chapter 13). The effects of curare (see Chapter 9), and local anesthetic drugs (see Chapter 11), reveal that the mind must use the mechanisms of the body to move and perceive sensations. The disembodied soul also cannot see and cannot hear (see Chapter 14). All these things mean that the conscious mind, or soul, only perceives through the senses of the body, and only manifests in this physical world through the mechanisms of the physical body. The soul also possesses no ability to form or retain memories. The combination of all these facts constitutes absolute proof of the illusory nature of a human soul with the properties claimed by the mind-model of dualism (see 1.123-1.135).

Filter function of the brain proves absence of the soul

15.115Supposed manifestations of the true nature of the soul revealed by near-death, and deathbed experiences, are expressions of the soul manifesting through the abnormally functioning mechanisms of the physical brain. The same is equally true for manifestations of control by the soul expressed through the normally functioning body. While these facts do not disprove the possible reality of a human soul, they do reveal that the cognitive, affective, transcendental, and paranormal experiences believed by many to be manifestations of the true nature of the human soul, are at best no more than expressions of a controlling influence manifesting through the mechanisms of the normally and abnormally functioning body (see 14.130). This reality means that the human soul evidently has very different properties to those proposed by many proponents of the mind-model of dualism. Therefore, the postulated filter function of the brain is a supplementary proof of the illusory nature of a human soul with the properties claimed by the mind-model of dualism (see 1.123-1.135).

Conclusion—the soul is an illusion

[15.116]The repeatedly confirmed observations summed up above, and discussed extensively throughout this book, prove that the soul does not possess the most essential and fundamental properties proposed by the mind-model of dualism. The immaterial soul has no memory, and has no superior intellect—it possesses none of the paranormal, cognitive, transcendental, or affective attributes believed by most people—and it can only perceive sensations through the sense organs of the body. As if this were not enough, other phenomena apparently proving the reality of the immaterial soul such as near-death experiences, and out-of-body experiences, are not manifestations of an immaterial soul. Instead, they are manifestations of natural laws and the functioning of the brain and body. Only one conclusion is possible. The ancient belief in the reality of the human soul is an illusion—an illusion derived from misinterpretation of sensations and observations—misinterpretations driven by a hope for a better eternal life, instead of the reality of an evanescent, possibly meaningless, and sometimes unpleasant life. Individual humans do not possess an immaterial soul with the properties explicitly and implicitly proposed by millennia of believers in the mind-model of dualism (see Chapter 1). So where does this leave us?

Illusory perceptions

[15.117]Anesthesia, medical practice, and natural laws prove there is no soul, no separable immaterial mind, no non-localized consciousness, or whatever one chooses to call it. Nonetheless, for many millennia, people have believed near-death experiences, out-of-body experiences, deathbed experiences, and other apparently paranormal experiences prove the reality of the human soul. But this millennia-old acceptance of the apparent meaning of these experiences is illusory. These experiences are actually manifestations of a malfunctioning, or differently functioning physical brain rather than anything else. So how was it possible for people to deceive themselves for so long, and to continue believing in this seemingly attractive idea of a soul?

[15.118]One of the most likely answers lies in the attractive nature of this belief. After all, it offers the possibility of an eternal life in some sort of paradise after death of the physical body. This would be very attractive, as well as being a source of strength and meaning to peoples cursed by unpleasant, short, or diseased lives. Another answer lies in the ways people interpret the world about them, seeking meaning in their perceptions. This is no new idea. A nineteenth century writer, William Hammond, once beautifully expressed it in a manner typical of his age.

[15.119]*Such persons have, probably, from a very early age, believed in the materiality of spirits; and having very little knowledge of the forces inherent in their own bodies, have no difficulty in ascribing occurrences, which do not accord with their experience, to the agency of disembodied individuals whom they imagine to be circulating through the world. In this respect they resemble those savages who regard the burning-lens, the mirror, and other things which produce unfamiliar effects, as being animated by deities. Their minds are decidedly fetish-worshipping in character, and are scarcely, in this respect, of a more elevated type than that of the Congo negro who endows the rocks and trees with higher mental attributes than he claims for himself. (pages 2-3 in Hammond 1876)*

[15.120]Very little has changed with the passage of more than 120 years. Modern psychological studies say the same of persons with a fervent belief in the paranormal, and the apparent reality of experiences undergone during near-death experiences and out-of-body experiences. For example, a study of the belief systems of 174 believers in the reality of paranormal perceptive abilities once concluded the following.

[15.121]*As predicted, individuals who reported a strong belief in the paranormal made more errors and displayed more delusional ideation than skeptical individuals. However, no differences were found with statements that were congruent with their belief system, confirming the domain-specificity of reasoning. This reasoning bias was limited to people who reported a belief in, rather than experience of, paranormal phenomena. These results suggest that reasoning abnormalities may have a causal role in the formation of unusual beliefs. (Lawrence 2004)*

[15.122]The conclusion of Emma Lawrence, and her colleague Emmanuelle Peters in the above citation is clear—believers in the paranormal and the mind-model of dualism often interpret the world differently to those skeptical of these phenomena. But this is no new knowledge. More than a century ago, Frank Podmore (1856-1910), recognized and eloquently expressed these differences between perceptions and interpretations among believers, and skeptics of the mind-model of dualism.

[15.123]*Man, as has been said by someone, is not naturally a veridical animal. It is not in fact an easy thing to tell the truth. It is the most difficult of all arts, and one of the latest acquirements of the most civilised races. There are in the first place defects and excesses in narration caused by self interest, or by the dramatic instinct, the love of telling a good story. But defects of this kind are generally recognised and proportionately easy to guard against. The real danger is more subtle. Not only our memory but our very acts of perception are shaped by our preconceptions and prejudices. To put it crudely, what we see and what we remember is not what actually happened, but what we think ought to have happened or what was likely to have happened. The retina supplies us with an imperfect photograph—a crude sensation. But this imperfect photograph is not "perceived" until it has been telegraphed up to higher brain centres, and it is the business of these higher centres to touch up the photograph, to fill in the lacunae, to select what seem the more salient and notable features, and to colour the whole with the emotion appropriate to the situation. It is likely that in most cases something is added to improve the picture. The result is no longer a photograph but a finished work of art, which contains at once more and less than the photograph—the original sensation. (pages 4-5 in Podmore 1909)*

[15.124]This statement is as true today as when Podmore penned these words more than one hundred years ago. Indeed, this book reveals just this—faulty interpretations of perceptions, uncritical belief in the reality of subjective experiences, coupled with an inability to distinguish between subjective experiences and external observations, are fertile breeding grounds for the pervasive belief in the reality of the human soul. Nonetheless, regardless of how such beliefs came to be, or are sustained, they are not proof of the reality of the existence of a human soul. Indeed, as the perspicacious William Hammond wrote more than a century ago, these latter phenomena are often merely illusory misinterpretations of otherwise natural phenomena.

[15.125]*Then it is possible for the most careful and experienced judgment to be deceived by false sensorial impressions of real objects, or by non-existing images created by the mind. In the first case a gleam of moonlight passes for a ghost, the stump of a tree becomes a robber, and the rustling of leaves blown by the wind is imagined to be the whispering of voices. No one possesses an absolute perfection of sensation, and thus things are never seen, or heard, or smelt, or tasted, or felt exactly as they exist. In the dark, or in the uncertain light of the moon, or of artificial illumination, the liability to self-deception is very much increased; and if, in addition to the defect of light, there are continual sounds and other means of engaging the attention, it is exceedingly easy to induce sensorial confusion and thus to impose upon the intellect. (page 3 in Hammond 1876)*

[15.126]As this book clearly demonstrates, the very reasons why people believe in the reality of a soul actually prove the illusory nature of this very same soul. The same is true for other indirect indications of the existence of the soul, such as paranormal sensory abilities, communication with the dead, ghosts, demonic possession, incubi and succubi, etc. All these things have natural explanations and are therefore not proof of the human soul or other immaterial forces. So what then?

Free at last

[15.128]Observations derived from anesthesiology, from other branches of medicine, and from the world about us, teach us the disappearance of the soul—banishing the soul forever to the realm of ancient superstitions and illusions. We have no individual souls. We have no separate immortal and immaterial conscious minds. We have no non-localized consciousness. The functioning of the brain generates consciousness and all the properties of the individual mind.

[15.129]Loss of the human soul as a belief system may seem terrifying to some people. But when carefully considered, acceptance of this proven fact actually means freedom. This knowledge frees us from the tyranny of a soul. We no longer need to live in fear of unending horrid torment in some everlasting life after death. We are spared the unspeakable tedium of eternity in some postmortem paradise. We no longer need fantasize about the logical idiocies of reincarnation. This may sound like substitution of a tyranny of the soul for the tyranny of the body. But this is not so. Knowledge of the absence of a soul teaches us that spiritual, cognitive, affective and transcendent experiences are wondrous products of the functioning of our bodies. Such experiences are part of the amazing reality of our being (Nelson 2011). Understanding of this knowledge frees us from subjugation to collective fantasies resulting from belief in the apparent immaterial reality of such experiences. This certain knowledge frees our minds from the cloying quagmire of baseless illusions and superstitions. Knowledge of the true nature of the conscious mind is the embodiment of a statement in the book, *Thus Spake Zarathustra*, written by the German philosopher Friedrich Nietzsche.

[15.130] *"Dead are all the Gods: now do we desire the Superman to live." (chapter XXII in Nietzsche 1914)*

[15.131]This triumphant statement of Friedrich Nietzsche can better be paraphrased as; "The soul is dead: now do we desire the Superman to live!" To acknowledge the absence of the immaterial soul is to welcome the dawn of the superman. This concept of the superman has nothing to do with brutish jackbooted blond Aryan beasts crushing supposedly inferior races underfoot. Nor does it have anything to do with a fictional muscle-bound man, who very curiously wears tight red underpants on top of blue pantyhose. Instead, the superman is a person whose mind is freed by knowledge of the reality of the true nature of the mind. The superman, or rather the knowledgeable enlightened individual, uses observation and logic to transcend mere sensation and existence to live a life fully cognizant of the four fundamental tenets of existence.

- [15.132]There is no life before birth, and there is no life after death. Life and consciousness exist only between birth and death.

409

- [15.133]Life, consciousness, and mind have a biological basis, because each person is a biological mechanism formed and sustained by food, water, and air. Accordingly, all thoughts, emotions, sensations, perceptions, speech, actions, and experiences are rooted in the biological nature of the body.
- [15.134]Each person is born of a father and a mother, and forms a link in a chain of reproduction from past ancestors to future progeny. We are each a link in a chain of biological existence, and this is our individual location in space and time.
- [15.135]Each person has a form of individual immortality due to the fact of their existence, the effects of their existence on the world and other people, and the memories they leave behind.

[15.136]This is the proven reality of our existence. This reality is unchanging and immutable. The brain is the form and the vehicle, and the mind is a product of the functioning of this form. Our minds are our being, our souls, and embodied within our physical brains. This knowledge is implicit recognition of the place of each individual in the continuity of the human biosystem in which we function. Individuals are never alone, but influence others by their conception and birth, their lives, and their legacies. Expressed another way, each individual is a link in a chain of existence extending from the past to the future. And as regards the influence, or legacy of each individual link, who would wish to leave a legacy such as that expressed centuries ago in a play by William Shakespeare (1564-1616).

[15.137]*Nothing in his life became him like the leaving it; (Macbeth Act 1, Scene IV, written by William Shakespeare)*

[15.138]Knowledge, understanding, and application of these four tenets of existence means freedom to develop wondrous new philosophical systems tailored precisely to our individual needs, the circumstances of our lives, and the societies in which we live. This certain knowledge frees the enlightened mind to soar and transcend the limitations of the physical body, to become more than a mere sentient and ephemeral biological mechanism. Knowledge of this reality is freedom.

References

A

Abramovich H, (1988), An Israeli account of a near-death experience: a case study of cultural dissonance. *Journal of Near-Death Studies,* 6: 175-184.

Adler LJ, et al, (1997), Regional brain activity changes associated with fentanyl analgesia elucidated by positron emission tomography. *Anesthesia & Analgesia,* 84: 120-126.

Alcock JE, (2003), Give the null hypothesis a chance. Reasons to remain doubtful about the existence of psi. *Journal of Consciousness Studies,* 10: 29-50.

Alkire MT, et al, (2000), Toward a unified theory of narcosis: brain evidence for a thalamocortical switch as the neurophysiologic basis of anesthetic-induced unconsciousness. *Consciousness and Cognition,* 9: 370-386.

Allen CW, (1920),. *Local and Regional Anesthesia.* 2nd edition, published by W.B. Saunders Company, Philadelphia, USA.

Allman JM, et al, (2001), The anterior cingulate cortex: the evolution of an interface between emotion and cognition. *Annals of the New York Academy of Sciences,*935: 107-117.

Almeida AN de, et al, (2006), Hemispherectomy: a schematic review of the current techniques. *Neurosurgical Review,* 29: 97-102.

Altman PL, et al, (1959),. *Handbook of Circulation,* published by W.B. Saunders Co., USA.

Alvarado CS, (2011), Prescribing for parapsychology: Note on J. B. Rhine's writings in the Journal of Parapsychology. *Australian Journal of Parapsychology,* 11: 89-99.

Aminoff MJ, et al, (1988), Electrocerebral accompaniments of syncope associated with malignant ventricular arrhythmias. *Annals of Internal Medicine,* 108: 791-796.

Andelman F, et al, (2006), Hippocampal memory function as reflected by the intracarotid sodium methohexital Wada Test. *Epilepsy & Behavior,* 9: 579-586.

Anderson SL, et al, (2008), Preliminary evidence for sensitive periods in the effect of childhood sexual abuse on regional brain development. *Journal of Neuropsychiatry and Clinical Neurosciences,* 20: 292-301.

Andina F von, (1937), Ueber Schwarzsehen als Ausdruck von Blutdruck-schwankungen bei Sturzflügen. *Schweizerische Medizinische Wochenschrift,* 67: 753-756.

Andrade J, et al, (2008), Awareness and memory function during paediatric anaesthesia. *British Journal of Anaesthesia,* 100: 389-396.

Angst MS, et al, (2012), Aversive and reinforcing opioid effects. A pharmacogenomic twin study. *Anesthesiology,* 117: 22-37.

Anonymous editorial, (1979), Editorial: On being aware. *British Journal of Anaesthesia,* 51: 711-712.

Ansari D, (2009), Effects of development and enculturation on number representation in the brain. *Nature Reviews - Neuroscience,* 9: 278-291.

Antognini JF, et al, (2003), Spinal anaesthesia indirectly depresses cortical activity associated with electrical stimulation of the reticular formation. *British Journal of Anaesthesia,* 91: 233-238.

Apple JK, et al, (1995), Effects of restraint and isolation stress and epidural blockade on endocrine and blood metabolite status, muscle glycogen metabolism, and incidence of dark-cutting longissimus muscle of sheep. *Journal of Animal Science,* 73: 2295-2307.

Arbous MS, et al, (2001), Mortality associated with anaesthesia: a qualitative analysis to identify risk factors. *Anaesthesia,* 56: 1141-1153.

Arias M, et al, (1996), Autoscopy and multiple sclerosis. *Neurologia,* 11: 230-232.

Ariskaka H, et al, (2008), Effects of spinal anesthesia on the electroencephalogram of the elderly. *Acta Anaesthetica Belgica,* 59: 15-17.

Aristotle, *De Anima,* in. *Aristotle's Psychology. A Treatise on the Principle of Life,* translated by W.A. Hammond, published by Swan Sonnenschein & Co, Lim, The MacMillan Co., New York, USA, 1902.

Arnette JK, (1992), The mind/body problem: the theory of essence. *Journal of Near-Death Studies,* 11: 5-19.

Aron A, et al, (2010), Temperament trait of sensory processing sensitivity moderates cultural differences in neural response. *Social Cognitive & Affective Neuroscience,* 5: 219-226.

Artusio JF, (1954), Di-ethyl Ether analgesia: a detailed description of the first stage of Ether anesthesia in man. *Journal of Pharmacology and Experimental Therapeutics,* 111: 343-348.

Arzy S, et al, (2006), Neural basis of embodiment: distinct contributions of temporoparietal junction and extrastriate body area. *Journal of Neuroscience,* 26: 8074-8081.

ASA, (2006), Practice advisory for intraoperative awareness and brain function monitoring. *Anesthesiology,* 104: 847-864.

Asher JE, et al, (2009), A Whole-Genome scan and fine-mapping linkage study of auditory-visual synesthesia reveals evidence of linkage to chromosomes 2q24, 5q33, 6p12, and 12p12. *American Journal of Human Genetics,* 84: 279-285.

Athappilly GK, et al, (2006), Do prevailing societal models influence reports of near-death experiences? A comparison of accounts reported before and after 1975. *Journal of Nervous and Mental Disease.* 194: 218-222.

Augustine A, *On the Soul and its Origin.* Volume XII,. *The Works of Aurelius Augustine, Bishop of Hippo,* edited by Rev. Marcus Dods, published by T&T Clark, Edinburgh, United Kingdom, 1874.

Austin KL, et al, (1980), Relationship between blood meperidine concentrations and analgesic response: a preliminary report. *Anesthesiology,* 53: 460-466.

Avidan MS, et al, (2008), Anesthesia awareness and the bispectral index. *New England Journal of Medicine,* 358: 1097-1108.

Avidan MS, et al, (2009), Long-term cognitive decline in older subjects was not attributable to noncardiac surgery or major illness. *Anesthesiology,* 111: 964-970.

B

Babenco DH, et al, (2000), The pharmacodynamic effect of a remifentanil bolus on ventilatory control. *Anesthesiology,* 92: 393-398.

Bachman GA, (1990), Hysterectomy. A critical review. *Journal of Reproductive Medicine,* 35: 839-862.

Beaulieu-Prevost D, Zadra A, (2007), Absorption, psychological boundaries and attitude towards dreams as correlates of dream recall: two decades of research seen through a meta-analysis. *Journal of Sleep Research,* 16: 51-59.

Balram B, (2009), Culture and the aging brain. *McGill Science Undergraduate Research Journal,* 4: 15-19.

Barach AL, Kagan J, (1940), Disorders of mental functioning produced by varying the oxygen tension of the atmosphere. I. Effects of low oxygen atmospheres on normal individuals and patients with psychoneurotic disease. *Psychosomatic Medicine,* II: 53-67.

Baraka A, et al, (1989), Awareness following different techniques of general anesthesia for caesarean section. *British Journal of Anaesthesia,* 62: 645-648.

Barker AE, (1908), A second report on clinical experiences with spinal analgesia: a second series of one hundred cases. *British Medical Journal,* February 1: 244-249.

Barrett W, (1926),. *Death-Bed Visions. Psychical Experiences of the Dying.* First published in 1926, facsimile edition published by Aquarian Press in 1986, ISBN 0850305209.

Bart G, et al, (2004), Substantial attributable risk related to a functional mu-opioid receptor gene polymorphism in association with heroin addiction in central Sweden. *Molecular Psychiatry,* 9: 547-549.

Bartels A, Seki S, (2000), The neural basis of romantic love. *NeuroReport,* 11: 3829-3834.

Bauer E, (1984), Criticism and controversy in parapsychology - an overview. *European Journal of Parapsychology,* 5: 141-166.

Baxendale S, (2009), The Wada Test. *Current Opinion in Neurology,* 22: 185-189.

Beaton M, (2005), What RoboDennett still doesn't know. *Journal of Consciousness Studies.* 12: 3-25.

Beauregard M, Paquette V, (2006), Neural correlates of a mystical experience in Carmelite nuns. *Neuroscience Letters,* 405: 186-190.

Becerra L, et al, (2006), Functional magnetic resonance imaging measures of the effects of morphine on central nervous system circuitry in opioid-naive healthy volunteers. *Anesthesia & Analgesia,* 103: 208-216.

Beckman NJ, et al, (2006), Within-subject comparison of the subjective and psychomotor effects of a gaseous anesthetic and two volatile anesthetics in healthy volunteers. *Drug and Alcohol Dependence,* 81: 89-95.

Beecher HK, Todd DP, (1954), A study of the deaths associated with anesthesia and surgery based on a study of 599,548 anesthesias in ten institutions 1948-1952, inclusive. *Annals of Surgery,* 140: 2-34.

Belanti J, et al, (2008), Phenomenology of near-death experiences: A cross-cultural perspective. *Transcultural Psychiatry,* 45: 121-133.

Bem DJ, Honorton C, (1994), Does psi exist? Replicable evidence for an anomalous process of information transfer. *Psychological Bulletin,* 115: 4-18.

Bem D, (2011), Feeling the future: Experimental evidence for anomalous retroactive influences on cognition and affect. *Journal of Personality and Social Psychology,* 100: 407-425.

Bendall JR, (2006), The effect of pre-treatment of pigs with curare on the post-mortem rate of pH fall and onset of rigor mortis in the musculature. *Journal of the Science of Food and Agriculture,* 17: 333-338.

Bennetts FE, (1995), Thiopentone anaesthesia at Pearl Harbour. *British Journal of Anaesthesia,* 75: 366-368.

Berek K, et al, (1995), Early determination of neurological outcome after prehospital cardiopulmonary resuscitation. *Stroke,* 26:543-549.

Berger EY, (1983), Introductory remarks. *Bulletin of the New York Academy of Medicine,* 59: 259-261.

Bethlehem J, (2009), Can we make official statistics with self-selection web surveys? *Proceedings of Statistics Canada Symposium 2008.* Data Collection: Challenges, Achievements and New Directions.

Bhagavad-Gita As It Is, translated by His Divine Grace A.C. Bhaktivedanta Swami Prabhupada.

Bhargava AK, et al, (2004), Correlation of Bispectral Index and Guedel's stages of Ether anesthesia. *Anesthesia & Analgesia,* 98: 132-134.

Bien CG, et al, (2000), Localizing value of epileptic visual auras. *Brain,* 123: 244-253.

Bier A, (1899), Versuche über Cocainisirung des Rückenmarkes. *Deutsche Zeitschrift für Chirurgie,* 51: 361-369.

Bier A, (1939),. *Die Seele.* Zweite Auflage, J.F. Lehmanns Verlag, München-Berlin.

Bihari S, Rajajee V, (2008), Prolonged retention of awareness during cardiopulmonary resuscitation for asystolic cardiac arrest. *Neurocritical Care,* 9: 382-386.

Binder JR, et al, (1996), Determination of language dominance using functional MRI : A comparison with the Wada Test. *Neurology,* 46:978-984.

Binkley CJ, et al, (2009), Genetic variations associated with red hair color and fear of dental pain, anxiety regarding dental care and avoidance of dental care. *Journal of the American Dental Association,* 140: 896-905.

Black DW, (1982), Psychosurgery,. *Southern Medical Journal,* 75: 453-458.

Blackmore S, (1993),. *Dying to Live. Near-death Experiences.* Published by Prometheus Books, USA, ISBN 0-87975-870-8

Blackmore S, (2004),. *Consciousness. An Introduction.* Oxford University Press, England, ISBN 019515343X.

Blanke O, et al, (2002), Stimulating illusory own-body perceptions. The part of the brain that can induce out-of-body experiences has been located. *Nature,* 419: 269-270.

Blanke O, et al, (2004), Out-of-body experience and autoscopy of neurological origin. *Brain,* 127: 243-258.

Blanke O, Arzy S, (2005), The out-of-body experience: disturbed self-processing at the temporo-parietal junction. *Neuroscientist,* 11: 16-24.

Blanke O, et al, (2005a), Linking out-of-body experience and self processing to mental own-body Imagery at the temporoparietal junction. *The Journal of Neuroscience,* 25: 550-557.

Blanke O, Dieguez C, (2009),. *Leaving Body and Life Behind: Out-of-Body and Near-Death Experience.* In Chapter 23,. *The Neurology of Consciousness,* Laureys S and Tononi G (Eds), Academic Press, New York, 440 pages, ISBN 0-12-374168-8.

Block RI, et al, (1990), Psychedelic effects of a subanesthetic concentration of nitrous oxide. *Anesthesia Progress,* 37:271-276.

Blussé van Oud-Alblas HJ, et al, (2008), A comparison in adolescents of Composite Auditory Evoked Potential Index and Bispectral Index during propofol-remifentanil anesthesia for scoliosis surgery with intraoperative wake-up test. *Anesthesia & Analgesia,* 107: 1683-1688.

BMJ, (1885), Berlin. [from our own correspondent.] Cucaine. - Dr. Koch's course on bacteriology. *British Medical Journal,* January 3: 47-48.

Bocka JJ,et al, (1988), Electromechanical dissociation in human beings: An echocardiographic evaluation. *Annals of Emergency Medicine,* 7: 450-452.

Bogen JE, (1995), On the neurophysiology of consciousness 1: an overview. *Consciousness and Cognition,* 4: 52-62.

Boland FK, (1950),. *The First Anesthetic. The Story of Crawford Long.* Published by the University of Georgia Press, USA, ISBN-13: 978-0-8203-3436-3.

Bond C, et al, (1998), Single-nucleotide polymorphism in the human mu opioid receptor gene alters β-endorphin binding and activity: Possible implications for opiate addiction. *Proceedings of the National Academy of Science*, 95: 9608-9613.

Bonnon M, et al, (2000), Effects of different stay durations on attentional performance during two mountain expeditions. *Aviation, Space, and Environmental Medicine*, 71: 678-684.

Booij J, et al, (1997), Assessment of endogenous dopamine release by methylphenidate challenge using iodine-123 iodobenzamide single-photon emission tomography. *European Journal of Nuclear Medicine*, 24: 674-677.

Booth JV, et al, (2002), Substance abuse among physicians: A survey of academic anesthesiology programs. *Anesthesia & Analgesia*, 95: 1024-1030.

Bosch FH, Schiltmans FHL, (2004), Stepwise sedation is safe and effective for the insertion of central venous catheters. *The Netherlands Journal of Medicine*, 62: 18-21.

Bösch H, et al, (2006), Examining psychokinesis: The interaction of human intention with random number generators - a meta-analysis. *Psychological Bulletin*, 132: 497-523.

Böttiger BW, et al, (2001), Astroglial protein S-100 is an early and sensitive marker of hypoxic brain damage and outcome after cardiac arrest in humans. *Circulation*, 103:2694-2698.

Bowdle TA, et al, (1998), Psychedelic effects of ketamine in healthy volunteers. Relationship to steady-state plasma concentrations. *Anesthesiology*, 88: 82-88.

Boyd R, (2008), Do people only use 10 percent of their brains? What's the matter with only exploiting a portion of our gray matter? *Scientific American.* Downloaded 16 April 2010 at: http://www.scientificamerican.com/article.cfm?id=people-only-use-10-percent-of-brain

Branco DM, et al, (2006), Functional MRI of memory in the hippocampus: Laterality indices may be more meaningful if calculated from whole voxel distributions. *NeuroImage*, 32: 592-602.

Bromage PR, Melzack R, (1974), Phantom limbs and the body schema. *Canadian Anaesthetists'Society Journal*, 21: 267-274.

Browne-Goode G, (1962), Sleep Paralysis. *Archives of Neurology*, 6: 228-234.

Brugger P, et al, (1999), Hallucinatory experiences in extreme-altitude climbers. *Neuropsychiatry, Neuropsychology, and Behavioral Neurology,* 12: 67-71.

Brugger P, Mohr C, (2009), Out of the body, but not out of mind. *Cortex,* 45: 137-140.

Bruhn J, et al, (2006), Depth of anaesthesia monitoring: what's available, what's validated and what's next? *British Journal of Anaesthesia,* 97: 85-94.

Brun CC, et al, (2009), Sex differences in brain structure in auditory and cingulate regions. *NeuroReport,* 20: 930-935.

Büchel C, et al, (1998), Different activation patterns in the visual cortex of late and congenitally blind subjects. *Brain,* 121: 409-419.

Buchtel HA, et al, (2002), Sodium methohexital (Brevital) as an anesthetic in the Wada Test. *Epilepsia,* 43: 1056-1061.

Budge W, (1913), *The Papyrus of Ani.* In Three Volumes, published by G.P. Putnam's Sons, New York, USA.

Bulach R, et al, (2005), Double-blind randomized controlled trial to determine extent of amnesia with midazolam given immediately before general anaesthesia. *British Journal of Anaesthesia,* 94: 300-305.

Burklund CW, Smith A, (1977), Language and the cerebral hemispheres. Observations of verbal and nonverbal responses during 18 months following left ("dominant") hemispherectomy. *Neurology,* 27: 627-633.

Bünning S, Blanke O, (2005), The out-of body experience: precipitating factors and neural correlates, in chapter 24 in. *Progress in Brain Research,* 150: 331-350.

Burns JM, et al, (2003), Right orbitofrontal tumor with pedophilia. Symptom and constructional apraxia sign. *Archives of Neurology,* 60: 437-440.

Byers GF, Muir JG, (1997), Detecting wakefulness in anaesthetised children. *Canadian Journal of Anesthesia,* 44: 486-488.

C

Cahn BR, Polich J, (2005), Meditation states and traits: EEG, ERP, and neuroimaging studies. *Psychological Bulletin,* 132: 180-211.

Calatayud J, Gonzalez A, (2003), History of the development and evolution of local anesthesia since the coca leaf. *Anesthesiology,* 98: 1503-1508.

Canfield MA, et al, (1996), Hispanic origin and neural tube defects in Houston/Harris County, Texas. I. Descriptive epidemiology. *American Journal of Epidemiology,* 143: 1-11.

Carter CD, (2010),. *Science and the Near-Death Experience: How Consciousness Survives Death.* Published by Inner Traditions, Vermont, USA, ISBN 978-1-59477-356-3.

Carus P, (1891),. *The Soul of Man. An Investigation of the Facts of Physiological and Experimental Psychology.* The Open Court Publishing Company, Chicago, USA.

Cassan A, et al, (2012), One or more bound planets per Milky Way star from microlensing observations. *Nature,* 481: 167-169.

Catani M, (2006), Diffusion tensor magnetic resonance imaging tractography in cognitive disorders. *Current Opinion in Neurology,* 19: 599-606.

Cave HA, (1931), Narcolepsy. *Archives of Neurology & Psychiatry,* 26: 50-101.

Chambers Encyclopaedia, 1901, Volume 7.

Chang J, et al, (2003), Pregnancy-Related Mortality Surveillance – United States, 1991-1999,. *Center for Disease Control, Surveillance Summaries,* 52(SS02): 1-8.

Cheyne JA, Girard TA, (2004), Spatial characteristics of hallucinations associated with sleep paralysis. *Cognitive Neuropsychiatry,* 9: 281-300.

Cheyne JA, (2005), Sleep paralysis episode frequency and number, types, and structure of associated hallucinations. *Journal of Sleep Research,* 14: 319-324.

Chi JH, et al, (2005), Time trends and demographics of deaths from congenital hydrocephalus in children in the United States: National Center for Health Statistics data, 1979 to 1998. *Journal of Neurosurgery (Pediatrics),* 103: 113-118.

Chiao JY, et al, (2008), Cultural specificity in amygdala response to fear faces. *Journal of Cognitive Neuroscience,* 20: 2167-2174.

Chisholm N, Gillett G, (2005), The patient's journey: Living with locked-in syndrome. *British Medical Journal,* 331: 94-97.

Chortkoff BS, et al, (1995), Subanesthetic concentrations of desflurane and propofol suppress recall of emotionally charged information. *Anesthesia & Analgesia,* 81: 728-736.

Christmas D, et al, (2004), Neurosurgery for mental disorder. *Advances in Psychiatric Treatment,* 10: 189-199.

419

Chudnofsky CR, (1997), Safety and efficacy of flumazenil in reversing conscious sedation in the emergency department. *Academic Emergency Medicine,* 4: 944-950.

Cicero MT,. *De Senectute,* [Translated by WA Falconer in Loeb Classical Library, Harvard University Press, 1996, ISBN 0-674-99170-2.]

Clute HL, Levy WJ, (1990), Electroencephalographic changes during brief cardiac arrest in humans. *Anesthesiology,* 73: 821-825.

Cobb JL, et al, (2000), Delirium in patients with cancer at the end of life. *Cancer Practice,* 8: 172-177.

Cobbe WR, (1895), *Doctor Judas. A Portrayal of the Opium Habit.* Published by S.C. Griggs and Company, Chicago, USA.

Collier BB, (1972), Ketamine and the conscious mind. *Anaesthesia,* 27: 120-134.

Combes X, et al, (2000), The effects of residual pain on oxygenation and breathing pattern during morphine analgesia. *Anesthesia & Analgesia,* 90: 156-160.

Comer SD, et al, (2008), Abuse liability of prescription opioids compared to heroin in morphine-maintained heroin abusers. *Neuropsychopharmacology,* 33: 1179-1191.

Cook TL, et al, (1978), Effect of subanesthetic concentrations of enflurane and halothane on human behavior. *Anesthesia & Analgesia,* 57:434-440.

Cook EW, et al, (1998), Do any near-death experiences provide evidence for the survival of human personality after death? Relevant features and illustrative case reports. *Journal of Scientific Exploration,* 12: 377-406.

Copeland JG, et al, (2004), Cardiac replacement with a total artificial heart as a bridge to transplantation. *New England Journal of Medicine,* 351: 859-867.

Cork RC, et al (1996), Is there implicit memory after propofol sedation? *British Journal of Anaesthesia,* 76: 492-498.

Corning JL, (1885), Spinal anaesthesia and local medication of the cord. *New York Medical Journal,* 42: 483-485.

Corning JL, (1894), *Pain in its Neuro-Pathological, Diagnostic, Medico-Legal, and Therapeutic Relations.* Published by J.B. Lippincott Company, Philadelphia, USA.

Cosgrove KP, et al, (2007), Evolving knowledge of sex differences in brain structure, function, and chemistry. *Biological Psychiatry,* 62: 847-855.

Council JR, Greyson B, (1985),. *Near-death experiences and the "fantasy-prone" personality: preliminary findings.* Paper presented at the annual convention of the American Psychological Association (93rd, Los Angeles, CA, August 23-27, 1985).

Cudaback DD, (1984), Four-km altitude effects on performance and health. *Publications of the Astronomical Society of the Pacific,* 96: 463-477.

Cullen SC, (1959), Clinical practice with muscle relaxants. *Anesthesiology,* 20: 530-534.

Cummings JL, (1993), Frontal-subcortical circuits and human behavior. *Archives of Neurology,* 50: 873-880.

D

Dahan A, et al, (2004), Simultaneous measurement and integrated analysis of analgesia and respiration after an intravenous morphine infusion. *Anesthesiology,* 101: 1201-1209.

Dahan A, et al, (2008), Sex-specific responses to opiates: animal and human studies. *Anesthesia & Analgesia,* 107: 83-95.

Dahan A, (2009), The importance of individual differences in response to opioid therapy. *Therapy,* 6: 633-635.

Dahan A, et al, (2010), Incidence, reversal and prevention of opioid-induced respiratory depression. *Anesthesiology,* 112: 226-238.

Dauvilliers Y, et al, (2003), Clinical aspects and pathophysiology of narcolepsy. *Clinical Neurophysiology,* 114: 2000-2017.

Davis KD, et al, (2005), Human anterior cingulate cortex neurons encode cognitive and emotional demands. *The Journal of Neuroscience,* 25: 8402-8406.

Davis JB, Marshall J, (1868), Contributions towards determining the Weight of the brain in different races of man. *Philosophical Transactions of the Royal Society of London,* 158: 505-527.

Davy H, (1800), *Researches, Chemical and Philosophical; Chiefly Concerning Nitrous Oxide, or Depholgisticated Nitrous Airs and its Respiration.* published by Biggs and Cottle, Bristol, England.

Day HB, (1868), *The Opium Habit, with Suggestions as to the Remedy.* Published by Harper & Brothers, New York, USA.

Deary IJ, et al, (2010), The neuroscience of human intelligence differences. *Nature Reviews. Neuroscience,* 11: 201-211.

Del Guercio LRM, et al, (1965), Comparison of blood flow during external and internal cardiac massage in man. *Circulation,* 31: suppl. 1: 171-180.

Demertzi A, et al, (2008), Is there anybody in there? Detecting awareness in disorders of consciousness. *Expert Review of Neurotherapeutics,* 8: 1719-1730.

Demertzi A,et al, (2009), Dualism persists in the science of mind,. *Annals of the New York Academy of Sciences,* 1157: 1-9.

Demorest FM, et al, (2010), An fMRI investigation of the cultural specificity of music memory. *Social Cognitive & Affective Neuroscience,* 5: 282-291.

Desmurget M, et al, (2007), Contrasting acute and slow-growing lesions: a new door to brain plasticity. *Brain,* 130: 898-914.

Devinsky O, Lai G, (2008), Spirituality and religion in epilepsy. *Epilepsy & Behavior,* 12: 636-643.

Devlin AM, et al, (2003), Clinical outcomes for hemispherectomy for epilepsy in childhood and adolescence. *Brain,* 126: 556-566.

Dewhurst K, Beard AW, (1970), Sudden Religious Conversions in Temporal Lobe Epilepsy,. *British Journal of Psychiatry,* 117: 497-507.

Dirksen L, et al, (2000), Fantoomsensaties tijdens plexus brachialis anesthesia. *Nederlands Tijdschrift voor Anesthesiologie,* 13: 81-86.

Dobelle WH, Mladejovsky MG, (1974), Phosphenes produced by electrical stimulation of human occipital cortex, and their application to the development of a prosthesis for the blind. *Brain,* 243: 553-576.

Doblin R, (1991), Pahnke's "Good Friday Experiment": A long-term follow-up and methodological critique. *Journal of Transpersonal Psychology,* 23: 1-28.

Doherty MJ, (2003), James Glaisher's 1862 account of balloon sickness: Altitude, decompression injury, and hypoxemia. *Neurology,* 60:1016-1018.

Dollfus P, et al, (1990), The locked-in syndrome: A review and presentation of two chronic cases. *Paraplegia,* 28: 5-16.

Domino KB, et al, (2012), Anaesthesia awareness registry: patient responses to awareness. *British Journal of Anaesthesia,* 108: 338P.

Dorgan JC, et al, (1984), Intra-operative awakening to monitor spinal cord function during scoliosis surgery. Description of the technique and a report of four cases. *Journal of Bone and Joint Surgery,* 66-B: 716-719.

Doufas AG, et al, (2004), Block-dependent sedation during epidural anaesthesia is associated with delayed brainstem conduction. *British Journal of Anaesthesia,* 93: 228-234.

Drummond H, (1908), *The Lowell Lectures on The Ascent of Man.* 14th edition, published by James Pott & Co., New York, USA.

Drummond JC, (2000), Monitoring depth of anesthesia. *Anesthesiology,* 93: 876-882.

Duane TD, (1966), Experimental blackout and the visual system. *Transactions of the American Opthalmological Society,* 64: 488-542.

Duarte R, et al, (2008), Comparison of the sedative, cognitive, and analgesic effects of nitrous oxide, sevoflurane, and ethanol. *British Journal of Anaesthesia,* 100: 203-210.

Duncum BM, (1947). *The Development of Inhalation Anaesthesia. With Special Reference to the Years 1846-1900.* Published for the Wellcome Historical Medical Museum, by Oxford University Press.

Dundee JW, (1952), Effect of controlled respiration on dosage of thiopentone and d-tubocurarine chloride required for abdominal surgery. *British Medical Journal,* 2: 893-896.

Dunn WT, (1920),. *The Opium Traffic in its International Aspects.* Published by Columbia University, New York, USA.

Dunne BJ, et al, (1994), Series position effects in random event generator experiments. *Journal of Scientific Exploration,* 8: 197-215.

Dupont S, et al, (2010), Functional MR imaging or Wada Test: Which is the better predictor of individual postoperative memory outcome? *Radiology,* 255: 128-134.

Dwyer R, et al, (1992s), Effects of isoflurane and nitrous oxide in subanesthetic concentrations on memory and responsiveness in volunteers. *Anesthesiology,* 77:888-898.

E

Easton S, et al, (2009), A putative implication for fronto-parietal connectivity in out-of-body experiences. *Cortex,* 45: 216-227.

Editorial, (1848), Suicide of Dr. Horace Wells, of Hartford, Connecticut. *Provincial Medical and Surgical Journal,* 31 May: 12: 305-306.

Eke N, (2000), Genital self-mutilation: there is no method in this madness. *BJU International,* 85: 295-298.

Elton CD, (1961), Cardiac arrest: A report on ten cases. *Canadian Anaesthetist's Society Journal,* 8: 64-69.

Encylopaedia Britannica, 1878, 9th edition, Volume 6.

Encylopaedia Britannica, 1911, 11th edition, Volume 20.

Errando CL, et al, (2008), Awareness with recall during general anaesthesia: a prospective observational evaluation of 4001 patients,. *British Journal of Anaesthesia*, 101: 178-185 (plus supplementary data table).

Etter J-F, Perneger TV, (2001), A comparison of cigarette smokers recruited through the internet or by mail. *International Journal of Epidemiology*, 30: 521-525.

Evans JM, et al, (1974), Degree and duration of reversal by naloxone of effects of morphine in conscious subjects. *British Medical Journal*, 2: 589-591.

Evans-Wentz WY, (1960),. *The Tibetan Book of the Dead.* 3rd edition, published by Oxford University Press, New York, USA.

F

Fagerlund MJ, Eriksson LI, (2009), Current concepts in neuromuscular transmission. *British Journal of Anaesthesia*, 103:108-114.

Fagiolini M, et al, (2009a), Epigenetic influences on brain development and plasticity. *Current Opinion in Neurobiology*, 19: 1-6.

Farley WF, (1992), Addiction and the anaesthesia resident. *Canadian Journal of Anesthesia*, 39: R11-R13.

Favrod-Coune T, Broers B, (2010), The health effect of psychostimulants: A literature review. *Pharmaceuticals*, 3: 2333-2361. (doi:10.3390/ph3072333).

Feldman MG, et al, (1994), Comparison of mortality rates for open and closed cholecystectomy in the elderly: Connecticut statewide survey. *Journal of Laparoendoscopic Surgery*, 4: 165-172.

Fell J,et al, (2006), Rhinal-hippocampal connectivity determines memory formation during sleep. *Brain*, 129: 108-114.

Fenwick P, Fenwick E, (1996),. *The Truth in the Light.* Published by Headline Book Publishing, United Kingdom, ISBN 0-7472-4668-8.

Feuillet L, et al, (2007), Brain of a white-collar worker. *Lancet*, 370: 262.

Fields RD, (2004), The other half of the brain. Mounting evidence suggests that glial cells, overlooked for half a century, may be nearly as critical to thinking and learning as neurons are. *Scientific American,* April 2004: 54-61.

Fillmore SJ, et al, (1970). Serial blood gas studies during cardiopulmonary resuscitation. *Annals of Internal Medicine,* 72: 465-469.

Finnerty FA, et al, (1954), Cerebral hemodynamics during cerebral ischemia induced by acute hypotension. *Journal of Clinical Investigation,* 33: 1227-1232.

Firestone LL, et al (1996), Human brain activity response to fentanyl imaged by positron emission tomography. *Anesthesia & Analgesia,* 82: 1247-1251.

Firth PG, Bolay H, (2004), Transient high altitude neurological dysfunction: an origin in the temporoparietal cortex. *High Altitude Medicine & Biology,* 5: 71-75.

Fitz-Ritson D, (1982), The anatomy and physiology of the muscle spindle,and its role in posture and movement: A review. *Journal of the Canadian Chiropractic Association,* 26: 144-150.

Flaishon R, et al (1997), Recovery of consciousness after thiopental or propofol Bispectral Index and the isolated forearm technique. *Anesthesiology,* 86: 613-619.

Fodden DI, et al, (1996), Doppler measurement of cardiac output during cardiopulmonary resuscitation. *Journal of Accident and Emergency Medicine,* 13: 379-382.

Foldes FF, et al, (1961), Studies with muscle relaxants in unanesthetized subjects. *Anesthesiology,* 22: 230-236.

Foldes FF, et al, (1971), Studies of pancuronium in conscious and anesthetized man. *Anesthesiology,* 35: 496-503.

Follette JW, (1992), Anesthesiologist addicted to propofol. *Anesthesiology,* 77: 817-818.

Foltin RW, Fischman MW, (1992), The cardiovascular and subjective effects of intravenous cocaine and morphine combinations in humans. *Journal of Pharmacology and Experimental Therapeutics,* 261: 623-632.

Font M, et al, (2003), Functional neuroimaging of auditory hallucinations in schizophrenia. *Actas Españolas de Psiquiatría,* 31: 3-9.

Forssmann W, (1972), *Selbstversuch. Erinnerungen eines Chirurgen.* Droste Verlag, Düsseldorf, Germany, ISBN 3770003136.

Fosse R, et al, (2001), Brain-mind states: reciprocal variations in thoughts and hallucinations. *Psychological Science,* 12: 30-36.

425

Fowler JS, et al, (2008), Fast uptake and long-lasting binding of methamphetamine in the human brain: Comparison with cocaine. *NeuroImage,* 43: 756-763.

Fox D, (2011), The limits of intelligence. *Scientific American,* July 2011, 305: 20-27.

Frazer JG, (1925),. *The Golden Bough: A study of Magic and Religion.* Published by The MacMillan Company, New York, USA.

Freeman W, (1949), Transorbital lobotomy. *American Journal of Psychiatry,* 105: 734-740.

Freeman W, (1958), Psychosurgery: present indications and future prospects. *California Medicine,*88: 429-434.

Freese L, et al, (2012), Non-medical use of methylphenidate: a review. *Trends in Psychiatry and Psychotherapy,* 34: 110-115.

Fröhlich F, et al, (1995), Conscious Sedation for Gastroscopy: Patient Tolerance and Cardiorespiratory Parameters. *Gastroenterology,* 108: 697-704.

G

Gabrielson A, et al, (2002), Non-invasive measurement of cardiac output in heart failure patients using a new foreign gas rebreathing technique. *Clinical Science,* 102: 247-252.

Gaitini L, et al, (1995), Awareness detection during Caesarean section under general anaesthesia using EEG spectrum analysis. *Canadian Journal of Anesthesia,* 42: 377-381.

Gal TJ, Goldberg SK, (1981), Relationship between respiratory muscle strength and vital capacity during partial curarization in awake subjects. *Anesthesiology,* 54: 141-147.

Galinkin JL, et al, (1997), Subjective, psychomotor, cognitive, and analgesic effects of subanesthetic concentrations of sevoflurane and nitrous oxide. *Anesthesiology,* 87:1082-1088.

Galton F, (1869), *Hereditary Genius. An Inquiry into its Laws and Consequences.* Published by Macmillan & Co, London, UK.

Gandevia SC, McCloskey DI, (1977), Changes in motor commands, as shown by changes in perceived heaviness, during partial curarization and peripheral anaesthesia in man. *Journal of Physiology,* 272: 673-689.

Gandevia SC, (1985), Illusory movements produced by electrical stimulation of low-threshold muscle afferents from the hand. *Brain,* 108: 965-981.

Gandevia SC, et al, (1993), Respiratory sensations, cardiovascular control, kinaesthesia and transcranial stimulation during paralysis in humans. *Journal of Physiology,* 470: 85-107.

Gandevia SC, et al, (1999), No laughing matter. *Lancet,* 354: 2086-2087.

Gardner WJ, et al, (1955), Residual function following hemispherectomy for tumour and for infantile hemiplegia. *Brain,* 78: 487-502.

Garland EL, et al, (2009), Nitrous oxide inhalation among adolescents: prevalence, correlates, and co-occurrence with volatile solvent inhalation. *Journal of Psychoactive Drugs,* 41: 337-347.

Gastaut H, Meyer JS, (1961),. *Cerebral anoxia and the Electroencephalogram,* Published Charles C. Thomas, USA.

Gastaut H, Fischer-Williams M, (1957), Electro-encephalographic study of syncope. Its differentiation from epilepsy. *Lancet,* II: 1018-1025.

Gawryluk JR, et al, (2010), Improving the clinical assessment of consciousness with advances in electrophysiological and neuroimaging techniques. *BMC Neurology,* 10: 11.

Gelder B de, (2010), Uncanny sight in the blind. *Scientific American,* May 2010: 42-47.

Gentili ME, et al, (2002), Clinical perception of phantom limb sensation in patients with brachial plexus block. *European Journal of Anaesthesiology,* 19: 105-108.

Georgi M,et al, (2012), Gender differences in dreaming in childhood and adolescence: The UK Library study. *International Journal of Dream Research,* 5: 125-129.

Gerra G, et al, (2007), Human Kappa opioid receptor gene (OPRK1) polymorphism is associated with opiate addiction. *American Journal of Medical Genetics Part B: Neuropsychiatric Genetics,* 144B: 771-775.

Ghoneim MM, Block RI, (1992), Learning and consciousness during general anesthesia. *Anesthesiology,* 76: 279-305.

Ghoneim MM, et al, (2009), Awareness during anesthesia: Risk factors, causes and sequelae: A review of reported cases in the literature. *Anesthesia & Analgesia,* 108: 527-535.

Gibson GE, et al, (1981), Brain dysfunction in mild to moderate hypoxia. *The American Journal of Medicine,* 70: 1247-1254.

Gil-Nagel A, Risinger W, (1997), Ictal semiology in hippocampal versus extrahippocampal temporal lobe epilepsy. *Brain,* 120: 183-192.

427

Gilron I, et al, (1996), Unintentional intraoperative awareness during sufentanil anaesthesia for cardiac surgery. *Canadian Journal of Anesthesia,* 43: 295-298.

Ginzberg L, (1913),. *The Legends of the Jews.* Published by The Jewish Publication Society of America, Philadelphia, USA.

Girardis M, et al, (2000), The hemodynamic and metabolic effects of tourniquet application during knee surgery. *Anesthesia & Analgesia,* 91: 727-731.

Girden E, (1962), A review of psychokinesis (PK). *Psychological Bulletin,* 59: 353-388.

Gläscher J, et al, (2010), Distributed neural system for general intelligence revealed by lesion mapping. *Proceedings of the National Academy of Sciences,* 107: 4705-4709.

Glenn GM, et al, (1987), Muscle blood flow and fiber activity in partially curarized rats during exercise. *Journal of Applied Physiology,* 63: 1450-1456.

Glicksohn J, (1990), Belief in the paranormal and subjective paranormal experience. *Personality and Individual Differences,* 11: 675-683.

Gloor P, et al, (1982), The role of the limbic system in experiential phenomena of temporal lobe epilepsy. *Annals of Neurology,* 12: 129-144.

Goldfine AM, Schiff ND, (2011), Consciousness: Its neurobiology and the major classes of impairment. *Neurological Clinics,* 29: 723-737.

Goldie EAG, (1941), The clinical manifestations of oxygen lack. *Proceedings of the Royal Society of Medicine,* 34: 631-632.

Gordon A, et al, (2005), Pediatric presence at cesarean section: Justified or not? *American Journal of Obstetrics and Gynecology,* 193: 599-605.

Gott P, (1973), Language after dominant hemispherectomy. *Journal of Neurology, Neurosurgery, and Psychiatry,* 36: 1082-1088.

Gourlay GK, et al, (1988), Fentanyl blood concentration-analgesic Response relationship in the treatment of postoperative pain. *Anesthesia & Analgesia,* 67: 329-337.

Gräff J, Mansuy IM, (2008), Epigenetic codes in cognition and behaviour. *Behavioural Brain Research,* 192: 70-87.

Grant SA, et al, (2000), Blood propofol concentration and psychomotor effects on driving skills. *British Journal of Anesthesia,* 85: 396-400.

Gray TC, Halton J, (1946), A milestone in anaesthesia? *Proceeding of the Royal Society of Medicine,(Section on Anaesthesia),* 34: 400-410.

Gray TC, Jackson Rees G, (1952), The role of apnoea in anaesthesia for major sugery. *British Medical journal,* 2: 891-892.

Greenberg JO, et al, (1977), Idiopathic normal pressure hydrocephalus - a report of 73 patients. *Journal of Neurology, Neurosurgery, and Psychiatry,* 40: 336-341.

Greenfield S, (2002), Mind, brain and consciousness. *British Journal of Psychiatry,* 181: 91-93.

Grey M, (1985), *Return from death. An Exploration of the Near-Death Experience.* published by Arkana, UK, ISBN 1-85063-019-4.

Greyson B, (1983), The Near-Death Experience Scale: Construction, reliability, and validity. *Journal of Nervous and Mental Disease,* 171: 369-375.

Greyson B, (1985), A typology of near-death experiences. *American Journal of Psychiatry,* 142: 967-969.

Greyson B, (2003), Incidence and correlates of near-death experiences in a cardiac care unit. *General Hospital Psychiatry,* 25: 269-276.

Greyson B, (2010), Seeing dead people not known to have died: "Peak in Darien" experiences. *Anthropology and Humanism,* 35: 159-171.

Griffith H, Davidson M, (1966), Long-term changes in intellect and behaviour after hemispherectomy,. *Journal of Neurology, Neurosurgery and Psychiatry,* 29: 571-576.

Griffith HR, et al, (1942), The use of curare in general anesthesia. *Anesthesiology,* 3: 418-420.

Griffiths RR, et al, (2006), Psilocybin can occasion mystical-type experiences having substantial and sustained personal meaning and spiritual significance. *Psychopharmacology,* 187: 268-283.

Griffiths RR, et al, (2008), Mystical-type experiences occasioned by psilocybin mediate the attribution of personal meaning and spiritual significance 14 months later. *Journal of Psychopharmacology,* 22: 621-632.

Griffiths RR, Grob CS, (2010), Hallucinogens as medicine. *Scientific American,* December 2010: 77-79.

Grim P, (1984), Psi phenomena and the Rosenthal effect. *New Ideas in Psychology,* 2: 35-45.

Grogaard HK,et al, (2007), Continuous mechanical chest compressions during cardiac arrest to facilitate restoration of coronary circulation with percutaneous coronary intervention. *Journal of the American College of Cardiology,* 50: 1093-1096.

Grön G, et al, (2000), Brain activation during human navigation: gender-different neural networks as substrate of performance. *Nature Neuroscience,* 3: 404-408.

Grondelle A van, et al, (1983), Thermodilution method overestimates low cardiac output in humans. *American Journal of Physiology - Heart and Circulatory Physiology,* 245: H690-H692.

Grossman N, (2002), Who's afraid of life after death? *Journal of Near Death Studies,* 21: 5-24.

Grottke O, et al, (2004), Intraoperative wake-up test and postoperative emergence in patients undergoing spinal surgery: A comparison of intravenous and inhaled anesthetic techniques using short-acting anesthetics. *Anesthesia & Analgesia,* 99: 1521-1527.

Grubb NR, et al, (1996), Chronic memory impairment after cardiac arrest outside hospital. *British Medical Journal,* 313: 143-146.

Grubb NR, et al, (2000), Memory impairment in out-of-hospital cardiac arrest survivors is associated with global reduction in brain volume, not focal hippocampal injury. *Stroke,* 31: 1509-1514.

Gutchess AH, et al, (2010), Neural differences in the processing of semantic relationships across cultures. *Social Cognitive & Affective Neuroscience,* 5: 254-263.

Gyulai FE, et al, (1996), In vivo imaging of human limbic responses to nitrous oxide inhalation. *Anesthesia & Analgesia,* 83: 291-298.

H

Haba M, et al, (2011), The evaluation of symptoms related to remifentanil effect-site concentrations in humans. Poster presentation at the 14th Eurosiva Annual Meeting, Apollo Hotel, Amsterdam, The Netherlands, 10 June 2011.

Haemmig RB, Tschacher W, (2001), Effects of high-dose heroin versus morphine in intravenous drug users: A randomised double-blind crossover study. *Journal of Psychoactive Drugs,* 33: 105-110.

Hagmann P, et al, (2007), Mapping human whole-brain Structural networks with diffusion MRI. *PLoS ONE* 2(7): e597. doi:10.1371/journal.pone.0000597.

Hagmann P, et al, (2008), Mapping the structural core of human cerebral cortex. *PLoS Biol* 6(7): e159. doi:10.1371/journal.pbio.0060159

Halford FJ, (1943), A critique of intravenous anesthesia in war surgery. *Anesthesiology,* 4: 67-69.

Hammond WA, (1876), *Spiritualism and Allied Causes of Nervous Derangement.* Published by G.B. Putnam's Sons, New York, USA.

Han S, Northoff G, (2008), Culture-sensitive neural substrates of human cognition: a transcultural neuroimaging approach. *Nature Reviews Neuroscience,* 9: 646-654.

Hanlon CA, Canterberry M, (2012), The use of brain imaging to elucidate neural circuit changes in cocaine addiction. *Substance Abuse and Rehabilitation,* 3: 115-128. (http://dx.doi.org/10.2147/SAR.S35153).

Hannan EL, et al, (1999), Laparoscopic and open cholecystectomy in New York State: Mortality, complications, and choice of procedure. *Surgery,* 125:223-231.

Hans P, et al, (2005), Comparative effects of ketamine on Bispectral Index and spectral entropy of the electroencephalogram under sevoflurane anaesthesia. *British Journal of Anaesthesia,* 94: 336-340.

Hansen BA, Brodtkorb E, (2003), Partial epilepsy with "ecstatic" seizures. *Epilepsy & Behavior,* 4: 667-673.

Harmsen P, et al, (1971), Acute controlled hypotension and EEG in patients with hypertension and cerebrovascular disease. *Journal of Neurology, Neurosurgery and Psychiatry,* 34: 300-307.

Harris Poll, (2008), More Americans believe in the Devil, Hell and Angels than in Darwin's Theory of Evolution. Survey published on the internet during 2010 at: http://www.harrisinteractive.com/harris_poll/printerfriend/index.asp?PID=9 82

Harroun P, et al, (1946), Curare and nitrous oxide anesthesia for lengthy operations. *Anesthesiology,* 7: 24-28.

Hasan D, et al, (1989), Management problems in acute hydrocephalus after subarachnoid hemorrhage. *Stroke,* 20: 747-753.

Hastings A, (2002), The resistance to belief. *Journal of Near Death Studies,* 21: 77-98.

Hawkins JV, (1867), On certain forms of blood poisoning. *British Medical Journal,* August 31: 179-180.

Heald G, (2000), The soul of Britain. Survey published on the internet during 2010 at: http://www.thetablet.co.uk/page/special-reports03

Heine L, et al, (2012), Resting state networks and consciousness: Alterations of multiple resting state network connectivity in physiological, pharmacological, and pathological consciousness states. *Frontiers in Psychology,* 3: article 295 (doi: 10.3389/fpsyg.2012.00295)

Heinke W, Schwarzbauer C, (2001), Subanesthetic isoflurane affects task-induced brain activation in a highly specific manner: A functional magnetic resonance imaging study. *Anesthesiology,* 94:973-981.

Heinke W, Schwarzbauer C, (2002), In vivo imaging of anaesthetic action in humans: approaches with positron emission tomography (PET) and functional magnetic resonance imaging (fMRI). *British Journal of Anaesthesia,* 89: 112-122.

Heinzen K, (1891), *The Rights of Women and the Sexual Relations.* Published Charles H. Kerr & Co., USA.

Heller H, et al, (2005), Bilateral bispectral index monitoring during suppression of unilateral hemispheric function. *Anesthesia & Analgesia,* 101: 235-241.

Henrie JR, et al, (1961), Alteration of human consciousness by nitrous oxide, as assessed by electroencephalography and psychological tests. *Anesthesiology,* 22: 247-259.

Hermann S, et al, (2004), Ictal pleasant sensations: Cerebral localization and lateralization. *Epilepsia,* 45: 35-40.

Hermle L,et al, (1992), Mescaline-induced psychopathological, neuropsychological, and neurometabolic effects in normal subjects: experimental psychosis as a tool for psychiatric research. *Biological Psychiatry,* 32: 976-991.

Hermle L, et al, (1998), Blood flow and cerebral laterality in the mescaline model of psychosis. *Pharmacopsychiatry,* 31(supplement): 85-91.

Hersch K, Borum R, (1998), Command hallucinations, compliance, and risk assessment. *Journal of the American Academy of Psychiatry and the Law,* 26: 353-359.

Heytens L, et al, (1989), Lazarus sign and extensor posturing in a brain-dead patient. *Journal of Neurosurgery,* 71:449-451.

Hilgenberg JC, (1981), Intraoperative awareness during high-dose fentanyl-oxygen anesthesia. *Anesthesiolgy,* 54: 341-343.

Hill K, et al, (2005), Estimates of maternal mortality for 1995. *Bulletin of the World Health Organization,* 79: 182-193.

Himmelseher S, Durieux ME, (2005), Ketamine for Perioperative pain management. *Anesthesiology,* 102: 211-220.

Ho JK, et al, (1992), Blood gas and electrolyte changes after tourniquet application in total knee replacement surgery. *Yonsei Medical Journal,* 32: 153-158.

Hobson JA, (2005), Sleep is of the brain, by the brain and for the brain. *Nature,* 437: 1254-1256.

Hobson JA, (2009), REM sleep and dreaming: towards a theory of protoconsciousness. *Nature Reviews: Neuroscience,* 10: 803-813.

Hocking G, et al, (2007), Ketamine: does life begin at 40? *Pain: Clinical Updates,* 15: 1-6.

Hoed J vd, et al, (1979), Hallucinatory experiences during cataplexy in patients with narcolepsy. *American Journal of Psychiatry,* 136: 1210-1211.

Hoeper MM, et al, (1999), Determination of cardiac output by the Fick method, thermodilution, and acetylene rebreathing in pulmonary hypertension. *American Journal of Respiratory and Critical Care Medicine,* 160: 535-541.

Hoffer JS, et al, (2007), Treatment of psychiatric symptoms associated with a frontal lobe tumor through surgical resection. *American Journal of Psychiatry,* 164: 877-882.

Holden JM, Greyson B, and James D, (Eds.) (2009), *The Handbook of Near-Death Experiences: Thirty Years of Investigation.* Published by Praeger/ABC-CLIO, Santa Barbara, California, USA, ISBN 978-0-313-35864-7.

Hollander B, (1920), *In Search of the Soul and the Mechanism of Thought, Emotion and Conduct.* published by Kegan Paul, Trench, Trubner & Co., Ltd., London.

Hollister LE, et al (1962), Mescaline, lysergic acid diethylamide and psilocybin: Comparison of clinical syndromes, effects on color perception and biochemical measures. *Comprehensive Psychiatry,* 3: 235-241.

Hölzel BK, et al, (2011), Mindfulness practice leads to increases in regional brain gray matter density. *Psychiatry Research: Neuroimaging,* 191: 36-43.

Holzinger B, et al, (2006), Psychophysiological correlates of lucid dreaming. *Dreaming,* 16: 88-95.

Honey GD, et al, (2005), Impairment of specific episodic memory processes by sub-psychotic doses of ketamine: The effects of levels of processing at encoding and of the subsequent retrieval task. *Psychopharmacology,* 181: 445-457.

Hong SB, et al, (2000), Contralateral EEG Slowing and amobarbital distribution in Wada Test: An intracarotid SPECT study. *Epilepsia,* 41: 207-212.

Honorton C, Ferrari D, (1989), "Future Telling": A meta-analysis of forced-choice precognition experiments, 1935-1987. *Journal of Parapsychology,* 53: 281-308.

Hornbein TF, et al, (1989), The cost to the central nervous system of climbing to extremely high altitude. *New England Journal of Medicine,* 321: 1714-1719.

Hornbein TF, (2001), The high-altitude brain. *The Journal of Experimental Biology,* 204: 3129-3132.

Horowitz I, McDonald AD, (1969), Anencephaly and spina bifida in the province of Quebec. *Canadian Medical Association Journal,* 100: 748-755.

Hosick EC, et al, (1971), Neurophysiological effects of different anesthetics in conscious man. *Journal of Applied Physiology,* 31: 892-898.

Hosie A, (1914), On the Trail of the Opium Poppy. A Narrative of Travel in the Chief Opium-Producing Provinces of China. Volumes I and II, Published by George Philip & Son Ltd., London, UK.

Hubbard EM, (2007), Neurophysiology of Synesthesia. *Current Psychiatry Reports,* 9:193-199.

Humboldt A von, (1852), *Personal Narrative of Travels to the Equinoctial Regions of America, During the Years 1799-1804.* translated from the French by Thomasina Ross, Volume 2, published by Henry G. Bohn, London, England.

Hurley RA, et al, (1999), Normal pressure hydrocephalus: Significance of MRI in a potentially treatable dementia. *Journal of Neuropsychiatry and Clinical Neurosciences,* 11: 297-300.

Hyde KL, et al, (2009), Musical training shapes structural brain development. *The Journal of Neuroscience,* 29: 3019-3025.

Hyman R, (1985), The ganzfeld psi experiment: A critical appraisal. *Journal of Parapsychology,* 49: 3-49.

Hyman R, (1988), Psi experiments: Do the best parapsychological experiments justify the claims for psi? *Experientia,* 44: 315-322.

I

Imani F, et al, (2006), Propofol-alfentanil vs propofol-remifentanil for posterior spinal fusion including wake-up test. *British Journal of Anaesthesia,* 96: 583-586.

Imberti R, et al, (2003), Cerebral perfusion pressure and cerebral tissue oxygen tension in a patient during cardiopulmonary resuscitation. *Intensive Care Medicine*, 29: 1016-1019.

Insel TR, (2010), Faulty circuits. Neuroscience is revealing the malfunctioning connections underlying psychological disorders and forcing psychiatrists to rethink the causes of mental illness. *Scientific American*, April 2010: 44-51.

Irwin HJ, (1993), Belief in the paranormal: A review of the empirical literature. *Journal of the American Society for Psychical Research*, 87: 1-39.

Isaacson SA, et al, (2000), Regulation of proprioceptive memory by subarachnoid regional anesthesia. *Anesthesiology*, 93: 55-61.

J

Jahn RG, (1982), The persistent paradox of psychic phenomena: An engineering perspective. *Proceedings of the IEEE*, 70: 136-170.

James W, (1898), *Human Immortality. Two Supposed Objections to the Doctrine.* Published by The Riverside Press, Cambridge, UK.

James W, (1902), *The Varieties of Religious Experience. A Study in Human Nature.* Published by Longmans, Green, and Co., New York.

James W, (1912), *The Will to Believe: and Other Essays in Popular Philosophy.* Published Longman, Green and Co., USA.

Janesewski DJ, et al, (1999), The effects of subanesthetic concentrations of sevoflurane and nitrous oxide, alone and in combination, on analgesia, mood, and psychomotor performance in healthy volunteers. *Anesthesia & Analgesia*, 88: 1149-1154.

Jansen KLR, (1997), The ketamine model of the near-death experience: a central role for the NMDA receptor. *Journal of Near-Death Studies*, 16: 5-26.

Jansen KLR, (2000), A Review of the Nonmedical Use of Ketamine: Use, Users and Consequences,. *Journal of Psychoactive Drugs*, 32: 419-433.

Jaquier M, et al, (2006), Spontaneous pregnancy outcome after prenatal diagnosis of anencephaly. *British Journal of Obstetrics & Gynaecology*, 113: 951-953.

Jasinski JR, Preston KL, (1986), Comparison of intravenously administered methadone, morphine and heroin. *Drug and Alcohol Dependence*, 17: 301-310.

Jensen EW, et al, (2004), Pitfalls and challenges when assessing the depth of hypnosis during general anaesthesia by clinical signs and electronic indices. *Acta Anaesthesiologica Scandinavica,* 48: 1260-1267.

Jones HE, et al, (1999), Assessment of opioid partial agonist activity with a three-choice hydromorphone dose-discrimination procedure. *Journal of Pharmacology and Experimental Therapeutics,* 289: 1350-1361.

Jones-Gotman M, et al, (1994), EEG slow waves and memory performance during the intracarotid amobarbital test. *Epilepsia,* 35: 61-69.

Jonnesco T, (1909), Remarks on general spinal analgesia. *British Medical Journal,* November 13: 1396-1401.

Jørgensen EO, (1973), Spinal man after brain death. *Acta Neurochirurgica,* 28: 259-273.

K

Kaiko RF, et al, (1981), Analgesic and mood effects of heroin and morphine in cancer patients with postoperative pain. *New England Journal of Medicine,* 304: 1501-1505.

Kammer T, et al, (2002), Propofol and sevoflurane in subanesthetic concentrations act preferentially on the spinal cord. *Anesthesiology,* 97: 1416-1425.

Kane HH, (1880), *The Hypodermic Injection of Morphia. Its History, Advantages and Dangers. (Based on the Experience of 360 Physicians).* published by Chas. L. Bermingham & Co., New York, USA.

Kaplan HG, et al, (1979), Hepatitis caused by halothane sniffing. *Annals of Internal Medicine,* 90: 797-798.

Karch SB, (1999), Cocaine: history, use, abuse. *Journal of the Royal Society of Medicine,* 92: 393-397.

Karl A, et al, (2001), Reorganization of motor and somatosensory cortex in upper extremity amputees with phantom limb pain. *The Journal of Neuroscience,* 21: 3609-3618.

Kashtan H, et al, (1990), Comparative evaluation of propofol and thiopentone for total intravenous anaesthesia. *Canadian Journal of Anesthesia,* 37: 170-176.

Kazemi AP, Amini A, (2006), A comparative study of remifentanil/propofol versus alfentanil/propofol for Wake-up Test in major spinal surgery. *Iranian Journal of Medical Sciences,* 31: 196-199.

Keeley LE, (1881), *The Morphine Eater, or, From Bondage to Freedom.* published by C.L. Palmer & Co. Publishers, Illinois, USA.

Kellehear A, (1993), Culture, biology and the near-death experience. *Journal of Nervous and Mental Disease,* 181: 148-156.

Kellehear A, (2001), An Hawaiian near-death experience. *Journal of Near-Death Studies,* 20: 31-35.

Kelley WM, et al, (2002), Wada Testing reveals frontal lateralization for the memorization of words and faces. *Journal of Cognitive Neuroscience,* 14: 116-125.

Kelly EF, et al, (2007), *Irreducible Mind. Toward a Psychology for the 21st Century.* Published by Rowman & Littlefield Publishers Inc., USA, ISBN 978-1-4422-0206-1.

Kennedy JE, (2001), Why is psi so elusive? A review and proposed model. *Journal of Parapsychology,* 65: 219-246.

Kennedy JE, (2003) The capricious, actively evasive, unsustainable nature of psi: A summary and hypothesis. *Journal of Parapsychology,* 67: 53-74.

Kennedy JE, (2004), A proposal and challenge for proponents and skeptics of psi. *Journal of Parapsychology,* 68: 157-167.

Kennedy JE, (2005), Personality and. *motivations* to believe, misbelieve, and disbelieve in paranormal phenomena. *Journal of Parapsychology,* 69: 263-292.

Kennedy JE, (2006), Letter on meta-analysis in parapsychology. *Journal of Parapsychology,* 70: 410-413.

Kenny CS, (1879), *The History of the Law of England as to the Effects of Marriage on Property and on the Wife's Legal Capacity.* Published Reeves and Turner, London, England.

Kent CD, et al, (2013), Psychological impact of unexpected explicit recall of events occurring during surgery performed under sedation, regional anaesthesia, and general anaesthesia: data from the Anesthesia Awareness Registry. *British Journal of Anaesthesia,* 110: 381-387.

Kerssens C, et al, (2005), Attenuated brain response to auditory word stimulation with sevoflurane: A functional magnetic resonance imaging study in humans. *Anesthesiology,* 103:11-19.

Kjaer TW, et al, (2002), Regional cerebral blood flow during light sleep - a $H_2^{15}O$-PET study. *Journal of Sleep Research,* 11: 201-207.

Klont RE, Lambooy E, (1995), Effects of preslaughter muscle exercise on muscle metabolism and meat quality studied in anesthetized pigs of different halothane genotypes. *Journal of Animal Science,* 73:108-117.

Knapp H, (1885), *Cocaine and its Use in Ophthalmic and General Surgery.* Published by G.P. Putnam's Sons, New York, USA.

Knoblauch H, et al, (2001), Different kinds of near-death experience: A report on a survey of near-death experiences in Germany. *Journal of Near Death Studies,* 20: 15-29.

Koller EA, et al, (1991), Respiratory, circulatory and neuropsychological responses to acute hypoxia in acclimatized and non-acclimatized subjects. *European Journal of Applied Physiology, and Occupational Physiology,* 62:67-72.

Kopman AF, et al, (1997), Relationship of the train-of-four fade ratio to clinical signs and symptoms of residual paralysis in awake volunteers. *Anesthesiology,* 86: 765-771.

Korttila K, et al, (1981), Time course of mental and psychomotor effects of 30 per cent nitrous oxide during inhalation and recovery. *Anesthesiology,* 54:220-226.

Korttila K, et al, (1992), Clinical recovery and psychomotor function after brief anesthesia with propofol or thiopental. *Anesthesiology,* 76: 676-681.

Kouwenhoven WB, et al, (1960), Closed chest cardiac massage. *Journal of the American Medical Association,* 173: 1064-1067.

Krahn LE, et al, (2001), Narcolepsy: New understanding of irresistible sleep. *Mayo Clinic Proceedings,* 76:185-194.

Krahn LE, et al, (2005), Characterizing the emotions that trigger cataplexy. The. *Journal of Neuropsychiatry and Clinical Neurosciences,* 17: 45-50.

Kramer W, (1963), From reanimation to deanimation. (Intravital death of the brain during artificial respiration). *Acta Neurologica Scandinavica,* 39:139-153.

Kreek MJ, et al, (2005), Genetic influences on impulsivity, risk taking, stress responsivity and vulnerability to drug abuse and addiction. *Nature Neuroscience,* 11: 1450-1457.

Krenz S, et al, (2003), Ether: a forgotten addiction. *Addiction,* 98: 1167-1168.

Krishnan V, (1993), The physical basis of out-of-body vision. *Journal of Near-Death Studies,* 11: 257-260.

Krystal JH, et al, (1998), Interactive effects of subanesthetic ketamine and subhypnotic lorazepam in humans. *Psychopharmacology,* 135: 213-229.

L

LaBerge S, (2010), Signal-verfied lucid dreaming proves that REM sleep can support reflective consciousness. *International Journal of Dream Research,* 3: 26-27.

Ladd LA, et al, (2005), Ventilatory responses of healthy subjects to intravenous combinations of morphine and oxycodone under imposed hypercapnic and hypoxaemic conditions. *British Journal of Clinical Pharmacology,* 59: 524-535.

Lallemand MA, et al, (2003), Bispectral index changes following etomidate induction of general anaesthesia and orotracheal intubation,. *British Journal of Anaesthesia,* 91: 341-346.

Lammer H, et al, (2010), Exoplanet status report: observation, characterization and evolution of exoplanets and their host stars. *Solar System Research,* 44: 290-310.

Landau R, et al, (2004), Genetic variability of μ-opioid receptor in an obstetric population. *Anesthesiology,* 100: 1030-1033.

Långsjö JW, et al, (2003), Effects of subanesthetic doses of ketamine on regional cerebral blood flow, oxygen consumption, and blood volume in humans. *Anesthesiology,* 99: 614-623.

Långsjö JW, et al, (2012), Returning from oblivion: imaging the neural core of consciousness. *Journal of Neuroscience,* 32: 4935-4943.

Langlois S, et al, (1987), Midazolam: kinetics and effects on memory, sensorium, and haemodynamics. *British Journal of Clinical Pharmacology,* 23: 273-278.

Large M, et al, (2009), Major self-mutilation in the first episode of psychosis. *Schizophrenia Bulletin,* 35: 1012-1021.

Lasagna L, et al, (1955), Drug-induced mood changes in man. 1. Observations on healthy subjects, chronically ill patients, and "post-addicts". *Journal of the American Medical Association,* 157: 1006-1020.

Lau HC, Passingham RE, (2006), Relative blindsight in normal observers and the neural correlate of visual consciousness. *Proceedings of the National Academy of Sciences of the United States of America,* 103: 18763-18768.

Laurence KM, Coates S, (1962), The natural history of hydrocephalus. Detailed analysis of 182 unoperated cases. *Archives of Disease in Childhood,* 37: 345-362.

Laureys S, et al, (2005), The locked-in syndrome: what is it like to be conscious but paralyzed and voiceless? In chapter 34,. *Progress in Brain Research*, 150: 495-511.

Laureys S, (2005a), The neural correlate of (un)awareness: lessons from the vegetative state. *Trends in Cognitive Sciences*, 9: 556-559.

Lawrence E, Peters E, (2004), Reasoning in believers in the paranormal. *Journal of Nervous and Mental Disease*, 192: 727-733.

Lazar SW, et al, (2010), Meditation experience is associated with increased cortical thickness. *NeuroReport*, 16: 1893-1897.

Lee JA, Atkinson RS, (1968),. *A Synopsis of Anaesthesia*, 6th edition, published by John Wright and Sons Ltd., Bristol, United Kingdom.

Lee JS, et al, (2004), Probabilistic map of blood flow distribution in the brain from the internal carotid artery. *NeuroImage*, 23: 1422-1431.

Lee TMY, et al, (2004a), Command hallucinations among asian patients With schizophrenia. *Canadian Journal of Psychiatry*, 49: 838-842.

Lemmens HJM, et al, (1988), Age has no effect on the pharmacodynamics of alfentanil. *Anesthesia & Analgesia*, 67: 956-960.

Lemmens HJM, et al, (1989), Alcohol consumption alters the pharmacodynamics of alfentanil. *Anesthesiology*, 71: 669-674.

Lempert T, et al, (1994), Syncope and near-death experience. *Lancet*, 344: 829-830.

Lempert T, et al, (1994a), Syncope: A videometric analysis of 56 episodes of transient cerebral hypoxia. *Annals of Neurology*, 36 : 233-237.

Lennmarken C, et al, (2002), Victims of awareness. *Acta Anaesthesiologica Scandinavica*, 46: 229-231.

Lennmarken C, Sydsjo G, (2007), Psychological consequences of awareness and their treatment. *Best Practice & Research Clinical Anaesthesiology*, 21: 357-367.

Levin HS, et al, (1994), Preliminary results of an incremental intracarotid amobarbital procedure: Evaluation of language and memory without sedation. *Journal of Epilepsy*, 7: 11-17.

Levin T, (2011), Holographic Trans-disciplinary Framework of Consciousness: An Integrative Perspective. *Journal of Consciousness Exploration & Research*, 2: 1385-1416.

Lewinter JR, et al, (1989), CPR-dependent consciousness: Evidence for cardiac compression causing forward flow. *Annals of Emergency Medicine*, 18: 1111-1115.

Liddon SC, (1967), Sleep paralysis and hypnagogic hallucinations. Their relationship to the nightmare. *Archives of General Psychiatry,* 17: 88-96.

Liem EB, et al, (2004), Anesthetic requirement is increased in redheads. *Anesthesiology,* 101: 279-283.

Liem EB, et al, (2005), Increased sensitivity to thermal pain and reduced subcutaneous lidocaine efficacy in redheads. *Anesthesiology,* 102:509-514.

Lienhart A, et al, (2006), Survey of Anesthesia-related Mortality in France. *Anesthesiology,* 105: 1087-1097.

Liere van EJ, Stickney JC, (1963), *Hypoxia,* published by the University of Chicago Press, U.S.A..

Lifetables, (2010), Data accessed from the internet from: http://www.lifetable.de

Lindeman M, et al, (2012), Distinguishing spirituality from other constructs. Not a matter of well-being but of belief in supernatural spirits. *Journal of Nervous and Mental Disease,* 200: 167-173.

Lipscomb KJ, et al, (1998), Subpectoral implantation of a cardioverter defibrillator under local anaesthesia. *Heart,* 79: 253-255.

Liu P, et al, (2002), Pump models assessed by transesophageal cardiography during cardiopulmonary resuscitation. *Chinese Medical Journal,* 115: 359-363.

Lommel P van, et al, (2001), Near-death experience in survivors of cardiac arrest: a prospective study in the Netherlands. *Lancet,* 358: 2039-2045.

Lommel P van, (2010), *Consciousness Beyond Life: The Science of the Near-Death Experience.* Published by HarperCollins, USA, ISBN 9780061777257.

Lommel P van, (2011), Setting the Record Straight: Correcting Two Recent Cases of Materialist Misrepresentation of My Research and Conclusions. *Journal of Near-Death Studies,* 30: 107-119.

London ED, et al, (1990), Morphine-induced metabolic changes in human brain. Studies With positron emission tomography and [Fluorine 18] fluorodeoxyglucose. *Archives of General Psychiatry,* 47: 73-81.

Long J, (2007), Does the arousal system contribute to near-death and out-of-body experiences? A summary and response. *Journal of Near-Death Studies,* 25: 135-169.

Long J, Perry P, (2010), *Evidence of the Afterlife. The Science of Near-Death Experiences.* Published by HarperOne, USA, ISBN 978-0-06-145255-0.

Lopez C, et al, (2008), Body ownership and embodiment: vestibular and multisensory mechanisms. *Clinical Neurophysiology,* 38: 149-161.

441

Lopez C, et al, (2010), Abnormal self-location and vestibular vertigo in a patient with right frontal lobe epilepsy. *Epilepsy & Behavior,* 17: 289-292.

Lopez U, et al, (2006), Near-death experience in a boy undergoing uneventful elective surgery under general anesthesia. *Pediatric Anesthesia,* 6: 85-88.

Lorber J, (1984), The family history of uncomplicated congenital hydrocephalus: an epidemiological study based on 270 probands. *British Medical Journal,* 289: 281-284.

Lorenz IH, et al, (2001), Influence of equianesthetic concentrations of nitrous oxide and isoflurane on regional cerebral blood flow, regional cerebral blood volume, and regional mean transit time in human volunteers. *British Journal of Anaesthesia.* 87: 691-698.

Lorenzi P, et al, (2004), False Proximate Awareness: an experience at the border of psychopathology. *Rivista di Psichiatria,* 39: 223-228.

Loring DW, et al, (1992), Amobarbital dose effects on Wada memory testing. *Journal of Epilepsy,* 5: 171-174.

Loring DW, et al, (1994), Stimulus timing effects on Wada memory testing. *Archives of Neurology,* 51: 806-810.

Losasso TJ, et al, (1992), Electroencephalographic monitoring of cerebral function during asystole and succesful cardiopulmonary resuscitation. *Anesthesia & Analgesia,* 75: 12-19.

Lotze M, et al, (2001), Phantom movements and pain. An fMRI study in upper limb amputees. *Brain,* 124: 2268-2277.

Louw JX, (1967), Specific mamba antivenom-report of survival of 2 patients with black mamba bites treated with this serum. *South African Medical Journal,* 2 December, 1175.

Lövblad KO, et al, (2003), Functional imaging of sleep. *Schweizer Archiv für Neurologie und Psychiatrie,* 154: 324-328.

Lowenstein E, (1971), Morphine "anesthesia" - a perspective. *Anesthesiology,* 35: 563-565.

Luders E, et al, (2009), The underlying anatomical correlates of long-term meditation: Larger hippocampal and frontal volumes of gray matter. *NeuroImage,* 45: 672-678.

Lundahl CR, Widdison HA, (1993), Social positions in the City of Light. *Journal of Near-Death Studies,* 11: 231-238.

Lutsky I, et al, (1994), Use of psychoactive substances in three medical specialties: anaesthesia, medicine and surgery. *Canadian Journal of Anesthesia,* 41: 561-567.

Luu BL, et al, (2009), The fusimotor and reafferent origin of the sense of force and weight. *Journal of Physiology*, 589: 3135-3147.

Luyendijk W, Treffers PDA, (1992), The smile in anencephalic infants. *Clinical Neurology and Neurosurgery*, 94: Supp. 1: 113-117.

Lysakowski C, et al, (2000), Memory functions during propofol sedation do not differ between smokers and non-smokers. *Schweizer Archiv für Neurologie und Psychiatrie*, 161: 96-99.

M

Macken E, et al, (1998), Midazolam versus diazepam in lipid emulsion as conscious sedation for colonoscopy with or without reversal of sedation with flumazenil. *Gastrointestinal Endoscopy*, 47: 57-61.

MacKenzie GJ, et al, (1964), Haemodynamic effects of external cardiac compression. *Lancet*, 1: 1342-1345.

Magnan V, (1876), *On Alcoholism: The Various Forms of Alcoholic Delirium and their Treatment.* Published by H.K. Lewis, London, UK.

Maguire EA, et al, (2000), Navigation-related structural change in the hippocampi of taxi drivers. *Proceedings of the National Academy of Sciences*, 97: 4398-4403.

Mahowald MW, Ettinger MG, (1990), Things that go bump in the night: The parasomnias revisited. *Journal of Clinical Neurophysiology*, 7: 119-143.

Mainzer J, (1979), Awareness, muscle relaxants and balanced anaesthesia. *Canadian Anaesthetic Society Journal*, 26: 386-393.

Malhotra AK, et al, (1996), NMDA receptor function and human cognition: The effects of ketamine in healthy volunteers. *Neuropsychopharmacology*, 14: 301-307.

Maltby JR, et al, (1980), Comparison of flunitrazepam and thiopentone for induction of general anaesthesia. *Canadian Anaesthetists Society Journal*, 27: 331-337.

Manchikanti L, Singh V, (2004), Managing phantom pain. *Pain Physician*, 7: 365-375.

Manousakis E, (2006), Founding quantum theory on the basis of consciousness. *Foundations of Physics*, 36: 795-838.

Marcet A, (1806), An account of the effects of a large dose of Laudanum taken internally and of the means used to counteract those effects. pages 77-82.

Mariani A, (1892), *Coca and its Therapeutic Application.* Second edition. Published by J.N. Jaros, New York, USA.

Marsh MN, (2012), *Out-of-Body and Near-Death Experiences: Brain-State Phenomena or Glimpses of Immortality?* published by Oxford University Press, UK, ISBN 978-0-19-957150-5.

Marsch LA, et al, (2001), Effects of infusion rate of intravenously administered morphine on physiological, psychomotor, and self-reported measures in humans. *Journal of Pharmacology and Experimental Therapeutics,* 299: 1056-1065.

Martens PR, (1994), Near-death-experiences in out-of-hospital cardiac arrest survivors. Meaningful phenomena or just fantasy of death? *Resuscitation,* 27: 171-175.

Martens PR, et al, (2010), External cardiac massage improved cerebral tissue oxygenation shown by near-infrared spectroscopy during transcatheter aortic valve implantation. *Resuscitation,* 81: 1590-1591.

Martin WR, Fraser HF, (1961), A comparative study of the physiological and subjective effects of heroin and morphine administered intravenously to postaddicts. *Journal of Pharmacology and Experimental Therapeutics,* 133: 388-399.

Marzano C,et al, (2011), Recalling and forgetting dreams: Theta and alpha oscillations during sleep predict subsequent dream recall. *The Journal of Neuroscience,* 31: 6674-6683.

Mashour GA, et al, (2005), Psychosurgery, past, present, and future. *Brain Research Reviews,* 48: 409-419.

Mashour GA, (2008), Integrating the science of consciousness and anesthesia. *Anesthesia & Analgesia,* 103: 975-982.

Mashour GA, (2010), Posttraumatic stress disorder after intraoperative awareness and high-risk surgery. *Anesthesia & Analgesia,* 110: 668-670.

Maupassant H. Guy de, *The Horla,* pages 1-35, in. *Short Stories of the Tragedy and Comedy of Life,* published by the Saint Dunstan Society, Akron, Ohio, USA, 1903.

Mayer-Gross W, (1951), Experimental psychoses and other mental abnormalities produced by drugs. *British Medical Journal,* August 11: 317-321.

McAleavy JC, et al, (1961), The effect of PCO_2 on the depth of anesthesia. *Anesthesiology,* 22: 260-264.

McCann ME, et al, (2002), The Bispectral Index and explicit recall during the intraoperative Wake-up Test for scoliosis surgery. *Anesthesia & Analgesia,* 94: 1474-1478.

McClelland S, Maxwell RE, (2007), Hemispherectomy for intractable epilepsy in adults: the first reported series. *Annals of Neurology*, 61: 372-376.

McCloskey DI, (1978), Kinesthetic sensibility. *Physiological Reviews*, 58: 763-820.

McDonald JL, (1982), Systolic and mean arterial pressures during manual and mechanical CPR in humans. *Annals of Emergency Medicine*, 11: 292-295.

McFie J, (1961), The effects of hemispherectomy on intellectual functioning in cases of infantile hemiplegia. *Journal of Neurology, Neurosurgery & Psychiatry*, 24: 240-249.

McGeer V, (2003), The trouble with Mary. *Pacific Philosophical Quarterly*, 84: 384-393.

McNamara P, et al, (2005), A "Jekyll and Hyde" within: aggressive versus friendly interactions in REM and Non-REM dreams. *Psychological Science*, 16: 130-136.

McNamara P, et al, (2007), Representation of the self in REM and NREM dreams. *Dreaming*, 17: 113-116.

McNicholas WT, (2002), Impact of sleep on respiratory muscle function. *Monaldi Archives for Chest Disease*, 57: 277-280.

McNiel DE, et al, (2000), The relationship between command hallucinations and violence. *Psychiatric Services*, 51: 1288-1292.

McQuaid KR, Laine L, (2008), A systematic review and meta-analysis of randomized, controlled trials of moderate sedation for routine endoscopic procedures. *Gastrointestinal Endoscopy*, 67: 910-23.

Mecklinger A, et al, (1998), Event-related potential evidence for a specific recognition memory defect in adult survivors of cerebral hypoxia. *Brain*, 121: 1919-1935.

Meehl PE, Scriven M, (1956), Compatibility of Science and ESP. *Science*, 123: 14-15.

Mehta MA, et al, (2009), Amygdala, hippocampal and corpus callosum size following severe early institutional deprivation: The English and Romanian Adoptees Study Pilot. *Journal of Child Psychology and Psychiatry*, 50: 943-951.

Meigs JA, (1857), *Catalogue of Human Crania.* Published by J.B. Lippincott & Co., Philadelphia, USA.

Melnick M, Myrianthopoulos NC, (1987), Studies in neural tube defects II. Pathologic findings in a prospectively collected series of anencephalics. *American Journal of Medical Genetics*, 26: 797-810.

Melzack R, (1992), Phantom limbs. *Scientific American*, April: 266: 90-96.

Merker B, (2007), Consciousness without a cerebral cortex: a challenge for neuroscience and medicine. *Behaviourial and Brain Sciences,* 30: 63-81.

Merwin S, (1908), *Drugging a Nation. The Story of China and the Opium Curse.* Published by Fleming H. Revell Company, UK.

Messner M, et al, (2003), The Bispectral Index declines during neuromuscular block in fully awake persons. *Anesthesia & Analgesia,* 97: 488-491.

Metzinger T, (2005), Out-of-body experiences as the origin of the concept of a "soul". *Mind & Matter,* 3: 57-84.

Mildh LH, et al, (2001), The concentration-effect relationship of the rerpiratory depressant effects of alfentanil and fentanyl. *Anesthesia & Analgesia,* 93: 939-946.

Miller JB, et al, (1961), The efficiency of cardiac massage in ventricular fibrillation. Description of an instance of recovery of consciousness without spontaneous heartbeat. *British Journal of Anaesthesia,* 33: 22-23.

Milton J, Wiseman R, (1999), Does psi exist? Lack of replication of an anomalous process of information transfer. *Psychological Bulletin,* 125: 387-391.

Milton J, Wiseman R, (2001), Does psi exist? Reply to Storm and Ertel (2001). *Psychological Bulletin,* 127: 434-438.

Min B-K, (2010), A thalamic reticular networking model of consciousness. *Theoretical Biology and Medical Modelling,* 7: 10.

Mirin SM, et al, (1976), Psychopathology and mood during heroin use: Acute vs chronic effects. *Archives of General Psychiatry,* 33: 1503-1508.

Mitchell SW, (1896), Remarks on the effects of Anhelonium Lewenii. (The Mescal button). *British Medical Journal,* December 5: 1625-1629.

Mlynash M, et al, (2010) Temporal and spatial profile of brain diffusion-weighted MRI after cardiac arrest. *Stroke,* 41: 1665-1672.

Moerman N, et al, (1993), Awareness and recall during general anesthesia. Facts and feelings. *Anesthesiology,* 79: 454-464.

Mogil JS, et al, (2003), The melanocortin-1 receptor gene mediates female-specific mechanisms of analgesia in mice and humans. *Proceedings of the National Academy of Science,* 100: 4867-4872.

Mohandas A, Chou SN, (1971), Brain death. A clinical and pathological study. *Journal of Neurosurgery,* 35: 211-218.

Moody RA, (1976), *Life after Life,* published Bantam, U.S.A., ISBN 0-553-27484-8.

Morgan H, (1990), Dostoevsky's epilepsy: A case report and comparison. *Surgical Neurology,* 33: 413-416.

Morgan HL, et al, (2010), Exploring the impact of ketamine on the experience of illusory body ownership. *Biological Psychiatry,* 69:35-41.

MORI, (1998), *Paranormal Survey.* From the internet during 2006, at internet address: http://www.mori.com/polls/1998/s980205.shtml

Mortimer WG, (1901), *Peru: History of Coca. "The Divine Plant" of the Incas.* Published by J.H. Vail & Company, New York, USA.

Morton LM, et al, (2006), Reporting participation in epidemiologic studies: A survey of practice. *American Journal of Epidemiology,* 163: 197-203.

Morton SG, (1839), *Crania Americana,* Published by J. Dobson, Philadelphia, USA.

Morton SG, (1868), *The Races of Man,* 9th edition, J.B. Lippincott & Co., Philadephia, USA.

Morton WA, Stockton GG, (2000), Methylphenidate abuse and psychiatric side-effects. *Primary Care Companion Journal of Clinical Psychiatry,* 2: 159-164.

Morton WJ, (1880), *The Invention of Anaesthetic Inhalation, or "Discovery of Anaesthesia".* D. Appleton and Company, New York.

Moulaert VRMP, et al, (2007), Activity and Life After Survival of a Cardiac Arrest (ALASCA) and the effectiveness of an early intervention service: design of a randomised controlled trial. *BMC Cardiovascular Disorders,* 7: 26. (doi:10.1186/1471-2261-7-26)

Muldoon SJ, Carrington H, (1973), *The Projection of the Astral Body.* Published by Samuel Weiser Inc, Maine, USA, ISBN 0-87728-069-X.

Müller FM, (1879), *The Sacred Books of the East: Translated by Various Oriental Scholars. The Upanishads, Part I. The Khandogya Upanishad.* Published by The Clarendon Press, Oxford, UK.

Munoz A, et al, (2007), Muscle glycogen depletion pattern and metabolic response in bulls after bullfighting. *Analecta Veterinaria,* 27: 5-10.

Murphy T, (2001), Near-death experiences in Thailand. *Journal of Near Death Studies,* 19: 161-178.

Murray CJL, Lopez AD, (1997), Mortality by cause for eight regions of the world: Global Burden of Disease Study. *Lancet,* 349: 1269-1276.

Mutangi T, (2008), Religion, law and human rights in Zimbabwe. *African Human Rights Law Journal,* 8: 526-545.

Myers FWH, (1903), *Human Personality and its Survival of Bodily Death.* Volume 1, published by Longmans, Green and Co., UK.

N

Nagdyman N, et al, (2003), Cerebral oxygenation measured by near-infrared spectroscopy during circulatory arrest and cardiopulmonary resuscitation. *British Journal of Anaesthesia,* 91: 438-442.

Nahm M, (2009), Terminal lucidity in people with mental illness and other mental disability: An overview and implications for possible explanatory models. *Journal of Near-Death Studies,* 28: 87-106.

Navalta CP, et al, (2006), Effects of childhood sexual abuse on neuropsychological and cognitive function in college women. *Journal of Neuropsychiatry and Clinical Neurosciences,* 18: 45-53.

Nelson H, (2006), Laparoscopic colectomy for cancer. A tale of two studies. *Annals of Surgery,* 245: 8-9.

Nelson KR, et al (2006a), Does the arousal system contribute to near death experience? *Neurology,* 66:1003-1009.

Nelson KR, et al (2007), Out-of-body experience and arousal. *Neurology,* 68: 794-795.

Nelson KR, (2011), *The Spiritual Doorway in the Brain: A Neurologist's Search for the God Experience.* Published by Dutton, New York, USA, ISBN 978-0-525-95188-9.

Nelson LE, et al, (2004), Rested and refreshed after anesthesia? Overlapping neurobiologic mechanisms of sleep and anesthesia. *Anesthesiology,* 100: 1341-1342.

Ng SH, et al, (2010), Dynamic bicultural brains: fMRI study of their flexible neural representation of self and significant others in response to culture primes. *Asian Journal of Social Psychology,* 13, 83-91.

Nichols DE, (2004), Hallucinogens. *Pharmacology & Therapeutics,* 101: 131-181.

Nielson JM, Sedgwick RP, (1949), Instincts and emotions in an anencephalic monster. *Journal of Nervous and Mental Disease,* 110: 387-94.

Nielsen T, (2012), Variations in dream recall frequency and dream theme diversity by age and sexs. *Frontiers in Neurology,* vol 3: pub 106, doi:10.3389/fneur.2012.00106

Nietzsche F, (1909), *Beyond Good and Evil,* Volume 5 in the. *Complete Works of Friedrich Nietzsche,* edited by Dr. Oscar Levy, published by T. N. Foulis, London, UK.

Nietzsche F, (1914), *Thus Spake Zarathustra*, Volume 11 in the. *Complete Works of Friedrich Nietzsche*, edited by Dr. Oscar Levy, published by The Macmillan Company, New York, USA.

Niu H,et al, (2012), Revealing topological organization of human brain functional networks with resting-state functional near infrared spectroscopy. *PLoS ONE* 7(9): e45771. doi:10.1371/journal.pone.0045771

Noirhomme Q, et al, (2010), Functional Neuroimaging approaches to the changing borders of consciousness. *Journal of Psychophysiology,* 24: 68-75.

Nolan JP, et al, (2008), Post-cardiac arrest syndrome: Epidemiology, pathophysiology, treatment, and prognostication A Scientific Statement from the International Liaison Committee on Resuscitation; the American Heart Association Emergency Cardiovascular Care Committee; the Council on Cardiovascular Surgery and Anesthesia; the Council on Cardiopulmonary, Perioperative, and Critical Care; the Council on Clinical Cardiology; the Council on Stroke. *Resuscitation,* 79: 350-379.

Norton JW, Corbett JJ, (2000), Visual perceptual abnormalities: hallucinations and illusions. *Seminars in Neurology,* 20: 111-121.

Novak P, (2002), Division of the self: life after death and the binary soul doctrine. *Journal of Near-Death Studies,* 20: 143-189.

O

Oehme P, Goerig M, (1998), Rückenmarksanästhesie mt Kokain. Die Prioritätskontroverse zur Lumbalanäesthesie. *Deutsches Ärzteblatt,* 41: A2556-A2558.

Ogawa K, et al, (2006), Cortical regions activated after rapid eye movements during REM sleep. *Sleep and Biological Rhythms,* 4: 63-71.

Ojemann JG, Kelley WM, (2002), The frontal lobe role in memory: a review of convergent evidence and implications for the Wada memory test. *Epilepsy & Behavior,* 3: 309-315.

Okawa K, et al, (2002), A comparison of propofol and dexmedetomidine for intravenous sedation: A randomized, crossover study of the effects on the central and autonomic nervous systems. *Anesthesia & Analgesia,* 110: 415-418.

Orenstein A, (2002), Religion and paranormal belief. *Journal for the Scientific Study of Religion,* 41, 301-311.

Oriol A, et al, (1968), Hemodynamic observations during closed-chest cardiac massage. *Canadian Medical Association Journal*, 98: 841-843.

Orser BA, et al, (2008), Awareness during anesthesia. *Canadian Medical Association Journal*, 178: 185-188.

Ortiz T, et al, (2011), Recruitment of occipital cortex during sensory substitution training linked to subjective experience of seeing in people with blindness. *PLoS ONE* 6(8): e23264. doi:10.1371/journal.pone.0023264

Osborn AG, et al, (1967), Effects of thiopental sedation on learning and memory. *Science,* 157: 574-576.

Osis K, Haraldsson E, (1986), *At the Hour of Death.* published by Hastings House, USA , ISBN 0-8038-9279-9.

Osterman JE, et al, (2001), Awareness under anesthesia and the development of posttraumatic stress disorder. *General Hospital Psychiatry,* 23: 198-204.

Oswald I, (1959), Sudden bodily jerks on falling asleep. *Brain,* 82: 92-103.

Otis AB, et al, (1946), Performance as related to the composition of alveolar air. *American Journal of Physiology,* 146: 207-221.

Oudiette D, et al, (2012), Dreaming without REM sleep. *Consciousness and Cognition,* 21: 1129-1140.

Overeem S, et al, (2004), Corticospinal excitability during laughter: implications for cataplexy and the comparison with REM sleep atonia. *Journal of Sleep Research,* 13: 257-264.

Oye I, et al, (1992), Effects of ketamine on sensory perception: Evidence for a role of N-Methyl-D-Aspartate receptors. *Journal of Pharmacology and Experimental Therapeutics,* 260: 1209-1213.

Ozan E, et al, (2010), Male genital self-mutilation as a psychotic solution. *Israel Journal of Psychiatry & Related Sciences,* 47: 297-303.

P

Pagani M, et al, (1998), Effect of acclimatization to altitude on learning. *Cortex,* 34: 243-251.

Paine T, (1831), *The Theological Works of Thomas Paine.* Published by "The Advocates for Common Sense", Boston, USA.

Pandit JJ, Cook TM, (2013), National Institute for Clinical Excellence guidance on measuring depth of anaesthesia: limitations of EEG-based technology. *British Journal of Anaesthesia,* 110: 325-328.

Paqueron X, et al, (2002), Is morphine-induced sedation synonymous with analgesia during intravenous morphine titration? *British Journal of Anaesthesia,* 89: 697-701.

Paqueron X, et al, (2003), The phenomenology of body image distortions induced by regional anesthesia. *Brain,* 126: 702-712.

Paqueron X, et al, (2004), Influence of sensory and proprioceptive Impairment on the development of phantom limb syndrome during regional anesthesia. *Anesthesiology,* 100: 979-986.

Parbrook GD, et al, (1989) Comparison of i.v. sedation with midazolam and inhalation sedation with isoflurane in dental outpatients. *British Journal of Anaesthesia,* 63, 81-86.

Parke AR, Horton CL, (2009), A re-examination of the interference hypothesis on dream recall and dream salience. *International Journal of Dream Research,* 2: 60-69.

Parkes JD, (1986). The parasomnias. *Lancet,* 2, 1021-1025.

Parkhouse J, et al, (1960), Nitrous oxide in relation to mental performance. *Journal of Pharmacology and Experimental Therapeutics,* 128: 44-54.

Parnia S, et al, (2001), A qualitative and quantitative study of the incidence, features and aetiology of near-death experiences in cardiac arrest survivors. *Resuscitation,* 48: 149-156.

Parnia S, (2006), *What Happens When We Die? A Groundbreaking Study into the Nature of Life and Death.* Published by Hay House, USA, ISBN 978-1-4019-0710-5.

Parnia S, (2007), Do reports of consciousness during cardiac arrest hold the key to discovering the nature of consciousness? *Medical Hypotheses,* 69: 933-937.

Pasricha S, Stevenson I, (1986), Near death experiences in India. *Journal of Nervous and Mental Disease,* 174: 165-170.

Patkl A, Shelgaonkar VC, (2011), A comparison of equisedative infusions of propofol and midazolam for conscious sedation during spinal anaesthesia - a prospective randomized study. *Journal of Anaesthesiology Clinical Pharmacology,* 27: 47-53.

Patterson JR, Grabois M, (1986), Locked-in syndrome: a review of 139 cases. *Stroke,* 17: 758-764.

Paul R, et al, (2008), The relationship between early life stress and microstructural integrity of the corpus callosum in a non-clinical population. *Neuropsychiatric Disease and Treatment*, 4: 193-201.

Payne EJ, (1880), Voyages of the Elizabethan Seamen to America. Thirteen Original Narratives Selected from the Collection of Hakluyt. Published by Thomas de la Rue & Co., London, England.

Pearson J, et al, (1978), Morphology of defectively perfused brains in patients with persistent extracranial circulation. *Annals of the New York Academy of Sciences*, 315: 265-271.

Penfield W, (1955), The role of the temporal cortex in certain psychical phenomena. *The Journal of Mental Science*, 101: 451-465.

Penfield W, Boldrey E, (1937), Somatic and sensory representation in the cerebral cortex of man as studied by electrical stimulation. *Brain*, 60: 389-443.

Pereira J, (1842), *The Elements of Materia Medica and Therapeutics*, Volume 1, 2nd edition, published by Longman, Brown, Green, and Longmans, London.

Perria L, et al, (1961), Determination of side of cerebral dominance with amybarbital. *Archives of Neurology*, 4: 173-181.

Petronis A, (2006), Epigenetics and twins: three variations on the theme. *Trends in Genetics*, 22: 347-350.

Pfenninger EG, et al, (2002), Cognitive impairment after small-dose ketamine isomers in comparison to equianalgesic racemic ketamine in human volunteers. *Anesthesiology*, 96:357-366.

Phillips AA, et al, (1993), Recall of intraoperative events after general anaesthesia and cardiopulmonary bypass. *Canadian Journal of Anesthesia*, 40: 922-926.

Picard F, Craig AD, (2009), Ecstatic epileptic seizures: A potential window on the neural basis for human self-awareness. *Epilepsy & Behavior*, 16: 539-546.

Plato, (1900), *Dialogues of Plato. Phaedo.* Translated by Benjamin Jowett, published by The Colonial Press, London and New York.

Podmore F, (1909), *Telepathic Hallucinations. The New View of Ghosts.* Published by Frederick A. Stokes Company, New York, USA.

Pollard RJ, et al, (2007), Intraoperative awareness in a regional medical system. *Anesthesiology*, 106: 269-274.

Pollock JE, et al, (2000), Sedation during spinal anesthesia. *Anesthesiology*, 93: 728-734.

Pomarol-Clotet E, et al, (2006), Psychological effects of ketamine in healthy volunteers. *British Journal of Psychiatry,* 189: 173-179.

Posner MI, et al, (2006), Analyzing and shaping human attentional networks. *Neural Networks,* 19: 1422-1429.

Potts M, (2002), The evidential value of near-death experiences for belief in life after death. *Journal of Near Death Studies,* 20: 233-258.

Prause G, et al, (1998), Die präklinische Blutgasanalyse. Teil 1: Der Stellenwert der präklinischen Blutgasanalyse. *Der Anaesthesist,* 47: 400-405.

Prescott F, et al, (1946), Tubocurarine hydrochloride as an adjunct to anaesthesia. Report on 180 cases. *Lancet,* 2: 80-84.

Prevoznik SJ, Eckenhoff JE, (1964), Phantom sensations during spinal anesthesia. *Anesthesiology,* 25: 767-770.

Proske U, Gandevia SC, (2009), The kinaesthetic senses. *Journal of Physiology,* 587: 4139-4146.

Proske U, Gandevia SC, (2012), The proprioceptive senses: Their roles in signalling body shape, body position and movement, and muscle force. *Physiological Reviews,* 92: 1651-1697.

Pryor KO, et al, (2004), Enhanced visual memory effect for negative versus positive emotional content is potentiated at sub-anaesthetic concentrations of thiopental. *British Journal of Anaesthesia,* 93: 348-355.

Pytliak M, et al, (2011), Serotonin receptors - from molecular biology to clinical applications. *Physiological Research,* 60: 15-25.

Q

Qin W, et al, (2013), The development of visual areas depends differently on visual experience. *PLoS ONE* 8(1): e53784. doi:10.1371/journal.pone.0053784

Quincey T de, (1823),. *Confessions of an English Opium-Eater.* 2nd edition, pub. Taylor and Hessey, London, UK.

Quintin L, et al, (1981), High dose fentanyl anaesthesia with oxygen for aorto-coronary bypass surgery. *Canadian Anaesthetists Society Journal,* 28: 314-320.

R

Radin DI, Nelson RD, (1989), Evidence for consciousness-related anomalies in random physical systems. *Foundations of Physics,* 19: 1499-1514.

Rains AJH, Ritchie HD, (eds.), (1981),. *Bailey & Love's Short Practice of Surgery.* 18th edition, published by H.K. Lewis & Co. Ltd., London, England, ISBN 0718604504.

Ramachandran VS, Hubbard EM, (2003), Hearing colors, tasting shapes. *Scientific American,* May 2003: 52-59.

Rampersad SE, Mulroy MF, (2005), A case of awareness despite an "Adequate Depth of Anesthesia" as indicated by a Bispectral Index® monitor. *Anesthesia & Analgesia,* 100: 1363-13644.

Ramsay MAE, et al, (1974), Controlled sedation with alphaloxone-alphadolone. *British Medical Journal,* 2: 656-659.

Ranta SOV, et al, (1998), Awareness with recall during general anesthesia: Incidence and risk factors. *Anesthesia & Analgesia,* 86: 1084-1089.

Rast E, (2012), De SE puzzles, the knowledge argument, and the formation of internal knowledge. *Analysis and Metaphysics,* 11: 25-52.

Rawlings M, (1979), *Beyond Death's Door.* Published by Bantam Books, New York, ISBN 0553229702.

Rechtschaffen A, (1978), The single-mindedness and isolation of dreams. *Sleep,* 1: 97-109.

Reder LM, et al, (2006), Midazolam does not inhibit association formation, just its storage and strengthening. *Psychopharmacology (Berlin),* 188: 462-471.

Rees G, et al, (2002), Neural correlates of consciousness in humans. *Nature Reviews: Neuroscience,* 3: 261-270.

Refsum HE, (1963), Relationship between state of consciousness and hypoxaemia and hypercapnia in patients with pulmonary insufficiency, breathing air. *Clinical Science,* 25: 361-367.

Reich DL, (1989), Ketamine: an update on the first twenty-five years of clinical experience. *Canadian Journal of Anesthesia,* 36: 186-197.

Reinstrup P, et al, (1997), Regional cerebral blood flow (SPECT), during anaesthesia with isoflurane and nitrous oxide anaesthesia in humans. *British Journal of Anaesthesia,* 78: 407-411.

Reinstrup P, et al, (2008), Regional cerebral metabolic rate (positron emission tomography) during inhalation of nitrous oxide 50% in humans. *British Journal of Anaesthesia*, 100: 66-71.

Reis A dos, (2009), Sigmund Freud (1856-1939) and Karl Köller (1857-1944) and the Discovery of Local Anesthesia. *Revista Brasileira de Anestesiologia*, 59: 244-257.

Report of the International Opium Commission, Shanghai, China, February 1 to February 26, 1909, Volume I,. *Report of the Proceedings*. Published by the North-China Daily News and Herald Limited, Shanghai, China, 1909.

Resnikoff S, et al, (2004), Global data on visual impairment in the year 2002. *Bulletin of the World Health Organization*, 82: 844-851.

Rhine JB, Pratt JG, (1957), *Parapsychology: Frontier Science of the Mind*. Published by Charles C. Thomas publisher, USA, ISBN 398-01580-5.

Ridder D de, et al, (2007), Visualizing out-of-body experience in the brain. *New England Journal of Medicine*, 357: 1829-1833.

Ring K, Lawrence M, (1993), Further evidence for veridical perception during near-death experiences. *Journal of Near-Death Studies*, 11: 223-229.

Ritchie SJ, et al, (2012), Failing the future: Three unsuccessful attempts to replicate Bem's 'retroactive facilitation of recall' effect. *PLoS ONE*, Volume 7, Issue 3, e33423.

Rivas T, (2003), The survivalist interpretation of recent studies into the near-death experience. *The Journal of Religion and Psychical Research*, 26: 27-31.

Rivas T, (2008), Een gesprek met TG over de Man met het Gebit. *Terugkeer*, 19: 12-21.

Ro T, Rafal R, (2006), Visual restoration in cortical blindness: Insights from natural and TMS-induced blindsight. *Neuropsychological Rehabilitation*, 16: 377-396.

Roberts PJP, Whelan WJ, (1960), The mechanism of carbohydrase action. 5. Action of human salivary α-amylase on amylopectin and glycogen. *Biochemical Journal*, 76: 246-253.

Robinson TE, Berridge KC, (2000), The psychology and neurobiology of addiction: an incentive-sensitization view. *Addiction*, 95 (Supplement 2): S91-S117.

Robson JG, et al, (1960), The effect of inhaling dilute nitrous oxide upon recent memory and time estimation. *Canadian Anaesthetic Society Journal*, 7: 399-410.

Rodin EA, (1980), The reality of death experiences. A personal perspective. *Journal of Nervous and Mental Disease,* 168: 259-263.

Rogo DS, (1989), *The Return from Silence. A Study of Near-Death Experiences.* Published by The Aquarian Press, UK, ISBN 0-85030-736-8.

Roode A de, et al, (2000), A comparison of the effects of propofol and midazolam on memory during two levels of sedation by using target-controlled infusion. *Anesthesia & Analgesia,* 91: 1056-1061.

Ropper AH, (1984), Unusual spontaneous movements in brain-dead patients. *Neurology,* 34: 1089-1092.

Rosadini G, Rossi GF, (1967), On the suggested cerebral dominance for consciousness. *Brain,* 90: 101-112.

Rosen DH, (1975), Suicide survivors – A follow-up study of persons who survived jumping from the Golden Gate and San Francisco-Oakland Bay bridges. *Western Journal of Medicine,* 122: 289-294.

Rosenberg H, et al, (1979) Abuse of nitrous oxide. *Anesthesia & Analgesia,* 58, 104-106.

Rosenberg K, et al, (2008), Language related reorganization in adult brain with slow growing glioma: fMRI prospective case-study. *Neurocase,* 14: 465-473.

Rossen R, et al, (1943), Acute arrest of cerebral circulation in man. *Archives of Neurology and Psychiatry,* 50: 510-528.

Rudski J, (2003), What does a "superstitious" person believe? Impressions of participants. *Journal of General Psychology,* 130: 431-435.

Russell IF, (1995), Intraoperative awareness and the isolated forearm technique. *British Journal of Anaesthesia,* 75: 819.

Russell IF, Wang M, (2001), Absence of memory for intra-operative information during surgery with total intravenous anaesthesia. *British Journal of Anaesthesia,* 86: 196-202.

S

Saavedra-Aguilar JC, Gomez-Jeria JS, (1989), A neurobiological model for near-death experiences. *Journal of Near-Death Studies,* 7: 205-222.

Saavedra-Aguilar JC, Gomez-Jeria JS, (1989a), Response to commentaries on "A Neurobiological Model for Near-Death Experiences". *Journal of Near-Death Studies,* 7: 265-272.

Sabom M, (1982), *Recollections of Death*. Published by Corgi Books, London, UK, ISBN 0552120537.

Sabom M, (1998), *Light & Death*. published by Zondervan Publishing House, USA, 1998, ISBN 0310219922.

Safar P, (1988), Resuscitation from clinical death: Pathophysiologic limits and therapeutic potentials. *Critical Care Medicine,* 16: 923-941.

Samuelsson P, et al, (2007), Late psychological symptoms after awareness among consecutively included surgical patients. *Anesthesiology,* 106: 26-32.

Sanders RD, et al, (2012), Unresponsiveness ≠ Unconsciousness. *Anesthesiology,* 116, 1-14.

Sandin RH, et al, (2000), Awareness during anaesthesia: a prospective case study. *Lancet,* 355: 707-711.

Sansom AE, (1865), *Chloroform: Its Action and Administration. A Handbook.* Published by John Churchill and Sons, London, UK.

Sarton E, et al, (2000), Sex differences in morphine analgesia. An experimental study in healthy volunteers. *Anesthesiology,* 93: 1245-1254.

Sartori P, et al, (2006), A prospectively studied near-death experience with corroborated out-of-body perceptions and unexplained healing. *Journal of Near-Death Studies,* 25: 69-84.

Sasselov DD, Valencia D, (2010), Planets we could call home. *Scientific American,* August 2010: 38-45.

Schell RM, Cole DJ, (2000), Cerebral monitoring: jugular venous oximetry. *Anesthesia & Analgesia,* 90: 559-566.

Searle WS, (1881), *A New Form of Nervous Disease together with An Essay on Erythroloxylon Coca.* Published by Fords, Howard & Hulbert, New York, USA.

Shadden BB, Holland AL, (1992), Linguistic performance of cardiac arrest survivors on a neuropsychological screening test. *Clinical Aphasiology,* 21: 343-356.

Shafer A, et al, (1988) Pharmacokinetics and pharmacodynamics of propofol infusions during general anesthesia. *Anesthesiology,* 69: 348-356.

Shanahan M, (2005), Global access, embodiment, and the conscious subject. *Journal of Consciousness Studies,* 12: 46-66.

Shephard RJ, (1956), Physiological changes and psychomotor performance during acute hypoxia. *Journal of Applied Physiology,* 9: 343-351.

Shewmon DA, et al, (1999), Consciousness in congenitally decorticate children: developmental vegetative state as a self-fulfilling prophecy. *Developmental Medicine & Child Neurology,* 41: 364-374.

Schiff ND, (2008), Central thalamic contributions to arousal regulation and neurological disorders of consciousness. *Annals of the New York Academy of Science,* 1129: 105-118.

Schiff PL, (2002), Opium and its alkaloids. *American Journal of Pharmaceutical Education,* 66: 186-194.

Schiller FCS, (1891),. *Riddles of the Sphinx.* Written under the pseudonym "Troglodyte", published by Swan Sonnenschein & Co., Paternoster Square, London, UK.

Schlaug G, et al, (2009), Evidence for plasticity in white-matter tracts of patients with chronic Broca's aphasia undergoing intense intonation-based speech therapy. *Annals of the New York Academy of Sciences,* 1169: 385-394.

Schnakers C, et al, (2008), Cognitive function in the locked-in syndrome. *Journal of Neurology,* 255: 323-330.

Schnakers C, et al, (2009), Detecting consciousness in a total locked-in syndrome: An active event-related paradigm. *Neurocase,* 15: 271-277.

Schneider G, (2003), Quality of perioperative AEP - variability of expert ratings. *British Journal of Anaesthesia,* 91: 905-908.

Schneider G, Kochs EF, (2007), The search for structures and mechanisms controlling anesthesia-induced unconsciousness. *Anesthesiology,* 107: 195-198.

Scholz J, et al, (2009), Training induces changes in white-matter architecture. *Nature Neuroscience,* 12: 1370-1371.

Schredl M, Wittman L, (2005), Dreaming: a psychological view. *Schweizer Archiv für Neurologie und Psychiatrie,* 156: 484-492.

Schredl M, Reinhard I, (2008), Gender differences in dream recall: a meta-analysis. *Journal of Sleep Research,* 17: 125-131.

Schredl M, (2009), Home dream recall in children and young adults. *International Journal of Dream Research,* 2: 58-59.

Schwabe L, Blanke O, (2007), Cognitive neuroscience of ownership and agency. *Consciousness and Cognition,* 16: 661-666.

Schwaninger J, et al, (2002), A prospective analysis of near-death experiences in cardiac arrest patients. *Journal of Near-Death Studies,* 20: 215-232.

Schwartz S, Maquet P, (2002), Sleep imaging and the neuropsychological assessment of dreams. *Trends in Cognitive Sciences,* 6: 23-30.

Schwender D, et al, (1998), Power spectral analysis of the electroencephalogram during increasing end-expiratory concentrations of isoflurane, desflurane and sevoflurane. *Anaesthesia,* 53: 335-342.

Sebel PS, et al, (2004), The incidence of awareness during anesthesia: A multicenter United States study. *Anesthesia & Analgesia,* 99: 833-839.

Seol TK, et al (2012), Bispectral index and their relation with consciousness of the patients who receive desflurane or sevoflurane anesthesia during wake-up test for spinal surgery for correction. *Korean Journal of Anesthesiology,* 62: 13-18.

Serafetinides EA, et al, (1965), Intracarotid sodium amylobarbitone and cerebral dominance for speech and consciousness. *Brain,* 88: 107-130.

Sharpless BA, et al, (2010), Isolated sleep paralysis and fearful isolated sleep paralysis in outpatients With panic attacks. *Journal of Clinical Psychology,* 66: 1292-1306.

Short EB, et al, (2010), Regional brain activation during meditation shows time and practice effects: an exploratory fMRI study. *Evidence-based Complementary and Alternative Medicine,* 7: 121-127.

Shulman RM, et al, (2007), A case of unusual substance abuse causing myeloneuropathy. *Spinal Cord,* 45: 314-317.

Silva R de, et al, (1999), Regional cerebral perfusion and Amytal distribution during the Wada Test. *Journal of Nuclear Medicine,* 40: 747-752.

Simner J, et al, (2006), Synaesthesia: The prevalence of atypical cross-modal experiences. *Perception,* 35: 1024-1033.

Simpson JY, (1847), Discovery of a new anaesthetic agent more efficient than sulphuric aether. *Provincial Medical and Surgical Journal,* 11: 656-658. This was exactly the same article as published in. *Lancet,* November 21, 1847: 549-550.

Sims JM, (1877), History of the Discovery of Anaesthesia. *Virginia Medical Monthly,* May 1877: 3-14.

Smit R, (2011), Almost brainless - yet lucid and intelligent: Implications for understanding NDEs and consciousness. *Journal of Near-Death Studies,* 29: 482-486.

Smith A, (1966), Speech and other functions after left (dominant) hemispherectomy. *Journal of Neurology, Neurosurgery and Psychiatry,* 29: 467-471.

Smith E, Delargy M, (2005), Locked-in syndrome. *British Medical Journal,* 330: 406-409.

Smith GM, Beecher HK, (1959), Measurement of "mental clouding" and other subjective effects of morphine. *Journal of Pharmacology and Experimental Therapeutics,* 126: 50-62.

459

Smith GM, Beecher HK, (1962), Subjective effects of heroin and morphine in normal subjects. *Journal of Pharmacology and Experimental Therapeutics,* 136: 47-52.

Smith GM, et al, (1962a), Objective evidence of mental effects of heroin, morphine and placebo in normal subjects. *Journal of Pharmacology and Experimental Therapeutics,* 136: 53-58.

Smith SM, et al, (1947), The lack of cerebral effects of d-tubocurarine. *Anesthesiology,* 8: 1-14.

Søgaard AJ, et al, (2004), The Oslo Health Study: The impact of self-selection in a large, population-based survey. . *International Journal for Equity in Health,* 3:3. (Article available at: http://www.equityhealthj.com/content/3/1/3)

Spencer JD, et al, (1976), Halothane Abuse in Hospital Personnel. *Journal of the American Medical Association,* 235: 1034-1035.

Spitzka EA, (1903), A study of the brain-weights of men notable in the professions, arts and sciences. *The Philadelphia Medical Journal,* May 2: 1-14.

Spitzka EA, (1907), A study of the brains of six eminent scientists and scholars belonging to the American Anthropometric Society, together with a description of the skull of Professor E. D. Cope. *Transactions of the American Philosophical Society, (New Series),* 21: 175-308.

Stanley TH, et al, (1973), The effects of high-dose morphine on fluid and blood requirements in open-heart operations. *Anesthesiology,* 38: 536-541.

Stanley TH, Lathrop GD, (1977), Urinary excretion of morphine during and after valvular and coronary-artery surgery. *Anesthesiology,* 46: 166-169.

Stanley TH, et al, (1979), Fentanyl-oxygen anesthesia for coronary artery surgery: cardiovascular and antidiuretic hormone responses. *Canadian Anaesthetists Society Journal,* 26: 168-172.

Statement of the Conference of Medical Royal Colleges, (1976), Diagnosis of brain death. *British Medical Journal,* 2: 1187-1188.

Steedman, D.J., Robertson, C.E. (1992). Acid base changes in arterial and central venous blood during cardiopulmonary resuscitation. *Archives of Emergency Medicine,* 9: 169-176.

Steinberg H, (1956), Abnormal behaviour induced by nitrous oxide. *British Journal of Psychology,* 47, 183-194.

Stoelting RK, et al, (1970), Minimum alveolar concentrations in man on awakening from methoxyflurane, halothane, ether, and fluroxene anesthesia: MAC awake. *Anesthesiology,* 33: 5-9.

Stoerig P, Cowey A, (1997), Blindsight in man and monkey. *Brain*, 120: 535-559.

Storm L, Ertel S, (2001), Does Psi Exist? Comments on Milton and Wiseman's (1999) meta-analysis of Ganzfeld research. *Psychological Bulletin*, 127: 424-433.

Storm L, Thalbourne MA, (2001a), Paranormal effects using sighted and vision-impaired participants in a quasi-ganzfeld task. *Australian Journal of Parapsychology*, 1: 133-170.

Storm L, (2006), Technical Paper No. 11: Meta-analysis in parapsychology: I. The Ganzfeld domain. *Australian Journal of Parapsychology*, 6: 35-53.

Storm L, Barrett-Woodbridge M, (2007), Psi as compensation for modality impairment - A replication study using sighted and blind participants. *European Journal of Parapsychology*, 22: 73-89.

Storm L, et al, (2010), Meta-analysis of free-response studies, 1992-2008: Assessing the noise reduction model in parapsychology. *Psychological Bulletin*, 136: 471-485.

Storrs RS, (1857). *The Constitution of the Human Soul. Six Lectures at the Brooklyn Institute.* Published by Robert Carter & Brothers, New York, USA.

Strandgaard S, (1976), Autoregulation of cerebral blood flow in hypertensive patients. The modifying influence of prolonged antihypertensive treatment on the tolerance to acute, drug-induced hypotension. *Circulation*, 53: 720-727.

Strandhagen E, et al, (2010), Selection bias in a population survey with registry linkage: potential effect on socioeconomic gradient in cardiovascular risk. *European Journal of Epidemiology*, 25: 163-172.

Streisand JB, et al, (1993), Fentanyl-induced rigidity and unconsciousness in human volunteers. Incidence, duration, and plasma concentrations. *Anesthesiology*, 78: 629-634.

Strickland RA, Butterworth JF, (2007), Sexual dreaming during anesthesia. *Anesthesiology*, 106: 1032-1036.

Studerus E, et al, (2010), Acute, subacute and long-term subjective effects of psilocybin in healthy humans: a pooled analysis of experimental studies. *Journal of Psychopharmacology*, September 20: Epub ahead of print: 1-19.

Swann A, et al, (2011), Recall after procedural sedation in the emergency department. *Emergency Medical Journal*, 24: 322-324.

Swenson RD, et al, (1988), Hemodynamics in humans during conventional and experimental cardiopulmonary resuscitation in humans. *Circulation*, 78: 630-639.

Sykes FH, (1908), *Coleridge's Ancient Mariner and Select Poems*, in The Scribner English Classics, USA.

T

Takayama M, et al, (2004), Intracarotid propofol test for speech and memory dominance in man. *Neurology,* 63: 510-515.

Tamietto M, Gelder B de, (2008), Affective blindsight in the intact brain: Neural interhemispheric summation for unseen fearful expressions. *Neuropsychologia,* 46: 820-828.

Tang YY, et al, (2010), Short-term meditation induces white matter changes in the anterior cingulate. *Proceedings of the National Academy of Sciences,* Aug 31;107(35):15649-52. Epub 2010 Aug 16.

Targ E, et al, (2000), *Psi-Related Experiences.* In Chapter 7, pages 219-252, in Cardena E, et al, (2000),. *Varieties of Anomalous Experience: Examining the Scientific Evidence.* Published by The American Psychological Association, USA, ISBN 1-55798-625-8.

Tart CT, (1969), A further psychophysiological study of out-of-the-body experiences in a gifted subject. *Proceedings of the Parapsychological Association,* 6: 43-44.

Tart CT, (1998), Six studies of out-of-body experiences. *Journal of Near-Death Studies,* 17: 73-99.

Teeple RC, et al, (2009), Visual hallucinations: differential diagnosis and treatment. *Primary Care Companion to The Journal of Clinical Psychiatry,* 11: 26-32.

Teicher MH, et al, (2004), Childhood neglect is associated with reduced corpus callosum area. *Biological Psychiatry,* 56: 80-85.

Teichtahl H, et al, (2005), Ventilatory responses to hypoxia and hypercapnia in stable methadone maintenance treatment patients. *Chest,* 128: 1339-1347.

Terhune DB, (2009), The incidence and determinants of visual phenomenology during out-of-body experiences. *Cortex,* 45: 236-242.

Tertullian, *A Treatise on the Soul,* translated by Peter Holmes in Volume III, of. *The Ante-Nicene Fathers,* editors A. Roberts and J. Donaldson, published by Charles Scribner's Sons, New York, USA, 1918.

Thalbourne MA, (1996), Belief in life after death: psychological origins and influences. *Personality and Individual Differences,* 21: 1043-1045.

Theos Ghosts Poll, (2009), Theos Gosts Poll published 13 April 2009. Results of a representative survey of belief in ghosts and the soul conducted in the UK. Retrieved from the internet at: http://www.comres.co.uk/page165141716.aspx

Thompson PM, et al, (2001), Mapping adolescent brain change reveals dynamic wave of accelerated gray matter loss in very early-onset schizophrenia. *Proceedings of the National Academy of Sciences*, 98: 11650-11655.

Tian SY, et al, (2010), Effect of midazolam on memory: a study of process dissociation procedure and functional magnetic resonance imaging. *Anaesthesia*, 65: 586-594.

Tiberi E, (1993), Extrasomatic emotions,. *Journal of Near-Death Studies*, 11: 149-170.

Ting CK, et al, (2004), Desflurane accelerates patient response during the wake-up test for scoliosis surgery. *Canadian Journal of Anesthesia*, 51: 393-397.

Tobias JD, (2008), Cerebral oximetry monitoring With near infrared spectroscopy detects alterations in oxygenation before pulse oximetry. *Journal of Intensive Care Medicine*, 23: 384-388.

Tobin JM, Mihm FG, (2009), A hemodynamic profile for consciousness during cardiopulmonary resuscitation. *Anesthesia & Analgesia*, 109: 1598-1599.

Topulos GP, et al, (1993), The experience of complete neuromuscular blockade in awake humans. *Journal of Clinical Anesthesia*, 5: 369-374.

Towbin A, (1973), The respirator brain death syndrome. *Human Pathology*, 4: 583-594.

Travis F, et al, (2009), Effects of transcendental meditation practice on brain functioning and stress reactivity in college students. *International Journal of Psychophysiology,* 71: 170-176.

Tsuang MT, et al, (1998), Co-occurrence of abuse of different drugs in men. The role of drug-specific and shared vulnerabilities. *Archives of General Psychiatry*, 55: 967-972.

Tuckett IL, (1932), *The Evidence for the Supernatural*. Published by "The Thinker's Library", United Kingdom.

Tunstall ME, (1977), Detecting wakefulness during general anaesthesia for caesarean section. *British Medical Journal*, 1: 1321.

Tusiewicz K, (1977), Mechanics of the rib cage and diaphragm during sleep. *Journal of Applied Physiology*, 43: 600-602.

Tuwir I, et al, (2005), Drug induced autoenucleation with resultant chiasmal damage. *British Journal of Ophthalmology,* 89: 121.

Twemlow SW, et al, (1982), The out-of-body experience: a phenomenological typology based on questionnaire responses. *American Journal of Psychiatry,* 139: 450-455.

U

UNAIDS, (2008), Report on the global AIDS epidemic. Published by the Joint United Nations Programme on HIV/AIDS, ISBN 9789291737116.

V

Vaitl D, et al, (2005), Psychobiology of altered states of consciousness. *Psychological Bulletin,* 131: 98-127.

Vanlancker-Sidtis D, (2004), When only the right hemisphere is left: Studies in language and communication. *Brain and Language,* 91: 199-211.

Vergauwen R, (2010), Will science and consciousness ever meat? Complexity, symmetry and qualia. *Symmetry,* 2: 1250-1269. doi:10.3390/sym2031250

Veselis RA, et al, (1994), Impaired memory and behavioral performance with fentanyl at low plasma concentrations. *Anesthesia & Analgesia,* 79: 952-960.

Veselis RA, et al, (1997), The comparative amnestic effects of midazolam, propofol, thiopental, and fentanyl at equisedative concentrations. *Anesthesiology,* 87: 749-764.

Veselis RA, et al, (2004), Thiopental and propofol affect different regions of the brain at similar pharmacologic effects. *Anesthesia & Analgesia,* 99: 399-408.

Veselis RA, et al, (2004a), Information loss over time defines the memory defect of propofol. A comparative response with thiopental and dexmedetomidine. *Anesthesiology,* 101: 831-841.

Veselis RA, et al, (2006), The remarkable memory effects of propofol. *British Journal of Anaesthesia,* 96: 289-291.

Veselis RA, et al, (2009), Propofol and midazolam inhibit conscious memory processes very soon after encoding: an event-related potential study of familiarity and recollection in volunteers. *Anesthesiology,* 110:295-312.

Vinson DR, Bradbury DR, (2002), Etomidate for procedural sedation in emergency medicine. *Annals of Emergency Medicine,* 39: 592-598.

Virués-Ortega J, et al, (2006), Human behaviour and development under high-altitude conditions. *Developmental Science,* 9: 400-410.

Visser GH, et al, (2001), The Development of Spectral EEG Changes During Short Periods of Circulatory Arrest. *Journal of Clinical Neurophysiology,* 18: 169-177.

Vogeler K, (1942), *August Bier. Leben und Werk.* published by J.F. Lehmanns Verlag, München-Berlin.

Vogt C, (1864), *Lectures on Man: His Place in Creation and in the History of the Earth.* Published by Longman, Green, Longman and Roberts, London, UK.

Volkow ND, et al, (2003), Expectation enhances the regional brain metabolic and the reinforcing effects of stimulants in cocaine abusers. *The Journal of Neuroscience,* 23: 11461-11468.

Volkow ND, et al, (2004), Dopamine in drug abuse and addiction: results from imaging studies and treatment implications. *Molecular Psychiatry,* 9: 557-569.

Volkow ND, et al, (2011), Addiction: Beyond dopamine reward circuitry. *Proceedings of the National Academy of Sciences,* 108: 15037-15042.

Vollenweider FX, et al, (1997), Positron Emission Tomography and Fluorodeoxyglucose studies of metabolic hyperfrontality and psychopathology in the psilocybin Model of psychosis. *Neuropsychopharmacology,* 16: 357-372.

Voracek M, (2009), Who wants to believe? Associations between digit ratio (2D:4D) and paranormal and superstitious beliefs. *Personality and Individual Differences,* 47: 105-109.

Voss U, et al, (2009), Lucid Dreaming: A State of Consciousness with Features of Both Waking and Non-Lucid Dreaming. *Sleep,* 32: 1191-1200.

Vuyk J, et al, (1992), Pharmacodynamics of propofol in female patients. *Anesthesiology,* 77: 3-9.

W

Wada J, Rasmussen T, (1960), Intracarotid injection of sodium amytal for the lateralization of cerebral speech dominance. *Journal of Neurosurgery,* 17: 266-282.

Wade J, (1998), Physically transcendent awareness: a comparison of the phenomenology of consciousness before birth and after death. *Journal of Near-Death Studies,* 16: 249-275.

Wagenmakers EJ, et al, (2011), Why psychologists must change the way they analyze their data: The case of psi: Comment on Bem (2011). *Journal of Personality and Social Psychology,* 100: 426-432.

Wagner KJ, et al, (2001), Dose-dependent regional cerebral blood flow changes during remifentanil infusion in humans. A positron emission tomography study. *Anesthesiology,* 94: 732-739.

Wain O, Spinella M, (2007), Executive functions in morality, religion, and paranormal beliefs. *International Journal of Neuroscience,* 117: 135-146.

Walker DJ, Zacny JP, (1998), Subjective, psychomotor, and analgesic effects of oral codeine and morphine in healthy volunteers. *Psychopharmacology,* 140: 191-201.

Walker DJ, Zacny JP, (1999), Subjective, psychomotor, and physiological effects of cumulative doses of opioid μ agonists in healthy volunteers. *Journal of Pharmacology and Experimental Therapeutics,* 289: 1454-1464.

Waller JL, et al, (1981), Hemodynamic changes during fentanyl-oxygen anesthesia for aortocoronary bypass operation. *Anesthesiology,* 55: 212-217.

Wang DS, et al, (2011), Inhibition of learning and memory by general anesthetics. *Canadian Journal of Anesthesia,* 58:167-177.

Wang M, Russell IF, (1995), Memory of intraoperative events. *British Medical Journal,* 310: 601.

Ward CF, et al, (1983), Drug abuse in anesthesia training programs. A survey: 1970 through 1980. *Journal of the American Medical Association,* 250: 922-925.

Warrell DA, (2010), Snake Bite. *Lancet,* 375, 77-88.

Waterton C, (1879), *Wanderings in South America.* published by Macmillan and Co., London, England.

Wei J, et al, (2006), Cardiopulmonary resuscitation in prone position: A simplified method for outpatients. *Journal of the Chinese Medical Association,* 69: 202-206.

Weil MH, et al, (1986). Difference in acid-base state between venous and arterial blood during cardiopulmonary resuscitation. *New England Journal of Medicine,* 315: 153-156.

Weinraub M, et al, (1972), Chloroformism - a new case of a bad old habit. *California Medicine,* 117: 63-65.

Wennervirta J, et al, (2002), Awareness and recall in outpatient anesthesia. *Anesthesia & Analgesia,* 95: 72-77.

Wettach GE, (2000), The near-death experience as a product of isolated subcortical brain function. *Journal of Near-death Studies,* 19: 71-90.

Whitacre RJ, Fisher AJ, (1945), Clinical observations on the use of curare in anesthesia. *Anesthesiology,* 6: 124-130.

White PF, et al, (1982), Ketamine - its pharmacology and therapeutic uses. *Anesthesiology,* 56: 119-136.

Whitworth B, (2010), The emergence of the physical world from information processing. *Quantum Biosystems,* 2: 221-249.

WHO, (2009), Fact Sheet No. 282. *Visual Impairment and blindness.* Published during May 2009.

WHO, (2010), Data from the life tables of the World Health Organization, accessed from the internet on 20 August 2010 at the address: http://www.who.int/healthinfo/statistics/mortality_life_tables/en/

Wijdicks EFM, (2001), The diagnosis of brain death. *New England Journal of Medicine,* 344: 1215-1221.

Wijdicks EFM, Pfeifer EA, (2008), Neuropathology of brain death in the modern transplant era. *Neurology,* 70: 1234-1237.

Williams BJ, (2011), Revisiting the Ganzfeld ESP debate: A basic review and assessment. *Journal of Scientific Exploration,* 25: 639-661.

Willoughby WW, (1925), *Opium as an International Problem, The Geneva Conferences.* Published by The Johns Hopkins Press, Baltimore, USA.

Wilm EC, (1914), *Henri Bergson: A Study in Radical Evolution.* Published by Sturgis & Walton Company, New York, USA.

Wilson JE, et al, (2008), A survey of inhalational anaesthetic abuse in anaesthesia training programmes. *Anaesthesia,* 63: 616-620.

Wilson ME, (1980), Awareness in general anaesthesia. *British Medical Journal,* 226: 1270.

Wilson RK, Williams MA, (2007), Evidence that congenital hydrocephalus is a precursor to idiopathic normal pressure hydrocephalus (INPH) in only a subset of patients. *Journal of Neurology, Neurosurgery & Psychiatry,* 78: 508-511.

Wilson RK, Williams MA, (2008a), What we gain by measuring head circumference. *Pediatrics,* 122: 219-220.

Wilson SAK, (1933), Cataplexy. *Journal of Neurology and Psychopathology,* 14: 45-51.

Winter JA, et al, (2005), Muscle spindle signals combine with the sense of effort to indicate limb position. *Journal of Physiology,* 568: 1035-1046.

Wischmeyer PE, et al, (2007), A survey of propofol abuse in academic anesthesia programs. *Anesthesia & Analgesia,* 105: 1066-1071.

Witelson SF, et al, (2006), Intelligence and brain size in 100 postmortem brains: sex, lateralization and age factors. *Brain,* 129: 386-398.

Wittenberg GF, (2009), Neural plasticity and treatment across the lifespan for motor deficits in cerebral palsy. *Developmental Medicine & Child Neurology,* 51 (Suppl. 4): 130-133.

Wittmann L, Schredl M, (2004), Does the mind sleep? An answer to "What is a dream generator?". *Sleep and Hypnosis,* 6: 177-178.

Wittmann L, et al, (2004a), NREM sleep dream recall, dream report length and cortical activation. *Sleep and Hypnosis,* 6: 43-47.

Wittmann M, et al, (2007), Effects of psilocybin on time perception and temporal control of behaviour in humans. *Journal of Psychopharmacology,* 21: 50-64.

Woerlee GM, (2005),. *Mortal Minds: The Biology of Near-death Experiences.* Published Prometheus, USA, ISBN 1591022835.

Woerlee GM, (2008),. *The Unholy Legacy of Abraham.* Published Booklocker, USA, ISBN: 978-1-60145-621-2

Wolfe RJ, (2000), *Tarnished Idol. William T.G. Morton and the Introduction of Surgical Anesthesia.* Published by Normal Publishing, USA, ISBN 0-930-405-81-1.

Woolsey CN, et al, (1979), Localization in somatic sensory and motor areas of human cerebral cortex as determined by direct recording of evoked potentials and electrical stimulation. *Journal of Neurosurgery,* 51: 476-506.

Wu CC, et al, (2001), EEG-Bispectral Index changes with ketamine versus Thiamylal induction of anesthesia. *Acta Anaesthesiologica Sinica,* 39:11-15.

Wulf HFV, (1998), The centennial of spinal anesthesia. *Anesthesiology,* 89: 500-506.

X

Xu J, et al, (2000), Gender effects on age-related changes in brain structure. *American Journal of Neuroradiology*, 21: 112-118.

Y

Yamamoto RT, et al, (2007), Effects of perceived cocaine availability on subjective and objective responses to the drug. *Substance Abuse Treatment, Prevention, and Policy*, 2:30 (doi:10.1186/1747-597X-2-30).

Yamashita M, et al, (1984), Illicit use of modern volatile anaesthetics. *Canadian Anaesthetists'Society Journal*, 31: 76-79.

Yentis SM, Vlassakov KV, (1999), Vassily von Anrep, forgotton pioneer of regional anesthesia. *Anesthesiology*, 90: 890-895.

Ying Han, et al, (2009), Gray matter density and white matter integrity in pianists' brain: A combined structural and diffusion tensor MRI study. *Neuroscience Letters*, 459: 3-6.

Yokota T, et al, (1992), F-response during cataplexy. *Journal of Neurology, Neurosurgery & Psychiatry*, 55: 75-76.

Yonelinas AP, et al, (2002), Effects of extensive temporal lobe damage or mild hypoxia on recollection and familiarity. *Nature Neuroscience*, 5: 1236-1241.

Yonelinas AP, et al, (2004), Mild hypoxia disrupts recollection, not familiarity. *Cognitive, Affective, & Behavioral Neuroscience*, 4: 393-400.

Young CJ, et al, (1997), Analgesic and psychomotor effects of thiopental at subanesthetic concentrations in human volunteers. *Acta Anaesthesiologica Scandinavica*, 41: 903-910.

Yung GL, et al, (2004), Comparison of impedance cardiography to direct Fick and thermodilution cardiac output determination in pulmonary arterial hypertension. *Congestive Heart Failure*, 10: (supplement 2): 7-10.

Z

Zacny JP, et al, (1992), Subjective and behavioral responses to intravenous fentanyl in healthy volunteers. *Psychopharmacology,* 107, 319-326.

Zacny JP, et al, (1992a), Subjective and psychomotor effects of subanesthetic doses of propofol in healthy volunteers. *Anesthesiology,* 76: 696-702.

Zacny JP, et al, (1993), Propofol at a subanesthetic dose may have abuse potential in healthy volunteers. *Anesthesia & Analgesia,* 77: 544-552.

Zacny JP, et al, (1994), The subjective, behavioral and cognitive effects of subanesthetic concentrations of isoflurane and nitrous oxide in healthy volunteers. *Psychopharmacology,* 114: 409-416.

Zacny JP, et al, (1997), Comparing the subjective, psychomotor and physiological effects of intravenous nalbuphine and morphine in healthy volunteers. *Journal of Pharmacology and Experimental Therapeutics,* 280: 1159-1169.

Zacny JP, et al, (1998), Comparing the subjective, psychomotor and physiological effects of intravenous pentazocine and morphine in normal volunteers. *Journal of Pharmacology and Experimental Therapeutics,* 286: 1197-1207.

Zaidi ZF, (2010), Gender differences in human brain: a review. *The Open Anatomy Journal,* 2: 37-55.

Zeman A, (2001), Consciousness. *Brain,* 124: 1263-1289.

Zhu Y, et al, (2007), Neural basis of cultural influence on self-representation. *NeuroImage,* 34: 1310-1316.

Zubieta JK, et al, (1999), Gender and age influences on human brain mu-opioid receptor binding measured by PET. *American Journal of Psychiatry,* 156: 842-848.

Zuckerman M, Cohen N, (1964), Sources of reports of visual and auditory sensations in perceptual-isolation experiments. *Psychological Bulletin,* 62: 1-20.

Index

A

B

C

477

D

481

G

Griffith and Johnson - introduction of Curare into anesthesia, 2.44
Guedel, Arthur, 6.88
- Guedel stages of ether anesthesia, 6.88-6.92
- Guedel stage ether anesthesia and BIS level, 6.93-6.96
- muscle paralysis during stage-1, 6.98-6.99
- pain free during stage-1, 6.89

H

Hallucinations:
- anesthetic gases and, 6.58, 6.113, 6.149
- command hallucinations, 3.33-3.38
- definition: see Definitions of terms
- due to brain disease, 5.65-5.66
- Mescaline and, see *Mescaline*
- Psilocybin and, see *Psilocybin*
- reality or abnormal brain function? 3.43, 15.95-15.104
Hammond, William Alexander, 1.148
- education and credulity, 1.149
- superstitious character and paranormal belief, 3.125
- paranormal beliefs and interpretation of perceptions, 15.119
- illusions and false conclusions, 15.125
Hamsters in heaven? 15.48
Hearing during out-of-body experiences, 14.26-14.28
Heart:
- a pump made of meat instead of metal, 12.20
- mechanical heart, 12.20
Heaven:
- 1423 animal souls per human soul, 15.62
- a hell of eternal repetition, 15.73
- absence of proven by anesthetic drugs, 7.93
- an eternal hallucination, 15.73
- animal and human consciousness, 15.63
- awareness during anesthesia proves illusory nature of, 10.95
- cuddly little hamsters in, 15.61
- eternity with your family in-law, 15.73
- evolutionary tree and admission to heaven, 15.63
- full of cackling chickens, 15.62
- Jesus repeatedly condemned to death on many planets, 15.68
- no babies in heaven, 15.63
- no extraterrestrial beings in heaven, 15.64-15.66

485

- no hamsters and no extraterrestrials - reasons why, 15.72
- no mentally retarded souls, 44015.63
- parochial nature of, 440X.001
- pigs in heaven, 15.62
Heroin: see *Opiates*
Hertz, Heinrich Rudolf, 13.40
- psi and radio waves - discovery and use, 13.40-13.41
Hexobarbital: see *Intravenous induction agents*
Hildebrandt, August, 11.30
- a reckless egoist, 11.33
- expulsion from Berlin Medical Association, 11.33
- house filled with plundered Chinese treasures, 11.33
- role in spinal anesthesia priority battle, 11.33
- spinal anesthesia experiments upon, 11.30-11.32
Hitler, and other malignant rulers, 15.35-15.39
Horla, the, 9.50
- monster experienced during sleep paralysis, 9.52
Humboldt, Alexander von, 9.7
- curare preparation by old women - the legend, 9.7-9.8
- curare preparation technique - the truth, 9.9
- curare used to kill meat animals, 9.11-9.13, 9.36
- travels in Orinoco area to study curare, 9.7
Hydrancephaly, 2.31-2.35, 5.49-5.53
- consciousness and, 2.32-2.34
- dualism and, 5.51-5.53
- electroencephalogram absent in hydrancephaly, 2.31-2.32
- mental function, 2.33-2.34, 5.50-5.51
- no brain except for brainstem and vestigial cortex, 2.31
Hydrocephalus, 5.24-5.53
- cause, 5.39
- cause of death, 5.39
- circumference of head, 5.40
- congenital, 5.37-5.40
- dualism and, 5.27-5.35
- electroencephalogram present in hydrocephaly, 5.36
- IQ range in hydrocephalus, 5.40-5.42
- IQ = 126 in man with hydrocephalus, 5.25, 5.37, 5.41-5.42
- Lorber studies, 5.37
- mortality, natural history, 5.38-5.40
Hypoxia, 4.36-4.93
- and near-death experiences, 12.85-12.108
- calm indifference during, 4.44
- clear mind, illusion of during, 4.64
- elation, euphoria due to, 4.64
- eyes more sensitive to hypoxia than brain, 4.34-4.35, 4.48, 4.63

I

J

K

M

Magnan, Valentin, 3.73
Mary and the color red, 3.6-3.12
 - knowledge argument, 3.6
 - and rejection of materialism, 3.8
 - physiology and poor reasoning, 3.10
 - subjective experience genesis of, 3.14-3.18
 - thought experiment, 3.7
Materialism: see Definitions of terms
 - more parsimonious than dualism, P.10
Maupassant, Henry Guy de, 9.50
 - "The Horla" short story, 9.50-9.51
Maxwell, James Clerk, 13.40
Meat:
 - annual per capita consumption in USA, 15.62
 - sweet tasting, 9.1, 9.32-9.36
Meigs, James Aitken, 5.8
 - skull capacities of Negroes born in slavery, 5.8
 - cranial capacity and race, 5.8
 - cranial capacity and racial superiority, 5.8
Memory:
 - absence of memory in soul, 15.112
 - absence of soul proven by absence of memory in soul, 15.112
 - location of memory and general anesthesia, 10.93-10.94
 - location of memory and dreams, 2.115
 - location of memory and dualism, 1.112-1.115
 - location of memory - ether and other gases, 6.131, 6.135-6.144
 - location of memory and hypoxia, 4.70, 4.84-4.93
 - location of memory and midazolam, 7.75-7.88
 - location of memory and nitrous oxide, 6.46-6.48
 - location of memory and propofol, 7.29, 7.91
 - location of memory and thiopental, 7.17
 - electrical stimulation of brain and, 4.99-4.105
 - fundamental property of soul, 15.110-15.111
 - mind without memory similar to dementia, 1.112
 - near-death experiences and, 1.95-1.104
 - out-of-body experiences and, 1.95-1.104
 - reincarnation and spiritual development require memory in the soul, 4.138
Mescaline, 4.17-4.21

N

O

P

Q

R

Romantic love - nitrous oxide and, 6.54
Rossen, Ralph, 4.36
   - amazing cardiac arrest experiment, 4.36-4.38
   - cardiac arrest simulation, 4.38
   - experience of sudden cardiac arrest, 4.39-4.50

S

Schiller, Ferdinand Cannon Scott, 1.78
Schizophrenia and command hallucinations, 3.33-3.35
Sensed presence:
   - hypoxia causing, 4.66
   - sleep paralysis and, 9.49-9.51
Separable conscious mind: see *Soul*
Sexual abuse:
   - brain structure in women and, 4.123-4.124
   - during general anesthesia, 6.102
Shakespeare, William, and personal legacy, 15.137
Simpson, James, 6.83
   - discovery chloroform, 6.83
Sleep:
   - a state of continuous mental activity, 2.79-2.80
   - and the soul, 1.41-1.43, 1.50-1.54, 1.77, 2.70-2.73, 2.94-2.97
   - belief in continual consciousness during sleep, 2.70-2.74
   - care of the soul during sleep, 2.72-2.73
   - death and sleep, similarity, 2.94-2.98
   - hypnic jerks during, 3.105-3.108
   - primitive societies and, 2.70-2.73
Sleep paralysis, 9.49
   - curare and, 9.52
   - Horla, the, 9.50-9.52
   - incidence, 9.49
   - experience of, 9.49-9.52
   - sensed presence during, 9.49
Slow Wave Sleep, see *NREM sleep*
Snakebite:
   - apparent unconsciousness, 2.68
   - artificial ventilation for, 2.66-2.67
   - Black Mamba, 2.66
   - Malayan Krait, 2.66
Soul:

- sedation and blood concentration, 7.15
- subjective effects, 7.11-7.14
- taste of garlic, 7.12
- time distortion due to, 7.21
Tibetan Book of the Dead, 17.70
- hallucinatory nature of afterlife, 15.71-15.73
- near-death experience and, 15.76-15.77
- retention of individuality, 15.75-15.76
Transcendental experiences: see Definitions of terms
- anesthetic vapors as cause, 6.115-6.121, 6.134
- brain tumors and, 5.65-5.66
- common pathway, 14.102
- epilepsy and, 5.70
Transorbital lobotomy: *see Lobotomy*

U

V

Vogt, Carl Christoph, 5.5
- no understanding of statistics, 5.7-5.8
- using dead soldiers for manure? 5.6-5.7

W

Wada Test, 2.25, 4.94
- anesthesia of half the brain, 2.25-2.26
- distribution of drug in brain, 2.26
- effects, 2.27
- memory and, 4.96
- no loss of consciousness, 2.26, 4.94
- proves soul cannot directly activate muscles, 4.97
- proves soul must use the brain to activate the body, 4.97
- technique, 2.26
Wada, Juhn Atsushi, 2.25

X

- an opium inspired poem, 8.1-8.2

Y

Z

Zimbabwe, 15.5
- government mismanagement, 15.5
- HIV incidence, 15.5
- increase in religious belief, 15.5
- life expectancy 2008, 15.5

<u>NOTES:</u>

Printed in Great Britain
by Amazon

18024368R00304